Good Housekeeping

Great Baking

600 recipes for cakes, cookies, breads, pies & pastries

Good Housekeeping

Great Baking

600 recipes for cakes, cookies, breads, pies & pastries

HEARST BOOKS
A Division of Sterling Publishing Co., Inc.
New York

Contents

This book was previously published under the title *Good Housekeeping Baking*.

Good Housekeeping

Ellen Levine	EDITOR IN CHIEF
Susan Westmoreland	FOOD DIRECTOR
Susan Deborah Goldsmith	ASSOCIATE FOOD DIRECTOR
Lisa Brainerd Burge, Sandra Rose Gluck,	
Gina Miraglia, Wendy Kalen, Sara Reynolds,	
Lori Perlmutter, Mary Ann Svec, Lisa Troland	RECIPE DEVELOPERS
Delia Hammock	NUTRITION DIRECTOR
Sharon Franke	FOOD APPLIANCES DIRECTOR
Richard Eisenberg	SPECIAL PROJECTS DIRECTOR
Gina Davis	ART DIRECTOR

Produced by Rebus, Inc.

Rodney M. Friedman	PUBLISHER
Kate Slate	EDITORIAL DIRECTOR, FOOD GROUP
Grace Young	PHOTOGRAPHY DIRECTOR
Evie Righter	PROJECT EDITOR
Bonnie J. Slotnick	WRITER
Timothy Jeffs	ART DIRECTOR
Hill Nutrition Associates	NUTRITIONISTS

All photography by Steven Mark Needham with the following exceptions: Mary Ellen Bartley: pages 33, 34. Simon Metz: page 105. Alan Richardson: pages 240, 312, 344, 346, 349. Ann Stratton: pages 180, 218, 249, 280, 282, 284, 318. Mark Thomas: pages 311, 314, 340. Farberware Classic Cookware provide by Meyer Corporation.

Library of Congress Cataloging-in-Publication Data
Available upon request.

10 9 8 7 6 5 4 3 2 1

First Paperback Edition 2003
Published by Hearst Books
A Division of Sterling Publishing Co., Inc.
387 Park Avenue South, New York, NY 10016

The Good Housekeeping Cookbook Seal guarantees that the recipes in this cookbook meet the strict standards of the Good Housekeeping Institute, a source of reliable information and a consumer advocate since 1900. Every recipe has been triple-tested for ease, reliability, and great taste.

Good Housekeeping and Hearst Books are trademarks owned by
Hearst Magazines Property, Inc., in USA, and Hearst Communications, Inc., in Canada.

www.goodhousekeeping.com

Distributed in Canada by Sterling Publishing
C/o Canadian Manda Group, One Atlantic Avenue, Suite 105
Toronto, Ontario, Canada M6K 3E7
Distributed in Australia by Capricorn Link (Australia) Pty. Ltd.
P.O. Box 704, Windsor, NSW 2756 Australia

Printed in China

ISBN 1-58816-259-1

WELCOME TO GOOD HOUSEKEEPING GREAT BAKING

Close your eyes and imagine your kitchen warmly perfumed with cinnamon and nutmeg; your kids' cheeks sweetly glazed with chocolate icing; your guests' eyes alight as you spoon into a lofty soufflé. If these simple pleasures sound inviting, we're here to help you discover (or rediscover) the joys of baking. Perhaps you're an expert cookie maker hoping to widen your horizons: *Good Housekeeping Great Baking* will help you master éclairs, chocolate truffle cake, apple strudel, and hundreds of other desserts. If a fragrant risen loaf is your goal, we'll take you step-by-step through the proofing, kneading, rising, shaping, and baking of a simple yeast bread; then you'll be ready to try your hand at our pizza, focaccia, pretzel, and stollen recipes. The recipes in *Good Housekeeping Great Baking* were chosen by the Food Editors of *Good Housekeeping* magazine to enhance your baking repertoire and your enjoyment of all things baked. We hope that you'll take pleasure in the process and the many delicious results.

Susan Westmoreland
Food Director,
Good Housekeeping

Baking Basics

Fine baking is undoubtedly an art, but it also calls for a more scientific approach. While adding a "pinch of this and a splash of that" is a wonderfully intuitive way to cook up a stew, baking requires more attention to detail. The only way to ensure success with a soufflé is to separate the eggs carefully so that not the smallest speck of yolk sullies the whites. A feathery-textured, fully risen cake depends on accurate measurement of the baking powder and use of the right size pan. This "glossary" of baking basics covers many of the utensils and ingredients you'll encounter in our recipes. Take a little time to browse these pages. Even experienced bakers are likely to learn one or two things they didn't know before.

Equipment

Our great-grandmothers baked with not much more than a bowl, a wooden spoon, and a rolling pin—and you don't have to invest your life savings in kitchen equipment in order to bake well. However, a few well-chosen tools and gadgets will make the job easier and more pleasurable. In many cases, inexpensive kitchen tools function just as well as top-of-the-line products, but a really good mixer and high-quality baking pans are two cases where the extra cost is well worth it.

APPLIANCES

A hundred years ago, "baking day" was a test of endurance that could last from dawn 'til dusk. Today, electrical kitchen appliances save time and muscle power, so you can decide to bake at 6 p.m. and serve a pie that same evening. Using a stand mixer to beat egg whites, a food processor to make graham-cracker crumbs, or a bread machine to knead dough frees you for the more creative aspects of the baking process—icing a cake, braiding a yeast dough, or adorning a piecrust with pastry cut-outs.

Blender A blender does some jobs better than a food processor—for example, mixing very liquid batters. Use your blender to mix popover and pancake batter (as well as smoothies and shakes, of course). You can also chop nuts very fine, puree fruits for dessert sauces, and crush ice in a blender. A machine with a "pulse" button helps you get precisely the results you're after.

Bread machine If you love homemade bread but don't have a lot of time for baking, consider a bread machine, which can virtually eliminate the hands-on work of mixing and kneading. You can even bake bread when you're not at home. If you choose, the machine can do the whole job from start to finish: You place the ingredients in the machine, which mixes them, kneads the dough, and signals when it has risen (some models also signal when it's time to add raisins or other ingredients). If you want a loaf shape, you can then let the machine continue the job of baking. Or, if you prefer, just use the machine for mixing, kneading, and rising; then remove the dough, shape it as you wish, let it rise a second time, and bake it in the oven.

Electric mixer A regular hand mixer is fine for making frostings, cake batters, and light- to medium-density cookie doughs. But for the greatest versatility, you will need a heavy-duty stand mixer. Its powerful motor can handle stiff cookie doughs and knead yeast breads; and because you don't have to hold a stand mixer, it saves your energy and leaves both hands free for adding ingredients. You can even walk away for a moment and let the mixer work completely on its own (keep an eye on things, though!). Heavy-duty stand mixers come with large stainless-steel bowls, a flat paddle for mixing batters, a wire "whip" attachment for beating cream or egg whites, and a dough hook for kneading bread dough.

Food processor For chopping or grinding nuts, making cookie or bread crumbs, chopping onions, or grating hard cheeses, a food processor fitted with a metal blade is a serious time-saver. This machine is also excellent for mixing and kneading some types of pastry and bread dough. A food processor with a 6-cup work bowl can knead dough made with up to 4 cups of flour. A larger machine, with an 8-cup capacity, can handle a dough made with 6 to 8 cups of flour. Mini processors are handy for small jobs, such as chopping a handful of nuts, and they take up little counter space.

Double Chocolate Bundt Cake
(page 312)

Immersion blender Also called a hand blender, this small appliance can be used for whipping cream. The blender consists of a handle (which contains a small motor) and a long shaft with a mixing blade (partially enclosed for safety) at the end. If your options for whipping cream are by hand or by immersion blender, the blender will save you some time. (An electric mixer will be the fastest of all.)

⚓ BAKING PANS, SHEETS & DISHES

Before you get serious about baking, take an inventory of your pans. If they're warped or rusted, it's time for new ones. Good-quality aluminum pans are among the best. You don't need nonstick pans for most recipes, but a durable nonstick finish is useful for some pans (see below). Be sure you have enough of each pan shape and size to bake, for instance, dozens and dozens of cookies (the pans need to cool down before re-use), a week's worth of muffins, or a three-layer cake.

Baking stone Short of building a brick oven, a baking stone is your best bet for achieving a perfect crust on breads and pizzas. You position the round or rectangular ceramic "stone" on the oven rack, and place the bread dough directly on it. The stone draws moisture from the dough so that the bottom crust browns and crisps. A set of thick terra-cotta tiles from a building-supply center works equally well; or, you can buy sets of baking tiles that come fitted into a metal tray.

Bundt pan This one-piece tube pan is curved on the bottom and deeply fluted, so it turns out cakes that look decorative even when you don't frost them. Standard Bundt pans come in 6-cup and 12-cup sizes. If you don't have a Bundt pan, you can substitute a tube pan.

Cookie sheets These are flat baking pans that do not have sides, although one or both ends may be slightly turned up to make it easier to handle the pans. In addition to cookie-baking, cookie sheets are used for hand-shaped loaves of bread. You'll definitely need heavy pans if you're using them for bread—flimsy ones won't hold up. Cookie sheets should also be placed under two-part pans (such as springform or tart) that may leak during baking. Double-bottom cookie sheets, which have a cushion of air between two layers of metal, help keep cookie bottoms from overbrowning. You can duplicate this effect by stacking two pans, but be very careful handling the doubled pans when they're hot. To ensure good air circulation, choose cookie sheets that fit your oven rack with 2 inches to spare on all sides.

Cooling racks Baked goods should be cooled on a wire rack both before and after you turn them out of the pan, or moisture may condense in the pan. Racks speed cooling, too, because air circulates all around. Round 10-inch racks are perfect for cooling cake layers; a nice big rectangular rack is good for cookies and breads. A rack is also useful when you're applying a thin glaze or icing to cakes, cookies, or pastries: The drips will fall through the wire grid (place a sheet of waxed paper underneath) instead of pooling around the cake.

Cupcake pans *see* Muffin pans

Jelly-roll pan This rectangular pan with low sides measures 15½" by 10½". Use it for sheets of sponge cake destined to become rolled cakes, and for baking rolls and pastries. Turned upside down, a jelly-roll pan can serve as an extra cookie sheet.

Layer cake pans It's worth the small extra investment to buy layer cake pans made of medium-weight aluminum. You'll need both 8- and 9-inch round pans; 8" by 8" and 9" by 9" pans are used for bar cookies as well as square layer cakes. Round layer

cake pans should be at least 1½ inches deep. Square pans are about 2 inches deep.

Loaf pans These deep rectangular pans, made in both metal and glass, are used for yeast breads, quick breads, and loaf cakes. They come in standard sizes of 8½" by 4½" and 9" by 5". A loaf baked in a glass pan will bake faster than one baked in a metal pan because of the radiant heat. Anticipate doneness accordingly.

Muffin pans Also called cupcake pans, these come in a range of sizes. The standard size, which measures 2½ inches across the top of an individual cup, holds about ½ cup of batter. With these traditional muffin pans, it's easiest to remove the finished baked goods if you line the pans with fluted paper cups. For muffins in fanciful shapes, such as flowers, fruits, or ears of corn (cornsticks), you can buy special pans of heavy cast iron or aluminum.

Pie plate Made of ovenproof glass, ceramic, or metal, pie plates come in 8-, 9-, and 10-inch sizes. A clear glass plate lets you check on how the bottom of the pie is browning, and the crust will actually brown better in a glass pan. Decorative stoneware pie plates may be of nonstandard sizes, so be sure to measure them before buying to see if they'll work with your recipes. Similarly, disposable foil pie pans, so useful when baking pies as gifts, have a smaller capacity than standard pie plates.

Pizza pan This shallow round pan is useful but not necessary for making pizza: You can simply mark a circle on a cookie sheet or baking stone and pat and stretch the dough to the right size. Some pizza pans have a perforated or mesh bottom to allow air to circulate. This helps the crust to bake up crisp.

Popover pans Popovers can be baked in muffin pans, but there are also special pans for them. These have deep cups that are flared at the top.

Sheetcake pan This 13" by 9" by 2" rectangular pan could prove to be the most versatile one in your repertoire. Use it for single-layer cakes and large batches of bar cookies, or as a *bain-marie,* or water bath, for custards. Available in both metal and glass.

Springform pan A springform is a deep, round, two-piece pan; our recipes call for a 9-inch springform. You'll need one if you're planning to bake cheesecakes or other cakes that are too delicate to turn out. The bottom and the side (or "collar") are separate pieces, and the side unlatches so that it can be removed from the cake for serving.

Lemon Soufflé Tart (page 238)

Tart pan Choose "loose bottom" tart pans, which comes in two parts. The fluted rim has just a slight edge around the inside bottom; the flat bottom rests on this edge. It's best to place a tart with a wet filling on a cookie sheet before baking it in case of leaks. To remove the tart from the side of the pan, stand the pan on a heavy can and ease the side down, leaving the tart on the pan bottom for serving. Tart pans come in many sizes and shapes.

Tube pan Sponge cakes and angel-food cakes require a pan with a "chimney" in the middle. This gives the batter something to latch onto as it rises. Tube pans come in one-piece and removable-bottom styles. The pan usually has little "feet" around the edge to allow you to stand it upside down for cooling, although many people like to invert the pan by slipping the center tube over the neck of a bottle.

BASICS, UTENSILS & GADGETS

When you bake, it seems that you can never have too many bowls. And if you have too few (or too few wooden spoons or spatulas), you'll constantly need to wash them in the middle of whatever you're doing. We're not suggesting that you go out and buy every single item listed here: Take into consideration the kinds of things you bake before buying gadgets and specialty items. The following, though, are true essentials: bowls, a chef's knife, dry and liquid measuring cups, measuring spoons, a rubber spatula, wooden spoon, vegetable peeler, and a timer.

Bowls A set of nesting bowls in graduated sizes from 1 to 3 quarts will see you through most baking projects; you may need a larger bowl for bread baking. A deep bowl is best for mixing, and a heavy one is less likely to skate around the counter. (Placing a damp kitchen towel under any bowl will also help.) Plastic bowls absorb fat, which is a problem when you need a grease-free bowl (for beating egg whites, for instance). Heat-proof glass, ceramic, and stainless-steel bowls are good choices. A collection of smaller bowls (cereal or dessert bowls, or custard cups, can double in this role) is useful for holding premeasured ingredients.

Cake tester Many cooks use a toothpick or bamboo skewer for testing whether cakes are done. But there is also a gadget sold specifically for this purpose. It consists of a small handle attached to a length of rigid metal wire that is inserted into the cake.

Citrus juicer The simplest citrus juicer is a one-piece gadget (of glass, ceramic, metal, or plastic) with a grooved, pointed dome in the center. You press and turn the halved citrus fruit on the dome and out flows the juice. Some juicers come in two parts, the bottom portion being a dish to catch the juice. Electrical citrus juicers work on the same principle, but the reamer revolves automatically. Perhaps the most economical juicer for lemons and limes is a wooden reamer—a small, hand-held device that you push into the halved fruit and twist.

Cookie cutters Made of tin, copper, aluminum, or plastic, these fanciful forms are used for cutting rolled-out dough into all sorts of shapes. Cookie cutters should have a smooth, sharp cutting edge; on metal cutters, the other side should have a finger-friendly rolled edge for safe handling. In a pinch, use the rim of a glass or cup—or the edge of a jar, can, or tin—to cut dough.

Gingerbread Cut-Outs (page 60)

Cookie press This tool, used for making spritz cookies from rich buttery dough, works something like a pastry bag. The press consists of a squat metal cylinder with a wide nozzle at the bottom. Perforated metal plates are fitted to the nozzle to make variously shaped cookies. A screw-operated plunger and a tight cover allow you to press out the dough onto the cookie sheet. Nowadays you can also buy electric cookie presses.

Dough scraper Also called a bench scraper, this functions like a big spatula: It's a rectangle of rigid metal or hard plastic about 4" by 5", with a rolled top (to serve as a handle) or a wooden handle. The metal edge is thin but not sharpened. Use this tool to clean your counter of bits of dough and mounds of flour; it also helps you turn and lift sticky doughs at

the start of kneading. A dough scraper is also good for transferring small pastries to a cookie sheet.

Dry measuring cups Used for measuring flour, sugar, cornmeal, cocoa, and the like, these come in sets of graduated sizes, usually ¼, ⅓, ½, and 1 cup. The cups are often joined with a ring but are easier to handle if you separate them. The cups (preferably stainless steel or hard plastic) should have straight sides and a straight top edge so you can level the contents with the back of a knife. When measuring flour, confectioner's sugar, and other light, powdery ingredients, spoon them into the cup, then level it by sweeping across the top with the back of a knife. Granulated sugar can be measured by dipping; brown sugar should be packed into the cup. Never use dry measuring cups for liquid (or vice versa); you won't get an accurate measurement.

Egg separator Rather than separating the yolk from the white by dropping the yolk from half-shell to half-shell (a time-honored but tricky process), use an egg separator. These may be saucer- or spoon-shaped; they have a little cup in the center to catch the yolk while the white slips through slots at the sides.

Eggbeater Although the electric mixer has taken over most of its tasks, the old-fashioned eggbeater—with its rotating beaters operated by a cranked handle—is handy for small jobs. Today's models run smoothly and quietly on nylon gears and make the most of your arm-power.

Flour sifter Resembling a big metal mug, the flour sifter has a wire-mesh bottom and, most commonly, a spring-action agitator that moves when you squeeze the "trigger" in the handle. The agitator aerates the flour and the mesh strainer eliminates any lumps. Be sure to stir the ingredients after sifting; while sifting lightens and refines dry ingredients, it doesn't mix them. You can also sift with a fine-mesh strainer, tapping the edge with a spoon to shake the dry ingredients through.

Grater A one-piece box grater has perforations of different sizes for shredding chocolate, cheese, carrots, citrus zest, or nutmeg all on one utensil. You can place the grater in a deep bowl while you use it, or on a plate or a sheet of waxed paper. Flat graters are like one side of a box grater, with a handle at the top. They come in different styles for different jobs, and you may need several graters. You can lay a flat grater across the top of a bowl for a neat job. For easy clean-up when grating sticky foods, spritz the face of the grater with nonstick spray before you begin. A rotary grater works like a little mill: The food to be grated (chocolate, cheese, or nuts, for instance) is placed in a little hopper, and by closing the handles on the grater you press the food against a crank-operated grating cylinder. Some rotary graters have interchangeable drums for different uses. It's virtually impossible to nick a knuckle or a fingernail on a rotary grater (as you may on a flat or box grater).

Knives There's plenty of chopping, slicing, and paring involved in baking, and it will go quickly and easily if you have several good knives to work with. For serious chopping, you'll need a chef's knife, which has a broad, wedge-shaped blade. An 8-inch chef's knife suits most home cooks. Look for a knife with a full tang—this means that the metal of the blade extends nearly all the way through the handle. A knife made this way is stronger, better balanced,

and safer to use. A small paring knife, with a blade about 4 inches long, is right for peeling and cutting up fresh fruit, peeling onions, and trimming vegetables. Though small, the knife should be strong and well made. Both the chef's knife and paring knife can be sharpened at home (if you know how) or professionally sharpened from time to time. A dull knife is frustrating and dangerous to use, because it will slip rather than bite into what it is meant to be cutting. To slice bread and light-textured cakes, and to split cake layers horizontally, use a long knife with a serrated blade, working it through with a firm or gentle sawing motion, depending on the texture of the bread or cake.

Liquid measuring cups Made of clear heatproof glass or plastic, these beaker-shaped cups have measurements marked on the sides. For accurate measurement, place the cup on the work surface, pour in the liquid, and then bend over so you can check the amount of liquid at eye level, without lifting or tipping the cup. Liquid measures in 1- and 2-cup sizes will serve most purposes. There are also 8-cup glass measuring cups that make excellent batter bowls (complete with handle for pouring). Don't measure dry ingredients in cups meant for liquids; it's not possible to level off the contents.

Measuring spoons These can be used for both dry ingredients (baking powder, salt, spices) and liquid ingredients (lemon juice, vanilla extract); but it's a good idea to have two sets. Stainless-steel spoons with deep bowls—the deeper the bowl, the more accurate—and smooth edges (for leveling) are the best choice. Like dry measuring cups, these come in sets joined with a ring. The standard sizes are ¼, ½, and 1 teaspoon, plus 1 tablespoon. Some sets have a ⅛-teaspoon measure as well.

Parchment paper Also called kitchen parchment or baker's parchment, this translucent, dull-finished paper is used for lining baking pans. Parchment paper comes in sheets and rolls.

Pastry bag For making cream puffs and éclairs, shaping meringue, and adorning cakes with whipped cream, you'll need a pastry bag with assorted tips. Nylon bags are easier to keep clean than canvas bags; they dry more quickly, and the fabric retains its flexibility better than canvas. A basic set of tips (also called tubes) will see you through the recipes in this book. A *decorating bag* is recommended when small quantities of icing or frosting are used on cakes and fine pastries.

Pastry blender If you find it difficult to use two knives to cut fat into dry ingredients to make dough of the right crumbly texture for pastry, try a pastry blender. Its straight handle is fitted with a curved sweep of tines or wires that are used with a punching/chopping motion. It's especially helpful for making biscuits and scones.

Saint-Honoré (page 273)

Pastry board A large (18" by 24"), sturdy wooden board makes an excellent work surface. Available, too, is a special board (hardwood or acrylic) with a deep lip at the front and back. The front lip, which faces down, hooks over the edge of the counter to keep the board from sliding away as you knead or roll dough; the lip at the back is turned up to act as a "backsplash" and keep flour from going everywhere. A marble pastry board, which stays cooler than any other work surface, is a luxury, but the smooth, cool surface is a pleasure to work on—worth the investment if you make pastry or candy often.

Pastry brush For smoothing on glazes and brushing off crumbs or excess flour, natural-bristle brushes should be set aside for baking (apart from brushes you use for basting savory foods). A 1-inch-wide brush is best for glazing; a wider brush works well for sweeping a surface clear of flour. A brand-new natural-bristle paintbrush can also be used.

Pastry cloth and rolling-pin cover Dusting the surface and dough with a lot of flour to keep dough from sticking will turn pastry crust tough. Instead, use a pastry cloth (a sheet of canvaslike cotton) and cover, sometimes called a sleeve, for your rolling pin. These need only a light dusting of flour. Some pastry cloths even have measured rounds marked on them to help you roll dough to just the size you need.

Pastry wheel, cutter, or jagger Like pizza cutters (which you can use if you already have one), these consist of a sharp-edged metal wheel mounted on the end of a wooden handle. These rolling cutters work much better than a knife for cutting uncooked dough. A jagger has a fluted wheel that produces a zigzag edge, as if you'd cut the dough with pinking shears; it's pretty for piecrust edges and crackers.

Pie weights A piecrust baked blind (without a filling) needs to be weighted in the center to keep it from buckling and bubbling. Packets of small, beanlike aluminum weights are sold for this purpose; you can also buy a 6-foot rope of small stainless-steel beads to coil in the crust before baking. Or, use real dried beans (and reuse them again and again) or uncooked rice. Line the bottom of the crust with a square of foil before placing the weights inside.

Rolling pins First, the American-style rolling pin—the kind with handles and a free-spinning roller: You want the weight of the pin to do the work, so choose a heavy pin (at least 4 pounds) and you'll never have to lean on it. The roller should turn smoothly on ball bearings; it should be of hardwood and nicely finished. If you prefer a European-style wooden pin—the one-piece kind—experiment with the tapered design (which may take some getting used to) as well as the straight kind (like a thick, heavy piece of broom handle). These are truly inexpensive, and it's nice to have both on hand.

Ruler An 18-inch wooden ruler with a steel edge (or a steel ruler) will help you roll piecrust to the right size, trim sheets of phyllo to fit a pan, and cut even-sized bar cookies and loaf-cake slices. And while some baking pans do have the size of the pan marked on the bottom, many do not. Estimating pan size can be risky; measuring with a ruler is not.

Scale Although American recipes call for ingredients by volume measures (e.g., cups), British and continental recipes give them by weight. If you bake from foreign recipes, you'll need a kitchen scale. In addition, a scale is useful for weighing out 3 ounces of chocolate from a large bar or 2 pounds of peaches from the half-bushel you've brought home. When dividing cake batter between two pans, weighing them ensures that they're filled equally; the same goes for dividing a batch of bread dough for two or more loaves. A battery-operated digital scale that shows both grams/kilograms and ounces/pounds, and can handle weights up to 5 pounds, is a good choice for all kitchen uses.

Spatulas Nylon or rubber spatulas in several sizes are a baking must; the narrower ones are great for getting the last bit of honey or jam out of the jar. Choose flexible spatulas with sturdy handles and heat-resistant blades. You'll also need a wide metal spatula or pancake turner for removing hot cookies from cookie sheets; it should have a thin edge to slip under fragile cookies without breaking them. You'll need icing spatulas for frosting cakes—one about 10 inches long overall, and a smaller one, with a blade about ½ inch wide and 4 inches long. An "offset" or "angled" spatula, on which the blade has a bend in it close to the handle, makes it easier to ice the sides of a cake. You can use an artist's palette knife instead.

Spoons Wooden spoons are nonreactive, gentle on food, and won't burn your fingers when you're stirring hot liquids. If you're stirring in a pot or stainless-steel bowl, a wooden spoon cuts down on clatter. Choose spoons made of hardwoods, such as maple; they should be smoothly finished and free of rough patches that may splinter off. Metal cooking spoons should have heatproof handles so that they can be used for stirring hot sauces as well as batters.

Thermometers Precise temperatures are important in baking. If you proof yeast in water that's too hot, or bake popovers in an oven that's too cool, neither will succeed. Every kitchen should be equipped with an *instant-read thermometer:* About the size of a pen (complete with sheath and pocket clip), it is used to check the temperature of liquids (up to 220° F), rising dough, roasting meat, or the inside of your freezer. Oven thermostats are sometimes miscalibrated, so the number you set on the dial or digital display may be far from the actual temperature of the oven. Check it with an *oven thermometer* that you can leave in while you're baking. If it's clear that your oven temperature is markedly off, call a service person and have the thermostat adjusted.

Timer Timing is too important in baking to risk relying on a glance at your watch. Many ranges and microwave ovens come equipped with timers—use them. If you work on several baking projects simultaneously, consider buying an electronic timer with multiple settings. If you're likely to be out of the room when the timer sounds, make sure it has a loud ring, chime, or buzz.

Whisk These days most bakers do their mixing with an electric mixer, but a whisk still has its uses. This classic French tool–a straight handle with looped wires at the "business end"–is intended for stirring sauces, whisking mixtures together, and beating eggs and cream. Whisks come in a variety of sizes, with the largest, the balloon whisk, used for beating egg whites until stiff.

Zester This little gadget is made to order for peeling the thin top portion of peel from citrus fruits. You can use a fine grater for grating zest, but with a zester you can cut long, thin strips for garnishes.

Ingredients

Baking is scientific, but it is also part magic. When carefully combined, an assortment of ingredients can be transformed into a toothsome cake, irresistible cookie, or crusty loaf. Cool, silky flour, moist brown sugar, freshly shelled nuts, plump raisins, a molten pour of melted chocolate—all should be of the best possible quality. Most baking ingredients are products you can keep on hand, whether in the cabinet, refrigerator, or freezer. With a good stock in your kitchen, you're always ready to produce home-baked treats. Buy baking ingredients in a store with a good turnover, and check freshness dates on any products that bear them.

CHOCOLATE & COCOA

Chocolate is the favorite flavor of millions, and fortunately there are many different ways to use it in baking. These ingredients are widely available in their many forms. Chocolate starts out as cocoa beans, which are dried, hulled, and roasted. The resulting pieces, called cocoa nibs, are then crushed to produce chocolate liquor—a mixture of cocoa butter and particles of cocoa. To make solid chocolate, the two elements are separated, refined, and then recombined in various proportions; other ingredients, such as flavorings or emulsifiers, may be added. Cocoa powder is made by removing most of the cocoa butter from chocolate liquor, resulting in a fine powder. Store solid chocolate, well wrapped, in a cool place (65° F is ideal). High temperatures are harder on chocolate than low ones, so if your kitchen is very warm, double-wrap the chocolate and keep it in the refrigerator.

Unsweetened chocolate Sold in 1-ounce squares, this is virtually pure chocolate liquor in solid form, with no sugar added. Sometimes flavoring and lecithin (an emulsifier) are incorporated.

Bittersweet chocolate In the United States, this term is used interchangeably with "semisweet" (see below) and you can substitute one for the other. When buying European chocolate, bittersweet will be less sweet than chocolate labeled semisweet.

Semisweet chocolate Some sugar (between 40 and 65 percent) has been added to this type of dark chocolate; the amount varies from one brand to another. Additional cocoa butter and vanilla flavor may be added as well. In general, American semisweet chocolate is sweeter than European brands.

This chocolate is sold in 1-ounce squares for baking, and in bars for eating. The bars are generally of better quality than the baking chocolate. Semisweet chocolate, chopped into chunks, can be substituted for semisweet chocolate chips.

Dark sweet chocolate Most notably used in German's chocolate cake, this is a sweet, highly "eatable" chocolate that does not have milk added. Look for bars in the baking aisle. Some chocolate companies also make bars of dark sweet chocolate for eating—you can use these successfully for baking, too.

Milk chocolate This type of chocolate, sold for eating, is made with milk solids, cream, or other dairy products and is usually quite sweet and soft-textured, with a mild cocoa flavor. Milk chocolate can't be substituted for other kinds of chocolate to flavor a cake batter or cookie dough, but a bar of milk chocolate can be cut into chunks and added to cookie or cake batter instead of chocolate chips.

Chocolate chips or morsels Originally available only in semisweet, chocolate chips now come in milk, dark, mint, and white versions, in different sizes. Try different brands until you find a favorite. Don't substitute chips when a recipe calls for squares or bars to be melted: Chips are formulated to hold their shape during baking and will behave differently in a batter or frosting.

White chocolate Most of what's sold as "white chocolate" is not, technically speaking, chocolate at all, and only recently have the rules been relaxed to allow manufacturers to label these products "choco-

Classic Devil's Food Cake
(page 308)

late." This is because white chocolate is usually made with a fat other than cocoa butter (often palm kernel oil). The best white "chocolate" is made with cocoa butter, although it contains no chocolate liquor.

Cocoa Cocoa powder is made by removing most of the fat from chocolate, drying the resulting paste, and then grinding it to a powder. *Dutch-process* or *European-style cocoa* has been treated with alkali to neutralize some of its acid. Use Dutch-process cocoa only if the recipe specifies it.

DAIRY PRODUCTS & EGGS

Creamy cheesecakes, delicate custards, mouth-watering shortcakes, towering soufflés—all depend on good, wholesome products from the dairy case. It's easy to be sure that you're getting fresh dairy products and eggs, because all these products are marked with a freshness or sell-by date of one kind or another. Be sure to check those dates and buy the freshest.

Butter *see* Fats, page 22

Cream cheese The main ingredient in cheesecakes and some frostings is a snowy white, soft but solid cheese. Use the kind that comes in a block, rather than in a tub, for best results. In addition to regular, full-fat cream cheese, you can buy *Neufchâtel*, which has about one-third less fat, and *light cream cheese*, with about half the fat. *Fat-free cream cheese* bears little resemblance to the real thing. It's best not to substitute anything else for full-fat cream cheese unless the recipe suggests it.

Cream With a milk-fat content of between 36 and 40 percent, *heavy cream* whips up to the dense, dreamy stuff of toppings, fillings, and frostings. *Medium or light whipping cream,* which can also be whipped, has 30 to 36 percent fat. *Light cream,* also called *coffee cream,* contains a mere (!) 18 to 30 percent fat. *Half-and-half,* with a fat content between 10.5 and 18 percent, can be substituted for light cream. Cream is easier to whip if the cream, bowl, and beaters are all ice cold. Chill them in the freezer before whipping.

Eggs Our recipes call for "large" grade eggs, which weigh approximately 2 ounces each. Substituting other sizes, such as small or jumbo, is not recommended because the results will be different. It's imperative to store eggs in the refrigerator, for both health and flavor reasons. Keep them in their original container, rather than putting them in the egg-holder in the refrigerator door; this will keep them colder and also protect them from picking up flavors from other foods (eggshells are porous). Eggs that are very fresh when you buy them will keep for up to five weeks.

Milk The dairy case presents lots of alternatives when it comes to milk: lactose-reduced, calcium-enriched, fruit-flavored—but for baking, the plain old-fashioned variety is perfect. *Whole milk,* naturally, brings the most richness to custards, puddings, and sauces; *reduced-fat milk* (2 percent fat) has nearly as much fat and can be substituted. You'll probably notice a difference in creamy desserts if you substitute *low-fat milk* (1 percent fat). Skim milk, now labeled *nonfat,* can be used in baked goods, but the result will be, predictably, less rich.

Classic Cheese Soufflé (page 172)

Buttermilk, made by culturing low-fat or skim milk, brings a hint of a tangy flavor to biscuits, muffins, and cakes. It also helps produce baked goods with a tender crumb. Don't substitute buttermilk or yogurt for whole milk. You can substitute yogurt for buttermilk, if necessary, in most recipes.

Sour cream Nothing can match the thickness and tangy richness of real dairy sour cream, which is made by culturing whole milk with lactic acid. *"Light" sour cream* can be substituted in some recipes, but don't bake with nondairy "sour dressings."

Yogurt This fermented dairy product is available plain or flavored, in whole-milk, low-fat, and nonfat versions. Low-fat yogurt—but not nonfat—can be substituted for full-fat in most recipes.

FLAVORINGS

Spices, herbs, and extracts play important roles in dessert-making. Vanilla extract is not only a lovely flavor on its own—it enhances the flavor of chocolate. Apple pie minus cinnamon would be bland, and without ginger, there would be no gingerbread. Keep an assortment of these flavorings in your kitchen, ready for use in our recipes.

Extracts It takes just a few drops of these concentrated flavorings to perfume a cake or quick bread. Use pure—not imitation—extracts whenever you can. *Vanilla* is the extract most used in American recipes. Try a few different brands and see which you prefer—they do vary. Other extracts to keep on hand are *almond, orange, lemon,* and *peppermint.*

Herbs & spices Beginning life as humble leaves, twigs, seeds, roots, and stalks, these supply a world of flavors for baking. Sweet spices for cookies, pungent herbs for pizza—they're all as close as your supermarket. If a recipe calls for fresh herbs and you have only dried, the usual substitution ratio is 3:1—if the recipe calls for 3 tablespoons of chopped fresh oregano, use a tablespoon of dried instead. Spices such as nutmeg and cardamom will stay fresh longer if you buy them whole and crush or grind them as needed. Herbs and spices lose their power over time: Before you use any dry seasoning, rub a bit between your fingers to be sure that the aroma and flavor are still vivid. Keep dried herbs and spices in tightly closed containers in a cool, dark place (not in a rack over the stove where they'll be exposed to heat and moisture). Here are some of the herbs and spices you'll encounter in this book: allspice, anise seeds, caraway seeds, cardamom, cinnamon, cloves, crushed red pepper, cumin, fennel seeds, ground ginger, nutmeg, mace, oregano, rosemary, thyme. Apple-pie spice and pumpkin-pie spice are blends that you can buy ready made; you can also prepare the same blends yourself, to taste.

Pepper Any recipe that calls for pepper deserves freshly ground pepper, either black or white. Both come from dried berries of the same plant, but white pepper is made from hulled berries. Use a peppermill to grind whole peppercorns as needed, and you'll always enjoy this spice at its flavorful best.

Salt If you've ever tasted bread made without salt, you know what even a pinch of this vital seasoning does for baked goods, and yeast bread needs salt to rise properly. Without a pinch of salt, sweet baked goods can taste flat. When not specified, use *table salt* for the recipes in this book. *Kosher salt*, specified

in some recipes, is much coarser grained. Because of the difference in texture, a teaspoon of one is not equal to a teaspoon of the other.

FLOURS & MEALS

What would baking be without flour? A hot oven and an empty pan! The right kind of flour (bread, cake, whole-wheat) is the key to fine baking, so be sure to use the type specified in the recipe. When you bring flour home from the store, transfer it from the bag or box to a canister or wide-mouth jar with a tight lid. Store flour in a cool place. Whole-grain flours and meals, which contain more fat than refined products, should be stored in the refrigerator or freezer to keep them from becoming rancid (in hot climates, store all flour in the refrigerator). Let flour return to room temperature before using. If the recipe says to sift the flour, do. If not, just stir the flour to aerate it slightly before measuring.

Wheat flour *All-purpose flour* is a blend of soft and hard wheats, giving it a balanced content of protein and starch that works in most recipes. *Cake flour* is made from soft wheat and ground very fine. Low in protein, it produces tender, fine-grained cakes. To substitute all-purpose flour for cake flour, subtract 2 tablespoons all-purpose flour from each cup. Do not substitute self-rising cake flour for plain cake flour. *Bread flour* is made from hard wheat; its higher protein content is needed to support the structure of the dough as it rises. *Semolina* is a coarse-grained flour made from durum wheat, which is very hard. It's used for making pasta and some Italian breads and cakes. *Whole-wheat flour* is made from the entire wheat kernel, with both the bran (outer covering) and germ (protein- and oil-rich nucleus) included.

Buckwheat flour Although its seeds look like grain, buckwheat is not a member of the grain family. The seeds are ground into grayish flour with an assertive flavor. Its most familiar use is in pancakes.

Cornmeal Dried kernels of field corn (different from the sweet corn we eat fresh) are ground into meal for baking. When metal grinders are used, most of the hull and germ are removed, and the meal emerges very smooth but somewhat characterless. Stone-ground cornmeal retains some of the hull and germ and because of that is coarser in texture. It brings a more interesting flavor and texture to baked goods. Yellow and white cornmeal are ground from different varieties of corn. Choosing one or the other will affect only the color of the finished product.

Cornstarch Made from the endosperm (the starchy portion) of the corn kernel, cornstarch is as fine and light as talcum powder. In baking, cornstarch is used in combination with wheat flour for very fine-textured cookies and cakes. It also serves as a thickener for puddings and sauces. If using cornstarch in quantity, sift it before adding it to the other ingredients.

Oatmeal Oats come in several forms. *Steel-cut oats* are whole oat kernels that have been chopped. *Old-fashioned oats* are steamed to soften them, then rolled into flakes. *Quick-cooking oats* are a similar product, but cut into smaller pieces. *Instant oatmeal* is made from the whole oat, but further processed so that it softens immediately when moistened. Old-fashioned and quick-cooking oats are suitable (and interchangeable) for most cookie and bread recipes.

Rye flour The flour of many of Europe's great peasant breads, rye has little gluten in it, so rye flour must be combined with wheat flour or it will be too

sticky to knead and too weak to hold its shape while rising. Rye flour comes in light, medium, and dark grades, depending on how much bran it has.

DRIED FRUIT & NUTS

From moist, spicy cookies studded with bits of pecan and apricot to a fluffy coconut frosting to a sophisticated hazelnut-chocolate cake, there are countless good reasons to keep your baking cupboard stocked with dried fruit and nuts. Buy them in boxes, bags, or in bulk (health-food stores usually have a good selection); store them airtight so they'll stay fresh and delicious longer.

Coconut Grating coconut from a whole nut is quite a project; fortunately, flaked sweetened coconut is sold in bags, ready to use. Refrigerate any leftovers. Unless a recipe calls for fresh coconut, do not substitute it; use the fresh only for garnish.

Dried fruit Joining the classic raisins, dates, currants, figs, dried apricots, and prunes are some tasty newcomers—chewy dried apple, peach, pear, pineapple, and mango as well as sweet dried cherries and tart cranberries. To keep it moist, store dried fruit in tightly closed bags or jars; it will keep longer in the refrigerator. When chopping dried fruit, lightly oil the blade of the knife or kitchen shears, and the fruit won't stick. To soften fruit that has gotten too dry and hard, place it in a shallow bowl, sprinkle with water, cover, and microwave for about 30 seconds.

Nuts & seeds Almonds, walnuts, pecans, macadamias, hazelnuts, and pine nuts—as well as sesame, sunflower, pumpkin, and poppy seeds—are some of the nuts and seeds most used in baking. Rich in fat (some types more than others), they are quite perishable. If the fat turns rancid, the nuts or seeds will have an unpleasant smell rather than their usual rich, toasty fragrance—and you should discard them. Nuts keep longest in the shell; next best is to buy shelled (but not chopped) nuts in airtight containers. Unless you're going to use them immediately, store nuts and seeds in the freezer, in sealed food-storage bags. For optimal flavor, toast nuts and seeds briefly before using. A final tip: When chopping nuts in a food processor or blender, run the machine in very quick pulses and watch carefully, as the nuts can quickly turn from finely chopped to nut butter.

LEAVENINGS

Bakers owe a huge "thank you" to their forebears who discovered and developed techniques for turning a soupy bowl of batter into a lofty cake, or a damp lump of dough into a tender loaf of bread. Yeast has been in use since ancient times, but baking powder dates back only to the mid-nineteenth century. Today, yeast and other leavenings come in convenient, ready-to use forms for nearly foolproof baking. Measure baking powder and baking soda carefully, levelling off the top of the spoon with the back of a knife or a metal spatula.

Baking powder This seemingly magical compound, used in cakes, cookies, and quick breads, works by releasing carbon dioxide gas into the batter. *Double-acting baking powder* is made from baking soda (see right) plus an acid ingredient (in most brands, sodium aluminum sulfate). When mixed with liquid, the baking powder begins to release car-

Easy Christmas Stollen
(page 100)

bon dioxide bubbles, and more is released when the batter is heated in the oven. Fresh baking powder is a must, so keep the container tightly closed—and always "keep your powder dry." To test baking powder for freshness, stir ½ teaspoon into a cup of warm water: It should foam up instantly. If you've had a can of baking powder for longer than a year, discard it and buy a fresh can.

Baking soda The chemical sodium bicarbonate, a base (the opposite of an acid), has long been used as a leavening. It has a single action: When combined with an acidic liquid, such as molasses, buttermilk, or fruit juice (or with a neutral liquid plus an acidic dry ingredient like brown sugar or cocoa powder), it releases carbon dioxide. Once baking soda starts to work, you must get the batter into the oven promptly, before it loses its "fizz." Store an opened box in an airtight container.

Cream of tartar A by-product of winemaking, this fine white powder is a chemical called potassium acid tartrate. It is sometimes added to egg whites while they're being beaten to help stabilize them, which makes them a more effective leavening.

Yeast This bread leavening is a living organism, a one-celled plant that, when encouraged to grow, has the power to puff a ball of dough to many times its original size. To do this, the yeast needs to be combined with liquid at just the right temperature (105° to 115° F), along with some starch to feed on. The yeast takes in the starch, turns it into sugar, releases bubbles of carbon dioxide—and grows. The carbon dioxide, trapped within the structure of the dough, causes it to rise. Cold will quickly stop the action of yeast, so be sure that all ingredients are at room temperature, and find a warm, draft-free place in which to leave the dough to rise. The recipes in this book use *active dry yeast*, which is a granular substance sold in ¼-ounce packages and in jars, and *quick-rise yeast*, sold in packages. Store yeast in the refrigerator, and check the freshness date on the package before you use it. If you're not sure the yeast is still good, stir it into the warm water called for in the recipe, and add a good pinch of sugar. After 5 to 10 minutes, the mixture should be bubbly.

FATS

If you've ever tried to cut down on the fat in a baking recipe, you know that it's no simple trick. That's because butter, oil, shortening, and other fats play several different roles in achieving delicious results. In pastry crust, fat coats particles of the protein in flour; if the dough is mixed properly (so that it's not totally blended), the fat will also separate the layers of dough to create a flaky texture. Fat keeps cookies, cakes, and quick breads soft and moist; traps the air bubbles that make them rise; and in all foods, it acts as a flavor carrier.

Overnight Sticky Buns
(page 152)

Butter The queen of all baking fats, butter brings a rich, sweet flavor to baked goods that nothing else can duplicate. Salted butter has been used in the development of all of the recipes in this book, unless otherwise noted. Some bakers may prefer to use unsalted butter. Butter should be at room temperature if it is to be creamed with sugar or blended into an already-mixed dough; but for flaky pie and tart crusts, butter should be well chilled. Butter will soften more quickly if you cut it into pieces. Be careful not to melt butter in trying to soften it over heat: Once melted—even if it is then chilled—it will not have the same properties for baking. Always keep butter covered in the refrigerator. You can store butter in the freezer for up to six months, but it must be well wrapped, preferably in its original box, over-wrapped with foil, and then placed in a plastic bag.

Margarine Although it looks a lot like butter, even the finest margarine cannot approach butter's taste. If you choose to bake with margarine (many of our recipes suggest it as an acceptable alternative to butter, while a few recipes specify butter only), use a solid stick type, with a fat content of at least 80%, not one that comes in a tub or squeeze bottle. Avoid "diet" margarines, which contain additional water and will greatly affect the outcome of the recipe.

Oil For some recipes, oil is the fat of choice. There are many different vegetable oils available, but for baking the main point is to use a flavorless oil. For most recipes, corn, safflower, sunflower, canola, soybean, and light olive oil are good choices. Like any fat, oil can become rancid, so store it in a cool place—not near the stove. Don't substitute oil for solid shortening in any baking recipes.

Vegetable shortening Made by treating vegetable oil with hydrogen to solidify it and make it stable at room temperature, vegetable shortening has a texture akin to that old-fashioned favorite, lard. Both shortening and lard are pure fat (butter and margarine contain some milk solids), which makes them ideal for pie and tart crusts. Vegetable shortening melts more slowly than butter, so cookies baked with it will be "taller" than those made with butter. Shortening will keep longer and remain fresher if stored in the refrigerator.

SWEETENERS

The pleasing sweetness of our favorite desserts has several sources: It may come from sugar cane, sugar beets, maple trees, or beehives. Each type of sweetener has its own delightful flavor and unique properties that affect the texture—crisp, crunchy, moist, smooth—of baked goods and other desserts.

Corn syrup This liquid sweetener is a thick, barely pourable liquid made from cornstarch. It comes in light (nearly colorless) and dark (clear brown) versions. In baking, corn syrup is used to help breads and cookies retain moisture; it also protects the satiny texture of some frostings and icings by preventing crystallization of sugar.

Honey Beloved for its old-country fragrance and flavor, honey, like all liquid sugars, helps keep baked goods moist. Depending on its source (what kinds of flowers the bees fed on), honey can vary in flavor. Sample a few and find a favorite. Because honey is acidic, baking recipes in which it is used will also include some baking soda to balance the acid.

Maple syrup Not just for pancakes, maple syrup is also a fine sweetener and flavoring for desserts. Be sure to buy pure maple syrup—not "table syrup" or "pancake syrup," which may contain no maple at all. Maple syrup's grade gives you an indication of its flavor, with AA or "Fancy" being the palest in color and most delicate in flavor. If you're a true maple fan, you may want to use a darker (and less expensive) grade, which will have more maple flavor.

Molasses Originally a by-product of sugar refining, the best (unsulfured) molasses is now made by refining boiled-down sugar-cane juice. Molasses is a very thick, brown syrup with a tangy undertone to its sweetness. The lighter the molasses, the milder and sweeter its flavor. Molasses is often used in spicy, old-fashioned desserts such as gingerbread and Indian pudding. Baked goods made with molasses have a tendency to brown quickly, so check them as they bake. Store molasses in a cool place; if too cold to pour, heat the jar of molasses in a pan of warm water.

Sugar There's more to sugar than just sweetness. In baking, sugar helps batters and doughs to rise by allowing more air to be captured as the mixture is beaten. Sugar also helps keep cakes and cookies tender and moist. *Granulated white sugar* is the baking basic; *superfine sugar*, also sold as bar sugar, dissolves more quickly, which is desirable for recipes in which a very smooth texture is desired. *Confectioners' sugar* (also called powdered sugar) is very finely ground and sifted white sugar; it's used for mixtures where a smooth texture is of primary importance, as in uncooked frostings. The designation 10X, often seen on confectioners' sugar, denotes the finest possible texture. A little cornstarch is added to confectioners' sugar to help keep it from lumping; still, the sugar is usually lumpy from being packed tightly in the box, and should be sifted and stirred before use. Many people think that *brown sugar* is somehow more "natural" than white sugar, but it is, in fact, simply granulated white sugar with varying amounts of molasses added to it. Dark brown and light brown sugar are interchangeable in our recipes.

Cookies

Cookies

large cookie sheet

13" by 9" metal baking pan

cookie press

Many great culinary careers begin with cookie baking—one of the easiest and most gratifying kitchen projects, and one "job" for which children readily volunteer. A batch of freshly baked cookies is a supreme crowd-pleaser, and cookies are always welcome in lunchboxes and at snack time. Be sure to keep a stash in the freezer for spur-of-the-moment treats. You don't need a lot of fancy equipment for cookie baking, but proper **cookie sheets** are recommended. These are rimless pans of various dimensions: 15" by 10" is a good size, but get smaller ones if your oven is tiny. Choose heavy-gauge pans, which won't buckle when heated and cooled. Some bakers prefer double-bottomed ("air-cushioned") pans; these do help keep cookies from burning. For baking bar cookies, you'll also need a **13" by 9" baking pan,** as well as an 8" by 8" and a 9" by 9" pan. A pan with square rather than rounded corners is best for cookies. Old-fashioned spritz cookies require a **cookie press,** which consists of a cylinder that you fill with dough, a plunger, and a selection of perforated plates and piping tips for shaping cookies. An assortment of **cookie cutters** lets you bake to suit any season or occasion. They can make a wonderful collection to display and to add decorative cheer to your kitchen.

Previous page: Checkerboard Cookies

Basic techniques

DROP AND SHAPED COOKIES

With practice, you'll become expert at scooping equal-size dollops of dough onto the spoon.

Rolling cookie dough in cinnamon sugar or plain granulated sugar gives the cookies a sparkly, crunchy finish.

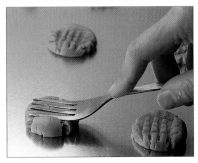

Flattening peanut-butter cookie dough criss-cross with a fork gives the cookies a pretty lattice pattern on the top.

BISCOTTI

Drop the dough by spoonfuls down the length of the cookie sheet. With lightly floured hands, flatten and shape it into a log of even thickness.

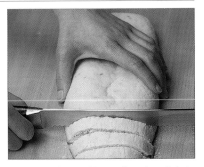

After the first baking, slice the slightly cooled loaf with a serrated knife, using a gentle but confident sawing motion.

ICEBOX COOKIES

Shape the dough roughly into a log shape, then use the waxed paper to roll and smooth it into a cylinder of even thickness.

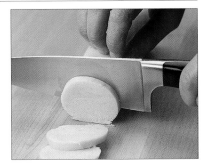

As you slice the log of dough, turn it every few cuts so that the bottom doesn't become flattened.

These are the easiest of cookies to make: Just mix the batter, spread it evenly in a pan, bake, and cut into squares or strips. Fancier bar cookies can have a sweet, short-bread-like base and a nut, fruit, or chocolate topping.

Cheesecake Swirl Brownies

PREP 30 MINUTES / BAKE 35 TO 40 MINUTES

A ribbon of creamy almond cheesecake winds its way through the middle of these super-chocolate brownies.

½ CUP BUTTER OR MARGARINE (1 STICK)
4 SQUARES (4 OUNCES) UNSWEETENED CHOCOLATE
4 SQUARES (4 OUNCES) SEMISWEET CHOCOLATE
2 CUPS SUGAR
5 LARGE EGGS
2½ TEASPOONS VANILLA EXTRACT
1¼ CUPS ALL-PURPOSE FLOUR
¾ TEASPOON BAKING POWDER
½ TEASPOON SALT
1½ PACKAGES (8 OUNCES EACH) CREAM CHEESE, CHILLED
¾ TEASPOON ALMOND EXTRACT

1 Preheat oven to 350° F. Grease 13" by 9" metal baking pan.

2 In 4-quart saucepan, melt butter and unsweetened and semisweet chocolates over low heat, stirring frequently. Remove saucepan from heat. With wooden spoon, beat in 1½ cups sugar. Add 4 eggs and 2 teaspoons vanilla and beat until well blended. Stir in flour, baking powder, and salt.

3 In small bowl, with mixer at medium speed, beat cream cheese until smooth; gradually beat in remaining ½ cup sugar. Beat in almond extract, remaining 1 egg, and remaining ½ teaspoon vanilla just until blended.

4 Spread 1½ cups chocolate batter in prepared pan. Spoon cream-cheese batter in 6 large dollops on top of chocolate mixture (cream-cheese mixture will cover much of chocolate batter). Spoon remaining chocolate batter in 6 large dollops over and between cream-cheese mixture. With tip of knife, cut and twist through mixtures to create marble design.

5 Bake 35 to 40 minutes, until toothpick inserted in center of pan comes out almost clean with a few crumbs attached. Cool completely in pan on wire rack.

6 When cool, cut lengthwise into 4 strips, then cut each strip crosswise into 6 pieces. *Makes 24 brownies.*

EACH BROWNIE: ABOUT 240 CALORIES, 4 G PROTEIN, 26 G CARBOHYDRATE, 14 G TOTAL FAT (8 G SATURATED), 1 G FIBER, 70 MG CHOLESTEROL, 160 MG SODIUM.

Blondies

PREP 10 MINUTES / BAKE 30 MINUTES

Don't ever think that a blondie is just a pale imitation of a brownie: It's a moist, butterscotchy, nut-filled bar cookie that stands on its own merits.

6 TABLESPOONS BUTTER OR MARGARINE
1¾ CUPS PACKED LIGHT BROWN SUGAR
2 TEASPOONS VANILLA EXTRACT
2 LARGE EGGS
1 CUP ALL-PURPOSE FLOUR
2 TEASPOONS BAKING POWDER
1 TEASPOON SALT
1½ CUPS PECANS, COARSELY CHOPPED

1 Preheat oven to 350° F. Grease 13" by 9" metal baking pan.

2 In 3-quart saucepan, melt butter over low heat. Remove saucepan from heat. With wooden spoon, stir in brown sugar and vanilla. Beat in eggs until well blended. In small bowl, combine flour, baking powder, and salt; stir into sugar mixture just until blended. Stir in pecans.

3 Spread batter evenly in prepared pan. Bake 30 minutes, or until toothpick inserted 2 inches from edge of pan comes out clean. Do not overbake; blondies will firm as they cool. Cool completely in pan on wire rack.

4 When cool, cut lengthwise into 4 strips, then cut each strip crosswise into 6 pieces. *Makes 24 blondies.*

EACH BLONDIE: ABOUT 160 CALORIES, 2 G PROTEIN, 21 G CARBOHYDRATE, 8 G TOTAL FAT (2 G SATURATED), 0.5 G FIBER, 25 MG CHOLESTEROL, 180 MG SODIUM.

Cheesecake Swirl Brownies

Midnight Snack Brownies

PREP 15 MINUTES / BAKE 18 TO 22 MINUTES

A few sneaky fat-cutting tricks make these dreamy low-fat mocha bars a reality. Using cocoa instead of solid chocolate makes a big difference; in addition, corn syrup replaces some of the fat, and egg whites take the place of whole eggs. A little butter in the batter ensures rich flavor.

1 TEASPOON INSTANT ESPRESSO-COFFEE POWDER
1 TEASPOON HOT WATER
¾ CUP ALL-PURPOSE FLOUR
½ CUP UNSWEETENED COCOA
½ TEASPOON BAKING POWDER
¼ TEASPOON SALT
3 TABLESPOONS BUTTER OR MARGARINE
¾ CUP SUGAR
¼ CUP DARK CORN SYRUP
1 TEASPOON VANILLA EXTRACT
2 LARGE EGG WHITES

1 Preheat oven to 350º F. Grease 8" by 8" metal baking pan. In cup, dissolve espresso-coffee powder in hot water.

2 In large bowl, with wire whisk, mix flour, cocoa, baking powder, and salt.

3 In 2-quart saucepan, melt butter over low heat. Remove saucepan from heat. With whisk, mix in sugar, corn syrup, vanilla, egg whites, and espresso-coffee mixture until blended. With wooden spoon, stir sugar mixture into flour mixture just until blended. Do not overmix.

4 Pour batter into prepared pan. Bake 18 to 22 minutes, until toothpick inserted in center of pan comes out almost clean. Cool in pan on wire rack at least 1 hour.

5 When cool, cut lengthwise into 4 strips, then cut each strip crosswise into 4 pieces. If brownies are difficult to cut, dip knife in hot water; dry and cut. *Makes 16 brownies.*

EACH BROWNIE: ABOUT 100 CALORIES, 2 G PROTEIN,
19 G CARBOHYDRATE, 3 G TOTAL FAT (2 G SATURATED),
1 G FIBER, 6 MG CHOLESTEROL, 90 MG SODIUM.

Fudgy Brownies

PREP 10 MINUTES / BAKE 30 MINUTES

What a great gift a pan of these brownies makes. Bake the brownies in a foil pan and then wrap the pan in colored cellophane and tie with a ribbon. You can make these well ahead of time and freeze them; in fact, they're delicious straight from the freezer.

¾ CUP BUTTER OR MARGARINE (1½ STICKS)
4 SQUARES (4 OUNCES) UNSWEETENED CHOCOLATE
4 SQUARES (4 OUNCES) SEMISWEET CHOCOLATE
2 CUPS SUGAR
1 TABLESPOON VANILLA EXTRACT
5 LARGE EGGS, BEATEN
1¼ CUPS ALL-PURPOSE FLOUR
½ TEASPOON SALT

1 Preheat oven to 350° F. Grease 13" by 9" metal baking pan.

2 In 3-quart saucepan, melt butter and unsweetened and semisweet chocolates over low heat, stirring frequently. Remove saucepan from heat. With wooden spoon, stir in sugar and vanilla. Beat in eggs until well blended. In small bowl, combine flour and salt; stir into chocolate mixture just until blended.

3 Spread batter evenly in prepared pan. Bake 30 minutes, or until toothpick inserted 1 inch from edge of pan comes out clean. Cool completely in pan on wire rack.

4 When cool, cut lengthwise into 4 strips, then cut each strip crosswise into 6 pieces. *Makes 24 brownies.*

EACH BROWNIE: ABOUT 205 CALORIES, 3 G PROTEIN,
26 G CARBOHYDRATE, 11 G TOTAL FAT (6 G SATURATED),
1 G FIBER, 60 MG CHOLESTEROL, 120 MG SODIUM.

CHOCOLATE MINT BROWNIES Prepare as above but spread half of batter in prepared pan. Sprinkle evenly with *2 boxes (5½ ounces each) miniature chocolate-covered soft mints*; spread remaining batter on top. Bake as directed.
EACH BROWNIE: ABOUT 255 CALORIES, 3 G PROTEIN,
37 G CARBOHYDRATE, 12 G TOTAL FAT (7 G SATURATED),
1.5 G FIBER, 60 MG CHOLESTEROL, 125 MG SODIUM.

Mississippi Mud Bars

PREP 20 MINUTES PLUS COOLING / BAKE 35 MINUTES

Even if you hadn't read the name, the pecans and coconut in this recipe would tip you off to its Southern origins. Mississippi Mud Bars may be the richest, gooiest, most ecstatically excessive chocolate cookies ever devised.

MUD CAKE:

¾ CUP BUTTER OR MARGARINE (1½ STICKS)

1¾ CUPS GRANULATED SUGAR

¾ CUP UNSWEETENED COCOA

4 LARGE EGGS

2 TEASPOONS VANILLA EXTRACT

½ TEASPOON SALT

1½ CUPS ALL-PURPOSE FLOUR

½ CUP PECANS, CHOPPED

½ CUP FLAKED SWEETENED COCONUT

3 CUPS MINI MARSHMALLOWS

FUDGE TOPPING:

5 TABLESPOONS BUTTER OR MARGARINE

1 SQUARE (1 OUNCE) UNSWEETENED CHOCOLATE

⅓ CUP UNSWEETENED COCOA

⅛ TEASPOON SALT

¼ CUP EVAPORATED MILK (NOT SWEETENED CONDENSED MILK) OR HEAVY OR WHIPPING CREAM

1 TEASPOON VANILLA EXTRACT

1 CUP CONFECTIONERS' SUGAR

½ CUP PECANS, COARSELY BROKEN

¼ CUP FLAKED SWEETENED COCONUT

1 Preheat oven to 350° F. Grease and flour 13" by 9" metal baking pan.

2 Prepare Mud Cake: In 3-quart saucepan, melt butter over low heat, stirring occasionally. With wire whisk, beat in granulated sugar and cocoa. Remove saucepan from heat. Beat in eggs, 1 at a time, vanilla, and salt until well blended. With wooden spoon, stir in flour just until blended. Stir in pecans and coconut (batter will be thick).

3 Spread batter in prepared pan. Bake 25 minutes. Remove pan from oven. Sprinkle marshmallows in even layer on top of cake. Return cake to oven and bake 10 minutes, or until marshmallows are puffed and golden. Cool completely in pan on wire rack.

4 When cake is cool, prepare Fudge Topping: In 2-quart saucepan, heat butter and chocolate over low heat, stirring constantly, until mixture melts. With wire whisk, beat in cocoa and salt until smooth. Beat in evaporated milk and vanilla (mixture will be thick). Beat in confectioners' sugar until smooth and blended.

5 Pour hot topping over cooled cake. Cool 20 minutes; sprinkle pecans and coconut on top.

6 To serve, cut lengthwise into 4 strips, then cut each strip crosswise into 8 pieces. *Makes 32 bars.*

EACH BAR: ABOUT 205 CALORIES, 3 G PROTEIN, 26 G CARBOHYDRATE, 11 G TOTAL FAT (5 G SATURATED), 1 G FIBER, 44 MG CHOLESTEROL, 125 MG SODIUM.

Cocoa Brownies

PREP 10 MINUTES / BAKE 25 MINUTES

These one-bowl brownies are made with pantry staples. If you don't have walnuts, use any other nuts that are on hand. Salted peanuts are wonderful in brownies.

½ CUP BUTTER OR MARGARINE (1 STICK)

1 CUP SUGAR

2 LARGE EGGS

1 TEASPOON VANILLA EXTRACT

½ CUP ALL-PURPOSE FLOUR

½ CUP UNSWEETENED COCOA

¼ TEASPOON BAKING POWDER

¼ TEASPOON SALT

1 CUP COARSELY CHOPPED WALNUTS (OPTIONAL)

1 Preheat oven to 350° F. Grease 9" by 9" metal baking pan.

2 In 3-quart saucepan, melt butter over low heat. Remove saucepan from heat. With wooden spoon, stir in sugar. Stir in eggs, 1 at a time, and vanilla until well blended. In medium bowl, combine flour, cocoa, baking powder, and salt; stir flour mixture into saucepan until blended. Stir in nuts, if you like.

3 Spread batter evenly in prepared pan. Bake 25 minutes, or until toothpick inserted 2 inches from center of pan comes out almost clean. Cool completely in pan on wire rack.

4 When cool, cut into 4 strips, then cut each strip crosswise into 4 pieces. *Makes 16 brownies.*

EACH BROWNIE WITHOUT NUTS: ABOUT 130 CALORIES, 2 G PROTEIN, 17 G CARBOHYDRATE, 7 G TOTAL FAT (4 G SATURATED), 1 G FIBER, 42 MG CHOLESTEROL, 110 MG SODIUM.

Macadamia Triangles

PREP 15 MINUTES PLUS COOLING
BAKE 35 TO 40 MINUTES

Macadamias are the most luxurious of nuts, and they're worth every penny of their rather high price.

SWEET PASTRY CRUST:

1 CUP ALL-PURPOSE FLOUR
¼ CUP GRANULATED SUGAR
⅛ TEASPOON SALT
6 TABLESPOONS COLD BUTTER OR MARGARINE
3 TABLESPOONS COLD WATER

MACADAMIA FILLING:

1 JAR (7 OUNCES) MACADAMIA NUTS
⅔ CUP PACKED LIGHT BROWN SUGAR
1 LARGE EGG
2 TEASPOONS VANILLA EXTRACT

1 Preheat oven to 425° F. Grease 9" by 9" metal baking pan. Line pan with foil; grease foil.

2 Prepare Sweet Pastry Crust: In medium bowl, combine flour, sugar, and salt. With pastry blender or 2 knives used scissor-fashion, cut in butter until mixture resembles coarse crumbs. Sprinkle water, about 1 tablespoon at a time, into flour mixture, mixing lightly with fork after each addition until dough is just moist enough to hold together.

3 With lightly floured hand, press dough evenly into bottom of prepared pan. With fork, prick dough in 1-inch intervals to prevent puffing and shrinking during baking. Bake crust 15 to 20 minutes, until golden (crust may crack slightly during baking). Cool completely in pan on wire rack. Turn oven off.

4 Prepare Macadamia Filling: Preheat oven to 375° F. Coarsely chop ½ cup macadamia nuts.

5 In food processor with knife blade attached, process remaining macadamia nuts with brown sugar until nuts are finely ground.

6 In medium bowl, with spoon, combine ground macadamia mixture with egg and vanilla. With small spatula, spread macadamia filling evenly over crust. Sprinkle reserved chopped macadamia nuts on top. Bake 20 minutes, or until filling is set. Cool completely in pan on wire rack.

7 When cool, transfer with foil to cutting board. Cut into 4 strips, then cut each strip crosswise into 4 squares. Cut each square diagonally in half. *Makes 32 triangles.*

EACH TRIANGLE: ABOUT 105 CALORIES, 1 G PROTEIN, 10 G CARBOHYDRATE, 7 G TOTAL FAT (2 G SATURATED), 0 G FIBER, 12 MG CHOLESTEROL, 35 MG SODIUM.

PECAN TRIANGLES Prepare dough as for Macadamia Triangles but use *2 cups pecans* for macadamia nuts. Bake as directed.
EACH TRIANGLE: ABOUT 105 CALORIES, 1 G PROTEIN, 10 G CARBOHYDRATE, 7 G TOTAL FAT (2 G SATURATED), 0.5 G FIBER, 12 MG CHOLESTEROL, 35 MG SODIUM.

Jam Crumble Bars

PREP 15 MINUTES
BAKE 40 TO 45 MINUTES

The food processor does most of the work here, mixing the dough that serves as both the base and topping. Experiment with your favorite jam flavors.

1¼ CUPS ALL-PURPOSE FLOUR
½ CUP PACKED LIGHT BROWN SUGAR
¼ TEASPOON BAKING SODA
¼ TEASPOON GROUND CINNAMON
½ CUP COLD BUTTER OR MARGARINE (1 STICK), CUT INTO 8 PIECES
½ CUP JAM (RASPBERRY, BLACKBERRY, OR OTHER FRUIT)
¼ CUP PECANS, CHOPPED

1 Preheat oven to 350° F. In food processor with knife blade attached, process flour, brown sugar, baking soda, and cinnamon until blended. Add butter and process until mixture resembles coarse crumbs and, when pressed, holds together. Remove ½ cup dough to small bowl and stir in pecans.

2 Press remaining dough firmly into bottom of ungreased 9" by 9" metal baking pan. Spread with jam up to ¼ inch from edges. With fingers, crumble reserved nut mixture over jam.

3 Bake 40 to 45 minutes, until browned at edges and on top. Cool completely in pan on wire rack.

4 When cool, cut into 4 strips; then cut each strip crosswise into 4 pieces. *Makes 16 bars.*

EACH BAR: ABOUT 150 CALORIES, 1 G PROTEIN, 21 G CARBOHYDRATE, 7 G TOTAL FAT (4 G SATURATED), 0 G FIBER, 16 MG CHOLESTEROL, 85 MG SODIUM.

Macadamia Triangles

Malted Milk Bars

PREP 15 MINUTES / BAKE 25 TO 30 MINUTES

Milkshake fans will adore these superlative bars. The frosting is made with malted milk powder and sprinkled with chopped malted milk balls.

CHOCOLATE BASE:

¾ CUP BUTTER OR MARGARINE (1½ STICKS)

4 SQUARES (4 OUNCES) SEMISWEET CHOCOLATE

2 SQUARES (2 OUNCES) UNSWEETENED CHOCOLATE

1½ CUPS GRANULATED SUGAR

1 TABLESPOON VANILLA EXTRACT

4 LARGE EGGS, BEATEN

1½ CUPS ALL-PURPOSE FLOUR

½ TEASPOON BAKING POWDER

½ TEASPOON SALT

MALTED MILK TOPPING:

¾ CUP MALTED MILK POWDER

3 TABLESPOONS MILK

1 TEASPOON VANILLA EXTRACT

3 TABLESPOONS BUTTER OR MARGARINE, SOFTENED

1 CUP CONFECTIONERS' SUGAR

1½ CUPS MALTED MILK BALL CANDIES (ABOUT 5 OUNCES), COARSELY CHOPPED

1 Preheat oven to 350° F. Grease 13" by 9" metal baking pan. Line pan with foil, extending it over short ends; grease foil.

2 Prepare Chocolate Base: In heavy 3-quart saucepan, melt butter and semisweet and unsweetened chocolates over low heat, stirring frequently. Remove saucepan from heat. With wooden spoon, stir in granulated sugar and vanilla. Beat in eggs until well blended. In small bowl, combine flour, baking powder, and salt; stir into chocolate mixture.

3 Spread batter evenly in prepared pan. Bake 25 to 30 minutes, until toothpick inserted 1 inch from edge of pan comes out clean. Cool in pan on wire rack.

4 Prepare Malted Milk Topping: In small bowl, stir together malted milk powder, milk, and vanilla until blended. Stir in butter and confectioners' sugar until blended. With small spatula, spread topping over cooled bars; top with chopped malted milk ball candies. Allow topping to set.

5 When topping is firm, transfer with foil to cutting board. Cut lengthwise into 4 strips, then cut each strip crosswise into 8 pieces. *Makes 32 bars.*

EACH BAR: ABOUT 200 CALORIES, 3 G PROTEIN, 27 G CARBOHYDRATE, 10 G TOTAL FAT (5 G SATURATED), 0.5 G FIBER, 42 MG CHOLESTEROL, 155 MG SODIUM.

Malted Milk Bars

Fig & Prune Bars

PREP **45** MINUTES PLUS CHILLING AND COOLING
BAKE **40** MINUTES

An elegant take on the storebought fig cookie, these lattice-topped bars offer a lovely contrast between dark, fruity filling and a buttery sugar-cookie crust. Calimyrna figs are the California-grown version of Turkish Smyrna figs. Small and golden-skinned, dried Calimyrna figs are widely available.

PAT-IN-PAN CRUST FOR 9-INCH TART (PAGE 209)
1 PACKAGE (10 OUNCES) CALIMYRNA FIGS
1 CUP PITTED PRUNES
⅓ CUP PACKED DARK BROWN SUGAR
1 CUP WATER
2 TABLESPOONS FRESH LEMON JUICE

1 Prepare dough as directed. Wrap smaller disk in plastic wrap and refrigerate. Grease 13" by 9" metal baking pan. Line pan with foil, extending it over short ends; grease foil. With fingertips, press remaining dough into bottom of prepared pan.

2 Meanwhile, with kitchen shears, cut stems from figs. In 2-quart saucepan, cook figs, prunes, brown sugar, and water over medium heat until mixture thickens and most of liquid has been absorbed, stirring occasionally, about 10 minutes.

3 Transfer warm fig mixture to food processor with knife blade attached; add lemon juice; process until almost smooth. Spoon fig mixture into bowl; refrigerate until cool, about 20 minutes.

4 Preheat oven to 375° F. Remove dough and filling from refrigerator. With small metal spatula, spread cooled filling evenly over dough. On lightly floured surface, cut remaining dough into 20 pieces. Gently roll pieces into ¼-inch-wide ropes (lengths will vary). Place 10 ropes diagonally across filling, about 1 inch apart; trim ends if necessary. Repeat with remaining 10 ropes, placing them at right angles. (If ropes break, press dough together.) Bake 40 minutes, or until crust is golden. Cool completely in pan on wire rack.

5 When cool, transfer with foil to cutting board. Cut lengthwise into 4 strips, then cut each strip crosswise into 6 pieces. *Makes 24 bars.*

EACH BAR: ABOUT 165 CALORIES, 2 G PROTEIN, 26 G CARBOHYDRATE, 6 G TOTAL FAT (4 G SATURATED), 2 G FIBER, 24 MG CHOLESTEROL, 90 MG SODIUM.

Apricot Bar Cookies

PREP **35** MINUTES PLUS COOLING / BAKE **40** MINUTES

APRICOT FILLING:
1½ CUPS DRIED APRICOTS (12 OUNCES)
1½ CUPS WATER
¼ CUP GRANULATED SUGAR

SHORTBREAD CRUST:
¾ CUP BUTTER OR MARGARINE (1½ STICKS), SOFTENED
½ CUP CONFECTIONERS' SUGAR
½ TEASPOON VANILLA EXTRACT
2 CUPS ALL-PURPOSE FLOUR

STREUSEL:
½ CUP OLD-FASHIONED OR QUICK-COOKING OATS,
    UNCOOKED
½ CUP PACKED LIGHT BROWN SUGAR
⅓ CUP ALL-PURPOSE FLOUR
4 TABLESPOONS BUTTER OR MARGARINE

1 Prepare Apricot Filling: In 1-quart saucepan, combine apricots and water. Heat to boiling over medium heat; reduce heat and simmer, covered, 25 minutes, or until tender (some water will remain). With wooden spoon or potato masher, mash until smooth. Stir in granulated sugar; cool to room temperature.

2 Prepare Shortbread Crust: Preheat oven to 375° F. Line 13" by 9" metal baking pan with foil, extending it over short ends. In large bowl, with mixer at medium speed, beat butter and confectioners' sugar until light and fluffy. Beat in vanilla. Stir in flour until well combined. With hand, pat dough firmly into bottom of prepared pan. Bake 15 minutes, or until golden brown and set. Cool to room temperature on wire rack.

3 Prepare Streusel: In medium bowl, stir together oats, brown sugar, and flour. With fingertips, mix in butter until mixture resembles coarse crumbs.

4 Spread cooled filling over crust. Scatter streusel on top. Bake 25 minutes, or until streusel is set. Cool completely in pan on wire rack.

5 When cool, transfer with foil to cutting board; peel foil from sides. Cut lengthwise into 5 strips, then cut each strip crosswise into 8 pieces. *Makes 40 bars.*

EACH BAR: ABOUT 110 CALORIES, 1 G PROTEIN, 17 G CARBOHYDRATE, 5 G TOTAL FAT (3 G SATURATED), 1 G FIBER, 12 MG CHOLESTEROL, 50 MG SODIUM.

Chocolate Pecan Bars

PREP 25 MINUTES / BAKE 45 TO 50 MINUTES

If you have the extra time, toast the pecans in the oven for 5 to 10 minutes; cool before using.

CRUST:

¾ CUP BUTTER OR MARGARINE (1½ STICKS), SOFTENED

½ CUP CONFECTIONERS' SUGAR

2 CUPS ALL-PURPOSE FLOUR

FILLING:

2 SQUARES (2 OUNCES) SEMISWEET CHOCOLATE

2 SQUARES (2 OUNCES) UNSWEETENED CHOCOLATE

2 TABLESPOONS BUTTER OR MARGARINE

⅔ CUP PACKED LIGHT BROWN SUGAR

⅔ CUP DARK CORN SYRUP

3 LARGE EGGS, LIGHTLY BEATEN

1 TEASPOON VANILLA EXTRACT

1½ CUPS PECANS, COARSELY CHOPPED

1 Preheat oven to 350° F. Line 13" by 9" metal baking pan with foil, extending it over short ends.

2 Prepare Crust: In medium bowl, with mixer at medium speed, beat butter and confectioners' sugar until combined. Reduce speed to low and beat in flour until combined. With lightly floured hand, press dough into bottom and 1 inch up side of prepared pan. Line pan with foil and fill with pie weights, dry beans, or uncooked rice. Bake 15 to 20 minutes, until lightly golden. Cool to room temperature on wire rack; remove foil and weights.

3 Meanwhile, prepare Filling: In 3-quart saucepan, melt semisweet and unsweetened chocolates and butter over very low heat. Cool to lukewarm. With rubber spatula, stir in brown sugar and corn syrup until smooth. Stir in eggs, vanilla, and pecans.

4 Pour filling over baked crust. Bake 30 minutes, or until set. Cool completely in pan on wire rack.

5 When cool, transfer with foil to cutting board. Cut lengthwise into 4 strips, then cut each strip crosswise into 8 pieces. *Makes 32 bars.*

EACH BAR: ABOUT 175 CALORIES, 2 G PROTEIN, 20 G CARBOHYDRATE, 10 G TOTAL FAT (4 G SATURATED), 1 G FIBER, 34 MG CHOLESTEROL, 70 MG SODIUM.

Fresh Lemon Bars

Fresh Lemon Bars

PREP 15 MINUTES
BAKE 30 TO 32 MINUTES

A lot of people call lemon bars (also known as lemon squares) "my specialty" and whip them up at the drop of a hat for coffee klatsches, bake sales, and potluck suppers. Try this recipe just once and you may join their ranks.

1½ CUPS PLUS 3 TABLESPOONS ALL-PURPOSE FLOUR
½ CUP PLUS 1 TABLESPOON CONFECTIONERS' SUGAR
¾ CUP COLD BUTTER OR MARGARINE (1½ STICKS), CUT
INTO SMALL PIECES
2 LARGE LEMONS
3 LARGE EGGS
1 CUP GRANULATED SUGAR
½ TEASPOON BAKING POWDER
½ TEASPOON SALT

1 Preheat oven to 350° F. Line 13" by 9" metal baking pan with foil, extending it over short ends; lightly grease foil.

2 In medium bowl, combine 1½ cups flour and ½ cup confectioners' sugar. With pastry blender or 2 knives used scissor-fashion, cut in butter until mixture resembles coarse crumbs.

3 Sprinkle dough evenly into prepared pan. With floured hand, pat dough firmly into bottom. Bake 15 to 17 minutes, until lightly browned.

4 Meanwhile, from lemons, grate 1 teaspoon and squeeze ⅓ cup juice. In large bowl, with mixer at high speed, beat eggs until thick and lemon-colored, about 3 minutes. Reduce speed to low; add lemon peel and juice, granulated sugar, baking powder, salt, and remaining 3 tablespoons flour, and beat until blended, scraping bowl occasionally.

5 Pour lemon filling over warm crust. Bake 15 minutes, or until filling is just set and golden around edges. Transfer pan to wire rack. Sift remaining 1 tablespoon confectioners' sugar over warm filling. Cool completely in pan on wire rack.

6 When cool, transfer with foil to cutting board. Cut lengthwise into 3 strips, then cut each strip crosswise into 12 pieces. *Makes 36 bars.*

EACH BAR: ABOUT 95 CALORIES, 1 G PROTEIN,
12 G CARBOHYDRATE, 4 G TOTAL FAT (3 G SATURATED),
0 G FIBER, 28 MG CHOLESTEROL, 85 MG SODIUM.

Peanut Butter Bar Cookies

PREP 15 MINUTES / BAKE 30 MINUTES

Put on the coffeepot, pour the milk, and get ready for a serious treat. Good as these cookies are just as they come from the oven, you may want to dress them up with a drizzle of chocolate. Use your favorite—milk, dark sweet, or semisweet chocolate. See the variation below for how to do it.

2¼ CUPS ALL-PURPOSE FLOUR
1 TEASPOON BAKING POWDER
⅛ TEASPOON SALT
1 CUP CHUNKY OR CREAMY PEANUT BUTTER
½ CUP BUTTER OR MARGARINE (1 STICK), SOFTENED
1 CUP PACKED DARK BROWN SUGAR
½ CUP GRANULATED SUGAR
1 TEASPOON VANILLA EXTRACT
⅛ TEASPOON ALMOND EXTRACT
2 LARGE EGGS

1 Preheat oven to 350° F. Grease 13" by 9" metal baking pan.

2 In medium bowl, stir together flour, baking powder, and salt.

3 In large bowl, with mixer at medium speed, beat peanut butter, butter, and brown and granulated sugars until light and fluffy. Beat in vanilla and almond extracts. Beat in eggs, 1 at a time, beating well after each addition. Reduce speed to low and beat in flour mixture until well combined.

4 Scrape batter into prepared pan. Bake 30 minutes, or until toothpick inserted in center of pan comes out clean. Cool completely in pan on wire rack.

5 When cool, cut lengthwise into 5 strips, then cut each strip crosswise into 8 pieces. *Makes 40 bars.*

EACH BAR: ABOUT 120 CALORIES, 3 G PROTEIN,
15 G CARBOHYDRATE, 6 G TOTAL FAT (2 G SATURATED),
1 G FIBER, 17 MG CHOLESTEROL, 80 MG SODIUM.

CHOCOLATE-TOPPED PEANUT BUTTER BARS Prepare as above but drizzle *2 ounces chocolate,* melted, over baked cake. Allow chocolate to set before cutting into bars.

EACH BAR: ABOUT 125 CALORIES, 3 G PROTEIN,
16 G CARBOHYDRATE, 6 G TOTAL FAT (2 G SATURATED),
1 G FIBER, 17 MG CHOLESTEROL, 80 MG SODIUM.

Lemon-Ginger Shortbread Bars

PREP 20 MINUTES PLUS COOLING
BAKE 30 TO 35 MINUTES

In contrast to the velvety smoothness of the Scottish Shortbread at right, these citrus-glazed bars are slightly crunchy because they're made with cornmeal. Shopping tip: If you can buy crystallized ginger in bulk (rather than from the spice rack), it is much cheaper.

1 LEMON
¾ CUP BUTTER OR MARGARINE (1½ STICKS), SOFTENED
¾ CUP GRANULATED SUGAR
2 CUPS ALL-PURPOSE FLOUR
⅓ CUP YELLOW CORNMEAL
1 JAR (2.7 OUNCES) CRYSTALLIZED GINGER, CHOPPED
   (½ CUP)
¼ TEASPOON SALT
1 LARGE EGG
¾ CUP CONFECTIONERS' SUGAR

1 Preheat oven to 350° F. Grease 13" by 9" metal baking pan. Line pan with foil, extending it over short ends; grease foil.

2 From lemon, grate ½ teaspoon peel and squeeze 3 tablespoons juice.

3 In large bowl, with mixer at low speed, beat butter, granulated sugar, and lemon peel until blended. Increase speed to high; beat until light and fluffy

about 2 minutes. Reduce speed to low and beat in flour, cornmeal, ginger, salt, and egg just until blended (mixture will be crumbly).

4 Sprinkle dough evenly into prepared pan. With hand, pat firmly into bottom. Bake 30 to 35 minutes, until golden around edges and toothpick inserted in center of pan comes out clean. Cool completely in pan on wire rack.

5 When shortbread is cool, in small bowl, with wire whisk or fork, mix lemon juice and confectioners' sugar until blended. Pour glaze over shortbread and, with small metal spatula, spread in even layer. Allow glaze to set, about 1 hour.

6 When glaze has set, transfer with foil to cutting board. Cut lengthwise into 4 strips, then cut each strip crosswise into 6 pieces. Cut each piece diagonally in half. *Makes 48 triangles.*

EACH TRIANGLE: ABOUT 75 CALORIES, 1 G PROTEIN,
11 G CARBOHYDRATE, 3 G TOTAL FAT (2 G SATURATED),
0 G FIBER, 12 MG CHOLESTEROL, 45 MG SODIUM.

Scottish Shortbread

PREP 20 MINUTES / BAKE 40 MINUTES

Shortbread recipes sometimes include some rice flour to give them the finest possible texture. As rice flour is not widely available, we use cake flour for a similar result. The predominant flavor in shortbread is butter, so be sure to use only fresh, sweet butter.

1½ CUPS CAKE FLOUR (NOT SELF-RISING)
1½ CUPS ALL-PURPOSE FLOUR
½ CUP SUGAR
¼ TEASPOON SALT
1½ CUPS BUTTER (3 STICKS), CUT UP AND SOFTENED

1 Preheat oven to 325° F.

2 In large bowl, combine cake and all-purpose flours, sugar, and salt. Knead butter into flour mixture until well blended and dough holds together. (Or, in food processor with knife blade attached, pulse cake and all-purpose flours and salt to blend. Add butter and pulse until mixture resembles coarse crumbs.) Divide dough in half.

3 With hand, pat each dough half evenly into bottom of ungreased 8-inch round cake pan. With fork,

---

SHAPELY SHORTBREAD

SHORTBREAD IS SOMETIMES FORMED USING A MOLD THAT SHAPES THE DOUGH AND CREATES RAISED PATTERNS ON ITS SURFACE. THE DOUGH IS PACKED INTO THE MOLD, WHICH LOOKS LIKE A THICK WOODEN PLATE WITH FLUTINGS AND DESIGNS CARVED DEEPLY INTO ITS INNER SURFACE. SINCE SHORTBREAD IS A SCOTTISH SPECIALTY, YOU'LL OFTEN SEE THESE ATTRACTIVE MOLDS DECORATED WITH A THISTLE MOTIF.

prick dough all over to make attractive pattern. Bake 40 minutes, or until golden. Transfer pans to wire racks; immediately run thin knife around edge of pans to loosen shortbread, and cut each round into 16 wedges. Cool completely in pans on wire racks.

4 When cool, carefully remove wedges from pans. *Makes 32 wedges.*

EACH WEDGE: ABOUT 130 CALORIES, 1 G PROTEIN, 12 G CARBOHYDRATE, 9 G TOTAL FAT (5 G SATURATED), 0 G FIBER, 23 MG CHOLESTEROL, 105 MG SODIUM.

Brown Sugar-Pecan Shortbread

PREP 20 MINUTES / BAKE 23 TO 25 MINUTES

Nut-topped shortbread makes a nifty holiday gift when packed in a pretty tin (it keeps well that way, too).

¾ CUP BUTTER OR MARGARINE (1½ STICKS), SOFTENED
⅓ CUP PACKED DARK BROWN SUGAR
3 TABLESPOONS GRANULATED SUGAR
1 TEASPOON VANILLA EXTRACT
1¾ CUPS ALL-PURPOSE FLOUR
1 CUP PECANS, CHOPPED

1 Preheat oven to 350° F.

2 In large bowl, with mixer at medium-low speed, beat butter, brown and granulated sugars, and vanilla until creamy. Reduce speed to low and beat in flour until blended (dough will be crumbly). With wooden spoon, stir dough until it holds together. Divide dough in half.

3 With hand, pat each dough half evenly into bottom of ungreased 8-inch round cake pan. Sprinkle with pecans; press lightly. Bake 23 to 25 minutes, until lightly browned at edges and firm in center. Transfer pans to wire racks. With small sharp knife, cut each round into 12 wedges. Cool completely in pans on wire racks. *Makes 24 wedges.*

EACH WEDGE: ABOUT 130 CALORIES, 1 G PROTEIN, 12 G CARBOHYDRATE, 9 G TOTAL FAT (4 G SATURATED), 0.5 G FIBER, 16 MG CHOLESTEROL, 60 MG SODIUM.

DROP COOKIES

It's always fun to watch little mounds of drop-cookie dough as they spread or puff or flatten or crisp (depending on the recipe) in the oven. Making drop cookies is a snap, but keep a few pointers in mind. A sheet of cookies will bake more evenly if they're all about equal size. Be sure the cookie sheets are cool when you drop the dough onto them; if they're warm, the dough may spread too quickly and the cookies will be flat. If necessary, cool the sheets between batches by running cool water over the bottoms.

Brown Sugar Drop Cookies

PREP 30 MINUTES / BAKE 10 MINUTES PER BATCH

1½ CUPS ALL-PURPOSE FLOUR
½ TEASPOON BAKING SODA
½ TEASPOON BAKING POWDER
¼ TEASPOON SALT
⅛ TEASPOON GROUND NUTMEG
¾ CUP BUTTER (1½ STICKS), CUT UP
1 CUP PACKED LIGHT BROWN SUGAR
2 LARGE EGGS
1½ TEASPOONS VANILLA EXTRACT

1 Preheat oven to 350° F. Grease and flour 2 large cookie sheets. On sheet of waxed paper, stir together flour, baking soda, baking powder, salt, and nutmeg.

2 In 3-quart saucepan, heat butter and brown sugar to boiling over low heat, stirring. Remove saucepan from heat. Stir in flour mixture, eggs, and vanilla until combined. Set pan in skillet of warm water.

3 Drop dough by rounded teaspoons, 1 inch apart, on prepared cookie sheets. Bake 10 minutes, rotating sheets between upper and lower racks halfway through baking, or until edges are browned and centers are set. Cool 1 minute on cookie sheets. With wide spatula, transfer cookies to wire racks to cool completely.

4 Repeat with remaining cookie dough. *Makes about 5 dozen cookies.*

EACH COOKIE: ABOUT 50 CALORIES, 1 G PROTEIN, 6 G CARBOHYDRATE, 3 G TOTAL FAT (2 G SATURATED), 0 G FIBER, 13 MG CHOLESTEROL, 50 MG SODIUM.

Chocolate Chip Cookies

PREP 15 MINUTES / BAKE 10 TO 12 MINUTES PER BATCH

In addition to the variation given below, there are all sorts of possibilities: milk-chocolate, mint-chocolate, or peanut-butter chips, or coarsely chopped chocolate bars; pecans, hazelnuts, peanuts, or almonds. It's up to you!

1¼ CUPS ALL-PURPOSE FLOUR
½ TEASPOON BAKING SODA
½ TEASPOON SALT
½ CUP BUTTER OR MARGARINE (1 STICK), SOFTENED
½ CUP PACKED LIGHT BROWN SUGAR
¼ CUP GRANULATED SUGAR
1 LARGE EGG
1 TEASPOON VANILLA EXTRACT
1 PACKAGE (6 OUNCES) SEMISWEET CHOCOLATE CHIPS
   (1 CUP)
½ CUP WALNUTS, CHOPPED (OPTIONAL)

1 Preheat oven to 375° F. On sheet of waxed paper, combine flour, baking soda, and salt.

2 In large bowl, with mixer at medium speed, beat butter and brown and granulated sugars until light and creamy. Beat in egg and vanilla until well combined. Reduce speed to low; beat in flour mixture until blended. With spoon, stir in chocolate pieces and walnuts, if you like.

3 Drop dough by rounded tablespoons, 2 inches apart, on ungreased large cookie sheet. Bake 10 to 12 minutes, until edges are golden. With wide spatula, transfer cookies to wire racks to cool completely.

4 Repeat with remaining cookie dough. *Makes about 3 dozen cookies.*

EACH COOKIE WITHOUT WALNUTS: ABOUT 80 CALORIES, 1 G PROTEIN, 11 G CARBOHYDRATE, 4 G TOTAL FAT (2 G SATURATED), 0.5 G FIBER, 13 MG CHOLESTEROL, 80 MG SODIUM.

WHITE CHOCOLATE-MACADAMIA COOKIES Prepare as above but use *¾ cup white chocolate chips* for semisweet chocolate chips and *1 cup macadamia nuts,* chopped, for walnuts. Bake as directed.
EACH COOKIE: ABOUT 110 CALORIES, 1 G PROTEIN, 11 G CARBOHYDRATE, 7 G TOTAL FAT (3 G SATURATED), 0 G FIBER, 13 MG CHOLESTEROL, 85 MG SODIUM.

Whoopie Pies

PREP 30 MINUTES PLUS COOLING
BAKE 12 TO 14 MINUTES

Two pillowy devil's-food cookies enclosing a cloudlike marshmallow filling—it's a child's dream of a cookie, but you'll no doubt find them quite tasty, too.

COOKIE DOUGH:

2 CUPS ALL-PURPOSE FLOUR
1 CUP SUGAR
¾ CUP MILK
½ CUP UNSWEETENED COCOA
6 TABLESPOONS BUTTER OR MARGARINE, MELTED
1 TEASPOON BAKING SODA
1 TEASPOON VANILLA EXTRACT
¼ TEASPOON SALT
1 LARGE EGG

MARSHMALLOW CREME FILLING:

6 TABLESPOONS BUTTER OR MARGARINE, SLIGHTLY
   SOFTENED
1 CUP CONFECTIONERS' SUGAR
1 JAR (7 TO 7½ OUNCES) MARSHMALLOW CREME
1 TEASPOON VANILLA EXTRACT

1 Preheat oven to 350° F. Grease 2 large cookie sheets.

2 Prepare Cookie Dough: In large bowl, with spoon, mix all dough ingredients until smooth.

3 Drop dough by heaping tablespoons, 2 inches apart, on each prepared cookie sheet. (There will be 12 rounds per sheet.)

4 Bake 12 to 14 minutes, rotating sheets between upper and lower racks halfway through baking, until puffy and toothpick inserted in center comes out clean. With wide spatula, transfer cookies to wire racks to cool completely.

5 When cool, prepare Marshmallow Creme Filling: In large bowl, with mixer at medium speed, beat butter until smooth. Reduce speed to low; gradually beat in confectioners' sugar. Beat in marshmallow creme and vanilla until smooth.

6 Spread 1 rounded tablespoon filling on flat side of 12 cookies. Top with remaining cookies. *Makes 12 whoopie pies.*

EACH WHOOPIE PIE: ABOUT 365 CALORIES, 4 G PROTEIN, 59 G CARBOHYDRATE, 14 G TOTAL FAT (8 G SATURATED), 1.5 G FIBER, 51 MG CHOLESTEROL, 290 MG SODIUM.

Whoopie Pies

Chewy Molasses Spice Cookies

PREP 15 MINUTES / BAKE 13 TO 15 MINUTES PER BATCH

What are ground mustard and black pepper doing in a cookie recipe? Time-honored ingredients in German and Scandinavian recipes for gingerbread and spice cookies, these seasonings add a lively "hotness" that plays against the sweetness.

2 CUPS ALL-PURPOSE FLOUR

1½ TEASPOONS BAKING SODA

1 TEASPOON GROUND GINGER

½ TEASPOON GROUND CINNAMON

¼ TEASPOON SALT

¼ TEASPOON FINELY GROUND BLACK PEPPER

⅛ TEASPOON GROUND CLOVES

⅛ TEASPOON GROUND MUSTARD

½ CUP BUTTER OR MARGARINE (1 STICK), SOFTENED

¾ CUP PACKED DARK BROWN SUGAR

½ CUP LIGHT (MILD) MOLASSES

1 LARGE EGG

1 TEASPOON VANILLA EXTRACT

1 Preheat oven to 350° F. On sheet of waxed paper, stir together flour, baking soda, ginger, cinnamon, salt, pepper, cloves, and mustard.

2 In large bowl, with mixer at medium speed, beat butter and brown sugar until smooth. Beat in molasses until combined. Reduce speed to low; beat in egg and vanilla until blended. Beat in flour mixture until combined, scraping bowl occasionally with rubber spatula.

3 Drop dough by rounded tablespoons, 3 inches apart, on ungreased large cookie sheet. Bake cookies 13 to 15 minutes, until flattened and evenly browned. Cool on cookie sheet on wire rack 2 minutes. With wide spatula, transfer cookies to wire rack to cool completely.

4 Repeat with remaining cookie dough. *Makes about 3½ dozen cookies.*

EACH COOKIE: ABOUT 70 CALORIES, 1 G PROTEIN, 11 G CARBOHYDRATE, 2 G TOTAL FAT (1 G SATURATED), 0 G FIBER, 11 MG CHOLESTEROL, 85 MG SODIUM.

Grandmother's Oatmeal-Raisin Cookies

PREP 15 MINUTES / BAKE 15 MINUTES PER BATCH

If you like crisp oatmeal cookies, bake these until the tops are golden. For softer, chewier cookies, bake only about 12 minutes, or just until the edges are golden. You can use either old-fashioned or quick-cooking oats, but don't use instant oatmeal, which is so fine that the cookies will not have much texture.

¾ CUP ALL-PURPOSE FLOUR

½ TEASPOON BAKING SODA

¼ TEASPOON SALT

½ CUP BUTTER OR MARGARINE (1 STICK), SOFTENED

½ CUP GRANULATED SUGAR

⅓ CUP PACKED BROWN SUGAR

1 LARGE EGG

2 TEASPOONS VANILLA EXTRACT

1½ CUPS OLD-FASHIONED OR QUICK-COOKING OATS, UNCOOKED

¾ CUP DARK SEEDLESS RAISINS OR CHOPPED PITTED PRUNES

1 Preheat oven to 350° F. On sheet of waxed paper, combine flour, baking soda, and salt.

2 In large bowl, with mixer at medium speed, beat butter and granulated and brown sugars until creamy. Beat in egg and vanilla until smooth. Reduce speed to low; beat in flour mixture. With spoon, stir in oats and raisins.

3 Drop dough by heaping tablespoons, 2 inches apart, on ungreased large cookie sheet. Bake 15 minutes, or until golden. With wide spatula, transfer cookies to wire racks to cool completely.

4 Repeat with remaining cookie dough. *Makes about 2 dozen cookies.*

EACH COOKIE: ABOUT 115 CALORIES, 2 G PROTEIN, 17 G CARBOHYDRATE, 4 G TOTAL FAT (2 G SATURATED), 1 G FIBER, 19 MG CHOLESTEROL, 95 MG SODIUM.

OATMEAL CHOCOLATE CHIP COOKIES Prepare as above but stir in *1 cup semisweet chocolate chips* with oats and raisins. Bake as directed.

EACH COOKIE: ABOUT 145 CALORIES, 2 G PROTEIN, 22 G CARBOHYDRATE, 6 G TOTAL FAT (4 G SATURATED), 1 G FIBER, 19 MG CHOLESTEROL, 95 MG SODIUM.

Black & White Cookies

PREP 20 MINUTES PLUS COOLING
BAKE 15 TO 17 MINUTES PER BATCH

New York City bakeries have long been famous for these cakelike, saucer-size beauties. Half of the top of each giant cookie is iced with a dark chocolate glaze, the other half with a vanilla icing.

2 CUPS ALL-PURPOSE FLOUR
½ TEASPOON BAKING SODA
¼ TEASPOON SALT
10 TABLESPOONS BUTTER OR MARGARINE (1¼ STICKS),
   SOFTENED
1 CUP GRANULATED SUGAR
2 LARGE EGGS
2 TEASPOONS VANILLA EXTRACT
½ CUP BUTTERMILK
1¾ CUPS CONFECTIONERS' SUGAR
¼ CUP UNSWEETENED COCOA
2 TABLESPOONS LIGHT CORN SYRUP
8 TO 10 TEASPOONS WARM WATER

1 Preheat oven to 350° F. In small bowl, stir together flour, baking soda, and salt.

2 In large bowl, with mixer at medium speed, beat butter and granulated sugar until creamy. Beat in eggs and vanilla until blended. Reduce speed to low; add flour mixture alternately with buttermilk, beginning and ending with flour mixture. Beat just until combined, scraping bowl occasionally with rubber spatula.

3 Drop dough by ¼ cups, about 3 inches apart, on 2 ungreased large cookie sheets. Bake 15 to 17 minutes, rotating sheets between upper and lower racks halfway through baking, until edges begin to brown and tops spring back when lightly touched with finger. With wide spatula, transfer cookies to wire racks to cool completely.

4 When cookies are cool, prepare glazes: In medium bowl, mix 1¼ cups confectioners' sugar, 1 tablespoon corn syrup, and 5 to 6 teaspoons water, 1 teaspoon at a time, to good spreading consistency. Turn cookies over, flat side up. With small spatula, spread glaze over half of each cookie. Allow glaze to set 20 minutes.

5 Meanwhile, prepare chocolate glaze: In small bowl, stir together remaining ½ cup confectioners' sugar, cocoa, remaining 1 tablespoon corn syrup, and remaining 3 to 4 teaspoons water, 1 teaspoon at a time, to good spreading consistency. With clean small spatula, spread chocolate glaze over remaining un-iced half of each cookie. Let glaze set completely, at least 1 hour. *Makes about 14 cookies.*

EACH COOKIE: ABOUT 280 CALORIES, 3 G PROTEIN,
46 G CARBOHYDRATE, 9 G TOTAL FAT (6 G SATURATED),
1 G FIBER, 53 MG CHOLESTEROL, 190 MG SODIUM.

Coconut Macaroons

PREP 10 MINUTES / BAKE 25 MINUTES PER BATCH

These cookies are traditional for Passover, when baked goods must be made without flour or leavening. But they're a special treat any time of year.

3 CUPS FLAKED SWEETENED COCONUT
4 LARGE EGG WHITES
¾ CUP SUGAR
1 TEASPOON VANILLA EXTRACT
¼ TEASPOON SALT
⅛ TEASPOON ALMOND EXTRACT

1 Preheat oven to 325° F. Line 2 large cookie sheets with cooking parchment or foil.

2 In large bowl, stir together coconut, egg whites, sugar, vanilla, salt, and almond extract until evenly combined.

3 Drop dough by rounded teaspoons, 1 inch apart, on prepared cookie sheets. Bake 25 minutes, rotating sheets between upper and lower racks halfway through baking, or until set and lightly golden. Cool 1 minute on cookie sheets. With wide spatula, transfer cookies to wire racks to cool completely.

4 Repeat with remaining cookie dough. *Makes about 3½ dozen cookies.*

EACH COOKIE: ABOUT 40 CALORIES, 1 G PROTEIN,
6 G CARBOHYDRATE, 2 G TOTAL FAT (2 G SATURATED),
0.5 G FIBER, 0 MG CHOLESTEROL, 30 MG SODIUM.

CHOCOLATE COCONUT MACAROONS Prepare as above but add *2 tablespoons unsweetened cocoa* and *1 square (1 ounce) semisweet chocolate*, grated, to dough. Bake as directed.
EACH COOKIE: ABOUT 45 CALORIES, 1 G PROTEIN,
7 G CARBOHYDRATE, 2 G TOTAL FAT (2 G SATURATED),
0.5 G FIBER, 0 MG CHOLESTEROL, 35 MG SODIUM.

Chocolate Hazelnut Macaroons

PREP 30 MINUTES / BAKE 10 MINUTES PER BATCH

Chocolate plus hazelnut equals gianduja—a flavor you may have encountered in fine Italian chocolates. These macaroons are a chocolate variation of an Italian recipe called "brutti ma buoni" (ugly but good)—a reference to the fact that the cookies are a bit lumpy and irregular in shape, though absolutely delicious.

1 CUP HAZELNUTS (FILBERTS)

1 CUP SUGAR

¼ CUP UNSWEETENED COCOA

1 SQUARE (1 OUNCE) UNSWEETENED CHOCOLATE, CHOPPED

⅛ TEASPOON SALT

2 LARGE EGG WHITES

1 TEASPOON VANILLA EXTRACT

1 Preheat oven to 350° F. Place hazelnuts in 9" by 9" metal baking pan. Bake 15 minutes, or until toasted. Wrap hot hazelnuts in clean cloth towel. With hands, roll hazelnuts back and forth to remove most of skins. Cool. Line 2 large cookie sheets with foil.

2 In food processor with knife blade attached, process hazelnuts, sugar, cocoa, chocolate, and salt until nuts and chocolate are finely ground. Add egg whites and vanilla and process until blended.

3 Drop dough by rounded teaspoons, using another spoon to release batter, 2 inches apart, on prepared cookie sheets. Bake 10 minutes, rotating sheets between upper and lower racks halfway through baking, or until tops feel firm when pressed lightly. Cool on cookie sheets on wire racks.

4 Repeat with remaining cookie dough. *Makes about 2½ dozen cookies.*

EACH COOKIE: ABOUT 60 CALORIES, 1 G PROTEIN, 8 G CARBOHYDRATE, 3 G TOTAL FAT (1 G SATURATED), 0.5 G FIBER, 0 MG CHOLESTEROL, 15 MG SODIUM.

Chocolate Hazelnut Macaroons

Triple Chocolate Chubbies

PREP 25 MINUTES
BAKE 14 MINUTES PER BATCH

Can the classic chocolate chip cookie be improved upon? The answer is "yes" if your definition of improvement is "more chocolate." There's melted chocolate as well as cocoa in the dough, and semisweet chocolate chips are dotted throughout these big cookies. If you don't want to use both pecans and walnuts, use 1 cup of either one.

¼ CUP ALL-PURPOSE FLOUR
¼ CUP UNSWEETENED COCOA
½ TEASPOON BAKING POWDER
¼ TEASPOON SALT
8 SQUARES (8 OUNCES) SEMISWEET CHOCOLATE, CHOPPED
6 TABLESPOONS BUTTER OR MARGARINE, CUT UP
1 CUP SUGAR
2 TEASPOONS VANILLA EXTRACT
2 LARGE EGGS
1 CUP SEMISWEET CHOCOLATE CHIPS
½ CUP PECANS, CHOPPED
½ CUP WALNUTS, CHOPPED

1 Preheat oven to 350° F. In small bowl, stir together flour, cocoa, baking powder, and salt.

2 In 3-quart saucepan, melt chopped chocolate and butter over low heat. Pour into large bowl; cool to lukewarm. Stir in sugar and vanilla until blended. Stir in eggs, 1 at a time, until well blended. Add flour mixture and stir until combined (batter will be thin). Stir in chocolate chips, pecans, and walnuts.

3 Drop batter by heaping tablespoons, 1½ inches apart, on ungreased large cookie sheet. Bake 14 minutes, or until set. Cool on cookie sheet on wire rack 2 minutes. With wide spatula, carefully transfer cookies to wire rack to cool completely.

4 Repeat with remaining cookie dough. *Makes about 2 dozen cookies.*

EACH COOKIE: ABOUT 180 CALORIES, 2 G PROTEIN,
21 G CARBOHYDRATE, 11 G TOTAL FAT (5 G SATURATED),
1 G FIBER, 26 MG CHOLESTEROL, 70 MG SODIUM.

MACAROONS

HAVE YOU EVER WONDERED WHY "MACAROON" AND "MACARONI" SOUND SO SIMILAR? YOU'RE NOT ALONE. ALTHOUGH BOTH WORDS SEEM TO BE DERIVED FROM THE ITALIAN WORD "MACCHERONI" OR THE SICILIAN "MACCARONE," SCHOLARS CAN'T SEEM TO AGREE ON THE REST OF THE STORY. MACAROONS WERE ORIGINALLY MADE FROM EGG WHITES, SUGAR, AND GROUND ALMONDS OR ALMOND PASTE; THE COCONUT MACAROON IS A LATER—BUT NO LESS DELICIOUS—DEVELOPMENT.

Brown Edge Wafers

PREP 20 MINUTES / BAKE 8 TO 10 MINUTES PER BATCH

A true classic, these vanilla-flavored cookies are delicate. Remove them from the cookie sheet promptly—while they're still warm and a little soft—or the cookies may break.

⅓ CUP BUTTER, MELTED (DO NOT USE MARGARINE)
½ CUP SUGAR
2 LARGE EGG WHITES
1 TEASPOON VANILLA EXTRACT
⅔ CUP ALL-PURPOSE FLOUR
⅛ TEASPOON SALT

1 Preheat oven to 375° F.

2 In large bowl, with wire whisk, beat melted butter, sugar, egg whites, and vanilla until blended. Beat in flour and salt until combined.

3 Drop dough by heaping teaspoons, 2 inches apart, on ungreased large cookie sheet. Bake 8 to 10 minutes, until edges are deep brown. With wide spatula, quickly transfer cookies to wire rack to cool completely.

4 Repeat with remaining cookie dough. *Makes about 3 dozen cookies.*

EACH COOKIE: ABOUT 35 CALORIES, 0 G PROTEIN,
5 G CARBOHYDRATE, 2 G TOTAL FAT (1 G SATURATED),
0 G FIBER, 5 MG CHOLESTEROL, 30 MG SODIUM.

Benne Wafers

PREP 30 MINUTES / BAKE 6 TO 7 MINUTES PER BATCH

½ CUP SESAME SEEDS
¾ CUP ALL-PURPOSE FLOUR
¼ TEASPOON SALT
½ CUP BUTTER (1 STICK), SOFTENED (DO NOT USE
   MARGARINE)
1 CUP PACKED LIGHT BROWN SUGAR
1 LARGE EGG
1 TEASPOON VANILLA EXTRACT

1 Preheat oven to 350° F. Grease large cookie sheet. Spread sesame seeds in even layer on jelly-roll pan. Bake 10 to 12 minutes, until light golden; cool on wire rack. On sheet of waxed paper, stir together flour and salt.

2 In medium bowl, with mixer at medium speed, beat butter and brown sugar until combined. Reduce speed to low; beat in egg and vanilla until well blended. Beat in flour mixture and sesame seeds until combined, scraping bowl occasionally with rubber spatula.

3 Drop dough by rounded half teaspoons, 3 inches apart, on prepared cookie sheet. Bake cookies 6 to 7 minutes, until light brown and lacy. Cool on cookie sheets on wire racks 1 minute. With wide spatula, transfer cookies to wire rack to cool completely.

4 Repeat with remaining cookie dough. *Makes about 10 dozen cookies.*

EACH COOKIE: ABOUT 20 CALORIES, 0 G PROTEIN,
3 G CARBOHYDRATE, 1 G TOTAL FAT (1 G SATURATED),
0 G FIBER, 4 MG CHOLESTEROL, 15 MG SODIUM.

Drop Sugar Cookies

PREP 25 MINUTES / BAKE 14 MINUTES PER BATCH

If you don't have the time (or the inclination) to make roll-and-cut sugar cookies, try this simple old-fashioned drop cookie recipe. The cookies can be varied by stirring in ½ cup chopped nuts, ½ cup chocolate mini-chips, or 1 tablespoon freshly grated lemon peel. You can also decorate them with piped icing after baking.

2 CUPS ALL-PURPOSE FLOUR
1 TEASPOON BAKING POWDER
¼ TEASPOON SALT
¾ CUP BUTTER OR MARGARINE (1½ STICKS), SOFTENED
1 CUP SUGAR
1 LARGE EGG
3 TABLESPOONS MILK
2 TEASPOONS VANILLA EXTRACT

1 Preheat oven to 350° F. On sheet of waxed paper, stir together flour, baking powder, and salt.

2 In large bowl, with mixer at medium-low speed, beat butter and sugar until creamy. Add egg, milk, and vanilla; beat until well blended. Reduce speed to low; beat in flour mixture just until blended.

3 Drop dough by rounded teaspoons, 2 inches apart, onto ungreased large cookie sheet. Bake 14 minutes, or until browned at edges. With wide spatula, transfer cookies to wire rack to cool completely.

4 Repeat with remaining cookie dough. *Makes about 3½ dozen cookies.*

EACH COOKIE: ABOUT 70 CALORIES, 1 G PROTEIN,
9 G CARBOHYDRATE, 3 G TOTAL FAT (2 G SATURATED),
0 G FIBER, 14 MG CHOLESTEROL, 60 MG SODIUM.

SHAPED COOKIES

An appealingly "hands on" project, shaped cookies are dense doughs that can be formed into balls or logs, knotted into pretzels, or, of course, rolled into sheets for using your favorite cookie cutters. Try not to work in a lot of extra flour when rolling these stiff doughs—it will make the cookies tough. If the mixture is too soft or sticky to handle, chilling will firm it up nicely. Another option is to roll the dough between sheets of waxed paper.

Peanut Butter Cookies

PREP 25 MINUTES / BAKE 10 TO 12 MINUTES PER BATCH

There's no mistaking the characteristic "tic-tac-toe" pattern on these cookie-jar favorites. Use the tines of a fork or one quick move with a potato masher to flatten and mark the dough. Kids love to help with this part!

1½ CUPS ALL-PURPOSE FLOUR
½ TEASPOON BAKING SODA
½ CUP BUTTER OR MARGARINE (1 STICK), SOFTENED
¾ CUP CREAMY OR CHUNKY PEANUT BUTTER
½ CUP PACKED BROWN SUGAR
½ CUP GRANULATED SUGAR
1 LARGE EGG
½ TEASPOON VANILLA EXTRACT

1 Preheat oven to 375° F. Grease 2 large cookie sheets. In small bowl, combine flour and baking soda.

2 In large bowl, with mixer at low speed, beat butter until creamy. Add peanut butter and brown and granulated sugars; beat until well blended. Beat in egg and vanilla. Reduce speed to low; beat in half of flour mixture until blended. With wooden spoon, stir in remaining flour mixture until combined.

3 With hands, shape dough into 1-inch balls. Place balls, 2 inches apart, on prepared cookie sheet. Press with floured tines of fork or potato masher ⅜ inch thick. Bake 10 to 12 minutes, until lightly browned at edges. Cool on cookie sheet on wire rack 2 minutes. With wide spatula, transfer cookies to wire rack to cool completely.

4 Repeat with remaining cookie dough. *Makes about 4 dozen cookies.*

EACH COOKIE: ABOUT 75 CALORIES, 2 G PROTEIN, 8 G CARBOHYDRATE, 4 G TOTAL FAT (2 G SATURATED), 0.5 G FIBER, 10 MG CHOLESTEROL, 55 MG SODIUM.

Snickerdoodles

PREP 25 MINUTES / BAKE 12 MINUTES PER BATCH

These cinnamon-spicy cookies are probably Pennsylvania-Dutch in origin—although nobody has come up with a definitive explanation of their name. Because the balls of dough are rolled in cinnamon sugar, the cookies come out with crinkly, crackly tops.

3 CUPS ALL-PURPOSE FLOUR
2 TEASPOONS CREAM OF TARTAR
1 TEASPOON BAKING SODA
1 CUP BUTTER OR MARGARINE (2 STICKS), SOFTENED
1⅓ CUPS PLUS ¼ CUP SUGAR
2 LARGE EGGS
1 TEASPOON VANILLA EXTRACT
1½ TEASPOONS GROUND CINNAMON

1 Preheat oven to 375° F. On sheet of waxed paper, stir together flour, cream of tartar, and baking soda.

2 In large bowl, with mixer at medium speed, beat butter and 1⅓ cups sugar until light and fluffy. Beat in eggs, 2 at a time, beating after each addition. Beat in vanilla. Reduce speed to low; beat in flour mixture until well combined.

3 In small bowl, combine cinnamon and remaining ¼ cup sugar. With hands, shape dough into 1-inch balls. Roll in cinnamon sugar to coat. Place balls, 1 inch apart, on ungreased large cookie sheet. Bake 12 minutes, or until set and lightly golden and slightly crinkly on top. Cool on cookie sheet on wire rack 1 minute. With wide spatula, transfer cookies to wire racks to cool completely.

4 Repeat with remaining cookie dough. *Makes about 4½ dozen cookies.*

EACH COOKIE: ABOUT 80 CALORIES, 1 G PROTEIN, 11 G CARBOHYDRATE, 4 G TOTAL FAT (2 G SATURATED), 0 G FIBER, 17 MG CHOLESTEROL, 60 MG SODIUM.

Raspberry Linzer Thumbprint Cookies

PREP 45 MINUTES / BAKE 20 MINUTES PER BATCH

The inspiration for these charming cookies is the Linzertorte, a traditional dessert from the Austrian city of Linz. The elaborate torte features a rich nut crust, raspberry filling, and a lattice top. Much simpler to prepare, this hazelnut cookie dough is made in the food processor; the jam fills a thumbprint indentation in each cookie. Raspberry jam is the classic Linzertorte filling, but you could use strawberry, blackberry, or another favorite flavor.

1⅓ CUPS HAZELNUTS (FILBERTS)
½ CUP SUGAR
¾ CUP BUTTER OR MARGARINE (1½ STICKS), CUT UP
1 TEASPOON VANILLA EXTRACT
¼ TEASPOON SALT
1¾ CUPS ALL-PURPOSE FLOUR
¼ CUP SEEDLESS RED RASPBERRY JAM

1 Preheat oven to 350° F. Place 1 cup hazelnuts in 9" by 9" metal baking pan. Bake 15 minutes, or until toasted. Wrap hot hazelnuts in clean cloth towel. With hands, roll hazelnuts back and forth to remove most of skins. Cool.

2 In food processor with knife blade attached, process toasted hazelnuts with sugar until nuts are finely ground. Add butter, vanilla, and salt and process until blended. Add flour and process until evenly combined. Remove knife blade and press dough together with hands.

3 Finely chop remaining ⅓ cup hazelnuts; spread on sheet of waxed paper. With hands, shape dough, 2 teaspoons at a time, into 1-inch balls (dough may be slightly crumbly). Roll balls in nuts, gently pressing nuts onto dough. Place balls, about 1½ inches apart, on ungreased large cookie sheet.

4 With thumb, make small indentation in center of each ball. Fill each indentation with ¼ teaspoon jam. Bake 20 minutes, or until lightly golden around edges. With wide spatula, transfer cookies to wire racks to cool completely.

5 Repeat with remaining balls and jam. *Makes about 4 dozen cookies.*

EACH COOKIE: ABOUT 75 CALORIES, 1 G PROTEIN, 7 G CARBOHYDRATE, 5 G TOTAL FAT (2 G SATURATED), 0.5 G FIBER, 8 MG CHOLESTEROL, 40 MG SODIUM.

Chocolate Crinkles

PREP 25 MINUTES PLUS CHILLING
BAKE 8 MINUTES PER BATCH

Rolling the dough in confectioners' sugar produces a snowy-looking finish appropriate for the winter holidays. For a change, roll the dough in granulated sugar, which gives the cookies a crackly-shiny coat.

1¾ CUPS ALL-PURPOSE FLOUR
½ CUP UNSWEETENED COCOA
1 TEASPOON BAKING SODA
½ TEASPOON BAKING POWDER
¼ TEASPOON SALT
½ CUP BUTTER OR MARGARINE (1 STICK), SOFTENED
1¼ CUPS GRANULATED SUGAR
2 TABLESPOONS LIGHT CORN SYRUP
2 SQUARES (2 OUNCES) UNSWEETENED CHOCOLATE,
    MELTED AND COOLED
2 LARGE EGGS
2 TEASPOONS VANILLA EXTRACT
½ CUP CONFECTIONERS' SUGAR

1 On sheet of waxed paper, stir together flour, cocoa, baking soda, baking powder, and salt.

2 In large bowl, with mixer at medium speed, beat butter, granulated sugar, and corn syrup until combined. Reduce speed to low and beat in chocolate, eggs, and vanilla until well blended. Beat in flour mixture until combined, scraping bowl occasionally with rubber spatula. Cover dough and refrigerate 1 hour.

3 Preheat oven to 350° F. Place confectioners' sugar in small bowl. Shape dough by level teaspoons into 1-inch balls; roll in confectioners' sugar.

4 Place cookies, 1 inch apart, on ungreased large cookie sheet. Bake 8 minutes. With wide spatula, transfer cookies to wire rack to cool completely.

5 Repeat with remaining cookie dough and confectioners' sugar. *Makes about 8 dozen cookies.*

EACH COOKIE: ABOUT 35 CALORIES, 1 G PROTEIN, 6 G CARBOHYDRATE, 1 G TOTAL FAT (1 G SATURATED), 0.5 G FIBER, 7 MG CHOLESTEROL, 35 MG SODIUM.

Raspberry Linzer Thumbprint Cookies

Pretzel Cookies

PREP 20 MINUTES / BAKE 25 TO 28 MINUTES

To give these clever cookies the look of salted pretzels, sprinkle them with coarse grains of pearl sugar, which remain crystalline, rather than melting, when baked. Look for this special decorating sugar at baking supply shops and in gourmet mail-order catalogues.

½ CUP BUTTER OR MARGARINE (1 STICK), SOFTENED
⅓ CUP GRANULATED SUGAR
1 TEASPOON FRESHLY GRATED LEMON OR ORANGE PEEL
¼ TEASPOON SALT
1 LARGE EGG
2 LARGE EGG YOLKS
2 CUPS ALL-PURPOSE FLOUR
½ TEASPOON WATER
COARSE OR GRANULATED SUGAR FOR SPRINKLING
2 SQUARES (2 OUNCES) SEMISWEET CHOCOLATE, MELTED
    (OPTIONAL)

1 Preheat oven to 350° F.

2 In large bowl, with mixer at medium speed, beat butter and granulated sugar until creamy. Add lemon or orange peel, salt, egg, and 1 egg yolk; beat until well blended. Add flour and beat until combined.

3 Gather dough into ball and knead on lightly floured surface. With hands, divide dough by heaping tablespoons into 20 pieces. Roll each piece into 11-inch-long rope. Shape each rope into pretzel, following directions for shaping soft pretzels (page 135). Place pretzels, 1 inch apart, on large ungreased cookie sheet.

4 In small cup, with fork, beat remaining egg yolk with water. Brush glaze on pretzels. Sprinkle with coarse sugar. Bake 25 to 28 minutes, until golden brown. Cool on cookie sheet on wire rack 3 minutes. With wide spatula, transfer cookies to wire rack to cool completely. When cool, drizzle melted chocolate over cookies, if you like; let chocolate set before serving. *Makes 20 cookies.*

EACH COOKIE WITHOUT CHOCOLATE: ABOUT 115 CALORIES, 2 G PROTEIN, 15 G CARBOHYDRATE, 5 G TOTAL FAT (3 G SATURATED), 0.5 G FIBER, 44 MG CHOLESTEROL, 80 MG SODIUM.

Sicilian Sesame Cookies

PREP 30 MINUTES / BAKE 30 TO 35 MINUTES PER BATCH

Toasted sesame seeds give these cookies from Sicily a deeply nutty flavor; they're not too sweet, so they can be served with a glass of sherry or with a glass of milk. Check (and stir) the sesame seeds often as they toast, as they can go from golden-and-fragrant to black-and-burnt in just a minute or so.

1 CUP (ABOUT 5 OUNCES) SESAME SEEDS
2¼ CUPS ALL-PURPOSE FLOUR
2 TEASPOONS BAKING POWDER
¾ CUP SUGAR
¼ TEASPOON SALT
3 LARGE EGGS, BEATEN
4 TABLESPOONS BUTTER OR MARGARINE, MELTED
1 TEASPOON VANILLA EXTRACT

1 Preheat oven to 350° F. Spread sesame seeds evenly on jelly-roll pan; bake 8 to 10 minutes, stirring once, or until golden. Cool on wire rack, then transfer to small bowl. In large bowl, stir together flour, baking powder, sugar, and salt.

2 In small bowl, stir together eggs, melted butter, and vanilla. Add to flour mixture, stirring just until blended.

3 Transfer dough to lightly floured surface. With hand, knead dough 5 or 6 times until smooth. Divide dough in quarters. Roll 1 piece into a 24-inch-long rope; with knife, cut into twelve 2-inch logs.

4 Fill small bowl with water. Dip each log in the water and roll in the sesame seeds until completely covered. Place logs, 1 inch apart, on 2 ungreased large cookie sheets. Bake 30 to 35 minutes, rotating sheets between upper and lower racks halfway through baking, until golden brown. With wide spatula, transfer cookies to wire racks to cool completely. (Cookies will harden as they cool.)

5 Repeat with remaining cookie dough and sesame seeds. *Makes 4 dozen cookies.*

EACH COOKIE: ABOUT 65 CALORIES, 2 G PROTEIN, 9 G CARBOHYDRATE, 3 G TOTAL FAT (1 G SATURATED), 0.5 G FIBER, 16 MG CHOLESTEROL, 45 MG SODIUM.

Anise Biscotti

PREP 20 MINUTES PLUS CHILLING / BAKE 30 MINUTES

Biscotti are crisp, dry Italian cookies intended for dunking—in wine, coffee, tea, or milk. If you're not planning to dunk, you can underbake them a bit the second time around so that they remain slightly soft. Store them in an airtight container so that the hard cookies stay hard and the softer cookies stay soft.

2½ CUPS ALL-PURPOSE FLOUR
1 TABLESPOON ANISE SEEDS
2 TEASPOONS BAKING POWDER
¼ TEASPOON SALT
1 CUP SUGAR
4 TABLESPOONS BUTTER OR MARGARINE, SOFTENED
3 LARGE EGGS

1 On sheet of waxed paper, stir together flour, anise seeds, baking powder, and salt.

2 In large bowl, with mixer at medium speed, beat sugar and butter until combined. Beat in eggs, 1 at a time. Reduce speed to low and beat in flour mixture.

3 Preheat oven to 375° F. Grease large cookie sheet. Divide dough in half and place on prepared cookie sheet. With floured hands, shape each half into 10" by 3" log, leaving about 2 inches in between. Bake 20 minutes.

4 Remove cookie sheet from oven. With serrated knife, immediately cut each log crosswise into ¾-inch-thick slices. Lay slices, cut sides down, on same cookie sheet, making sure they do not touch. Return to oven and bake 5 minutes, or until lightly golden. Turn each slice over and bake 5 minutes longer, or until golden on second side. With wide spatula, transfer biscotti to wire racks to cool completely. *Makes about 2½ dozen biscotti.*

EACH BISCOTTO: ABOUT 90 CALORIES, 2 G PROTEIN, 15 G CARBOHYDRATE, 2 G TOTAL FAT (1 G SATURATED), 0.5 G FIBER, 25 MG CHOLESTEROL, 75 MG SODIUM.

Chocolate-Cherry Biscotti

PREP 30 MINUTES PLUS COOLING
BAKE 50 TO 55 MINUTES

These sophisticated cookies are dotted with bits of dried tart cherries. Serve them with strong hot coffee—or with bowls of coffee ice cream.

2½ CUPS ALL-PURPOSE FLOUR
¾ CUP UNSWEETENED COCOA
1 TABLESPOON BAKING POWDER
½ TEASPOON SALT
1⅓ CUPS SUGAR
½ CUP BUTTER OR MARGARINE (1 STICK), SOFTENED
3 LARGE EGGS
2 SQUARES (2 OUNCES) SEMISWEET CHOCOLATE, MELTED
1 TEASPOON INSTANT ESPRESSO-COFFEE POWDER
1 TEASPOON HOT WATER
¾ CUP DRIED TART CHERRIES, COARSELY CHOPPED

1 Preheat oven to 350° F. Grease and flour large cookie sheet. In medium bowl, stir together flour, cocoa, baking powder, and salt.

2 In large bowl, with mixer at medium speed, beat sugar and butter until creamy. Reduce speed to low; add eggs, 1 at a time, beating after each addition. Beat in chocolate until blended.

3 Dissolve espresso-coffee powder in water; beat into chocolate mixture. Add flour mixture and beat just until blended. With hands, knead in cherries until combined.

4 Divide dough in half; drop each half by spoonfuls down length of prepared cookie sheet. With floured hands, shape each half into 12" by 3" log, leaving about 3 inches in between. With pastry brush, brush off excess flour. Bake 30 minutes. Cool on cookie sheet on wire rack 10 minutes, or until cool enough to handle.

5 Place logs on cutting board. With serrated knife, cut each log crosswise into ¾-inch-thick diagonal slices. Place slices, cut side down, on 2 cookie sheets. Bake 20 to 25 minutes, turning slices over and rotating sheets between upper and lower racks halfway through baking, until dry. With wide spatula, transfer biscotti to wire racks to cool completely. *Makes about 3 dozen biscotti.*

EACH BISCOTTO: ABOUT 110 CALORIES, 2 G PROTEIN, 18 G CARBOHYDRATE, 4 G TOTAL FAT (2 G SATURATED), 1 G FIBER, 25 MG CHOLESTEROL, 105 MG SODIUM.

Mandelbrot

PREP 30 MINUTES PLUS COOLING
BAKE 37 TO 38 MINUTES

Mandelbrot, or "almond bread," is a favorite Jewish cookie that resembles biscotti, but the slices are not baked quite as crisp. There are thousands of recipes, but many have in common the use of oil as a shortening, and most are made with almonds (although some bakers substitute or add walnuts, dried fruit, chocolate pieces, or a swirl of cocoa).

3¾ CUPS ALL-PURPOSE FLOUR
2 TEASPOONS BAKING POWDER
½ TEASPOON SALT
3 LARGE EGGS
1 CUP SUGAR
¾ CUP VEGETABLE OIL
2 TEASPOONS VANILLA EXTRACT
¼ TEASPOON ALMOND EXTRACT
1 TEASPOON FRESHLY GRATED ORANGE PEEL
1 CUP BLANCHED ALMONDS, COARSELY CHOPPED, TOASTED
   UNTIL GOLDEN

1 Preheat oven to 350° F. On sheet of waxed paper, stir together flour, baking powder, and salt.

2 In large bowl, with mixer at medium speed, beat eggs with sugar until light lemon-colored. Add oil, vanilla and almond extracts, and orange peel and beat until blended. With wooden spoon, beat in flour mixture until combined. Stir in almonds

3 Divide dough in half; drop each half by spoonfuls down length of ungreased large cookie sheet. With lightly floured hands, shape each half into 12-inch-long log, leaving 4 inches in between (dough will be slightly sticky). Bake 30 minutes, or until dough is lightly colored and firm. Cool on cookie sheet on wire rack 10 minutes, or until easy to handle.

4 Place logs on cutting board. With serrated knife, cut each log crosswise into ½-inch-thick slices. Place slices, cut side down, on 2 ungreased cookie sheets. Bake 7 to 8 minutes, rotating sheets between upper and lower racks halfway through baking, until golden. With wide spatula, transfer cookies to wire racks to cool completely. *Makes about 4 dozen cookies.*

EACH COOKIE: ABOUT 105 CALORIES, 2 G PROTEIN,
12 G CARBOHYDRATE, 5 G TOTAL FAT (1 G SATURATED),
0.5 G FIBER, 13 MG CHOLESTEROL, 50 MG SODIUM.

Ginger Biscotti

PREP 25 MINUTES PLUS COOLING
BAKE 48 TO 50 MINUTES

Flecked with morsels of crystallized ginger, these crunchy "biscuits" have a powerful gingery bite. If you buy sliced crystallized ginger and find it too dry and tough to chop, steam it over boiling water for 5 minutes or so to tenderize it.

3 CUPS ALL-PURPOSE FLOUR
1 TABLESPOON GROUND GINGER
2 TEASPOONS BAKING POWDER
¼ TEASPOON SALT
½ CUP BUTTER OR MARGARINE (1 STICK), SOFTENED
½ CUP GRANULATED SUGAR
½ CUP PACKED BROWN SUGAR
3 LARGE EGGS
½ CUP FINELY CHOPPED CRYSTALLIZED GINGER

1 Preheat oven to 350° F. Grease large cookie sheet. In medium bowl, stir together flour, ground ginger, baking powder, and salt.

2 In large bowl, with mixer at medium speed, beat butter with granulated and brown sugars until light and creamy. Beat in eggs, 1 at a time. Reduce speed to low and beat in flour mixture until combined. Stir in crystallized ginger.

3 Divide dough in half; drop each half by spoonfuls down length of prepared cookie sheet. With floured hands, shape each half into 12-inch-long log, leaving about 3 inches in between. Bake 30 minutes, or until toothpick inserted in center of logs comes out clean. Cool on cookie sheet on wire rack 10 minutes, until easy to handle.

4 Place logs on cutting board. With serrated knife, cut each log crosswise into ½-inch-thick diagonal slices. Place slices, cut side down, on 2 ungreased cookie sheets. Bake 20 minutes, turning slices over and rotating sheets between upper and lower racks halfway through baking, until golden. With wide spatula, transfer biscotti to wire racks to cool completely. *Makes about 3½ dozen biscotti.*

EACH BISCOTTO: ABOUT 90 CALORIES, 1 G PROTEIN,
15 G CARBOHYDRATE, 3 G TOTAL FAT (2 G SATURATED),
0.5 G FIBER, 21 MG CHOLESTEROL, 65 MG SODIUM.

Mexican Wedding Cookies

These two-bite "pastelitas de boda" may be made with almonds, walnuts, or toasted, skinned hazelnuts instead of pecans. The cookies should be rolled in confectioners' sugar twice: once while they're still slightly warm (so that the sugar sticks) and again after they've cooled, for a pristine, snowy finish.

1 CUP PECANS
1¾ CUPS CONFECTIONERS' SUGAR
1 CUP BUTTER (2 STICKS), CUT INTO 16 PIECES, SOFTENED
   (DO NOT USE MARGARINE)
1 TEASPOON VANILLA EXTRACT
2 CUPS ALL-PURPOSE FLOUR

1 Preheat oven to 325° F.

2 In food processor with knife blade attached, process pecans and ¼ cup sugar until nuts are finely chopped. Add butter and vanilla and process until smooth, scraping down sides of processor with rubber spatula. Add flour and process until combined and dough holds together.

3 With floured hands, shape dough by heaping teaspoons into 1-inch balls. Place balls, 1½ inches apart, on ungreased large cookie sheet. Bake 20 to 22 minutes, until bottoms are lightly browned and cookies are very light golden brown. With wide spatula, transfer to wire rack to cool.

4 Place remaining 1½ cups sugar in pie plate. While cookies are still warm, roll in sugar until coated and place on wire rack to cool completely. When cool, reroll cookies in sugar until thoroughly coated.

5 Repeat with remaining dough and sugar. *Makes about 4 dozen cookies.*

EACH COOKIE: ABOUT 85 CALORIES, 1 G PROTEIN,
9 G CARBOHYDRATE, 5 G TOTAL FAT (3 G SATURATED),
0.5 G FIBER, 10 MG CHOLESTEROL, 40 MG SODIUM.

Hermits

Moist and wonderfully chewy, hermits seem to have been so named because they keep well. Although they're sometimes made as drop cookies, the dough is more traditionally formed into long slabs that are cut into cookie-size pieces after baking.

2 CUPS ALL-PURPOSE FLOUR
1 TEASPOON BAKING POWDER
½ TEASPOON BAKING SODA
¼ TEASPOON SALT
1 TEASPOON GROUND CINNAMON
½ TEASPOON GROUND GINGER
¼ TEASPOON GROUND NUTMEG
⅛ TEASPOON GROUND CLOVES
½ CUP BUTTER OR MARGARINE (1 STICK), SOFTENED
1 CUP PACKED LIGHT BROWN SUGAR
¼ CUP LIGHT (MILD) MOLASSES
1 LARGE EGG
1 CUP DARK SEEDLESS RAISINS
1 CUP PECANS, TOASTED AND CHOPPED

1 Preheat oven to 350° F. Grease and flour 2 large cookie sheets.

2 On sheet of waxed paper, stir together flour, baking powder, baking soda, salt, cinnamon, ginger, nutmeg, and cloves.

3 In large bowl, with mixer at medium speed, beat butter and sugar until light and fluffy. Beat in molasses until well combined. Beat in egg. Reduce speed to low and beat in flour mixture until blended. With rubber spatula, fold in raisins and pecans.

4 Divide dough in thirds. With lightly floured hands, on prepared cookie sheets, shape each third into 12" by 1½" log. On one prepared cookie sheet, place 2 logs spaced widely apart; place third log on remaining cookie sheet. Bake 22 minutes, rotating sheets between upper and lower racks halfway through baking, until logs are set and tops are firm to touch. Cool on cookie sheets on wire racks 20 minutes. With serrated knife, slice each log in half lengthwise, then cut crosswise into 2-inch pieces. *Makes 3 dozen cookies.*

EACH COOKIE: ABOUT 115 CALORIES, 1 G PROTEIN,
17 G CARBOHYDRATE, 5 G TOTAL FAT (2 G SATURATED),
0.5 G FIBER, 13 MG CHOLESTEROL, 80 MG SODIUM.

ICEBOX COOKIES

It's hard to make a case for buying refrigerated cookie dough when you can make your own—in a scrumptious variety of flavors—and have it on hand for baking any time the spirit moves you.

Spicy Almond Slices

PREP 25 MINUTES PLUS CHILLING
BAKE 10 TO 12 MINUTES PER BATCH

3½ CUPS ALL-PURPOSE FLOUR
1 TABLESPOON GROUND CINNAMON
1 TEASPOON BAKING SODA
½ TEASPOON SALT
½ TEASPOON GROUND CLOVES
½ TEASPOON GROUND NUTMEG
1 CUP BUTTER OR MARGARINE (2 STICKS), SOFTENED
1 CUP GRANULATED SUGAR
¾ CUP PACKED DARK BROWN SUGAR
2 LARGE EGGS
1 TEASPOON VANILLA EXTRACT
2 CUPS SLICED BLANCHED ALMONDS

1 In medium bowl, stir together flour, cinnamon, baking soda, salt, cloves, and nutmeg. In large bowl, with mixer at medium speed, beat butter and granulated and brown sugars until creamy. Beat in eggs and vanilla. Reduce speed to low; beat in flour mixture. With wooden spoon, stir in almonds, with hands, if necessary (dough will be stiff).

2 Divide dough in half. On separate sheets of waxed paper, shape each half into 10" by 3" by 1" brick; wrap each brick tightly in the waxed paper. Refrigerate overnight or freeze at least 2 hours, or until very firm.

3 Preheat oven to 375° F. Keeping remaining dough refrigerated, cut 1 brick into ¼-inch-thick slices. Place slices, 1 inch apart, on ungreased large cookie sheet. Bake 10 to 12 minutes, until browned at edges. With wide spatula, transfer cookies to wire racks to cool completely.

4 Repeat with remaining cookie dough. *Makes about 6½ dozen cookies.*

EACH COOKIE: ABOUT 75 CALORIES, 1 G PROTEIN,
9 G CARBOHYDRATE, 4 G TOTAL FAT (2 G SATURATED),
0.5 G FIBER, 12 MG CHOLESTEROL, 60 MG SODIUM.

Coconut Thins

PREP 30 MINUTES PLUS CHILLING
BAKE 8 TO 9 MINUTES PER BATCH

The perfect "tea" cookie, these are lovely as is or delicately zebra-striped with melted chocolate.

2 CUPS (6 OUNCES) FLAKED SWEETENED COCONUT
1¾ CUPS ALL-PURPOSE FLOUR
¼ CUP CORNSTARCH
½ TEASPOON BAKING POWDER
⅛ TEASPOON GROUND NUTMEG
⅛ TEASPOON SALT
¾ CUP BUTTER OR MARGARINE (1½ STICKS), SOFTENED
1 CUP SUGAR
1 LARGE EGG
½ TEASPOON VANILLA EXTRACT
¼ TEASPOON ALMOND EXTRACT

1 Preheat oven to 350° F. In jelly-roll pan, toast coconut 9 to 10 minutes, stirring occasionally, until lightly golden. On sheet of waxed paper, stir together flour, cornstarch, baking powder, nutmeg, and salt.

2 In large bowl, with mixer at medium speed, beat butter and sugar until light and fluffy. Beat in egg and vanilla and almond extracts until well combined. Reduce speed to low and beat in flour mixture until well combined.

3 Divide dough in half. On separate sheets of waxed paper, shape each half into 14" by 1½" log. Wrap each log in the waxed paper, rolling it up tightly. Refrigerate several hours until very firm; or label, date, and freeze.

4 Preheat oven to 350° F. Keeping remaining dough refrigerated, cut 1 log into ¼-inch-thick slices. Place slices, 1 inch apart, on 2 ungreased large cookie sheets. Bake 8 to 9 minutes, rotating sheets between upper and lower racks halfway through baking, until edges are golden brown. Cool on cookie sheets on wire rack 1 minute. With wide spatula, transfer to wire racks to cool completely.

5 Repeat with remaining cookie dough. *Makes about 10 dozen cookies.*

EACH COOKIE: ABOUT 30 CALORIES, 0 G PROTEIN,
4 G CARBOHYDRATE, 2 G TOTAL FAT (1 G SATURATED),
0 G FIBER, 5 MG CHOLESTEROL, 20 MG SODIUM.

Lemon Slices

PREP 30 MINUTES PLUS OVERNIGHT TO CHILL
BAKE 12 MINUTES PER BATCH

Using half confectioners' sugar and half granulated sugar gives the cookies a melt-in-your-mouth texture.

2 CUPS ALL-PURPOSE FLOUR
¼ TEASPOON BAKING POWDER
¼ TEASPOON SALT
2 TO 3 LARGE LEMONS
¾ CUP BUTTER OR MARGARINE (1½ STICKS), SOFTENED
½ CUP PLUS 2 TABLESPOONS GRANULATED SUGAR
½ CUP CONFECTIONERS' SUGAR
½ TEASPOON VANILLA EXTRACT

1 On sheet of waxed paper, stir together flour, baking powder, and salt. From lemons, grate 1 tablespoon peel and squeeze 2 tablespoons juice.

2 In large bowl, with mixer at medium speed, beat butter, ½ cup granulated sugar, and confectioners' sugar until creamy. Beat in lemon peel and juice and vanilla until blended. Reduce speed to low and beat in flour mixture just until combined.

3 Divide dough in half. Shape each half into 6-inch-long log. Wrap each log in waxed paper and refrigerate dough overnight. (If using margarine, freeze overnight.)

4 Preheat oven to 350° F. Keeping remaining log refrigerated, cut 1 log into scant ¼-inch-thick slices. Place slices, 1½ inches apart, on ungreased large cookie sheet. Sprinkle lightly with some of remaining 2 tablespoons granulated sugar. Bake 12 minutes, or until lightly browned at edges. Cool on cookie sheet on wire rack 2 minutes. With wide spatula, transfer to wire rack to cool completely.

5 Repeat with remaining cookie dough and granulated sugar. *Makes about 5 dozen cookies.*

EACH COOKIE: ABOUT 50 CALORIES, 0 G PROTEIN,
6 G CARBOHYDRATE, 2 G TOTAL FAT (1 G SATURATED),
0 G FIBER, 6 MG CHOLESTEROL, 35 MG SODIUM.

LEMON-POPPYSEED SLICES Prepare as above but add *2 tablespoons poppyseeds* when beating in lemon peel and juice, and vanilla. Bake as directed.
EACH COOKIE: ABOUT 50 CALORIES, 1 G PROTEIN,
6 G CARBOHYDRATE, 2 G TOTAL FAT (1 G SATURATED),
0 G FIBER, 6 MG CHOLESTEROL, 35 MG SODIUM.

Lemon Slices

MINI LEMON SLICES Prepare dough as for Lemon Slices; divide into 4 pieces. Roll each piece into 12-inch-long log; wrap and refrigerate. Cut into ¼-inch-thick slices and place, 1 inch apart, on ungreased cookie sheet. Bake 10 to 12 minutes, until lightly browned at edges Repeat with remaining dough. *Makes about 16 dozen cookies.*

EACH COOKIE: ABOUT 15 CALORIES, 0 G PROTEIN, 2 G CARBOHYDRATE, 1 G TOTAL FAT (0 G SATURATED), 0 G FIBER, 2 MG CHOLESTEROL, 11 MG SODIUM.

Lime Icebox Cookies

PREP 30 MINUTES PLUS CHILLING
BAKE 12 TO 15 MINUTES PER BATCH

A drift of powdered sugar tops these thin, crisp citrus rectangles. For even more delicate cookies, slice the dough ⅛ inch thick and bake for 10 to 12 minutes.

3 LIMES
½ CUP BUTTER OR MARGARINE (1 STICK), SOFTENED
¾ CUP GRANULATED SUGAR
1 LARGE EGG
1¾ CUPS ALL-PURPOSE FLOUR
ABOUT ½ CUP CONFECTIONERS' SUGAR

1 From limes, grate 1 teaspoon peel and squeeze 3 tablespoons juice. In medium bowl, with mixer at medium speed, beat butter and granulated sugar until creamy. Reduce speed to low; beat in egg and lime peel and juice until blended. Beat in flour until combined.

2 Divide dough in half. On separate sheets of waxed paper, shape each half into 6" by 2½" by 1½" brick. Wrap each brick in the waxed paper and freeze 3 hours, or up to 1 month.

3 Preheat oven to 350° F. Slice 1 brick into ¼-inch-thick slices. Place slices, 1 inch apart, on ungreased large cookie sheet. Bake cookies 12 to 15 minutes, until edges are golden brown. With wide spatula, transfer to wire racks. Sift confectioners' sugar over hot cookies.

4 Repeat with remaining cookie dough and confectioners' sugar. *Makes about 4 dozen cookies.*

EACH COOKIE: ABOUT 50 CALORIES, 1 G PROTEIN, 8 G CARBOHYDRATE, 2 G TOTAL FAT (1 G SATURATED), 0 G FIBER, 10 MG CHOLESTEROL, 20 MG SODIUM.

Oatmeal Icebox Cookies

PREP 35 MINUTES PLUS CHILLING
BAKE 14 MINUTES PER BATCH

Try these if you like thin, crunchy, almost candylike oatmeal cookies, as opposed to the thick, soft kind.

1½ CUPS ALL-PURPOSE FLOUR
1 TEASPOON BAKING POWDER
½ TEASPOON BAKING SODA
¼ TEASPOON SALT
1 CUP BUTTER OR MARGARINE (2 STICKS), SOFTENED
1 CUP PACKED DARK BROWN SUGAR
¾ CUP GRANULATED SUGAR
2 LARGE EGGS
2 TEASPOONS VANILLA EXTRACT
3 CUPS OLD-FASHIONED OATS, UNCOOKED
1 CUP PECANS
1 CUP RAISINS

1 On sheet of waxed paper, stir together flour, baking powder, baking soda, and salt until blended.

2 In large bowl, with mixer at low speed, beat butter and brown and granulated sugars until creamy. Beat in eggs, 1 at a time, until well blended. Beat in vanilla. Reduce speed to low and beat in flour mixture until combined. With wooden spoon, stir in oats, pecans, and raisins.

3 Divide dough in half. On separate sheets of waxed paper, shape each half into 12-inch-long log. Wrap each log in the waxed paper, rolling it up tightly, and refrigerate 4 hours or overnight, until firm.

4 Preheat oven to 350° F. With serrated knife, using a sawing motion, cut each log into ⅜-inch-thick slices. Place slices, 2 inches apart, on ungreased large cookie sheets. Bake 14 minutes, rotating sheets between upper and lower racks halfway through baking, until golden brown. Cool on cookie sheets on wire racks 2 minutes. With wide spatula, transfer to wire racks to cool completely.

5 Repeat with remaining cookie dough. *Makes about 5 dozen cookies.*

EACH COOKIE: ABOUT 100 CALORIES, 1 G PROTEIN, 13 G CARBOHYDRATE, 5 G TOTAL FAT (2 G SATURATED), 0.5 G FIBER, 15 MG CHOLESTEROL, 65 MG SODIUM.

Chocolate Icebox Cookies

PREP 25 MINUTES PLUS CHILLING
BAKE 10 TO 11 MINUTES PER BATCH

Pair two of these thin rounds with your favorite frosting (or a thin layer of raspberry jam) to make some very classy sandwich cookies.

1⅔ CUPS ALL-PURPOSE FLOUR
½ CUP UNSWEETENED COCOA
1 TEASPOON BAKING POWDER
½ TEASPOON BAKING SODA
¼ TEASPOON SALT
¾ CUP BUTTER OR MARGARINE (1½ STICKS), SOFTENED
½ CUP PACKED LIGHT BROWN SUGAR
½ CUP GRANULATED SUGAR
2 SQUARES (2 OUNCES) SEMISWEET CHOCOLATE, MELTED
   AND COOLED
1 TEASPOON VANILLA EXTRACT
1 LARGE EGG

1 On sheet of waxed paper, stir together flour, cocoa, baking powder, baking soda, and salt.

2 In large bowl, with mixer at medium speed, beat butter and brown and granulated sugars until light and fluffy. Beat in chocolate and vanilla until well combined. Beat in egg. Reduce speed to low and beat in flour mixture until well combined.

3 Divide dough in half. On separate sheets of waxed paper, shape each half into 12" by 1½" log. Wrap each log in the waxed paper and slide onto small cookie sheet for easier handling. Refrigerate dough at least 2 hours, or overnight, until firm enough to slice. (If using margarine, freeze overnight.)

4 Preheat oven to 350° F. Keeping remaining log refrigerated, cut log into scant ¼-inch-thick slices. Place slices, 1 inch apart, on 2 ungreased large cookie sheets. Bake 10 to 11 minutes, rotating sheets between upper and lower racks halfway through baking. Cool on cookie sheets on wire racks 1 minutes. With wide spatula, transfer to wire racks to cool completely. Repeat with remaining cookie dough. *Makes about 10 dozen cookies.*

EACH COOKIE: ABOUT 25 CALORIES, 0 G PROTEIN,
4 G CARBOHYDRATE, 1 G TOTAL FAT (1 G SATURATED),
0 G FIBER, 5 MG CHOLESTEROL, 25 MG SODIUM.

CHOCOLATE SPICE COOKIES Prepare dough as for Chocolate Icebox Cookies and add *¼ teaspoon finely ground black pepper*, *¾ teaspoon ground cinnamon*, and *⅛ teaspoon ground allspice* to flour mixture. Chill, cut, and bake as directed.
EACH COOKIE: ABOUT 25 CALORIES, 0 G PROTEIN,
4 G CARBOHYDRATE, 1 G TOTAL FAT (1 G SATURATED),
0 G FIBER, 5 MG CHOLESTEROL, 25 MG SODIUM.

CHOCOLATE WALNUT COOKIES Prepare dough as for Chocolate Icebox Cookies and beat *1 cup coarsely chopped walnuts* into dough after adding flour mixture. Chill, cut, and bake as directed.
EACH COOKIE: ABOUT 35 CALORIES, 0 G PROTEIN,
4 G CARBOHYDRATE, 2 G TOTAL FAT (1 G SATURATED),
0 G FIBER, 5 MG CHOLESTEROL, 25 MG SODIUM.

Almond Cookies

PREP 25 MINUTES PLUS CHILLING
BAKE 15 MINUTES PER BATCH

These elegant little cookies are glossed with a shiny egg glaze and each is topped with a whole almond.

1⅓ CUPS ALL-PURPOSE FLOUR
2 TEASPOONS BAKING POWDER
¼ TEASPOON SALT
½ CUP BUTTER OR MARGARINE (1 STICK), SOFTENED
¾ CUP SUGAR
2 LARGE EGGS
½ TEASPOON VANILLA EXTRACT
¼ TEASPOON ALMOND EXTRACT
1 TABLESPOON WATER
30 WHOLE BLANCHED ALMONDS

1 In small bowl, stir together flour, baking powder, and salt. In large bowl, with mixer at medium speed, beat butter and sugar until creamy. Beat in 1 egg and vanilla and almond extracts until blended. Reduce speed to low and beat in flour mixture just until combined, scraping bowl with rubber spatula.

2 On sheet of waxed paper, shape dough into 8" by 1½" log; wrap in waxed paper and refrigerate 2 hours, or until firm enough to slice. (If using margarine, freeze overnight.)

3 Preheat oven to 350° F. Cut log into ¼-inch-thick slices. Place slices, 1 inch apart, on ungreased large cookie sheet. Whisk together remaining egg and water. Brush cookies with egg glaze. Lightly press 1 almond in the center of each cookie. Bake 15 minutes, or until lightly browned. With wide spatula, transfer to wire racks to cool completely. Repeat with remaining cookie dough. *Makes 2½ dozen cookies.*

EACH COOKIE: ABOUT 80 CALORIES, 1 G PROTEIN,
10 G CARBOHYDRATE, 4 G TOTAL FAT (2 G SATURATED),
0 G FIBER, 22 MG CHOLESTEROL, 85 MG SODIUM.

Checkerboard Cookies

PREP 40 MINUTES PLUS CHILLING
BAKE 10 TO 12 MINUTES PER BATCH

The little bit of extra effort required to make these fanciful cookies is worthwhile when you see the impression they make on children of all ages.

2 CUPS ALL-PURPOSE FLOUR
1 TEASPOON BAKING POWDER
¼ TEASPOON SALT
½ CUP (1 STICK) PLUS 1 TABLESPOON BUTTER OR
    MARGARINE, SOFTENED
1 CUP SUGAR
1 LARGE EGG
1 TEASPOON VANILLA EXTRACT
1 SQUARE (1 OUNCE) SEMISWEET CHOCOLATE
3 TABLESPOONS UNSWEETENED COCOA
MILK FOR ASSEMBLING COOKIES

1 On sheet of waxed paper, combine flour, baking powder, and salt. In medium bowl, with mixer at medium speed, beat ½ cup butter and sugar until creamy. Reduce speed to low and beat in egg and vanilla until blended. Beat in flour mixture until combined, scraping bowl occasionally with rubber spatula. Remove half of dough.

2 In 1-quart saucepan, melt chocolate and remaining 1 tablespoon butter over very low heat. Stir in cocoa until combined. Add to dough in bowl, stirring until blended. Shape chocolate and vanilla doughs each into 12" by 2" by 1" block.

3 Slice each block lengthwise into two 12" by 1" by 1" strips (see top photo). Brush one side of one chocolate strip with milk. Place brushed side next to one vanilla strip. Repeat with remaining 2 strips. Brush top of one of the vanilla/chocolate rectangles with milk. Place second vanilla/chocolate rectangle on top, reversing colors so end forms checkerboard (see bottom photo). Wrap in waxed

paper, using paper to square edges. Refrigerate 4 hours or overnight. (If using margarine, freeze overnight.)

4 Preheat oven to 375° F. Grease 2 large cookie sheets. Cut dough into ¼-inch-thick slices. Place slices, ½ inch apart, on prepared cookie sheets. Bake 10 to 12 minutes, until golden. Cool on cookie sheets on wires racks 5 minutes. With wide spatula, transfer to wire racks to cool completely. Repeat with remaining dough. *Makes about 4½ dozen cookies.*

EACH COOKIE: ABOUT 55 CALORIES, 1 G PROTEIN,
8 G CARBOHYDRATE, 2 G TOTAL FAT (1 G SATURATED),
0 G FIBER, 9 MG CHOLESTEROL, 40 MG SODIUM.

Forming Checkerboard Cookies

Cut each 12" by 2" by 1" block of dough in half lengthwise to make two 1"-thick sticks.

Brush one side of a chocolate stick with milk and "stick" it to a vanilla strip. Brush the top of the two-tone block with milk and place the remaining sticks of dough on top as shown.

ROLLED COOKIES

Once the dough is rolled out, you're on your way to lots of different kinds of cookies. Cookie cutters are one option, or try your hand at freehand shaping. Rolled dough can also go into three dimensions, formed into tiny jam-filled crescents or folded into fruit-filled triangular pastries.

Brown Sugar Cut-Out Cookies

PREP 35 MINUTES PLUS CHILLING
BAKE 10 MINUTES PER BATCH

Sprinkle the cookies with sugar before baking for a sparkly finish (as below); or leave them plain and decorate them with Ornamental Frosting (page 359) as we do in Ultimate Sugar Cookies (page 63).

2 CUPS ALL-PURPOSE FLOUR
½ TEASPOON BAKING SODA
¼ TEASPOON SALT
½ CUP BUTTER OR MARGARINE (1 STICK), SOFTENED
¾ CUP PACKED LIGHT BROWN SUGAR
1 LARGE EGG
¼ CUP GRANULATED SUGAR

1 On sheet of waxed paper, stir together flour, baking soda, and salt. In large bowl, with mixer at medium speed, beat butter and brown sugar until combined. Reduce speed to low and beat in egg until blended. Beat in flour mixture until combined, scraping bowl occasionally with rubber spatula.

2 Shape dough into 2 balls; flatten each slightly. Wrap 1 ball in waxed paper and refrigerate while working with remaining half.

3 Preheat oven to 350° F. On lightly floured surface, with floured rolling pin, roll dough ⅛ inch thick With floured 2-inch cookie cutters, cut as many cookies as possible; reserve trimmings. Place cookies, about ½ inch apart, on ungreased large cookie sheet.

4 Sprinkle granulated sugar over cookies. Bake 10 minutes. Transfer cookies to wire rack to cool completely. Repeat with remaining dough, trimmings, and granulated sugar. *Makes about 6½ dozen cookies.*

EACH COOKIE: ABOUT 35 CALORIES, 0 G PROTEIN,
5 G CARBOHYDRATE, 1 G TOTAL FAT (1 G SATURATED),
0 G FIBER, 6 MG CHOLESTEROL, 30 MG SODIUM.

Gingerbread Cut-Outs

PREP 45 MINUTES PLUS COOLING AND DECORATING
BAKE 12 MINUTES PER BATCH

These cut-out cookies are sturdy enough to use as ornaments on the Christmas tree.

½ CUP SUGAR
½ CUP LIGHT (MILD) MOLASSES
1½ TEASPOONS GROUND GINGER
1 TEASPOON GROUND ALLSPICE
1 TEASPOON GROUND CINNAMON
1 TEASPOON GROUND CLOVES
2 TEASPOONS BAKING SODA
½ CUP BUTTER OR MARGARINE (1 STICK), CUT UP
1 LARGE EGG, BEATEN
3½ CUPS ALL-PURPOSE FLOUR
ORNAMENTAL FROSTING (PAGE 358)

1 In 3-quart saucepan, heat sugar, molasses, ginger, allspice, cinnamon, and cloves to boiling over medium heat, stirring occasionally with wooden spoon. Remove pan from heat; stir in baking soda (mixture will foam up in pan). Stir in butter until melted. Stir in egg; add flour and stir until dough forms.

2 On floured surface, knead dough until combined. Divide dough in half; wrap 1 half in waxed paper and refrigerate.

3 Preheat oven to 325° F. With floured rolling pin, roll dough half a scant ¼ inch thick. With floured 3- to 4-inch assorted cookie cutters, cut as many cookies as possible; reserve trimmings. Place cookies, 1 inch apart, on ungreased large cookie sheet. If you like, with skewer, make ¼-inch hole near edge of each cookie for hanging as an ornament.

4 Bake 12 minutes, or until edges begin to brown. With wide spatula, transfer cookies to wire racks to cool. Repeat with remaining cookie dough and trimmings.

5 When cookies are cool, prepare Ornamental Frosting. Use frosting to decorate cookies; let dry completely, about 1 hour, before serving. *Makes about 3 dozen cookies.*

EACH COOKIE WITHOUT FROSTING: ABOUT 95 CALORIES,
2 G PROTEIN, 16 G CARBOHYDRATE, 3 G TOTAL FAT
(2 G SATURATED), 0.5 G FIBER, 13 MG CHOLESTEROL,
100 MG SODIUM.

Gingerbread Cut-Outs

Rugelach

PREP 1 HOUR PLUS CHILLING / BAKE 30 MINUTES

A specialty of Jewish bakeries (and Jewish grandmothers), rugelach are cookie-size rolled pastries. The dough may be prepared days or weeks ahead of time and frozen; you can also shape the rugelach in advance and refrigerate or freeze them. They can then be baked without thawing.

1 CUP BUTTER OR MARGARINE (2 STICKS), SOFTENED

1 PACKAGE (8 OUNCES) CREAM CHEESE, SOFTENED

1 TABLESPOON PLUS ½ CUP SUGAR

1 TEASPOON VANILLA EXTRACT

1 TEASPOON FRESHLY GRATED ORANGE PEEL (OPTIONAL)

2 CUPS ALL-PURPOSE FLOUR

1½ TEASPOONS GROUND CINNAMON

8 TEASPOONS BUTTER, MELTED

1 CUP WALNUTS, CHOPPED

1 CUP DRIED CURRANTS

1 LARGE EGG YOLK

1 TABLESPOON WATER

1 In large bowl, with mixer at low speed, beat butter and cream cheese until blended and smooth. Beat in 1 tablespoon sugar, vanilla, and orange peel, if using. Beat in flour until blended. Divide dough into 4 equal pieces. Wrap each in waxed paper and refrigerate until firm, at least 2 hours or overnight. (If using margarine, freeze overnight.)

2 Preheat oven to 325° F. Line 2 large cookie sheets with foil; grease foil. In small bowl, stir together cinnamon and remaining ½ cup sugar.

3 Keeping remaining dough refrigerated, on lightly floured surface, with floured rolling pin, roll 1 piece of chilled dough into 10½-inch round. Brush dough with 2 teaspoons melted butter. Sprinkle a generous 2 tablespoons cinnamon-sugar mixture over dough. Sprinkle one-fourth of nuts and one-fourth of currants over top; gently press filling onto dough.

4 With pastry wheel or sharp knife, cut dough into 12 wedges. Starting at curved edge, roll up each wedge jelly-roll fashion (see photo opposite page). Place, point-side down, about ½ inch apart., on prepared cookie sheets. Repeat with remaining dough, melted butter, and fillings, one-fourth at a time.

5 In cup, stir together egg yolk and water. Lightly brush egg-yolk mixture over rugelach.

6 Bake about 30 minutes, rotating sheets between upper and lower racks halfway through baking, until golden. Immediately transfer rugelach to wire racks to cool. *Makes 4 dozen rugelach.*

EACH RUGELACH: ABOUT 110 CALORIES, 1 G PROTEIN, 9 G CARBOHYDRATE, 8 G TOTAL FAT (4 G SATURATED), 0.5 G FIBER, 22 MG CHOLESTEROL, 60 MG SODIUM.

Apricot-Raspberry Rugelach

PREP 1 HOUR PLUS CHILLING / BAKE 35 TO 40 MINUTES

1 CUP BUTTER OR MARGARINE (2 STICKS), SOFTENED

1 PACKAGE (8 OUNCES) CREAM CHEESE, SOFTENED

1 TEASPOON VANILLA EXTRACT

¼ TEASPOON SALT

2 CUPS ALL-PURPOSE FLOUR

¾ CUP GRANULATED SUGAR

1 CUP WALNUTS, CHOPPED

¾ CUP DRIED APRICOTS, CHOPPED

¼ CUP PACKED LIGHT BROWN SUGAR

1½ TEASPOONS GROUND CINNAMON

½ CUP SEEDLESS RASPBERRY PRESERVES

1 TABLESPOON MILK

1 In large bowl, with mixer at low speed, beat butter and cream cheese until blended and smooth. Beat in vanilla, salt, 1 cup flour, and ¼ granulated cup sugar until blended. With spoon, stir in remaining 1 cup flour. Divide dough into 4 equal pieces. Wrap each in waxed paper and refrigerate until firm, at least 2 hours or overnight. (If using margarine, freeze overnight.)

2 In medium bowl, with spoon, stir walnuts, apricots, brown sugar, ¼ cup plus 2 tablespoons granulated sugar, and ½ teaspoon cinnamon until well mixed.

3 Preheat oven to 325° F. Line 2 large cookies sheets with foil; grease foil. Keeping remaining dough refrigerated, on lightly floured surface, with floured rolling pin, roll 1 piece chilled dough into 9-inch round. Spread dough with 2 tablespoons raspberry preserves. Sprinkle with about ¼ cup apricot filling; gently press filling onto dough. With pastry wheel or sharp knife, cut dough into 12 equal wedges. Starting at curved edge, roll up each wedge jelly-roll fashion (see photo below). Place, point-side down, about ½ inch apart, on prepared cookie sheets. Repeat with remaining dough, preserves, and fillings, one-fourth at a time.

4 In cup, mix remaining 2 tablespoons sugar with 1 teaspoon cinnamon. With pastry brush, brush rugelach with milk. Sprinkle with cinnamon-sugar.

5 Bake about 35 to 40 minutes, rotating sheets between upper and lower racks halfway through baking, until golden. With wide spatula, immediately transfer rugelach to wire racks to cool. *Makes 4 dozen rugelach.*

EACH RUGELACH: ABOUT 115 CALORIES, 1 G PROTEIN, 12 G CARBOHYDRATE, 7 G TOTAL FAT (4 G SATURATED), 0.5 G FIBER, 16 MG CHOLESTEROL, 65 MG SODIUM.

Forming Rugelach

Spread the dough with butter and sprinkle it with cinnamon-sugar, currants, and nuts. Cut the round into 12 wedges and roll each one up, starting from the wide end.

Ultimate Sugar Cookies

PREP 1 HOUR 30 MINUTES PLUS CHILLING
BAKE 12 TO 15 MINUTES PER BATCH

Classic holiday cookies like these are sure to become a family tradition. They can be dressed up with colored sugar crystals (before baking) or decorated with Ornamental Frosting (page 358) after baking.

3 CUPS ALL-PURPOSE FLOUR
½ TEASPOON BAKING POWDER
½ TEASPOON SALT
1 CUP BUTTER (2 STICKS), SOFTENED (DO NOT USE MARGARINE)
1½ CUPS SUGAR
2 LARGE EGGS
1 TEASPOON VANILLA EXTRACT

1 On sheet of waxed paper, stir together flour, baking powder, and salt. In large bowl, with mixer at low speed, beat butter and sugar until blended. Increase speed to high; beat until light and creamy, about 5 minutes. Reduce speed to low; beat in eggs and vanilla until mixed. Beat in flour mixture, scraping bowl occasionally with rubber spatula, just until mixed. Shape dough into 4 balls; flatten each slightly. Wrap each in waxed paper and refrigerate overnight, until firm enough to roll.

2 Preheat oven to 350° F. Keeping remaining dough refrigerated, on lightly floured surface, with floured rolling pin, roll 1 piece of dough a scant ¼ inch thick. With floured 3- to 4-inch assorted cookie cutters, cut dough into as many cookies as possible; reserve trimmings. Place cookies, about 1 inch apart, on ungreased large cookie sheet.

3 Bake 12 to 15 minutes, until golden around edges. With wide spatula, transfer cookies to wire racks to cool.

4 Repeat with remaining cookie dough and trimmings. *Makes about 6 dozen cookies.*

EACH COOKIE WITHOUT SUGAR CRYSTALS OR FROSTING: ABOUT 60 CALORIES, 1 G PROTEIN, 8 G CARBOHYDRATE, 3 G TOTAL FAT (2 G SATURATED), 0 G FIBER, 13 MG CHOLESTEROL, 45 MG SODIUM.

SANDWICH SUGAR COOKIES Prepare, chill, and roll dough as for Ultimate Sugar Cookies (page 63). With fluted round or other decorative cutter, cut dough into 2½-inch rounds; with smaller cutter, cut out and remove centers from half of rounds. Reserve centers for rerolling. Bake as directed; cool. Spread whole rounds with thin layer of *warmed seedless raspberry jam* (you will need about 1 cup). Top each with 1 cut-out round. *Makes 3 dozen filled cookies.*

EACH COOKIE: ABOUT 145 CALORIES, 2 G PROTEIN, 23 G CARBOHYDRATE, 5 G TOTAL FAT (3 G SATURATED), 0.5 G FIBER, 26 MG CHOLESTEROL, 100 MG SODIUM.

Simple Sugar Cookies

PREP 30 MINUTES PLUS CHILLING
BAKE 9 TO 10 MINUTES PER BATCH

2 CUPS ALL-PURPOSE FLOUR
½ TEASPOON BAKING POWDER
¼ TEASPOON SALT
1 STICK BUTTER OR MARGARINE (½ CUP), SOFTENED
1 CUP SUGAR
1 LARGE EGG
1 TEASPOON VANILLA EXTRACT

1 On sheet of waxed paper, stir together flour, baking powder, and salt.

2 With mixer at medium speed, beat butter and sugar until light and fluffy. Beat in egg and vanilla. Reduce speed to low and beat in flour mixture until well combined. Divide dough in half. Wrap each half in waxed paper and refrigerate at least 1 hour or overnight.

3 Preheat oven to 375° F. On lightly floured surface, with floured rolling pin, roll 1 piece of dough ⅛-inch thick. With 2½-inch cookie cutters, cut as many cookies as possible; reserve trimmings. Place, 1 inch apart, on 2 ungreased large cookie sheets. Bake 9 to 10 minutes, rotating sheets between upper and lower racks halfway through baking, or until lightly browned. Cool cookie sheets on wire racks 1 minute. With wide spatula, transfer to racks to cool completely.

4 Repeat with remaining cookie dough and trimmings. *Makes about 5 dozen cookies.*

EACH COOKIE: ABOUT 45 CALORIES, 1 G PROTEIN, 7 G CARBOHYDRATE, 2 G TOTAL FAT (1 G SATURATED), 0 G FIBER, 8 MG CHOLESTEROL, 30 MG SODIUM.

Biscochitos

PREP 18 MINUTES / BAKE 11 MINUTES PER BATCH

Lard is the traditional shortening used in these Mexican sugar cookies; we've substituted butter and vegetable shortening for a flaky texture and buttery flavor.

3 CUPS ALL-PURPOSE FLOUR
1½ TEASPOONS BAKING POWDER
¼ TEASPOON SALT
½ CUP BUTTER OR MARGARINE (1 STICK), SOFTENED
½ CUP VEGETABLE SHORTENING
1 CUP SUGAR
2 TEASPOONS ANISE SEEDS
1 LARGE EGG YOLK
¼ CUP SHERRY OR SWEET WINE
4 TEASPOONS GROUND CINNAMON

1 Preheat oven to 375° F. On sheet of waxed paper, stir together flour, baking powder, and salt.

2 In large bowl, with mixer at medium speed, beat butter, shortening, and ½ cup sugar until light and fluffy. Beat in anise seeds and egg yolk until well combined. Beat in sherry until smooth.

3 Reduce speed to low and beat in flour mixture until well combined. Divide dough into 4 equal pieces. On lightly floured surface, working with 1 piece of dough at a time, roll out ¼ inch thick.

4 In small bowl, stir together remaining ½ cup sugar and cinnamon. Sprinkle one-fourth of the sugar mixture over dough. With 2-inch decorative cookie cutter, cut out as many cookies as possible. (Cut each cookie as close to the other as possible; do not reroll scraps). Repeat with remaining cookie dough and cinnamon sugar.

5 Place cookies, 1 inch apart, on ungreased large cookie sheets. Bake 11 minutes, rotating sheets between upper and lower racks halfway through baking, until set. Cool on cookie sheets on wire racks 1 minute. With wide spatula, transfer to wire racks to cool completely.

6 Repeat with remaining cookie dough. *Makes about 6½ dozen cookies.*

EACH COOKIE: ABOUT 50 CALORIES, 1 G PROTEIN, 6 G CARBOHYDRATE, 3 G TOTAL FAT (1 G SATURATED), 0 G FIBER, 6 MG CHOLESTEROL, 30 MG SODIUM.

Hamantaschen

PREP 1 HOUR PLUS CHILLING
BAKE 12 MINUTES PER BATCH

The three-cornered pastries called "Haman's pockets" are the culinary symbol of the Jewish holiday of Purim. Both prune and poppyseed fillings are traditional.

2 CUPS ALL-PURPOSE FLOUR

¾ TEASPOON BAKING POWDER

⅛ TEASPOON SALT

1 LEMON

½ CUP BUTTER OR MARGARINE (1 STICK), SOFTENED

⅔ CUP GRANULATED SUGAR

1 LARGE EGG

1 LARGE EGG YOLK

1 TEASPOON VANILLA EXTRACT

1½ CUPS PRUNE BUTTER (LEKVAR)

4 TEASPOONS PACKED LIGHT BROWN SUGAR

1 On sheet of waxed paper, stir together flour, baking powder, and salt. From lemon, grate 1 teaspoon peel and squeeze 1 teaspoon juice.

2 In large bowl, with mixer at medium speed, beat butter until creamy. Beat in granulated sugar until light and fluffy. Beat in egg, egg yolk, vanilla, and ½ teaspoon lemon peel until well combined.

3 Reduce speed to low and beat in flour mixture until well combined. Divide dough in half. Wrap each half in waxed paper and refrigerate several hours or overnight.

4 Preheat oven to 375° F. Line 2 large cookie sheets with foil. In small bowl, stir together prune butter, brown sugar, lemon juice, and remaining ½ teaspoon lemon peel. Keeping remaining dough refrigerated, on lightly floured surface, with floured rolling pin, roll dough ⅛ inch thick. With 2½-inch round biscuit cutter, cut 20 rounds; reserve trimmings.

5 Spoon 1 teaspoon of prune mixture into center of each round (see top photo at right). To make triangular pocket, fold 2 "sides" up and pinch corners to seal (see bottom photo at right). Fold third side up to meet folded sides and pinch corner to seal (leave small opening in center). Place 1 inch apart on prepared cookie sheets. Bake 1 sheet at a time 12 min-utes, or until pastries are lightly browned. Cool 1 minute on cookie sheet on wire rack. With wide spatula, transfer to wire rack to cool completely.

6 Repeat with remaining dough, trimmings, and filling. *Makes about 3½ dozen cookies.*

EACH COOKIE: ABOUT 95 CALORIES, 1 G PROTEIN, 17 G CARBOHYDRATE, 2 G TOTAL FAT (1 G SATURATED), 0.5 G FIBER, 16 MG CHOLESTEROL, 45 MG SODIUM.

Forming Hamantaschen

Place a teaspoonful of filling in the center of each round of dough.

Bring two "sides" of the dough round up over the filling and pinch them together, then bring up the third side to form a triangular pastry. Leave a little open space in the center to show the filling.

Pinwheels

Pinwheels

PREP **35** MINUTES PLUS CHILLING
BAKE **9** MINUTES PER BATCH

1⅓ CUPS ALL-PURPOSE FLOUR
¼ TEASPOON BAKING POWDER
⅛ TEASPOON SALT
6 TABLESPOONS BUTTER OR MARGARINE, SOFTENED
½ CUP SUGAR
1 LARGE EGG
1 TEASPOON VANILLA EXTRACT
¼ CUP DAMSON PLUM, SEEDLESS RASPBERRY,
   OR OTHER JAM

1 On sheet of waxed paper, stir together flour, baking powder, and salt.

2 In large bowl, with mixer at medium speed, beat butter and sugar until light and fluffy. Beat in egg and vanilla until well combined. Reduce speed to low and beat in flour mixture until combined. Divide dough in half, wrap each half in waxed paper, and refrigerate at least 1 hour, or overnight. (If using margarine, freeze overnight.)

3 Preheat oven to 375° F. Keeping remaining dough refrigerated, on floured surface, with floured rolling pin, roll half of dough into 10" by 7½" rectangle. With jagged-edged pastry wheel or sharp knife, cut into twelve 2½" by 2½" squares. Place 1 square at a time, 1 inch apart, on 2 ungreased cookie sheets. Make a 1½-inch cut from each corner toward center. Spoon ½ teaspoon jam in center of each square. Fold every other tip in to center. Repeat with remaining squares.

4 Bake 9 minutes, rotating sheets between upper and lower racks halfway through baking, or until lightly browned around the edges and set. With wide spatula, transfer to wire racks to cool completely.

5 Repeat with remaining dough and jam. *Makes 2 dozen cookies.*

EACH COOKIE: ABOUT 80 CALORIES, 1 G PROTEIN,
12 G CARBOHYDRATE, 3 G TOTAL FAT (2 G SATURATED),
0 G FIBER, 17 MG CHOLESTEROL, 50 MG SODIUM.

Sour Cream Cut-Out Sugar Cookies

PREP 35 MINUTES PLUS CHILLING
BAKE 8 MINUTES PER BATCH

1¾ CUPS ALL-PURPOSE FLOUR
½ TEASPOON BAKING SODA
¼ TEASPOON SALT
½ CUP BUTTER OR MARGARINE (1 STICK), SOFTENED
1 CUP PLUS ABOUT 2 TABLESPOONS SUGAR
1 LARGE EGG
1 TEASPOON VANILLA EXTRACT
½ CUP SOUR CREAM

1 On sheet of waxed paper, stir together flour, baking soda, and salt.

2 In large bowl, with mixer at medium speed, beat butter and 1 cup sugar until combined. Reduce speed to low and beat in egg and vanilla until blended. Beat in sour cream. Beat in flour mixture until combined, scraping bowl occasionally with rubber spatula. Shape dough into 4 balls; flatten each slightly. Wrap each in waxed paper and refrigerate at least 2 hours, or overnight, until dough is firm enough to roll. (If using margarine, refrigerate overnight.)

2 Preheat oven to 350° F. Keeping remaining dough refrigerated, on lightly floured surface, with floured rolling pin, roll 1 piece of dough ⅛ inch thick. With floured 2-inch cookie cutters, cut as many cookies as possible; reserve trimmings. Place cookies, about 1½ inches apart, on ungreased large cookie sheet. Sprinkle with some of remaining sugar. Bake 8 minutes. With wide spatula, transfer cookies to wire racks to cool completely.

3 Repeat with remaining dough, trimmings, and sugar. *Makes about 6½ dozen cookies.*

EACH COOKIE: ABOUT 35 CALORIES, 0 G PROTEIN,
5 G CARBOHYDRATE, 2 G TOTAL FAT (1 G SATURATED),
0 G FIBER, 7 MG CHOLESTEROL, 30 MG SODIUM.

PRESSED & PIPED COOKIES

You could call these methods elaborations on the drop cookie—the dough is placed on the sheet by piping it through a pastry bag tip or "extruding" it through the decorative plates of a cookie press. Cookie-press dough is very buttery yet firm so that it neither crumbles nor runs when "spritzed" onto the baking sheet. Soft, almost batterlike doughs based on almond paste or meringue are suitable for piping with a pastry bag.

Spritz Cookies

PREP 15 MINUTES / BAKE 10 TO 12 MINUTES PER BATCH

1 CUP BUTTER OR MARGARINE (2 STICKS), SOFTENED
¾ CUP CONFECTIONERS' SUGAR
1 TEASPOON VANILLA EXTRACT
⅛ TEASPOON ALMOND EXTRACT
2 CUPS ALL-PURPOSE FLOUR
⅛ TEASPOON SALT

1 Preheat oven to 350° F.

2 In large bowl, with mixer at medium speed, beat butter and sugar until light and fluffy. Beat in vanilla and almond extracts. Reduce speed to low; add flour and salt and beat until well combined.

3 Spoon one-third of dough into cookie press fitted with pattern of your choice. Press cookies, 1 inch apart, on ungreased large cookie sheet. Bake 10 to 12 minutes, until golden brown around edges. With wide spatula, transfer cookies to wire racks to cool completely.

4 Repeat with remaining cookie dough. *Makes about 5 dozen cookies.*

EACH COOKIE: ABOUT 50 CALORIES, 0 G PROTEIN,
5 G CARBOHYDRATE, 3 G TOTAL FAT (2 G SATURATED),
0 G FIBER, 8 MG CHOLESTEROL, 35 MG SODIUM.

CHOCOLATE SPRITZ COOKIES Prepare as above but use *1 cup confectioners' sugar* and add *2 squares (2 ounces) unsweetened chocolate*, melted and cooled, after combining butter and sugar. Bake as directed.
EACH COOKIE: ABOUT 55 CALORIES, 1 G PROTEIN,
5 G CARBOHYDRATE, 4 G TOTAL FAT (2 G SATURATED),
0 G FIBER, 8 MG CHOLESTEROL, 35 MG SODIUM.

ALMOND SPRITZ COOKIES In food processor with knife blade attached, process *¾ cup whole natural almonds*, toasted, and *¼ cup confectioners' sugar* until nuts are finely ground. Prepare dough as for Spritz Cookies (page 67) but use *¼ teaspoon almond extract* and *2¼ cups flour*. Add ground almond mixture with flour (dough will be quite stiff). Bake as directed.

EACH COOKIE: ABOUT 60 CALORIES, 1 G PROTEIN, 6 G CARBOHYDRATE, 4 G TOTAL FAT (2 G SATURATED), 0.5 G FIBER, 8 MG CHOLESTEROL, 35 MG SODIUM.

Almond Macaroons

PREP 15 MINUTES / BAKE 20 MINUTES PER BATCH

These are light, delicate macaroons. If it's the more substantial coconut version you crave, see page 43.

1 TUBE OR CAN (7 TO 8 OUNCES) ALMOND PASTE
½ CUP CONFECTIONERS' SUGAR, PLUS ADDITIONAL (OPTIONAL)
2 LARGE EGG WHITES
½ TEASPOON VANILLA EXTRACT

1 Preheat oven to 300° F. Line 2 large cookie sheets with parchment paper.

2 In large bowl, knead almond paste and sugar until combined (a few small lumps will remain). Add egg whites and vanilla. With mixer at medium speed, beat until well combined.

3 Spoon batter into pastry bag fitted with ¼-inch plain tip. Pipe mounds 1 inch in diameter, about 1 inch apart, onto prepared cookie sheets. Dust with confectioners' sugar, if you like.

4 Bake 20 minutes, rotating sheets between upper and lower racks halfway through baking, or until cookies start to color around the edges. Cool completely on cookie sheets on wire racks.

5 Repeat with remaining batter and confectioners' sugar, if using. *Makes about 4 dozen macaroons.*

EACH COOKIE: ABOUT 25 CALORIES, 1 G PROTEIN, 3 G CARBOHYDRATE, 1 G TOTAL FAT (0 G SATURATED), 0 G FIBER, 0 MG CHOLESTEROL, 5 MG SODIUM.

Pignoli Cookies

PREP 25 MINUTES / BAKE 10 TO 12 MINUTES PER BATCH

Pignoli are the sweet, oily seeds of a certain type of pine tree. They're used in Italian desserts as well as in savory recipes such as pesto.

1 TUBE OR CAN (7 TO 8 OUNCES) ALMOND PASTE
¾ CUP CONFECTIONERS' SUGAR
1 LARGE EGG WHITE
1 TABLESPOON PLUS 1 TEASPOON HONEY
½ CUP PINE NUTS (PIGNOLI)

1 Preheat oven to 350° F. Line 2 large cookie sheets with parchment paper.

2 Crumble almond paste into food processor with knife blade attached. Add sugar and process until paste is texture of fine meal. Transfer to large bowl. Add egg white and honey. With mixer at low speed, beat until blended. Increase speed to medium-high and beat 5 minutes, or until very smooth.

3 Spoon batter into pastry bag fitted with ½-inch round tip. Pipe 1¼-inch rounds, 2 inches apart, on prepared cookie sheets. Brush cookies lightly with water and cover cookies completely with pine nuts, pressing nuts lightly to stick.

4 Bake 10 to 12 minutes, rotating sheets between upper and lower rack halfway through baking, until golden brown. Slide parchment paper onto wire racks and let cookies cool on parchment paper.

5 Repeat with remaining dough and pine nuts. *Makes about 2 dozen cookies.*

EACH COOKIE: ABOUT 75 CALORIES, 2 G PROTEIN, 9 G CARBOHYDRATE, 4 G TOTAL FAT (0 G SATURATED), 0.5 G FIBER, 0 MG CHOLESTEROL, 5 MG SODIUM.

MERINGUE COOKIES

MERINGUES ARE USUALLY "LIGHTER" THAN OTHER COOKIES BECAUSE THEY ARE MADE WITHOUT EGG YOLKS OR BUTTER; HOWEVER, ADDING NUTS AND ALMOND PASTE INCREASES FAT AND CALORIES.

Meringue Fingers

PREP 25 MINUTES PLUS COOLING
BAKE 1 HOUR PER BATCH

Meringues, made from beaten egg whites, sugar, and very little else, are baked slowly in a very low oven. Don't try to speed up the process by turning up the heat. As a whimsical touch, we've half-dipped these piped cookies into semisweet chocolate.

3 LARGE EGG WHITES
¼ TEASPOON CREAM OF TARTAR
⅛ TEASPOON SALT
½ CUP SUGAR
1 TEASPOON VANILLA EXTRACT
2 SQUARES (2 OUNCES) SEMISWEET CHOCOLATE
1 TEASPOON VEGETABLE SHORTENING

1 Preheat oven to 200° F. Line 2 large cookie sheets with foil.

2 In small bowl, with mixer at high speed, beat egg whites, cream of tartar, and salt until soft peaks form when beaters are lifted. Increase speed to high and gradually sprinkle in sugar, 2 tablespoons at a time, beating until sugar has dissolved. Add vanilla; continue beating until meringue stands in stiff, glossy peaks when beaters are lifted.

3 Spoon meringue into pastry bag fitted with ½-inch star tip. Pipe meringue into 3" by ½" fingers, about 1 inch apart, on prepared cookie sheets.

4 Bake cookies 1 hour, rotating sheets between upper and lower racks halfway through baking, or until set. Cool 10 minutes on cookie sheets on wire racks. With small spatula, transfer cookies to wire racks to cool completely.

5 When cookies have cooled, in small saucepan, heat chocolate and shortening over low heat, stirring occasionally, until melted and smooth. Remove saucepan from heat. Dip one end of each cookie into melted chocolate mixture; let dry on wire racks over sheet of waxed paper. *Makes about 4 dozen cookies.*

EACH COOKIE: ABOUT 15 CALORIES, 0 G PROTEIN,
3 G CARBOHYDRATE, 0 G TOTAL FAT (0 G SATURATED),
0 G FIBER, 0 MG CHOLESTEROL, 10 MG SODIUM.

Meringue Fingers

SPECIAL COOKIES

Drop, bar, and icebox cookies are fine for filling the cookie-jar and livening up lunchboxes. But special occasions call for fancier sweets that may take a little more time or call for slightly trickier techniques. The response usually goes beyond the usual "Yum!" to "You *made* these?"

Pecan Tassies

PREP 40 MINUTES PLUS CHILLING / BAKE 30 MINUTES

The South is home to these diminutive pecan tarts. In a pinch, bake the nut filling in storebought miniature tart shells rather than making the pastry yourself.

1 PACKAGE (3 OUNCES) CREAM CHEESE, SOFTENED
½ CUP (1 STICK) PLUS 1 TABLESPOON BUTTER OR
  MARGARINE, SOFTENED
1 CUP ALL-PURPOSE FLOUR
2 TABLESPOONS GRANULATED SUGAR
1 CUP PECANS, TOASTED AND FINELY CHOPPED
⅔ CUP PACKED LIGHT BROWN SUGAR
1 LARGE EGG
1 TEASPOON VANILLA EXTRACT

1 Preheat oven to 350° F. In large bowl, with mixer at high speed, beat cream cheese with ½ cup butter until creamy. Reduce speed to low and add flour and granulated sugar; beat until well mixed. Cover bowl with plastic wrap; refrigerate 30 minutes.

2 In medium bowl, with spoon, combine pecans, brown sugar, egg, vanilla, and remaining 1 tablespoon butter.

3 With floured hands, divide chilled dough into 24 equal pieces (dough will be very soft). With floured fingertips, gently press each piece of dough evenly onto bottom and up side of twenty-four 1¾" by 1" ungreased miniature muffin-pan cups. Spoon pecan filling, by heaping teaspoons, into each pastry cup.

4 Bake 30 minutes, or until filling is set and crust is golden. With small thin knife, loosen cookie cups from muffin-pan cups and transfer to wire racks to cool completely. *Makes 2 dozen cookies.*

EACH COOKIE: ABOUT 135 CALORIES, 1 G PROTEIN,
12 G CARBOHYDRATE, 9 G TOTAL FAT (4 G SATURATED),
0.5 G FIBER, 24 MG CHOLESTEROL, 60 MG SODIUM.

Brandy Snaps

PREP 25 MINUTES / BAKE 5 MINUTES PER BATCH

It's best to wait for dry weather before attempting to bake these lacy delights. When they're cooled, store them in an airtight container.

½ CUP BUTTER (1 STICK) (DO NOT USE MARGARINE)
3 TABLESPOONS LIGHT (MILD) MOLASSES
½ CUP ALL-PURPOSE FLOUR
½ CUP SUGAR
1 TEASPOON GROUND GINGER
¼ TEASPOON SALT
2 TABLESPOONS BRANDY

1 Preheat oven to 350° F. Grease large cookie sheet.

2 In small saucepan, heat butter and molasses over medium heat, stirring occasionally, until butter has melted. Remove saucepan from heat; with spoon, stir in flour, sugar, ginger, and salt until smooth. Stir in brandy until blended. Place saucepan in skillet of hot water to keep warm.

3 Drop 1 teaspoon batter on prepared cookie sheet; with back of spoon, spread in circular motion to make 4-inch round (batter spreads during baking to fill in any thin areas). Repeat to make 3 more rounds, about 2 inches apart. (Do not place more than 4 rounds on cookie sheet because, after baking, cookies must be shaped quickly before they harden.)

4 Bake about 5 minutes, or until golden brown. Cool on cookie sheet on wire rack, 30 to 60 seconds only, until edges set. With wide spatula, flip cookies over quickly so lacy texture will be on outside after rolling.

5 Working as quickly as possible, roll each cookie into cylinder around handle of wooden spoon or dowel (about ½ inch in diameter). If cookies become too hard to shape, return to oven briefly to soften. As each cookie is shaped, remove from spoon handle; cool on wire rack.

6 Repeat with remaining batter. *Makes about 2 dozen cookies.*

EACH COOKIE: ABOUT 70 CALORIES, 0 G PROTEIN,
8 G CARBOHYDRATE, 4 G TOTAL FAT (2 G SATURATED),
0 G FIBER, 10 MG CHOLESTEROL, 65 MG SODIUM.

Almond Tuiles

PREP 30 MINUTES / BAKE 5 TO 7 MINUTES PER BATCH

Gracefully curved French terracotta roof tiles–"tuiles"– inspired the shape of these cookies. If the curling step seems too time-consuming, serve them as flat wafers.

3 LARGE EGG WHITES
¾ CUP CONFECTIONERS' SUGAR
½ CUP ALL-PURPOSE FLOUR
6 TABLESPOONS BUTTER, MELTED (DO NOT USE
   MARGARINE)
¼ TEASPOON SALT
¼ TEASPOON ALMOND EXTRACT
⅔ CUP SLICED NATURAL ALMONDS

1 Preheat oven to 350° F. Grease large cookie sheet.

2 In large bowl, with wire whisk, beat egg whites, sugar, and flour until blended and smooth. Beat in melted butter, salt, and almond extract.

3 Drop 1 heaping teaspoon batter on prepared cookie sheet; with back of spoon (see top photo at right), spread in circular motion to make 3-inch round (batter spreads during baking to fill in any thin areas). Repeat to make 3 more rounds, about 3 inches apart. (Do not place more than 4 rounds on cookie sheet because, after baking, cookies must be shaped quickly before they harden.) Sprinkle with some almonds in single layer over each cookie.

4 Bake 5 to 7 minutes, until edges are golden. With wide spatula, quickly remove cookies from cookie sheet and drape over rolling pin to curve (see bottom photo at right). If cookies become too hard to shape, return to oven briefly to soften. When firm, transfer to wire racks to cool. (If you like, omit shaping cookies and cool flat.)

5 Repeat with remaining batter and almonds. (Batter will become slightly thicker upon standing.) *Makes about 2½ dozen cookies.*

EACH COOKIE: ABOUT 60 CALORIES, 1 G PROTEIN,
5 G CARBOHYDRATE, 4 G TOTAL FAT (2 G SATURATED),
0 G FIBER, 6 MG CHOLESTEROL, 50 MG SODIUM.

Shaping Almond Tuiles

Spread the batter for the Almond Tuiles into even 3-inch rounds on well-greased cookie sheets.

After baking, carefully lift each cookie while still hot from the sheet and drape it over a rolling pin or other cylindrical object so that it cools in a curved shape.

Quick Palmiers

PREP 35 MINUTES PLUS CHILLING
BAKE 15 MINUTES PER BATCH

Palmiers (palm trees) are clever French pastries made by cutting slices from a doubly scrolled sheet of dough. Palmiers are usually made with puff pastry; our version uses a simple but rich sour-cream dough.

1½ CUPS COLD BUTTER (3 STICKS), CUT UP (DO NOT USE
    MARGARINE)
3 CUPS ALL-PURPOSE FLOUR
¾ CUP SOUR CREAM
1 CUP SUGAR

1 In large bowl, with pastry blender or 2 knives used scissor-fashion, cut butter into flour until mixture resembles coarse crumbs. Stir in sour cream. On lightly floured surface, knead just until dough holds together. Flatten dough to 8" by 6" rectangle. Wrap in waxed paper and refrigerate until firm enough to roll, at least 2½ hours, or overnight.

2 Preheat oven to 400° F. Cut dough in half. Sprinkle ½ cup sugar on surface of one half. Keeping remaining dough refrigerated, with floured rolling pin, roll dough half into 14" by 14" square. Using side of your hand, make indentation down center of dough. Starting at one side, roll dough tightly up to indentation. Repeat with other side until it meets first in center, incorporating as much of sugar as possible into dough. Refrigerate scroll.

3 Repeat with remaining chilled dough and ½ cup sugar. With serrated knife, cut scroll crosswise into ¼-inch-thick slices. (Refrigerate scroll if too soft to slice.) Place slices, 2 inches apart, on ungreased cookie sheet. Bake 10 minutes. With wide spatula, carefully turn cookies over and bake 5 minutes longer, or until sugar has caramelized and cookies are deep golden. Cool on cookie sheet 1 minute. With wide spatula, transfer cookies to wire racks to cool completely.

4 Repeat with remaining scroll and sugar. *Makes about 6 dozen cookies.*

EACH COOKIE: ABOUT 70 CALORIES, 1 G PROTEIN,
7 G CARBOHYDRATE, 4 G TOTAL FAT (3 G SATURATED),
0 G FIBER, 11 MG CHOLESTEROL, 40 MG SODIUM.

Florentines

PREP 40 MINUTES PLUS COOLING
BAKE 10 MINUTES PER BATCH

Made with very little flour—but lots of almonds and candied orange peel—these elegant cookies are perfect for a reception or as a special gift. Handle the cookies carefully when icing them, as they are quite fragile. For an even more lavish treat, sandwich two cookies together with a layer of chocolate in between.

6 TABLESPOONS BUTTER, CUT UP (DO NOT USE
    MARGARINE)
¼ CUP HEAVY OR WHIPPING CREAM
1 TABLESPOON LIGHT CORN SYRUP
½ CUP SUGAR
2 TABLESPOONS ALL-PURPOSE FLOUR
1 CUP SLIVERED ALMONDS, FINELY CHOPPED
½ CUP CANDIED ORANGE PEEL, FINELY CHOPPED
8 SQUARES (8 OUNCES) SEMISWEET CHOCOLATE, MELTED

1 Preheat oven to 350° F. Line large cookie sheet with cooking parchment.

2 In 1-quart saucepan, combine butter, cream, corn syrup, sugar, and flour and heat to boiling over medium heat, stirring frequently. Remove saucepan from heat; stir in almonds and candied orange peel.

3 Drop batter by rounded teaspoons, 3 inches apart, on prepared cookie sheet. Do not place more than 6 on cookie sheet. Bake 10 minutes, or just until set. Cool on cookie sheet 1 minute. With wide metal spatula, transfer to wire racks to cool. If cookies become too hard to remove, return sheet to oven briefly to soften. Repeat with remaining batter.

4 With small metal spatula or butter knife, spread flat side of each cookie with melted chocolate. Return to wire racks, chocolate side up, and let stand until chocolate has set. *Makes about 4 dozen cookies.*

EACH COOKIE: ABOUT 70 CALORIES, 1 G PROTEIN,
8 G CARBOHYDRATE, 5 G TOTAL FAT (2 G SATURATED),
0.5 G FIBER, 6 MG CHOLESTEROL, 15 MG SODIUM.

Almond Leaves

PREP 65 MINUTES PLUS COOLING
BAKE 7 TO 9 MINUTES PER BATCH

A spatula-like stencil with a leaf-shaped cut-out is used to make these autumnal almond cookies.

⅓ CUP ALMOND PASTE (3½ OUNCES), CRUMBLED
¼ CUP SUGAR
3 TABLESPOONS BUTTER OR MARGARINE, SOFTENED
¼ TEASPOON ALMOND EXTRACT
1 LARGE EGG, SLIGHTLY BEATEN
⅓ CUP PLUS 2 TABLESPOONS ALL-PURPOSE FLOUR

1 In small bowl, with mixer at medium speed, beat almond paste until softened. Add sugar and beat until smooth (a few small lumps will remain). Add butter and beat until well blended. Reduce speed to low and beat in egg and almond extract until incorporated. Stir in flour until just combined, scraping bowl occasionally with rubber spatula.

2 Preheat oven to 350° F. Generously butter 2 large cookie sheets. Spread a teaspoonful of batter through leaf spatula and smooth ⅛ inch thick with small wet metal spatula Repeat with remaining batter, leaving 2 inches in between leaves. Bake 7 to 9 minutes, rotating sheets between upper and lower racks halfway through baking, until edges are golden. With wide spatula, transfer cookies to wire rack to cool completely.

3 Repeat with remaining cookie batter. *Makes about 3 dozen cookies.*

EACH COOKIE: ABOUT 35 CALORIES, 1 G PROTEIN,
4 G CARBOHYDRATE, 2 G TOTAL FAT (1 G SATURATED),
0 G FIBER, 9 MG CHOLESTEROL, 15 MG SODIUM.

CHOCOLATE-ALMOND LEAVES Prepare as above; cool. Melt *3½ squares (3½ ounces) semisweet chocolate.* Spread chocolate in thin layer over cooled cookies, marking veins of leaves with edge of thin metal spatula. Let stand on wire racks until chocolate has set.
EACH COOKIE: ABOUT 50 CALORIES, 1 G PROTEIN,
6 G CARBOHYDRATE, 3 G TOTAL FAT (1 G SATURATED),
0 G FIBER, 9 MG CHOLESTEROL, 15 MG SODIUM.

Madeleines

PREP 25 MINUTES PLUS COOLING
BAKE 10 TO 12 MINUTES PER BATCH

1 CUP ALL-PURPOSE FLOUR
½ TEASPOON BAKING POWDER
10 TABLESPOONS BUTTER (1¼ STICKS), SOFTENED (DO NOT USE MARGARINE)
¾ CUP SUGAR
3 LARGE EGGS
1 LARGE EGG YOLK
1½ TEASPOONS VANILLA EXTRACT

1 Preheat oven to 400° F. Generously grease and flour madeleine pan. On sheet of waxed paper, mix flour and baking powder.

2 In large bowl, with mixer at medium speed, beat butter and sugar until creamy, about 2 minutes. Add eggs, egg yolk, and vanilla. Increase speed to high; beat until pale yellow, about 3 minutes. Reduce speed to low and beat in flour just until blended, scraping bowl with rubber spatula.

3 Spoon batter by rounded measuring tablespoons into prepared pan. Bake 10 to 12 minutes, until browned at edges and tops spring back when lightly pressed. Let madeleines cool in pan 1 minute. With the tip of a table knife, release onto wire rack to cool completely.

4 Wash, grease, and flour pan. Repeat with remaining batter. *Makes 2 dozen madeleines.*

EACH MADELEINE: ABOUT 105 CALORIES, 2 G PROTEIN,
11 G CARBOHYDRATE, 6 G TOTAL FAT (3 G SATURATED),
0 G FIBER, 48 MG CHOLESTEROL, 65 MG SODIUM.

THE LITERARY COOKIE

MADELEINES—SMALL FRENCH SPONGE CAKES BAKED IN A PAN WITH SHALLOW, SHELL-SHAPED CUPS—WERE MADE WORLD-FAMOUS BY MARCEL PROUST (1871–1922) IN HIS 4-VOLUME NOVEL, REMEMBRANCE OF THINGS PAST. THE NOVEL OPENS WITH THE WRITER HAVING MADELEINES WITH AFTERNOON TEA. THE SHAPE AND FLAVOR OF THE LITTLE CAKES EVOKE LONG-FORGOTTEN EVENTS OF HIS YOUTH AND LIFE.

Almond Leaves

Quick Breads &
Crackers

Quick Breads & Crackers

loaf pans (8½" by 4½" and 9" by 5")

muffin pan

cornstick pan

biscuit cutter

Baking bread doesn't have to be an all-day affair. You can mix up the batter quickly for a tea bread or a batch of muffins, or the dough for biscuits or scones, in 20 minutes or less, and the baking time is not very long, either. Homemade crackers are slightly more time-consuming but a highly rewarding project. Most quick breads freeze well, and very few of them require any sophisticated skills or techniques. Basic equipment for quick breads includes a couple of **loaf pans,** which come in several sizes. Batter for a standard 9" by 5" loaf can also be baked in three mini (5½" by 3") pans. If you're giving quick breads as gifts, bake them in disposable foil pans; slip the breads out of the pans to cool, then slip them back in, and wrap. **Muffin pans** come in several sizes, too. Standard pans have cups 2½" in diameter and 1¼" deep; there are also mini and "Texas size" muffin-pan cups. Used to bake loaflets in the shape of ears of corn, **cornstick pans** are an American tradition. They're usually made of cast iron. Finally, you may want to buy a **biscuit cutter,** which is like a cookie cutter but deeper. Old-time cooks often used the edge of an empty metal baking-powder can or a jelly glass to cut out biscuits.

Previous page: Orange-Cranberry Bread

Basic techniques

BISCUITS

With a pastry blender (or 2 knives used scissor-fashion), "chop" the shortening into the dry ingredients until crumblike.

On a lightly floured surface, pat or roll the dough out into a round. The less you "work" the dough at this point, the more tender it will be.

Use a 2-inch cutter to cut out the biscuits. If you don't have one, cut the dough with the rim of a drinking glass that's roughly the right size.

SCONES

After patting the dough into a round, score it with a sharp knife into 8 wedges, without cutting all the way through the dough.

After scoring the dough, brush it with an egg-white wash for a glossy finish.

MUFFINS

Combine the dry ingredients in a bowl and stir until well mixed. Then add the liquid ingredients all at once.

Stir the wet ingredients into the dry ingredients just until the flour mixture is moistened. The batter will be slightly lumpy. Avoid overmixing.

Use a tablespoon to spoon the batter into prepared muffin cups. For most recipes, the cups should be about two-thirds full.

BISCUITS

The old Southern saying is that biscuit baking requires "a good heart and a light hand." You'll have to take responsibility for the first part, but the second is a simple matter of restraint: Don't stir the dough too long or too hard, knead it too vigorously (it's a far gentler process than kneading yeast dough), or overhandle the dough as you cut it. Avoid these pitfalls and you'll be duly rewarded with tender, flaky biscuits. To give biscuits their due, eat them piping hot straight out of the oven.

Baking-Powder Biscuits

PREP 10 MINUTES / BAKE 12 TO 15 MINUTES

There's nothing like a fresh, hot biscuit, dripping with butter or doused with gravy. For a little headstart, you can prepare the flour/shortening mixture ahead of time; when you're ready to bake, just stir in the milk.

2 CUPS ALL-PURPOSE FLOUR
1 TABLESPOON BAKING POWDER
½ TEASPOON SALT
¼ CUP COLD VEGETABLE SHORTENING
¾ CUP MILK

1 Preheat oven to 450° F. In large bowl, stir together flour, baking powder, and salt. With pastry blender or 2 knives used scissor-fashion, cut in shortening until mixture resembles coarse crumbs. Stir in milk, stirring just until mixture forms soft dough that leaves side of bowl.

2 Turn dough onto lightly floured surface; knead 6 to 8 times, just until smooth. With floured rolling pin, roll dough ½ inch thick for high, fluffy biscuits or ¼ inch thick for thin, crusty ones.

3 With floured 2-inch biscuit cutter, cut out biscuits. With wide spatula, place biscuits on ungreased large cookie sheet, 1 inch apart for crusty biscuits, or nearly touching for soft-sided ones.

4 Press trimmings together; reroll and cut. Bake 12 to 15 minutes, until golden. Serve warm. *Makes about 1½ dozen high biscuits or 3 dozen thin biscuits.*

EACH HIGH BISCUIT: ABOUT 85 CALORIES, 2 G PROTEIN, 12 G CARBOHYDRATE, 3 G TOTAL FAT (1 G SATURATED), 0.5 G FIBER, 1 MG CHOLESTEROL, 150 MG SODIUM.
EACH THIN BISCUIT: ABOUT 40 CALORIES, 1 G PROTEIN, 6 G CARBOHYDRATE, 2 G TOTAL FAT (0 G SATURATED), 0 G FIBER, 1 MG CHOLESTEROL, 75 MG SODIUM.

BUTTERMILK BISCUITS Prepare dough as for Baking-Powder Biscuits but use *2½ teaspoons baking powder* and add *½ teaspoon baking soda* to flour mixture. Use *¾ cup buttermilk* for milk. Cut biscuits and bake as directed.
EACH HIGH BISCUIT: ABOUT 85 CALORIES, 2 G PROTEIN, 12 G CARBOHYDRATE, 3 G TOTAL FAT (1 G SATURATED), 0.5 G FIBER, 0 MG CHOLESTEROL, 180 MG SODIUM.

SESAME BISCUITS Prepare dough as for Baking-Powder Biscuits but, in Step 4, brush biscuits with *1 egg,* slightly beaten, and sprinkle with *2 tablespoons sesame seeds,* toasted. Cut biscuits and bake as directed.
EACH HIGH BISCUIT: ABOUT 95 CALORIES, 2 G PROTEIN, 12 G CARBOHYDRATE, 4 G TOTAL FAT (1 G SATURATED), 1 G FIBER, 13 MG CHOLESTEROL, 155 MG SODIUM.

BACON-GREEN ONION BISCUITS Prepare dough as for Baking-Powder Biscuits but, in Step 1, use *3 tablespoons vegetable shortening* and *1 tablespoon bacon drippings,* chilled. Stir *3 slices bacon,* cooked and crumbled, and *2 tablespoons chopped green onion* into flour mixture. Cut biscuits and bake as directed.
EACH HIGH BISCUIT: ABOUT 90 CALORIES, 2 G PROTEIN, 12 G CARBOHYDRATE, 4 G TOTAL FAT (1 G SATURATED), 0.5 G FIBER, 3 MG CHOLESTEROL, 170 MG SODIUM.

CHEDDAR-JALAPEÑO BISCUITS Prepare dough as for Baking-Powder Biscuits but cut *4 ounces Cheddar cheese,* shredded (1 cup), into flour mixture with shortening; stir in *3 tablespoons pickled jalapeño chiles,* drained and chopped, with milk. Cut biscuits and bake as directed.
EACH HIGH BISCUIT: ABOUT 110 CALORIES, 3 G PROTEIN, 12 G CARBOHYDRATE, 5 G TOTAL FAT (2 G SATURATED), 0.5 G FIBER, 8 MG CHOLESTEROL, 210 MG SODIUM.

DROP BISCUITS Prepare dough as for Baking-Powder Biscuits but use *1 cup milk;* stir dough just until blended. Drop dough by heaping tablespoons, 1 inch apart, on ungreased cookie sheet. Bake as directed. *Makes about 20 biscuits.*
EACH BISCUIT: ABOUT 75 CALORIES, 2 G PROTEIN, 5 G CARBOHYDRATE, 3 G TOTAL FAT (1 G SATURATED), 0.5 G FIBER, 2 MG CHOLESTEROL, 135 MG SODIUM.

Cornmeal Biscuits

PREP 10 MINUTES / BAKE 17 TO 18 MINUTES

For the tastiest, most nutritious biscuits, choose stone-ground cornmeal, which retains the protein-rich portion of the grain called the germ. As far as yellow or white cornmeal goes—use what you have on hand.

1¼ CUPS ALL-PURPOSE FLOUR
¾ CUP CORNMEAL
2 TABLESPOONS SUGAR
2 TEASPOONS BAKING POWDER
½ TEASPOON BAKING SODA
¼ TEASPOON SALT
6 TABLESPOONS COLD BUTTER OR MARGARINE, CUT UP
¾ CUP BUTTERMILK
1 LARGE EGG

1 Preheat oven to 375° F. In large bowl, stir together flour, cornmeal, sugar, baking powder, baking soda, and salt. With pastry blender or 2 knives used scissor-fashion, cut in butter until mixture resembles coarse crumbs.

2 In medium bowl, whisk together buttermilk and egg. Stir buttermilk mixture into flour mixture just until mixture holds together.

3 Turn dough onto lightly floured surface and, with floured rolling pin, roll dough ¾ inch thick.

4 With 2-inch biscuit cutters, cut out biscuits. Place, 1 inch apart, on ungreased large cookie sheet. Press trimmings together; reroll and cut as above.

5 Bake 17 to 18 minutes, until golden and baked through. With wide spatula, transfer to wire rack to cool briefly. Serve warm. *Makes 1 dozen biscuits.*

EACH BISCUIT: ABOUT 155 CALORIES, 3 G PROTEIN,
21 G CARBOHYDRATE, 7 G TOTAL FAT (4 G SATURATED),
1 G FIBER, 34 MG CHOLESTEROL, 260 MG SODIUM.

CORNMEAL-CHEDDAR BISCUITS Prepare as above but use *1 tablespoon sugar*, add *½ teaspoon ground red pepper (cayenne)* and *4 ounces sharp Cheddar cheese*, shredded (1 cup), to flour mixture, stirring until combined. Cut biscuits and bake as directed.
EACH BISCUIT: ABOUT 190 CALORIES, 6 G PROTEIN,
20 G CARBOHYDRATE, 10 G TOTAL FAT (6 G SATURATED),
1 G FIBER, 44 MG CHOLESTEROL, 320 MG SODIUM.

SCONES

These humble but rich British tea breads have been transformed in recent years: They've grown in size, and for "mix-ins" have gone beyond traditional currants or raisins to fresh fruit, cheese, herbs—even chocolate chips.

Blueberry Hill Scones

PREP 15 MINUTES / BAKE 22 TO 25 MINUTES

Blueberries are sturdy enough to stir into this dough, but if you'd like to use more fragile fruits, such as raspberries or blackberries, don't mix them in: Instead, gently press the berries into the top of the dough.

2 CUPS ALL-PURPOSE FLOUR
¼ CUP PACKED BROWN SUGAR
1 TABLESPOON BAKING POWDER
¼ TEASPOON SALT
4 TABLESPOONS COLD BUTTER OR MARGARINE, CUT UP
1 CUP BLUEBERRIES, PICKED OVER
⅔ CUP HEAVY OR WHIPPING CREAM
1 LARGE EGG
½ TEASPOON FRESHLY GRATED LEMON PEEL

1 Preheat oven to 375° F. In large bowl, stir together flour, brown sugar, baking powder, and salt. With pastry blender or 2 knives used scissor-fashion, cut in butter until mixture resembles coarse crumbs. Add blueberries and toss to mix.

2 In small bowl, with fork, mix cream, egg, and lemon peel until blended. Slowly pour into flour mixture, stirring with rubber spatula just until soft dough forms.

3 With lightly floured hand, knead dough in bowl 3 to 4 times, just until it holds together; do not overmix. Divide dough in half. On lightly floured surface, shape each half into 6-inch round. With floured knife, cut each round into 6 wedges. With wide spatula, place wedges, 1 inch apart, on ungreased large cookie sheet.

4 Bake 22 to 25 minutes, until golden brown. Serve scones warm, or transfer to wire rack to cool. *Makes 1 dozen scones.*

EACH SCONE: ABOUT 190 CALORIES, 3 G PROTEIN,
24 G CARBOHYDRATE, 9 G TOTAL FAT (6 G SATURATED),
1 G FIBER, 46 MG CHOLESTEROL, 220 MG SODIUM.

Simple Scones

PREP 15 MINUTES / BAKE 22 TO 25 MINUTES

2 CUPS ALL-PURPOSE FLOUR

2 TABLESPOONS PLUS 2 TEASPOONS SUGAR

2½ TEASPOONS BAKING POWDER

¼ TEASPOON SALT

½ CUP COLD BUTTER OR MARGARINE (1 STICK), CUT UP

⅔ CUP MILK

1 LARGE EGG, SEPARATED

1 Preheat oven to 375° F. In large bowl, stir together flour, 2 tablespoons sugar, baking powder, and salt. With pastry blender or 2 knives used scissor-fashion, cut in butter until mixture resembles coarse crumbs.

2 In small cup, with fork, mix milk and egg yolk. Make well in center of flour mixture, pour in milk mixture, and stir just until combined.

3 Transfer dough to ungreased large cookie sheet. With floured hands, shape into 7½-inch round. With floured knife, cut round into 8 wedges, but do not separate wedges. Brush wedges with egg white and sprinkle remaining 2 teaspoons sugar on top.

4 Bake 22 to 25 minutes, until golden brown and just cooked through. Separate scones and serve warm, or transfer to wire rack to cool. *Makes 8 scones.*

EACH SCONE: ABOUT 255 CALORIES, 5 G PROTEIN, 29 G CARBOHYDRATE, 13 G TOTAL FAT (8 G SATURATED), 1 G FIBER, 60 MG CHOLESTEROL, 360 MG SODIUM.

BRITISH TEA BREADS

THE BRITISH TRADITION OF AFTERNOON TEA IS ENHANCED BY THE MULTIPLICITY OF BREADS AND BUNS THAT APPEAR ALONGSIDE THE STEAMING KETTLE. OVEN-BAKED SCONES AND GRIDDLE SCONES, COOKED ON THE STOVETOP, ARE TWO FAVORITES. THEN THERE ARE CRUMPETS (SIMILAR TO WHAT WE CALL ENGLISH MUFFINS) AND PIKELETS (MINIATURE CRUMPETS); CURRANT-STUDDED BATH BUNS AND CINNAMON-RAISIN-FILLED CHELSEA BUNS; SNOW-WHITE IRISH SODA BREAD AND WELSH BARA BRITH (BURSTING WITH DRIED FRUIT). CAKES AND BISCUITS FOLLOW, FOR THOSE WITH ANY APPETITE REMAINING.

BUTTERMILK SCONES Prepare dough as for Simple Scones but use *2 teaspoons baking powder.* Add *½ teaspoon baking soda* and use *⅔ cup buttermilk* in place of milk. Bake as directed.

EACH SCONE: ABOUT 250 CALORIES, 5 G PROTEIN, 30 G CARBOHYDRATE, 13 G TOTAL FAT (8 G SATURATED), 1 G FIBER, 58 MG CHOLESTEROL, 420 MG SODIUM.

DRIED FRUIT SCONES Prepare dough as for Simple Scones and add *¾ cup dried fruit* (apricots, cherries, dates, or figs), coarsely chopped, or *¾ cup dark or golden raisins* to milk mixture. Bake as directed.

EACH SCONE: ABOUT 290 CALORIES, 5 G PROTEIN, 39 G CARBOHYDRATE, 13 G TOTAL FAT (8 G SATURATED), 2 G FIBER, 60 MG CHOLESTEROL, 360 MG SODIUM.

ORANGE SCONES Prepare dough as for Simple Scones and add *1 teaspoon freshly grated orange peel* to flour mixture. Bake as directed.

EACH SCONE: ABOUT 255 CALORIES, 5 G PROTEIN, 29 G CARBOHYDRATE, 13 G TOTAL FAT (8 G SATURATED), 1 G FIBER, 60 MG CHOLESTEROL, 360 MG SODIUM.

CHOCOLATE CHIP SCONES Prepare dough as for Simple Scones and add *¾ cup semisweet chocolate chips* to flour mixture. Bake as directed.

EACH SCONE: ABOUT 330 CALORIES, 5 G PROTEIN, 40 G CARBOHYDRATE, 17 G TOTAL FAT (10 G SATURATED), 1 G FIBER, 61 MG CHOLESTEROL, 360 MG SODIUM.

JAM-FILLED SCONES Prepare dough for Simple Scones; divide dough in half. On ungreased large cookie sheet, shape 1 dough half into 7½-inch round. Spread with *¼ cup jam,* leaving ½-inch rim. On lightly floured surface, with lightly floured hands, shape remaining dough half into 7½-inch round; place on top of jam. When cutting into wedges, do not cut through to jam. Bake as directed.

EACH SCONE: ABOUT 285 CALORIES, 5 G PROTEIN, 37 G CARBOHYDRATE, 13 G TOTAL FAT (8 G SATURATED), 1 G FIBER, 60 MG CHOLESTEROL, 365 MG SODIUM.

CURRANT SCONES Prepare dough as for Simple Scones; stir *1 cup dried currants* into flour mixture before adding milk mixture. Pat out into 9" by 5" by ¾" rectangle. Brush with egg white and remaining sugar. With 2-inch round biscuit cutter, cut 14 rounds. Bake, 2 inches apart, on ungreased large cookie sheet 18 minutes, or until just baked through. *Makes 14 scones.*

EACH ROUND SCONE: ABOUT 175 CALORIES, 3 G PROTEIN, 24 G CARBOHYDRATE, 7 G TOTAL FAT (4 G SATURATED), 1 G FIBER, 35 MG CHOLESTEROL, 205 MG SODIUM.

Oatmeal Scones

PREP 20 MINUTES / BAKE 20 TO 25 MINUTES

Hearty and just slightly sweet, these nutritious scones are delicious with jam or marmalade for breakfast, or with a slice of sharp Cheddar and a dab of chutney at any time of day.

1 CUP OLD-FASHIONED OR QUICK-COOKING OATS,
   UNCOOKED
1¾ CUPS ALL-PURPOSE FLOUR
3 TABLESPOONS SUGAR
2 TEASPOONS BAKING POWDER
½ TEASPOON BAKING SODA
¼ TEASPOON SALT
6 TABLESPOONS COLD BUTTER OR MARGARINE, CUT UP
½ CUP PECANS, TOASTED AND COARSELY CHOPPED
⅔ CUP BUTTERMILK
1 LARGE EGG, SEPARATED
2 TEASPOONS WATER

1 Preheat oven to 400° F. On jelly-roll pan, toast oats 5 to 7 minutes, until lightly browned. Cool. Grease large cookie sheet; dust with flour.

2 In large bowl, stir together flour, 2 tablespoons sugar, baking powder, baking soda, salt, and oats. With pastry blender or 2 knives used scissor-fashion, cut in butter until mixture resembles coarse crumbs. Stir in pecans.

3 In small bowl, with fork, mix buttermilk and egg yolk. Make well in center of flour mixture, pour in buttermilk mixture, and stir until combined. Lightly knead in bowl until dough just holds together.

4 Transfer dough to prepared cookie sheet. Shape into 7½-inch round. With floured knife, cut round into 8 wedges, but do not separate into wedges. In small bowl, stir together egg white and water. Brush over top of round. Sprinkle with remaining 1 tablespoon sugar.

5 Bake 20 to 25 minutes, until toothpick inserted in center of round comes out clean. Separate scones and serve warm, or transfer to wire rack to cool. *Makes 8 scones.*

EACH SCONE: ABOUT 305 CALORIES, 7 G PROTEIN, 36 G CARBOHYDRATE, 15 G TOTAL FAT (6 G SATURATED), 2 G FIBER, 51 MG CHOLESTEROL, 390 MG SODIUM.

Oatmeal Scones

Cream Scones

Destined for the afternoon tea table, these are the most elegant members of scone society. In berry season, melt a pat of sweet butter on a split, still-warm cream scone, then cover with thinly sliced sugared strawberries. The best strawberry jams can't match this.

2 CUPS ALL-PURPOSE FLOUR
2 TEASPOONS BAKING POWDER
½ TEASPOON SALT
¼ CUP PLUS 1½ TEASPOONS SUGAR
4 TABLESPOONS COLD BUTTER OR MARGARINE, CUT UP
1 LARGE EGG
⅔ CUP PLUS 1½ TEASPOONS HEAVY OR WHIPPING CREAM

1 Preheat oven to 400° F. In large bowl, stir together flour, baking powder, salt, and ¼ cup sugar. With pastry blender or 2 knives used scissor-fashion, cut in butter until mixture resembles coarse crumbs.

2 Stir egg and ⅔ cup cream into flour mixture just until dough holds together.

3 Transfer dough to ungreased large cookie sheet. With lightly floured hands, shape dough into 8-inch round. Brush remaining 1½ teaspoons cream over dough and sprinkle with remaining 1½ teaspoons sugar. With floured knife, cut round into 8 wedges, but do not separate wedges.

4 Bake 20 minutes, or until golden. Separate scones and serve warm, or transfer to wire rack to cool. *Makes 8 scones.*

EACH SCONE: ABOUT 275 CALORIES, 5 G PROTEIN, 33 G CARBOHYDRATE, 14 G TOTAL FAT (9 G SATURATED), 1 G FIBER, 71 MG CHOLESTEROL, 340 MG SODIUM.

Olive-Rosemary Scones

A British tradition meets the flavors of Italy with fabulous results. These rich, crumbly scones are redolent of rosemary with bits of tangy olives in every bite. Serve the scones warm, alongside a bowl of minestrone or tomato soup. Or make scone sandwiches with smoked provolone and strips of roasted pepper.

3 CUPS ALL-PURPOSE FLOUR
4 TABLESPOONS COLD BUTTER OR MARGARINE, CUT UP
1 TABLESPOON SUGAR
1 TABLESPOON BAKING POWDER
2 TEASPOONS FRESH CHOPPED ROSEMARY OR ¼ TEASPOON DRIED ROSEMARY, CRUMBLED
1 TEASPOON BAKING SODA
½ TEASPOON SALT
¼ CUP PLUS 1 TABLESPOON OLIVE OIL
1 CUP MILK
1 LARGE EGG
½ CUP KALAMATA OLIVES, PITTED AND COARSELY CHOPPED

1 Preheat oven to 425° F. Grease large cookie sheet. In food processor with knife blade attached, pulse flour, butter, sugar, baking powder, rosemary, baking soda, salt, and ¼ cup oil until mixture resembles coarse crumbs.

2 In small bowl, with fork, mix milk and egg. Pour mixture through feed tube and pulse just until dough forms.

3 Turn dough onto lightly floured surface. With floured hands, press olives into dough. Place dough on prepared cookie sheet. With floured hands, pat dough into 10-inch round. With floured knife, cut round into 12 wedges, but do not separate wedges. Brush tops with remaining 1 tablespoon oil.

4 Bake 20 to 25 minutes, until golden. Separate scones and serve warm, or transfer to wire rack to cool. *Makes 1 dozen scones.*

EACH SCONE: ABOUT 245 CALORIES, 5 G PROTEIN, 28 G CARBOHYDRATE, 13 G TOTAL FAT (4 G SATURATED), 1 G FIBER, 31 MG CHOLESTEROL, 480 MG SODIUM.

MUFFINS

Breakfast favorites and satisfying snacks, muffins are the quickest of quick breads. They freeze very well (wrap them individually), so you don't have to worry about eating up a dozen muffins before they get stale.

Basic Muffins

PREP 10 MINUTES / BAKE 20 TO 25 MINUTES

2½ CUPS ALL-PURPOSE FLOUR
½ CUP SUGAR
1 TABLESPOON BAKING POWDER
½ TEASPOON SALT
1 LARGE EGG
1 CUP MILK
½ CUP BUTTER OR MARGARINE (1 STICK), MELTED
1 TEASPOON VANILLA EXTRACT

1 Preheat oven to 400° F. Grease twelve 2½" by 1¼" muffin-pan cups or line with paper baking liners. In large bowl, stir together flour, sugar, baking powder, and salt. In medium bowl, with wire whisk or fork, mix egg, milk, melted butter, and vanilla; stir egg mixture into flour mixture just until flour is moistened (batter will be lumpy).

2 Spoon batter into prepared muffin-pan cups. Bake 20 to 25 minutes, until toothpick inserted in center of muffin comes out clean. Immediately remove muffins from pan; serve warm. Or cool on wire rack to serve later. *Makes 1 dozen muffins.*

EACH MUFFIN: ABOUT 225 CALORIES, 4 G PROTEIN, 30 G CARBOHYDRATE, 10 G TOTAL FAT (6 G SATURATED), 0.5 G FIBER, 41 MG CHOLESTEROL, 310 MG SODIUM.

BROWN SUGAR MUFFINS Prepare as above but use ⅓ *cup packed dark brown sugar* for sugar. Make streusel topping: Combine ⅔ *cup pecans*, chopped, ¼ *cup packed dark brown sugar*, and ½ *teaspoon ground cinnamon*. Sprinkle mixture on top of muffins. Bake as directed, but cover loosely with foil after 20 minutes to prevent overbrowning.
EACH MUFFIN: ABOUT 275 CALORIES, 4 G PROTEIN, 33 G CARBOHYDRATE, 14 G TOTAL FAT (6 G SATURATED), 1 G FIBER, 41 MG CHOLESTEROL, 315 MG SODIUM.

CRANBERRY-ORANGE MUFFINS Prepare batter as for Basic Muffins and add ½ *teaspoon freshly grated orange peel* to flour mixture. After adding liquid ingredients, fold in *1½ cups chopped cranberries.* Sprinkle muffins with *2 tablespoons sugar.* Bake as directed.
EACH MUFFIN: ABOUT 240 CALORIES, 4 G PROTEIN, 33 G CARBOHYDRATE, 10 G TOTAL FAT (6 G SATURATED), 1 G FIBER, 41 MG CHOLESTEROL, 310 MG SODIUM.

JAM-FILLED MUFFINS Prepare batter as for Basic Muffins; fill each muffin-pan cup one-third full; drop *1 rounded teaspoon strawberry or raspberry preserves* in center of each cup; top with remaining batter. Bake as directed.
EACH MUFFIN: ABOUT 250 CALORIES, 4 G PROTEIN, 36 G CARBOHYDRATE, 10 G TOTAL FAT (6 G SATURATED), 1 G FIBER, 41 MG CHOLESTEROL, 315 MG SODIUM.

CHOCOLATE CHIP MUFFINS Prepare batter as for Basic Muffins and fold in ¾ *cup semisweet chocolate chips.* Bake as directed.
EACH MUFFIN: ABOUT 275 CALORIES, 4 G PROTEIN, 37 G CARBOHYDRATE, 13 G TOTAL FAT (7 G SATURATED), 0.5 G FIBER, 41 MG CHOLESTEROL, 315 MG SODIUM.

BLUEBERRY OR RASPBERRY MUFFINS Prepare batter as for Basic Muffins and gently fold in *1 cup blueberries or raspberries.* Bake as directed.
EACH BLUEBERRY MUFFIN: ABOUT 230 CALORIES, 4 G PROTEIN, 31 G CARBOHYDRATE, 10 G TOTAL FAT (6 G SATURATED), 1 G FIBER, 41 MG CHOLESTEROL, 315 MG SODIUM.

LEMON MUFFINS Prepare batter as for Basic Muffins; add *1½ teaspoons freshly grated lemon peel* to egg mixture. Bake as directed. Meanwhile, combine ¼ *cup confectioners' sugar* and *1 tablespoon fresh lemon juice*; brush glaze onto muffins while they are hot.
EACH MUFFIN: ABOUT 235 CALORIES, 4 G PROTEIN, 32 G CARBOHYDRATE, 10 G TOTAL FAT (6 G SATURATED), 1 G FIBER, 41 MG CHOLESTEROL, 310 MG SODIUM.

LEMON-POPPYSEED MUFFINS Prepare batter as for Lemon Muffins and fold in ¼ *cup poppyseeds.* Bake and glaze muffins as directed.
EACH MUFFIN: ABOUT 250 CALORIES, 4 G PROTEIN, 33 G CARBOHYDRATE, 11 G TOTAL FAT (6 G SATURATED), 0.5 G FIBER, 41 MG CHOLESTEROL, 315 MG SODIUM.

Lemon-Ricotta Muffins

PREP 15 MINUTES / BAKE 20 TO 22 MINUTES

Ricotta cheese gives these muffins a terrific, tender texture and helps keep them moist. If you have some cottage cheese on hand, you can substitute it for the ricotta.

2 CUPS ALL-PURPOSE FLOUR

½ CUP PLUS 2 TABLESPOONS SUGAR

2½ TEASPOONS BAKING POWDER

½ TEASPOON SALT

1 CUP RICOTTA CHEESE

⅓ CUP MILK

6 TABLESPOONS BUTTER OR MARGARINE, MELTED

2 LARGE EGGS

2 TEASPOONS FRESHLY GRATED LEMON PEEL

1 Preheat oven to 400° F. Grease twelve 2½" by 1¼" muffin-pan cups or line with paper baking liners. In large bowl, stir together flour, ½ cup sugar, baking powder, and salt.

2 In medium bowl, with wire whisk or fork, mix together ricotta, milk, melted butter, eggs, and lemon peel. Make well in center of flour mixture and pour in ricotta mixture; stir just until flour is moistened.

3 Spoon batter into prepared muffin-pan cups. Sprinkle remaining 2 tablespoons sugar over muffins. Bake 20 to 22 minutes, until muffins are golden brown, tops spring back when lightly touched, and toothpick inserted in center of muffin comes out clean. Immediately remove from pan; serve warm. Or cool on wire rack to serve later. *Makes 1 dozen muffins.*

EACH MUFFIN: ABOUT 230 CALORIES, 6 G PROTEIN, 28 G CARBOHYDRATE, 11 G TOTAL FAT (6 G SATURATED), 0.5 G FIBER, 62 MG CHOLESTEROL, 290 MG SODIUM.

Lemon-Ricotta Muffins

Pumpkin Muffins

PREP 15 MINUTES / BAKE 25 TO 30 MINUTES

Pumpkin muffins are perfect Halloween party fare and are always welcome on the autumn breakfast table or the Thanksgiving bread basket. For a change, add 1 cup raisins or 1 cup chopped walnuts or pecans.

3½ CUPS ALL-PURPOSE FLOUR

1 TABLESPOON BAKING POWDER

2 TEASPOONS PUMPKIN-PIE SPICE*

1 TEASPOON BAKING SODA

1 TEASPOON SALT

3 LARGE EGGS

1 CAN (16 OUNCES) SOLID PACK PUMPKIN (NOT PUMPKIN PIE MIX)

¾ CUP BUTTER OR MARGARINE (1½ STICKS), MELTED

⅔ CUP PLUS 2 TABLESPOONS PACKED BROWN SUGAR

⅔ CUP HONEY

⅔ CUP MILK

1 TEASPOON GROUND CINNAMON

1 Preheat oven to 400° F. Grease twenty-four 2½" by 1¼" muffin-pan cups or line with paper baking liners. In large bowl, stir together flour, baking powder, pumpkin-pie spice, baking soda, and salt.

2 In medium bowl, with wire whisk or fork, mix eggs, pumpkin, melted butter, ⅔ cup brown sugar, honey, and milk. Stir egg mixture into flour mixture just until flour is moistened (batter will be lumpy).

3 Spoon batter into prepared muffin-pan cups. In small cup, combine remaining 2 tablespoons brown sugar and cinnamon; sprinkle over muffins. Bake 25 to 30 minutes, rotating pans between upper and lower racks halfway through baking, or until tops of muffins are browned and toothpick inserted in center of muffin comes out clean. Immediately remove muffins from pan; serve warm. Or cool on wire rack to serve later. *Makes 2 dozen muffins.*

*Or use 1 teaspoon ground cinnamon, ¾ teaspoon ground ginger, ¼ teaspoon ground nutmeg, and ⅛ teaspoon ground cloves.

EACH MUFFIN: ABOUT 205 CALORIES, 3 G PROTEIN, 31 G CARBOHYDRATE, 8 G TOTAL FAT (4 G SATURATED), 1 G FIBER, 43 MG CHOLESTEROL, 285 MG SODIUM.

Apple Streusel Muffins

PREP 25 MINUTES / BAKE 25 MINUTES

Because the muffin cups are completely filled with batter, the tops of the muffins will run together; you'll need to cut them apart with a sharp knife before turning them out. It's easiest to cut the muffin tops apart in straight lines—squaring them off—rather than trying to round them.

⅓ CUP PACKED LIGHT BROWN SUGAR

3 TABLESPOONS PLUS ½ CUP BUTTER OR MARGARINE

2⅔ CUPS ALL-PURPOSE FLOUR

1½ TEASPOONS GROUND CINNAMON

½ CUP GRANULATED SUGAR

2 TEASPOONS BAKING POWDER

½ TEASPOON BAKING SODA

½ TEASPOON SALT

1 CUP BUTTERMILK

1 LARGE EGG

1 LARGE GRANNY SMITH APPLE, PEELED, CORED, AND FINELY CHOPPED (1 HEAPING CUP)

1 In medium bowl, with pastry blender or fingertips, mix brown sugar, 3 tablespoons butter, cut into pieces, ⅓ cup flour, and 1 teaspoon cinnamon until mixture resembles coarse crumbs.

2 Preheat oven to 400° F. Grease twelve 2½" by 1¼" muffin-pan cups or line with paper baking liners. Melt remaining ½ cup butter. In large bowl, stir together remaining 2 cups flour, ½ teaspoon cinnamon, granulated sugar, baking powder, baking soda, and salt. In medium bowl, with wire whisk or fork, mix buttermilk, egg mixture, and melted butter until blended. Stir in apple. Stir egg mixture into flour mixture just until flour is moistened.

3 Spoon batter into prepared muffin-pan cups (cups will be full). Sprinkle streusel over muffins, pressing it down lightly. Bake 25 minutes, or until toothpick inserted in center of muffin comes out clean. Cool in cups 10 minutes. Cut through tops to separate and run a knife around sides to release; remove muffins to wire rack to cool. If using paper liners, cool muffins in pan 5 minutes, then remove to wire rack. Serve warm or cool on wire rack to serve later. *Makes 1 dozen muffins.*

EACH MUFFIN: ABOUT 270 CALORIES, 4 G PROTEIN, 36 G CARBOHYDRATE, 12 G TOTAL FAT (7 G SATURATED), 1 G FIBER, 47 MG CHOLESTEROL, 365 MG SODIUM.

Bran Muffins

PREP 10 MINUTES / BAKE 20 TO 25 MINUTES

Muffins made with bran cereal do not have a heavy "health-foody" flavor. Add raisins or prunes, if you like.

1 CUP MILK
1 LARGE EGG, LIGHTLY BEATEN
¼ CUP VEGETABLE OIL
¼ CUP LIGHT (MILD) MOLASSES
1 CUP WHOLE BRAN CEREAL (NOT BRAN FLAKES)
1 CUP ALL-PURPOSE FLOUR
¼ CUP SUGAR
1 TABLESPOON BAKING POWDER
½ TEASPOON SALT

1 Preheat oven to 400° F. Grease twelve 2½" by 1¼" muffin-pan cups or line with paper liners. In medium bowl, with wire whisk, mix milk, egg, oil, molasses, and cereal until blended; let stand 10 minutes.

2 Meanwhile, in large bowl, stir together flour, sugar, baking powder, and salt. Stir egg mixture into flour mixture just until flour is moistened (batter will be lumpy).

3 Spoon batter into prepared muffin-pan cups. Bake 20 to 25 minutes, until golden and toothpick inserted in center of muffin comes out almost clean. Immediately remove muffins from pan; serve warm. Or cool on rack to serve later. *Makes 1 dozen muffins.*

EACH MUFFIN: ABOUT 155 CALORIES, 3 G PROTEIN, 22 G CARBOHYDRATE, 7 G TOTAL FAT (1 G SATURATED), 2 G FIBER, 21 MG CHOLESTEROL, 285 MG SODIUM.

Sour Cream Muffins

PREP 10 MINUTES / BAKE 15 MINUTES

2 CUPS ALL-PURPOSE FLOUR
⅓ CUP PLUS 2 TABLESPOONS SUGAR
2 TEASPOONS BAKING POWDER
½ TEASPOON BAKING SODA
½ TEASPOON SALT
1 CONTAINER (8 OUNCES) SOUR CREAM
2 LARGE EGGS
1 TEASPOON VANILLA EXTRACT
½ TEASPOON GROUND CINNAMON
⅓ CUP COARSELY CHOPPED PECANS OR WALNUTS

1 Preheat oven to 400° F. Grease twelve 2½" by 1¼" muffin-pan cups or line with paper liners. In large bowl, stir together flour, ⅓ cup sugar, baking powder, baking soda, and salt.

2 In medium bowl, with wire whisk or fork, stir together sour cream, eggs, and vanilla. Stir sour cream mixture into flour mixture just until flour is moistened.

3 Spoon batter into prepared muffin-pan cups. In small bowl, stir together cinnamon and remaining 2 tablespoons sugar. Sprinkle over muffins; sprinkle nuts on top. Bake 15 minutes, or until toothpick inserted in the center of muffin comes out clean. Immediately remove muffins from pan; serve warm. Or cool on wire rack to serve later. *Makes 1 dozen muffins.*

EACH MUFFIN: ABOUT 190 CALORIES, 4 G PROTEIN, 25 G CARBOHYDRATE, 8 G TOTAL FAT (3 G SATURATED), 1 G FIBER, 44 MG CHOLESTEROL, 250 MG SODIUM.

Applesauce Muffins

PREP 15 MINUTES / BAKE 25 TO 30 MINUTES

A sprinkling of cinnamon sugar on top before baking gives these muffins a crunchy "crust." Serve them with a pot of coffee or a jug of ice-cold cider; for breakfast, and spread them with soft cream cheese.

2 CUPS ALL-PURPOSE FLOUR
2 TEASPOONS BAKING POWDER
½ TEASPOON SALT
1½ TEASPOONS GROUND CINNAMON
1 LARGE EGG
1 CUP UNSWEETENED APPLESAUCE
½ CUP PLUS 2 TABLESPOONS PACKED BROWN SUGAR
⅓ CUP (5⅓ TABLESPOONS) BUTTER OR MARGARINE, MELTED
½ TEASPOON VANILLA EXTRACT
1 CUP DARK SEEDLESS RAISINS

1 Preheat oven to 400° F. Grease twelve 2½" by 1¼" muffin-pan cups or line with paper baking liners. In large bowl, stir together flour, baking powder, salt, and ½ teaspoon cinnamon.

2 In medium bowl, with wire whisk or fork, mix egg, applesauce, ½ cup brown sugar, melted butter, and vanilla, stirring well until combined. Stir egg mixture into flour mixture just until flour is moistened (batter will be lumpy). Stir in raisins.

3 Spoon batter into prepared muffin-pan cups. In small cup, combine remaining 2 tablespoons sugar and remaining 1 teaspoon cinnamon; sprinkle over muffins. Bake 25 to 30 minutes, until browned and toothpick inserted in center of muffin comes out clean. Immediately remove muffins from pan; serve warm. Or cool on wire rack to serve later. *Makes 1 dozen muffins.*

EACH MUFFIN: ABOUT 225 CALORIES, 3 G PROTEIN, 39 G CARBOHYDRATE, 7 G TOTAL FAT (4 G SATURATED), 2 G FIBER, 31 MG CHOLESTEROL, 240 MG SODIUM.

Lemon-Yogurt Muffins

PREP 10 MINUTES / BAKE 20 MINUTES

Nonfat yogurt is one of those magical ingredients that can take the place of butter and egg yolks in certain (not all) baked goods. The yogurt's slight tartness is a pleasing complement to the muffins' lemony zing.

2 CUPS ALL-PURPOSE FLOUR
½ CUP PLUS 1 TABLESPOON SUGAR
2 TEASPOONS BAKING POWDER
½ TEASPOON BAKING SODA
½ TEASPOON SALT
2 LARGE EGG WHITES
1 CONTAINER (8 OUNCES) NONFAT PLAIN YOGURT
2 TABLESPOONS VEGETABLE OIL
2 TEASPOONS FRESHLY GRATED LEMON PEEL
1 TEASPOON VANILLA EXTRACT

1 Preheat oven to 400° F. Grease twelve 2½" by 1¼" muffin-pan cups or line with paper baking liners. In large bowl, stir together flour, ½ cup sugar, baking powder, baking soda, and salt.

2 In medium bowl, with wire whisk or fork, mix egg whites, yogurt, vegetable oil, grated lemon peel, and vanilla. Stir yogurt mixture into flour mixture just until flour is moistened (batter will be lumpy).

3 Spoon batter into prepared muffin-pan cups. Sprinkle over muffins with remaining 1 tablespoon sugar. Bake 20 minutes, or until toothpick inserted in center of muffin comes out clean. Immediately remove muffins from pan; serve warm. Or cool on wire rack to serve later. *Makes 1 dozen muffins.*

EACH MUFFIN: ABOUT 155 CALORIES, 4 G PROTEIN, 27 G CARBOHYDRATE, 4 G TOTAL FAT (1 G SATURATED), 0.5 G FIBER, 0 MG CHOLESTEROL, 255 MG SODIUM.

LEMON-YOGURT MUFFINS WITH BLUEBERRIES Prepare batter as for Lemon-Yogurt Muffins and gently fold in *1½ cups fresh blueberries.* Bake 20 to 25 minutes, until toothpick comes out clean.
EACH MUFFIN: ABOUT 165 CALORIES, 4 G PROTEIN, 30 G CARBOHYDRATE, 4 G TOTAL FAT (1 G SATURATED), 1 G FIBER, 0 MG CHOLESTEROL, 255 MG SODIUM.

Blueberry-Corn Muffins

PREP 15 MINUTES / BAKE 20 TO 25 MINUTES

1 CUP ALL-PURPOSE FLOUR
1 CUP CORNMEAL
½ CUP SUGAR
2 TEASPOONS BAKING POWDER
1 TEASPOON BAKING SODA
½ TEASPOON SALT
1 CUP BUTTERMILK
¼ CUP VEGETABLE OIL
2 TEASPOONS VANILLA EXTRACT
1 LARGE EGG
1½ CUPS BLUEBERRIES OR 1½ CUPS FRESH RASPBERRIES (½ PINT)

1 Preheat oven to 400° F. Grease twelve 2½" by 1¼" muffin-pan cups or line with paper baking liners. In large bowl, stir together flour, cornmeal, sugar, baking powder, baking soda, and salt.

2 In small bowl, with wire whisk or fork, beat buttermilk, oil, vanilla, and egg until blended. Stir egg mixture into flour mixture just until flour is moistened (batter will be lumpy). Fold in berries.

3 Spoon batter into prepared muffin-pan cups. Bake 20 to 25 minutes, until toothpick inserted in center of muffin comes out clean. Immediately remove muffins from pan; serve warm. Or cool on wire rack to serve later. *Makes 1 dozen muffins.*

EACH MUFFIN: ABOUT 190 CALORIES, 3 G PROTEIN, 29 G CARBOHYDRATE, 7 G TOTAL FAT (1 G SATURATED), 1 G FIBER, 19 MG CHOLESTEROL, 310 MG SODIUM.

Oatmeal Muffins

PREP 20 MINUTES / BAKE 20 TO 25 MINUTES

A sweet and crunchy blend of chopped walnuts, toasted oats, and brown sugar crowns these fruit-filled muffins. Serve them in a napkin-lined basket with a bowl of apple, peach, or pumpkin butter.

1¼ CUPS OLD-FASHIONED OR QUICK-COOKING OATS, UNCOOKED

1½ CUPS ALL-PURPOSE FLOUR

½ CUP GRANULATED SUGAR

2 TEASPOONS BAKING POWDER

½ TEASPOON BAKING SODA

¼ TEASPOON SALT

1 CUP BUTTERMILK

⅓ CUP BUTTER OR MARGARINE, MELTED

1 LARGE EGG

1 TEASPOON VANILLA EXTRACT

½ CUP DRIED CRANBERRIES OR RAISINS

¼ CUP PACKED LIGHT BROWN SUGAR

¼ CUP TOASTED WALNUTS, COARSELY CHOPPED

1 Preheat oven to 400° F. Grease twelve 2½" by 1¼" muffin-pan cups or line with paper baking liners. On jelly-roll pan, toast oats 5 to 7 minutes, until lightly browned. Cool.

2 In large bowl, stir together flour, granulated sugar, baking powder, baking soda, salt, and 1 cup oats. In small bowl, with wire whisk or fork, mix buttermilk, melted butter, egg, and vanilla. Stir buttermilk mixture into flour mixture until flour is moistened (batter will be lumpy). Fold in cranberries.

3 Spoon batter into prepared muffin-pan cups. In small bowl, stir together brown sugar, walnuts, and remaining ¼ cup oats; sprinkle over muffins. Bake 20 to 25 minutes, until toothpick inserted in center of muffin comes out clean. Immediately remove muffins from pan; serve warm. Or cool on wire rack to serve later. *Makes 1 dozen muffins.*

EACH MUFFIN: ABOUT 230 CALORIES, 4 G PROTEIN, 34 G CARBOHYDRATE, 9 G TOTAL FAT (2 G SATURATED), 2 G FIBER, 18 MG CHOLESTEROL, 260 MG SODIUM.

Morning Glory Muffins

PREP 20 MINUTES / BAKE 25 MINUTES

Here is the ultimate breakfast muffin—a carrot cakelike batter with coconut, sunflower seeds, and raisins. Toasting the coconut and sunflower seeds is key: A few minutes in the oven brings out the flavor of the seeds and totally transforms the coconut, turning it a tawny tan, crisping it, and increasing its sweetness.

½ CUP FLAKED SWEETENED COCONUT

¼ CUP HULLED SUNFLOWER SEEDS

2 CUPS ALL-PURPOSE FLOUR

2 TEASPOONS BAKING POWDER

½ TEASPOON BAKING SODA

½ TEASPOON SALT

½ TEASPOON GROUND CINNAMON

½ CUP PLAIN LOW-FAT YOGURT

½ CUP PACKED LIGHT BROWN SUGAR

¼ CUP VEGETABLE OIL

1 LARGE EGG

1½ CUPS SHREDDED CARROTS (2 TO 3 CARROTS)

½ CUP DARK SEEDLESS RAISINS

1 Preheat oven to 375° F. Grease twelve 2½" by 1¼" muffin-pan cups or line with paper baking liners. On jelly-roll pan, toast coconut and sunflower seeds 7 minutes, stirring occasionally, or until coconut is golden brown. Cool.

2 In large bowl, stir together flour, baking powder, baking soda, salt, and cinnamon. In small bowl, with wire whisk or fork, mix yogurt, brown sugar, oil, and egg. Stir egg mixture into flour mixture just until flour is moistened. Stir in carrots, raisins, and coconut and sunflower seeds until combined.

3 Spoon batter into prepared muffin-pan cups. Bake 25 minutes, or until toothpick inserted in center of muffin comes out clean. Immediately remove muffins from pan; serve warm. Or cool on wire rack to serve later. *Makes 1 dozen muffins.*

EACH MUFFIN: ABOUT 240 CALORIES, 5 G PROTEIN, 36 G CARBOHYDRATE, 9 G TOTAL FAT (4 G SATURATED), 2 G FIBER, 32 MG CHOLESTEROL, 260 MG SODIUM.

CORN BREADS

Breads made with cornmeal are in a class by themselves. The meal has a slightly sweet, rich flavor and most corn quick breads are dense and almost cakelike. Use yellow or white cornmeal, as you like. It's said that Southerners prefer white meal and Northerners, yellow. (Of course, the "golden" breads will not be golden if you bake them with white cornmeal, but they'll be just as delicious.) Try to get stone-ground meal, which is more nutritious than bolted cornmeal and adds interesting texture to the bread.

Golden Corn Bread

PREP 10 MINUTES / BAKE 20 TO 25 MINUTES

You probably have the ingredients for a pan of basic corn bread or a dozen muffins in your kitchen right now, and these versatile breads fit right in at breakfast, lunch, or dinner. Our two variations are flavored with bacon or peppery cheese, and we also give you the methods for baking the batter as muffins or as cornsticks—slender mini-loaves shaped like ears of corn.

1 CUP ALL-PURPOSE FLOUR

¾ CUP CORNMEAL

3 TABLESPOONS SUGAR

1 TABLESPOON BAKING POWDER

¾ TEASPOON SALT

1 LARGE EGG

⅔ CUP MILK

4 TABLESPOONS BUTTER OR MARGARINE, MELTED

1 Preheat oven to 425° F. Grease 8" by 8" metal baking pan. In medium bowl, stir together flour, cornmeal, sugar, baking powder, and salt. In small bowl, with fork, beat egg, milk, and melted butter until blended.

2 Add egg mixture to flour mixture; stir just until flour is moistened (batter will be lumpy).

3 Spread batter evenly in prepared pan. Bake 20 to 25 minutes, until golden and toothpick inserted in center of bread comes out clean. Cut corn bread into 9 squares; serve warm. *Makes 9 servings.*

EACH SERVING: ABOUT 180 CALORIES, 4 G PROTEIN, 25 G CARBOHYDRATE, 7 G TOTAL FAT (4 G SATURATED), 1 G FIBER, 40 MG CHOLESTEROL, 425 MG SODIUM.

GOLDEN CORN BREAD WITH BACON & PEPPER Prepare flour mixture as for Golden Corn Bread. In 10-inch skillet, cook *5 slices bacon* over medium heat until browned. Drain bacon on paper towel. Pour *¼ cup bacon fat* into measuring cup (if necessary, add enough vegetable oil to equal ¼ cup). Crumble bacon; stir crumbled bacon and *½ teaspoon freshly ground black pepper* into flour mixture. Use bacon fat in place of melted butter. Combine batter and bake as directed.

EACH SERVING: ABOUT 195 CALORIES, 5 G PROTEIN, 25 G CARBOHYDRATE, 8 G TOTAL FAT (3 G SATURATED), 1 G FIBER, 33 MG CHOLESTEROL, 460 MG SODIUM.

GOLDEN CORN BREAD WITH PEPPERJACK Prepare flour mixture as for Golden Corn Bread and stir in *4 ounces Monterey jack cheese with jalapeños,* shredded (1 cup), and *¾ teaspoon mild to medium chili powder.* Use only *3 tablespoons melted butter.* Combine batter and bake as directed.

EACH SERVING: ABOUT 220 CALORIES, 7 G PROTEIN, 26 G CARBOHYDRATE, 10 G TOTAL FAT (5 G SATURATED), 1 G FIBER, 50 MG CHOLESTEROL, 825 MG SODIUM.

CORN MUFFINS Grease twelve 2½" by 1¼" muffin-pan cups. Prepare flour mixture as for Golden Corn Bread but use *1 cup milk.* Spoon batter into prepared muffin-pan cups, filling each two-thirds full. Bake about 20 minutes, or until golden and toothpick inserted in center of muffin comes out clean. Immediately remove muffins from pans; serve warm. *Makes 1 dozen muffins.*

EACH MUFFIN: ABOUT 145 CALORIES, 3 G PROTEIN, 19 G CARBOHYDRATE, 6 G TOTAL FAT (3 G SATURATED), 0.5 G FIBER, 31 MG CHOLESTEROL, 320 MG SODIUM.

CORNSTICKS Grease 14 cornstick molds with vegetable oil. Heat molds in oven 15 minutes, until hot. Meanwhile, prepare batter as for Golden Corn Bread. Remove molds from oven; spoon batter into hot molds. Bake 15 to 20 minutes, until toothpick inserted in center of cornstick comes out clean. Cool in molds on wire rack 10 minutes. Remove cornsticks from molds; serve warm. *Makes 14 cornsticks.*

EACH CORNSTICK: ABOUT 120 CALORIES, 2 G PROTEIN, 16 G CARBOHYDRATE, 5 G TOTAL FAT (3 G SATURATED), 0.5 G FIBER, 26 MG CHOLESTEROL, 275 MG SODIUM.

Buttermilk Corn Bread

PREP 10 MINUTES / BAKE 15 TO 20 MINUTES

Buttermilk or clabbered (soured) milk appears as an ingredient in many Southern corn bread recipes., and we've take the Northern liberty of adding a bit of sugar.

2 LARGE EGGS
⅓ CUP BUTTER OR MARGARINE, MELTED AND COOLED
1½ CUPS BUTTERMILK
1⅓ CUPS CORNMEAL
⅔ CUP ALL-PURPOSE FLOUR
1 TABLESPOON SUGAR
2 TEASPOONS BAKING POWDER
½ TEASPOON BAKING SODA
½ TEASPOON SALT

1 Preheat oven to 400° F. Grease 9" by 9" metal baking pan. In medium bowl, with wire whisk or fork, mix eggs, melted butter, and buttermilk until blended. In large bowl, stir together cornmeal, flour, sugar, baking powder, baking soda, and salt.

2 Stir buttermilk mixture into flour mixture just until flour is moistened.

AN AMERICAN TRADITION

CORNMEAL MAY NOT BE AS VERSATILE AS WHEAT FLOUR, BUT INVENTIVE AMERICAN COOKS OVER THE CENTURIES HAVE DEVISED QUITE A VARIETY OF CORN BREADS. ONE OF THE EARLIEST WAS ASHCAKE, OR HOECAKE, WHICH WAS BAKED RIGHT IN THE COALS OF THE COOKING FIRE. OTHER OLD-TIME FAVORITES INCLUDE CORN DODGERS—A SORT OF FREE-FORM DROP BISCUIT MADE WITH BACON DRIPPINGS; CORN PONE (THICK, STURDY CORN CAKES BAKED ON A GRIDDLE); HUSH PUPPIES, WHICH ARE SPOONFULS OF CORN BATTER COOKED IN DEEP FAT, LIKE FRITTERS; AND ELEGANT, AIRY SPOONBREAD.

---

3 Spread batter evenly in prepared pan. Bake 15 to 20 minutes, until toothpick inserted in center of bread comes out clean. Cut corn bread into 9 squares; serve warm. Or cool in pan on wire rack to serve later. *Makes 9 servings.*

EACH SERVING: ABOUT 210 CALORIES, 5 G PROTEIN, 27 G CARBOHYDRATE, 9 G TOTAL FAT (5 G SATURATED), 1 G FIBER, 67 MG CHOLESTEROL, 435 MG SODIUM.

Spoonbread

PREP 15 MINUTES / BAKE 40 MINUTES

A Southern standby since Colonial times, this is more of a soufflé than a bread. Rather than cutting it into slices, bring the spoonbread to the table in its baking dish and spoon it out—steaming hot—as a dinner side dish.

3 CUPS MILK
½ TEASPOON SALT
¼ TEASPOON GROUND BLACK PEPPER
1 CUP CORNMEAL
4 TABLESPOONS BUTTER OR MARGARINE, CUT UP
3 LARGE EGGS, SEPARATED

1 Preheat oven to 400° F. Grease shallow 1½-quart ceramic or glass baking dish.

2 In 4-quart saucepan, heat milk, salt, and pepper to boiling. Remove saucepan from heat; with wire whisk or fork, mix in cornmeal. Whisk in butter until melted. Let stand 5 minutes.

3 Whisk egg yolks, 1 at a time, into cornmeal mixture. In small bowl, with mixer at medium speed, beat egg whites until soft peaks form when beaters are lifted. Fold half of whites into cornmeal mixture; fold in remaining whites.

4 Pour batter into prepared baking dish and spread evenly with rubber spatula. Bake 40 minutes, or until set. Serve immediately. *Makes 8 servings.*

EACH SERVING: ABOUT 205 CALORIES, 7 G PROTEIN, 18 G CARBOHYDRATE, 11 G TOTAL FAT (6 G SATURATED), 1 G FIBER, 108 MG CHOLESTEROL, 270 MG SODIUM.

POPOVERS

Far more than the sum of their parts, popovers are made from just 5 ingredients: eggs, milk, butter, flour, and salt. But the batter puffs into an astonishingly high dome, and although they look like overgrown muffins, popovers are almost completely hollow. These light, appealing quick breads are great with soup or salads; or, halve popovers and fill them with tuna or chicken salad. Special popover pans can be found at kitchenware shops, but custard cups or muffins tins will do fine.

Popovers

PREP 10 MINUTES / BAKE 1 HOUR

Theories of popover perfection vary. Some recipes start the batter in a cold oven, while others specify that both oven and pans be hot before pouring in the batter. We find the latter method to work perfectly. Don't open the oven for the first 50 minutes of baking time.

3 LARGE EGGS
1 CUP MILK
3 TABLESPOONS BUTTER OR MARGARINE, MELTED
1 CUP ALL-PURPOSE FLOUR
½ TEASPOON SALT

1 Preheat oven to 375° F. Grease well with melted butter or vegetable oil eight 6-ounce custard cups or twelve 2½" by 1¼" muffin-pan cups. Set custard cups on jelly-roll pan for easier handling.

2 In medium bowl, with mixer at low speed, beat eggs until frothy; beat in milk and melted butter until blended. Gradually beat in flour and salt. Or, combine all ingredients in blender; blend until smooth.

3 Pour about ⅓ cup batter into each prepared custard cup or fill muffin-pan cups half full. Bake 50 minutes, then quickly cut small slit in top of each popover to let out steam; bake 10 minutes longer. Immediately remove popovers from cups, loosening with spatula if necessary. Serve hot. *Makes 8 medium or 12 small popovers.*

EACH MEDIUM POPOVER: ABOUT 160 CALORIES, 5 G PROTEIN, 14 G CARBOHYDRATE, 9 G TOTAL FAT (5 G SATURATED), 0.5 G FIBER, 101 MG CHOLESTEROL, 250 MG SODIUM.
EACH SMALL POPOVER: ABOUT 105 CALORIES, 3 G PROTEIN, 9 G CARBOHYDRATE, 6 G TOTAL FAT (3 G SATURATED), 0.5 G FIBER, 67 MG CHOLESTEROL, 165 MG SODIUM.

PARMESAN POPOVERS Prepare batter as for Popovers and add *½ cup freshly grated Parmesan cheese* and *⅛ teaspoon coarsely ground black pepper*; use only *¼ teaspoon salt.* Bake as directed.
EACH MEDIUM POPOVER: ABOUT 185 CALORIES, 8 G PROTEIN, 14 G CARBOHYDRATE, 11 G TOTAL FAT (6 G SATURATED), 0.5 G FIBER, 106 MG CHOLESTEROL, 290 MG SODIUM.
EACH SMALL POPOVER: ABOUT 125 CALORIES, 5 G PROTEIN, 9 G CARBOHYDRATE, 7 G TOTAL FAT (4 G SATURATED), 0.5 G FIBER, 70 MG CHOLESTEROL, 190 MG SODIUM.

HERB POPOVERS Prepare batter as for Popovers and add *2 tablespoons chopped chives or green onion.* Bake as directed.
EACH MEDIUM POPOVER: ABOUT 160 CALORIES, 5 G PROTEIN, 14 G CARBOHYDRATE, 9 G TOTAL FAT (5 G SATURATED), 0.5 G FIBER, 101 MG CHOLESTEROL, 250 MG SODIUM.
EACH SMALL POPOVER: ABOUT 105 CALORIES, 3 G PROTEIN, 9 G CARBOHYDRATE, 6 G TOTAL FAT (3 G SATURATED), 0.5 G FIBER, 67 MG CHOLESTEROL, 165 MG SODIUM.

LOW-FAT POPOVERS Prepare batter as for Popovers but use *1 whole large egg* and *3 large egg whites* in place of the 3 whole eggs, *1 tablespoon melted butter* and *1 cup low-fat milk* in place of the whole milk. Bake as directed.
EACH MEDIUM POPOVER: ABOUT 115 CALORIES, 5 G PROTEIN, 14 G CARBOHYDRATE, 4 G TOTAL FAT (2 G SATURATED), 0.5 G FIBER, 37 MG CHOLESTEROL, 225 MG SODIUM.
EACH SMALL POPOVER: ABOUT 80 CALORIES, 3 G PROTEIN, 9 G CARBOHYDRATE, 3 G TOTAL FAT (2 G SATURATED), 0.5 G FIBER, 25 MG CHOLESTEROL, 150 MG SODIUM.

GIANT POPOVERS Grease well six 8-ounce deep ceramic custard cups; place on jelly-roll pan. Prepare batter as for Popovers but use *6 eggs, 2 cups milk, 6 tablespoons butter or margarine,* melted, *2 cups flour,* and *1 teaspoon salt.* Bake 1 hour before cutting slits in top, then bake 10 minutes longer, as directed. *Makes 6 large popovers.*
EACH GIANT POPOVER: ABOUT 410 CALORIES, 13 G PROTEIN, 36 G CARBOHYDRATE, 23 G TOTAL FAT (13 G SATURATED), 1 G FIBER, 265 MG CHOLESTEROL, 650 MG SODIUM.

TEA BREADS & COFFEE CAKES

Lovely loaves of sweet fruit and nut bread, country-style soda bread, buttery streusel-topped cakes—here are some great ideas for what to bake for a company brunch, morning coffee klatsch, afternoon tea, a special snack, or potluck bring-along. Baked in foil loaf pans and over-wrapped with foil or cellophane, tea breads are gracious gifts for a holiday or housewarming. Most are quickly made, and many of these breads and cakes freeze well, so that unexpected guests can always be welcomed with a home-baked treat. And leftover portions of loaf-shaped tea breads are excellent for toasting.

Orange-Cranberry Bread

PREP 20 MINUTES / BAKE 55 TO 60 MINUTES

An obvious choice for Thanksgiving, this orange-scented bread is packed with fresh cranberries. Like many tea breads, it's best to bake it a day ahead of time to allow the flavors to develop. You may want to make several loaves—one to serve with dinner, and one or more extras for the holiday weekend breakfasts that follow.

1 LARGE ORANGE
2½ CUPS ALL-PURPOSE FLOUR
1 CUP SUGAR
2 TEASPOONS BAKING POWDER
½ TEASPOON BAKING SODA
½ TEASPOON SALT
2 LARGE EGGS
4 TABLESPOONS BUTTER OR MARGARINE, MELTED
2 CUPS CRANBERRIES, COARSELY CHOPPED
¾ CUP WALNUTS, CHOPPED (OPTIONAL)

1 Preheat oven to 375° F. Grease 9" by 5" metal loaf pan. From orange, grate 1 teaspoon peel and squeeze ½ cup juice.

2 In large bowl, stir together flour, sugar, baking powder, baking soda, and salt. In small bowl, with whisk or fork, beat eggs, melted butter, and orange peel and juice. Add egg mixture to flour mixture; with spoon, stir until batter is just mixed (batter will be stiff). Fold in cranberries and walnuts, if you like.

3 Pour batter into prepared loaf pan. Bake 55 to 60 minutes, until toothpick inserted in center of bread comes out clean. Cool loaf in pan on wire rack 10 minutes; remove from pan and cool completely on wire rack. *Makes 1 loaf, 12 slices.*

EACH SLICE WITHOUT WALNUTS: ABOUT 225 CALORIES, 4 G PROTEIN, 40 G CARBOHYDRATE, 5 G TOTAL FAT (3 G SATURATED), 1.5 G FIBER, 46 MG CHOLESTEROL, 280 MG SODIUM.

Banana Bread

PREP 20 MINUTES / BAKE 1 HOUR 10 MINUTES

Really ripe bananas (fully golden and covered with brown "freckles") are a must for a naturally sweet bread. Leave unripe bananas in a plastic bag at room temperature for a few days to ripen. Once ripe, bananas can be frozen for future baking.

2½ CUPS ALL-PURPOSE FLOUR
2 TEASPOONS BAKING POWDER
¾ TEASPOON SALT
½ TEASPOON BAKING SODA
1½ CUPS MASHED BANANAS (3 LARGE RIPE BANANAS)
¼ CUP MILK
2 TEASPOONS VANILLA EXTRACT
½ CUP BUTTER OR MARGARINE (1 STICK), SOFTENED
1 CUP SUGAR
2 LARGE EGGS

1 Preheat oven to 350° F. Grease 9" by 5" metal loaf pan. In medium bowl, stir together flour, baking powder, salt, and baking soda. In small bowl, stir together bananas, milk, and vanilla until blended.

2 In large bowl, with mixer at medium speed, beat butter and sugar until light and creamy. Beat in eggs, 1 at a time. Reduce speed to low; add flour mixture alternately with milk mixture, beginning and ending with flour mixture, scraping bowl occasionally.

3 Pour batter into prepared loaf pan. Bake 1 hour 10 minutes, or until toothpick inserted in center of bread comes out clean. Cool loaf in pan on wire rack 10 minutes; remove from pan and cool completely on wire rack. *Makes 1 loaf, 16 slices.*

EACH SLICE: ABOUT 205 CALORIES, 3 G PROTEIN, 33 G CARBOHYDRATE, 7 G TOTAL FAT (4 G SATURATED), 1 G FIBER, 43 MG CHOLESTEROL, 280 MG SODIUM.

BANANA-NUT BREAD Prepare batter as for Banana Bread and fold in *1 cup walnuts or pecans*, coarsely chopped. Bake as directed.
EACH SLICE: ABOUT 255 CALORIES, 4 G PROTEIN, 34 G CARBOHYDRATE, 12 G TOTAL FAT (4 G SATURATED), 1 G FIBER, 43 MG CHOLESTEROL, 280 MG SODIUM.

Zucchini Bread

PREP 15 MINUTES / BAKE 1 HOUR 10 MINUTES

The salvation of the home gardener, zucchini bread offers the tastiest solution to the question, "What are we ever going to do with all this zucchini?" Fortunately, the bread doesn't actually taste like zucchini—cinnamon and orange are the predominant flavors. The shredded squash makes the bread delectably moist.

1½ CUPS ALL-PURPOSE FLOUR
¾ CUP SUGAR
2¼ TEASPOONS BAKING POWDER
½ TEASPOON SALT
½ TEASPOON GROUND CINNAMON
½ CUP WALNUTS, CHOPPED
2 LARGE EGGS
⅓ CUP VEGETABLE OIL
1½ CUPS SHREDDED ZUCCHINI (1 MEDIUM)
½ TEASPOON FRESHLY GRATED ORANGE PEEL

1 Preheat oven to 350° F. Grease 8½" by 4½" metal loaf pan. In large bowl, stir together flour, sugar, baking powder, salt, cinnamon, and walnuts.

2 In medium bowl, with whisk or fork, mix eggs, oil, zucchini, and orange peel. Stir zucchini mixture into flour mixture just until flour is moistened.

3 Pour batter into prepared loaf pan. Bake 1 hour 10 minutes, or until toothpick inserted in center of loaf comes out clean. Cool loaf in pan on wire rack 10 minutes; remove from pan and cool completely on wire rack. *Makes 1 loaf, 12 slices.*

EACH SLICE: ABOUT 210 CALORIES, 4 G PROTEIN, 26 G CARBOHYDRATE, 10 G TOTAL FAT (1 G SATURATED), 1 G FIBER, 35 MG CHOLESTEROL, 200 MG SODIUM.

Traditional Irish Soda Bread

PREP 15 MINUTES / BAKE 1 HOUR

Don't save this recipe for St. Patrick's Day. In Ireland, soda bread is enjoyed every day—with butter, jam, honey, or in its perfectly splendid simplicity.

4 CUPS ALL-PURPOSE FLOUR, PLUS ADDITIONAL
    FOR DUSTING
¼ CUP SUGAR
1 TABLESPOON BAKING POWDER
1½ TEASPOONS SALT
1 TEASPOON BAKING SODA
6 TABLESPOONS BUTTER OR MARGARINE
1½ CUPS BUTTERMILK

1 Preheat oven to 350° F. Grease large cookie sheet. In large bowl, stir together flour, sugar, baking powder, salt, and baking soda. With pastry blender or 2 knives used scissor-fashion, cut in butter until mixture resembles coarse crumbs. Stir in buttermilk just until flour is moistened (dough will be sticky).

2 Turn dough onto well-floured surface. With floured hands, knead 8 to 10 times until combined. (Do not overmix, or bread will be tough.) Shape into ball; place on prepared cookie sheet.

3 Sprinkle ball lightly with flour. In center, cut 4-inch cross about ¼ inch deep. Bake 1 hour, or until toothpick inserted in center of loaf comes out clean. Remove loaf from cookie sheet and cool completely on wire rack. *Makes 1 loaf, 12 slices.*

EACH SLICE: ABOUT 235 CALORIES, 5 G PROTEIN, 38 G CARBOHYDRATE, 7 G TOTAL FAT (4 G SATURATED), 1 G FIBER, 17 MG CHOLESTEROL, 610 MG SODIUM.

WHOLE-WHEAT SODA BREAD Prepare as above but use *1½ cups whole-wheat flour* and only *2½ cups all-purpose flour* for 4 cups all-purpose flour. Bake as directed.
EACH SLICE: ABOUT 290 CALORIES, 6 G PROTEIN, 37 G CARBOHYDRATE, 7 G TOTAL FAT (4 G SATURATED), 3 G FIBER, 17 MG CHOLESTEROL, 610 MG SODIUM.

SODA BREAD WITH CURRANTS & CARAWAY SEEDS Prepare dough as for Traditional Irish Soda Bread and add *1½ cups dried currants* and *2 teaspoons caraway seeds* to crumb mixture. Bake as directed.
EACH SLICE: ABOUT 300 CALORIES, 6 G PROTEIN, 52 G CARBOHYDRATE, 7 G TOTAL FAT (4 G SATURATED), 2 G FIBER, 17 MG CHOLESTEROL, 610 MG SODIUM.

Zucchini Cheese Loaf

PREP 15 MINUTES / BAKE 55 TO 60 MINUTES

Here's another zucchini bread, but this one, made with Cheddar and Parmesan, is savory rather than sweet. The ½ teaspoon of pepper gives the bread a spicy bite, but you can reduce the amount of pepper or leave it out.

2½ CUPS ALL-PURPOSE FLOUR

4 TEASPOONS BAKING POWDER

1 TABLESPOON SUGAR

1½ TEASPOONS SALT

½ TEASPOON FRESHLY GROUND BLACK PEPPER

4 OUNCES SHARP CHEDDAR CHEESE, SHREDDED (1 CUP)

½ CUP FRESHLY GRATED PARMESAN CHEESE

2 CUPS COARSELY SHREDDED ZUCCHINI (1 MEDIUM-TO-LARGE)

3 GREEN ONIONS, FINELY CHOPPED

2 LARGE EGGS

¾ CUP MILK

⅓ CUP OLIVE OIL

1 Preheat oven to 350° F. Grease 9" by 5" metal loaf pan. In large bowl, stir together flour, baking powder, sugar, salt, and pepper.

2 In small bowl, combine ¼ cup Cheddar and 2 tablespoons Parmesan; set aside. Stir together remaining ¾ cup Cheddar and 6 tablespoons Parmesan into flour mixture. Add zucchini and green onions. In medium bowl with a fork, beat eggs; stir in milk and oil. Add egg mixture to flour mixture, stirring just until dry ingredients are moistened (batter will be very thick).

3 Scrape batter into prepared loaf pan and spread evenly; sprinkle with reserved cheese mixture. Bake 55 to 60 minutes, until toothpick inserted in center of loaf comes out clean. Cool loaf in pan on wire rack 5 minutes. Remove from pan and cool completely on wire rack. *Makes 1 loaf, 12 slices.*

EACH SLICE: ABOUT 240 CALORIES, 9 G PROTEIN, 23 G CARBOHYDRATE, 12 G TOTAL FAT (4 G SATURATED), 1 G FIBER, 51 MG CHOLESTEROL, 610 MG SODIUM.

Zucchini Cheese Loaf

Oatmeal Quick Bread

PREP 15 MINUTES / BAKE 55 TO 60 MINUTES

This is a particularly easy bread to mix and bake. Stirred up in one bowl, with no sifting, creaming, or folding, it's a good choice a novice bread baker.

1 CUP MILK

1 CUP PLUS 1 TABLESPOON QUICK-COOKING OATS, UNCOOKED

2 LARGE EGGS, LIGHTLY BEATEN

6 TABLESPOONS BUTTER OR MARGARINE, MELTED

¼ CUP PACKED LIGHT BROWN SUGAR

2 CUPS ALL-PURPOSE FLOUR

2¼ TEASPOONS BAKING POWDER

½ TEASPOON SALT

1 Preheat oven to 350° F. Grease 8½" by 4½" or 9" by 5" metal loaf pan. In large bowl, combine milk and 1 cup oats; let stand 5 minutes.

2 Stir eggs, melted butter, and brown sugar into oat mixture and combine well, making sure there are no lumps of brown sugar. Stir in flour, baking powder, and salt just until blended.

3 Pour batter into prepared loaf pan. Sprinkle top with remaining 1 tablespoon oats. Bake 55 to 60 minutes for 8½" by 4½" pan, 35 to 40 minutes for 9" by 5" pan, until toothpick inserted in center of loaf comes out clean. Cool loaf in pan on wire rack 10 minutes; remove from pan and cool completely on wire rack. *Makes 1 loaf, 12 slices.*

EACH SLICE: ABOUT 200 CALORIES, 5 G PROTEIN, 26 G CARBOHYDRATE, 8 G TOTAL FAT (4 G SATURATED), 1 G FIBER, 54 MG CHOLESTEROL, 270 MG SODIUM.

OATMEAL OPTIONS

BECAUSE OF THE OAT KERNEL'S STRUCTURE, YOU GET THE WHOLE GRAIN, COMPLETE WITH ITS CHOLESTEROL-LOWERING SOLUBLE FIBER, IN ALL FORMS OF OAT CEREAL. WHETHER THE OATS ARE STEEL-CUT OR ROLLED, OLD-FASHIONED, QUICK-COOKING, OR INSTANT—IT'S IN THERE. OLD-FASHIONED OR QUICK-COOKING OATS ARE BEST FOR BAKING RECIPES.

Toasted Coconut Bread

PREP 15 MINUTES / BAKE 50 TO 60 MINUTES

Coconut, coconut milk, and lime juice combine to give this indulgently rich tea bread a refreshingly exotic taste. Serve it for brunch or breakfast with a tropical fruit salad made with pineapple, mango, and kiwifruit.

1 CUP FLAKED SWEETENED COCONUT

2 CUPS ALL-PURPOSE FLOUR

1 TEASPOON BAKING POWDER

½ TEASPOON BAKING SODA

¼ TEASPOON SALT

3 LIMES

½ CUP BUTTER OR MARGARINE (1 STICK), SOFTENED

½ CUP PACKED LIGHT BROWN SUGAR

½ CUP PLUS 1 TABLESPOON GRANULATED SUGAR

2 LARGE EGGS

½ CUP WELL-STIRRED LIGHT COCONUT MILK (NOT CREAM OF COCONUT)

1 Preheat oven to 350° F. On jelly-roll pan, toast coconut 7 minutes, or until golden brown, stirring occasionally.

2 Grease and flour 9" by 5" metal loaf pan. On sheet of waxed paper, stir together flour, baking powder, baking soda, and salt. From limes, grate 2 teaspoons peel and squeeze 1 tablespoon juice.

3 In large bowl, with mixer at medium speed, beat butter, brown sugar, and ½ cup granulated sugar until light and fluffy. Beat in eggs, 1 at a time, beating well after each addition (mixture may appear curdled). Beat in lime peel and juice. Reduce speed to low; add flour mixture alternately with coconut milk, beginning and ending with flour mixture. Fold in toasted coconut.

4 Scrape batter into prepared loaf pan. Sprinkle with remaining 1 tablespoon granulated sugar. Bake 50 to 60 minutes, or until toothpick inserted in center of loaf comes out clean. Cool loaf in pan on wire rack 10 minutes. Run a metal spatula around edges of pan to loosen bread. Remove from pan and cool completely on wire rack. *Makes 1 loaf, 12 slices.*

EACH SLICE: ABOUT 280 CALORIES, 4 G PROTEIN, 38 G CARBOHYDRATE, 13 G TOTAL FAT (9 G SATURATED), 1 G FIBER, 56 MG CHOLESTEROL, 250 MG SODIUM.

Date-Nut Bread

A famous New York City coffee shop chain made its reputation on a trademark sandwich of cream cheese on date-nut bread. You, too, can be famous for this lunch-time classic when you bake a loaf of moist, fruited quick bread. Slather on the cream cheese and enjoy!

1½ CUPS CHOPPED PITTED DATES
6 TABLESPOONS BUTTER OR MARGARINE, CUT UP
1¼ CUPS BOILING WATER
2 CUPS ALL-PURPOSE FLOUR
¾ CUP SUGAR
1 TEASPOON BAKING POWDER
½ TEASPOON BAKING SODA
½ TEASPOON SALT
1 LARGE EGG, LIGHTLY BEATEN
1 CUP WALNUTS, COARSELY CHOPPED

1 In medium bowl, combine dates and butter; stir in boiling water and let stand until cool.

2 Preheat oven to 325° F. Grease 9" by 5" metal loaf pan. In large bowl, stir together flour, sugar, baking powder, baking soda, and salt. Stir egg into date mixture, then stir date mixture into flour mixture just until moistened. Stir in walnuts.

3 Pour batter into prepared loaf pan. Bake 1 hour 15 minutes, or until toothpick inserted in center of loaf comes out clean. Cool loaf in pan on wire rack 10 minutes; remove from pan and cool completely on wire rack. *Makes 1 loaf, 16 slices.*

EACH SLICE: ABOUT 230 CALORIES, 3 G PROTEIN,
35 G CARBOHYDRATE, 10 G TOTAL FAT (3 G SATURATED),
2 G FIBER, 25 MG CHOLESTEROL, 190 MG SODIUM.

PRUNE BREAD Prepare as above but use *1½ cups pitted prunes*, coarsely chopped, in place of chopped pitted dates. Bake as directed.
EACH SLICE: ABOUT 225 CALORIES, 4 G PROTEIN,
32 G CARBOHYDRATE, 10 G TOTAL FAT (3 G SATURATED),
2 G FIBER, 25 MG CHOLESTEROL, 190 MG SODIUM.

FIG BREAD Prepare as above but use *1½ cups dried figs*, coarsely chopped, in place of chopped pitted dates. Bake as directed.
EACH SLICE: ABOUT 235 CALORIES, 4 G PROTEIN,
35 G CARBOHYDRATE, 10 G TOTAL FAT (3 G SATURATED),
3 G FIBER, 25 MG CHOLESTEROL, 195 MG SODIUM.

Easy Christmas Stollen

If baking a yeast-raised stollen (page 162) takes too much time, try this easy variation, which is made with baking powder and requires no rising. With stollen, there's no fancy shaping, anyway—just roll the dough into an oval and fold it in half. Lots of dried and candied fruit and nuts dot the dough, which is thick and easy to handle.

2¼ CUPS ALL-PURPOSE FLOUR
½ CUP SUGAR
1½ TEASPOONS BAKING POWDER
¼ TEASPOON SALT
½ CUP COLD BUTTER OR MARGARINE (1 STICK)
1 CUP RICOTTA CHEESE
½ CUP CANDIED LEMON PEEL OR COARSELY CHOPPED RED
    CANDIED CHERRIES
½ CUP DARK SEEDLESS RAISINS
⅓ CUP SLIVERED BLANCHED ALMONDS, TOASTED
1 TEASPOON VANILLA EXTRACT
½ TEASPOON FRESHLY GRATED LEMON PEEL
1 LARGE EGG
1 LARGE EGG YOLK

1 Preheat oven to 325° F. Grease large cookie sheet. In large bowl, stir together flour, sugar, baking powder, and salt. With pastry blender or 2 knives used scissor-fashion, cut in 6 tablespoons butter until mixture resembles fine crumbs. With spoon, stir in ricotta until moistened. Stir in candied peel, raisins, almonds, vanilla, lemon peel, egg, and egg yolk until well combined.

2 Turn dough onto lightly floured surface; gently knead dough 2 or 3 times to blend. With floured rolling pin, roll dough into 10" by 8" oval. Fold lengthwise almost in half, letting bottom dough extend about 1 inch beyond edge of top dough.

3 Place stollen on prepared cookie sheet. Bake 1 hour, or until toothpick inserted in center of bread comes out clean. Remove stollen from cookie sheet to wire rack. Melt remaining 2 tablespoons butter and brush over stollen. Cool completely on wire rack. Sprinkle with confectioners' sugar, if you like. *Makes 1 loaf, 12 servings.*

EACH SERVING: ABOUT 300 CALORIES, 7 G PROTEIN,
38 G CARBOHYDRATE, 14 G TOTAL FAT (7 G SATURATED),
1 G FIBER, 67 MG CHOLESTEROL, 210 MG SODIUM.

Easy Christmas Stollen ✦

New England Brown Bread

PREP 15 MINUTES / BAKE 55 TO 60 MINUTES

Look up a recipe for Brown Bread in an old cookbook and you'll find complicated directions for pouring the batter into 1-pound coffee cans, covering them with foil tied on with string, and steaming the loaves in a big kettle of water for two to three hours. We think you'll prefer our updated version.

1 CUP ALL-PURPOSE FLOUR
1 CUP WHOLE-WHEAT FLOUR
¾ CUP DARK SEEDLESS RAISINS
¼ CUP SUGAR
1¼ TEASPOONS BAKING SODA
½ TEASPOON SALT
1¼ CUPS BUTTERMILK OR PLAIN LOW-FAT YOGURT
¾ CUP LIGHT (MILD) MOLASSES
1 LARGE EGG

1 Preheat oven to 350° F. Grease 9" by 5" metal loaf pan. In large bowl, stir together all-purpose and whole-wheat flours, raisins, sugar, baking soda, and salt. Stir in buttermilk, molasses, and egg until batter is just mixed (batter will be very wet).

2 Pour batter into prepared loaf pan. Bake 55 to 60 minutes, until toothpick inserted in center of loaf comes out clean. With thin metal spatula, loosen bread from sides of pan. Remove loaf from pan to wire rack and cool slightly to serve warm. Or cool completely to serve later. *Makes 1 loaf, 12 slices.*

EACH SLICE: ABOUT 190 CALORIES, 4 G PROTEIN, 42 G CARBOHYDRATE, 1 G TOTAL FAT (0 G SATURATED), 2 G FIBER, 19 MG CHOLESTEROL, 270 MG SODIUM.

BOSTON BROWN BREAD

THE ORIGINAL BOSTON BROWN BREAD WAS MADE WITH THREE DIFFERENT GRAINS: WHOLE-WHEAT FLOUR, CORNMEAL, AND RYE FLOUR (RYE GREW READILY IN NEW ENGLAND'S COLD CLIMATE). IT'S THE TRADITIONAL ACCOMPANIMENT FOR A SUNDAY MEAL OF SAVORY, SLOW-COOKED BAKED BEANS.

Sour Cream Tea Bread

PREP 25 MINUTES / BAKE 1 HOUR 5 MINUTES

This light, fine-textured cake (or any of the ten variations that follow) may be baked in four 5¾" by 3¼" mini loaf pans for 40 minutes, or until the bread tests done with a toothpick. These mini-loaves make great gifts.

2½ CUPS ALL-PURPOSE FLOUR
1½ TEASPOONS BAKING POWDER
½ TEASPOON BAKING SODA
½ TEASPOON SALT
½ CUP BUTTER OR MARGARINE (1 STICK), SOFTENED
1¼ CUPS SUGAR
2 LARGE EGGS
1 CONTAINER (8 OUNCES) SOUR CREAM
1 TEASPOON VANILLA EXTRACT

1 Preheat oven to 350° F. Grease 9" by 5" metal loaf pan; dust with flour. In medium bowl, stir together flour, baking powder, baking soda, and salt. In large bowl, with mixer at low speed, beat butter until smooth. Add sugar and beat until creamy.

2 Reduce speed to low and add eggs, 1 at a time, beating after each addition until well blended, scraping bowl occasionally with rubber spatula. Add flour mixture alternately with sour cream, beginning and ending with flour mixture.

3 Spoon batter into prepared loaf pan. Bake 1 hour 5 minutes, or until toothpick inserted in center of loaf comes out clean. Cool loaf in pan on wire rack 10 minutes; remove loaf from pan and cool completely on wire rack. *Makes 1 loaf, 16 slices.*

EACH SLICE: ABOUT 225 CALORIES, 3 G PROTEIN, 31 G CARBOHYDRATE, 10 G TOTAL FAT (6 G SATURATED), 0.5 G FIBER, 48 MG CHOLESTEROL, 230 MG SODIUM.

ROSEMARY & GOLDEN RAISIN TEA BREAD Prepare as above but omit vanilla. Combine *1½ teaspoons finely chopped dried rosemary* with *½ teaspoon vegetable oil*; stir into batter after adding eggs. Fold *¾ cup golden raisins* into batter before spooning into pan. Bake as directed.
EACH SLICE: ABOUT 245 CALORIES, 4 G PROTEIN, 37 G CARBOHYDRATE, 10 G TOTAL FAT (6 G SATURATED), 1 G FIBER, 48 MG CHOLESTEROL, 235 MG SODIUM.

CHERRY-ALMOND TEA BREAD Prepare as above and add *½ teaspoon almond extract* with vanilla. Fold *1 cup dried tart cherries,* coarsely chopped, into batter before spooning into pan. Before baking, sprinkle ¼ cup sliced almonds on top of batter. Bake as directed, covering loaf with foil after 45 minutes of baking to prevent overbrowning.

EACH SLICE: ABOUT 255 CALORIES, 4 G PROTEIN, 38 G CARBOHYDRATE, 11 G TOTAL FAT (6 G SATURATED), 0.5 G FIBER, 48 MG CHOLESTEROL, 230 MG SODIUM.

BLUEBERRY STREUSEL TEA BREAD Prepare batter as for Sour Cream Tea Bread and fold in *1½ cups blueberries*. In small bowl, with fingertips, mix *¼ cup all-purpose flour, ¼ cup packed light brown sugar, 2 tablespoons chopped pecans, ⅛ teaspoon ground cinnamon, 2 tablespoons butter or margarine*, softened, until blended. Sprinkle streusel over batter. Bake 1 hour 15 to 25 minutes.

EACH SLICE: ABOUT 270 CALORIES, 4 G PROTEIN, 38 G CARBOHYDRATE, 12 G TOTAL FAT (7 G SATURATED), 1 G FIBER, 52 MG CHOLESTEROL, 250 MG SODIUM.

CURRANT & SPICE TEA BREAD Prepare batter as for Sour Cream Tea Bread and add *¾ teaspoon each ground ginger and cinnamon* and *⅛ teaspoon ground nutmeg* to flour mixture. In 1-quart sauce-pan, heat *¼ cup water* and *1 cup dried currants* over high heat 5 minutes, or until water has been absorbed; cool and fold into batter. Bake as directed.

EACH SLICE: ABOUT 250 CALORIES, 4 G PROTEIN, 38 G CARBOHYDRATE, 10 G TOTAL FAT (6 G SATURATED), 1 G FIBER, 48 MG CHOLESTEROL, 230 MG SODIUM.

GINGER TEA BREAD Prepare batter as for Sour Cream Tea Bread and add *1 teaspoon ground ginger* to flour mixture. Fold *½ cup crystallized ginger*, coarsely chopped, into batter. Bake as directed.

EACH SLICE: ABOUT 250 CALORIES, 3 G PROTEIN, 38 G CARBOHYDRATE, 10 G TOTAL FAT (6 G SATURATED), 1 G FIBER, 48 MG CHOLESTEROL, 240 MG SODIUM.

APRICOT-ALMOND TEA BREAD Prepare batter as for Sour Cream Tea Bread and add *½ teaspoon almond extract* with vanilla. Fold *1 cup dried apricots*, coarsely chopped, into batter. Before baking, sprinkle *¼ cup sliced almonds* over batter. Bake as directed, covering loaf with foil after 45 minutes of baking to prevent overbrowning.

EACH SLICE: ABOUT 255 CALORIES, 4 G PROTEIN, 37 G CARBOHYDRATE, 11 G TOTAL FAT (6 G SATURATED), 1 G FIBER, 48 MG CHOLESTEROL, 235 MG SODIUM.

Blueberry Streusel Tea Bread

CHOCOLATE CHIP TEA BREAD Prepare batter as for Sour Cream Tea Bread (page 102) and add *1 cup chocolate mini-chips* to batter. Bake as directed.

EACH SLICE: ABOUT 275 CALORIES, 4 G PROTEIN, 38 G CARBOHYDRATE, 13 G TOTAL FAT (8 G SATURATED), 1 G FIBER, 48 MG CHOLESTEROL, 235 MG SODIUM.

LEMON TEA BREAD Prepare batter as for Sour Cream Tea Bread (page 102) and add *2 teaspoons freshly grated lemon peel* to butter-sugar mixture. Bake as directed.

EACH SLICE: ABOUT 225 CALORIES, 3 G PROTEIN, 31 G CARBOHYDRATE, 10 G TOTAL FAT (6 G SATURATED), 0.5 G FIBER, 48 MG CHOLESTEROL, 230 MG SODIUM.

ANISE-RAISIN TEA BREAD Prepare batter as for Sour Cream Tea Bread (page 102) and add *2 teaspoons anise seeds*, crushed, to flour mixture. Fold *1 cup dark seedless raisins* into batter. Bake as directed.

EACH SLICE: ABOUT 255 CALORIES, 4 G PROTEIN, 39 G CARBOHYDRATE, 10 G TOTAL FAT (6 G SATURATED), 1 G FIBER, 48 MG CHOLESTEROL, 235 MG SODIUM.

CRANBERRY TEA BREAD Bake batter as for Sour Cream Tea Bread (page 102) and add *2 teaspoons freshly grated orange peel* to butter-sugar mixture. Fold *1 cup cranberries*, coarsely chopped, into batter. Bake as directed.

EACH SLICE: ABOUT 230 CALORIES, 3 G PROTEIN, 32 G CARBOHYDRATE, 10 G TOTAL FAT (6 G SATURATED), 1 G FIBER, 48 MG CHOLESTEROL, 230 MG SODIUM.

1 Preheat oven to 350° F. Grease and flour a 9- to 10-inch tube pan with removable bottom.

2 In large bowl, with mixer at low speed, beat butter, 1 cup sugar, and cinnamon until blended. Increase speed to high and beat until light and fluffy. Add 2 cups flour. Reduce speed to low, and beat, scraping bowl with rubber spatula, until well blended and crumbly. Set aside 1 cup of mixture.

3 In small bowl, mix remaining 1½ cups flour, baking powder, baking soda, and salt until blended. Add remaining ½ cup sugar, sour cream, eggs, and vanilla to mixture in large bowl. With mixer at low speed, beat until blended, scraping bowl with rubber spatula. Increase speed to high and beat 2 minutes, scraping bowl occasionally. Reduce speed to low; add flour mixture and beat just until blended. With rubber spatula, gently fold in 1½ cups blueberries.

4 Spoon batter into prepared tube pan. Sprinkle with remaining ½ cup blueberries, then reserved crumb mixture. Bake 60 to 65 minutes, until toothpick inserted in center of cake comes out clean. Cool cake in pan on wire rack 10 minutes. With small metal spatula, loosen cake from side of pan; remove pan side. Cool cake completely on wire rack. To remove, run a knife around center and bottom of pan. Gently lift cake from bottom of pan onto rack, crumb side up. *Makes 1 cake, 16 slices.*

EACH SLICE: ABOUT 340 CALORIES, 5 G PROTEIN, 44 G CARBOHYDRATE, 16 G TOTAL FAT (10 G SATURATED), 1 G FIBER, 77 MG CHOLESTEROL, 310 MG SODIUM.

Blueberry Crumb Ring

PREP 25 MINUTES / BAKE 1 HOUR TO 1 HOUR 5 MINUTES

A mixture of utter, sugar, and cinnamon forms the base of the batter and serves as the crumb topping.

1 CUP BUTTER OR MARGARINE (2 STICKS), SOFTENED

1½ CUPS SUGAR

1 TEASPOON GROUND CINNAMON

3½ CUPS ALL-PURPOSE FLOUR

2 TEASPOONS BAKING POWDER

½ TEASPOON BAKING SODA

½ TEASPOON SALT

1 CONTAINER (8 OUNCES) SOUR CREAM

3 LARGE EGGS

2 TEASPOONS VANILLA EXTRACT

2 CUPS FRESH BLUEBERRIES, RINSED AND DRIED

Classic Crumb Cake

PREP 40 MINUTES / BAKE 40 TO 45 MINUTES

CRUMB TOPPING:

2 CUPS ALL-PURPOSE FLOUR

½ CUP GRANULATED SUGAR

½ CUP PACKED LIGHT BROWN SUGAR

1½ TEASPOONS GROUND CINNAMON

1 CUP BUTTER OR MARGARINE (2 STICKS), SOFTENED

CAKE:

2¼ CUPS ALL-PURPOSE FLOUR

2¼ TEASPOONS BAKING POWDER

½ TEASPOON SALT

1¼ CUPS GRANULATED SUGAR

½ CUP BUTTER OR MARGARINE (1 STICK), SOFTENED

3 LARGE EGGS

¾ CUP MILK

2 TEASPOONS VANILLA EXTRACT

1 Prepare Crumb Topping: In medium bowl, mix flour, granulated and brown sugars, and cinnamon until well blended. With fingertips, work in butter until mixture resembles coarse crumbs.

2 Prepare Cake: Preheat oven to 350° F. Grease two 9-inch round cake pans; dust with flour. In medium bowl, stir together flour, baking powder, and salt.

3 In large bowl, with mixer at low speed, beat granulated sugar and butter until blended, scraping bowl often with rubber spatula. Increase speed to medium; beat about 2 minutes, until well mixed, scraping bowl occasionally. Reduce speed to low; add eggs, 1 at a time, beating well after each addition.

4 In cup, combine milk and vanilla. With mixer at low speed, add flour mixture alternately with milk mixture, beginning and ending with flour mixture, scraping bowl occasionally, until batter is smooth.

5 Pour batter into prepared pans. With hand, press crumb topping into large chunks; sprinkle evenly over batter. Bake 40 to 45 minutes, until toothpick inserted in centers of cakes comes out clean. Cool cakes in pans on wire racks 15 minutes. With small metal spatula, loosen cakes from side of pans. Invert each cake onto plate; remove pan. Immediately invert cakes onto wire racks to cool completely, with crumb topping up. *Makes 2 coffee cakes, 10 servings each.*

EACH SERVING: ABOUT 330 CALORIES, 4 G PROTEIN, 45 G CARBOHYDRATE, 16 G TOTAL FAT (9 G SATURATED), 0.5 G FIBER, 70 MG CHOLESTEROL, 270 MG SODIUM.

Classic Crumb Cake

Sour Cream Coffee Cake

PREP 30 MINUTES / BAKE 1 HOUR 20 MINUTES

This is a real tried-and-true American classic that your grandmother may well have served to her friends. Baked in a tube pan, the cake has a layer of walnuts and cinnamon sugar in the middle and a topping of the same spicy-sweet mixture. In the variations, this filling/topping is replaced with a cinnamon-chocolate layer or a ribbon of raspberry jam and walnuts. Or create your own combinations.

⅔ PLUS 1¾ CUPS SUGAR
⅔ CUP WALNUTS, FINELY CHOPPED
1 TEASPOON GROUND CINNAMON
3¾ CUPS ALL-PURPOSE FLOUR
2 TEASPOONS BAKING POWDER
1 TEASPOON BAKING SODA
¾ TEASPOON SALT
½ CUP BUTTER OR MARGARINE (1 STICK), SOFTENED
3 LARGE EGGS
1 CONTAINER (16 OUNCES) SOUR CREAM
2 TEASPOONS VANILLA EXTRACT

1 Preheat oven to 350° F. Grease 9- to 10-inch tube pan with removable bottom; dust with flour. In small bowl, mix ⅔ cup sugar, walnuts, and cinnamon. In medium bowl, stir together flour, baking powder, baking soda, and salt.

SOUR CREAM SELECTION

JUST A FEW YEARS AGO THERE WAS NO CHOICE IN SOUR CREAMS—IT WAS THE REAL (CREAMY, DELICIOUS, TANGY) STUFF OR NOTHING. BUT THEN CAME THE ADVENT OF SOUR HALF-AND-HALF, FOLLOWED BY "LITE," LOW-FAT, FAT-FREE, CHOLESTEROL-FREE, AND EVEN NONDAIRY RENDITIONS. FOR BAKING, YOUR BEST BET IS TO STICK TO THE REAL THING. ITS BUTTERFAT CONTENT AND AUTHENTIC DAIRY FLAVOR HELP ENSURE THE SUCCESS OF CAKES AND BREADS.

---

2 In large bowl, with mixer at low speed, beat remaining 1¾ cups sugar and butter until blended, scraping bowl with rubber spatula. Increase speed to high; beat until creamy, about 2 minutes, scraping bowl occasionally. Reduce speed to low; add eggs, 1 at a time, beating well after each addition.

3 With mixer at low speed, add flour mixture alternately with sour cream, beginning and ending with flour mixture, beating until batter is smooth, occasionally scraping bowl. Beat in vanilla.

4 Spoon one-third of batter into prepared tube pan. Sprinkle ½ cup nut mixture evenly over batter, then spread half of remaining batter on top. Sprinkle with ½ cup more nut mixture; layer with remaining batter, then remaining nut mixture.

5 Bake cake 1 hour 20 minutes, or until toothpick inserted in center comes out clean. Cool cake in pan on wire rack 10 minutes. With small metal spatula, loosen cake from side of pan and lift cake from pan bottom. Invert cake onto plate; remove bottom of pan. Immediately invert cake onto wire rack to cool completely, with nut mixture on top. *Makes 1 coffee cake, 16 servings.*

EACH SERVING: ABOUT 390 CALORIES, 6 G PROTEIN, 55 G CARBOHYDRATE, 17 G TOTAL FAT (8 G SATURATED), 1 G FIBER, 68 MG CHOLESTEROL, 335 MG SODIUM.

CHOCOLATE-CHERRY COFFEE CAKE Prepare batter as above but omit nut mixture in Step 1. Stir ⅔ cup *dried tart cherries* into batter after adding vanilla in Step 3. In small bowl, mix *½ cup semisweet chocolate mini-chips, 1 tablespoon unsweetened cocoa, 2 teaspoons ground cinnamon,* and *⅓ cup sugar.* Spoon one-third of batter into prepared pan; sprinkle with half of chocolate mixture. Top with half of remaining batter; sprinkle with remaining chocolate mixture. Spread remaining batter on top. Bake as directed. To serve, sprinkle with *confectioners' sugar.*
EACH SERVING: ABOUT 380 CALORIES, 5 G PROTEIN, 58 G CARBOHYDRATE, 15 G TOTAL FAT (9 G SATURATED), 1 G FIBER, 68 MG CHOLESTEROL, 335 MG SODIUM.

RASPBERRY-WALNUT SOUR CREAM COFFEE CAKE Prepare batter as above but omit nut mixture in Step 1. Spoon three-fourths of batter into prepared pan. Spread *½ cup seedless red raspberry jam* over batter, spread remaining batter over jam. Sprinkle *½ cup walnuts,* toasted and chopped, over top of batter. Bake as directed.
EACH SERVING: ABOUT 370 CALORIES, 6 G PROTEIN, 53 G CARBOHYDRATE, 16 G TOTAL FAT (8 G SATURATED), 1 G FIBER, 68 MG CHOLESTEROL, 340 MG SODIUM.

Raspberry-Walnut Sour Cream Coffee Cake

Fruit-Streusel Coffee Cake

PREP 25 MINUTES / BAKE 50 TO 55 MINUTES

Here's a coffee-time treat to suit every season. You can cover the buttery cake with just about any fruit you please, from summer's berries, peaches, nectarines, or plums to autumn's pears and apples, to an unexpected midwinter treat—frozen rhubarb.

STREUSEL TOPPING:

¾ CUP ALL-PURPOSE FLOUR

½ CUP LIGHT BROWN SUGAR

1 TEASPOON GROUND CINNAMON

4 TABLESPOONS BUTTER OR MARGARINE, CHILLED
    AND CUT UP

CAKE:

2¼ CUPS ALL-PURPOSE FLOUR

1½ TEASPOONS BAKING POWDER

½ TEASPOON BAKING SODA

½ TEASPOON SALT

1½ CUPS GRANULATED SUGAR

¾ CUP BUTTER OR MARGARINE (1½ STICKS), SOFTENED

3 LARGE EGGS

1 CUP MILK

1 TEASPOON VANILLA EXTRACT

1¼ POUNDS RIPE PEARS, APPLES, OR PEACHES, PEELED
    AND THINLY SLICED, OR NECTARINES OR PLUMS, THINLY
    SLICED (3 CUPS), OR FRESH OR FROZEN RHUBARB, CUT
    INTO 1-INCH PIECES (4 CUPS), OR 1 PINT BLUEBERRIES

1 Prepare Streusel Topping: In medium bowl, with fingertips, stir together flour, brown sugar, cinnamon, and butter until mixture resembles coarse crumbs.

2 Prepare Cake: Preheat oven to 350° F. Grease 13" by 9" metal baking pan; dust with flour. In medium bowl, stir together flour, baking powder, baking soda, and salt.

3 In large bowl, with mixer at low speed, beat sugar and butter until blended, scraping bowl often with rubber spatula. Increase speed to high; beat until creamy, about 2 minutes, scraping bowl occasionally. Reduce speed to low; add eggs, 1 at a time, beating well after each addition.

4 In cup, combine milk and vanilla. With mixer at low speed, add flour mixture alternately with milk mixture, beginning and ending with flour mixture, scraping bowl occasionally, until batter is smooth.

5 With metal spatula, spread batter evenly in prepared pan. Arrange pear slices or other fruit slices, overlapping slightly, on top. Sprinkle streusel topping over fruit.

6 Bake cake 50 to 55 minutes, until toothpick inserted in center of cake comes out clean. Cool cake in pan on wire rack 10 minutes to serve warm. Or, cool completely in pan. *Makes 1 coffee cake, 15 servings.*

EACH SERVING: ABOUT 355 CALORIES, 5 G PROTEIN, 53 G CARBOHYDRATE, 14 G TOTAL FAT (8 G SATURATED), 2 G FIBER, 78 MG CHOLESTEROL, 315 MG SODIUM.

CRACKERS & FLATBREADS

Why make crackers at home? After all, the supermarket shelves have all sorts of crackers. But homemade crackers are fun to bake and you can make them just the way you want—a bit thicker or thinner, bigger or smaller, with more or less cheese, seeds, or salt sprinkled on top. Bake them for your next party, and don't worry too much about the toppings—the crackers themselves will take center stage.

Sesame Thins

PREP 50 MINUTES / BAKE 8 TO 10 MINUTES PER BATCH

The sesame seeds don't sit on top of these crackers—they're incorporated into the dough. A combination of cornmeal and flour gives the crackers a sturdy texture, and a brushing of melted butter crisps the tops. Store these—all crackers, for that matter—in airtight containers.

1¾ CUPS ALL-PURPOSE FLOUR

½ CUP CORNMEAL

2 TABLESPOONS SESAME SEEDS

2 TABLESPOONS SUGAR

½ TEASPOON BAKING SODA

½ TEASPOON SALT

6 TABLESPOONS COLD BUTTER OR MARGARINE

½ CUP WATER

2 TABLESPOONS DISTILLED WHITE VINEGAR

1 In large bowl, stir together flour, cornmeal, sesame seeds, sugar, baking soda, and salt. With pastry blender or 2 knives used scissor-fashion, cut in 4 tablespoons butter until mixture resembles coarse crumbs. Stir in water and vinegar; mix just until soft dough forms. Turn dough onto lightly floured surface and knead 8 to 10 times, just until blended. (Do not overmix dough or crackers will be tough.)

2 Preheat oven to 375° F. Divide dough into 30 balls. On floured surface, with rolling pin, roll each of 5 balls (keeping remaining dough balls covered so they will not dry out) into a 5-inch paper-thin circle (edges may be ragged). Place circles, 1 inch apart, on ungreased cookie sheet.

3 Melt remaining 2 tablespoons butter or margarine. Lightly brush each circle with butter.

4 Bake 8 to 10 minutes, until browned. With wide spatula, immediately transfer crackers to wire racks to cool.

5 Repeat with remaining dough and melted butter. *Makes 2½ dozen crackers.*

EACH CRACKER: ABOUT 65 CALORIES, 1 G PROTEIN,
9 G CARBOHYDRATE, 3 G TOTAL FAT (1 G SATURATED),
0.5 G FIBER, 6 MG CHOLESTEROL, 85 MG SODIUM.

Wine Biscuits

PREP 20 MINUTES PLUS CHILLING
BAKE 12 TO 15 MINUTES PER BATCH

With cheese, fruit, and a glass of wine, these cookielike biscuits make a simple and very elegant dessert.

1 CUP DRY RED WINE
2 CUPS ALL-PURPOSE FLOUR
2 TEASPOONS BAKING POWDER
¼ CUP SUGAR
½ TEASPOON SALT
½ TEASPOON COARSELY GROUND BLACK PEPPER
¼ CUP OLIVE OIL

1 In 1-quart saucepan, heat wine to boiling over medium-high heat; boil 10 minutes, or until reduced to ½ cup. Chill to room temperature.

2 Meanwhile, in large bowl, stir together flour, baking powder, sugar, salt, and pepper. With fork, stir olive oil into cool wine.

3 Add wine mixture to flour mixture and stir until combined. Turn dough onto lightly floured surface and knead gently, about 10 times, until smooth.

Divide dough in half. Roll each half into 14½" by 1½" rope (dough will be crumbly). Wrap each rope in waxed paper and freeze 1 hour, or until firm.

4 Preheat oven to 400° F. Grease 2 large cookie sheets. On cutting board, with serrated knife, cut each rope into ¼-inch-thick slices. Place, ½ inch apart, on prepared cookie sheets. Bake 12 to 15 minutes, rotating sheets between upper and lower racks halfway through baking, or until edges begin to brown. With wide spatula, remove biscuits to wire rack to cool completely.

5 Repeat with remaining dough *Makes about 10 dozen biscuits.*

EACH BISCUIT: ABOUT 15 CALORIES, 0 G PROTEIN,
2 G CARBOHYDRATE, 1 G TOTAL FAT (0 G SATURATED),
0 G FIBER, 0 MG CHOLESTEROL, 20 MG SODIUM.

Caraway-Cheese Crisps

PREP 10 MINUTES / BAKE 10 TO 12 MINUTES PER BATCH

1½ CUPS ALL-PURPOSE FLOUR
½ CUP BUTTER OR MARGARINE (1 STICK), SOFTENED
½ TEASPOON CARAWAY SEEDS
¼ TEASPOON SALT
12 OUNCES EXTRA SHARP CHEDDAR CHEESE, SHREDDED
  (3 CUPS)

1 Preheat oven to 425° F. In large bowl, with hand, knead all ingredients until blended into a dough.

2 Shape dough into ½-inch balls. Place balls, 2 inches apart, on ungreased large cookie sheet. With fingers, flatten balls ¼ inch thick. Bake 10 to 12 minutes, until lightly browned. With wide spatula, transfer crisps to wire racks to cool.

3 Repeat with remaining balls. *Makes about 4½ dozen crackers.*

EACH CRACKER: ABOUT 55 CALORIES, 2 G PROTEIN,
3 G CARBOHYDRATE, 4 G TOTAL FAT (2 G SATURATED),
0 G FIBER, 11 MG CHOLESTEROL, 65 MG SODIUM.

SWISS CHEESE ROUNDS Prepare as above but use *12 ounces Swiss cheese*, shredded, and add *⅛ teaspoon ground red pepper (cayenne)*. Bake as directed.
EACH CRACKER: ABOUT 50 CALORIES, 2 G PROTEIN,
3 G CARBOHYDRATE, 3 G TOTAL FAT (2 G SATURATED),
0 G FIBER, 10 MG CHOLESTEROL, 45 MG SODIUM.

Spicy Cornmeal Cheddar Wafers

PREP 25 MINUTES PLUS CHILLING
BAKE 18 MINUTES PER BATCH

The food processor mixes the dough for these irresistibly savory crackers, zesty with Cheddar, Parmesan, and Dijon mustard. Serve the wafers with tomato bisque or cream of broccoli soup, or alongside a green salad. Be careful when removing the wafers from the cooling rack as they are quite fragile.

1 CUP ALL-PURPOSE FLOUR
¼ CUP CORNMEAL
¼ CUP FRESHLY GRATED PARMESAN OR ROMANO CHEESE
½ TEASPOON COARSELY GROUND BLACK PEPPER
½ TEASPOON BAKING POWDER
¼ TEASPOON GROUND RED PEPPER (CAYENNE)
½ CUP BUTTER (1 STICK), CUT INTO 8 PIECES, SOFTENED
1 TABLESPOON DIJON MUSTARD
8 OUNCES SHARP CHEDDAR CHEESE, SHREDDED (2 CUPS)

1 In food processor with knife blade attached, combine flour, cornmeal, Parmesan cheese, pepper, baking powder, and ground red pepper; process until blended. Add butter and process until mixture resembles fine meal. Add mustard and Cheddar and process until mixture is blended and begins to form a ball.

2 Turn dough onto lightly floured surface and knead to blend. With hands, shape into 10-inch-long log. Wrap in waxed paper and refrigerate 4 hours, or overnight.

3 Preheat oven to 350° F. With serrated knife, cut log into scant ¼-inch-thick slices. Place, 1½ inches apart, on 2 ungreased large cookie sheets. Bake 18 minutes, rotating sheets between upper and lower racks halfway through baking, or until lightly browned and crisp. While hot, with wide spatula, remove to wire rack to cool completely. *Makes about 4 dozen wafers.*

EACH WAFER: ABOUT 50 CALORIES, 2 G PROTEIN,
3 G CARBOHYDRATE, 4 G TOTAL FAT (2 G SATURATED),
0 G FIBER, 11 MG CHOLESTEROL, 70 MG SODIUM.

Romano Cheese Flatbread Crisps

PREP 45 MINUTES / BAKE 15 TO 18 MINUTES PER BATCH

No dip is called for when you offer these peppery, cheese-topped strips. They're perfect any time you'd serve breadsticks. For a different flavor, sprinkle the dough with sesame or poppyseeds (or a mixture of the two).

2¼ CUPS ALL-PURPOSE FLOUR
1½ TEASPOONS BAKING POWDER
1 TEASPOON SALT
1 TEASPOON COARSELY GROUND BLACK PEPPER
¾ CUP WATER
1 TABLESPOON OLIVE OR VEGETABLE OIL
½ CUP FRESHLY GRATED ROMANO CHEESE

1 In medium bowl, stir together flour, baking powder, salt, and pepper. Stir in water, stirring until dough comes together in a ball. With hand, knead dough in bowl until smooth, about 2 minutes. (Or, in food processor with knife blade attached, blend flour, baking powder, salt, and pepper, pulsing processor just until ingredients are blended. With processor running, pour water through feed tube; continue to process about 30 seconds, until dough forms smooth ball.) Divide dough in half; cover half of dough.

2 Preheat oven to 350° F. On floured surface, with floured rolling pin, roll dough half into paper-thin rectangle, about 20" by 12" (edges may be ragged). With pizza wheel or sharp knife, cut dough lengthwise in half to form two 20" by 6" rectangles. Cut rectangles crosswise into 2-inch-wide strips.

3 Place strips, ½ inch apart, on 2 ungreased large cookie sheets; let rest 10 minutes. With pastry brush, brush strips lightly with oil; sprinkle with half of grated cheese. Bake strips 15 to 18 minutes, until lightly browned, rotating sheets between upper and lower racks halfway through baking. With wide spatula, immediately transfer crisps to wire racks to cool.

4 Repeat with remaining dough, oil, and cheese. *Makes about 3 dozen crisps.*

EACH CRISP: ABOUT 40 CALORIES, 1 G PROTEIN,
6 G CARBOHYDRATE, 1 G TOTAL FAT (0 G SATURATED),
0 G FIBER, 1 MG CHOLESTEROL, 100 MG SODIUM.

Lemon-Pepper Crisps

PREP 50 MINUTES / BAKE 15 TO 18 MINUTES PER BATCH

You will love the fresh flavor of these crisps whether you roll them out on a well-floured counter, using a thin setting of your pasta machine, or with a rolling-pin sleeve and a pastry cloth. It's almost inevitable that the rectangles of dough will stretch a bit as you transfer them from the counter to the cookie sheet.

2¼ CUPS ALL-PURPOSE FLOUR
1 CUP PACKED FRESH PARSLEY LEAVES, FINELY CHOPPED
1 TABLESPOON FRESHLY GRATED LEMON PEEL
1½ TEASPOONS BAKING POWDER
¼ TEASPOON COARSELY GROUND BLACK PEPPER
2½ TEASPOONS KOSHER SALT
¾ CUP WATER
2 TABLESPOONS OLIVE OIL

1 In medium bowl, mix flour, parsley, lemon peel, baking powder, pepper, and 2 teaspoons salt. Stir in water, stirring just until dough comes together in a ball. With hand, knead dough in bowl until smooth, about 2 minutes. Divide dough in half; cover each half with waxed paper and let rest 10 minutes.

2 Preheat oven to 350° F. On floured surface, with floured rolling pin, roll half of dough into a paper-thin rectangle, about 18" by 12" (edges may be ragged). With pizza wheel or sharp knife, cut dough lengthwise in half to form two 18" by 6" rectangles. Cut rectangles crosswise into 2-inch-wide strips.

3 Place strips, ½ inch apart, on 2 ungreased large cookie sheets; let rest 10 minutes. With pastry brush, brush strips lightly with 1 tablespoon oil; sprinkle with ¼ teaspoon salt. Bake 15 to 18 minutes, until lightly browned, rotating sheets between upper and lower racks halfway through baking. With wide metal spatula, immediately transfer crisps to wire racks to cool.

4 Repeat with remaining dough, oil, and salt. *Makes 3 dozen crisps.*

EACH CRISP: ABOUT 40 CALORIES, 1 G PROTEIN,
7 G CARBOHYDRATE, 1 G TOTAL FAT (0 G SATURATED),
0.5 G FIBER, 0 MG CHOLESTEROL, 125 MG SODIUM.

Scandinavian Rye Flatbread

PREP 45 MINUTES PLUS RISING
BAKE 25 TO 30 MINUTES PER BATCH

Serve these tangy, caraway-scented rye crisps with softened butter and Scandinavian cheeses, such as Havarti, Jarlsberg, and Danish blue.

1 PACKAGE ACTIVE DRY YEAST
¼ CUP WARM WATER (105° TO 115° F)
1 TABLESPOON SUGAR
1 CUP BUTTERMILK, HEATED TO LUKEWARM (105 TO 115°)
ABOUT 2 CUPS MEDIUM RYE FLOUR
1½ CUPS WHOLE-WHEAT FLOUR
3 TABLESPOONS BUTTER OR MARGARINE, SOFTENED
1½ TEASPOONS CARAWAY SEEDS
1 TEASPOON SALT
CORNMEAL AND RYE FLOUR FOR DUSTING

1 In large bowl, combine yeast, warm water, and sugar to dissolve. Let stand 5 minutes, or until foamy.

2 Add warm buttermilk, 1½ cups rye flour, 1 cup whole-wheat flour, butter, caraway seeds, and salt. With wooden spoon, beat until well blended. Gradually stir in remaining ½ cup whole-wheat flour.

3 Turn dough onto floured surface. Knead 8 minutes, until smooth and elastic, adding remaining ½ cup rye flour as needed to keep dough from sticking. Place dough in greased bowl, cover with plastic wrap, and let rise in warm place (80 to 85° F) until doubled, about 1 hour.

4 Preheat oven to 300° F. Punch down dough. Divide in half; cover half with plastic wrap. On surface dusted lightly with cornmeal and rye flour, with floured rolling pin, roll half of dough into a 17" by 16" rectangle. With pizza cutter or knife cut dough crosswise into 8 strips, then cut each strip into 4 pieces, making 32 crackers. Prick all over with fork. Place, 1 inch apart, on ungreased large cookie sheets.

5 Bake 25 to 30 minutes, until golden brown, removing crackers as they brown. With wide spatula, transfer to wire racks to cool completely.

6 Repeat with remaining dough. *Makes 64 crackers.*

EACH CRACKER: ABOUT 30 CALORIES, 1 G PROTEIN,
5 G CARBOHYDRATE, 1 G TOTAL FAT (0 G SATURATED),
1 G FIBER, 2 MG CHOLESTEROL, 45 MG SODIUM.

Pappadams

Pappadams

PREP 45 MINUTES / BAKE 10 TO 12 MINUTES PER BATCH

Indian meals frequently begin with small bowls of chutney and a platter of crisp, peppery pappadams.

1½ TEASPOONS CUMIN SEEDS

2 TABLESPOONS BUTTER OR MARGARINE

1 CUP FINELY CHOPPED ONION

1 TABLESPOON FINELY CHOPPED GARLIC

1 TEASPOON SALT

½ TEASPOON FRESHLY GROUND PEPPER

¼ TEASPOON GROUND RED PEPPER (CAYENNE)

ABOUT ¾ CUP ALL-PURPOSE FLOUR

½ CUP WHOLE-WHEAT FLOUR

2 TABLESPOONS VEGETABLE SHORTENING

2 TABLESPOONS WATER

1 In medium skillet, toast cumin seeds over medium heat until fragrant, about 4 minutes; cool. In same skillet, melt butter over medium heat. Add onion, garlic, ½ teaspoon salt, pepper, and ground red pepper; cook, stirring, 5 minutes, or until onion softens; cool.

2 In food processor with knife blade attached, combine ½ cup all-purpose flour, whole-wheat flour, remaining ½ teaspoon salt, and cumin seeds; pulse until combined. Add shortening and process until mixture resembles fine meal. Add onion mixture and process until blended. With motor running, pour water through feed tube, processing dough 1 minute.

3 Turn dough onto well floured surface. Knead 4 minutes, until smooth, adding remaining ¼ cup all-purpose flour to keep dough from sticking.

4 Preheat oven to 325° F. Divide dough into 8 pieces. Keeping remaining dough covered, shape 1 piece of dough into disk. On well-floured surface, with floured rolling pin, roll into paper-thin circle, about 9 inches in diameter. (Every time dough is rolled, lift it up and sprinkle surface and dough lightly with flour.)

5 Place circles, 2 inches apart, on ungreased cookie sheet. Bake 8 minutes; turn and bake 2 to 4 minutes, until edges curl up and circles are golden brown and crisp. Remove to wire racks to cool completely.

6 Repeat with remaining dough. *Makes 8 crackers.*

EACH CRACKER: ABOUT 145 CALORIES, 3 G PROTEIN, 20 G CARBOHYDRATE, 6 G TOTAL FAT (3 G SATURATED), 2 G FIBER, 8 MG CHOLESTEROL, 325 MG SODIUM.

Whole-Wheat Digestive Biscuits

PREP 15 MINUTES / BAKE 16 TO 18 MINUTES

Something between a cracker and a cookie, the "whole-meal digestive" is a staple on grocers' shelves in the United Kingdom. Try making some at home to serve alongside fruit and cheese, or with a spoonful of natural-style peanut butter.

2 CUPS WHOLE-WHEAT FLOUR
½ CUP FIRMLY PACKED BROWN SUGAR
⅓ CUP QUICK-COOKING OR OLD-FASHIONED OATS, UNCOOKED
1 TEASPOON BAKING POWDER
¼ TEASPOON SALT
½ CUP COLD BUTTER OR MARGARINE (1 STICK), CUT INTO 8 PIECES
⅓ CUP MILK

1 Preheat oven to 350° F. In food processor with knife blade attached, combine flour, brown sugar, oats, baking powder, and salt. Process until combined. Add butter and process until mixture resembles texture of cornmeal. Add milk and process until dough begins to hold together.

2 Turn mixture onto surface. With hand, knead lightly, about 30 seconds; gather into ball. Lightly flour surface. With floured rolling pin, roll dough a scant ¼-inch thick. With 2½-inch round cookie cutter, cut out rounds; reserve trimmings.

3 With wide spatula, place rounds, 1 inch apart, on ungreased large cookie sheet. Bake 16 to 18 minutes, until light brown. With metal spatula, transfer biscuits to wire racks to cool completely.

4 Repeat with remaining dough and trimmings. *Makes about 3 dozen biscuits.*

EACH BISCUIT: ABOUT 65 CALORIES, 1 G PROTEIN, 9 G CARBOHYDRATE, 3 G TOTAL FAT (2 G SATURATED), 1 G FIBER, 7 MG CHOLESTEROL, 60 MG SODIUM.

CAN THIS BE HEALTH FOOD?

ALTHOUGH THEIR NAME MAKES THEM SOUND PRIMLY HEALTHFUL AND BRITISH (THEY ARE BRITISH), "DIGESTIVES" HAVE THE SAME SIMPLE, UNIVERSAL APPEAL AS GRAHAM CRACKERS—WHICH WERE ORIGINALLY INTENDED AS A HEALTH FOOD. BAKED WITH WHOLE-WHEAT FLOUR, OATS, AND BROWN SUGAR—PLUS PLENTY OF BUTTER—DIGESTIVES ARE THICK BUT TENDER CRACKERS THAT GO BEAUTIFULLY WITH CHEESE. IN BRITAIN, DIGESTIVE BISCUITS COATED WITH CHOCOLATE (MILK OR DARK) ARE ALSO A POPULAR ITEM. SO MUCH FOR HEALTH FOOD!

Yeast Breads

instant-read thermometer

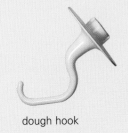

dough hook

dough scraper

bread knife

The most important tools for the gratifying task of baking yeast breads are your own two hands and sufficient time to practice. Whether the dough has been adequately kneaded, how much flour to add, when the dough has risen enough—these are things no meter or gauge can tell you; your fingertips—and a bit of experience—will be your guides. In addition to a large bowl, a good-size board, and a wooden spoon, a few pieces of more specialized equipment do help. In the pocket of every professional chef is an **instant-read thermometer,** the right kind to confirm that water is the right temperature for starting yeast (it's also the best thermometer to use when roasting meat). A **heavy-duty stand mixer with a dough hook** makes bread-making easier because the machine does the kneading. (A regular hand mixer is not nearly strong enough.) A powerful mixer kneads dough very fast, so be careful not to overwork it. Use the slow speed the first few times you make bread so that you can keep a close eye on things. A **dough scraper** helps you gather and knead dough; it's especially useful when you're handling a sticky dough. When you're done, the metal edge does a great job of cleaning the surface. To preserve the look of your perfect loaf, slice it with a sharp **serrated bread knife,** using a gentle sawing motion.

Previous page: Crescent Rolls

Basic techniques

PROOFING YEAST AND KNEADING DOUGH

Stir the yeast and a spoonful of sugar into warm water (105° to 115° F). If the yeast is active, the mixture will bubble. This is called proofing yeast.

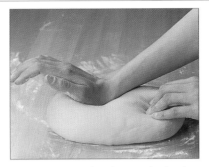

To knead yeast dough, use the heel of one hand to push the dough away from you. The dough may be soft at first, but will firm up as you knead it.

After each kneading stroke, fold the dough over and give it a quarter turn. Start the next kneading stroke on top of the folded-over portion of dough.

PUNCHING DOWN DOUGH

The dough is fully risen if, when you poke your finger into it, the indentation remains. At this point, deflate the dough with your fist.

SLASHING TOP OF LOAF

If the recipe calls for slashes to be made in the dough before baking, use a single-edge razor blade or a French baker's tool called a *lame* ("lahm").

SHAPING A PIZZA CRUST

Pizza doesn't have to be round: You can make it on a rectangular baking sheet. Roll out the dough on the cornmeal-dusted sheet.

Turn the outer inch or so of the dough inward all around to form a rim

WHITE BREADS

It's time to put aside your old image of "white bread." Sliced storebought loaves bear little or no resemblance to the firm, crusty white breads you can make in your own kitchen. Your homemade loaves will be free of additives such as the dough conditioners and preservatives often used in supermarket breads. "White bread" doesn't just mean sandwich bread—it comes in many shapes, sizes, textures, and flavors, including French baguettes, sturdy sourdoughs, peasant loaves studded with olives and scented with rosemary, roasted-garlic and cheese bread, and Italian-style loaves made with semolina, a coarsely ground durum wheat flour.

Farmhouse White Bread

PREP 24 HOURS FOR STARTER PLUS 1 HOUR 30 MINUTES
PLUS RISING / BAKE 25 MINUTES

This two-loaf recipe is a "plan-ahead" bread that requires two overnight risings. First, a sponge starter is made of flour, water, and yeast; after 24 hours in the refrigerator, it's light and bubbly. Once the starter is combined with the remaining ingredients, the dough requires two 1-hour rises at warm room temperature, then another 3 to 24 hours in the refrigerator. Don't imagine that you need to spend the whole time in the kitchen, though! While the dough is rising, it doesn't need any attention at all.

SPONGE STARTER:

3 CUPS ALL-PURPOSE FLOUR OR 2½ CUPS BREAD FLOUR
½ TEASPOON ACTIVE DRY YEAST
1⅓ CUPS WARM WATER (105° TO 115° F)

DOUGH:

1 CUP WARM WATER (105° TO 115° F)
¾ TEASPOON ACTIVE DRY YEAST
¼ TEASPOON SUGAR
1 TABLESPOON PLUS 1 TEASPOON SALT
ABOUT 3⅓ CUPS ALL-PURPOSE FLOUR OR 3¼ CUPS BREAD
    FLOUR

1 Prepare Sponge Starter: In large bowl, combine flour, yeast, and warm water. With mixer at low speed, beat 3 minutes to develop a smooth, elastic batter. Cover bowl and refrigerate at least 15 hours, or up to 24 hours. Starter is ready to use when it has thinned out slightly, the volume has tripled, and small bubbles appear on the surface.

2 Next day, let starter stand, covered, at room temperature 30 minutes before using. Meanwhile, prepare Dough: In very large bowl, combine warm water, yeast. and sugar; stir to dissolve. Let stand 5 minutes, or until foamy.

3 Add starter to yeast mixture in bowl, breaking up starter with hand (it will not be completely blended). Stir in salt and 3 cups flour. With floured hand, knead to combine in bowl.

4 Turn dough onto lightly floured surface and knead 10 to 12 minutes, until smooth and elastic, working in about ¼ cup more all-purpose flour or ⅓ cup more bread flour as necessary to keep dough from sticking. Shape dough into ball and place in greased large bowl, turning dough over to grease top. Cover bowl and let dough rise in warm place (80° to 85° F) until doubled, about 1 hour.

5 Punch down dough. In same bowl, shape dough into ball. Cover bowl and let dough rise again until doubled, about 1 hour.

6 Turn dough onto floured surface and cut in half; cover and let rest 15 minutes for easier shaping. Sprinkle large cookie sheet with flour.

7 Shape each dough half into 7-inch round loaf. Place loaves at opposite corners on prepared cookie sheet. Cover and let dough rise in refrigerator at least 3 hours, or up to 24 hours.

8 Preheat oven to 500° F. Remove loaves from refrigerator. Sprinkle loaves with flour. With serrated knife or single-edge razor blade, cut 2 parallel slashes, 1½ inches apart, on top of each loaf, then cut 2 more slashes, perpendicular to first lines (final effect will be a grid, like tic-tac-toe box). Place 12 ice cubes in 13" by 9" metal baking pan. Place pan in bottom of oven. Bake loaves on middle rack 10 minutes. Turn oven control to 400° F. Bake 15 minutes longer, or until loaves are golden and bottoms sound hollow when lightly tapped with fingers. Transfer to wire racks to cool. *Makes 2 loaves, 12 slices each.*

EACH SLICE: ABOUT 125 CALORIES, 4 G PROTEIN, 26 G CARBOHYDRATE, 0 G TOTAL FAT (0 G SATURATED), 1 G FIBER, 0 MG CHOLESTEROL, 385 MG SODIUM.

Farmhouse White Bread

Ciabatta

PREP 30 MINUTES PLUS RISING / BAKE 25 TO 30 MINUTES

Ciabatta means "slipper" in Italian, and you may detect the resemblance in these long, oval, flattish loaves. Serve ciabatta with soup or salad, or slice it in half to make sandwiches. The soft, sticky dough requires a heavy-duty stand mixer—or a very strong stirring arm.

2¼ CUPS WARM WATER (105° TO 115° F)
1 PACKAGE ACTIVE DRY YEAST
1 TEASPOON SUGAR
5 CUPS ALL-PURPOSE FLOUR OR 4½ CUPS BREAD FLOUR
1 TABLESPOON SALT
2 TABLESPOONS MILK
2 TABLESPOONS EXTRAVIRGIN OLIVE OIL

1 In cup, combine ¼ cup warm water, yeast, and sugar; stir to dissolve. Let stand 5 minutes, or until foamy.

2 In bowl of heavy-duty mixer, combine flour and salt. With wooden spoon, stir in milk, oil, yeast mixture, and remaining 2 cups warm water until blended. With dough hook, mix at medium speed 15 minutes, or until dough becomes elastic. Or, if mixing by hand, in very large bowl, combine ingredients as above and stir with wooden spoon 15 minutes, or until dough becomes elastic. (This is a very sticky and moist dough; do not add more flour, and do not knead or stir for less than the suggested time.)

3 Scrape dough into greased large bowl; with greased hand, pat top of dough to coat. Cover bowl and let dough rise in warm place (80° to 85° F) until doubled, about 1 hour to 1 hour 30 minutes.

4 Sprinkle large cookie sheet with flour. With floured hand, punch down dough and cut in half. Places halves, about 3 inches apart, on prepared cookie sheet; cover and let rest 15 minutes for easier shaping.

5 With hands, pull 1 piece of dough into 14" by 4" oval. Repeat with remaining piece of dough, keeping loaves 3 inches apart. With floured fingers, make deep indentations all over each loaf, making sure to press all the way down to cookie sheet. Sprinkle loaves lightly with flour. Cover and let dough rise in warm place until doubled, about 30 minutes.

6 Preheat oven to 425° F. Place 12 ice cubes in 13" by 9" metal baking pan. Place pan in bottom of oven. Bake loaves on middle rack 25 to 30 minutes, until golden, using spray bottle to spritz loaves with water 3 times during first 10 minutes of baking, being careful to avoid oven light bulb. Transfer loaves to wire racks to cool. *Makes 2 loaves, 12 slices each.*

EACH SLICE: ABOUT 115 CALORIES, 3 G PROTEIN,
21 G CARBOHYDRATE, 2 G TOTAL FAT (0 G SATURATED),
1 G FIBER, 0 MG CHOLESTEROL, 290 MG SODIUM.

Buttermilk Bread

PREP 20 MINUTES PLUS RISING / BAKE 25 TO 30 MINUTES

A half-cup of butter makes this a rich bread; the buttermilk adds a slight tang. Use storebought buttermilk (rather than plain milk soured with vinegar).

¼ CUP WARM WATER (105° TO 115° F)
1 PACKAGE ACTIVE DRY YEAST
1 TEASPOON PLUS ¼ CUP SUGAR
1½ CUPS BUTTERMILK
½ CUP BUTTER OR MARGARINE (1 STICK)
2 TEASPOONS SALT
ABOUT 4¾ CUPS ALL-PURPOSE FLOUR OR BREAD FLOUR

1 In cup, combine warm water, yeast, and 1 teaspoon sugar; stir to dissolve. Let stand 5 minutes, or until foamy.

2 Meanwhile, in 1-quart saucepan, heat buttermilk, remaining ¼ cup sugar, and 6 tablespoons butter over medium-low heat until warm (105° to 115° F) (Butter does not need to melt completely.)

3 In large bowl, combine salt and 4½ cups flour. Gradually add yeast mixture and buttermilk mixture and, with wooden spoon, beat until blended.

4 Turn dough onto lightly floured surface and knead about 10 minutes, until smooth and elastic, working in about ¼ cup more flour as necessary just to keep dough from sticking. Shape dough into ball and place in greased large bowl, turning dough over to grease top. Cover bowl and let dough rise in warm place (80° to 85° F) until doubled, about 1 hour.

5 Punch down dough. Turn dough onto lightly floured surface and cut in half; cover and let rest 15 minutes. Grease two 8½" by 4½" metal loaf pans.

6 Shape each half into a loaf; place, seam side down, in prepared loaf pans. Cover and let rise in warm place until doubled, about 1 hour.

7 Preheat oven to 375° F. Melt remaining 2 table-spoons butter. Just before baking, with serrated knife or single-edge razor blade, slash top of each loaf lengthwise, cutting about ¼ inch deep. Brush slashes with melted butter. Bake 25 to 30 minutes, until loaves are golden and bottoms sound hollow when lightly tapped with fingers. Transfer loaves to wire racks to cool. *Makes 2 loaves, 12 slices each.*

EACH SLICE: ABOUT 145 CALORIES, 3 G PROTEIN, 22 G CARBOHYDRATE, 5 G TOTAL FAT (3 G SATURATED), 1 G FIBER, 11 MG CHOLESTEROL, 250 MG SODIUM.

Olive-Rosemary Loaves

PREP 30 MINUTES PLUS RISING / BAKE 30 MINUTES

Kalamata olives—deep purple, brine-cured Greek olives—and woodsy fresh rosemary flavor these robust peasant loaves. Kalamata olives are sold at Middle-Eastern grocery stores and gourmet shops, and can also be found in cans in many supermarkets.

1½ CUPS WARM WATER (105° TO 115° F)
4 TABLESPOONS EXTRAVIRGIN OLIVE OIL
2 PACKAGES ACTIVE DRY YEAST
1 TABLESPOON SUGAR
1 CUP KALAMATA OR GREEN OLIVES, PITTED AND CHOPPED
2 TABLESPOONS FINELY CHOPPED FRESH ROSEMARY
2 TEASPOONS SALT
ABOUT 4½ CUPS BREAD FLOUR OR 5 CUPS ALL-PURPOSE FLOUR

1 In small bowl, combine ½ cup warm water, 3 tablespoons oil, yeast, and sugar; stir to dissolve. Let stand 5 minutes, or until foamy.

2 Meanwhile, in large bowl, with wooden spoon, mix olives, rosemary, salt, and 4 cups flour. Add yeast mixture and remaining 1 cup warm water; stir until combined.

3 Turn dough onto lightly floured surface and knead about 8 minutes, until smooth and elastic, working in ½ to 1 cup more flour as necessary just to keep dough from sticking.

4 Shape dough into ball and place in greased large bowl, turning dough over to grease top. Cover bowl and let dough rise in warm place (80° to 85° F) until doubled, about 1 hour.

5 Punch down dough. Turn dough onto lightly floured surface and cut in half; cover and let rest 15 minutes for easier shaping. Grease large cookie sheet.

6 Shape each half into 7½" by 4" oval and place at least 4 inches apart on prepared cookie sheet. Cover and let rise in warm place until doubled, about 1 hour.

7 Preheat oven to 400° F. Brush tops of loaves with remaining 1 tablespoon oil. With serrated knife or single-edge razor, cut 3 diagonal slashes across top of each loaf. Bake 30 minutes, or until golden. Transfer loaves to wire racks. to cool. *Makes 2 loaves, 12 slices each.*

EACH SLICE: ABOUT 150 CALORIES, 4 G PROTEIN, 23 G CARBOHYDRATE, 5 G TOTAL FAT (1 G SATURATED), 1 G FIBER, 0 MG CHOLESTEROL, 295 MG SODIUM.

FREEZING BREAD

IF TWO LOAVES OF BREAD ARE ONE TOO MANY FOR YOUR FAMILY TO FINISH UP WITHIN A COUPLE DAYS, YOU'LL WANT TO FREEZE THE EXTRA LOAF FOR FUTURE USE. IF PROPERLY WRAPPED—PROTECTED FROM THE DEHYDRATING EFFECT OF A FROST-FREE FREEZER—THE BREAD WILL TASTE JUST-BAKED WHEN IT EMERGES FROM THE FREEZER. COOL THE LOAF COMPLETELY, THEN WRAP IT WELL IN ALUMINUM FOIL. SLIP THE FOIL-WRAPPED LOAF INTO A FREEZER-SAFE BAG, SQUEEZE OUT AS MUCH AIR AS POSSIBLE, AND SEAL THE BAG. LABEL THE PACKAGE AND DATE IT. WHEN YOU WANT TO SERVE THE LOAF, LET IT THAW AT ROOM TEMPERATURE IN ITS WRAPPINGS (SO NO MOISTURE IS LOST). BEFORE SERVING, HEAT THE BREAD IN A PREHEATED 350° F OVEN FOR 15 MINUTES.

Baguettes

PREP 20 MINUTES PLUS RISING
BAKE 30 TO 35 MINUTES

This is the bread Parisians carry home every day from the local boulangerie. It tastes best the day it's baked, and becomes stale rather quickly—so freeze one loaf.

2 CUPS WARM WATER (105° TO 115° F)

1 PACKAGE ACTIVE DRY YEAST

1 TABLESPOON SUGAR

1 TABLESPOON PLUS ¼ TEASPOON SALT

ABOUT 5 CUPS ALL-PURPOSE FLOUR OR 4½ CUPS BREAD
    FLOUR

1 LARGE EGG WHITE

1 In large bowl, combine warm water, yeast, and sugar; stir to dissolve. Let stand 5 minutes, or until foamy. Add 1 tablespoon salt and 3 cups flour. Beat well with wooden spoon until smooth. Gradually stir in 1½ cups flour to make soft dough.

2 Turn dough onto lightly floured surface and knead 6 to 8 minutes, until smooth and elastic, working in remaining flour as necessary just to keep dough from sticking. Shape dough into ball and place in greased large bowl, turning dough over to grease top. Cover bowl with greased plastic wrap and let dough rise in warm place (80° to 85° F) until doubled, about 1 hour 30 minutes.

3 Grease 2 large cookie sheets. Punch down dough. Turn dough onto lightly floured surface and cut in half. Roll each half into 18" by 7" rectangle. From one long side, roll up tightly, rolling dough with hands to taper ends. Place 1 loaf diagonally on each cookie sheet. Cover loosely with greased plastic wrap and let rise in warm place until almost doubled, about 1 hour.

4 Preheat oven to 400° F. With serrated knife or single-edge razor blade, cut 5 diagonal slashes in each loaf. In small cup, with fork, beat egg white and remaining ¼ teaspoon salt. Brush loaves with egg white. Bake 30 to 35 minutes, rotating sheets between upper and lower racks halfway through baking, until well browned. Transfer loaves to wire racks to cool. *Makes 2 loaves, 8 slices each.*

EACH SLICE: ABOUT 160 CALORIES, 5 G PROTEIN,
32 G CARBOHYDRATE, 1 G TOTAL FAT (0 G SATURATED),
1 G FIBER, 0 MG CHOLESTEROL, 475 MG SODIUM.

WHOLE-WHEAT BAGUETTES Prepare dough as for Baguettes but, in Step 1, use *2 cups whole-wheat flour* and *1 cup all-purpose flour* for 3 cups all-purpose flour. Gradually stir in *1½ cups all-purpose flour* to make soft, sticky dough. Let rise, shape, brush with egg white, and bake as directed.
EACH SLICE: ABOUT 150 CALORIES, 5 G PROTEIN,
30 G CARBOHYDRATE, 1 G TOTAL FAT (0 G SATURATED),
3 G FIBER, 0 MG CHOLESTEROL, 480 MG SODIUM.

EPI Epi is the French name for a loaf shaped as a wheat stalk. Prepare as for Baguettes but, in Step 3, let loaves rise only 30 minutes. Using scissors 3 inches long, beginning at end farthest from you, cut almost all the way through dough. Pull flap to one side, stretching the tip of "wheat" from the "stalk."

Shaping Epi Loaves

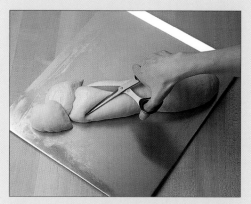

Holding scissors at 30° angle, make cut almost all the way through dough. Pull flap of dough to one side, stretching out tip.

Continue making cuts in the dough, at 1½-inch intervals, down length of the loaf, alternately pulling the dough left and right.

Make another cut (see top photo opposite) and pull dough to opposite side (see bottom photo opposite). Repeat cutting, leaving 1½-inch intervals, alternately pulling each flap of dough left and right, to end of loaf. Let loaf rise 30 minutes. Brush with egg white and bake as directed.

EACH SLICE: ABOUT 160 CALORIES, 5 G PROTEIN, 32 G CARBOHYDRATE, 1 G TOTAL FAT (0.5 G SATURATED), 1 G FIBER, 0 MG CHOLESTEROL, 475 MG SODIUM.

HARD ROLLS Prepare dough as for Baguettes. Divide into 24 pieces and shape each into smooth round or oblong ball; place, 2½ inches apart, on greased large cookie sheets. Let rise and brush with egg white as directed. Bake 25 minutes. *Makes 24 rolls.*

EACH ROLL: ABOUT 105 CALORIES, 3 G PROTEIN, 21 G CARBOHYDRATE, 1 G TOTAL FAT (0 G SATURATED), 1 G FIBER, 0 MG CHOLESTEROL, 320 MG SODIUM.

Potato Bread

PREP 35 MINUTES PLUS RISING
BAKE 25 TO 30 MINUTES

Day-old slices of potato bread make superb toast or French toast. If you like, you can let the dough slow-rise in the refrigerator overnight (see Step 5).

3 MEDIUM ALL-PURPOSE POTATOES (ABOUT 1 POUND), PEELED AND CUT INTO 1-INCH CHUNKS

1 CUP WARM WATER (105° TO 115° F)

2 PACKAGES ACTIVE DRY YEAST

2 TABLESPOONS SUGAR

4¼ TEASPOONS SALT

4 TABLESPOONS BUTTER OR MARGARINE, SOFTENED

ABOUT 9¾ CUPS ALL-PURPOSE FLOUR OR 8¾ CUPS BREAD FLOUR

2 LARGE EGGS

1 In 2-quart saucepan, heat potatoes and *4 cups water* to boiling over high heat. Reduce heat; cover and simmer 15 minutes, or until potatoes are fork-tender. Drain potatoes, reserving 1 cup potato cooking water. Return potatoes to saucepan. With potato masher, mash potatoes until smooth.

2 In large bowl, combine warm water, yeast, and 1 tablespoon sugar; stir to dissolve. Let stand 5 minutes, or until foamy. Stir in remaining 1 tablespoon sugar, 4 teaspoons salt, butter, reserved potato cooking water, and 3 cups flour.

3 With mixer at low speed, beat just until blended. Increase speed to medium; beat 2 minutes, scraping bowl occasionally with rubber spatula. Separate 1 egg and reserve white, covered, in refrigerator. Gradually beat in 1 egg, 1 egg yolk, and 1 cup flour to make a thick batter; continue beating 2 minutes, scraping bowl often. With wooden spoon, stir in mashed potatoes, then 5 cups all-purpose flour or 4 cups bread flour, 1 cup at a time, to make a soft dough. (You may want to transfer mixture to a larger bowl for easier mixing.)

4 Turn dough onto well-floured surface and knead about 10 minutes, until smooth and elastic, working in remaining ¾ cup flour (or less if using bread flour) as necessary just to keep dough from sticking. Shape dough into ball; place in greased large bowl, turning dough over to grease top. Cover bowl and let rise in warm place (80° to 85° F) until doubled, about 1 hour.

5 Grease two 9" by 5" metal loaf pans. Punch down dough. Turn dough onto lightly floured surface and cut in half. Shape each half into loaf; place, seam side down, in prepared pans. Cover pans and let rise in warm place until doubled, about 40 minutes. Or, cover pans with greased plastic wrap and refrigerate overnight.

6 Preheat oven to 400° F. (If loaves are refrigerated, remove plastic wrap; let stand 10 minutes before baking.) With fork, beat reserved egg white with remaining ¼ teaspoon salt. Brush tops of loaves with egg white. Bake 25 to 30 minutes, until golden and bottoms sound hollow when lightly tapped with fingers. Transfer loaves to wire racks. Serve warm or cool completely. *Makes 2 loaves, 12 slices each.*

EACH SLICE: ABOUT 235 CALORIES, 6 G PROTEIN, 44 G CARBOHYDRATE, 3 G TOTAL FAT (2 G SATURATED), 2 G FIBER, 23 MG CHOLESTEROL, 440 MG SODIUM.

REFRIGERATOR POTATO ROLLS Prepare dough as above. Grease 17" by 11½" roasting pan. In Step 5, cut dough into 24 equal pieces. Shape each into a ball and place, slightly touching each other, in prepared roasting pan. Cover pan with greased plastic wrap and let rise until doubled. Or refrigerate overnight. Bake as directed in Step 6. Invert baked rolls onto wire rack; cool 15 minutes before separating to serve warm, or cool completely. *Makes 24 rolls.*

EACH ROLL: ABOUT 235 CALORIES, 6 G PROTEIN, 44 G CARBOHYDRATE, 3 G TOTAL FAT (2 G SATURATED), 2 G FIBER, 23 MG CHOLESTEROL, 440 MG SODIUM.

Sourdough Starter

PREP 10 MINUTES PLUS 3 TO 4 DAYS

Old-fashioned sourdough starters (it's an ancient concept) were created by leaving a flour-and-water mixture in an open crock, allowing wild yeasts to find their way in on a passing breeze. Colonized by yeast, the mixture would bubble, thicken, and soon become the basis of a distinctively chewy, tangy bread. This starter, made with packaged yeast, is more predictable, but still gives rise to great bread. It's preferable to use bottled spring water for the starter, but tap water can be used: Let it stand at room temperature overnight to allow the chlorine to evaporate before using.

2 CUPS WARM WATER (105° TO 115° F)
1 PACKAGE ACTIVE DRY YEAST
1 TABLESPOON HONEY
2 CUPS UNBLEACHED ALL-PURPOSE FLOUR OR BREAD
    FLOUR

1 In large glass or ceramic bowl, combine warm water, yeast, and honey; stir to dissolve. Let stand 5 minutes, or until foamy. Gradually stir in flour. Cover bowl with clean kitchen towel and let stand in warm place (80° to 85° F) 3 to 4 days, until starter stops bubbling and has a pleasant yeasty, sour aroma. A clear amber liquid will separate from mixture; stir this back into starter once a day. Pour starter into a clean jar with a lid. Place lid loosely on jar and refrigerate starter until ready to use.

2 To maintain starter, it should be fed once every 2 weeks. Remove jar from refrigerator and pour starter into large glass or ceramic bowl. Whisk in liquid that has separated. Measure out amount of starter needed for recipe. Replace amount used with equal amounts of flour and water. For example, if recipe uses 1 cup starter, stir in 1 cup unbleached flour and 1 cup water. Let starter sit at room temperature 8 to 12 hours to become active again. Use immediately or refrigerate to use within 2 weeks before feeding again.

3 If not baking with starter every 2 weeks, 1 cup should be discarded or given away before feeding, otherwise volume will become too large. If at any point starter seems sluggish and breads are not rising well, then stir 1 teaspoon active dry yeast dissolved in 1/4 cup warm water (105° to 115° F) into starter and let sit at room temperature overnight. *Makes about 2 2/3 cups starter.*

Sourdough Bread

PREP 30 MINUTES PLUS 3 TO 4 DAYS TO MAKE STARTER,
8 TO 24 HOURS FOR SPONGE, PLUS RISING
BAKE 25 TO 30 MINUTES PER LOAF

This is where the starter gets to do its stuff, raising two hearty round loaves. The dough is quite soft, but don't add a lot of flour in an attempt to firm it up. The shaped balls of dough may even spread a bit on the baking sheets during the second rising, but they will spring back up when baked. Crisscross slashes in the top of each loaf add extra crunchy texture to the delightfully crisp crust.

1 CUP SOURDOUGH STARTER (AT LEFT)
1¾ CUPS WARM WATER (105° TO 115° F)
5½ TO 6 CUPS UNBLEACHED ALL-PURPOSE FLOUR OR
    BREAD FLOUR
1 TEASPOON ACTIVE DRY YEAST
1 TABLESPOON SUGAR
1 TABLESPOON PLUS ¼ TEASPOON SALT
CORNMEAL FOR SPRINKLING
1 LARGE EGG WHITE

1 Measure starter into large glass or ceramic bowl. Add 1½ cups warm water and 3 cups flour; stir vigorously with wooden spoon. Cover bowl with plastic wrap and let stand in draft-free place 8 to 24 hours. The longer the sponge sits, the more tangy the flavor of the bread will be.

2 In small bowl, combine remaining 1/4 cup warm water, yeast, and sugar; stir to dissolve. Let stand 5 minutes, or until foamy. Stir 2 cups flour, yeast mixture, and 1 tablespoon salt into sponge to make a soft dough. Turn dough onto floured surface and knead 8 minutes, until smooth and elastic, working in enough remaining flour, 1/2 to 3/4 cup, to make a firm dough. Shape dough into ball and place in greased large bowl, turning dough over to grease top. Cover bowl and let dough rise in warm place (80° to 85° F) until doubled, about 2 hours.

3 Grease 2 large cookie sheets and sprinkle with cornmeal. Punch down dough. Turn dough onto lightly floured surface and cut in half. Shape each half into smooth round ball. Place 1 loaf on each prepared cookie sheet. Cover with greased plastic wrap and let rise until doubled, about 1 hour 30 minutes.

4 Preheat oven to 425° F. In small bowl, beat egg white with remaining 1/4 teaspoon salt. Brush 1 loaf with the egg white. With serrated knife or single-edge razor blade, cut six 1/4-inch-deep slashes in top of loaf to make a criss-cross pattern. Place 12 ice cubes in 13" by 9" metal baking pan. Place pan in bottom of oven. Bake loaf with slashes 25 to 30 minutes, until well browned and bottom sounds hollow when lightly tapped with fingers. Transfer loaf to wire rack to cool completely. Glaze, slash, and bake remaining loaf; cool completely. *Makes 2 loaves, 8 slices each.*

EACH SLICE: ABOUT 205 CALORIES, 6 G PROTEIN,
41 G CARBOHYDRATE, 1 G TOTAL FAT (0 G SATURATED),
2 G FIBER, 0 MG CHOLESTEROL, 475 MG SODIUM.

SOURDOUGH ROLLS Prepare dough as for Sourdough Bread through Step 2. After first rising, cut dough into 24 equal pieces. Shape each piece into a smooth round ball and place, 2 inches apart, on greased cookie sheets. Cover with greased plastic wrap and let rise until doubled, about 1 hour. Brush with egg-white glaze. Bake 20 to 25 minutes, until well browned. Cool on wire rack. *Makes 24 rolls.*
EACH ROLL: ABOUT 135 CALORIES, 4 G PROTEIN,
28 G CARBOHYDRATE, 1 G TOTAL FAT (0 G SATURATED),
1 G FIBER, 0 MG CHOLESTEROL, 320 MG SODIUM.

SOURDOUGH RYE BREAD Prepare dough as for Sourdough Bread but use 3 to 3½ cups all-purpose flour. In Step 2, add *3 cups rye flour* and *1 tablespoon caraway seeds* when stirring flour into sponge. Shape, glaze, slash, and bake loaves as directed. *Makes 2 loaves, 8 slices each.*
EACH SLICE: ABOUT 200 CALORIES, 6 G PROTEIN,
41 G CARBOHYDRATE, 2 G TOTAL FAT (0 G SATURATED),
4 G FIBER, 0 MG CHOLESTEROL, 480 MG SODIUM.

SAN FRANCISCO SOURDOUGH

SAN FRANCISCO HAS HAD A LONG LOVE AFFAIR WITH SOURDOUGH BREAD, AND SOURDOUGH FROM THAT CITY'S FEW REMAINING SMALL BAKERIES HAS A FLAVOR ALL ITS OWN. THE RECIPE IS NOT REALLY UNUSUAL, BUT THE COMBINATION OF THE LOCAL CLIMATE AND WATER—AND THE LOCAL AIRBORNE YEASTS THAT LEAVEN THE BREAD—DISTINGUISH IT FROM ALL OTHERS. FEEL FREE TO NAME YOUR STARTER-BASED BREAD AFTER YOUR HOME TOWN!

Anadama Bread

PREP 25 MINUTES PLUS RISING / BAKE 30 TO 35 MINUTES

Maybe a Gloucester fisherman did once exclaim, "Anna, damn her!" and thus give this bread its name. Maybe not. It's a time-honored but questionable story about an unquestionably delicious molasses-sweetened bread.

½ CUP YELLOW CORNMEAL
1½ CUPS COLD WATER
½ CUP WARM WATER (105° TO 115° F.)
2 PACKAGES ACTIVE DRY YEAST
2 TEASPOONS SUGAR
½ CUP LIGHT (MILD) MOLASSES
6 TABLESPOONS BUTTER OR MARGARINE, SOFTENED
1 LARGE EGG
2 TEASPOONS SALT
5½ CUPS ALL-PURPOSE FLOUR

1 In medium bowl, stir together cornmeal and 1 cup cold water until well combined. In 2-quart saucepan, heat remaining ½ cup water to boiling over medium heat. Stir in cornmeal mixture and cook 3 to 5 minutes, stirring constantly, until thickened. Cool to room temperature.

2 In large bowl, combine warm water, yeast, and sugar; stir to dissolve. Let stand 5 minutes, or until foamy. Stir in cornmeal mixture, molasses, butter, egg, salt, and 3 cups flour until well combined. Gradually stir in 2 cups flour. Turn dough onto floured surface and knead 5 to 8 minutes, until smooth and elastic, adding remaining ½ cup flour if necessary. Place in greased large bowl, turning dough over to grease top. Cover bowl and let rise in warm place until doubled, 1 hour 30 minutes.

3 Punch down dough; let rest 10 minutes. Grease two 9" by 5" metal loaf pans. Divide dough in half; shape each half into a loaf. Place in prepared pans. Cover with lightly greased plastic wrap and let rise until almost doubled, 45 to 60 minutes.

4 Preheat oven to 375° F. Bake 30 to 35 minutes, or until loaves are golden and sound hollow when bottoms are lightly tapped with fingers. Transfer to wire racks to cool. *Makes 2 loaves, 12 slices each.*

EACH SLICE: ABOUT 170 CALORIES, 4 G PROTEIN,
30 G CARBOHYDRATE, 4 G TOTAL FAT (2 G SATURATED),
1 G FIBER 17 MG CHOLESTEROL, 230 MG SODIUM.

Fig-Walnut Bread

PREP 25 MINUTES PLUS RISING
BAKE 30 TO 35 MINUTES

Breads like this are loved in Europe. A popular Portuguese version is studded with almonds and raisins.

1½ CUPS WARM WATER (105° TO 115° F)
1 PACKAGE ACTIVE YEAST
1 TEASPOON SUGAR
ABOUT 4¼ CUPS ALL-PURPOSE FLOUR
2 TABLESPOONS OLIVE OIL
1 TABLESPOON HONEY
2 TEASPOONS SALT
2 CUPS DRIED FIGS, FINELY CHOPPED
1 CUP WALNUTS, TOASTED AND COARSELY CHOPPED

1 In large bowl, combine 1 cup warm water, yeast, and sugar; stir to dissolve. Let stand 5 minutes, or until foamy. Stir in 1 cup flour. Cover bowl and let stand at room temperature 45 minutes, or until mixture is thick and bubbly.

2 Stir in 3 cups flour, 1 tablespoon olive oil, honey, salt, and remaining ½ cup warm water until well combined. Turn dough onto lightly floured surface and knead 5 to 8 minutes, adding additional ¼ cup flour as needed, until smooth and elastic. Flatten dough; press figs and walnuts into dough. Fold dough over onto fruit and nuts and knead until well combined. Place in greased large bowl, turning dough over to grease top.

3 Cover bowl and let rise in warm place (80° to 85° F) until doubled, about 2 hours. Punch down dough; cover and let rest 10 minutes. Grease large cookie sheet. Divide dough in half. Shape each half into 6-inch round loaf. Place loaves at opposite corners on prepared cookie sheet. Cover and let rise until doubled, about 45 minutes.

4 Preheat oven to 425° F. With serrated knife or single-edge razor blade, make several slashes in top of each loaf. Brush loaves with remaining 1 tablespoon oil. Bake loaves 30 to 35 minutes, or until bottoms sound hollow when lightly tapped with fingers. Cool 10 minutes on cookie sheet. Transfer to wire racks to cool completely. *Makes 2 loaves, 12 slices each.*

EACH SLICE: ABOUT 170 CALORIES, 4 G PROTEIN,
30 G CARBOHYDRATE, 5 G TOTAL FAT (1 G SATURATED),
2 G FIBER, 0 MG CHOLESTEROL, 195 MG SODIUM.

Roasted Garlic & Cheese Bread

PREP 1 HOUR 10 MINUTES PLUS RISING
BAKE 35 TO 40 MINUTES

After you've roasted the garlic cloves, taste one—and discover how roasting has mellowed it.

1 WHOLE HEAD GARLIC
¾ CUP WARM WATER (105° TO 115° F)
1 PACKAGE ACTIVE DRY YEAST
1 TEASPOON SUGAR
ABOUT 3½ CUPS ALL-PURPOSE FLOUR
½ CUP WHOLE-WHEAT FLOUR
¼ CUP OLIVE OIL
1 TEASPOON SALT
8 OUNCES GRUYÈRE CHEESE, SHREDDED (2 CUPS)

1 Preheat oven to 400° F. Wrap garlic in foil, place on cookie sheet, and roast 35 to 40 minutes, until packet can be easily squeezed. When cool, separate cloves; squeeze pulp from each clove into small bowl.

2 In large bowl, combine ¼ cup warm water, yeast, and sugar; stir to dissolve. Let stand 5 minutes, or until foamy. Stir in 2½ cups all-purpose flour, whole-wheat flour, oil, salt, garlic pulp, and remaining ½ cup warm water until well combined. Stir in remaining ½ cup flour if dough is sticky. Turn dough onto floured surface and knead 5 to 8 minutes, until smooth and elastic. Knead in cheese (dough will be slightly sticky). Shape dough into ball; place in greased large bowl, turning dough over to grease top. Cover bowl and let rise in warm place (80° to 85° F) until doubled, about 1 hour 30 minutes.

3 Punch down dough. Cover bowl and let rest 10 minutes. Cut dough into 4 pieces. Shape each piece into 12-inch loaf, tapering ends slightly. Place 2 loaves, 3 inches apart, on 2 ungreased large cookie sheets. Cover, and let rise in warm place until doubled, about 45 minutes. With serrated knife or single-edge razor blade, make several slashes on top of each loaf.

4 Preheat oven to 375° F. Bake loaves 35 to 40 minutes, rotating sheets between upper and lower racks halfway through baking, until bottoms sound hollow when lightly tapped with fingers. Transfer to wire racks to cool. *Makes 4 loaves, 6 slices each.*

EACH SLICE: ABOUT 140 CALORIES, 5 G PROTEIN,
17 G CARBOHYDRATE, 6 G TOTAL FAT (2 G SATURATED),
1 G FIBER, 10 MG CHOLESTEROL, 130 MG SODIUM.

Fig-Walnut Bread

Semolina Bread

PREP 20 MINUTES PLUS RISING / BAKE 30 MINUTES

Semolina flour is widely used in Italy to make pasta.
This semolina bread is a staple in Sicily.

1¾ CUPS WARM WATER (105° TO 115° F)
1 PACKAGE ACTIVE DRY YEAST
1 TABLESPOON SUGAR
3¾ TO 4 CUPS FINE SEMOLINA FLOUR
2¼ TEASPOONS SALT
2 TABLESPOONS SESAME SEEDS

1 In large bowl, combine ¼ cup warm water, yeast, and 1 teaspoon sugar; stir to dissolve. Let stand 5 minutes, or until foamy.

2 Stir in remaining 1½ cups warm water, 3 cups semolina flour, salt, and remaining 2 teaspoons sugar. Stir in remaining ¾ cup semolina flour. Turn dough onto floured surface and knead until smooth and elastic, working in remaining ¼ cup flour if dough is very sticky. Shape dough into ball and place in greased large bowl, turning dough over to grease top. Cover and let rise in warm place (80° to 85° F) until doubled, about 1 hour.

3 Punch down dough. Turn dough onto lightly floured surface and cut in half. Cover and let rest 10 minutes. Shape dough into 2 rounds, 2 long loaves, or one of each. Transfer to 2 large ungreased cookie sheets. Brush tops of loaves with water and sprinkle 1 tablespoon sesame seeds over each. Cover and let rise in warm place until doubled, about 45 minutes.

4 Preheat oven to 400° F. Place cookie sheets in oven and use spray bottle to spritz loaves with water (avoid spraying oven light bulb). Spray 2 more times during first 5 minutes of baking. Bake loaves 30 minutes, rotating sheets between upper and lower racks halfway through baking, or until bottoms sound hollow when lightly tapped with fingers. Transfer loaves to wire racks to cool. *Makes 2 loaves, 12 slices each.*

EACH SLICE: ABOUT 105 CALORIES, 4 G PROTEIN, 21 G CARBOHYDRATE, 1 G TOTAL FAT (0 G SATURATED), 1 G FIBER, 0 MG CHOLESTEROL, 220 MG SODIUM.

FENNEL-GOLDEN RAISIN SEMOLINA BREAD Prepare dough as for Semolina Bread through Step 2, then knead in *⅔ cup golden raisins* and *4 teaspoons fennel seeds*. Shape, let rise, and bake as directed.
EACH SLICE: ABOUT 120 CALORIES, 4 G PROTEIN, 24 G CARBOHYDRATE, 1 G TOTAL FAT (0 G SATURATED), 2 G FIBER, 0 MG CHOLESTEROL, 220 MG SODIUM.

Fennel-Golden Raisin Semolina Bread

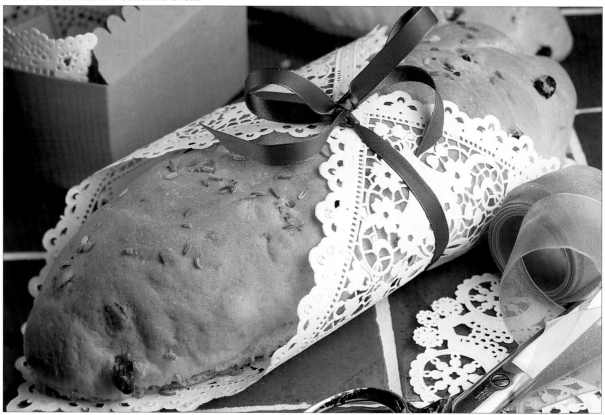

WHOLE-GRAIN BREADS

Whole grains have a lot to offer the bread baker. Of course, there's the full, nutlike flavor and hearty texture that make a sandwich—or a simple buttered slice—so satisfying. And there's the substantial health benefit of the fiber in whole grains: White flour is enriched with many nutrients after it's refined, but fiber is not added to it. Because whole-wheat flour tends to make heavy breads, many recipes call for a combination of whole-wheat and all-purpose flours. This is true of breads made with rye flour, too: Rye is low in gluten, so wheat flour helps make the dough less sticky and more resilient and manageable.

Multi-Grain Bread

PREP 25 MINUTES PLUS RISING / BAKE 35 MINUTES

A health-food store is a likely place to find whole-grain rye flour (supermarket rye flour is refined). And it's also the place to buy flax seed, a nutty-tasting seed that's rich in omega-3 oils (heart-healthy polyunsaturates). You can substitute hulled sunflower seeds if you like. Because of the oats and rye flour, this dough is slightly sticky; resist the temptation to stir or knead in additional flour.

1 CUP OLD-FASHIONED OATS, UNCOOKED
2 CUPS WARM WATER (105° TO 115° F)
2 PACKAGES ACTIVE DRY YEAST
1 TABLESPOON SUGAR
4 TABLESPOONS BUTTER OR MARGARINE, SOFTENED
¼ CUP LIGHT (MILD) MOLASSES
1 CUP WHOLE-WHEAT FLOUR
1 CUP RYE FLOUR
⅓ CUP FLAX SEEDS OR SUNFLOWER SEEDS
2½ TEASPOONS SALT
ABOUT 3½ CUPS ALL-PURPOSE FLOUR OR 3 CUPS
   BREAD FLOUR

1 Preheat oven to 350° F. On jelly-roll pan, toast oats 10 minutes, or until lightly browned. Cool to room temperature.

2 In large bowl, combine ½ cup warm water, yeast, and sugar; stir to dissolve. Let stand 5 minutes, or until foamy.

3 Stir in butter, molasses, whole-wheat and rye flours, flax seeds, salt, remaining 1½ cups warm water, and oats until smooth. Gradually stir in 3 cups all-purpose flour or 2½ cups bread flour. Knead in bowl until dough holds together.

4 Turn dough onto lightly floured surface and knead 7 to 10 minutes, until smooth and elastic, working in remaining ½ cup flour as necessary (dough will be slightly sticky). Shape dough into ball and place in greased large bowl, turning dough over to grease top. Cover bowl and let rise in warm place (80° to 85° F) until doubled, about 1 hour.

5 Punch down dough. Turn dough onto floured surface and cut in half. Flatten each half into 10" by 8" rectangle. Fold over lengthwise, pressing edges to seal, and shape each into 10" by 4" rectangle. Place, seam side down, on 2 ungreased large cookie sheets. Cover loosely and let rise in warm place until doubled, about 30 minutes. With serrated knife or single-edge razor blade, cut six 3-inch-long diagonal slashes across top of each loaf.

6 Preheat oven to 350° F. Sprinkle loaves lightly with all-purpose flour. Bake 35 minutes, or until loaves sound hollow when bottoms are lightly tapped with fingers. Transfer loaves to wire racks to cool. *Makes 2 loaves, 12 slices each.*

EACH SLICE: ABOUT 155 CALORIES, 4 G PROTEIN, 27 G CARBOHYDRATE, 3 G TOTAL FAT (1 G SATURATED), 2 G FIBER, 5 MG CHOLESTEROL, 265 MG SODIUM.

MULTI-GRAIN ROLLS Prepare dough as for Multi-Grain Bread but, in Step 5, cut dough into 24 equal pieces; roll each into a ball. Place, 3 inches apart, on 2 ungreased large cookie sheets. Cover and let rise until doubled, about 30 minutes. Bake 25 minutes, rotating sheets between upper and lower racks halfway through baking. *Makes 2 dozen rolls.*
EACH ROLL: ABOUT 155 CALORIES, 4 G PROTEIN, 27 G CARBOHYDRATE, 3 G TOTAL FAT (1 G SATURATED), 2 G FIBER, 5 MG CHOLESTEROL, 265 MG SODIUM.

Whole-Wheat Oatmeal Bread

PREP 45 MINUTES PLUS RISING / BAKE 35 TO 40 MINUTES

We don't want to give the impression that this bread is just healthful (it's both healthful and delicious), but the combination of whole wheat and oats yields a loaf that's rich in both soluble and insoluble fiber. Spread thick slices of the bread with honey or berry jam.

2 CUPS WARM WATER (105° TO 115° F)

2 PACKAGES ACTIVE DRY YEAST

½ TEASPOON SUGAR

4 CUPS WHOLE-WHEAT FLOUR

1 CUP QUICK-COOKING OR OLD-FASHIONED OATS, UNCOOKED

1 TABLESPOON SALT

½ CUP HONEY

4 TABLESPOONS BUTTER OR MARGARINE, SOFTENED AND CUT UP

1 LARGE EGG

ABOUT 2½ CUPS ALL-PURPOSE FLOUR OR 2 CUPS BREAD FLOUR

1 In large bowl, combine ½ cup warm water, yeast, and sugar; stir to dissolve. Let stand 5 minutes, or until foamy.

2 Stir in 2 cups whole-wheat flour, remaining 1½ cups warm water, oats, salt, honey, and butter until smooth. Stir in egg. Gradually stir in remaining 2 cups whole-wheat flour, then 2 cups all-purpose flour or 1½ cups bread flour.

3 Turn dough onto lightly floured surface and knead 7 minutes, until smooth but slightly sticky, working in remaining ½ cup all-purpose or bread flour as necessary just to keep dough from sticking. Shape dough into ball and place in greased large bowl, turning dough over to grease top. Cover bowl and let rise in warm place (80° to 85° F) until doubled, about 1 hour.

4 Punch down dough. Turn dough onto lightly floured surface and cut in half; cover and let rest 15 minutes. Grease large cookie sheet.

5 Shape each half into 7" by 4" oval, tapering ends slightly; place on prepared cookie sheet. Cover and let rise in warm place until doubled, about 1 hour.

6 Preheat oven to 350° F. With serrated knife or single-edge razor blade, cut 3 to 5 criss-cross slashes across top of each loaf; lightly dust tops of loaves

with all-purpose flour. Bake loaves 35 to 40 minutes, until bottoms sound hollow when lightly tapped with fingers. Transfer loaves to wire racks to cool. *Makes 2 oval loaves, about 12 slices each.*

EACH SLICE: ABOUT 175 CALORIES, 5 G PROTEIN, 34 G CARBOHYDRATE, 3 G TOTAL FAT (1 G SATURATED), 3 G FIBER, 14 MG CHOLESTEROL, 315 MG SODIUM.

Walnut-Oatmeal Bread

PREP 25 MINUTES PLUS RISING / BAKE 35 TO 40 MINUTES

This rustic loaf is made with brown sugar for a touch of sweetness. To be sure that the walnuts are sweet, too, buy them from a store with a rapid turnover; because nuts are high in fat, they can turn rancid and bitter if left at room temperature. Store walnuts (and all nuts) in a tightly closed container in the freezer.

1 CUP OLD-FASHIONED OR QUICK-COOKING OATS, UNCOOKED

1 PACKAGE QUICK-RISE YEAST

⅓ CUP PACKED LIGHT BROWN SUGAR

1½ TEASPOONS SALT

ABOUT 4½ CUPS ALL-PURPOSE FLOUR OR 4 CUPS BREAD FLOUR

1¼ CUPS VERY WARM WATER (120° TO 130° F)

2 TABLESPOONS BUTTER OR MARGARINE, SOFTENED

1 LARGE EGG

1 CUP WALNUTS (ABOUT 4 OUNCES), COARSELY CHOPPED

1 TABLESPOON MILK

1 Reserve 1 tablespoon oats for top of loaf. In large bowl, combine remaining oats, yeast, brown sugar, salt, and 1½ cups flour. With spoon or with mixer at low speed, gradually stir warm water and butter into flour mixture.

2 Beat in egg and 1 cup flour to make thick batter. Increase speed to medium and beat 2 minutes longer, scraping bowl often with rubber spatula. With spoon, stir in walnuts and 1½ cups all-purpose flour or 1¼ cups bread flour to make soft dough.

3 Turn dough onto lightly floured surface and knead about 10 minutes, until smooth and elastic, working in remaining ½ cup all-purpose flour or 2 to 4 tablespoons bread flour as necessary just to keep dough from sticking. Grease large cookie sheet.

4 Shape dough into 5-inch ball; place on prepared cookie sheet. Cover loosely with greased plastic wrap and let rise in warm place (80° to 85° F) until doubled, about 45 minutes.

5 Preheat oven to 350° F. With serrated knife or single-edge razor blade, cut 3 slashes across top of loaf. Brush with milk; sprinkle with reserved 1 tablespoon oats. Bake loaf 35 to 40 minutes, until bottom sounds hollow when lightly tapped with fingers. Transfer to wire rack to cool. *Makes 1 loaf, 12 slices.*

EACH SLICE: ABOUT 305 CALORIES, 8 G PROTEIN, 48 G CARBOHYDRATE, 9 G TOTAL FAT (2 G SATURATED), 3 G FIBER, 23 MG CHOLESTEROL, 320 MG SODIUM.

Pumpernickel Bread

PREP 30 MINUTES PLUS RISING / BAKE 40 MINUTES

There's no such thing as "pumpernickel flour." Pumpernickel is a hearty rye bread that can be colored with a number of different ingredients (we've used four of them in this recipe for a really dark bread).

¾ CUP WARM WATER (105° TO 115° F)

2 PACKAGES ACTIVE DRY YEAST

1 TABLESPOON DARK BROWN SUGAR

2 TEASPOONS INSTANT ESPRESSO-COFFEE POWDER

1 CUP PRUNE JUICE

3 CUPS RYE FLOUR, PREFERABLY DARK

½ CUP WHOLE-WHEAT FLOUR

1 TABLESPOON SALT

1 TABLESPOON CARAWAY SEEDS

⅓ CUP LIGHT (MILD) MOLASSES

4 TABLESPOONS BUTTER OR MARGARINE, SOFTENED AND CUT UP

1 SQUARE (1 OUNCE) UNSWEETENED CHOCOLATE, MELTED

ABOUT 2½ CUPS ALL-PURPOSE FLOUR

1 LARGE EGG WHITE

1 TEASPOON WATER

1 In large bowl, combine ½ cup warm water, yeast, and brown sugar; stir to dissolve. Let stand 5 minutes, or until foamy.

2 Meanwhile, dissolve espresso-coffee powder in remaining ¼ cup warm water. Stir into yeast mixture along with prune juice. Stir in rye and whole-wheat flours, salt, caraway seeds, molasses, butter, and chocolate until smooth. Gradually stir in 2 cups all-purpose flour. Knead mixture in bowl until dough holds together.

3 Turn dough onto lightly floured surface and knead about 10 minutes, until smooth and elastic, working in remaining ½ cup all-purpose flour as necessary just to keep dough from sticking (dough will be slightly sticky). Shape dough into ball and place in greased large bowl, turning dough over to grease top. Cover bowl and let rise in warm place (80° to 85° F) until doubled, about 1 hour.

4 Grease 2 large cookie sheets. Punch down dough. Turn dough onto floured surface; cut in half. Shape each half into ball. Place 1 ball on each prepared cookie sheet. Cover and let rise in warm place until doubled, about 1 hour.

5 Preheat oven to 350° F. With serrated knife or single-edge razor blade, cut 3 slashes in top of each loaf. In small bowl, whisk together egg white and water. Brush each loaf with egg-white mixture. Bake 40 minutes, or until loaves sound hollow when bottoms are lightly tapped with fingers. Transfer loaves to wire racks to cool. *Makes 2 loaves, 12 slices each.*

EACH SLICE: ABOUT 160 CALORIES, 5 G PROTEIN, 29 G CARBOHYDRATE, 4 G TOTAL FAT (2 G SATURATED), 5 G FIBER, 5 MG CHOLESTEROL, 315 MG SODIUM.

COLOR ME PUMPERNICKEL

DARK RYE FLOUR CAN'T GIVE A LOAF THE DEEP COLOR WE ASSOCIATE WITH PUMPERNICKEL. SO BAKERS ADD SOMETHING TO DARKEN THE DOUGH— COFFEE, MOLASSES, CHOCOLATE, COCOA, POWDERED CARAMEL COLOR, OR EVEN THE FINELY GRATED CRUMBS OF A PREVIOUSLY BAKED LOAF. OUR RECIPE CALLS FOR ESPRESSO POWDER, PRUNE JUICE, MOLASSES, AND CHOCOLATE.

Marble Rye Bread

PREP 30 MINUTES PLUS RISING / BAKE 35 MINUTES

A handsome two-tone rye looks great on a buffet table. Slices of this old-country bread would fit right in with a hearty offering of cold meats, cheeses, mustards, chutneys, pickles—and beer.

1¼ CUPS MEDIUM RYE FLOUR

ABOUT 2¼ CUPS ALL-PURPOSE FLOUR OR 2 CUPS BREAD
   FLOUR

¼ CUP WARM WATER (105° TO 115° F)

1 PACKAGE ACTIVE DRY YEAST

1 TEASPOON SUGAR

¾ CUP MILK, HEATED TO LUKEWARM (105° TO 115° F)

3 TABLESPOONS BUTTER OR MARGARINE, SOFTENED

3 TEASPOONS CARAWAY SEEDS

1½ TEASPOONS SALT

½ CUP WHOLE-WHEAT FLOUR

2 TABLESPOONS DARK MOLASSES

2 TEASPOONS UNSWEETENED COCOA

1 TEASPOON INSTANT COFFEE POWDER

CORNMEAL

1 LARGE EGG, LIGHTLY BEATEN

1 In medium bowl, combine rye flour and 1¼ cups all-purpose or bread flour.

2 In large bowl, combine warm water, yeast, and sugar; stir to dissolve. Let stand 5 minutes, or until foamy. With wooden spoon, stir in 1½ cups of the rye-flour mixture, heated milk, butter, 2½ teaspoons caraway seeds, and salt; beat well. Remove ¾ cup batter to medium bowl.

3 To mixture in large bowl, add whole-wheat flour, molasses, cocoa, and coffee powder and beat well with wooden spoon. Gradually stir in ¾ cup of the rye-flour mixture until dough forms and leaves side of bowl.

4 Turn dough onto lightly floured surface and knead 5 minutes, until smooth and elastic, working in additional ¼ cup all-purpose flour or 2 tablespoons bread flour if necessary just to keep dough from sticking. Shape dough into ball and place in greased medium bowl, turning dough over to grease top. Cover.

5 To batter in medium bowl, stir in remaining ¼ cup rye-flour mixture and ½ cup all-purpose flour or ¼ cup bread flour until dough leaves side of bowl. Turn dough onto floured surface and knead 5 minutes, until smooth and elastic, working in remaining

¼ cup all-purpose flour or 2 tablespoons bread flour as necessary just to keep dough from sticking. Place dough in greased bowl, turning dough over to grease top. Cover. Let both doughs rise in warm place (80° to 85° F) until doubled, about 1 hour 30 minutes.

6 Grease large cookie sheet and sprinkle with cornmeal. Punch down doughs. Divide each into 6 pieces. Lightly knead pieces together, alternating light and dark pieces. Shape into 10-inch-long loaf. Place loaf on prepared cookie sheet, cover with greased plastic wrap, and let rise until almost doubled, about 45 minutes.

7 Preheat oven to 375° F. With serrated knife or single-edge razor blade, make 4 diagonal slashes across top of loaf. Brush with beaten egg, avoiding slashes. Sprinkle with remaining ½ teaspoon caraway seeds. Bake loaf 35 minutes, or until browned and bottom sounds hollow when lightly tapped with fingers. Transfer to wire rack to cool. *Makes 1 loaf, 16 slices.*

EACH SLICE: ABOUT 160 CALORIES, 4 G PROTEIN,
26 G CARBOHYDRATE, 4 G TOTAL FAT (2 G SATURATED),
2 G FIBER, 21 MG CHOLESTEROL, 250 MG SODIUM.

RYE REMARKS

IMMIGRANTS TO AMERICA FROM EASTERN EUROPE SPREAD THE POPULARITY OF THEIR BELOVED RYE BREADS (INCLUDING PUMPERNICKEL) THROUGHOUT THEIR NEW HOMELAND. GERMAN, JEWISH, RUSSIAN, AND SCANDINAVIAN RYES ARE FOUND ALL OVER THE UNITED STATES, WITH CITIES SUCH AS NEW YORK AND MILWAUKEE HAVING A PARTICULARLY RICH TRADITION OF THESE BREADS. IF YOU CAN GET ONLY SLICED SUPERMARKET RYE BREADS WHERE YOU LIVE, IT'S DEFINITELY WORTH THE TROUBLE TO MAKE YOUR OWN AT HOME.

Marble Rye Bread

Swedish Limpa

PREP 35 MINUTES PLUS RISING / BAKE 30 MINUTES

Swedish rye bread is flavored lightly with orange peel, cardamom, caraway, fennel, and anise seeds.

¼ CUP WARM WATER (105° TO 115° F)
1 PACKAGE ACTIVE DRY YEAST
1 TEASPOON SUGAR
ABOUT 5½ CUPS ALL-PURPOSE OR BREAD FLOUR
1 CUP RYE FLOUR
1 TEASPOON ANISE SEEDS
1 TEASPOON FENNEL SEEDS
1 TEASPOON CARAWAY SEEDS
½ TEASPOON GROUND CARDAMOM (OPTIONAL)
1 TABLESPOON FRESHLY GRATED ORANGE PEEL
1½ TEASPOONS SALT
2 CUPS MILK
2 TABLESPOONS PLUS 1 TABLESPOON BUTTER OR
  MARGARINE, MELTED AND COOLED
¼ CUP HONEY
¼ CUP DARK BROWN SUGAR

1 In large bowl, combine water, yeast, and sugar; stir to dissolve. Let stand 5 minutes, or until foamy.

2 In medium bowl, with wire whisk, combine 5 cups all-purpose or bread flour, rye flour, anise seeds, fennel seeds, caraway seeds, cardamom, if you like, orange peel, and salt. Into yeast mixture, stir milk, 2 tablespoons melted butter, honey, and brown sugar. Stir in flour mixture until dough forms.

3 Turn dough onto floured surface and knead about 10 minutes, until smooth and elastic, working in remaining ½ cup flour as necessary (dough will be slightly sticky). Shape dough into ball and place in greased large bowl, turning dough over to grease top. Cover bowl and let rise in warm place (80° to 85° F) until doubled, about 1 hour.

4 Grease large cookie sheet. Punch down dough; divide in half. Shape halves into rounds and place, 3 inches apart on prepared cookie sheet. Brush tops with remaining 1 tablespoon melted butter. Cover and let rise until doubled, about 45 minutes.

5 Preheat oven to 375° F. Bake loaves 30 minutes, or until bottoms sound hollow when lightly tapped with fingers. Transfer loaves to wire racks to cool. *Makes 2 loaves, 12 slices each.*

EACH SLICE: ABOUT 170 CALORIES, 4 G PROTEIN,
32 G CARBOHYDRATE, 3 G TOTAL FAT (1 G SATURATED),
2 G FIBER, 7 MG CHOLESTEROL, 170 MG SODIUM.

BATTER BREAD

Batter bread is made with yeast, but the ingredients form a soft, spoonable mixture rather than a dense dough. Instead of kneading the dough, you beat it— either with a mixer or by hand.

Sally Lunn

PREP 20 MINUTES PLUS RISING / BAKE 40 TO 45 MINUTES

Rich with butter and eggs, and slightly sweet, Sally Lunn may have been named for an English baker who was famed for the recipe in the eighteenth century. It became a favorite in the American South.

⅓ CUP WARM WATER (105° TO 115° F)
1 PACKAGE ACTIVE DRY YEAST
1 TEASPOON PLUS ⅓ CUP SUGAR
½ CUP MILK, HEATED TO LUKEWARM (105° TO 115° F)
½ CUP BUTTER OR MARGARINE (1 STICK), SOFTENED
1¼ TEASPOONS SALT
3¼ CUPS ALL-PURPOSE FLOUR
3 LARGE EGGS

1 In large bowl, combine warm water, yeast, and 1 teaspoon sugar; stir to dissolve. Let stand 5 minutes, or until foamy.

2 With mixer at low speed or with wooden spoon, stir warm milk, butter, salt, remaining ⅓ cup sugar, and 1¼ cups flour into yeast mixture. Increase speed to medium; beat 2 minutes, scraping bowl occasionally with rubber spatula. Beat in eggs, 1 at a time, and 1 cup flour; continue beating 2 minutes, scraping bowl occasionally. With spoon, stir in remaining 1 cup flour.

3 Cover bowl with slightly damp towel and let dough rise in warm place (80° to 85° F) until doubled, about 1 hour.

4 Grease and flour a 9- to 10-inch tube pan. With spoon, stir down dough; spoon dough into tube pan. With well-greased hands, pat dough evenly into pan. Cover pan with slightly damp towel and let rise in warm place until doubled, about 45 minutes.

5 Preheat oven to 350° F. Bake bread 40 to 45 minutes, until golden and bottom sounds hollow when lightly tapped with fingers. With thin metal spatula, loosen bread from side of pan; remove from pan to cool on wire rack. *Makes 1 loaf, 16 slices.*

EACH SLICE: ABOUT 190 CALORIES, 4 G PROTEIN, 25 G CARBOHYDRATE, 8 G TOTAL FAT (4 G SATURATED), 1 G FIBER, 56 MG CHOLESTEROL, 255 MG SODIUM.

PRETZELS, BREADSTICKS, BISCUITS & ROLLS

Now the fun really begins—the fun of shaping dough into rings, twists, sticks, clover leaves, knots, and crescents, topping it with seeds, coarse salt, or a shiny egg glaze, and watching it bake up golden brown. There's nothing difficult about it (yes, even you can knot a pretzel), and your achievements will be all the more impressive because "*nobody* makes those at home anymore!"

Soft Pretzels

PREP 30 MINUTES PLUS RISING / BAKE 16 TO 18 MINUTES

Like the big pretzels sold by street vendors, these are best when eaten hot, with mustard for dipping. Freeze unbaked pretzels on a cookie sheet, covered tightly with foil. Just thaw and proceed from Step 5. Try mixing the coarse salt with sesame or poppy seeds.

2 CUPS WARM WATER (105° TO 115° F)

1 PACKAGE ACTIVE DRY YEAST

1 TEASPOON SUGAR

ABOUT 4 CUPS ALL-PURPOSE FLOUR

1 TEASPOON TABLE SALT

2 TABLESPOONS BAKING SODA

1 TABLESPOON KOSHER OR COARSE OR SEA SALT

1 In large bowl, combine 1½ cups warm water, yeast, and sugar; stir to dissolve. Let stand 5 minutes, or until foamy. Add 2 cups flour and table salt. Beat well with wooden spoon. Gradually stir in 1½ cups flour to make soft dough.

2 Turn dough onto floured surface and knead 6 minutes, until smooth and elastic, kneading in remaining ½ cup flour as necessary just to keep dough from sticking.

3 Shape dough into ball; place in greased large bowl, turning dough over to grease top. Cover bowl and let rise in warm place (80° to 85° F) until doubled, about 30 minutes.

4 Preheat oven to 400° F. Grease 2 large cookie sheets. Punch down dough and cut into 12 pieces. Roll each piece into 24-inch-long rope. Shape ropes into loop-shaped pretzels (see photo below).

5 In small bowl, whisk remaining ½ cup warm water and baking soda until soda has dissolved.

6 Dip pretzels in baking-soda mixture and place 1½ inches apart, on prepared cookie sheets. Sprinkle lightly with kosher salt. Bake pretzels 16 to 18 minutes, rotating sheets between upper and lower racks halfway through baking, until browned. Transfer to wire racks to cool. Serve warm or at room temperature. *Makes 12 pretzels.*

EACH PRETZEL: ABOUT 165 CALORIES, 5 G PROTEIN, 33 G CARBOHYDRATE, 1 G TOTAL FAT (0 G SATURATED), 1 G FIBER, 0 MG CHOLESTEROL, 1190 MG SODIUM.

SOFT PRETZEL STICKS Prepare dough as for Soft Pretzels; cut into 12 pieces. On lightly floured surface, with hands, roll each piece into 8-inch-long rope. Dip ropes into baking-soda mixture; place, 2 inches apart, on greased cookie sheets. Sprinkle with 1 teaspoon coarse salt. Bake as directed.

EACH PRETZEL STICK: ABOUT 170 CALORIES, 5 G PROTEIN, 33 G CARBOHYDRATE, 1 G TOTAL FAT (0 G SATURATED), 1 G FIBER, 0 MG CHOLESTEROL, 945 MG SODIUM.

Shaping Pretzels

Form each rope of dough into an open loop. Then cross the ends and rest each one on the bottom of the loop.

Taralli

PREP 1 HOUR PLUS RISING
BAKE 35 TO 40 MINUTES PER BATCH

Taralli and bagels are boiled before baking. But taralli are small and crunchy—more cracker than bread.

1 CUP WARM WATER (105° 115° F)
1 PACKAGE ACTIVE DRY YEAST
1 TEASPOON SUGAR
¼ CUP OLIVE OIL
ABOUT 3½ CUPS ALL-PURPOSE FLOUR
1½ TEASPOONS SALT
1 TABLESPOON PLUS 1 TEASPOON FENNEL SEEDS, CRUSHED
½ TEASPOON COARSELY GROUND BLACK PEPPER
1 LARGE EGG
1 TABLESPOON WATER

1 In large bowl, combine ¼ cup warm water, yeast, and sugar; stir to dissolve. Let stand 5 minutes, or until foamy. With wooden spoon, stir in remaining ¾ cup warm water, oil, 3 cups flour, salt, fennel seeds, and pepper until combined.

2 Turn dough onto floured surface and knead 10 minutes, working in about ½ cup more flour, until smooth and elastic. Shape dough into ball; place in greased large bowl, turning dough over to grease top. Cover bowl and let rise in warm place (80° to 85° F) until doubled, about 1 hour 30 minutes.

3 Punch down dough. Turn onto lightly floured surface; divide dough into 4 pieces. Working with 1 piece at a time, keeping remaining dough covered with clean towel, divide dough into 10 pieces. Roll each piece into 12" by ¼" rope, with slightly tapering ends. Form rope into a ring, overlapping tapered ends, slipping over fingers and roll seam to seal.

4 Preheat oven to 350° F. In a 5-quart saucepan, heat *4 quarts water* to boiling over medium-high heat. Meanwhile, in small bowl, with fork, mix egg and 1 tablespoon water. Grease 2 large cookie sheets.

5 Drop rings, 3 at a time, into rapidly boiling water. When rings float to top, boil 30 seconds. With slotted spoon, remove from water and place on clean surface. Repeat with remaining rings.

6 Place rings, about 2 inches apart, on prepared cookie sheets. With pastry brush, brush rings with egg mixture. Bake taralli 35 to 40 minutes, rotating sheets between upper and lower racks halfway through baking, until golden on top and deep golden on bottom. With wide metal spatula, transfer taralli to wire racks to cool.

7 Repeat with remaining dough and egg mixture. *Makes 40 taralli.*

EACH TARALLE: ABOUT 60 CALORIES, 1 G PROTEIN,
9 G CARBOHYDRATE, 2 G TOTAL FAT (0 G SATURATED),
0.5 G FIBER, 5 MG CHOLESTEROL, 90 MG SODIUM.

RINGS AND THINGS

THE ITALIANS USE THE WORD "TARALLI" TO DESCRIBE A NUMBER OF DIFFERENT RING-SHAPED BAKED GOODS. SOME OF THEM ARE SWEET BISCUITS, SUCH AS THE SUGARED SICILIAN TARALLI MADE OF PUFF PASTRY. THE RECIPE ON THIS PAGE IS FOR SAVORY TARALLI, WHICH ARE OFTEN SERVED WITH WINE. THE COOKING METHOD RESEMBLES THAT USED FOR BAGELS IN THAT THE DOUGH IS SHAPED INTO RINGS, THEN BOILED BRIEFLY IN WATER BEFORE BAKING. TARALLI SHOULD BE QUITE HARD AND CRUNCHY—LIKE PRETZELS—AFTER BAKING.

Breadsticks

PREP 15 MINUTES PLUS RISING
BAKE 20 MINUTES PER BATCH

You can make these ahead of time. They keep very well for up to 2 weeks stored in an airtight container.

2 PACKAGES QUICK-RISE YEAST
2½ TEASPOONS SALT
ABOUT 4¾ CUPS ALL-PURPOSE FLOUR
1⅓ CUPS VERY WARM WATER (120° TO 130° F)
½ CUP OLIVE OIL
3 TABLESPOONS CARAWAY SEEDS, SESAME SEEDS, OR
  POPPYSEEDS

1 In large bowl, combine yeast, salt, and 2 cups flour. With wooden spoon, stir in warm water; beat vigorously 1 minute. Stir in oil. Gradually stir in 2¼ cups flour. Stir in caraway seeds, if using.

2 Turn dough onto floured surface and knead about 8 minutes, until smooth and elastic, working in about ½ cup more flour. Cover dough loosely; let rest 10 minutes.

3 Preheat oven to 375° F. Grease 2 large cookie sheets. Cut dough in half. Keeping remaining dough covered, cut 1 dough half into 32 pieces. Shape each piece into a 12-inch-long rope. Place ropes, about 1 inch apart, on prepared cookie sheets. If not using caraway seeds, sprinkle with sesame seeds or poppyseeds.

4 Bake breadsticks 20 minutes, rotating cookie sheets between upper and lower racks halfway through baking, or until golden and crisp throughout. Transfer breadsticks to wire racks to cool.

5 Repeat with remaining dough and seeds. *Makes 64 breadsticks.*

EACH BREADSTICK: ABOUT 50 CALORIES, 1 G PROTEIN, 7 G CARBOHYDRATE, 2 G TOTAL FAT (0 G SATURATED), 0.5 G FIBER, 0 MG CHOLESTEROL, 90 MG SODIUM.

ROSEMARY-FENNEL BREADSTICKS Prepare dough for Breadsticks but omit caraway, sesame, or poppyseeds, or Parmesan. In Step 1, stir *2 teaspoons fennel seeds*, crushed, *1 teaspoon dried rosemary leaves*, crumbled, and *½ teaspoon coarsely ground black pepper* into dough. Shape breadsticks and bake as directed.
EACH BREADSTICK: ABOUT 50 CALORIES, 1 G PROTEIN, 7 G CARBOHYDRATE, 2 G TOTAL FAT (0 G SATURATED), 0.5 G FIBER, 0 MG CHOLESTEROL, 90 MG SODIUM.

PARMESAN BREADSTICKS Prepare dough as for Rosemary-Fennel Breadsticks but omit fennel seeds and rosemary. Roll each 12-inch-long rope in *1 slightly rounded teaspoon freshly grated Parmesan cheese.* (You will need about 2½ cups grated Parmesan in all.) Bake as directed.
EACH BREADSTICK: ABOUT 70 CALORIES, 3 G PROTEIN, 7 G CARBOHYDRATE, 3 G TOTAL FAT (1 G SATURATED), 0.5 G FIBER, 3 MG CHOLESTEROL, 160 MG SODIUM.

Soft Breadsticks

PREP 15 MINUTES PLUS RISING
BAKE 15 TO 20 MINUTES PER BATCH

The perfect companion for a salad or bowl of soup, these puffy breadsticks can be topped with sesame, poppy, caraway, or fennel seeds, or simply sprinkled with coarse salt.

1 CUP WARM WATER (105° TO 115° F)
1 PACKAGE ACTIVE DRY YEAST
1 TEASPOON SUGAR
2 TABLESPOONS OLIVE OIL
1½ TEASPOONS SALT
ABOUT 3 CUPS PLUS 2 TABLESPOONS ALL-PURPOSE FLOUR
1 LARGE EGG
1 TABLESPOON WATER
3 TABLESPOONS SESAME SEEDS, POPPYSEEDS, CARAWAY SEEDS, OR FENNEL SEEDS, OR 1 TABLESPOON COARSE SALT

1 In large bowl, combine ¼ cup warm water, yeast, and sugar; stir to dissolve. Let stand 5 minutes, or until foamy. With wooden spoon, stir in remaining ¾ cup water, oil, salt, and 3 cups flour until combined.

2 Turn dough onto lightly floured surface and knead 10 minutes, until smooth and elastic, working in about 2 tablespoons more flour to keep dough from sticking.

3 Shape dough into ball; place in greased large bowl, turning dough to grease top. Cover bowl and let rise in warm place (80° to 85° F) until doubled, about 45 minutes.

4 In bowl, stir together egg and 1 tablespoon water.

5 Preheat oven to 400° F. Grease 2 large cookie sheets. Punch down dough and turn onto lightly floured surface; divide into 32 pieces. Working with 1 piece at a time (keep remaining dough covered with clean towel), roll each piece into 10" by ¼" rope. Place ropes, about 2 inches apart, on prepared cookie sheets. With pastry brush, brush each rope with egg mixture; sprinkle with seeds or salt.

6 Bake breadsticks 15 to 20 minutes, rotating sheets between upper and lower rack halfway through baking, until golden brown. With wide metal spatula, transfer breadsticks to wire racks to cool. *Makes 32 breadsticks.*

EACH BREADSTICK: ABOUT 65 CALORIES, 2 G PROTEIN, 10 G CARBOHYDRATE, 2 G TOTAL FAT (0 G SATURATED), 0.5 G FIBER, 7 MG CHOLESTEROL, 110 MG SODIUM.

Dinner Rolls

PREP 30 MINUTES PLUS RISING / BAKE 10 TO 12 MINUTES

½ CUP WARM WATER (105° TO 115° F)

2 PACKAGES ACTIVE DRY YEAST

1 TEASPOON PLUS ⅓ CUP SUGAR

¾ CUP MILK, HEATED TO LUKEWARM (105° TO 115° F)

4 TABLESPOONS BUTTER OR MARGARINE, SOFTENED

ABOUT 3¾ CUPS ALL-PURPOSE FLOUR

1½ TEASPOONS SALT

2 LARGE EGGS

1 EGG YOLK MIXED WITH 1 TABLESPOON WATER

1 In large bowl, combine warm water, yeast, and 1 teaspoon sugar; stir to dissolve. Let stand 5 minutes, until foamy.

2 With wooden spoon, or mixer at low speed, beat in warm milk, butter, ½ cup flour, remaining ⅓ cup sugar, salt, and eggs to make a thick batter; continue beating 2 minutes, scraping bowl often. Gradually stir in 3 cups flour to make soft dough.

3 Turn dough onto lightly floured surface and knead about 10 minutes, until smooth and elastic, working in remaining ¼ cup more flour as necessary just to keep dough from sticking. Shape dough into ball; place in greased large bowl, turning dough over to grease top. Cover bowl and let rise in warm place (80° to 85° F) until doubled, about 1 hour.

4 Punch down dough. Turn onto lightly floured surface; cover and let rest 15 minutes.

5 Grease large cookie sheets or muffin-pan cups, depending on type of rolls. Shape dough into rolls as directed on right. Cover and let rise in warm place, until doubled, about 30 minutes.

6 Preheat oven to 400° F. Brush rolls with egg-yolk mixture or melted butter. Bake rolls 10 to 12 minutes, rotating sheets between upper and lower racks halfway through baking, until golden and bottoms sound hollow when lightly tapped with fingers. Transfer to wire racks. Serve warm or let cool to serve later. *Makes 24 rolls.*

EACH ROLL WITH EGG GLAZE: ABOUT 120 CALORIES, 3 G PROTEIN, 19 G CARBOHYDRATE, 4 G TOTAL FAT (2 G SATURATED), 0.5 G FIBER, 33 MG CHOLESTEROL, 175 MG SODIUM.

EACH ROLL WITH MELTED BUTTER: ABOUT 130 CALORIES, 3 G PROTEIN, 19 G CARBOHYDRATE, 4 G TOTAL FAT (2 G SATURATED), 0.5 G FIBER, 27 MG CHOLESTEROL, 185 MG SODIUM.

CLOVERLEAF ROLLS Prepare dough as for Dinner Rolls through Step 4. Grease twenty-four 2½-inch muffin-pan cups. Divide dough in half. Cut 1 dough half into 36 equal pieces; shape each piece into ball. Place 3 balls in each prepared muffin-pan cup. Repeat with remaining dough. Let rolls rise; brush with egg-yolk mixture or melted butter. Bake as directed.

EACH ROLL WITH EGG GLAZE: ABOUT 130 CALORIES, 3 G PROTEIN, 19 G CARBOHYDRATE, 4 G TOTAL FAT (2 G SATURATED), 0.5 G FIBER, 33 MG CHOLESTEROL, 175 MG SODIUM.

DINNER BUNS Prepare dough as for Dinner Rolls through Step 4. Grease 2 large cookie sheets. Cut dough into 24 equal pieces. Shape each piece into 2-inch ball; with floured hands, roll each ball 4 inches long, tapering ends slightly. Place rolls, 2 inches apart, on prepared cookie sheets. With serrated knife or single-edge razor blade, make slash lengthwise through center of each roll. Let buns rise; brush with egg-yolk mixture. Bake as directed. *Makes 24 rolls.*

EACH ROLL WITH EGG GLAZE: ABOUT 120 CALORIES, 3 G PROTEIN, 19 G CARBOHYDRATE, 4 G TOTAL FAT (2 G SATURATED), 0.5 G FIBER, 33 MG CHOLESTEROL, 175 MG SODIUM.

CRESCENT ROLLS Prepare dough as for Dinner Rolls through Step 4. Grease 2 large cookie sheets. Melt *2 tablespoons butter or margarine*. Divide dough in half. Roll dough half into 9-inch circle. With serrated knife, cut circle into 8 wedges; brush wedges with melted butter. Starting at wide base, roll up each wedge toward point. Curve ends toward each other and place, point side up, on prepared cookie sheet. Repeat with remaining dough and butter. Let rolls rise; brush with egg-yolk mixture. Bake as directed. *Makes 16 rolls.*

EACH ROLL: ABOUT 195 CALORIES, 5 G PROTEIN, 28 G CARBOHYDRATE, 7 G TOTAL FAT (3 G SATURATED), 1 G FIBER, 53 MG CHOLESTEROL, 275 MG SODIUM.

KNOTS Prepare dough as for Dinner Rolls through Step 4. Grease large cookie sheet. Cut dough into 18 equal pieces. With hands, roll each piece into 6-inch-long rope. Carefully tie each rope into loose knot. Place knots, 2 inches apart, on prepared cookie sheet. Let knots rise; brush with egg-yolk mixture. Bake as directed *Makes 18 rolls.*

EACH ROLL WITH EGG GLAZE: ABOUT 160 CALORIES, 4 G PROTEIN, 25 G CARBOHYDRATE, 5 G TOTAL FAT (2 G SATURATED), 1 G FIBER, 44 MG CHOLESTEROL, 235 MG SODIUM.

Cloverleaf Rolls

Angel Biscuits

PREP 15 MINUTES PLUS RISING / BAKE 17 TO 20 MINUTES

Sometimes called "Bride's Biscuits," these triple-leavened treats are supposedly failsafe. Made with yeast, baking powder, and baking soda, they're virtually guaranteed to be feather-light.

¼ CUP WARM WATER (105° TO 115° F)
1 PACKAGE ACTIVE DRY YEAST
1 TEASPOON SUGAR
3 CUPS ALL-PURPOSE FLOUR
1½ TEASPOONS BAKING POWDER
½ TEASPOON BAKING SODA
¼ TEASPOON SALT
4 TABLESPOONS COLD BUTTER OR MARGARINE, CUT UP
2 TABLESPOONS VEGETABLE SHORTENING
1 CUP PLUS 2 TABLESPOONS BUTTERMILK

1 In small bowl, combine warm water, yeast, and sugar; stir to dissolve. Let stand 5 minutes, or until foamy.

2 In large bowl, stir together flour, baking powder, baking soda, and salt until well combined. With pastry blender or 2 knives used scissor-fashion, cut in butter and shortening until mixture resembles coarse crumbs. Make well in center of mixture and pour in buttermilk and yeast mixture. Stir until well combined.

3 Turn dough onto lightly floured surface and knead several times until it holds together and is smooth and elastic. Place in greased bowl, turning dough over to grease top. Cover bowl and let stand in warm place (80° to 85° F) until doubled, 1 hour.

4 Punch down dough. Cover dough and let stand 10 minutes. On lightly floured surface, with floured hands, pat dough out ¾-inch thick. With 2-inch round biscuit cutters, cut out biscuits; place 2 inches apart on 2 large ungreased cookie sheets. Reserve trimmings for rerolling. Cover and let rise until almost doubled, about 30 minutes.

5 Preheat oven to 400° F. Bake biscuits 17 to 20 minutes, rotating sheets between upper and lower racks halfway through baking. Serve warm. *Makes 2 dozen biscuits.*

EACH BISCUIT: ABOUT 95 CALORIES, 2 G PROTEIN, 14 G CARBOHYDRATE, 3 G TOTAL FAT (2 G SATURATED), 0.5 G FIBER, 6 MG CHOLESTEROL, 110 MG SODIUM.

Bagels

PREP 40 MINUTES PLUS RISING / BAKE 20 MINUTES

Boiling bagels prior to baking helps produce a chewy, glossy crust. Choose your favorite topping from those suggested below, or bake the bagels plain.

1¼ CUPS WARM WATER (105° TO 115° F)
1 PACKAGE ACTIVE DRY YEAST
1 TEASPOON PLUS 2 TABLESPOONS SUGAR
¼ CUP MILK
1 TABLESPOON SALT
ABOUT 6 CUPS BREAD FLOUR OR ALL-PURPOSE FLOUR
1 TABLESPOON HONEY
1 TABLESPOON LIGHT (MILD) OR DARK MOLASSES
4 TEASPOONS POPPYSEEDS, SESAME SEEDS, OR KOSHER SALT

1 In large bowl, combine ¼ cup warm water, yeast, and 1 teaspoon sugar; stir to dissolve. Let stand 5 minutes, or until foamy. Stir in remaining 1 cup warm water, remaining 2 tablespoons sugar, milk, salt, and 4 cups flour until combined. Stir in enough of remaining 2 cups flour to make a stiff dough.

2 Turn dough onto lightly floured surface and knead 5 to 8 minutes until smooth and elastic.

3 Shape dough into ball; place in greased large bowl, turning dough over to grease top. Cover bowl and let rise in warm place (80° to 85° F) until doubled, about 1 hour 30 minutes.

4 Punch down dough. Cut into 12 pieces. Cover and let rest 10 minutes. With floured hands, roll each piece into 14-inch-long rope. Wrap each rope around your hand, overlapping the ends, and pinch to seal. Place on surface, cover, and let rise in warm place until puffy and almost doubled, about 25 minutes.

5 Preheat oven to 450° F. In 5-quart saucepan, heat *3 quarts water*, honey, and molasses to boiling. Drop 3 bagels at a time into pan and poach 20 seconds, turning bagels over midway. With slotted spoon, transfer bagels to ungreased cookie sheets. Repeat with remaining bagels. Sprinkle bagels with poppyseeds, sesame seeds, or kosher salt.

6 Bake bagels 20 minutes, rotating sheets between upper and lower racks halfway through baking, or until crusty and baked through (a toothpick inserted into bagel comes out clean). *Makes 12 bagels.*

EACH BAGEL: ABOUT 270 CALORIES, 9 G PROTEIN, 54 G CARBOHYDRATE, 2 G TOTAL FAT (0 G SATURATED), 2 G FIBER, 1 MG CHOLESTEROL, 585 MG SODIUM.

PIZZA, CALZONES, FOCACCIA & FLATBREAD

Although pizza and focaccia are among the most famous flatbreads, these doughy delights are not just Italian. They're also found in Israel and Syria, India and Pakistan, France and Greece, and many other places. Pizza, of course, needs no introduction; stromboli and calzone are stuffed breads made from pizza dough. Focaccia is a thick slab of rich pizza dough, baked with or without toppings; it makes a wonderful meal accompaniment or, if split horizontally, a superlative sandwich bread. Fougasse is the handsomely shaped Provençal version of focaccia. Pissaladière, also from southern France, is a flatbread topped with sautéed onions, olives, and anchovies.

Basic Pizza Dough

PREP 15 MINUTES PLUS RISING
BAKE 15 TO 20 MINUTES

This recipe makes enough dough for two pizzas so you can try at least two of the toppings on the right, at one time, if you like. Or freeze one ball for another time, perhaps to serve small wedges as appetizers.

1¼ CUPS WARM WATER (105° TO 115° F)
1 PACKAGE ACTIVE DRY YEAST
1 TEASPOON SUGAR
2 TABLESPOONS OLIVE OIL
2 TEASPOONS SALT
ABOUT 4 CUPS ALL-PURPOSE FLOUR OR 3½ CUPS BREAD
    FLOUR
CORNMEAL

1 In large bowl, combine ¼ cup warm water, yeast, and sugar; stir to dissolve. Let stand 5 minutes, or until foamy. With wooden spoon, stir in remaining 1 cup warm water, oil, and salt; gradually add 1½ to 2 cups flour until smooth. Gradually add 2 cups flour, stirring until dough comes away from sides of bowl.

2 Turn dough onto lightly floured surface and knead 10 minutes, working in about ½ cup more flour. Shape dough into ball; place in greased large bowl, turning dough over to grease top. Cover bowl and let rise in warm place (80° to 85° F) until doubled, about 1 hour.

3 Punch down dough. Turn onto lightly floured surface and cut in half; cover and let rest 15 minutes. If not using right away, place in greased large bowl, cover loosely with greased plastic wrap, and refrigerate up to 24 hours until ready to use.

4 Preheat oven to 450° F. Sprinkle 2 large cookie sheets with cornmeal. Shape each half into a ball. On prepared cookie sheet, with floured rolling pin, roll 1 ball into 14" by 10" rectangle, folding edge in to make 1-inch rim. Add topping (see below). Repeat with remaining dough. Let rest 20 minutes. Bake 15 to 20 minutes, until golden, or as directed. *Makes enough dough for 2 pizzas, 4 main-dish servings each.*

EACH SERVING: ABOUT 280 CALORIES, 7 G PROTEIN, 51 G CARBOHYDRATE, 5 G TOTAL FAT (1 G SATURATED), 2 G FIBER, 0 MG CHOLESTEROL, 585 MG SODIUM.

WHOLE-WHEAT PIZZA DOUGH Prepare dough as for Basic Pizza Dough, adding 2 cups all-purpose flour in Step 1. Add *1 tablespoon dark molasses* with oil and *2½ cups whole-wheat flour* for remaining all-purpose flour. Let rise, shape, and bake as directed.
EACH SERVING: ABOUT 270 CALORIES, 8 G PROTEIN, 50 G CARBOHYDRATE, 5 G TOTAL FAT (1 G SATURATED), 6 G FIBER, 0 MG CHOLESTEROL, 585 MG SODIUM.

CHEESE PIZZA Prepare dough as for Basic Pizza Dough. Shape 1 ball of dough as directed. Sprinkle round with *2 tablespoons freshly grated Parmesan cheese*, spread with *1 cup Pizza Sauce* (page 142), and sprinkle with *1 cup shredded mozzarella*. Let rest 20 minutes before baking as directed. *Makes 1 pizza, 4 main-dish servings.*
EACH SERVING: ABOUT 400 CALORIES, 14 G PROTEIN, 56 G CARBOHYDRATE, 13 G TOTAL FAT (5 G SATURATED), 2 G FIBER, 25 MG CHOLESTEROL, 900 MG SODIUM.

PIZZA CARBONARA Prepare dough as for Basic Pizza Dough. Shape 1 ball of dough as directed. In skillet, cook *6 slices bacon* over medium-high heat 5 minutes, or until brown. Transfer to paper towels to drain. Reserve *1 tablespoon fat* in skillet. Stir *2 tablespoons flour*, *¼ teaspoon salt*, and *¼ teaspoon ground black pepper* into pan. Cook 30 seconds; do not brown. Whisk in *1½ cups warmed milk* and heat to boiling over medium-high heat. Reduce heat to low and simmer 3 minutes. Remove saucepan from heat and stir in *¼ cup freshly grated Parmesan cheese* and *2 tablespoons chopped parsley*. Spoon sauce over dough; crumble bacon on top. Let rest 20 minutes before baking as above. *Makes 1 pizza, 4 main-dish servings.*
EACH SERVING: ABOUT 450 CALORIES, 15 G PROTEIN, 59 G CARBOHYDRATE, 16 G TOTAL FAT (6 G SATURATED), 2 G FIBER, 27 MG CHOLESTEROL, 1035 MG SODIUM.

PIZZA PUTTANESCA Prepare dough as for Basic Pizza Dough (page 141). Shape 1 ball of dough as directed. In 12-inch skillet, heat *1 tablespoon olive oil* over medium-high heat. Stir in *2 garlic cloves, minced, 4 anchovy fillets, minced,* and *⅛ teaspoon crushed red pepper.* Cook, stirring often, 1 minute, until garlic is pale golden. Add *1½ pounds plum tomatoes,* coarsely chopped, and *⅛ teaspoon ground black pepper.* Simmer 4 minutes. Remove from heat; stir in *¼ cup pitted Kalamata or pimiento-stuffed olives,* chopped, and *1 tablespoon capers,* chopped. Sprinkle *3 tablespoons freshly grated Parmesan cheese* over dough. Spread with sauce. Let rest 20 minutes before baking as directed. *Makes 1 pizza, 4 main-dish servings.*

EACH SERVING: ABOUT 400 CALORIES, 11 G PROTEIN, 61 G CARBOHYDRATE, 14 G TOTAL FAT (2 G SATURATED), 4 G FIBER, 5 MG CHOLESTEROL, 1065 MG SODIUM.

Pizza Sauce

PREP 5 MINUTES / COOK 20 MINUTES

You can find jars of pizza sauce at the supermarket, but it's so easy to make your own. For the best flavor, use imported Italian plum tomatoes. If you really love garlic, add as much as you like.

1 TABLESPOON OLIVE OIL
1 LARGE GARLIC CLOVE, FINELY CHOPPED
1 CAN (28 OUNCES) TOMATOES IN THICK PUREE, CHOPPED
¼ TEASPOON SALT

In 2-quart saucepan, heat oil over medium-high heat. Stir in garlic and cook, stirring often, 30 seconds, or until golden. Add tomatoes with puree and salt; heat to boiling over high heat. Reduce heat and simmer, uncovered, 10 minutes. *Makes about 3 cups.*

EACH ¼ CUP: ABOUT 30 CALORIES, 1 G PROTEIN, 4 G CARBOHYDRATE, 1 G TOTAL FAT (0 G SATURATED), 0.5 G FIBER, 0 MG CHOLESTEROL, 155 MG SODIUM.

Sicilian Pizza

PREP 25 MINUTES PLUS RISING / BAKE 25 TO 30 MINUTES

A thick crust and plenty of cheese comprise this classic pizza. If you like, add chopped anchovies, artichoke hearts, and thin slices of prosciutto.

1½ CUPS WARM WATER (105° TO 115° F)
1 PACKAGE ACTIVE DRY YEAST
1 TEASPOON SUGAR
2 TABLESPOONS EXTRAVIRGIN OLIVE OIL
1½ TEASPOONS SALT
3½ CUPS BREAD FLOUR OR ALL-PURPOSE FLOUR
¼ CUP FRESHLY GRATED PARMESAN CHEESE
PINCH GROUND BLACK PEPPER
1½ CUPS PIZZA SAUCE (ON LEFT)
6 OUNCES MOZZARELLA CHEESE, SHREDDED (1½ CUPS)

1 In large bowl, combine ½ cup warm water, yeast, and sugar; stir to dissolve. Let stand 5 minutes, or until foamy. With wooden spoon, add remaining warm water, oil, salt, and flour; stir to combine.

2 Turn dough onto lightly floured surface and knead 7 minutes, or until smooth and elastic (dough may be slightly soft; do not add more flour). Shape dough into ball; place in greased large bowl, turning dough over to coat top. Cover bowl and let stand in warm place (80° to 85° F) until doubled, about 1 hour.

3 Lightly oil 15½" by 10½" jelly-roll pan. Punch down dough. Pat dough evenly into prepared pan. Sprinkle dough with Parmesan and pepper; spoon pizza sauce evenly on top. Sprinkle with mozzarella. Cover pizza and let rise in warm place until doubled, about 45 minutes.

4 Preheat oven to 450° F. Bake pizza on lowest oven rack 25 to 30 minutes, until bottom is crusty and cheese is lightly browned. *Makes 6 main-dish servings.*

EACH SERVING: ABOUT 480 CALORIES, 18 G PROTEIN, 65 G CARBOHYDRATE, 16 G TOTAL FAT (6 G SATURATED), 3 G FIBER, 25 MG CHOLESTEROL, 920 MG SODIUM.

Pissaladière

PREP 45 MINUTES PLUS RISING
BAKE 25 MINUTES

This version of a Provençal onion pizza is baked in a rectangular pan and cut into squares—which make great appetizers. You can prepare the dough in advance, let rise once, then freeze for up to 3 months.

1 CUP WARM WATER (105° TO 115° F)
1 PACKAGE ACTIVE DRY YEAST
3 CUPS ALL-PURPOSE FLOUR
1¾ TEASPOONS SALT
2 TABLESPOONS OLIVE OIL
2 POUNDS LARGE YELLOW ONIONS, CUT INTO ½-INCH
   PIECES
1 CAN (2 OUNCES) ANCHOVY FILLETS, RINSED, DRAINED,
   AND COARSELY CHOPPED
⅓ CUP PITTED AND HALVED KALAMATA OR GAETA OLIVES

1 In cup, combine ¼ cup warm water and yeast; stir to dissolve. Let stand about 5 minutes, or until foamy.

2 In large bowl, stir together flour and 1½ teaspoons salt. Stir in yeast mixture, remaining ¾ cup warm water, and 1 tablespoon oil.

3 Turn dough onto lightly floured surface and knead about 8 minutes, until smooth and elastic. Shape dough into ball and place in greased large bowl, turning dough over to grease top. Cover bowl and let rise in warm place (80° to 85° F) until doubled, about 45 minutes.

4 Meanwhile, in 12-inch skillet, heat remaining 1 tablespoon oil over low heat. Add onions and remaining ¼ teaspoon salt and cook, stirring frequently, about 30 minutes, or until onions are soft. Cool to room temperature.

5 Oil 15½" by 10½" jelly-roll pan. Punch down dough. Pat dough evenly into prepared pan. Cover loosely and let rise until almost doubled, 30 minutes.

6 Preheat oven to 425° F. With fingertips, make indentations, 1 inch apart, over surface of dough. Add anchovies to onion mixture and spread mixture on top. Place olives at 2-inch intervals on onion mixture. Bake pizza on lowest oven rack 25 minutes, or until crust is golden. Cut into 2-inch squares. Cool in pan on wire rack. *Makes 32 appetizer servings.*

EACH SERVING: ABOUT 70 CALORIES, 2 G PROTEIN,
12 G CARBOHYDRATE, 2 G TOTAL FAT (0 G SATURATED),
1 G FIBER, 1 MG CHOLESTEROL, 205 MG SODIUM.

Stromboli

PREP 30 MINUTES PLUS RISING / BAKE 30 TO 35 MINUTES

Any combination of thinly sliced deli meats or cheeses can be used to fill this rolled "sandwich." Depending upon how you slice it (thick or thin), the stromboli can be served as an appetizer, snack, or light meal. It can be served warm or at room temperature; store leftovers in the refrigerator and reheat as needed. To reheat, place on cookie sheet in preheated 375° F oven for about 10 minutes.

BASIC PIZZA DOUGH (PAGE 141)
¼ POUND THINLY SLICED SALAMI
¼ POUND THINLY SLICED PROVOLONE CHEESE
¼ POUND THINLY SLICED SMOKED BAKED HAM OR
   PROSCIUTTO
¼ CUP FRESHLY GRATED PARMESAN CHEESE
¼ CUP BLACK OLIVES, PITTED AND FINELY CHOPPED
¼ CUP GREEN OLIVES, PITTED AND FINELY CHOPPED
1 LARGE EGG

1 Preheat oven to 375° F. Grease large cookie sheet.

2 Prepare Basic Pizza Dough through Step 2. Punch down dough. On lightly floured surface, with floured rolling pin, roll dough into 16" by 12" rectangle. Arrange salami slices on dough up to ½ inch from edges, overlapping slices slightly if necessary. Repeat with Provolone and ham. Sprinkle with Parmesan and black and green olives. Roll up dough, from a long side, jelly-roll style. Pinch seam and ends to seal and tuck ends under slightly. Place loaf, seam side down, diagonally on prepared cookie sheet. Cover with oiled plastic wrap and let dough rest 15 minutes.

3 In small cup, with fork, beat egg. With serrated knife or single-edge razor blade, cut 5 long diagonal slashes in top of loaf, each about ½ inch deep. Brush loaf with beaten egg, but do not brush slashes. Bake stromboli 30 to 35 minutes, until browned. With metal spatula, loosen bottom of loaf and slide loaf onto wire rack. Let cool slightly and serve warm or at room temperature. *Makes 16 slices.*

EACH SLICE: ABOUT 225 CALORIES, 9 G PROTEIN,
26 G CARBOHYDRATE, 9 G TOTAL FAT (3 G SATURATED),
1 G FIBER, 28 MG CHOLESTEROL, 690 MG SODIUM.

Semolina Focaccia with Golden Raisins & Fennel

PREP 20 MINUTES PLUS RISING AND COOLING
BAKE ABOUT 20 MINUTES

If you have a bread machine, you can effortlessly bake this focaccia in loaf form rather than as a flatbread. Add the ingredients to the pan in the order specified in the instruction manual, with these adjustments: Use only 1½ cups patent durum or semolina flour; increase the olive oil in the dough to ¼ cup, and don't drizzle oil over the dough. Patent durum and semolina flours are high-protein flours milled from hard (durum) wheat. Semolina flour is sold in Italian grocery stores.

1 CUP WARM WATER (105° TO 115° F)

6 TABLESPOONS OLIVE OIL

1 PACKAGE ACTIVE DRY YEAST

1 TEASPOON PLUS 2 TABLESPOONS SUGAR

2 TEASPOONS SALT

1½ CUPS PLUS 2 TABLESPOONS PATENT DURUM OR FINELY
   GROUND SEMOLINA FLOUR

ABOUT 1½ CUPS ALL-PURPOSE FLOUR

¾ CUP GOLDEN RAISINS

1 TABLESPOON FENNEL SEEDS, CRUSHED

1 In large bowl, combine ¼ cup warm water, 3 tablespoons oil, yeast, and 1 teaspoon sugar; stir to dissolve. Let stand 5 minutes, or until foamy.

2 Stir in remaining ¾ cup warm water, salt, 1½ cups patent durum or semolina flour, 1 cup all-purpose flour, and remaining 2 tablespoons sugar. With floured hands, knead to combine.

3 Turn dough onto lightly floured surface and knead 8 minutes, or until smooth and elastic, working in about ½ cup more remaining all-purpose flour as necessary just to keep dough from sticking. Knead in raisins and fennel seeds.

4 Shape dough into ball and place in greased large bowl, turning dough over to grease top. Cover bowl and let dough rise in warm place (80° to 85° F) until doubled, about 40 minutes.

5 Grease 15½" by 10½" jelly-roll pan; sprinkle with remaining 2 tablespoons patent durum or semolina flour. With floured rolling pin, roll dough evenly in prepared pan; with fingers, press dough into corners. Cover and let rise in warm place until doubled, about 30 minutes.

6 Preheat oven to 425° F. With fingertips, make deep indentations, about 1 inch apart, over entire surface of dough, almost to bottom of pan. Drizzle with remaining 3 tablespoons oil. Bake focaccia 20 minutes, or until golden. With wide spatula, transfer focaccia to wire rack to cool. *Makes 12 servings.*

EACH SERVING: ABOUT 250 CALORIES, 5 G PROTEIN,
39 G CARBOHYDRATE, 8 G TOTAL FAT (1 G SATURATED),
2 G FIBER, 0 MG CHOLESTEROL, 390 MG SODIUM.

Focaccia

PREP 25 MINUTES PLUS RISING / BAKE 18 MINUTES

The triple rising gives focaccia its satisfying, chewy texture. Whether plain, herbed, or embellished with a topping, focaccia is the ideal accompaniment for an Italian meal; it also makes irresistible sandwiches when filled with meats, cheeses, or grilled vegetables. And squares of focaccia make fine crusts for mini-pizzas.

1½ CUPS WARM WATER (105° TO 115° F)

1 PACKAGE ACTIVE DRY YEAST

1 TEASPOON SUGAR

ABOUT 3¾ CUPS ALL-PURPOSE FLOUR OR 3½ CUPS
   BREAD FLOUR

5 TABLESPOONS EXTRAVIRGIN OLIVE OIL

1½ TEASPOONS TABLE SALT

1 TEASPOON KOSHER SALT OR COARSE SEA SALT

1 In large bowl, combine ½ cup warm water, yeast, and sugar; stir to dissolve. Let stand 5 minutes, or until foamy. Add remaining 1 cup warm water, flour, 2 tablespoons oil, and table salt; stir to combine.

2 Turn dough onto lightly floured surface and knead 7 minutes, or until smooth and elastic (dough will be soft; do not add more flour). Shape dough into ball; place in greased large bowl, turning dough over to coat. Cover bowl and let stand in warm place (80° to 85° F) until doubled, about 1 hour.

3 Lightly oil 15½" by 10½" jelly-roll pan. Punch down dough and pat into prepared pan. Cover and let rise in warm place until doubled, about 45 minutes. With fingertips, make deep indentations, 1 inch apart, over entire surface of dough, almost to bottom of pan. Drizzle with remaining 3 tablespoons oil; sprinkle with kosher salt. Cover loosely and let rise in warm place until doubled, about 45 minutes.

4 Preheat oven to 450° F. Bake focaccia on lowest rack 18 minutes, or until bottom is crusty and top is lightly browned. With wide spatula, transfer focaccia from pan to wire rack to cool. *Makes 12 servings.*

EACH SERVING: ABOUT 205 CALORIES, 4 G PROTEIN, 31 G CARBOHYDRATE, 7 G TOTAL FAT (1 G SATURATED), 1 G FIBER, 0 MG CHOLESTEROL, 415 MG SODIUM.

RED PEPPER FOCACCIA Prepare dough as for Focaccia but do not sprinkle with kosher salt. In 12-inch skillet, heat *1 tablespoon olive oil* over medium heat. Add *4 red peppers,* sliced, and *¼ teaspoon salt* and cook, stirring frequently, 20 minutes, or until tender. Cool to room temperature. Spoon peppers over dough. Bake as directed.

EACH SERVING: ABOUT 220 CALORIES, 5 G PROTEIN, 32 G CARBOHYDRATE, 8 G TOTAL FAT (1 G SATURATED), 2 G FIBER, 0 MG CHOLESTEROL, 340 MG SODIUM.

ONION FOCACCIA Prepare dough as for Focaccia but do not sprinkle with kosher salt. In 12-inch skillet, heat *2 teaspoons olive oil* over medium heat. Add *2 large onions (about 1 pound),* halved and sliced, *1 teaspoon sugar,* and *½ teaspoon salt* and cook, stirring frequently, 20 minutes, or until golden brown. Cool to room temperature. Spoon onions over dough. Bake as directed.

EACH SERVING: ABOUT 225 CALORIES, 5 G PROTEIN, 34 G CARBOHYDRATE, 8 G TOTAL FAT (1 G SATURATED), 2 G FIBER, 0 MG CHOLESTEROL, 390 MG SODIUM.

HERB FOCACCIA Prepare dough as for Focaccia; just before baking, sprinkle dough with either *2 tablespoons chopped fresh sage* or *1 tablespoon chopped fresh rosemary.* Bake as directed.

EACH SERVING: ABOUT 205 CALORIES, 4 G PROTEIN, 31 G CARBOHYDRATE, 7 G TOTAL FAT (1 G SATURATED), 1 G FIBER, 0 MG CHOLESTEROL, 415 MG SODIUM.

DRIED TOMATO & OLIVE FOCACCIA Prepare dough as for Focaccia but sprinkle with only *½ teaspoon kosher salt.* Pit *½ cup Gaeta olives* and coarsely chop with *¼ cup oil-packed dried tomatoes,* drained. Sprinkle mixture over dough. Bake as directed.

EACH SERVING: ABOUT 235 CALORIES, 5 G PROTEIN, 33 G CARBOHYDRATE, 10 G TOTAL FAT (1 G SATURATED), 2 G FIBER, 0 MG CHOLESTEROL, 570 MG SODIUM.

Red Pepper Focaccia

Fougasse

PREP 25 MINUTES PLUS RISING / BAKE 20 TO 25 MINUTES

Baked in the form of a big, handsome leaf, fougasse is a simple yet festive bread. Vary it with different flavorings (see below), and use only white flour (bread or all-purpose) if you'd rather not use whole-wheat.

1¾ CUPS WARM WATER (105° TO 115° F)

1½ TEASPOONS ACTIVE DRY YEAST

ABOUT 4½ CUPS ALL-PURPOSE FLOUR OR 4 CUPS BREAD
   FLOUR

½ CUP WHOLE-WHEAT FLOUR

1½ TEASPOONS TABLE SALT

¼ CUP OLIVE OIL

½ TEASPOON KOSHER OR COARSE SEA SALT

1 In large bowl, combine 1½ cups warm water, 1 teaspoon yeast, 1 cup all-purpose or bread flour, and whole-wheat flour. Whisk until smooth. Cover bowl with plastic wrap and set aside to let sponge rise 2 to 4 hours or overnight. If letting sponge rise overnight, refrigerate.

2 In cup, combine remaining ¼ cup warm water and remaining ½ teaspoon yeast; stir to dissolve. Add yeast mixture, 1½ cups all-purpose or bread flour, table salt, and 2 tablespoons olive oil to sponge. Beat vigorously with wooden spoon. Gradually stir in 1½ cups all-purpose flour or 1 cup bread flour to make a soft sticky dough.

3 Turn dough onto lightly floured surface. Knead 8 minutes, until smooth and elastic, working in remaining ½ cup flour as needed just to keep dough from sticking (dough should be soft). Place dough in a greased large bowl, and turn to grease top. Cover bowl and let rise in a warm place (80° to 85° F) until doubled, about 1 hour.

4 Grease 2 large cookie sheets. Punch down dough and divide in half. Knead each half into a smooth ball, cover, and let rest 5 minutes. On lightly floured

Olive Fougasse

surface, with floured rolling pin, roll 1 piece at a time into 13" by 8" oval. Place on prepared cookie sheet. With serrated knife, make three 3-inch-long slits lengthwise down center of oval, leaving 1 inch between slits. Make 5 diagonal 2½-inch slits on each side of center slit to resemble leaf pattern. Stretch dough to widen slashes so they will remain open during baking. Repeat with remaining dough. Cover and let rise 20 minutes.

5 Preheat oven to 425° F. Gently brush each loaf with 1 tablespoon remaining olive oil and sprinkle with kosher salt. Bake 20 to 25 minutes, rotating sheets between upper and lower racks halfway through baking, until browned. Transfer to wire rack to cool. *Makes 2 loaves, 8 slices each.*

EACH SLICE: ABOUT 180 CALORIES, 4 G PROTEIN, 30 G CARBOHYDRATE, 5 G TOTAL FAT (1 G SATURATED), 2 G FIBER, 0 MG CHOLESTEROL, 265 MG SODIUM.

OLIVE FOUGASSE Prepare dough as for Fougasse through Step 3. Pit and chop *1 cup mixed Kalamata, salt-cured, and green olives.* After punching down dough in Step 4, knead in olives. Shape loaves, cut slits, and brush with oil, but omit kosher salt. Bake as directed.
EACH SLICE: ABOUT 200 CALORIES, 4 G PROTEIN, 31 G CARBOHYDRATE, 6 G TOTAL FAT (1 G SATURATED), 2 G FIBER, 0 MG CHOLESTEROL, 395 MG SODIUM.

BACON FOUGASSE Prepare dough as for Fougasse through Step 3. In large skillet, cook *8 ounces slab or thick-sliced bacon,* cut into ⅜-inch pieces, over medium heat, 8 to 10 minutes, until browned. With slotted spoon, transfer to plate and cool. After punching down dough in Step 4, knead in bacon. Shape loaves, cut slits, and brush with oil, but omit kosher salt. Bake as directed.
EACH SLICE: ABOUT 205 CALORIES, 6 G PROTEIN, 30 G CARBOHYDRATE, 7 G TOTAL FAT (1 G SATURATED), 2 G FIBER, 3 MG CHOLESTEROL, 280 MG SODIUM.

HERB FOUGASSE Prepare dough as for Fougasse through Step 3. After punching down dough in Step 4, knead in *1 tablespoon chopped fresh rosemary, sage, or thyme (or 1 teaspoon each).* Shape loaves, cut slits, brush with oil, and sprinkle with kosher salt. On each loaf, place *6 fresh sage leaves.* Bake as directed.
EACH SLICE: ABOUT 185 CALORIES, 4 G PROTEIN, 31 G CARBOHYDRATE, 5 G TOTAL FAT (1 G SATURATED), 2 G FIBER, 0 MG CHOLESTEROL, 220 MG SODIUM.

Sausage Calzones

PREP 45 MINUTES PLUS RISING / BAKE 30 TO 35 MINUTES

A pizza-parlor specialty, these half-moon turnovers are stuffed with a "three-cheese-plus" filling—the plus is either sausage, as here, or spinach (see page 148). Served hot from the oven, with a salad alongside, calzones make an excellent supper.

BASIC PIZZA DOUGH (PAGE 141)
8 OUNCES SWEET OR HOT ITALIAN SAUSAGE LINKS, CASINGS REMOVED
1 SMALL ONION, FINELY CHOPPED
1 GARLIC CLOVE, FINELY CHOPPED
1 CONTAINER (15 OUNCES) PART-SKIM RICOTTA CHEESE
2 OUNCES PART-SKIM MOZZARELLA CHEESE, SHREDDED (½ CUP)
⅓ CUP FRESHLY GRATED PARMESAN CHEESE
⅛ TEASPOON GROUND BLACK PEPPER
CORNMEAL
1 TABLESPOON OLIVE OIL

1 Prepare Basic Pizza Dough as directed through Step 3.

2 While dough is rising, prepare filling: In 10-inch skillet, cook sausage, onion, and garlic over medium heat, stirring to break up sausage, about 8 minutes, or until browned. With slotted spoon, transfer sausage mixture to large bowl. Stir in ricotta, mozzarella, Parmesan, and pepper until blended.

3 Preheat oven to 450° F. Sprinkle large cookie sheet with cornmeal.

4 Divide dough into 6 equal pieces. On lightly floured surface, with floured rolling pin, roll each piece of dough into 6-inch round. Spoon about ⅔ cup filling onto half of each round, leaving ½-inch border. Fold uncovered half over filling and pinch edges together firmly. With back of fork, press edges to seal. Brush with oil. Repeat with remaining dough, filling, and oil.

5 Place turnovers on prepared cookie sheet on bottom rack in oven. Bake 30 to 35 minutes, until golden. Transfer to wire rack and let cool 5 minutes before serving. *Makes 6 main-dish servings.*

EACH SERVING: ABOUT 670 CALORIES, 28 G PROTEIN, 77 G CARBOHYDRATE, 27 G TOTAL FAT (10 G SATURATED), 3 G FIBER, 57 MG CHOLESTEROL, 1280 MG SODIUM.

SPINACH-CHEESE CALZONES Prepare dough as for Basic Pizza Dough (page 141) through Step 3. In Step 2 (page 147), omit sausage. In 10-inch skillet, cook onion and garlic in *1 tablespoon olive oil* over medium heat 8 minutes, or until onion is tender. Meanwhile, cook *1 package (10 ounces) frozen chopped spinach* as label directs; squeeze dry. Add spinach to skillet and cook, stirring, 5 minutes, until heated through. Transfer mixture to large bowl; stir in ricotta, mozzarella, Parmesan, and pepper as directed in Step 2; add *¼ teaspoon salt* and *pinch ground nutmeg*. Roll dough, fill, and bake as directed.

EACH SERVING: ABOUT 590 CALORIES, 24 G PROTEIN, 79 G CARBOHYDRATE, 20 G TOTAL FAT (7 G SATURATED), 4 G FIBER, 32 MG CHOLESTEROL, 1145 MG SODIUM.

SWEET BREADS & BUNS

Sweet yeast breads are always the center of attention at brunch or coffee time. Some of our recipes are for loaves that are only mildly sweet; they could even be used for sandwich bread. Others—pastries and cakes like the Overnight Sticky Buns and Coffee Cake Braid—are unabashedly rich and sweet.

Chocolate-Cherry Bread

PREP 25 MINUTES PLUS RISING / BAKE 20 MINUTES

This contemporary classic is unique: Not overly rich, sweet, or "desserty," it nonetheless satisfies a chocolate-craver's deepest needs! Dutch-process cocoa gives the bread a darker brown color than natural cocoa.

¼ CUP WARM WATER (105° TO 115° F)

1 PACKAGE ACTIVE DRY YEAST

3 TEASPOONS GRANULATED SUGAR

⅓ CUP UNSWEETENED DUTCH-PROCESS COCOA

⅓ CUP PACKED DARK BROWN SUGAR

1¾ TEASPOONS SALT

ABOUT 3½ CUPS ALL-PURPOSE FLOUR

1 CUP FRESHLY BREWED COFFEE, COOLED TO LUKEWARM (105° TO 115° F)

4 TABLESPOONS BUTTER OR MARGARINE, SOFTENED

1 LARGE EGG, SEPARATED

¾ CUP DRIED TART CHERRIES

3 OUNCES BITTERSWEET CHOCOLATE, COARSELY CHOPPED

1 TEASPOON WATER

1 In small cup, combine warm water, yeast, and 1 teaspoon granulated sugar; stir to dissolve. Let stand 5 minutes, or until foamy.

2 In large bowl, combine cocoa, brown sugar, salt, and 3 cups flour and stir to blend.

3 With wooden spoon, stir warm coffee, butter, egg yolk (cover and refrigerate egg white to use later), and yeast mixture into flour mixture. With floured hands, knead to combine.

4 Turn dough onto lightly floured surface and knead about 10 minutes, until smooth and elastic, working in about ½ cup more remaining flour as necessary just to keep dough from sticking. Knead in cherries and chocolate.

5 Place dough in greased large bowl, turning dough over to grease top. Cover bowl and let dough rise in warm place (80° to 85° F) until doubled, about 1 hour 30 minutes.

6 Punch down dough. Turn dough onto lightly floured surface and cut in half; cover and let rest 15 minutes. Shape each dough half into 5-inch round loaf. Place loaves, about 3 inches apart, in opposite corners on ungreased large cookie sheet. Cover and let rise in warm place until doubled, about 1 hour.

7 Preheat oven to 400° F. In cup, mix reserved egg white with water. Brush egg-white mixture on tops of loaves. Sprinkle loaves with remaining 2 teaspoons granulated sugar. With serrated knife or single-edge razor blade, cut shallow "X" on top of each loaf. Bake loaves 20 minutes, or until crusty and bottoms sound hollow when lightly tapped with fingers. Transfer loaves to wire racks to cool. *Makes 2 loaves, 12 slices each.*

EACH SLICE: ABOUT 135 CALORIES, 3 G PROTEIN, 24 G CARBOHYDRATE, 4 G TOTAL FAT (2 G SATURATED), 0.5 G FIBER, 14 MG CHOLESTEROL, 200 MG SODIUM.

Portuguese Sweet Bread

PREP 15 MINUTES PLUS RISING / BAKE 35 MINUTES

Rich with eggs and butter, delicate in texture, this sweet Portuguese bread is wonderful plain or toasted.

⅓ CUP WARM WATER (105° TO 115° F)

2 PACKAGES ACTIVE DRY YEAST

1 TEASPOON PLUS ¾ CUP SUGAR

⅓ CUP MILK, HEATED TO LUKEWARM (105° TO 115° F), PLUS 2 TABLESPOONS MILK

¾ CUP BUTTER OR MARGARINE (1½ STICKS), SOFTENED

1 TEASPOON SALT

6 LARGE EGGS

ABOUT 4½ CUPS ALL-PURPOSE FLOUR

1 In large bowl, combine warm water, yeast, and 1 teaspoon sugar; stir to dissolve. Let stand 5 minutes, or until foamy.

2 With wooden spoon or mixer at low speed, stir in remaining ¾ cup sugar, ⅓ cup warm milk, butter, and salt just until blended. Stir in eggs and 1½ cups flour to make a thick batter; beat 3 minutes, scraping bowl often with rubber spatula. Stir in 2½ cups flour to make a very soft dough.

3 Turn dough onto well-floured surface and knead about 10 minutes, until smooth and elastic, working in about ½ cup more remaining flour. Shape dough into ball; place in greased large bowl, turning dough over to grease top. Cover and let rise in warm place (80° to 85° F) until doubled, about 1 hour.

4 Punch down dough. Turn dough onto lightly floured surface; cut in half. Cover and let rest 15 minutes. Grease 2 large cookie sheets.

5 Shape dough into two 6-inch round loaves. Place each loaf on a prepared cookie sheet. Cover and let rise in warm place until doubled, about 1 hour.

6 Preheat oven to 350° F. With serrated knife or single-edge razor blade, cut 3 long slashes in top of each loaf. With pastry brush, gently brush loaves with remaining milk. Bake 35 minutes, or until loaves are golden and bottoms sound hollow when lightly tapped with fingers, rotating sheets between upper and lower racks halfway through baking. Transfer to wire racks to cool. *Makes 2 loaves, 16 slices each.*

EACH SLICE: ABOUT 145 CALORIES, 3 G PROTEIN, 19 G CARBOHYDRATE, 6 G TOTAL FAT (3 G SATURATED), 0.5 G FIBER, 52 MG CHOLESTEROL, 130 MG SODIUM.

Bee-Sting Cake

PREP 40 MINUTES PLUS RISING / BAKE 20 TO 25 MINUTES

This generously sized German coffee cake is topped with a honey glaze—hence its name ("Bienenstich" in German). This cake is more traditionally baked in a round pan, but spreading the dough over a larger area gives you a greater proportion of glaze to cake—yum!

CAKE:

¼ CUP WARM WATER (105° TO 115° F)

1 PACKAGE ACTIVE DRY YEAST

1 TEASPOON PLUS ⅓ CUP SUGAR

6 TABLESPOONS BUTTER OR MARGARINE, SOFTENED

1 LARGE EGG

1 LARGE EGG YOLK

⅓ CUP MILK

1 TEASPOON VANILLA EXTRACT

¼ TEASPOON SALT

ABOUT 3 CUPS ALL-PURPOSE FLOUR

GLAZE:

⅔ CUP SUGAR

½ CUP BUTTER OR MARGARINE (1 STICK)

½ CUP HONEY

¼ CUP HEAVY OR WHIPPING CREAM

2 TEASPOONS FRESH LEMON JUICE

1⅓ CUPS SLICED NATURAL ALMONDS

1 Prepare Cake: In cup, combine warm water, yeast, and 1 teaspoon sugar; stir to dissolve. Let stand 5 minutes, or until foamy.

2 In large bowl, with mixer at low speed, beat butter with remaining ⅓ cup sugar, scraping bowl often with rubber spatula, until blended. Increase speed to high; beat, occasionally scraping bowl, about 3 minutes, until creamy. Reduce speed to low; beat in whole egg and egg yolk (mixture may look curdled). Beat in yeast mixture, milk, vanilla, salt, and 2½ cups flour until blended.

3 Turn dough onto lightly floured surface and knead about 5 minutes, until smooth and elastic, working in about ½ cup more remaining flour (dough will be slightly sticky).

4 Shape dough into ball; place in greased large bowl, turning dough over to grease top. Cover bowl and let rise in warm place (80° to 85° F) until doubled, about 45 minutes.

5 Punch down dough. Cover and let rest 15 minutes. Meanwhile, grease 15½" by 10½" jelly-roll pan. Line bottom and sides of pan with foil; grease foil.

6 Turn dough into pan. With hands, press dough evenly into prepared pan, making sure to press dough into corners. Cover pan and let rise in warm place until doubled, about 45 minutes.

7 Preheat oven to 375° F. Prepare Glaze: In 2-quart saucepan, heat sugar, butter, honey, and cream to boiling over medium heat, stirring frequently. Remove saucepan from heat; stir in lemon juice. Set aside 5 minutes to cool slightly.

8 Pour glaze over dough and scatter almonds over top. Place 2 sheets of foil underneath pan; crimp edges of foil to form a rim to catch any overflow during baking. Bake cake 20 to 25 minutes, until top is golden. Cool in pan on wire rack 15 minutes. Run small knife between foil and edge of pan to loosen, then invert cake onto large cookie sheet. Gently peel off foil and discard. Immediately invert cake onto wire rack to cool, almond side up. *Makes 1 cake, 16 servings.*

EACH SERVING: ABOUT 335 CALORIES, 5 G PROTEIN, 42 G CARBOHYDRATE, 17 G TOTAL FAT (8 G SATURATED), 1 G FIBER, 60 MG CHOLESTEROL, 150 MG SODIUM.

Kugelhopf

PREP 25 MINUTES PLUS RISING / BAKE 35 MINUTES

Cousin to both brioche and panettone, this rich, sweet bread is made with eggs and butter, studded with raisins, crusted with almonds, and flavored with liquor. If you don't have a Kugelhopf mold (see box at right), a Bundt or tube pan will do fine. You'll note that the butter is beaten into the already-mixed dough: Be sure to have the butter at room temperature (nice and soft) or it will be difficult to work in.

1 PACKAGE ACTIVE DRY YEAST

¾ CUP MILK, HEATED TO LUKEWARM (105° TO 115° F)

4 CUPS ALL-PURPOSE FLOUR

1 CUP GOLDEN OR DARK SEEDLESS RAISINS

2 TABLESPOONS RUM, BOURBON, OR BRANDY

⅔ CUP GRANULATED SUGAR

4 LARGE EGGS

1¼ TEASPOONS SALT

¾ CUP BUTTER OR MARGARINE (1½ STICKS), SOFTENED

½ CUP SLICED BLANCHED ALMONDS

CONFECTIONERS' SUGAR (OPTIONAL)

1 In large bowl, combine yeast, warm milk, and 1 cup flour. Whisk until smooth. Cover bowl with plastic wrap and let sponge rise in warm place 1 hour.

2 In saucepan, combine raisins and liquor of choice. Heat to boiling over high heat. Cover and cool.

3 Add 1 cup flour, granulated sugar, eggs, and salt to sponge. Beat well with wooden spoon until smooth. Gradually stir in 1½ cups flour, beating vigorously with wooden spoon. Add remaining ½ cup flour and butter, and beat well with wooden spoon, pulling and stretching dough until butter is blended in. Stir in raisins with any liquid. Cover bowl with plastic wrap and let rise in warm place (80° to 85° F) until almost doubled, about 1 hour 30 minutes.

4 Stir down dough. Generously butter 9-inch (12-cup) fluted Kugelhopf mold or Bundt pan. Sprinkle bottom and sides with almonds, covering evenly. Spoon dough into prepared pan, smoothing top. Cover pan with greased plastic wrap. Let rise in warm place until doubled and dough comes up to ½ inch from top of pan, about 1 hour 30 minutes.

5 Preheat oven to 375° F. Bake 35 minutes, covering top loosely with foil after about 30 minutes to prevent overbrowning. Cool in pan on wire rack 3 minutes. Turn out onto wire rack. Let cool completely. Before serving, sprinkle confectioners' sugar lightly on top, if desired. *Makes 1 loaf, 16 slices.*

EACH SLICE: ABOUT 300 CALORIES, 6 G PROTEIN, 41 G CARBOHYDRATE, 13 G TOTAL FAT (7 G SATURATED), 2 G FIBER, 80 MG CHOLESTEROL, 300 MG SODIUM.

Kugelhopf Mold

A traditional Austrian Kugelhopf (or Gugelhupf) mold is a deep, fluted pan with a tube in the middle. The fluting creates a handsome pattern on the surface of the bread.

Overnight Sticky Buns

PREP 1 HOUR PLUS RISING AND 12 TO 20 HOURS
REFRIGERATING / BAKE 30 MINUTES

Not just sticky but also spicy, nutty, and downright delectable, these breakfast treats should be started the night before you plan to serve them. The shaped buns slowly rise overnight in the refrigerator, all you do in the morning is bake them for 30 minutes. Wrap leftovers in foil and freeze. When you're ready for a quick breakfast or snack, reheat the still-wrapped buns in a preheated 350° F oven 15 to 20 minutes.

DOUGH:

¼ CUP WARM WATER (105° TO 115° F)

1 PACKAGE ACTIVE DRY YEAST

1 TEASPOON PLUS ¼ CUP GRANULATED SUGAR

¾ CUP MILK

4 TABLESPOONS BUTTER OR MARGARINE, SOFTENED

1 TEASPOON SALT

3 LARGE EGG YOLKS

ABOUT 4 CUPS ALL-PURPOSE FLOUR

FILLING:

½ CUP PACKED DARK BROWN SUGAR

¼ CUP DRIED CURRANTS

1 TABLESPOON GROUND CINNAMON

4 TABLESPOONS BUTTER OR MARGARINE, MELTED

TOPPING:

⅔ CUP PACKED DARK BROWN SUGAR

3 TABLESPOONS BUTTER OR MARGARINE

2 TABLESPOONS LIGHT CORN SYRUP

2 TABLESPOONS HONEY

1¼ CUPS PECANS, COARSELY CHOPPED

1 Prepare Dough: In cup, combine warm water, yeast, and 1 teaspoon granulated sugar; stir to dissolve. Let stand 5 minutes, or until foamy.

2 In large bowl, with mixer at low speed, blend yeast mixture with milk, butter, salt, egg yolks, 3 cups flour, and remaining ¼ cup granulated sugar until blended. With wooden spoon, stir in ¾ cup flour.

3 Turn dough onto lightly floured surface and knead about 5 minutes, until smooth and elastic, working in about ¼ cup more flour as necessary just to keep dough from sticking.

4 Shape dough into ball; place in greased large bowl, turning dough over to grease top. Cover bowl and let dough rise in warm place (80° to 85° F) about 1 hour.

5 Meanwhile, prepare Filling: In small bowl, combine brown sugar, currants, and cinnamon. Reserve melted butter.

6 Prepare Topping: In 1-quart saucepan, heat brown sugar, butter, corn syrup, and honey over low heat, stirring occasionally, until butter has melted. Grease 13" by 9" metal baking pan; pour melted brown-sugar mixture into pan and sprinkle evenly with pecans; set aside.

7 Punch down dough. Turn dough onto lightly floured surface; cover and let rest 15 minutes. On lightly floured surface, with floured rolling pin, roll dough into 18" by 12" rectangle. Brush dough with reserved melted butter and sprinkle with currant mixture. Starting at one long side, roll up dough jelly-roll fashion; place, seam side down, on surface. Cut dough crosswise into 20 slices.

8 Place slices, cut side down, on topping in baking pan in 4 rows of 5 slices each. Cover pan and refrigerate at least 12 or up to 20 hours.

9 Preheat oven to 375° F. Bake buns 30 minutes, or until golden. Remove pan from oven. Immediately place serving tray or jelly-roll pan over top of baking pan and invert; remove baking pan. Let buns cool slightly to serve warm or cool completely to serve later. *Makes 20 buns.*

EACH BUN: ABOUT 290 CALORIES, 4 G PROTEIN,
42 G CARBOHYDRATE, 12 G TOTAL FAT (5 G SATURATED),
1 G FIBER, 50 MG CHOLESTEROL, 195 MG SODIUM.

CINNAMON BUNS Prepare dough and shape buns as for Overnight Sticky Buns. Omit topping but bake as directed. Invert baked buns onto cookie sheet; remove baking pan and invert buns onto wire rack. In small bowl, mix *1 cup confectioners' sugar* with *5 teaspoons water* until smooth; drizzle over hot buns.
EACH BUN: ABOUT 215 CALORIES, 4 G PROTEIN,
36 G CARBOHYDRATE, 6 G TOTAL FAT (3 G SATURATED),
1 G FIBER, 46 MG CHOLESTEROL, 170 MG SODIUM.

Old-Fashioned Crumb Cake

PREP 30 MINUTES PLUS RISING / BAKE 30 TO 35 MINUTES

Inviting guests for brunch doesn't mean you need to be up at dawn. You can give this cake its final rising in the refrigerator overnight, and bake it while you set the table and arrange a bowl of fruit. The cake will need extra baking time if it has been refrigerated.

CAKE:

¼ CUP WARM WATER (105° TO 115° F)

1 PACKAGE ACTIVE DRY YEAST

1 TEASPOON PLUS ½ CUP GRANULATED SUGAR

½ CUP MILK, HEATED TO LUKEWARM (105° TO 115° F)

½ CUP BUTTER (1 STICK), SOFTENED (DO NOT USE MARGARINE)

1 LARGE EGG

1 LARGE EGG YOLK

1½ TEASPOONS VANILLA EXTRACT

1 TEASPOON SALT

ABOUT 3¾ CUPS ALL-PURPOSE FLOUR

CRUMB TOPPING:

1 CUP ALL-PURPOSE FLOUR

⅓ CUP GRANULATED SUGAR

⅓ CUP PACKED LIGHT BROWN SUGAR

1½ TEASPOONS GROUND CINNAMON

½ CUP BUTTER (1 STICK), CUT UP AND SOFTENED (DO NOT USE MARGARINE)

1 Prepare Cake: In small bowl, combine warm water, yeast, and 1 teaspoon granulated sugar; stir to dissolve. Let stand 5 minutes, or until foamy. With wooden spoon, stir in warm milk.

2 In large bowl, with mixer at medium speed, beat remaining ½ cup granulated sugar with butter until blended, scraping bowl often with rubber spatula. Increase speed to high; beat until creamy, about 2 minutes, scraping bowl occasionally. Reduce speed to low; add egg, egg yolk, vanilla, and salt, beating well after each addition. Add yeast mixture and 1¼ cups flour until combined. Stir in 2¼ cups flour.

3 Turn dough onto lightly floured surface and knead 5 to 8 minutes, working in about ¼ cup remaining flour. Shape dough into ball; place in greased large bowl, turning dough over to grease top. Cover and let rise in warm place (80° to 85° F) until doubled, about 1 hour 30 minutes. Grease 13" by 9" metal baking pan.

4 Prepare Crumb Topping: In medium bowl, combine flour, granulated and brown sugars, and cinnamon until well blended. With fingers, work in butter until mixture resembles coarse crumbs.

5 Preheat oven to 350° F. Punch down dough. Turn dough into pan. With hands, press dough evenly into pan, making sure to press into corners. Sprinkle topping evenly over dough. Cover and let rise in warm place until doubled, about 1 hour. (Or wrap pan with plastic wrap and refrigerate overnight. The next day, remove wrap and bake 40 to 45 minutes.) Bake 30 to 35 minutes until cake and crumbs are golden brown. *Makes 16 servings.*

EACH SERVING: ABOUT 315 CALORIES, 5 G PROTEIN, 44 G CARBOHYDRATE, 13 G TOTAL FAT (8 G SATURATED), 1 G FIBER, 59 MG CHOLESTEROL, 275 MG SODIUM.

ALMOND CRUMB CAKE Prepare dough as for Old-Fashioned Crumb Cake. In Step 4, for Crumb Topping, use only *6 tablespoons butter* and add *⅓ cup almond paste*. With fingers, work mixture until it resembles coarse crumbs. Sprinkle topping over dough; let rise and bake cake as directed.

EACH SERVING: ABOUT 325 CALORIES, 5 G PROTEIN, 47 G CARBOHYDRATE, 13 G TOTAL FAT (7 G SATURATED), 1 G FIBER, 55 MG CHOLESTEROL, 260 MG SODIUM.

Coffee Cake Dough

PREP 40 MINUTES PLUS RISING / BAKE 30 TO 35 MINUTES

This sweet yeast dough is used for the Wreath and the Braid coffee cakes and for Kolaches. Whichever one you make, it will take about 4 hours—but only about 40 minutes is for hands-on work.

½ CUP WARM WATER (105° TO 115° F)

2 PACKAGES ACTIVE DRY YEAST

1 TEASPOON PLUS ½ CUP SUGAR

½ CUP BUTTER OR MARGARINE (1 STICK), SOFTENED

1 LARGE EGG

½ TEASPOON SALT

ABOUT 3¼ CUPS ALL-PURPOSE FLOUR

1 In 2-cup glass measuring cup, combine warm water, yeast, and 1 teaspoon sugar; stir to dissolve. Let stand 5 minutes, or until foamy.

2 In large bowl, with mixer at low speed, beat butter with remaining ½ cup sugar until blended. Increase speed to high; beat until creamy, about 2 minutes, scraping bowl occasionally with rubber spatula. Reduce speed to low; beat in egg until blended. Beat in yeast mixture, salt, and ½ cup flour (batter will look curdled) just until blended. With wooden spoon, stir in 2½ cups flour until blended.

3 Turn dough onto lightly floured surface and knead about 8 minutes, until smooth and elastic, working in about ¼ cup more flour as necessary just to keep dough from sticking.

4 Shape dough into ball. Place in greased large bowl, turning dough over to grease top. Cover and let rise in warm place (80° to 85° F) until doubled, about 1 hour. Follow directions for the cake shape of your choice.

Coffee Cake Wreath

PREP **40** MINUTES PLUS RISING
BAKE **30** TO **35** MINUTES

Bake this handsome wreath with your choice of fillings, then drizzle a sugar glaze on the top if you like.

COFFEE CAKE DOUGH (OPPOSITE)
CHOICE OF FILLING: LEMON-POPPYSEED (PAGE 157),
   PRUNE (PAGE 157), OR APRICOT-ORANGE (PAGE 157)
COFFEE CAKE GLAZE (OPTIONAL, AT RIGHT)

1 Prepare Coffee Cake Dough. Meanwhile, prepare filling of choice.

2 Punch down dough. Turn dough onto lightly floured surface; cover and let rest 15 minutes. Meanwhile, grease 17" by 14" cookie sheet.

3 With floured rolling pin, roll dough into 18" by 12" rectangle. Spread filling over dough to within ½ inch of edges. Starting at one long side, roll up dough jelly-roll fashion. Carefully lift roll and place, seam side down, on prepared cookie sheet. Shape roll into ring; press ends together to seal. With kitchen shears or clean scissors, cut ring at 1½-inch intervals, up to but not through inside edge (see photo at right). Gently pull and twist each cut piece to show spiral filling. Cover and let stand in warm place (80° to 85° F) until dough has risen slightly,

about 1 hour. (Dough will continue to rise during baking.)

4 Preheat oven to 350° F. Bake 30 to 35 minutes, until golden. Transfer wreath to wire rack to cool completely. When cool, drizzle with Coffee Cake Glaze, if desired. *Makes 16 servings.*

EACH SERVING WITH LEMON-POPPYSEED FILLING,
WITHOUT GLAZE: ABOUT 265 CALORIES, 5 G PROTEIN,
41 G CARBOHYDRATE, 9 G TOTAL FAT (4 G SATURATED),
3 G FIBER, 29 MG CHOLESTEROL, 155 MG SODIUM.

EACH SERVING WITH PRUNE FILLING, WITHOUT GLAZE:
ABOUT 245 CALORIES, 4 G PROTEIN, 44 G CARBOHYDRATE,
7 G TOTAL FAT (4 G SATURATED), 2 G FIBER,
29 MG CHOLESTEROL, 135 MG SODIUM.

EACH SERVING WITH APRICOT-ORANGE FILLING,
WITHOUT GLAZE: ABOUT 240 CALORIES, 4 G PROTEIN,
42 G CARBOHYDRATE, 7 G TOTAL FAT (4 G SATURATED),
2 G FIBER, 29 MG CHOLESTEROL, 140 MG SODIUM.

COFFEE CAKE GLAZE In small bowl, mix *1 cup confectioners' sugar* with *2 tablespoons milk* until smooth. With spoon, drizzle over cooled coffee cake. *Makes about 6 tablespoons.*
EACH TABLESPOON: ABOUT 80 CALORIES, 0 G PROTEIN,
20 G CARBOHYDRATE, 0 G TOTAL FAT (0 G SATURATED),
0 G FIBER, 1 MG CHOLESTEROL, 5 MG SODIUM.

Coffee Cake Wreath

To make the "petals" of the wreath, first cut deeply into the cake at 1½-inch intervals, without cutting all the way through. Then gently turn each section onto its side.

Coffee Cake Braid

PREP 40 MINUTES PLUS RISING / BAKE 30 TO 35 MINUTES

COFFEE CAKE DOUGH (PAGE 154)

CHOICE OF FILLING: CHERRY-CHEESE, SWEET ALMOND, OR
   CHOCOLATE-WALNUT (ALL ON OPPOSITE PAGE)

1 LARGE EGG

COFFEE CAKE GLAZE (OPTIONAL, PAGE 155)

1 Prepare Coffee Cake Dough. Meanwhile, prepare filling of choice.

2 Punch down dough. Turn dough onto lightly floured surface; cover and let rest 15 minutes. Meanwhile, grease large cookie sheet.

3 Place dough on prepared cookie sheet. Place damp towel under cookie sheet to keep it from moving. With floured rolling pin, roll dough into 14" by 10" rectangle. With metal spatula, spread filling in 3-inch-wide strip lengthwise down center of rectangle, leaving 1-inch border at both ends. Sprinkle walnuts over chocolate filling (or spoon cherries over cheese filling). With sharp knife, cut dough on both sides of filling crosswise into 1-inch-wide strips just to filling.

4 Fold strips at an angle across filling, alternating sides for braided effect and making sure that end of each strip is covered by the next strip so strips stay in place as dough rises. Pinch both ends of braid to seal. Cover and let stand in warm place (80° to 85° F) until dough has risen slightly, about 1 hour.

5 Preheat oven to 350° F. In cup, lightly beat egg. Brush braid with beaten egg. Bake braid 30 to 35 minutes, until golden. Transfer to wire rack to cool. Drizzle with Coffee Cake Glaze, if desired. *Makes 16 servings.*

EACH SERVING WITH SWEET ALMOND FILLING, WITHOUT GLAZE: ABOUT 260 CALORIES, 6 G PROTEIN, 34 G CARBOHYDRATE, 11 G TOTAL FAT (4 G SATURATED), 1 G FIBER, 42 MG CHOLESTEROL, 150 MG SODIUM.

EACH SERVING WITH CHOCOLATE-WALNUT FILLING, WITHOUT GLAZE: ABOUT 290 CALORIES, 6 G PROTEIN, 40 G CARBOHYDRATE, 12 G TOTAL FAT (6 G SATURATED), 2 G FIBER, 44 MG CHOLESTEROL, 155 MG SODIUM.

EACH SERVING WITH CHERRY-CHEESE FILLING, WITHOUT GLAZE: ABOUT 275 CALORIES, 6 G PROTEIN, 35 G CARBOHYDRATE, 12 G TOTAL FAT (7 G SATURATED), 1 G FIBER, 72 MG CHOLESTEROL, 210 MG SODIUM.

Coffee Cake Braid

Coffee Cake Fillings

PREP 10 TO 30 MINUTES

Customize your coffee cakes and other pastries with a variety of fillings. Fruits, nuts, cheese, spices, chocolate—they're all here, just waiting for you to choose.

SWEET ALMOND FILLING In food processor, with knife blade attached, process *½ cup whole blanched almonds* with *¼ cup packed dark brown sugar* until almonds are finely ground. Add *4 ounces almond paste* (about half 7- to 8-ounce can or tube) and *2 large egg whites* and process until mixture is smooth. *Makes about 1 cup.*

EACH TABLESPOON: ABOUT 75 CALORIES, 2 G PROTEIN, 7 G CARBOHYDRATE, 4 G TOTAL FAT (0 G SATURATED), 0.5 G FIBER, 0 MG CHOLESTEROL, 10 MG SODIUM.

LEMON-POPPYSEED FILLING In small bowl, stir *1 can (12½ ounces) poppyseed filling* with *1 teaspoon freshly grated lemon peel. Makes about 1 cup.*

EACH TABLESPOON: ABOUT 85 CALORIES, 1 G PROTEIN, 15 G CARBOHYDRATE, 2 G TOTAL FAT (0 G SATURATED), 2 G FIBER, 0 MG CHOLESTEROL, 20 MG SODIUM.

CHOCOLATE-WALNUT FILLING In 1-quart saucepan, melt *3 squares (3 ounces) semisweet chocolate* and *1 square (1 ounce) unsweetened chocolate* with *¾ cup low-fat sweetened condensed milk* over low heat until smooth. Cool to room temperature. Toast and chop *½ cup walnuts* and reserve for assembling coffee cake. *Makes about 1 cup.*

EACH TABLESPOON: ABOUT 105 CALORIES, 2 G PROTEIN, 13 G CARBOHYDRATE, 5 G TOTAL FAT (2 G SATURATED), 1 G FIBER, 2 MG CHOLESTEROL, 15 MG SODIUM.

CHEESE FILLING Into medium bowl, press *½ cup creamed cottage cheese* through fine sieve. Add *1 package (8 ounces) cream cheese*, softened, *½ cup confectioners' sugar, 1 teaspoon freshly grated lemon peel*, and *1 large egg yolk*; with mixer at low speed, beat until smooth. *Makes about 1½ cups.*

EACH TABLESPOON: ABOUT 50 CALORIES, 1 G PROTEIN, 3 G CARBOHYDRATE, 4 G TOTAL FAT (2 G SATURATED), 0 G FIBER, 20 MG CHOLESTEROL, 45 MG SODIUM.

CHERRY-CHEESE FILLING Prepare Cheese Filling (above). After spreading on dough, spoon *1 cup canned cherry-pie filling* on top. *Makes 2½ cups.*

EACH TABLESPOON: ABOUT 35 CALORIES, 1 G PROTEIN, 3 G CARBOHYDRATE, 2 G TOTAL FAT (1 G SATURATED), 0 G FIBER, 12 MG CHOLESTEROL, 30 MG SODIUM.

PRUNE FILLING In 2-quart saucepan, heat *1 cup pitted prunes*, chopped, *1¼ cups water*, and *2 strips lemon peel* (each 3" by ¾") to boiling over high heat. Reduce heat to medium-low; cook, uncovered, 12 to 15 minutes, stirring occasionally. Remove lemon peel. In food processor with knife blade attached, or blender, blend prune mixture with *6 tablespoons sugar* to form thick puree. *Makes 1 cup.*

EACH TABLESPOON: ABOUT 45 CALORIES, 0 G PROTEIN, 12 G CARBOHYDRATE, 0 G TOTAL FAT (0 G SATURATED), 1 G FIBER, 0 MG CHOLESTEROL, 0 MG SODIUM.

CINNAMON-SUGAR FILLING In small bowl, combine *½ cup packed brown sugar, ½ cup blanched almonds*, toasted and chopped, and *½ teaspoon ground cinnamon*. After rolling out dough, brush with *2 tablespoons melted butter or margarine* and sprinkle with sugar mixture. *Makes about 1 cup.*

EACH TABLESPOON: ABOUT 65 CALORIES, 1 G PROTEIN, 8 G CARBOHYDRATE, 4 G TOTAL FAT (1 G SATURATED), 0.5 G FIBER, 4 MG CHOLESTEROL, 20 MG SODIUM.

APPLE FILLING In 10-inch skillet, melt 2 tablespoons butter or margarine over medium-high heat. Add *2 medium Rome Beauty or Crispin apples (about 1¼ pounds)*, peeled, cored, and finely chopped; *¼ cup dark seedless raisins, ¼ teaspoon ground cinnamon*, and *¼ cup sugar* and cook about 10 minutes, until apples are tender. Remove from skillet and cool. *Makes about 2 cups.*

EACH TABLESPOON: ABOUT 25 CALORIES, 0 G PROTEIN, 5 G CARBOHYDRATE, 1 G TOTAL FAT (0 G SATURATED), 0.5 G FIBER, 2 MG CHOLESTEROL, 5 MG SODIUM.

APRICOT-ORANGE FILLING In 1-quart saucepan, heat *1 cup dried apricots (7 ounces)* and *1 cup water* to boiling over high heat. Reduce heat to low; cover and simmer, stirring occasionally, about 25 minutes, or until apricots have softened. Remove saucepan from heat; mash apricots with potato masher or fork until almost smooth. Stir in *⅓ cup sweet orange marmalade*, cover and refrigerate until ready to use. *Makes about 1 cup.*

EACH TABLESPOON: ABOUT 50 CALORIES, 0 G PROTEIN, 12 G CARBOHYDRATE, 0 G TOTAL FAT (0 G SATURATED), 1 G FIBER, 0 MG CHOLESTEROL, 0 MG SODIUM.

Scandinavian Tea Ring

PREP 35 MINUTES PLUS RISING / BAKE 25 MINUTES

½ CUP WARM WATER (105° TO 115° F)

1 PACKAGE ACTIVE DRY YEAST

1 TEASPOON PLUS ½ CUP GRANULATED SUGAR

½ CUP MILK

½ CUP BUTTER OR MARGARINE (1 STICK) CUT UP AND AT
    ROOM TEMPERATURE, PLUS 2 TABLESPOONS

4½ CUPS ALL-PURPOSE FLOUR

1 TEASPOON GROUND CARDAMOM (OPTIONAL)

½ TEASPOON SALT

2 LARGE EGGS

CINNAMON-SUGAR FILLING (PAGE 157)

CONFECTIONERS' GLAZE (AT RIGHT)

1 In large bowl with mixer, combine warm water, yeast, and 1 teaspoon sugar; stir to dissolve. Let stand, about 5 minutes, or until foamy.

2 In 1-quart saucepan, bring milk and ½ cup butter to simmer over medium heat. (Butter does not need to melt.)

3 With mixer at low speed, gradually beat 1 cup flour into yeast mixture. Beat in milk mixture, remaining 3½ cups flour, cardamom, if you like, and salt. Beat in eggs, beating until well combined.

4 Turn dough onto lightly floured surface and knead about 10 minutes, until smooth and elastic. Shape dough into ball; place in greased large bowl, turning dough over to grease top. Cover bowl; let rise in warm place (80° to 85° F) until doubled, about 1 hour.

5 Meanwhile, prepare Cinnamon-Sugar Filling. Punch down dough. Turn dough onto lightly floured surface; cover and let rest 15 minutes. Grease large cookie sheet. In 1-quart saucepan, melt remaining 2 tablespoons butter over medium heat.

6 On lightly floured surface, with floured rolling pin, roll dough into 18-inch square. With pastry brush, brush dough with melted butter; sprinkle with cinnamon-sugar filling. Starting at one side, roll dough up jelly-roll fashion; place, seam side down, on prepared cookie sheet. Shape roll into ring; press ends together to seal. With kitchen shears or clean scissors, cut ring at 1-inch intervals up to but not through inside edge. Gently pull and twist each cut piece to show spiral filling, arranging in slightly overlapping pattern. Cover and let rise in warm place until doubled, about 45 minutes.

7 Preheat oven to 375° F. Bake ring 25 minutes, or until golden and bread tests done. Transfer ring to wire rack to cool. When cool, drizzle with Confectioners' Glaze. *Makes 16 servings.*

EACH SERVING: ABOUT 320 CALORIES, 6 G PROTEIN, 49 G CARBOHYDRATE, 12 G TOTAL FAT (6 G SATURATED), 2 G FIBER, 49 MG CHOLESTEROL, 170 MG SODIUM.

CONFECTIONERS' GLAZE In small saucepan, melt *1 tablespoon butter* or margarine; stir in *1 cup confectioners' sugar, 2 tablespoons milk*, and *¼ teaspoon vanilla extract*. and stir until smooth. *Makes about ⅓ cup.*
EACH TABLESPOON: ABOUT 120 CALORIES, 0 G PROTEIN, 24 G CARBOHYDRATE, 3 G TOTAL FAT (2 G SATURATED), 0 G FIBER, 7 MG CHOLESTEROL, 25 MG SODIUM.

Kolaches

PREP 1 HOUR PLUS RISING / BAKE 20 MINUTES

These delicious Czechoslovakian breakfast treats can be made as triangular turnovers or round pastries.

COFFEE CAKE DOUGH (PAGE 154)

CHOICE OF FILLING: LEMON-POPPYSEED (PAGE 157),
    PRUNE (PAGE 157), OR APPLE (PAGE 157)

1 LARGE EGG

1 TEASPOON WATER

1 Prepare Coffee Cake Dough. Meanwhile, prepare filling of choice. Grease 2 large cookie sheets.

2 For foldover pastries: Divide dough in half. On lightly floured surface, with floured rolling pin, roll 1 dough half into 12-inch square. With knife, cut into 3 strips. Cut each strip crosswise into 3 squares. Place 1 rounded tablespoon filling in center of each square. Fold one corner in 2 inches to cover filling; fold opposite corner to edge. Place 2 inches apart, on prepared cookie sheets. Repeat with remaining dough and filling.

3 For round pastries: Divide dough into 12 equal pieces and shape each piece into ball. Place, 2 inches apart, on prepared cookie sheets; flatten balls slightly. With thumb, make indentation in middle of each ball and fill with 1 rounded tablespoon filling. Cover dough and let stand in warm place (80° to 85° F) until dough has risen slightly.

4 Preheat oven to 350° F. Beat egg with water; brush egg-yolk mixture over pastries. Bake 20 minutes, or until golden. Transfer to wire racks to cool. *Makes 18 foldover pastries or 12 round pastries.*

EACH FOLDOVER PASTRY WITH PRUNE FILLING: ABOUT 225 CALORIES, 4 G PROTEIN, 39 G CARBOHYDRATE, 6 G TOTAL FAT (3 G SATURATED), 2 G FIBER, 37 MG CHOLESTEROL, 125 MG SODIUM.

EACH FOLDOVER PASTRY WITH APPLE FILLING: ABOUT 205 CALORIES, 4 G PROTEIN, 32 G CARBOHYDRATE, 7 G TOTAL FAT (4 G SATURATED), 1 G FIBER, 41 MG CHOLESTEROL, 140 MG SODIUM.

EACH ROUND PASTRY WITH LEMON-POPPYSEED FILLING: ABOUT 360 CALORIES, 7 G PROTEIN, 55 G CARBOHYDRATE, 12 G TOTAL FAT (5 G SATURATED), 4 G FIBER, 56 MG CHOLESTEROL, 210 MG SODIUM.

EACH ROUND PASTRY WITH PRUNE FILLING: ABOUT 335 CALORIES, 6 G PROTEIN, 59 G CARBOHYDRATE, 9 G TOTAL FAT (5 G SATURATED), 3 G FIBER, 56 MG CHOLESTEROL, 190 MG SODIUM.

Moravian Sugar Cake

PREP 35 MINUTES PLUS RISING AND REFRIGERATING OVERNIGHT / BAKE 35 TO 40 MINUTES

Moravians (members of a Protestant sect that originated in Czechoslovakia) settled in Pennsylvania and North Carolina, bringing with them a fine heritage of baking that lives on to this day. This cake, which is made with an unusual potato-based dough, is at its most luscious when served warm.

CAKE:
12 OUNCES ALL-PURPOSE POTATOES
¼ CUP WARM WATER (105° TO 115° F)
1 PACKAGE ACTIVE DRY YEAST
1 TEASPOON PLUS ½ CUP GRANULATED SUGAR
½ CUP BUTTER OR MARGARINE (1 STICK), SOFTENED
1 LARGE EGG
¾ CUP MILK
½ TEASPOON SALT
ABOUT 5 CUPS ALL-PURPOSE FLOUR

TOPPING:
4 TABLESPOONS BUTTER OR MARGARINE, MELTED AND COOLED
1 CUP PACKED LIGHT BROWN SUGAR
2 TEASPOONS GROUND CINNAMON

1 Prepare Cake: Peel potatoes and cut into ½-inch pieces. In 2-quart saucepan, heat potatoes and enough water to cover to boiling over high heat. Reduce heat, cover, and simmer 15 minutes, or until fork-tender; drain. Mash with potato masher. You should have 1 cup mashed potatoes. Cool to room temperature.

2 Meanwhile, in cup, combine warm water, yeast, and 1 teaspoon granulated sugar; stir to dissolve. Let stand 5 minutes, or until foamy.

3 In large bowl, with mixer at low speed, beat 6 tablespoons butter until creamy. Add remaining ½ cup granulated sugar and beat until combined. Add egg, beating just until mixed. Beat in potatoes, beating just until blended. With wooden spoon, stir in milk, yeast mixture, and salt. Gradually stir in 4½ cups flour. Turn dough onto floured surface and knead 5 to 10 minutes, until smooth and elastic, working in only as much remaining ½ cup flour as necessary to keep dough from sticking (dough will be fairly sticky).

4 Shape dough into ball; place in greased large bowl, turning dough over to grease top. Cover dough and let rise in warm place (80° to 85° F) until doubled, about 1 hour 45 minutes.

5 Grease two 9-inch square metal baking pans. Melt remaining 2 tablespoons butter; cool. Punch down dough; divide in half. Pat 1 dough half into each prepared baking pan. Brush with melted butter. Cover and let rise in warm place until doubled, about 1 hour 30 minutes. With fingertips, punch holes at 1-inch intervals almost to bottom of pan.

6 Prepare Topping: Pour melted butter over both doughs. Mix brown sugar and cinnamon. Sprinkle mixture over both doughs. Cover and refrigerate overnight. (It is not necessary to bring dough to room temperature before baking the next day.)

7 Preheat oven to 350° F. Bake 35 to 40 minutes, until browned and toothpick inserted in center of cake comes out clean. Cool in pans on wire racks 10 minutes. Serve warm. *Makes 2 cakes, 12 servings each.*

EACH SERVING: ABOUT 220 CALORIES, 4 G PROTEIN, 36 G CARBOHYDRATE, 7 G TOTAL FAT (4 G SATURATED), 1 G FIBER, 25 MG CHOLESTEROL, 120 MG SODIUM.

SPECIAL YEAST BREADS

These holiday and special-occasion breads are well worth the time and effort required. Master one or more of these glorious breads, and friends and family will look forward to enjoying it every time the season rolls around.

Greek Christmas Bread

PREP 35 MINUTES PLUS RISING
BAKE 40 TO 45 MINUTES PER BATCH

Fragrant with anise, this rich holiday bread is baked as two round loaves topped with decorative crosses. The bread is delicious warm—a wonderful idea for brunch.

¾ CUP WARM WATER (105° TO 115° F)

2 PACKAGES ACTIVE DRY YEAST

1 TEASPOON PLUS 1 CUP SUGAR

1¼ CUPS MILK, HEATED TO LUKEWARM (105° TO 115° F)

1 CUP BUTTER OR MARGARINE (2 STICKS), SOFTENED

1½ TEASPOONS SALT

1 TEASPOON ANISE SEEDS, CRUSHED (OPTIONAL)

3 LARGE EGGS

ABOUT 7½ CUPS ALL-PURPOSE FLOUR

1½ CUPS DARK SEEDLESS RAISINS

2 TABLESPOONS SLICED BLANCHED ALMONDS

1 In large bowl, combine warm water, yeast, and 1 teaspoon sugar; stir to dissolve. Let stand 5 minutes, or until foamy. Add remaining 1 cup sugar, warm milk, butter, salt, anise seeds, if you like, 2 eggs, and 3 cups flour. Beat well with wooden spoon. Stir in raisins. Gradually stir in enough remaining flour (about 4 cups) to make soft dough.

2 Turn dough onto lightly floured surface and knead about 10 minutes, until smooth and elastic, working in about ½ cup more remaining flour as necessary, just to keep dough from sticking.

3 Shape dough into ball; place in greased large bowl, turning dough over to grease top. Cover bowl and let rise in warm place (80° to 85° F) until doubled, about 1 hour 30 minutes.

4 Grease 2 large cookie sheets. Punch down dough. Divide dough into 2 pieces; cover and refrigerate 1 piece. Turn dough onto lightly floured surface and cut in half. Reserve ½ cup dough from 1 piece. Shape larger piece into a smooth ball. Place in center of 1 prepared cookie sheet and press into 8-inch

Greek Christmas Bread

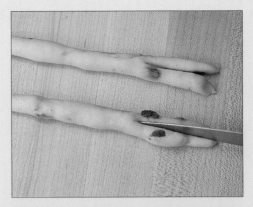

To make the decorative cross for the tops of the breads, roll balls of dough into 10-inch ropes. Split each end to a depth of 2 inches.

Place one rope of dough on the loaf, then cross it with the second rope. Shape the split tips of the ropes in a graceful curl.

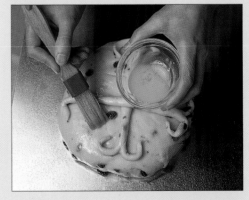

An egg wash gives the loaf a shiny finish and helps the sliced almonds to adhere.

round. Cut ½ reserved cup dough into 4 equal pieces. With hands, roll each piece into long 10-inch rope. With knife, cut 2-inch-long split in each end (see top photo opposite). Arrange ropes on loaf to form a cross; curl ends (see middle photo opposite). Cover loaf loosely with greased plastic wrap and let rise in warm place (80° to 85° F) until doubled, 45 to 60 minutes. After 45 minutes, remove remaining dough from refrigerator and repeat shaping; place on remaining cookie sheet. Cover and let rise in warm place until doubled, 45 to 60 minutes.

5 Preheat oven to 350° F. In small cup, with fork, beat remaining egg. Brush first loaf with beaten egg (see bottom photo opposite); sprinkle with half of sliced almonds. Bake 40 to 45 minutes, until bottom sounds hollow when lightly tapped with fingers, covering loaf loosely with foil to prevent overbrowning after 30 minutes. Transfer loaf to wire rack to cool. When second loaf has risen, brush with egg and sprinkle with remaining almonds; bake as above. *Makes 2 loaves, 12 slices each.*

EACH SLICE: ABOUT 295 CALORIES, 6 G PROTEIN, 47 G CARBOHYDRATE, 10 G TOTAL FAT (5 G SATURATED), 2 G FIBER, 49 MG CHOLESTEROL, 240 MG SODIUM.

Baba au Rhum

PREP 25 MINUTES PLUS RISING AND STANDING
BAKE 25 MINUTES

It's kin to Kugelhopf and to the Polish yeast cake called babka, but baba au rhum has a major difference. It's soaked with a rum syrup after baking.

CAKE:
⅔ CUP MILK, HEATED TO LUKEWARM (105° F TO 115° F)
1 TEASPOON ACTIVE DRY YEAST
1 TEASPOON PLUS 1 TABLESPOON SUGAR
2 CUPS ALL-PURPOSE FLOUR
1 TEASPOON SALT
3 LARGE EGGS
6 TABLESPOONS BUTTER OR MARGARINE, MELTED AND
    COOLED

SYRUP:
1½ CUPS WATER
1 CUP SUGAR

6 STRIPS (3" BY ½" EACH) ORANGE PEEL
⅓ CUP DARK RUM
1 TEASPOON VANILLA EXTRACT

1 Prepare Cake: In large bowl, combine warm milk, yeast, and 1 teaspoon sugar; stir to dissolve. Let stand 5 minutes, or until foamy. Stir in flour, salt, and eggs until well combined. Cover and let rise in warm place (80° F to 85° F) until doubled, about 1 hour. With wooden spoon, stir in melted butter, stirring about 5 minutes, until batter is thick, smooth, and elastic.

2 Grease and flour 9- to 10-inch tube pan. Spoon batter into pan, cover, and let rise in warm place until doubled, about 45 minutes.

3 Preheat oven to 375° F. Bake cake 25 minutes, or until golden brown and toothpick inserted in center of cake comes out clean. Cool in pan on wire rack 5 minutes; remove from pan to wire rack.

4 Prepare Syrup: In 3-quart saucepan, stir together water, sugar, and orange peel over medium heat. Heat to boiling; boil 1 minute. Strain and discard orange peel. Stir in rum and vanilla.

5 Transfer warm cake to deep-dish pie plate. With skewer or toothpick, prick cake several times. Spoon 1½ cups warm syrup over cake. Continue spooning syrup over top. Let stand 20 minutes before serving. Serve warm or at room temperature. Pass remaining syrup with cake. *Makes 12 servings.*

EACH SERVING: ABOUT 250 CALORIES, 4 G PROTEIN, 36 G CARBOHYDRATE, 8 G TOTAL FAT (4 G SATURATED), 0.5 G FIBER, 71 MG CHOLESTEROL, 275 MG SODIUM.

THE STORY OF BABA

IT'S A RATHER COMPLICATED TALE THAT BEGINS WITH A POLISH KING (STANISLAS) IN EXILE IN FRANCE. HE FOUND THE TRADITIONAL SWEET YEAST BREADS (SUCH AS KUGELHOPF) TOO DRY FOR HIS TASTE AND CAME UP WITH THE IDEA OF SOAKING THEM IN RUM. AS REFINED BY HIS PASTRY CHEF, THE RECIPE BECAME A BRIOCHE DOUGH BAKED IN A CYLINDRICAL MOLD (OR MOLDS, FOR INDIVIDUAL SERVINGS); AFTER BAKING, THE BABA IS DRENCHED IN A SWEET RUM SYRUP.

Stollen

As holiday breads go, a stollen is modest in appearance—no fancy braids, just a gracefully folded oval of dough—and it is dear to the hearts of Germans and German-Americans at Christmas.

½ CUP WARM WATER (105° TO 115° F)

2 PACKAGES ACTIVE DRY YEAST

1 TEASPOON PLUS ½ CUP GRANULATED SUGAR

2 LARGE EGGS

1 CUP MILK, HEATED TO LUKEWARM (105° TO 115° F)

¾ CUP BUTTER OR MARGARINE (1½ STICKS), SOFTENED

1½ TEASPOONS SALT

ABOUT 6 CUPS ALL-PURPOSE FLOUR

1 CUP SLIVERED ALMONDS, TOASTED

1 CUP CANDIED CHERRIES, COARSELY CHOPPED

½ CUP DICED CANDIED CITRON OR CANDIED LEMON PEEL

½ CUP GOLDEN RAISINS

CONFECTIONERS' SUGAR

1 In large bowl, combine warm water, yeast, and 1 teaspoon granulated sugar; stir to dissolve. Let stand 5 minutes, or until foamy. Add remaining ½ cup granulated sugar, eggs, warm milk, butter, salt, and 4 cups flour; beat well with wooden spoon until combined. Gradually stir in enough flour (about 1½ cups) to make soft dough.

2 Turn dough onto floured surface and knead 8 minutes, until smooth and elastic, working in ½ cup more remaining flour as necessary just to keep dough from sticking. Knead in almonds, cherries, citron, and raisins.

3 Shape dough into ball. Place in greased bowl, turning dough over to grease top. Cover bowl and let dough rise in warm place (80° to 85° F) until doubled, about 1 hour 30 minutes.

4 Grease 1 large and 1 small cookie sheet. Punch down dough. Turn dough onto lightly floured surface and cut into thirds. Cover and refrigerate 1 piece of dough. With floured rolling pin, shape each remaining piece of dough into 12" by 7" oval. Fold each oval lengthwise in half. Place, about 3 inches apart, on large cookie sheet. Cover and let rise in warm place until doubled, 1 hour to 1 hour 30 minutes. After 30 minutes of rising, remove remaining dough from refrigerator and repeat shaping; place on small cookie sheet. Cover and let rise in warm place until doubled, 1 hour to 1 hour 30 minutes.

5 Preheat oven to 350° F. Bake 25 to 30 minutes, until browned. Cool on wire racks. Bake remaining loaf 25 to 30 minutes, until golden brown; cool on wire rack. Sprinkle with confectioners' sugar before serving. *Makes 3 loaves, 8 slices each.*

EACH SLICE: ABOUT 285 CALORIES, 6 G PROTEIN, 43 G CARBOHYDRATE, 10 G TOTAL FAT (4 G SATURATED), 1 G FIBER, 35 MG CHOLESTEROL, 230 MG SODIUM.

MARZIPAN STOLLEN Prepare dough as for Stollen through Step 3. Prepare filling: Crumble *1 tube or can (7 to 8 ounces) almond paste* into food processor with knife blade attached. Add *2 tablespoons butter or margarine, 2 tablespoons sugar,* and *1 large egg;* process until smooth. Shape dough into ovals. Spread one-third of filling lengthwise on half of each oval, leaving ½-inch border. Fold lengthwise in half, let loaves rise, and bake as directed.

EACH SLICE: ABOUT 340 CALORIES, 7 G PROTEIN, 48 G CARBOHYDRATE, 14 G TOTAL FAT (5 G SATURATED), 1 G FIBER, 46 MG CHOLESTEROL, 245 MG SODIUM.

Hot Cross Buns

Topped with a cross rendered in white icing, these buns are traditionally eaten during Lent. By arranging the buns into a tree shape (see Festive Christmas Tree Buns, opposite), they are perfect for the Yuletide, too.

1 CUP WARM WATER (105° TO 115° F)

2 PACKAGES ACTIVE DRY YEAST

1 TEASPOON PLUS ½ CUP GRANULATED SUGAR

1½ TEASPOONS GROUND CARDAMOM

1½ PLUS ⅛ TEASPOON SALT

½ CUP BUTTER OR MARGARINE (1 STICK), SOFTENED

ABOUT 4¾ CUPS ALL-PURPOSE FLOUR

2 LARGE EGGS

½ CUP GOLDEN RAISINS

½ CUP DICED MIXED CANDIED FRUIT

1 CUP CONFECTIONERS' SUGAR

4 TEASPOONS WATER

1 In large bowl, combine warm water, yeast, and 1 teaspoon granulated sugar; stir to dissolve. Let stand 5 minutes, or until foamy. Stir in cardamom, 1½ teaspoons salt, butter, remaining ½ cup granulated sugar, and 1½ cups flour. With mixer at low speed, beat just until blended.

2 Separate 1 egg and reserve white, covered, in refrigerator. Beat remaining egg, egg yolk, and ½ cup flour into flour mixture. With wooden spoon, stir in 2¼ cups flour to make soft dough.

3 Turn dough onto lightly floured surface and knead about 10 minutes, until smooth and elastic, working in about ½ cup more remaining flour as necessary just to keep dough from sticking.

4 Shape dough into a ball; place in greased large bowl, turning dough over to grease top. Cover bowl and let rise in warm place (80° to 85° F) until doubled, about 1 hour.

5 Punch down dough. Knead in raisins and candied fruit. Cut dough into 25 equal pieces; let rest 15 minutes on surface for easier shaping.

6 Grease large cookie sheet. Shape dough into balls. Arrange balls, ½ inch apart, in square, on prepared cookie sheet. Cover loosely and let rise in warm place until doubled, about 40 minutes.

7 Preheat oven to 375° F. In cup, with fork, beat reserved egg white with remaining ⅛ teaspoon salt. Brush buns with egg white. Bake 20 to 25 minutes, until golden and bottoms sound hollow when lightly tapped with fingers. Transfer to wire rack to cool.

8 When buns are cool, prepare icing: In small bowl, mix confectioners' sugar and water until smooth. Spoon icing into small zip-tight plastic bag; snip off one corner and pipe a cross on each bun. Let icing set before serving. *Makes 25 buns.*

EACH BUN: ABOUT 190 CALORIES, 3 G PROTEIN, 34 G CARBOHYDRATE, 5 G TOTAL FAT (3 G SATURATED), 1 G FIBER, 27 MG CHOLESTEROL, 210 MG SODIUM.

FESTIVE CHRISTMAS TREE BUNS Prepare dough as for Hot Cross Buns and shape into 25 balls as directed. To make Christmas tree: Place 1 dough ball at top of lightly greased large cookie sheet. Make a second row by centering 2 dough balls directly under first ball and placing balls about ¼ inch apart to allow space for rising. Continue making rows by increasing each row by 1 ball and centering balls directly under previous row, until there are 6 rows in all. Leave space to allow for rising. Use last 4 balls to make trunk of tree. Cover and let rise until doubled, about 40 minutes. Brush with egg-white mixture and bake as directed. When buns are cool, prepare icing and pipe in zigzag pattern over tree.

EACH BUN: ABOUT 190 CALORIES, 3 G PROTEIN, 34 G CARBOHYDRATE, 5 G TOTAL FAT (3 G SATURATED), 1 G FIBER, 27 MG CHOLESTEROL, 210 MG SODIUM.

Hot Cross Buns

Challah

PREP 30 MINUTES PLUS RISING / BAKE 30 TO 35 MINUTES

Challah is served on the Jewish sabbath and holidays.

¾ CUP WARM WATER (105° TO 115° F)
1 PACKAGE ACTIVE DRY YEAST
1 TEASPOON PLUS ¼ CUP SUGAR
3 LARGE EGGS, LIGHTLY BEATEN
¼ CUP VEGETABLE OIL
1 TEASPOON SALT
ABOUT 4¼ CUPS ALL-PURPOSE FLOUR OR ABOUT 3½ CUPS
　　BREAD FLOUR

1 In large bowl, combine warm water, yeast, and 1 teaspoon sugar; stir to dissolve. Let stand 5 minutes, or until foamy. Measure 1 tablespoon beaten egg into small cup; cover and refrigerate. Add remaining eggs, remaining ¼ cup sugar, oil, salt, and 2 cups flour to yeast mixture. Beat well with wooden spoon. Stir in about 1¾ cups all-purpose flour or 1¼ cups bread flour to make a soft dough.

2 Turn dough onto lightly floured surface and knead about 8 minutes, until smooth and elastic, working in ¼ to ½ cup more remaining all-purpose or bread flour just to keep dough from sticking.

3 Shape dough into ball; place in greased large bowl, turning dough over to grease top. Cover and let dough rise in warm place (80° to 85° F) until doubled, about 1 hour.

4 Punch down dough. Grease large cookie sheet. Turn dough onto lightly floured surface and cut two-thirds of dough into 3 equal pieces; with hands, roll each piece into a 13-inch-long rope. Place ropes side by side on cookie sheet and braid, pinching ends to seal (see top photo at right). Cut remaining one-third dough into 3 pieces. With hands, roll each piece into a 14-inch-long rope. Place ropes side by side and braid; pinch ends to seal. Place small braid on top of large braid on cookie sheet. Tuck ends of top braid under bottom braid, stretching top braid if necessary, and pinch ends to seal (see bottom photo at right). Cover loosely with greased plastic wrap and let rise in warm place until doubled, about 45 minutes.

5 Preheat oven to 375° F. Brush reserved beaten egg over top and sides of loaf. Bake loaf 30 to 35 minutes, covering loaf loosely with foil to prevent over-browning after 20 minutes if necessary, until bottom sounds hollow when lightly tapped with fingers. Transfer to wire rack to cool. *Makes 1 loaf, 12 slices.*

EACH SLICE: ABOUT 250 CALORIES, 6 G PROTEIN, 40 G CARBOHYDRATE, 7 G TOTAL FAT (1 G SATURATED), 1 G FIBER, 53 MG CHOLESTEROL, 210 MG SODIUM.

Shaping Challah

To make a double-braided challah, start by forming a large braid, using two-thirds of the dough. Form the dough into three ropes and braid them together. Pinch the ends together.

Divide the remaining portion of dough into three pieces and roll them into rope. Braid these and pinch the ends together, then place the small braid on top of the large one and tuck the ends under the bottom braid.

Croissants

PREP 1 HOUR PLUS REFRIGERATING AND RISING
BAKE 15 TO 20 MINUTES

This recipe makes 32 croissants (64 minis). A half, or quarters, of the dough could be wrapped and frozen, then thawed and baked at another time.

2 CUPS UNSALTED BUTTER (4 STICKS), CHILLED (DO NOT USE SALTED BUTTER OR MARGARINE)
½ CUP WARM WATER (105° TO 115° F)
2 PACKAGES ACTIVE DRY YEAST
2 TEASPOONS PLUS ¼ CUP SUGAR
ABOUT 4⅓ CUPS ALL-PURPOSE FLOUR
2 TEASPOONS SALT
¾ CUP MILK, HEATED TO LUKEWARM (105° TO 115° F)
1 LARGE EGG
1 TEASPOON WATER

1 Cut 2 sticks butter lengthwise in half. On sheet of waxed paper dusted with 1½ teaspoons flour, place 4 halves of butter side by side; dust butter with ½ tablespoon flour and cover with waxed paper. With rolling pin, shape butter into 6" by 9" rectangle. Place in refrigerator. Repeat with remaining 2 sticks butter and 1 tablespoon flour.

2 In cup, combine warm water, yeast, and 2 teaspoons sugar; stir to dissolve. Let stand 5 minutes, or until foamy.

3 In large bowl, with wire whisk, combine 4 cups flour, remaining ¼ cup sugar, and salt. Make well in center and stir in yeast mixture and warm milk. Turn dough onto lightly floured surface and knead 4 to 5 minutes working in just enough flour (about 2 tablespoons) to keep dough from sticking to hands. Cover with plastic wrap and let rest 10 minutes.

4 On lightly floured surface, with floured rolling pin, roll dough into 24" by 12" rectangle. Take 1 of the pieces of rolled butter, place in middle third of dough, and fold top third over it to completely cover. Place the remaining chilled butter on top of dough that covers butter and fold bottom third of dough up and over; pinch the edges together to seal the butter completely.

5 Roll the dough into 24" by 10" rectangle. Fold in short ends to meet in middle of dough, then fold in half to make 10" by 6" rectangle. Wrap dough in plastic wrap; refrigerate 20 minutes (long enough to relax the gluten in the flour but not so long that the butter becomes too hard). Roll dough to 24" by 10"

rectangle and repeat turn; refrigerate 20 minutes. Repeat rolling, folding, and refrigerating 2 more times, or 4 turns in all. Label after each turn. After fourth turn, refrigerate at least 2 hours or overnight (or freeze up to 3 months; thaw in refrigerator overnight).

6 Cut dough crosswise into 4 pieces, each about 6" by 2¼". On lightly floured surface, with floured rolling pin, roll 1 piece of dough into 18" by 6" rectangle (keep remaining dough refrigerated). On long sides, with knife, mark nicks in dough every 2¼ inches. Use nicks as guides to cut dough into isosceles triangles with 4½" bases. Enlarge nicks in center of each base to ½-inch nick for easier curving. Roll up triangles from base to point. Place croissants, 2 inches apart, on ungreased cookie sheet and curve into crescent shape. Piece remaining end scraps together to form croissant. Repeat with remaining dough. Cover and let rise at room temperature in draft-free area until slightly puffy, about 1 hour 30 minutes. (The area should not be so warm that the butter melts.)

7 Preheat oven to 375° F. In cup, with fork, mix egg and water. Brush croissants with egg mixture. Bake 15 to 20 minutes, until golden brown. Transfer to wire racks to cool. *Makes 32 croissants.*

EACH CROISSANT: ABOUT 180 CALORIES, 2 G PROTEIN, 16 G CARBOHYDRATE, 12 G TOTAL FAT (7 G SATURATED), 0.5 G FIBER, 39 MG CHOLESTEROL, 270 MG SODIUM.

MINI CROISSANTS Prepare dough as for Croissants but, in Step 6, marks nicks in dough every *1⅛ inches*; cut triangles with 2¼-inch bases. Shape and bake as directed. *Makes 64 mini croissants.*
EACH MINI CROISSANT: ABOUT 90 CALORIES, 1 G PROTEIN, 8 G CARBOHYDRATE, 6 G TOTAL FAT (4 G SATURATED), 0.5 G FIBER, 19 MG CHOLESTEROL, 135 MG SODIUM.

ALMOND CROISSANTS Prepare dough as for Croissants through Step 5. In medium bowl, with mixer at medium speed, beat *2 tubes or cans (7 or 8 ounces each) almond paste* until crumbly. Add *2 large eggs*; beat until smooth. Cut dough into triangles as directed. Place 1 tablespoon almond mixture over each triangle and spread with small flexible spatula. Roll as directed. Let rise at room temperature until puffy, 1 hour to 1 hour 30 minutes. Preheat oven to 375° F. Brush with egg mixture; sprinkle with *sliced almonds*. Bake 15 to 20 minutes, until golden brown. *Makes 32 croissants.*
EACH CROISSANT: ABOUT 265 CALORIES, 5 G PROTEIN, 22 G CARBOHYDRATE, 18 G TOTAL FAT (8 G SATURAT, 0.5 G FIBER, 58 MG CHOLESTEROL, 275 MG SODIUM

PAINS AU CHOCOLAT Prepare dough as for Croissants (page 165) through Step 5. Chop *1 pound chocolate bars, preferably bittersweet.* Cut dough into 4 pieces. Keeping remaining dough refrigerated, on floured board, with floured rolling pin, roll 1 dough piece into 16" by 9" rectangle. Cut lengthwise into 3 strips. Cut each strip crosswise into 4 rectangles, each 3" by 4". Place 1 scant tablespoon chocolate ½ inch from one short end of each rectangle. From the chocolate end, roll each up jelly-roll fashion. Place, 2 inches apart, on ungreased large cookie sheet. Repeat with remaining dough and chocolate. Let rise at room temperature until puffy, 1 hour to 1 hour 30 minutes. Preheat oven to 375° F. Brush pastries with egg mixture and sprinkle with *4 teaspoons sugar.* Bake 15 to 20 minutes, until golden brown. *Makes 48 pains au chocolat.*

EACH PAIN AU CHOCOLAT: ABOUT 165 CALORIES, 2 G PROTEIN, 16 G CARBOHYDRATE, 11 G TOTAL FAT (7 G SATURATED), 0.5 G FIBER, 26 MG CHOLESTEROL, 180 MG SODIUM.

Brioche

PREP 25 MINUTES PLUS RISING AND OVERNIGHT TO CHILL
BAKE 30 MINUTES

You really do need a heavy-duty stand mixer for this rich French classic. It's an overnight recipe—all you need to do before serving is bake the breads for 30 minutes. So knock 'em dead with brioche at brunch!

¾ CUP MILK, HEATED TO LUKEWARM (105° TO 115° F)
1 PACKAGE ACTIVE DRY YEAST
1 TEASPOON PLUS ¼ CUP SUGAR
4 CUPS BREAD OR ALL-PURPOSE FLOUR
1 TEASPOON SALT
6 LARGE EGGS
1 CUP (2 STICKS) BUTTER, SOFTENED AND CUT INTO 4
    PIECES (DO NOT USE MARGARINE)

1 In large bowl of heavy-duty mixer, combine warm milk, yeast, and 1 teaspoon sugar; stir to dissolve. Let stand 5 minutes, or until foamy.

2 Stir in 1 cup flour, remaining 1 cup sugar, and salt until blended. With mixer at low speed, beat in 1 egg. Continue alternately beating in 3 remaining cups flour, 1 cup at a time, and eggs until well incorporated. Gradually beat in butter until smooth.

3 Place dough in lightly buttered bowl. Cover with greased plastic wrap and let rise in warm place (80° to 85° F) until doubled, about 2 hours 30 minutes.

4 Meanwhile, lightly grease two 8½" by 4½" metal loaf pans. Punch down dough. Divide dough evenly between prepared pans. Cover pans with lightly greased plastic wrap; refrigerate overnight.

5 Preheat oven to 350° F. Uncover and bake loaves 30 minutes, or until toothpick inserted in center of loaves comes out clean. Remove loaves from pans and cool on wire racks. *Makes 2 loaves, 12 slices each.*

EACH SLICE: ABOUT 190 CALORIES, 5 G PROTEIN, 19 G CARBOHYDRATE, 10 G TOTAL FAT (6 G SATURATED), 0.5 G FIBER, 75 MG CHOLESTEROL, 195 MG SODIUM.

Individual Brioches

PREP 45 MINUTES PLUS RISING AND OVERNIGHT TO CHILL
BAKE 17 TO 20 MINUTES

BRIOCHE (AT LEFT)
1 LARGE EGG
1 TABLESPOON WATER

1 Prepare Brioche dough as directed through Step 3. Place dough in buttered bowl, cover, and refrigerate overnight. Punch down dough. Divide dough into 2 equal pieces. Roll each piece into 16-inch-long rope. Cut each rope into 12 equal pieces. Roll each piece into tight ball.

2 Lightly butter twenty-four ½-cup fluted individual brioche molds. Place 1 ball in front of you and, with side of hand, press almost but not quite through ⅓ of the ball., to form attached large and small balls. With your fingers, push smaller ball of dough inside larger one, pressing all around so that small ball is deeply set into large ball. Place ball, larger section down, in each prepared mold. Repeat with remaining dough. Cover molds with lightly greased plastic wrap and let rise in warm place (80° to 85° F) until doubled, about 45 minutes.

3 Preheat oven to 400° F. In cup, beat egg with water until combined. Brush tops of brioche with egg mixture, being careful not to let egg drip down sides of mold as this could inhibit rising. Place molds on 2 large cookie sheets for easier handling. Bake 17 to 20 minutes, rotating sheets between upper and

lower racks halfway through baking. until golden brown. Remove brioche from molds and cool on wire rack. *Makes 24 individual brioches.*

Almond Slices

PREP 45 MINUTES PLUS RISING AND OVERNIGHT TO CHILL
BAKE 30 MINUTES

A baked loaf of brioche is the basis for this unbelievably indulgent take on French toast.

1 BRIOCHE LOAF (OPPOSITE PAGE)
1 TUBE OR CAN (7 TO 8 OUNCES) ALMOND PASTE,
    CRUMBLED
1 TABLESPOON WATER
2 TEASPOONS VANILLA EXTRACT
3 LARGE EGGS
⅔ CUP MILK
2 TABLESPOONS GRANULATED SUGAR
½ CUP SLICED ALMONDS
1 TABLESPOON CONFECTIONERS' SUGAR

1 Prepare 1 Brioche Loaf and let cool. Trim crusts from ends; slice loaf into 8 slices.

2 Preheat oven to 350° F. Butter large cookie sheet.

3 In large bowl, with mixer at medium speed, beat almond paste, water, and 1 teaspoon vanilla until well combined and smooth. Spread a scant tablespoon of almond mixture on one side of each brioche slice, spreading almost to edges.

4 In shallow bowl, whisk together eggs, milk, granulated sugar, and remaining 1 teaspoon vanilla. Dip both sides of brioche slices in egg mixture, until soaked, but not falling apart (about 1 minute total). Place, almond paste side up, on prepared cookie sheet; sprinkle with almonds. Bake 30 minutes, or until golden brown and firm. Sprinkle confectioners' sugar over slices. Transfer slices to wire rack and cool 10 minutes. Sprinkle with confectioners' sugar. *Makes 8 servings.*

Panettone

PREP 35 MINUTES PLUS RISING
BAKE 30 TO 35 MINUTES

Tall, domed loaves of panettone are often given as Christmas gifts. Commercially-made versions of this festive bread are widely available—which makes homemade panettone all the more special. Beat the dough by hand or use a heavy-duty stand mixer.

½ CUP MILK, HEATED TO LUKEWARM (105° TO 115° F)
1 PACKAGE ACTIVE DRY YEAST
3¼ CUPS ALL-PURPOSE FLOUR
½ CUP BUTTER OR MARGARINE (1 STICK), SOFTENED
½ CUP SUGAR
1 TABLESPOON FRESHLY GRATED ORANGE PEEL
1½ TEASPOONS VANILLA EXTRACT
½ TEASPOON SALT
3 LARGE EGGS
½ CUP GOLDEN RAISINS
⅓ CUP CHOPPED CANDIED LEMON PEEL
VEGETABLE SHORTENING FOR GREASING COFFEE CANS

1 In medium bowl, combine warm milk, yeast, and ½ cup flour. Cover bowl and let stand 45 minutes. (Mixture will bubble and rise.)

2 In bowl of heavy-duty stand mixer, with mixer at medium speed, beat butter, sugar, orange peel, vanilla, and salt until light and fluffy. Alternately beat in eggs and remaining 2¾ cups flour until well combined. Beat in yeast mixture. Stir in raisins and candied lemon peel. Place dough in greased large bowl, turning dough over to grease top. Cover bowl and let rise in warm place (80° to 85° F) until doubled, about 2 hours.

3 Meanwhile, brush insides of 2 clean 11½-ounce coffee cans with shortening. Punch down dough and divide between 2 cans. Cover cans and let rise in warm place until doubled and dough has risen almost to top of cans, 1 hour 15 minutes to 2 hours.

4 Preheat oven to 350° F. Bake breads about 30 to 35 minutes, until golden brown and skewer inserted in center of each loaf comes out clean. Remove from cans to cool on wire rack. To serve, cut into wedges. *Makes 2 loaves, 8 wedges each.*

Soufflés, Custards & Baked Desserts

Soufflés, Custards & Baked Desserts

soufflé dish

ramekins

baking dish

When a cake or pie isn't elegant enough, it's time for a high and handsome soufflé. And when a plate of cookies doesn't warm your soul, you may crave a soothing custard or pudding. Although a bread pudding or a cobbler can be baked in any sizeable glass or ceramic baking dish, some desserts call for more specific items. For the soufflés in this chapter, you'll need a 2-quart **soufflé dish**. Shown here is the classic French white porcelain model, but soufflé dishes also come in stoneware and glass (these make attractive salad bowls, too). The porcelain **ramekins** are miniatures of the larger soufflé dish and come in various sizes. Available, too, are other small ovenproof dishes made of clear glass. The heatproof glass **custard cups** are just right for individual servings of pudding or crème caramel. They all are extremely handy in the kitchen for storing leftovers and for holding pre-measured ingredients at the ready—no doubt you've seen television chefs using them. Sturdy **baking dishes** can go directly from oven to table holding a family-size cobbler or crisp. Milk-based desserts and those made with acidic fruits should be baked in glass or ceramic. Standard sizes are 8" by 8", 11" by 7", and 13" by 9".

Previous page: Rhubarb-Strawberry Cobbler

Basic techniques

SOUFFLÉS

Coating the greased soufflé dish with sugar or bread crumbs gives the batter something to "hold onto" as it rises.

A soufflé begins with a "white sauce" made from milk and flour that is enriched with egg yolks. Then stiffly beaten egg whites are folded in.

Tracing a circle around the top of the soufflé mixture will help it pouf to the maximum impressive height.

CRÈME CARAMEL

When making crème caramel, pour the hot caramel into the dishes first; then prepare the custard and pour it on top. When the custards are turned out, the caramel will be on top.

BAKING IN A BAIN-MARIE

Set the custard cups in a roasting pan and place it in the oven. Carefully pour boiling water from a teakettle into the pan until the water reaches half the height of the cups.

MERINGUE SHELL

Depending on the recipe, sugar is added to the egg whites after they've been beaten until foamy, or when they've reached the soft-peak stage. Either way, add the sugar gradually, just a tablespoonful or two at a time.

Using a toothpick, trace a circle onto a sheet of foil (use a plate as a pattern). Spoon the meringue onto the foil, then spread it to the size of the circle, using the back of a spoon.

After baking and cooling the meringue completely, carefully peel off the foil.

SOUFFLÉS

To repeat the oft-quoted (but eternally true) maxim about serving a soufflé: "You wait for the soufflé, the soufflé doesn't wait for you." These high-rise creations must be served as soon as they come out of the oven, or they'll deflate. A deflated soufflé is perfectly delicious, but it's hardly a show-stopper, so plan to have your guests (or lucky family) sitting at the table when the timer goes off. If you put a sweet soufflé in the oven when you serve the entrée, your dessert should be ready at just the right moment for serving.

Classic Cheese Soufflé

PREP 25 MINUTES / BAKE 55 TO 60 MINUTES

The flavor of this classic soufflé can be varied by using different cheeses. Well-aged Cheddar adds bold, sharp flavor, while nutty-sweet Gruyère is more subtle (and more traditionally French). Stirring some of the hot cheese sauce into the egg yolks before adding the slightly warmed yolks to the sauce helps keep the eggs from curdling. Don't short-cut this step!

4 TABLESPOONS BUTTER OR MARGARINE
¼ CUP ALL-PURPOSE FLOUR
¼ TEASPOON SALT
⅛ TEASPOON GROUND RED PEPPER (CAYENNE)
1½ CUPS MILK
8 OUNCES SHARP CHEDDAR CHEESE, SHREDDED (2 CUPS)
5 LARGE EGGS, SEPARATED
2 TABLESPOONS PLAIN DRIED BREAD CRUMBS OR FRESHLY
   GRATED PARMESAN CHEESE
1 LARGE EGG WHITE

1 In 3-quart saucepan, melt butter over low heat. Stir in flour, salt, and ground red pepper until blended; cook, stirring, 1 minute. Gradually stir in milk; cook, stirring constantly, until mixture boils and thickens. Stir in Cheddar; cook, stirring, just until cheese melts. Remove saucepan from heat.

2 In small bowl, with wire whisk or fork, beat egg yolks slightly; stir in small amount hot cheese sauce. Gradually pour egg-yolk mixture into cheese sauce, stirring rapidly to prevent curdling. Cool slightly.

3 Preheat oven to 325° F. Grease 2-quart soufflé dish; sprinkle with bread crumbs or Parmesan.

4 In large bowl, with mixer at high speed, beat egg whites until stiff peaks form when beaters are lifted. With rubber spatula, gently fold one-third of whites into cheese mixture. Fold cheese mixture gently back into remaining whites.

5 Pour mixture into prepared soufflé dish. With back of spoon, about 1 inch from edge of dish, make 1-inch-deep indentation all around in soufflé mixture. Bake 55 to 60 minutes, until knife inserted under "top hat" comes out clean. Serve immediately. *Makes 6 main-dish servings.*

EACH SERVING: ABOUT 355 CALORIES, 18 G PROTEIN, 9 G CARBOHYDRATE, 27 G TOTAL FAT (15 G SATURATED), 0 G FIBER, 246 MG CHOLESTEROL, 520 MG SODIUM.

CORN & PEPPERJACK SOUFFLÉ Grease 2½- to 3-quart soufflé dish. Prepare as for Classic Cheese Soufflé but, in Step 1, after mixture boils and thickens, cook 2 minutes, stirring frequently. Use *8 ounces Monterey Jack cheese with jalapeño chiles,* shredded (2 cups), for Cheddar; stir *1 cup fresh corn kernels* into cheese mixture before folding in egg whites. Bake as directed.
EACH SERVING: ABOUT 375 CALORIES, 19 G PROTEIN, 15 G CARBOHYDRATE, 27 G TOTAL FAT (14 G SATURATED), 1 G FIBER, 246 MG CHOLESTEROL, 540 MG SODIUM.

GRUYÈRE-SPINACH SOUFFLÉ Prepare as for Classic Cheese Soufflé but use *8 ounces Gruyère cheese,* shredded (2 cups), for Cheddar; stir *1 package (10 ounces) frozen chopped spinach,* thawed and squeezed dry, into cheese mixture before folding in egg whites. Use *pinch ground nutmeg* for ground red pepper. Bake as directed.
EACH SERVING: ABOUT 370 CALORIES, 21 G PROTEIN, 11 G CARBOHYDRATE, 27 G TOTAL FAT (15 G SATURATED), 1 G FIBER, 248 MG CHOLESTEROL, 445 MG SODIUM.

SOUTHWESTERN SOUFFLÉ Prepare as for Classic Cheese Soufflé but use *8 ounces Monterey Jack cheese,* shredded (2 cups), for Cheddar and stir *½ cup chopped cooked ham* into cheese mixture before folding in egg whites. Bake as directed.
EACH SERVING: ABOUT 365 CALORIES, 21 G PROTEIN, 9 G CARBOHYDRATE, 27 G TOTAL FAT (15 G SATURATED), 0 G FIBER, 253 MG CHOLESTEROL, 660 MG SODIUM.

Tomato Soufflé

Serve this rosy soufflé as the main dish for a light (but impressive) summer supper; or offer it as a side dish with simply cooked chicken or fish. This is really a summer recipe—you wouldn't want to bother making it without fresh, flavorful, vine-ripened tomatoes.

1 TABLESPOON VEGETABLE OIL
1 MEDIUM ONION, CHOPPED
2 POUNDS RIPE TOMATOES, PEELED AND FINELY CHOPPED,
    JUICES RESERVED
½ TEASPOON SUGAR
¼ TEASPOON GROUND BLACK PEPPER
1¼ TEASPOONS SALT
4 TABLESPOONS BUTTER OR MARGARINE
¼ CUP ALL-PURPOSE FLOUR
1¼ CUPS MILK
1 TABLESPOON PLAIN DRIED BREAD CRUMBS
6 LARGE EGGS, SEPARATED
2 TABLESPOONS FRESHLY GRATED PARMESAN CHEESE

1 In 12-inch skillet, heat oil over medium heat. Add onion and cook, stirring, 10 minutes, or until tender. Add tomatoes with their juice, sugar, pepper, and ½ teaspoon salt. Increase heat to high and cook, stirring, 15 minutes, or until all juices have evaporated.

2 Meanwhile, in 2-quart saucepan, melt butter over low heat. Stir in flour and remaining ¾ teaspoon salt until blended; cook, stirring, 1 minute. Gradually stir in milk and cook, stirring constantly, until mixture boils and thickens. Remove saucepan from heat; stir in tomato mixture until blended.

3 Preheat oven to 325° F. Grease 2-quart soufflé dish; sprinkle evenly with bread crumbs.

4 In large bowl, with wire whisk or fork, beat egg yolks slightly; stir in small amount hot tomato mixture. Gradually pour egg-yolk mixture into tomato mixture, stirring rapidly to prevent curdling. Pour mixture back into bowl.

5 In clean large bowl, with mixer at high speed, beat egg whites until stiff peaks form when beaters are lifted. With rubber spatula, gently fold beaten egg whites, one-third at a time, into tomato mixture just until blended.

6 Pour mixture into prepared soufflé dish. Sprinkle with Parmesan. With back of spoon, about 1 inch from edge of dish, make 1-inch-deep indentation all around in soufflé mixture. Bake 45 minutes, or until soufflé is puffy and brown and knife inserted under "top hat" comes out clean. Serve immediately. *Makes 8 accompaniment or 4 main-dish servings.*

EACH ACCOMPANIMENT SERVING: ABOUT 205 CALORIES,
8 G PROTEIN, 13 G CARBOHYDRATE, 14 G TOTAL FAT,
(6 G SATURATED), 2 G FIBER, 181 MG CHOLESTEROL,
530 MG SODIUM.

Ginger Soufflé

A gingery dessert is the perfect finale to a meal featuring Asian flavors. Though French in conception, this soufflé would be a welcome dessert after a Chinese, Japanese, Thai, or Indian dinner.

GINGER SYRUP:
⅓ CUP WATER
¼ CUP GRANULATED SUGAR
¼ CUP THINLY SLICED, UNPEELED FRESH GINGER

SOUFFLÉ:
4 TABLESPOONS BUTTER OR MARGARINE
⅓ CUP ALL-PURPOSE FLOUR
⅛ TEASPOON SALT
1 CUP MILK
½ CUP PLUS 2 TABLESPOONS GRANULATED SUGAR
4 LARGE EGGS, SEPARATED
⅓ CUP CRYSTALLIZED GINGER, FINELY CHOPPED
2 LARGE EGG WHITES
CONFECTIONERS' SUGAR
WHIPPED CREAM (OPTIONAL)

1 Prepare Ginger Syrup: In 1-quart saucepan, heat water, granulated sugar, and fresh ginger to boiling over medium heat; boil 2 minutes. Remove saucepan from heat, cover, and let stand 10 minutes. Strain and cool syrup to room temperature.

2 Prepare Soufflé: In 2-quart saucepan, melt butter over low heat. Stir in flour and salt until blended. Gradually stir in milk and cook, stirring constantly, until mixture boils and thickens; cook 1 minute. Remove saucepan from heat.

3 With wire whisk, beat ¼ cup granulated sugar into milk mixture. Beat in egg yolks until well blended. Cool to lukewarm, stirring occasionally. Stir in ginger syrup and crystallized ginger.

4 Preheat oven to 375° F. Grease one 2-quart soufflé dish or ten 6-ounce custard cups or ramekins; sprinkle lightly with 2 tablespoons granulated sugar.

5 In large bowl, with mixer at high speed, beat egg whites until soft peaks form when beaters are lifted. Add remaining ¼ cup granulated sugar, 1 tablespoon at a time, and beat until whites hold stiff peaks when beaters are lifted. With rubber spatula, gently fold one-third of whites into yolk mixture. Fold yolk mixture gently back into remaining whites.

6 Pour mixture into prepared soufflé dish. With back of spoon, about 1 inch from edge of dish, make 1-inch-deep indentation all around in soufflé mixture. Bake 30 to 35 minutes for large soufflé, 25 to 30 minutes for individual soufflés, until set.

7 When soufflé is done, sprinkle with confectioners' sugar. Serve immediately. Pass whipped cream in bowl, if you like. *Makes 8 servings.*

EACH SERVING WITHOUT WHIPPED CREAM: ABOUT 260 CALORIES, 6 G PROTEIN, 37 G CARBOHYDRATE, 10 G TOTAL FAT (5 G SATURATED), 0.5 G FIBER, 126 MG CHOLESTEROL, 165 MG SODIUM.

SOUFFLÉ SECRETS

IF YOU'VE NEVER MADE A SOUFFLÉ BEFORE, YOU MAY WANT TO TRY ONE FOR "PRIVATE CONSUMPTION" BEFORE ATTEMPTING ONE FOR COMPANY. SOME POINTERS: BEAT THE EGG WHITES UNTIL STIFF BUT NOT DRY. FOLD THE EGG WHITES INTO THE SOUFFLÉ BASE QUICKLY BUT GENTLY, SO AS NOT TO DEFLATE THE BEATEN WHITES. BE SURE TO USE A STRAIGHT-SIDED DISH FOR MAXIMUM HEIGHT. GET THE SOUFFLÉ TO THE TABLE QUICKLY! TO SERVE, INSERT TWO SERVING FORKS, BACK-TO-BACK, INTO THE CENTER. GENTLY DIVIDE THE SOUFFLÉ INTO PORTIONS, THEN SERVE WITH A LARGE SPOON.

Lemon Soufflé

PREP 20 MINUTES / BAKE 35 TO 40 MINUTES

For the juiciest lemons, look for heavy fruits with fine-grained skins. Warming the lemons briefly (under hot tap water or in the microwave) will help to maximize the amount of juice. When grating the peel from the lemons, be careful to remove only the colored portion, not the spongy white pith that's under it.

4 TABLESPOONS BUTTER OR MARGARINE
⅓ CUP ALL-PURPOSE FLOUR
⅛ TEASPOON SALT
1 CUP MILK
⅔ CUP PLUS 2 TABLESPOONS GRANULATED SUGAR
4 LARGE EGGS, SEPARATED
2 LARGE LEMONS
2 LARGE EGG WHITES
CONFECTIONERS' SUGAR

1 In 2-quart saucepan, melt butter over low heat. Stir in flour and salt until blended; gradually stir in milk. Cook, stirring constantly, until mixture thickens and boils; cook 1 minute. Remove saucepan from heat.

2 With wire whisk, beat ⅓ cup granulated sugar into milk mixture. Beat in egg yolks until well blended. Cool to lukewarm, stirring occasionally. Meanwhile, from lemons, grate 1 tablespoon peel and squeeze ⅓ cup juice. Stir peel and juice into egg-yolk mixture.

3 Preheat oven to 375° F. Grease 2-quart soufflé dish; sprinkle with 2 tablespoons granulated sugar.

4 In large bowl, with mixer at high speed, beat egg whites until soft peaks form when beaters are lifted. Gradually sprinkle in remaining ⅓ cup granulated sugar and beat until egg whites hold stiff peaks when beaters are lifted. With rubber spatula, gently fold one-third of whites into egg-yolk mixture. Fold egg-yolk mixture gently back into remaining whites.

5 Pour mixture into prepared soufflé dish. With back of spoon, about 1 inch from edge of dish, make 1-inch-deep indentation all around in soufflé mixture. Bake 35 to 40 minutes, until set.

6 When soufflé is done, sprinkle with confectioners' sugar. Serve immediately. *Makes 8 servings.*

EACH SERVING: ABOUT 215 CALORIES, 6 G PROTEIN, 27 G CARBOHYDRATE, 10 G TOTAL FAT (5 G SATURATED), 0 G FIBER, 126 MG CHOLESTEROL, 155 MG SODIUM.

Hazelnut Soufflé

PREP 25 MINUTES / BAKE 45 MINUTES

½ CUP HAZELNUTS (FILBERTS)
2 TABLESPOONS PLUS ½ CUP GRANULATED SUGAR
1½ CUPS MILK
4 TABLESPOONS BUTTER OR MARGARINE
¼ CUP ALL-PURPOSE FLOUR
¼ TEASPOON SALT
4 LARGE EGGS, SEPARATED
2 LARGE EGG WHITES
2 TABLESPOONS HAZELNUT-FLAVORED LIQUEUR
CONFECTIONERS' SUGAR

1 Preheat oven to 350° F. Place hazelnuts in 9" by 9" metal baking pan. Bake 15 minutes, or until toasted. Wrap hot hazelnuts in clean cloth towel. With hands, roll hazelnuts back and forth to remove most of skins. Cool completely. In food processor with knife blade attached, process hazelnuts with ¼ cup granulated sugar until very finely ground.

2 In 1-quart saucepan, heat milk to boiling. In 3-quart saucepan, melt butter over low heat. Stir in flour and salt and cook, stirring frequently, 2 minutes. Gradually stir in milk and heat to boiling; cook, stirring, 1 minute. Remove saucepan from heat. Whisk in egg yolks until well blended. Stir in ground hazelnut mixture and hazelnut liqueur. Cool to lukewarm, stirring occasionally.

3 Preheat oven to 375° F. Grease 2½-quart soufflé dish; sprinkle with 2 tablespoons granulated sugar.

4 In large bowl, with mixer at high speed, beat egg whites until soft peaks form when beaters are lifted. Sprinkle in remaining ¼ cup granulated sugar, 1 tablespoon at a time, and beat until whites hold stiff, glossy peaks when beaters are lifted. With rubber spatula, gently fold one-third of beaten egg whites into hazelnut mixture. Fold hazelnut mixture gently into remaining egg whites.

5 Pour mixture into prepared soufflé dish. With back of spoon, about 1 inch from edge of dish, make 1-inch-deep indentation all around in soufflé mixture. Bake 45 minutes, or until just set.

6 When soufflé is done, sprinkle with confectioners' sugar. Serve immediately. *Makes 6 servings.*

EACH SERVING: ABOUT 335 CALORIES, 9 G PROTEIN,
32 G CARBOHYDRATE, 20 G TOTAL FAT (8 G SATURATED),
1 G FIBER, 171 MG CHOLESTEROL, 265 MG SODIUM.

Banana Rum Soufflé

PREP 15 MINUTES / BAKE 55 TO 60 MINUTES

The starch in bananas turns to sugar as they ripen, so for maximum flavor, the fruit must be fully ripe. This means that the skin will be thoroughly dotted with brown freckles. To speed up ripening, put bananas in a bag along with half an apple (or even an apple core).

2 MEDIUM-LARGE BANANAS
4 TABLESPOONS BUTTER OR MARGARINE
⅓ CUP ALL-PURPOSE FLOUR
⅛ TEASPOON SALT
1 CUP MILK
¼ CUP PACKED BROWN SUGAR
4 LARGE EGGS, SEPARATED
¼ CUP DARK RUM
2 TABLESPOONS PLUS ¼ CUP GRANULATED SUGAR
2 LARGE EGG WHITES
CONFECTIONERS' SUGAR

1 In blender or food processor with knife blade attached, puree bananas until smooth (you should have 1 cup). In 2-quart saucepan, melt butter over low heat. Stir in flour and salt until blended; gradually stir in milk. Cook, stirring constantly, until mixture boils and thickens; cook 1 minute. Remove saucepan from heat.

2 With wire whisk, beat brown sugar into milk mixture. Beat in egg yolks until well blended. Stir in pureed bananas and rum. Cool to lukewarm, stirring mixture occasionally.

3 Preheat oven to 350° F. Grease 2½-quart soufflé dish; sprinkle with 2 tablespoons granulated sugar.

4 In large bowl, with mixer at high speed, beat egg whites until soft peaks form. Sprinkle in remaining ¼ cup granulated sugar, 1 tablespoon at a time, and beat until whites hold stiff peaks when beaters are lifted. With rubber spatula, gently fold one-third of beaten egg whites into banana mixture. Fold banana mixture gently into remaining whites.

5 Pour mixture into prepared soufflé dish. With back of spoon, about 1 inch from edge of dish, make 1-inch-deep indentation all around in soufflé mixture. Bake 55 to 60 minutes, until just set.

6 When soufflé is done, sprinkle with confectioners' sugar. Serve immediately. *Makes 8 servings.*

EACH SERVING: ABOUT 225 CALORIES, 6 G PROTEIN,
29 G CARBOHYDRATE, 10 G TOTAL FAT (5 G SATURATED),
0.5 G FIBER, 126 MG CHOLESTEROL, 160 MG SODIUM.

Chocolate Soufflés

PREP 20 MINUTES PLUS COOLING
BAKE 20 TO 30 MINUTES

Make as eight individual desserts or as one delectably tall, dark, and handsome soufflé.

1¼ CUPS PLUS 2 TABLESPOONS GRANULATED SUGAR
¼ CUP ALL-PURPOSE FLOUR
1 TEASPOON INSTANT ESPRESSO-COFFEE POWDER
1 CUP MILK
3 TABLESPOONS BUTTER OR MARGARINE, SOFTENED
5 SQUARES (5 OUNCES) UNSWEETENED CHOCOLATE,
  COARSELY CHOPPED
4 LARGE EGGS, SEPARATED
2 TEASPOONS VANILLA EXTRACT
2 LARGE EGG WHITES
¼ TEASPOON SALT
CONFECTIONERS' SUGAR

1 In 3-quart saucepan, combine 1¼ cups granulated sugar, flour, and espresso powder; gradually stir in milk until blended. Cook over medium heat, stirring constantly, until mixture thickens and boils; boil, stirring, 1 minute. Remove saucepan from heat.

2 Stir in butter and chocolate until smooth. With wire whisk, beat in egg yolks until well blended. Stir in vanilla. Cool to lukewarm, stirring mixture occasionally.

3 Preheat oven to 350° F. Grease eight 6-ounce ramekins or custard cups, or one 2-quart soufflé dish; sprinkle with remaining 2 tablespoons granulated sugar.

4 In large bowl, with mixer at high speed, beat egg whites and salt until stiff peaks form when beaters are lifted. With rubber spatula, gently fold one-third of beaten whites into chocolate mixture. Fold chocolate mixture gently back into remaining whites.

5 Pour into prepared ramekins or soufflé dish. (If using individual ramekins, place in jelly-roll pan for easier handling.) Bake ramekins 20 to 25 minutes (centers will still be glossy). If using 2-quart soufflé dish, bake 25 to 30 minutes.

6 When soufflés are done, sprinkle with confectioners' sugar. Serve immediately. *Makes 8 servings.*

EACH SERVING: ABOUT 365 CALORIES, 7 G PROTEIN,
45 G CARBOHYDRATE, 20 G TOTAL FAT (10 G SATURATED),
3 G FIBER, 122 MG CHOLESTEROL, 180 MG SODIUM.

Chocolate Soufflés

Orange Liqueur Soufflé

PREP 20 MINUTES / BAKE 30 TO 35 MINUTES

Grand Marnier, Cointreau, and Triple Sec are the most famous names in orange liqueur; you can also use any brand of curaçao.

4 TABLESPOONS BUTTER OR MARGARINE
⅓ CUP ALL-PURPOSE FLOUR
⅛ TEASPOON SALT
1½ CUPS MILK
½ CUP PLUS 2 TABLESPOONS GRANULATED SUGAR
4 LARGE EGGS, SEPARATED
⅓ CUP ORANGE-FLAVORED LIQUEUR
1 TABLESPOON FRESHLY GRATED ORANGE PEEL
2 LARGE EGG WHITES
CONFECTIONERS' SUGAR
WHIPPED CREAM (OPTIONAL)

1 In 2-quart saucepan, melt butter over low heat. Stir in flour and salt until blended; gradually stir in milk. Cook, stirring constantly, until mixture thickens and boils; boil 1 minute. Remove saucepan from heat.

2 With wire whisk, beat ½ cup granulated sugar into milk mixture. Beat in egg yolks until well blended. Cool to lukewarm, stirring occasionally. Stir in orange liqueur and orange peel.

3 Preheat oven to 375° F. Grease 2-quart soufflé dish with butter; sprinkle with remaining 2 tablespoons granulated sugar.

4 In large bowl, with mixer at high speed, beat egg whites until stiff peaks form when beaters are lifted. With rubber spatula, gently fold one-third of whites into egg-yolk mixture; fold egg-yolk mixture gently back into remaining whites.

5 Pour mixture into prepared soufflé dish. With back of spoon, about 1 inch from edge of dish, make 1-inch-deep indentation all around in soufflé mixture. Bake 30 to 35 minutes, until just set.

6 When soufflé is done, sprinkle with confectioners' sugar. Serve immediately. Serve whipped cream in bowl, if desired. *Makes 8 servings.*

EACH SERVING WITHOUT WHIPPED CREAM: ABOUT
220 CALORIES, 6 G PROTEIN, 26 G CARBOHYDRATE,
10 G TOTAL FAT (5 G SATURATED), 0 G FIBER,
128 MG CHOLESTEROL, 160 MG SODIUM.

CUSTARD DESSERTS

Despite plain custard's well-deserved role as a nursery food, these sweet smoothies can also be absolutely elegant: Pôts de crème, crème brûlée, and crème caramel are definitely dinner-party fare. They all require chilling time, making them ideal make-ahead desserts. These creamy custards need gentle handling—the egg-rich mixture must be protected from direct heat—so they're baked in a *bain- marie,* or water bath. This is easy to do as long as you remember to put the pan of custards in the oven before pouring in the boiling water. After baking, remove the custard cups from the pan one by one.

Crème Brûlée

PREP 20 MINUTES PLUS CHILLING
BAKE 35 TO 40 MINUTES

A thin covering of brown sugar is scattered over the surface of the cooled custard, and then it is broiled. A shatteringly crisp, totally irresistible layer results.

½ VANILLA BEAN, OR 2 TEASPOONS VANILLA EXTRACT
1½ CUPS HEAVY OR WHIPPING CREAM
1½ CUPS HALF-AND-HALF OR LIGHT CREAM
8 LARGE EGG YOLKS
⅔ CUP GRANULATED SUGAR
⅓ TO ½ CUP PACKED BROWN SUGAR

1 Preheat oven to 325° F. With knife, cut vanilla bean lengthwise in half. Scrape out and reserve seeds. In 3-quart saucepan, heat cream, half-and-half, and vanilla bean and seeds over medium heat, until tiny bubbles form around edge of pan. Remove saucepan from heat. With slotted spoon, remove vanilla bean from saucepan.

2 Meanwhile, in large bowl, with wire whisk or fork, mix egg yolks with granulated sugar until blended. Slowly stir in warm cream mixture until well combined. Pour mixture into ten 4- to 5-ounce broiler-safe ramekins or custard cups, or one 2½-quart shallow broiler-safe casserole.

3 Place ramekins or casserole in 17" by 11½" roasting pan; place in oven. Carefully pour *boiling water* into roasting pan to come halfway up sides of ramekins or casserole. Bake 35 to 40 minutes, or just until set (mixture will still be slightly soft in center).

Remove ramekins or casserole from roasting pan; cool to room temperature on wire rack. Cover and refrigerate at least 2 hours, until well chilled.

4 Up to 4 hours before serving, preheat broiler. Place brown sugar in small sieve; with spoon, press sugar through sieve to cover top of chilled custard.

5 Place ramekins or casserole in jelly-roll pan for easier handling. With broiler rack at closest position to heat source, broil custard 3 to 4 minutes, just until sugar melts. (The melted brown sugar will form a shiny, crisp crust.) Refrigerate until ready to serve. Serve within 4 hours, or brown sugar topping will lose its crispness. *Makes 10 servings.*

EACH SERVING: ABOUT 305 CALORIES, 4 G PROTEIN, 25 G CARBOHYDRATE, 21 G TOTAL FAT (12 G SATURATED), 0 G FIBER, 232 MG CHOLESTEROL, 40 MG SODIUM.

Chocolate Pôts de Crème

PREP 15 MINUTES PLUS CHILLING
BAKE 30 TO 35 MINUTES

This old-fashioned dessert is sometimes served in porcelain cups specially made for the purpose (the cups themselves are also called "pôts de crème").
If you have some pretty china teacups and saucers—a matching set or not—they could be used instead.

3 SQUARES (3 OUNCES) SEMISWEET CHOCOLATE
2½ CUPS MILK
2 LARGE EGGS
2 LARGE EGG YOLKS
¼ CUP SUGAR
1 TEASPOON VANILLA EXTRACT

1 Preheat oven to 350° F. Arrange six 6-ounce ramekins or custard cups in 14" by 10" roasting pan. In 3-quart saucepan, heat chocolate and ¼ cup milk over low heat, stirring often, until chocolate is melted. Remove saucepan from heat. In 2-quart saucepan, heat remaining 2¼ cups milk to boiling over medium-high heat; stir into chocolate mixture.

2 In large bowl, with wire whisk or fork, beat whole eggs, egg yolks, sugar, and vanilla until blended. Gradually whisk in chocolate mixture until well combined. Pour mixture evenly into ramekins.

3 Place ramekins in roasting pan; place in oven. Carefully pour *boiling water* into roasting pan to come halfway up sides of ramekins. Bake 30 to 35 minutes, until knife inserted halfway between edge and center of custards comes out clean. Transfer ramekins to wire rack to cool. Cover and refrigerate at least 3 hours, until well chilled. *Makes 6 servings.*

EACH SERVING: ABOUT 210 CALORIES, 7 G PROTEIN, 22 G CARBOHYDRATE, 11 G TOTAL FAT (6 G SATURATED), 1 G FIBER, 156 MG CHOLESTEROL, 75 MG SODIUM.

MOCHA PÔTS DE CRÈME Prepare as for Chocolate Pôts de Crème but heat *2¼ cups milk* to boiling with *1 tablespoon instant coffee powder.* Bake, cool, and chill as directed.
EACH SERVING: ABOUT 204 CALORIES, 7 G PROTEIN, 22 G CARBOHYDRATE, 11 G TOTAL FAT (5 G SATURATED), 1 G FIBER, 155 MG CHOLESTEROL, 70 MG SODIUM.

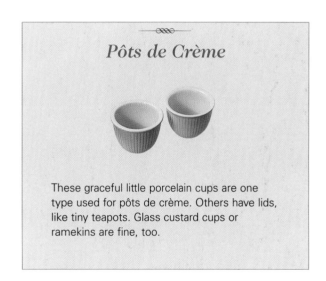

Pôts de Crème

These graceful little porcelain cups are one type used for pôts de crème. Others have lids, like tiny teapots. Glass custard cups or ramekins are fine, too.

Pumpkin Crème Caramel

PREP 30 MINUTES PLUS OVERNIGHT TO CHILL
BAKE 55 MINUTES

You might consider a change in your Thanksgiving menu after tasting this luscious caramel-drenched pumpkin custard. Be sure to used canned solid pack pumpkin, not pumpkin-pie mix, for this recipe.

6 STRIPS (3" BY 1" EACH) ORANGE PEEL
1¼ CUPS SUGAR
¼ CUP WATER
1 CAN (12 OUNCES) EVAPORATED MILK
1 CUP HEAVY OR WHIPPING CREAM
1 CUP SOLID PACK PUMPKIN (NOT PUMPKIN-PIE MIX)
6 LARGE EGGS
¼ CUP ORANGE-FLAVORED LIQUEUR
1 TEASPOON VANILLA EXTRACT
1 TEASPOON GROUND CINNAMON
PINCH GROUND NUTMEG
PINCH SALT

1 In 1-quart saucepan, heat orange peel, ¾ cup sugar, and water to boiling over high heat; cover and cook 10 minutes. With fork, remove orange peel and discard. Continue cooking sugar mixture about 3 minutes longer, until amber in color. Pour caramel into 9" by 5" loaf pan, swirling to coat bottom. (Hold pan with pot holders to protect hands from heat of caramel.) Set pan aside.

2 In heavy 2-quart saucepan, heat evaporated milk, cream, and remaining ½ cup sugar just to boiling over medium-high heat.

3 Meanwhile, preheat oven to 350° F. In large bowl, with wire whisk, mix pumpkin, eggs, liqueur, vanilla, cinnamon, nutmeg, and salt until combined.

4 Gradually whisk hot milk mixture into pumpkin mixture until combined. Pour pumpkin mixture through medium-mesh sieve into prepared loaf pan. Place loaf pan in 13" by 9" roasting pan; place in oven. Carefully pour *boiling water* into roasting pan to come three-quarters up side of loaf pan. Bake 55 minutes, or until knife inserted 1 inch from edge of custard comes out clean (center will jiggle slightly). Remove loaf pan from roasting pan to cool on wire rack 1 hour. Cover and refrigerate crème caramel overnight.

5 To unmold, run small metal spatula around sides of loaf pan; invert crème caramel onto serving plate, allowing caramel syrup to drip from pan onto loaf (some caramel may remain in loaf pan). *Makes 12 servings.*

EACH SERVING: ABOUT 245 CALORIES, 6 G PROTEIN, 28 G CARBOHYDRATE, 12 G TOTAL FAT (7 G SATURATED), 0.5 G FIBER, 143 MG CHOLESTEROL, 85 MG SODIUM.

Crème Caramel

PREP 15 MINUTES PLUS CHILLING
BAKE 50 TO 55 MINUTES

This is sometimes called "crème renversée" because it's "reversed" or inverted onto plates for serving, allowing the rich caramel to cascade over the custard as a sauce.

¼ CUP PLUS ⅓ CUP SUGAR
4 LARGE EGGS
2 CUPS MILK
1½ TEASPOONS VANILLA EXTRACT
¼ TEASPOON SALT

1 Preheat oven 325° F. In small saucepan, heat ¼ cup sugar over medium heat, swirling pan occasionally, until sugar is melted and amber in color. Immediately pour into six 6-ounce custard cups.

2 In large bowl, with wire whisk or fork, mix eggs and ⅓ cup sugar until well blended. Whisk in milk, vanilla, and salt until well combined. Pour mixture into prepared custard cups. Place custard cups in 13" by 9" roasting pan; place in oven. Carefully pour *boiling water* into pan to come halfway up sides of cups. Bake 50 to 55 minutes, until knife inserted in center of custards comes out clean. Transfer cups to wire rack to cool. Cover and refrigerate about 2 hours, until chilled.

3 To unmold, run small metal spatula around side of each custard cup; invert cup onto dessert plate, allowing caramel syrup to drip from cup onto custard. *Makes 6 servings.*

EACH SERVING: ABOUT 180 CALORIES, 7 G PROTEIN, 24 G CARBOHYDRATE, 6 G TOTAL FAT (3 G SATURATED), 0 G FIBER, 153 MG CHOLESTEROL, 175 MG SODIUM.

Pumpkin Crème Caramel

BAKED PUDDINGS

RIce pudding, bread pudding, and Indian pudding are just a few of the dense, satisfying desserts that come under this heading. They're all easy to make—perfect as do-ahead family or company desserts—and are destined to become favorites. Puddings are wonderful served warm, especially when topped with a dollop of whipped cream or a scoop of ice cream.

Bread-and-Butter Pudding

PREP 10 MINUTES PLUS STANDING
BAKE 50 TO 60 MINUTES

This old-fashioned favorite is simply flavored with cinnamon and vanilla.

½ CUP SUGAR
¾ TEASPOON GROUND CINNAMON
4 TABLESPOONS BUTTER OR MARGARINE, SOFTENED
12 SLICES FIRM WHITE BREAD
3 CUPS MILK
1½ TEASPOONS VANILLA EXTRACT
4 LARGE EGGS
WHIPPED CREAM (OPTIONAL)

1 Preheat oven to 325° F. Grease 8" by 8" baking dish. In cup, combine 1 tablespoon sugar and cinnamon. Spread butter on bread slices. Arrange 4 bread slices in 1 layer in prepared dish, overlapping slightly if necessary; sprinkle lightly with cinnamon sugar. Repeat to make 2 more layers.

2 In medium bowl, with wire whisk or fork, beat milk, remaining 7 tablespoons sugar, vanilla, and eggs until well combined. Pour egg mixture over bread slices. Let stand 20 minutes, occasionally pressing bread into egg mixture.

3 Bake 50 to 60 minutes, until knife inserted in center of pudding comes out clean. Cool on wire rack 15 minutes. Serve pudding warm, or cover and refrigerate to serve cold later. Top with whipped cream, if desired. *Makes 8 servings.*

EACH SERVING WITHOUT WHIPPED CREAM: ABOUT 315 CALORIES, 10 G PROTEIN, 38 G CARBOHYDRATE, 13 G TOTAL FAT (7 G SATURATED), 1 G FIBER, 135 MG CHOLESTEROL, 365 MG SODIUM.

BREAD-AND-BUTTER PUDDING WITH DRIED FRUIT Chop *¾ cup mixed dried fruit* (such as apricots, prunes, and/or pears). Prepare bread as for Bread-and-Butter Pudding; sprinkle first bread layer with some cinnamon sugar and half of dried fruit. Repeat over second bread layer. Top with remaining bread and sugar. Bake as directed.
EACH SERVING: ABOUT 350 CALORIES, 10 G PROTEIN, 48 G CARBOHYDRATE, 13 G TOTAL FAT (7 G SATURATED), 2 G FIBER, 135 MG CHOLESTEROL, 365 MG SODIUM.

BREAD-AND-BUTTER PUDDING WITH BERRIES In bowl, combine *1 cup strawberries,* hulled and sliced, *½ cup blueberries,* picked over, *½ cup raspberries,* and *1 tablespoon sugar.* Prepare bread as for Bread-and-Butter Pudding. Sprinkle first bread layer with some cinnamon sugar and half of berry mixture. Repeat over second bread layer. Top with remaining bread and sugar. Bake as directed.
EACH SERVING: ABOUT 335 CALORIES, 10 G PROTEIN, 43 G CARBOHYDRATE, 13 G TOTAL FAT (7 G SATURATED), 2 G FIBER, 135 MG CHOLESTEROL, 365 MG SODIUM.

BREAD-AND-BUTTER PUDDING WITH JAM Prepare bread as for Bread-and-Butter Pudding. Spread with *2 generous tablespoons seedless raspberry jam.* Sprinkle with cinnamon sugar. Repeat over second bread layer. Top with remaining bread layer and sugar. Bake as directed.
EACH SERVING: ABOUT 330 CALORIES, 10 G PROTEIN, 43 G CARBOHYDRATE, 13 G TOTAL FAT (7 G SATURATED), 1 G FIBER, 135 MG CHOLESTEROL, 365 MG SODIUM.

BREAD PUDDING BREADS

FIRM WHITE BREAD IS USED FOR MOST OF OUR BREAD PUDDINGS. IF YOU'RE BUYING SLICED BREAD IN THE SUPERMARKET, LOOK FOR ONE WITH DENSE TEXTURE. WORDS LIKE "HEARTY," "TRADITIONAL," AND "BRICK OVEN-BAKED" ARE CUES TO GOOD TEXTURE. THE BREAD NEED NOT BE FRESH; IN FACT, SLIGHTLY STALE BREAD IS PREFERABLE. EXCELLENT OPTIONS FOR PUDDING ARE FRENCH OR ITALIAN BREAD, CHALLAH, BRIOCHE, AND RAISIN BREAD.

Chocolate Bread Pudding

PREP 25 MINUTES PLUS CHILLING / BAKE 50 MINUTES

For this pudding, cubes of bread are steeped in chocolate custard and then layered with ribbons of melted semisweet chocolate.

8 SLICES STALE FIRM WHITE BREAD
3 TABLESPOONS PLUS ⅓ CUP SUGAR
8 SQUARES (8 OUNCES) SEMISWEET CHOCOLATE, MELTED
3 LARGE EGGS
3 CUPS MILK
1½ TEASPOONS VANILLA EXTRACT

1 Grease 8" by 8" baking dish. Cut bread into 1-inch squares. Scatter one-third of bread in prepared dish in 1 layer; sprinkle with 1 tablespoon sugar and drizzle with 2 tablespoons melted chocolate. Make a second layer. Top with remaining bread.

2 In 2-quart saucepan, heat milk to boiling over medium-high heat. Meanwhile, in medium bowl, with wire whisk, combine eggs and ⅓ cup sugar. While whisking, slowly pour milk into egg mixture. Add remaining melted chocolate and vanilla; stir to combine.

3 Pour egg mixture over bread. Refrigerate, gently stirring mixture occasionally, 3 hours, or until bread is soaked with chocolate mixture.

4 Preheat oven to 325° F. Sprinkle pudding with remaining 1 tablespoon sugar. Place dish in 13" by 9" roasting pan; place in oven. Carefully pour *boiling water* into roasting pan to come halfway up sides of dish. Bake 50 minutes, or until knife inserted in center of pudding comes out clean. Transfer dish from roasting pan to wire rack to cool 15 minutes. Serve pudding warm, or cover and refrigerate to serve cold later. *Makes 8 servings.*

EACH SERVING: ABOUT 355 CALORIES, 9 G PROTEIN, 49 G CARBOHYDRATE, 15 G TOTAL FAT (8 G SATURATED), 2 G FIBER, 93 MG CHOLESTEROL, 225 MG SODIUM.

Sticky Toffee Pudding

PREP 20 MINUTES PLUS STANDING / BAKE 30 MINUTES

Britishers often refer to any sort of dessert as "pudding" (as in, "what's for pudding?"). This is a very British pudding indeed, with a gooey, butterscotch topping.

1 CUP CHOPPED PITTED DATES
1 TEASPOON BAKING SODA
1½ CUPS BOILING WATER
10 TABLESPOONS (1¼ STICKS) BUTTER OR MARGARINE, SOFTENED
1 CUP GRANULATED SUGAR
1 LARGE EGG
1 TEASPOON VANILLA EXTRACT
1 TEASPOON BAKING POWDER
2 CUPS ALL-PURPOSE FLOUR
1 CUP PACKED BROWN SUGAR
¼ CUP HEAVY OR WHIPPING CREAM
WHIPPED CREAM (OPTIONAL)

1 Preheat oven to 350° F. Grease 13" by 9" broiler-safe baking pan. In medium bowl, combine dates, baking soda, and boiling water; let stand 15 minutes.

2 In large bowl, with mixer at medium speed, beat 6 tablespoons butter until creamy. Beat in granulated sugar. Add egg and vanilla; beat until blended. Reduce speed to low and add baking powder and flour, beating to combine. Add date mixture and beat until evenly combined (batter will be very thin).

3 Pour batter into prepared pan. Bake 30 minutes, or until golden and toothpick inserted in center of pudding comes out clean.

4 Meanwhile, in 2-quart saucepan, heat brown sugar, cream, and remaining 4 tablespoons butter to boiling over medium heat; boil 1 minute.

5 Turn oven control to broil. Spread brown-sugar mixture evenly over top of hot pudding. Broil at position closest to source of heat until bubbly, about 30 seconds. Cool in pan on wire rack 15 minutes. Serve warm with whipped cream, if desired. *Makes 12 servings.*

EACH SERVING WITHOUT WHIPPED CREAM: ABOUT 360 CALORIES, 3 G PROTEIN, 62 G CARBOHYDRATE, 12 G TOTAL FAT (7 G SATURATED), 1 G FIBER, 50 MG CHOLESTEROL, 260 MG SODIUM.

Nantucket Indian Pudding

PREP 30 MINUTES / BAKE 2 HOURS

Native Americans introduced the European settlers to cornmeal, which the grateful newcomers subsequently referred to as "Indian meal." That's how this specialty of New England got its name.

⅔ CUPS CORNMEAL

4 CUPS MILK

½ CUP LIGHT (MILD) MOLASSES

4 TABLESPOONS BUTTER OR MARGARINE, CUT UP

¼ CUP SUGAR

1 TEASPOON GROUND GINGER

1 TEASPOON GROUND CINNAMON

½ TEASPOON SALT

¼ TEASPOON GROUND NUTMEG

WHIPPED CREAM OR VANILLA ICE CREAM (OPTIONAL)

1 Preheat oven to 350° F. Grease shallow 1½-quart glass or ceramic baking dish.

2 In small bowl, combine cornmeal and 1 cup milk. In 4-quart saucepan, heat remaining 3 cups milk to boiling over high heat. Stir in cornmeal mixture; heat to boiling. Reduce heat and simmer, stirring often to prevent lumps, 20 minutes (mixture will be very thick). Remove saucepan from heat; stir in molasses, butter, sugar, ginger, cinnamon, salt, and nutmeg until well combined.

3 Pour batter evenly into prepared dish. Cover with foil and place dish in 13" by 9" roasting pan; place in oven. Carefully pour *boiling water* into roasting pan to come halfway up sides of baking dish. Bake 1 hour. Remove foil and bake pudding 1 hour longer, or until lightly browned and just set.

4 Carefully remove baking dish from water and cool on wire rack 30 minutes. Serve pudding warm with whipped cream or vanilla ice cream, if desired. *Makes 8 servings.*

EACH SERVING WITHOUT WHIPPED CREAM OR ICE CREAM: ABOUT 255 CALORIES, 5 G PROTEIN, 35 G CARBOHYDRATE, 11 G TOTAL FAT (6 G SATURATED), 0.5 G FIBER, 33 MG CHOLESTEROL, 270 MG SODIUM.

New Orleans Bread Pudding

PREP 20 MINUTES PLUS STANDING AND COOLING
BAKE 45 TO 50 MINUTES

Bourbon, French bread, and pecan-praline sauce are the key Louisianan features in this slightly "tipsy" pudding. (Don't worry as most of the alcohol will burn off in the baking.)

½ CUP DARK SEEDLESS RAISINS

2 TABLESPOONS BOURBON

⅓ CUP GRANULATED SUGAR

⅛ TEASPOON GROUND NUTMEG

⅛ TEASPOON GROUND CINNAMON

3 LARGE EGGS

2 TEASPOONS VANILLA EXTRACT

1 PINT HALF-AND-HALF OR LIGHT CREAM

3 CUPS DAY-OLD FRENCH BREAD CUBES (½ INCH)

¼ CUP PACKED DARK BROWN SUGAR

2 TABLESPOONS BUTTER OR MARGARINE

1 TABLESPOON CORN SYRUP

⅓ CUP PECANS, TOASTED AND CHOPPED

1 In small bowl, combine raisins and bourbon; let stand 15 minutes. Meanwhile, grease 8" by 8" glass or ceramic baking dish.

2 In large bowl, stir together granulated sugar, nutmeg, and cinnamon until blended. Whisk in eggs and vanilla until combined. Measure and set aside 1 tablespoon half-and-half. Add remaining half-and-half to egg mixture and whisk until well blended. Stir in bread cubes. Let stand 15 minutes, stirring occasionally. Stir in raisin mixture.

3 Preheat oven to 325° F. Pour bread mixture into prepared dish. Bake 45 to 50 minutes, until knife inserted near center of pudding comes out clean. Cool on wire rack 30 minutes.

4 In 1-quart saucepan, heat reserved 1 tablespoon half-and-half, brown sugar, butter, and corn syrup to boiling over medium heat. Reduce heat and simmer 2 minutes, stirring occasionally. Remove saucepan from heat and stir in pecans. Serve pudding drizzled with praline sauce. *Makes 8 servings.*

EACH SERVING: ABOUT 300 CALORIES, 6 G PROTEIN, 36 G CARBOHYDRATE, 16 G TOTAL FAT (7 G SATURATED), 1 G FIBER, 110 MG CHOLESTEROL, 175 MG SODIUM.

Brownie Cake Pudding

PREP 20 MINUTES / BAKE 30 MINUTES

It's one of those culinary miracles: You fill a pan with batter, pour what seems like an awful lot of boiling water over it, and it comes out of the oven—quite astonishingly—as a light cake with a warm, custardy layer of pudding underneath.

2 TEASPOONS INSTANT COFFEE GRANULES OR POWDER
 (OPTIONAL)
2 TABLESPOONS PLUS 1¾ CUPS BOILING WATER
1 CUP ALL-PURPOSE FLOUR
½ CUP GRANULATED SUGAR
2 TEASPOONS BAKING POWDER
¼ TEASPOON SALT
¾ CUP UNSWEETENED COCOA
½ CUP MILK
4 TABLESPOONS BUTTER OR MARGARINE, MELTED
1 TEASPOON VANILLA EXTRACT
½ CUP PACKED LIGHT BROWN SUGAR
WHIPPED CREAM OR VANILLA ICE CREAM (OPTIONAL)

1 Preheat oven to 350° F. In cup, dissolve instant coffee, if you like, in 2 tablespoons boiling water.

2 In medium bowl, stir together flour, granulated sugar, baking powder, salt, and ½ cup cocoa. In 2-cup measuring cup, combine milk, melted butter, vanilla, and dissolved instant coffee, if using. With spoon, stir milk mixture into flour mixture until just blended. Pour batter into ungreased 8" by 8" glass or ceramic baking dish.

3 In small bowl, combine brown sugar and remaining ¼ cup cocoa; sprinkle over batter. Carefully pour remaining 1¾ cups boiling water over batter; do not stir.

4 Bake 30 minutes (batter will separate into cake and pudding layers). Cool on wire rack 10 minutes. Serve immediately or pudding will be absorbed by cake. Serve with whipped cream or ice cream, if desired. *Makes 8 servings.*

EACH SERVING WITHOUT WHIPPED CREAM OR ICE CREAM:
ABOUT 240 CALORIES, 4 G PROTEIN, 43 G CARBOHYDRATE,
7 G TOTAL FAT (5 G SATURATED), 3 G FIBER, 18 MG
CHOLESTEROL, 265 MG SODIUM.

Lemon Pudding Cake

PREP 20 MINUTES PLUS COOLING / BAKE 40 MINUTES

In this recipe, the oven's heat again works its spell, dividing a fluffy batter into two delectable parts: a light lemon sponge cake and rich lemon pudding. Eat it warm from the oven, or chill to serve later.

3 LEMONS
¾ CUP SUGAR
¼ CUP ALL-PURPOSE FLOUR
1 CUP MILK
3 LARGE EGGS, SEPARATED
4 TABLESPOONS BUTTER OR MARGARINE, MELTED
⅛ TEASPOON SALT

1 Preheat oven to 350° F. Grease 8" by 8" glass or ceramic baking dish. From lemons, grate 1 tablespoon peel and squeeze ⅓ cup juice. In large bowl, combine sugar and flour. With wire whisk or fork, beat in milk, egg yolks, melted butter, and lemon peel and juice.

2 In small bowl, with mixer at high speed, beat egg whites with salt until soft peaks form when beaters are lifted. With rubber spatula, fold one-fourth of egg whites into lemon mixture; gently fold in remaining egg whites. Pour batter into prepared dish.

3 Place baking dish in 13" by 9" roasting pan; place on rack in oven. Carefully pour *boiling water* into roasting pan to come halfway up sides of dish. Bake 40 minutes, or until top is golden and set (batter will separate into cake and pudding layers). Transfer dish from roasting pan to wire rack to cool 10 minutes. Serve immediately. *Makes 6 servings.*

EACH SERVING: ABOUT 255 CALORIES, 5 G PROTEIN,
32 G CARBOHYDRATE, 12 G TOTAL FAT (7 G SATURATED),
0 G FIBER, 133 MG CHOLESTEROL, 180 MG SODIUM.

ORANGE PUDDING CAKE Prepare as above but, in Step 1, squeeze *¼ cup fresh lemon juice*. From 1 large orange, grate *2 teaspoons peel* and squeeze *¼ cup juice*. Make batter and bake as directed.

EACH SERVING: ABOUT 260 CALORIES, 5 G PROTEIN,
33 G CARBOHYDRATE, 12 G TOTAL FAT (7 G SATURATED),
0 G FIBER, 133 MG CHOLESTEROL, 180 MG SODIUM.

Persimmon-Date Pudding

PREP 25 MINUTES / BAKE 50 TO 60 MINUTES

Puddings like this go way back in the South and the Midwest, where native persimmons grow. Fortunately for the rest of us, Asian persimmons are now widely available. The fruit must be fully ripe—soft to the point of mushiness—or the flavor will not be sweet.

1 CUP ALL-PURPOSE FLOUR

1 CUP SUGAR

2 TEASPOONS BAKING SODA

1½ TEASPOONS BAKING POWDER

¼ TEASPOON GROUND CINNAMON

⅛ TEASPOON GROUND GINGER

PINCH GROUND CLOVES

1 CUP WALNUTS, COARSELY CHOPPED

½ CUP CHOPPED PITTED DATES

½ CUP DARK SEEDLESS RAISINS

½ TEASPOON FRESHLY GRATED ORANGE PEEL

1 CUP PERSIMMON PULP, FROM 1 TO 2 LARGE, RIPE
   HACHIYA PERSIMMONS

½ CUP MILK

2 TABLESPOONS BUTTER OR MARGARINE, MELTED

1 TEASPOON VANILLA EXTRACT

HARD SAUCE (PAGE 363) OR WHIPPED CREAM

1 Preheat oven to 325° F. Grease 8" by 8" glass or ceramic baking dish.

2 In large bowl, stir together flour, sugar, baking soda, baking powder, cinnamon, ginger, and cloves. Stir in walnuts, dates, raisins, and orange peel. Stir in persimmon pulp, milk, melted butter, and vanilla until well combined. Spoon batter evenly into prepared dish.

3 Bake 50 to 60 minutes, until toothpick inserted in center of pudding comes out clean. Serve warm with Hard Sauce or whipped cream. *Makes 8 servings.*

EACH SERVING WITHOUT HARD SAUCE OR WHIPPED CREAM: ABOUT 375 CALORIES, 5 G PROTEIN, 63 G CARBOHYDRATE, 14 G TOTAL FAT (3 G SATURATED), 2 G FIBER, 10 MG CHOLESTEROL, 445 MG SODIUM.

COBBLERS, CRISPS & CRUMBLES

Seasonal fruits are the inspiration for these country-style desserts. Bake them with the specified fruits or, if those are not in season, experiment with other choices—the best that the orchard or berry patch has to offer. You can even use frozen, unsweetened fruits in these desserts.

Rhubarb-Apple Crumble

PREP 20 MINUTES / BAKE 45 MINUTES

Rhubarb is often combined with strawberries, since the two share a growing season and the sweet berries help compensate for the rhubarb's tartness. This innovative recipe pairs rhubarb with sweet Golden Delicious apples, which are available year round.

⅓ CUP GRANULATED SUGAR

1 TABLESPOON CORNSTARCH

1¼ POUNDS RHUBARB, CUT INTO ½-INCH PIECES (ABOUT
   4 CUPS)

3 MEDIUM GOLDEN DELICIOUS APPLES (ABOUT 1¼
   POUNDS), PEELED, CORED, AND CUT INTO 1-INCH
   PIECES

½ CUP PACKED BROWN SUGAR

4 TABLESPOONS BUTTER OR MARGARINE, SOFTENED

¼ TEASPOON GROUND CINNAMON

½ CUP OLD-FASHIONED OR QUICK-COOKING OATS,
   UNCOOKED

⅓ CUP ALL-PURPOSE FLOUR

1 Preheat oven to 375° F. In large bowl, combine granulated sugar and cornstarch. Add rhubarb and apples and toss to coat. Spoon fruit mixture into 11" by 7" glass baking dish or shallow 2-quart casserole.

2 In medium bowl, with fingers, mix brown sugar, butter, and cinnamon until mixture resembles coarse crumbs. Stir in oats and flour. Sprinkle over fruit.

3 Bake 45 minutes, or until filling is bubbly. Serve warm. *Makes 6 servings.*

EACH SERVING: ABOUT 300 CALORIES, 3 G PROTEIN, 56 G CARBOHYDRATE, 9 G TOTAL FAT (5 G SATURATED), 2 G FIBER, 21 MG CHOLESTEROL, 90 MG SODIUM.

Rhubarb-Strawberry Cobbler

PREP 25 MINUTES / BAKE 20 TO 25 MINUTES

The basic formula works beautifully with just about any fruit filling you can dream up. How about nectarine-blackberry, raspberry-peach, apple-cranberry, or fresh apricot? If your fruit is particularly tart, you may want to add an extra tablespoon or two of sugar.

FILLING:

1¼ POUNDS RHUBARB, CUT INTO 1-INCH CHUNKS (4 CUPS)

½ CUP SUGAR

1 TABLESPOON CORNSTARCH

¼ CUP COLD WATER

1 PINT STRAWBERRIES, HULLED AND QUARTERED

BISCUITS:

1½ CUPS ALL-PURPOSE FLOUR

¼ CUP PLUS 1 TEASPOON SUGAR

1½ TEASPOONS BAKING POWDER

½ TEASPOON BAKING SODA

¼ TEASPOON SALT

¼ TEASPOON GROUND CINNAMON

¼ TEASPOON GROUND NUTMEG

4 TABLESPOONS COLD BUTTER OR MARGARINE, CUT UP

¾ CUP PLUS 1 TABLESPOON HEAVY OR WHIPPING CREAM

1 Prepare Filling: In 3-quart saucepan, heat rhubarb and sugar to boiling over high heat, stirring constantly. Reduce heat to medium-low and simmer until rhubarb is tender, about 8 minutes.

2 In cup, blend cornstarch and water until smooth. Stir cornstarch mixture and strawberries into rhubarb mixture; continue cooking 2 minutes, or until mixture boils. Remove saucepan from heat.

3 Preheat oven to 400° F. Prepare Biscuits: In bowl, stir together flour, ¼ cup sugar, baking powder, baking soda, salt, cinnamon, and nutmeg. With pastry blender or 2 knives used scissor-fashion, cut in butter until mixture resembles coarse crumbs. Add ¾ cup cream, stirring just until mixture forms soft dough that pulls away from side of bowl.

4 Turn dough onto lightly floured surface; knead 6 to 8 times to blend thoroughly. With floured rolling pin, roll dough into 10½" by 6½" rectangle, ½ inch thick. Cut dough lengthwise in half, then crosswise 3 times to make 8 biscuits. Brush biscuits with remaining 1 tablespoon cream and sprinkle with remaining 1 teaspoon sugar.

5 Reheat filling until hot. Pour into 11" by 7" glass or ceramic baking dish or shallow 2-quart casserole.

6 Place biscuits on top of filling. Place sheet of foil under baking dish; crimp edges to form rim to catch any overflow during baking. Bake 20 to 25 minutes, until biscuits are lightly browned and filling is bubbly. Cool on wire rack 30 minutes; serve warm. *Makes 8 servings.*

EACH SERVING: ABOUT 330 CALORIES, 4 G PROTEIN, 46 G CARBOHYDRATE, 15 G TOTAL FAT (9 G SATURATED), 2 G FIBER, 49 MG CHOLESTEROL, 315 MG SODIUM.

BLUEBERRY COBBLER Prepare biscuits as for Rhubarb-Strawberry Cobbler but use blueberry filling for rhubarb-strawberry filling: In 3-quart saucepan, stir together *½ cup sugar* and *2 tablespoons cornstarch*. Stir in *1 tablespoon fresh lemon juice, ¼ cup water,* and *6 cups fresh blueberries,* picked over. Heat to boiling over medium-high heat, stirring frequently. Remove saucepan from heat. Assemble and bake as directed.

EACH SERVING: ABOUT 370 CALORIES, 4 G PROTEIN, 56 G CARBOHYDRATE, 15 G TOTAL FAT (9 G SATURATED), 3 G FIBER, 49 MG CHOLESTEROL, 315 MG SODIUM.

PEACH COBBLER Prepare biscuits as for Rhubarb-Strawberry Cobbler but use peach filling for rhubarb-strawberry filling: In 3-quart saucepan, stir together *½ cup sugar* and *3 tablespoons cornstarch*. Stir in *1 tablespoon fresh lemon juice* and *3 pounds (about 8 large) ripe peaches,* peeled, pitted, and thickly sliced. Heat to boiling over medium-high heat, stirring. Remove from heat. Assemble and bake as directed.

EACH SERVING: ABOUT 365 CALORIES, 4 G PROTEIN, 56 G CARBOHYDRATE, 15 G TOTAL FAT (9 G SATURATED), 3 G FIBER, 49 MG CHOLESTEROL, 310 MG SODIUM.

SLUMP, GRUNT, AND ENJOY

SOME FAVORITE FRUIT DESSERTS HAVE INEXPLICABLE BUT ENDEARING NAMES—LIKE COBBLERS (OVEN-BAKED FRUIT WITH A SUGARED BISCUIT TOPPING); SLUMPS AND GRUNTS (KETTLE-STEAMED FRUIT WITH BISCUIT TOPPING); FLUMMERY (CORNSTARCH-THICKENED FRUIT PUDDING); BETTYS (LAYERS OF FRUIT AND BUTTERY BREAD CRUMBS); AND BUCKLES (STREUSEL-TOPPED, FRUIT-STUDDED COFFEE CAKES).

Rhubarb-Strawberry Cobbler

Apple Brown Betty

PREP 35 MINUTES / BAKE 50 MINUTES

Brown Betty is an old-fashioned American dessert that combines fruit with buttery bread crumbs. You can use any flavorful variety of apples you like—Granny Smiths are just a suggestion. You could also try a combination of thinly sliced apples and pears.

8 SLICES FIRM WHITE BREAD, TORN INTO ½-INCH PIECES
½ CUP BUTTER OR MARGARINE (1 STICK), MELTED
1 TEASPOON GROUND CINNAMON
2½ POUNDS GRANNY SMITH APPLES (6 MEDIUM), PEELED, CORED, AND THINLY SLICED
⅔ CUP PACKED LIGHT BROWN SUGAR
2 TABLESPOONS FRESH LEMON JUICE
1 TEASPOON VANILLA EXTRACT
¼ TEASPOON GROUND NUTMEG

1 Preheat oven to 400° F. In 15½" by 10½" jelly-roll pan, bake bread pieces, stirring occasionally, about 12 to 15 minutes, until very lightly toasted. Grease shallow 2-quart glass or ceramic baking dish.

2 In medium bowl, combine melted butter and ½ teaspoon cinnamon. Add toasted bread; toss gently until evenly moistened.

3 In large bowl, combine apples, brown sugar, lemon juice, vanilla, nutmeg, and remaining ½ teaspoon cinnamon; toss to coat.

4 Place ½ cup bread pieces in prepared dish. Top with half of apple mixture, then 1 cup bread pieces. Place remaining apple mixture on top; sprinkle with remaining bread pieces, leaving 1-inch border all around edge.

5 Cover dish with foil and bake 40 minutes. Remove foil and bake 10 minutes longer, or until apples are tender and bread on top is brown. Cool on wire rack 10 minutes before serving warm. *Makes 8 servings.*

EACH SERVING: ABOUT 325 CALORIES, 3 G PROTEIN, 51 G CARBOHYDRATE, 13 G TOTAL FAT (8 G SATURATED), 3 G FIBER, 31 MG CHOLESTEROL, 275 MG SODIUM.

BANANA BROWN BETTY Prepare as above but use *6 ripe medium bananas,* sliced ¼ inch thick (about 4 cups), for apples, *½ teaspoon ground ginger* for nutmeg, and *6 tablespoons melted butter.* Bake as directed.
EACH SERVING: ABOUT 410 CALORIES, 3 G PROTEIN, 53 G CARBOHYDRATE, 22 G TOTAL FAT (13 G SATURATED), 2 G FIBER, 55 MG CHOLESTEROL, 365 MG SODIUM.

Plum Kuchen

PREP 20 MINUTES / BAKE 30 TO 35 MINUTES

A kuchen is a simple cake made from a sweet dough topped with halved or whole fruits. Plum kuchen is the most popular; small, egg-shaped European prune plums are especially suitable for this German recipe.

5 LARGE PLUMS OR 16 PRUNE PLUMS, PITTED
½ CUP SUGAR
1 CUP ALL-PURPOSE FLOUR
¼ CUP PLUS 3 TABLESPOONS BUTTER OR MARGARINE, SOFTENED
¼ CUP MILK
1 LARGE EGG
1½ TEASPOONS BAKING POWDER
¼ TEASPOON SALT
¼ TEASPOON GROUND CINNAMON
PINCH GROUND NUTMEG
⅓ CUP APRICOT JAM OR CURRANT JELLY
1 TABLESPOON BOILING WATER

1 Preheat oven to 400° F. Grease 11" by 7" glass or ceramic baking dish. Cut large plums into 8 wedges each; cut prune plums in half.

2 In large bowl, combine ¼ cup sugar, flour, ¼ cup butter, milk, egg, baking powder, and salt. With mixer at low speed, beat, scraping bowl frequently with rubber spatula, until mixture leaves sides of bowl and clings to beaters, about 2 minutes

3 Spread dough evenly in prepared dish. Arrange plums, skin side up, in slightly overlapping rows on dough.

4 In small saucepan, melt remaining 3 tablespoons butter over medium heat. Stir in remaining ¼ cup sugar, cinnamon, and nutmeg; spoon over plums. Bake 30 to 35 minutes, until plums are tender.

5 In small bowl, with fork, stir together jam and water until smooth. Brush glaze over hot fruit. Cool kuchen on wire rack 10 minutes before serving warm. *Makes 10 servings.*

EACH SERVING: ABOUT 220 CALORIES, 3 G PROTEIN, 32 G CARBOHYDRATE, 10 G TOTAL FAT (5 G SATURATED), 1 G FIBER, 44 MG CHOLESTEROL, 225 MG SODIUM.

BLUEBERRY KUCHEN Prepare as above but use *1 pint blueberries* for plums. Bake as directed.
EACH SERVING: ABOUT 215 CALORIES, 2 G PROTEIN, 31 G CARBOHYDRATE, 9 G TOTAL FAT (5 G SATURATED), 1 G FIBER, 44 MG CHOLESTEROL, 230 MG SODIUM.

Sweet Cherry Kuchen Prepare as for Plum Kuchen but use *1 pound sweet cherries,* pitted, for plums. Bake as directed.
EACH SERVING: ABOUT 225 CALORIES, 3 G PROTEIN, 34 G CARBOHYDRATE, 10 G TOTAL FAT (5 G SATURATED), 1 G FIBER, 44 MG CHOLESTEROL, 225 MG SODIUM.

Apple Kuchen Prepare as for Plum Kuchen but use *3 Golden Delicious apples (1¼ pounds),* peeled, cored, and thinly sliced, for plums. Bake as directed.
EACH SERVING: ABOUT 230 CALORIES, 2 G PROTEIN, 35 G CARBOHYDRATE, 9 G TOTAL FAT (5 G SATURATED), 2 G FIBER, 44 MG CHOLESTEROL, 225 MG SODIUM.

Pear Crisp Prepare as for Apple-Oatmeal Crisp but use *6 large firm-ripe pears* (2¾ pounds), peeled, cored, and cut into ½-inch slices, for apples. Toss in large bowl instead of baking dish. Bake as directed.
EACH SERVING: ABOUT 380 CALORIES, 3 G PROTEIN, 68 G CARBOHYDRATE, 13 G TOTAL FAT (7 G SATURATED), 6 G FIBER, 31 MG CHOLESTEROL, 130 MG SODIUM.

Pear-Cranberry Crisp Prepare as above but add *1 cup fresh or frozen cranberries* with pear slices. Bake as directed.
EACH SERVING: ABOUT 390 CALORIES, 3 G PROTEIN, 70 G CARBOHYDRATE, 13 G TOTAL FAT (7 G SATURATED), 6 G FIBER, 31 MG CHOLESTEROL, 130 MG SODIUM.

Apple-Oatmeal Crisp

PREP 20 MINUTES / BAKE 30 TO 35 MINUTES

Oats add extra nutrition to this fragrant fall dessert; the apples, of course, are plenty healthful in themselves. As with a cobbler, you can try the topping with many different fruit fillings.

2¾ POUNDS GRANNY SMITH APPLES (7 MEDIUM), PEELED, CORED, AND CUT INTO ¼-INCH SLICES
2 TABLESPOONS FRESH LEMON JUICE
¾ CUP PACKED DARK BROWN SUGAR
2 TABLESPOONS PLUS ⅓ CUP ALL-PURPOSE FLOUR
½ CUP OLD-FASHIONED OR QUICK-COOKING OATS, UNCOOKED
¼ TEASPOON GROUND CINNAMON
6 TABLESPOONS BUTTER OR MARGARINE, CUT UP

1 Preheat oven to 425° F. In 1½-quart glass or ceramic baking dish, combine apples, lemon juice, ½ cup brown sugar, and 2 tablespoons flour, tossing to coat.

2 In small bowl, stir together oats, remaining ⅓ cup flour, and remaining ¼ cup brown sugar. With pastry blender or 2 knives used scissor-fashion, cut in butter until mixture resembles coarse crumbs. Sprinkle over apple mixture.

3 Bake 30 to 35 minutes, until apples are tender and topping is lightly browned. Cool crisp slightly on wire rack before serving warm. *Makes 6 servings.*

EACH SERVING: ABOUT 370 CALORIES, 2 G PROTEIN, 65 G CARBOHYDRATE, 13 G TOTAL FAT (7 G SATURATED), 4 G FIBER, 31 MG CHOLESTEROL, 130 MG SODIUM.

Cherry-Almond Clafouti

PREP 20 MINUTES / BAKE 40 TO 45 MINUTES

Clafouti—or clafoutis—is a French country specialty that's rather like a thick, fruit-studded pancake.

1 POUND DARK SWEET CHERRIES, PITTED
2 CUPS HALF-AND-HALF OR LIGHT CREAM
⅓ CUP SUGAR
2 TABLESPOONS AMARETTO (ALMOND-FLAVORED LIQUEUR)
4 LARGE EGGS
⅔ CUP ALL-PURPOSE FLOUR
CONFECTIONERS' SUGAR

1 Preheat oven to 350° F. Grease 10" by 1½" round ceramic baking dish.

2 Place cherries in prepared dish. In medium bowl, with wire whisk or fork, beat half-and-half, sugar, amaretto, and eggs until well blended. Whisk in flour, a little at a time, until smooth. Or, in blender, process half-and-half, sugar, amaretto, eggs, and flour until smooth.

3 Pour egg mixture over cherries in prepared dish. Bake 40 to 45 minutes, until custard is set and knife inserted 1 inch from edge comes out clean (center will still jiggle). Sprinkle with confectioners' sugar. Serve hot. *Makes 12 servings.*

EACH SERVING: ABOUT 155 CALORIES, 4 G PROTEIN, 20 G CARBOHYDRATE, 7 G TOTAL FAT (4 G SATURATED), 0.5 G FIBER, 86 MG CHOLESTEROL, 40 MG SODIUM.

Pear Dumplings
à la Crème

PREP 35 MINUTES PLUS CHILLING
BAKE 40 TO 45 MINUTES

*This dressed-up dumpling provides a happy ending to
a very special dinner party. The photos at right will
help you shape the dumplings as well as decorate them
with delicate pastry leaves.*

1½ CUPS ALL-PURPOSE FLOUR
½ CUP BUTTER OR MARGARINE (1 STICK), SOFTENED
1 PACKAGE (3 OUNCES) CREAM CHEESE, SOFTENED
3 MEDIUM BARTLETT OR BOSC PEARS (1 POUND)
¼ CUP PACKED DARK BROWN SUGAR
¼ TEASPOON GROUND CINNAMON
1 LARGE EGG WHITE, LIGHTLY BEATEN
2 TEASPOONS GRANULATED SUGAR
6 WHOLE CLOVES
CUSTARD SAUCE (PAGE 363)

1 In food processor with knife blade attached,
process flour, butter, and cream cheese until mixture
forms ball. Remove ball from processor; flatten into
small disk. Refrigerate for 30 minutes.

2 Line large cookie sheet with foil. Peel pears, leaving stem intact; cut each pear lengthwise in half and
remove core. Set pear halves aside. On floured surface, with floured rolling pin, roll half of pastry ⅛
inch thick. Using 7-inch round plate as guide, cut 3
rounds from pastry. Reserve trimmings.

3 In cup, combine brown sugar and cinnamon.
Sprinkle pastry rounds with half of sugar mixture.
Place 1 pear half, core side up, on each pastry round.
Fold pastry over pears; pinch edges to seal (see top
photo opposite). Place pastry-covered pears, seam
side down, on prepared cookie sheet. Repeat with
remaining pastry, sugar mixture, and pear halves to
make 6 dumplings.

4 Preheat oven to 375° F. Reroll pastry trimmings;
cut to make leaves (see bottom photo opposite).
Brush pastry-covered pears with egg white; decorate
with pastry leaves and brush with egg white. Sprin-

Pear Dumplings à la Crème

kle dumplings with granulated sugar. Place 2 sheets foil under cookie sheet; crimp edges to form rim to catch any overflow during baking. Bake 40 to 45 minutes, until pastry is golden (there will be some leakage). With spatula, immediately transfer dumplings to wire rack. Cool slightly.

5 While pears bake, prepare Custard Sauce.

6 To serve; insert 1 whole clove in tip of each pear half without stem to resemble stems. Serve warm with Custard Sauce. *Makes 6 servings.*

EACH SERVING: ABOUT 490 CALORIES, 9 G PROTEIN, 56 G CARBOHYDRATE, 26 G TOTAL FAT (15 G SATURATED), 3 G FIBER, 206 MG CHOLESTEROL, 240 MG SODIUM.

Making Pear Dumplings

After cutting the pastry into 7-inch circles, lay a pear half on each one. Bring the sides of the pastry up over the pear and pinch them together to seal.

Place the pastry-wrapped pears, seam side down, on the cookie sheet. Decorate each one with leaves cut from the remaining pastry, then glaze the pastry with egg white and sprinkle with sugar.

Nectarine & Cherry Crisp with Oatmeal Topping

PREP 30 MINUTES / BAKE 60 TO 75 MINUTES

½ CUP GRANULATED SUGAR

3 TABLESPOONS CORNSTARCH

10 RIPE MEDIUM NECTARINES (3 POUNDS), EACH CUT INTO 6 WEDGES

1½ POUNDS DARK SWEET CHERRIES, PITTED

2 TABLESPOONS FRESH LEMON JUICE

2 TABLESPOONS COLD BUTTER OR MARGARINE, CUT INTO SMALL PIECES

⅔ CUP PACKED LIGHT BROWN SUGAR

6 TABLESPOONS BUTTER OR MARGARINE, SOFTENED

1 LARGE EGG

2 TEASPOONS VANILLA EXTRACT

1½ CUPS OLD-FASHIONED OR QUICK-COOKING OATS, UNCOOKED

¾ CUP ALL-PURPOSE FLOUR

¼ TEASPOON SALT

¼ TEASPOON BAKING SODA

1 Preheat oven to 375° F. In small bowl, stir together granulated sugar and cornstarch. In large bowl, toss nectarines, cherries, lemon juice, and sugar mixture until fruit is evenly coated.

2 Spoon mixture into 13" by 9" glass or ceramic baking dish; dot with butter. Place sheet of foil under baking dish; crimp edges to form rim to catch overflow during baking. Cover dish with foil and bake 40 to 50 minutes, until gently bubbling.

3 Meanwhile, in large bowl, with mixer, beat brown sugar and butter until smooth. Beat in egg and vanilla until light and fluffy. With spoon, stir in oats, flour, salt, and baking soda. Chill until ready to use.

4 Drop oat mixture by scant ¼ cups over hot filling. Bake, uncovered, 20 to 25 minutes, until topping is browned. Cool slightly on wire rack before serving warm. *Makes 12 servings.*

EACH SERVING: ABOUT 315 CALORIES, 5 G PROTEIN, 56 G CARBOHYDRATE, 10 G TOTAL FAT (5 G SATURATED), 4 G FIBER, 38 MG CHOLESTEROL, 160 MG SODIUM.

MERINGUES

The desserts in this section are all made with meringue that has been slowly baked until crisp. Make meringues when the humidity is very low. The oven temperatures are notably low; you could say that the meringues are really dried rather than baked. Don't try to speed things up with higher heat, which will dry and brown the outer surface too quickly, leaving the inside undercooked.

Pavlova

PREP 30 MINUTES / BAKE 2 HOURS PLUS DRYING TIME

Sometimes referred to as the "national dessert of Australia," this gorgeous dessert was created to honor prima ballerina Anna Pavlova, who was renowned for her leading role in Swan Lake. *Swanlike in its enchanting delicacy and pristine whiteness, the meringue shell is filled with fresh fruit and whipped cream.*

⅔ CUP PLUS 2 TABLESPOONS SUGAR

1 TABLESPOON CORNSTARCH

4 LARGE EGG WHITES (½ CUP)

¼ TEASPOON SALT

2 TEASPOONS DISTILLED WHITE VINEGAR

1½ TEASPOONS VANILLA EXTRACT

1 CUP HEAVY OR WHIPPING CREAM

3 KIWIFRUIT, PEELED, QUARTERED LENGTHWISE, AND
    THICKLY SLICED

½ PINT RASPBERRIES

1 RIPE PASSIONFRUIT, PULP SCOOPED OUT IN SMALL
    PIECES (OPTIONAL)

1 Preheat oven to 225° F. Line large cookie sheet with foil. Grease foil; dust with flour. Using bottom of 9-inch round plate or cake pan as a guide, with toothpick, trace a circle in center of foil on cookie sheet.

2 In bowl, combine ⅔ cup sugar and cornstarch.

3 In large bowl, with mixer at medium speed, beat egg whites and salt until foamy. Beat in sugar-cornstarch mixture, 1 tablespoon at a time, beating well after each addition, until mixture completely

dissolves and whites stand in stiff, glossy peaks when beaters are lifted. Beat in vinegar and 1 teaspoon vanilla. Spoon egg-white mixture into circle on foil. With spoon, spread mixture to edge of circle, forming 2-inch-high edge all around (see photo below).

4 Bake 2 hours, or until set. Turn oven off; leave meringue in oven 2 hours or up to overnight to dry.

5 In small bowl, with mixer at medium speed, beat cream and remaining 2 tablespoons sugar to soft peaks. Beat in remaining ½ teaspoon vanilla.

6 Transfer cooled meringue to cake plate. Spoon whipped cream into center and top with fruits. *Makes 8 servings.*

EACH SERVING: ABOUT 225 CALORIES, 3 G PROTEIN, 29 G CARBOHYDRATE, 12 G TOTAL FAT (7 G SATURATED), 2 G FIBER, 41 MG CHOLESTEROL, 110 MG SODIUM.

Forming a Meringue Nest

Spoon the meringue mixture onto the foil and spread it to the edges of the circle. Then push the meringue from the center toward the outer edge of the circle to form a rim. Use the same technique for the Coconut Meringue Nest (page 197) and Meringue Shells (page 196).

Meringue Shells

PREP 15 MINUTES / BAKE 2 HOURS PLUS DRYING TIME

These versatile shells are made of crisp meringue that is quite different from the soft meringue used on lemon pies. For perfect results, make sure that the sugar is completely dissolved in the egg whites. To test, rub a bit of the meringue mixture between your fingers: It should feel perfectly smooth, not grainy. By the way, if you love pies and tarts but want to avoid the extra fat in pie dough, meringue shells may be your salvation.

3 LARGE EGG WHITES
⅛ TEASPOON CREAM OF TARTAR
¾ CUP SUGAR
½ TEASPOON VANILLA EXTRACT

1 Preheat oven to 200° F. Line large cookie sheet with foil or parchment paper. In medium bowl, with mixer at high speed, beat egg whites and cream of tartar until soft peaks begin to form when beaters are lifted. Gradually sprinkle in sugar, 2 tablespoons at a time, beating well after each addition until sugar dissolves and egg whites stand in stiff, glossy peaks when beaters are lifted. Beat in vanilla.

2 Onto prepared cookie sheet, spoon meringue to make 6 equal mounds, 4 inches apart. With back of tablespoon, spread each mound into a 4-inch round. Make well in center of each meringue round to form a nest (see photo page 194).

3 Bake 2 hours, or until meringues are crisp but not brown. Turn oven off; leave meringues in oven 1 hour or overnight to dry. If not leaving overnight, cool completely on cookie sheet on wire rack. Store shells in airtight container for up to 1 month. *Makes 6 meringue shells.*

EACH SHELL: ABOUT 105 CALORIES, 2 G PROTEIN,
25 G CARBOHYDRATE, 0 G TOTAL FAT (0 G SATURATED),
0 G FIBER, 0 MG CHOLESTEROL, 30 MG SODIUM.

MERINGUE SHELLS WITH LEMON FILLING & STRAW-BERRIES Prepare Meringue Shells as above. In medium bowl, toss *1 pint strawberries,* hulled and quartered, with *1 tablespoon strawberry preserves.* Spoon Lemon Curd Cream (page 361) into cooled shells. Top with strawberry mixture. Garnish with fresh mint leaves. *Makes 6 servings.*

EACH SERVING: ABOUT 275 CALORIES, 3 G PROTEIN,
42 G CARBOHYDRATE, 11 G TOTAL FAT (6 G SATURATED),
1 G FIBER, 93 MG CHOLESTEROL, 105 MG SODIUM.

MINIATURE MERINGUE SHELLS Line 2 large cookie sheets with foil or parchment paper. Prepare meringue as for Meringue Shells in Step 1. Drop meringue by rounded teaspoons, 2 inches apart, on prepared cookie sheets. With back of teaspoon, make well in center of each meringue to form a nest. (Nests will be about 1½ inches in diameter.) Bake 1 hour, or until meringues are crisp but not brown. Turn off oven; leave meringues in oven 1 hour, or overnight to dry. If not leaving overnight, cool completely on cookie sheet on wire rack. *Makes 20 miniature meringue shells.*

EACH SHELL: ABOUT 30 CALORIES, 1 G PROTEIN,
8 G CARBOHYDRATE, 0 G TOTAL FAT (0 G SATURATED),
0 G FIBER, 0 MG CHOLESTEROL, 10 MG SODIUM.

STRAWBERRIES & CREAM MERINGUE SHELLS Prepare Miniature Meringue Shells. In small bowl, with mixer at medium speed, beat *½ cup heavy or whipping cream* and *2 teaspoons sugar* until soft peaks form; stir in *1 to 2 teaspoons orange-flavored liqueur.* Spoon flavored cream into cooled shells. Top each with *1 whole hulled strawberry. Makes 20 servings.*

EACH SERVING: ABOUT 55 CALORIES, 1 G PROTEIN,
9 G CARBOHYDRATE, 2 G TOTAL FAT (1 G SATURATED),
0 G FIBER, 8 MG CHOLESTEROL, 10 MG SODIUM.

ANGEL PIE Line 9-inch pie plate with foil. Generously grease and flour foil. Prepare meringue as for Meringue Shells in Step 1. Spoon into prepared plate and, with rubber spatula, spread evenly up sides of pan. Bake 1 hour, or until dry and set. Turn off oven; leave shell in oven 1 hour 30 minutes, or overnight

---

ANGEL PIE

NOT JUST A SWEET-TALKER'S ENDEARMENT, ANGEL PIE IS ALSO A BOON TO THE FAT-CONSCIOUS. THE MERINGUE CRUST IS, OF COURSE, FAT-FREE, AND IF THE FILLING IS NOT TOO RICH, YOU CAN SERVE UP QUITE A FABULOUS LOW-FAT DESSERT. ONE POSSIBILITY IS JUICY FRESH BERRIES—PUREE SOME OF THE FRUIT, THEN MIX THE WHOLE BERRIES INTO IT. SPOON THE MIXTURE INTO THE MERINGUE SHELL AND TOP WITH DOLLOPS OF VANILLA YOGURT. OR TRY A NEW TAKE ON AN ICE-CREAM CAKE: FILL THE SHELL WITH SCOOPS OF TROPICAL SORBETS, LIKE MANGO, LIME, AND PASSIONFRUIT. THEN COVER AND FREEZE.

---

to dry. Meanwhile, prepare Lemon Curd Cream (page 361). To serve, lift shell out of pan and carefully remove foil. Place on plate and fill with Lemon Curd Cream or softened ice cream. *Makes 8 servings.*

EACH SERVING WITH LEMON CURD CREAM: ABOUT 205 CALORIES, 2 G PROTEIN, 29 G CARBOHYDRATE, 9 G TOTAL FAT (5 G SATURATED), 0 G FIBER, 70 MG CHOLESTEROL, 80 MG SODIUM.

Coconut Meringue Nest with Mango Filling

PREP 45 MINUTES
BAKE 1 HOUR 15 MINUTES PLUS DRYING TIME

Don't set your heart on this wonderful dessert unless you can get ripe mangoes. The flowery fragrance of the ripe fruit is unmistakable. If necessary, get a headstart: Buy a mango that's at least slightly aromatic and keep it in a loosely closed plastic bag at cool room temperature for a few days. It will soften, develop a pinkish or orange-yellow blush, and become sweeter and juicier.

MERINGUE NEST:
¾ CUP FLAKED SWEETENED COCONUT
3 LARGE EGG WHITES
¼ TEASPOON SALT
¼ TEASPOON CREAM OF TARTAR
¾ CUP GRANULATED SUGAR

FILLING:
2 LARGE RIPE MANGOES (2 POUNDS)
4 TO 6 LIMES
1 CAN (14 OUNCES) SWEETENED CONDENSED MILK
1 ENVELOPE UNFLAVORED GELATIN
¼ CUP COLD WATER
1 CUP HEAVY OR WHIPPING CREAM
2 TABLESPOONS CONFECTIONERS' SUGAR
1 CUP RASPBERRIES

1 Preheat oven to 325° F. Prepare Meringue Nest: Spread coconut on large cookie sheet. Bake 8 to 10 minutes, until toasted. Let coconut and cookie sheet cool. Turn oven control to 275° F.

2 Line cookie sheet with foil. Using bottom of 9-inch round plate or cake pan as a guide, with toothpick, trace a circle in center of foil on cookie sheet.

3 In large bowl, with mixer at high speed, beat egg whites and salt until foamy. Beat in cream of tartar. Increase speed to high and gradually beat in granulated sugar, 1 tablespoon at a time, beating well after each addition until whites stand in stiff, glossy peaks when beaters are lifted. With hands, crush coconut slightly. Fold into egg-white mixture. Spoon egg-white mixture into circle on foil. With back of spoon, spread mixture to edge of circle, forming 1½-inch-high edge all around (see photo, page 194).

4 Bake 1 hour 15 minutes. Turn oven off; leave meringue in oven 1 hour to dry. Transfer meringue on foil to wire rack; cool completely.

5 Prepare Filling: Slice each mango down both sides of long, flat seed. Run small paring knife between skin and flesh of each half, cutting away peel. Dice ½ cup mango and refrigerate. Cut remaining mango into chunks. In food processor, with knife blade attached, puree mango chunks until smooth (you should have about 1¼ cups puree).

6 From limes, grate 2 teaspoons peel and squeeze ½ cup juice. In medium bowl, combine condensed milk, and lime peel and juice until blended. Stir in mango puree until combined.

7 In 1-quart saucepan, sprinkle gelatin evenly over cold water; let stand 1 minute to soften. Heat over low heat, stirring frequently, about 2 to 3 minutes, until gelatin completely dissolves; do not boil. Whisk into mango mixture.

8 Set bowl filled with mango mixture in larger bowl filled with ice water. With rubber spatula, stir occasionally until mixture thickens enough to mound without loosing its shape, 20 to 30 minutes. Remove bowl with filling from bowl of ice water.

9 With metal spatula, carefully loosen and remove meringue from foil. Place meringue shell on serving plate. Pour mango mixture into shell; refrigerate at least 1 hour or up to 6 hours, until filling is firm enough to slice.

10 In small bowl, with mixer on high speed, beat cream and confectioners' sugar until soft peaks form. Garnish filling with whipped cream, reserved diced mango, and raspberries. *Makes 10 servings.*

EACH SERVING: ABOUT 360 CALORIES, 6 G PROTEIN, 55 G CARBOHYDRATE, 14 G TOTAL FAT (9 G SATURATED), 2 G FIBER, 46 MG CHOLESTEROL, 150 MG SODIUM.

Meringue Mushrooms

PREP **45** MINUTES
BAKE **1** HOUR **45** MINUTES PLUS DRYING TIME

Charming little meringue mushrooms are a traditional finishing touch on a Bûche de Noël (page 328). And you can make them well in advance, saving a bit of last-minute fuss at holiday time.

4 LARGE EGG WHITES
¼ TEASPOON CREAM OF TARTAR
¾ CUP SUGAR
¼ TEASPOON ALMOND EXTRACT
2 SQUARES (2 OUNCES) SEMISWEET CHOCOLATE, MELTED
UNSWEETENED COCOA

1 Preheat oven to 200° F. Line large cookie sheet with foil or parchment paper.

2 In medium bowl, with mixer at high speed, beat egg whites and cream of tartar until soft peaks form when beaters are lifted. Gradually sprinkle in sugar, 2 tablespoons at a time, beating well after each addition, until sugar completely dissolves and whites stand in stiff, glossy peaks when beaters are lifted. Beat in almond extract.

3 Spoon meringue into large pastry bag with ½-inch plain tip. Pipe meringue onto cookie sheet in 30 mounds, each about 1½ inches in diameter, to resemble mushroom caps (see top photo at right). Pipe remaining meringue upright in thirty 1¼-inch lengths to resemble mushroom stems.

4 Bake 1 hour 45 minutes. (If there is extra meringue, pipe additional stems in case of breakage.) Turn off oven; leave meringues in oven 30 minutes to dry. Cool completely on cookie sheet on wire rack.

5 With tip of small knife, cut small hollow in center of underside of each mushroom cap (see middle photo at right). Place small amount of melted chocolate in hollow; spread underside of cap with chocolate. Attach stem to cap by inserting pointed end of stem into hollow in underside of cap (see bottom photo at right). Repeat with remaining stems, caps, and chocolate. Let chocolate set, about 1 hour.

6 Store meringue mushrooms in airtight container at room temperature up to 1 month. Just before serving, sprinkle lightly with unsweetened cocoa. *Makes 30 mushrooms.*

EACH MUSHROOM: ABOUT 30 CALORIES, 1 G PROTEIN,
6 G CARBOHYDRATE, 1 G TOTAL FAT (0 G SATURATED),
0 G FIBER, 0 MG CHOLESTEROL, 10 MG SODIUM.

Forming Meringue Mushrooms

Pipe the meringue for the mushroom caps onto a sheet of foil, using a ½-inch plain tip. The mounds of meringue don't have be be regular in shape, just nicely rounded.

After baking, remove the caps from foil. Use a paring knife to carve a small hollow in the bottom of each cap.

Spoon a few drops of melted chocolate into the hollow and insert one of the stems, pointed side up. Leave at room temperature until the chocolate has set, about 1 hour.

FRUIT SHORTCAKES

Most people would confirm the validity of the following equation: Fruit plus cake plus cream equals ambrosia. The fruits—and they must be at their ripe, sweet peak—are the shortcake's reason for being, and the whipped cream elevates it to a sublime status. However, opinions diverge when it comes to the cake. There are those who believe that a true shortcake must be made with still-warm baking-powder biscuits, while others prefer to complement the fruit and cream with layers of vanilla-scented butter cake. Both factions are well served with the two recipes that follow. The filling variations presented with the first (biscuit) recipe will work equally well with the second (butter cake) version.

Strawberry Shortcake

PREP 25 MINUTES / BAKE 20 TO 22 MINUTES

This recipe is for the biscuit partisans; the variations will keep you happy for many seasons to come. You can bake the biscuit in an 8-inch pan for one large shortcake, or cut the dough into small rounds for individual servings. For truly superb shortcake, assemble and serve the dessert while the biscuits are still warm.

2 CUPS ALL-PURPOSE FLOUR
6 TABLESPOONS PLUS ⅓ CUP SUGAR
2 TEASPOONS BAKING POWDER
¼ TEASPOON SALT
⅓ CUP COLD BUTTER OR MARGARINE, CUT UP
⅔ CUP MILK
6 CUPS STRAWBERRIES
1 CUP HEAVY OR WHIPPING CREAM

1 Preheat oven to 425° F. Grease 8-inch round cake pan.

2 In medium bowl, stir together flour, 3 tablespoons sugar, baking powder, and salt. With pastry blender or 2 knives used scissor-fashion, cut in butter until mixture resembles coarse crumbs. Stir in milk and stir just until mixture forms soft dough that leaves side of bowl.

3 On lightly floured surface, knead dough about 10 times, just to mix. Pat dough evenly into prepared pan and sprinkle top with 1 tablespoon sugar. Bake 20 to 22 minutes, until dough is lightly golden.

4 Meanwhile, reserve 4 whole strawberries for garnish; hull and halve or quarter remaining strawberries. In medium bowl, mix cut-up strawberries with ⅓ cup sugar until sugar has dissolved.

5 Invert shortcake onto surface. With long serrated knife, carefully split hot shortcake horizontally. In bowl, with mixer at medium speed, beat cream just until soft peaks form. Beat in remaining 2 tablespoons sugar.

6 Place bottom half of shortcake, cut side up, on cake plate; top with half of strawberry mixture and half of whipped cream. Place cake top, cut side down, on strawberry mixture. Spoon remaining strawberry mixture on top and then spoon whipped cream on top of strawberries. Garnish with reserved whole strawberries. *Makes 10 servings.*

EACH SERVING: ABOUT 325 CALORIES, 4 G PROTEIN, 42 G CARBOHYDRATE, 16 G TOTAL FAT (10 G SATURATED), 3 G FIBER, 51 MG CHOLESTEROL, 235 MG SODIUM.

SUMMER FRUIT SHORTCAKE Prepare and bake dough as for Strawberry Shortcake. Use *6 cups (about 3 pounds) mixed summer fruit* (such as sliced nectarines, sliced peeled peaches, blueberries, blackberries, and/or raspberries) for strawberries; toss with *⅓ cup sugar* and *1 to 2 tablespoons fresh lemon juice.* Assemble shortcake as directed.
EACH SERVING: ABOUT 370 CALORIES, 4 G PROTEIN, 53 G CARBOHYDRATE, 16 G TOTAL FAT (10 G SATURATED), 2 G FIBER, 51 MG CHOLESTEROL, 235 MG SODIUM.

INDIVIDUAL SHORTCAKES Prepare dough as for Strawberry Shortcake. On lightly floured surface, pat dough 1 inch thick. With 2½-inch floured cutter, cut 8 biscuits. Transfer to cookie sheet and bake 15 to 20 minutes, or until bottoms are golden brown. Split biscuits horizontally, place bottom halves on 8 dessert plates, and top evenly with fruit mixture and whipped cream. Replace tops. *Makes 8 servings.*
EACH SERVING: ABOUT 410 CALORIES, 5 G PROTEIN, 53 G CARBOHYDRATE, 21 G TOTAL FAT (12 G SATURATED), 4 G FIBER, 64 MG CHOLESTEROL, 295 MG SODIUM.

PECAN SHORTCAKES Prepare dough as for Strawberry Shortcake and add *1 cup pecans,* toasted and coarsely chopped, to flour-butter mixture in Step 2. Cut into Individual Shortcakes as above; bake and fill as directed. *Makes 8 servings.*
EACH SERVING: ABOUT 500 CALORIES, 6 G PROTEIN, 55 G CARBOHYDRATE, 30 G TOTAL FAT (13 G SATURATED), 5 G FIBER, 64 MG CHOLESTEROL, 295 MG SODIUM.

BROWN SUGAR-PEAR SHORTCAKES Prepare Individual Shortcakes (page 199). Meanwhile, in 12-inch nonstick skillet, melt *4 tablespoons butter* over medium-high heat. Add *2¼ pounds ripe Bosc pears (6)*, peeled, cored, and cut lengthwise into ¾-inch wedges. Cook, uncovered, stirring gently and frequently, 10 to 15 minutes, until pears are browned and tender. Stir in *¼ cup packed light brown sugar, ¼ teaspoon ground cinnamon, 2 strips (2½" by ½" each) lemon peel,* and *¼ cup water.* Cook 1 minute; discard peels. Spoon mixture onto bottom of each shortcake. Top each with whipped cream and biscuit top.

EACH SERVING: ABOUT 525 CALORIES, 5 G PROTEIN, 70 G CARBOHYDRATE, 26 G TOTAL FAT (16 G SATURATED), 3.5 G FIBER, 80 MG CHOLESTEROL, 355 MG SODIUM.

TART CHERRY SHORTCAKES Prepare Individual Shortcakes (page 199). In 3-quart saucepan, stir *⅔ cup sugar* with *1 tablespoon cornstarch* until evenly blended. Working over bowl to catch juices, with cherry pitter or paring knife, remove pits from *1 quart tart cherries.* Stir cherries and any juice into sugar mixture. Heat to boiling over medium-high heat, stirring, and cook until mixture has thickened. Reduce heat and simmer, stirring, 1 minute. Remove saucepan from heat. Spoon warm cherry mixture onto bottom of each shortcake. Top each with whipped cream and biscuit top.

EACH SERVING: ABOUT 470 CALORIES, 5 G PROTEIN, 69 G CARBOHYDRATE, 20 G TOTAL FAT (12 G SATURATED), 1 G FIBER, 64 MG CHOLESTEROL, 295 MG SODIUM.

BLUEBERRY-PEACH SHORTCAKES Prepare Individual Shortcakes (page 199). Meanwhile, in 3-quart nonreactive saucepan, stir together *2 tablespoons fresh lemon juice* and *1 tablespoon cornstarch.* Add *1½ pints blueberries,* picked over, and *⅔ cup sugar* and heat to boiling over medium heat. Boil 1 minute. Remove saucepan from heat and stir in *6 medium peaches,* peeled, pitted, and each sliced into 8 wedges. Spoon warm fruit mixture onto bottom of each shortcake. Top each with whipped cream and biscuit top.

EACH SERVING: ABOUT 520 CALORIES, 6 G PROTEIN, 82 G CARBOHYDRATE, 20 G TOTAL FAT (12 G SATURATED), 4 G FIBER, 64 MG CHOLESTEROL, 295 MG SODIUM.

Berries & Cream Shortcake

PREP 40 MINUTES PLUS COOLING
BAKE 25 TO 30 MINUTES

½ CUP BUTTER OR MARGARINE (1 STICK), SOFTENED
1 CUP PLUS 1 TABLESPOON SUGAR
1½ CUPS CAKE FLOUR (NOT SELF-RISING)
½ CUP MILK
1½ TEASPOONS BAKING POWDER
1 TEASPOON VANILLA EXTRACT
¼ TEASPOON SALT
2 LARGE EGGS
1 PINT BLUEBERRIES
½ PINT STRAWBERRIES, HULLED AND HALVED
½ PINT RASPBERRIES
½ PINT BLACKBERRIES
¼ CUP SEEDLESS STRAWBERRY JAM
1 CUP HEAVY OR WHIPPING CREAM

1 Preheat oven to 350° F. Grease and flour two 8-inch round cake pans.

2 In large bowl, with mixer at low speed, beat butter and 1 cup sugar just until blended. Increase speed to high; beat until light and fluffy, about 5 minutes. Reduce speed to low; add flour, milk, baking powder, vanilla, salt, and eggs; beat until well mixed, scraping bowl constantly with rubber spatula. Increase speed to high; beat 2 minutes, scraping bowl occasionally.

3 Spoon batter into pans. Bake 25 to 30 minutes, until toothpick inserted in centers of cakes comes out clean. Cool cake layers in pans on wire racks 10 minutes; remove from pans and cool completely on racks.

4 Meanwhile, in large bowl, toss all the berries with strawberry jam.

5 In small bowl, with mixer at medium speed, beat cream and remaining 1 tablespoon sugar until stiff peaks form.

6 Place 1 cake layer on cake plate; spread with half the whipped cream and half the berry mixture. Place second cake layer on berry mixture; top with remaining whipped cream and fruit. *Makes 10 servings.*

EACH SERVING: ABOUT 395 CALORIES, 4 G PROTEIN, 50 G CARBOHYDRATE, 21 G TOTAL FAT (12 G SATURATED), 2 G FIBER, 102 MG CHOLESTEROL, 255 MG SODIUM.

Pies & Tarts

glass pie plate

pie weights

9-inch tart pan with removable bottom

tartlet pan

mini-muffin pan

Pies & Tarts

The tools of pie-making are the stuff of heirlooms, and no kitchen is complete without them. Perhaps you have some of your mother's or grandmother's pie-baking equipment. If not, start by getting some good **pie plates.** Oven-safe glass speeds baking because in addition to conducting heat, it allows radiant energy to pass through to the crust. You can easily check on how the bottom crust is browning, and glass is easy to clean. For metal pans, heavy aluminum is a good choice. (Pie plates, by the way, are measured across their diameter from rim to rim, not across the bottom.) Metal **pie weights** are required when you're baking an unfilled crust (called "baking blind"), to keep the dough from puffing or blistering. Dry beans can be used instead of metal weights (you can reuse the beans indefinitely for pie-baking, but they'll dry out too much to cook), as can uncooked rice. For tarts and quiches, you'll need a **tart pan** with a removable bottom. After baking and cooling the tart, remove the side of the pan to display the tart's fluted crust. Individual **tartlet pans** allow you to make tempting mini-tarts and quiches. Here, too, pans with removable bottoms are preferable. Diminutive pastry shells can be baked in a **mini-muffin pan,** which is also used for doll-size muffins and cupcakes.

Previous page: Peach Pie

Basic techniques

MAKING PIE CRUST

With a pastry blender (or 2 knives used scissor-fashion), "chop" the shortening into the dry ingredients until crumb-like.

Before rolling, let chilled dough stand at room temperature 5 minutes. With a floured rolling pin on a floured surface, flatten the dough into a round.

Roll out the dough until it's the right size. Give the round an occasional quarter-turn; if it sticks, sprinkle the surface with a bit more flour.

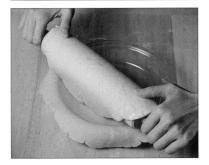

Fold half of the dough round over the rolling pin. Center the rolling pin over the pie plate and let the dough roll off the pin onto the plate.

BAKING BLIND

When baking an unfilled crust, prick the bottom of the crust all over with a fork. This will help keep the crust from blistering as it bakes.

To prevent crust from puffing up and shrinking, bake it blind: Line it with foil and fill it with dry beans, metal pie weights, or uncooked rice.

DOUBLE-CRUST PIE

Fold under both edges to seal them, then create a decorative edge, if you like (see page 212). Cut several 1-inch slits in the top to let steam escape.

TRIMMING A TART CRUST

With a tart pan, you don't have to worry about finishing the edges. Just press the dough gently into the rim; let the dough hang over the edge.

To trim off the excess dough, simply roll a rolling pin over the edges of the pan; the rim will act as a cutting edge and the dough will fall away.

PASTRY & PIE DOUGHS

Depending on which type and size pie you're making, you'll want to choose your pastry accordingly. Classic fruit pies are very nice with a straightforward double-crust pastry. The butter adds great flavor. For single-crust tarts, a sweeter or shortbread crust is a good choice. A pat-in-the pan crust is a great choice when baking with children.

Pastry for Double-Crust Pie

PREP 10 MINUTES PLUS CHILLING

2¼ CUPS ALL-PURPOSE FLOUR
½ TEASPOON SALT
½ CUP COLD BUTTER OR MARGARINE (1 STICK), CUT UP
¼ CUP VEGETABLE SHORTENING
4 TO 6 TABLESPOONS ICE WATER

1 In large bowl, mix flour and salt. With pastry blender or 2 knives used scissor-fashion, cut in butter and shortening until mixture resembles coarse crumbs.

2 Sprinkle in ice water, 1 tablespoon at a time, mixing lightly with fork after each addition, until dough is just moist enough to hold together.

3 Shape dough into 2 disks, one slightly larger than the other. Wrap each in plastic wrap and refrigerate 30 minutes, or overnight. If chilled overnight, let stand at room temperature 30 minutes before rolling.

4 On lightly floured surface, with floured rolling pin, roll larger disk into 12-inch round. Roll dough round gently onto rolling pin; ease into pie plate. Trim edge, leaving a 1-inch overhang. Reserve trimmings for decorating pie, if you like. Fill piecrust.

5 Roll remaining disk into 12-inch round. Cut ¾-inch circle out of center and cut 1-inch slits to allow steam to escape during baking; center over filling or make desired pie top (see photos on page 211). Fold overhang under; make desired decorative edge (see photos on page 212). Bake pie as directed in recipe. *Makes one 9-inch double crust.*

EACH ⅒ PASTRY: ABOUT 240 CALORIES, 3 G PROTEIN, 24 G CARBOHYDRATE, 15 G TOTAL FAT (7 G SATURATED), 1 G FIBER, 25 MG CHOLESTEROL, 210 MG SODIUM.

FOOD PROCESSOR METHOD In food processor with knife blade attached, pulse flour and salt. Add butter and shortening; pulse until mixture resembles coarse crumbs. With processor running, pour *¼ cup ice water* through feed tube. Stop motor and pinch dough; it should be just moist enough to hold together. If not, add up to *2 tablespoons more ice water*, mixing with fork. Wrap, refrigerate, and roll as directed.

ALL-SHORTENING PASTRY Prepare dough as at left but omit butter and use *¾ cup vegetable shortening* and *1 teaspoon salt.*
EACH ⅒ PASTRY: ABOUT 250 CALORIES, 3 G PROTEIN, 24 G CARBOHYDRATE, 16 G TOTAL FAT (4 G SATURATED), 1 G FIBER, 0 MG CHOLESTEROL, 235 MG SODIUM.

VINEGAR PASTRY Prepare dough as at left but use *1 tablespoon distilled white vinegar* for 1 tablespoon ice water.
EACH ⅒ PASTRY: ABOUT 240 CALORIES, 3 G PROTEIN, 24 G CARBOHYDRATE, 15 G TOTAL FAT (7 G SATURATED), 1 G FIBER, 25 MG CHOLESTEROL, 210 MG SODIUM.

WHOLE-WHEAT PASTRY Prepare dough as at left but use *1½ cups all-purpose flour* and *¾ cup whole-wheat flour.*
EACH ⅒ PASTRY: ABOUT 235 CALORIES, 4 G PROTEIN, 23 G CARBOHYDRATE, 15 G TOTAL FAT (7 G SATURATED), 2 G FIBER, 25 MG CHOLESTEROL, 210 MG SODIUM.

Pastry for Single-Crust Pie

PREP 10 MINUTES PLUS CHILLING

1¼ CUPS ALL-PURPOSE FLOUR
¼ TEASPOON SALT
4 TABLESPOONS COLD BUTTER OR MARGARINE, CUT UP
2 TABLESPOONS VEGETABLE SHORTENING
3 TO 5 TABLESPOONS ICE WATER

1 Prepare dough as for Pastry for Double-Crust Pie, Steps 1 through 4, making 1 disk of dough. Do not fill pie shell.

2 Make desired decorative edge (see photos on page 212). Refrigerate or freeze 10 to 15 minutes to firm pastry before baking. Fill and bake pie as directed in recipe. *Makes one 9-inch crust.*

EACH ⅒ PASTRY: ABOUT 125 CALORIES, 2 G PROTEIN, 13 G CARBOHYDRATE, 7 G TOTAL FAT (4 G SATURATED), 0.5 G FIBER, 12 MG CHOLESTEROL, 105 MG SODIUM.

Pastry for 11-Inch Tart

PREP 10 MINUTES PLUS CHILLING

1½ CUPS ALL-PURPOSE FLOUR
½ TEASPOON SALT
½ CUP COLD BUTTER OR MARGARINE (1 STICK), CUT UP
2 TABLESPOONS VEGETABLE SHORTENING
3 TO 4 TABLESPOONS ICE WATER

1 Prepare dough as for Pastry for Double-Crust Pie (opposite page), Steps 1 through 3, making 1 disk of dough.

2 On lightly floured surface, with floured rolling pin, roll dough into 14-inch round. Fit dough into 11" by 1" round tart pan with removable bottom. Fold overhang in and press against side of tart pan to form ⅛-inch rim above edge of pan. Refrigerate or freeze 10 to 15 minutes to firm pastry before baking. Fill and bake tart as directed in recipe. *Makes one 11-inch tart crust.*

EACH ¹/₁₂ PASTRY: ABOUT 145 CALORIES, 2 G PROTEIN, 12 G CARBOHYDRATE, 10 G TOTAL FAT (5 G SATURATED), 0.5 G FIBER, 21 MG CHOLESTEROL, 175 MG SODIUM.

Pastry for 9-Inch Tart

PREP 10 MINUTES PLUS CHILLING

1 CUP ALL-PURPOSE FLOUR
¼ TEASPOON SALT
6 TABLESPOONS COLD BUTTER OR MARGARINE, CUT UP
1 TABLESPOON VEGETABLE SHORTENING
2 TO 3 TABLESPOONS ICE WATER

Prepare dough as for Pastry for 11-Inch Tart (above). Roll dough into 11-inch round and fit into 9" by 1" round tart pan with removable bottom. Fold overhang in and press against side of tart pan to form ⅛-inch rim above edge of pan. Refrigerate or freeze 10 to 15 minutes to firm pastry before baking. Fill and bake tart as directed in recipe. *Makes one 9-inch tart crust.*

EACH ⅛ PASTRY: ABOUT 145 CALORIES, 2 G PROTEIN, 12 G CARBOHYDRATE, 10 G TOTAL FAT (6 G SATURATED), 0.5 G FIBER, 23 MG CHOLESTEROL, 160 MG SODIUM.

Italian Sweet Pastry

PREP 15 MINUTES PLUS CHILLING

This pastry is called "pasta frolla" in Italy—frolla means "tender." This rich, all-butter dough is sometimes cut into rounds and baked as sugar cookies.

2 CUPS ALL-PURPOSE FLOUR
¼ CUP SUGAR
1 TEASPOON BAKING POWDER
¼ TEASPOON SALT
½ CUP COLD BUTTER OR MARGARINE (1 STICK), CUT UP
2 LARGE EGGS

1 In large bowl, mix flour, sugar, baking powder, and salt. With pastry blender or 2 knives used scissor-fashion, cut in butter until mixture resembles coarse crumbs.

2 In small bowl, with fork, lightly beat eggs. Make a well in flour mixture and add beaten eggs. Mix lightly with fork until dough is just moist enough to hold together. Shape dough into disk.

3 Wrap in plastic wrap and refrigerate 30 minutes, or overnight. If chilled overnight, let stand at room temperature 30 minutes before rolling. *Makes one 9- or 10-inch lattice-crust tart.*

EACH ¹/₁₂ PASTRY: ABOUT 175 CALORIES, 3 G PROTEIN, 21 G CARBOHYDRATE, 9 G TOTAL FAT (5 G SATURATED), 0.5 G FIBER, 56 MG CHOLESTEROL, 175 MG SODIUM.

FAT FACTS

WHICH FAT IS BEST FOR PASTRY CRUST? MANY BAKERS PREFER LARD, WHICH, BECAUSE OF ITS FAT CONTENT (100%), GIVES A FLAKY TEXTURE, BUT HAS A PRONOUNCED AFTERTASTE. VEGETABLE SHORTENING (ALSO 100% FAT) GIVES A FLAKY TEXTURE, BUT HAS A NEUTRAL FLAVOR. BUTTER, AT 80 TO 85% FAT, ADDS A DELICATE SWEETNESS, BUT A LESS FLAKY TEXTURE. A GOOD SOLUTION IS TO USE A COMBINATION OF BUTTER AND SHORTENING. (IF YOU USE MARGARINE, BE SURE IT IS STICK MARGARINE—AT LEAST 80% FAT—NOT SOFT, WHIPPED, OR DIET.)

Sweet Pastry Crust for 11-Inch Tart

PREP 15 MINUTES PLUS CHILLING
BAKE 27 TO 30 MINUTES

Known as "pate sucrée" in France, this cross between a cookie and a pastry shell is the perfect foil for pastry cream and berries.

1½ CUPS ALL-PURPOSE FLOUR
¼ CUP SUGAR
¼ TEASPOON SALT
10 TABLESPOONS COLD BUTTER, CUT UP (DO NOT USE MARGARINE)
1 LARGE EGG YOLK
¼ CUP COLD WATER

1 In large bowl, stir together flour, sugar, and salt. With pastry blender or 2 knives used scissor-fashion, cut in butter until mixture resembles coarse crumbs. In small bowl, with fork, stir together egg yolk and water. Pour into flour mixture and stir together until dough just forms a ball. Shape into a disk, wrap, and refrigerate at least 1 hour, or overnight.

2 Place disk between 2 layers of lightly floured waxed paper. Roll into 14-inch round. If dough becomes too soft to handle, return to refrigerator for 5 minutes. Remove top sheet of waxed paper and invert pastry into 11-inch tart pan with removable bottom, gently pressing dough into bottom and up side of pan. Remove second sheet of waxed paper. If dough cracks, gently press together. Run rolling pin over top of pan to trim excess dough. Refrigerate or freeze 10 to 15 minutes to firm pastry before baking. Prick bottom all over with fork. *Makes one 11-inch tart shell.*

EACH ¹/₁₂ PASTRY: ABOUT 165 CALORIES, 2 G PROTEIN, 17 G CARBOHYDRATE, 10 G TOTAL FAT (6 G SATURATED), 0.5 G FIBER, 44 MG CHOLESTEROL, 145 MG SODIUM.

BAKED SWEET PASTRY CRUST Prepare Sweet Pastry Crust and use to line 9- or 11-inch tart pan with removable bottom; refrigerate or freeze 10 to 15 minutes. Preheat oven to 375° F. Line shell with foil and fill foil with pie weights, dry beans, or uncooked rice. Bake 20 minutes. Remove foil and weights and bake 7 to 10 minutes longer, or until golden. If crust puffs up during baking, gently press it to tart pan with back of spoon. Cool in pan on wire rack. Fill as directed. *Makes one 9- or 11-inch baked tart shell.*

Sweet Pastry Crust for 9-Inch Tart

PREP 15 MINUTES PLUS CHILLING

1¼ CUPS ALL-PURPOSE FLOUR
3 TABLESPOONS SUGAR
⅛ TEASPOON SALT
½ CUP (1 STICK) COLD BUTTER, CUT UP (DO NOT USE MARGARINE)
1 LARGE EGG YOLK
2 TABLESPOONS COLD WATER

1 In large bowl, stir together flour and sugar. With pastry blender or 2 knives used scissor-fashion, cut in butter until mixture resembles coarse crumbs. In small bowl, with fork, stir together egg yolk and water. Pour into flour mixture and stir together until dough just forms a ball. Shape into a disk, wrap, and refrigerate at least 1 hour, or overnight.

2 Place disk between 2 layers of lightly floured waxed paper. Roll into 11-inch round. Remove top sheet of waxed paper and invert pastry into 9-inch tart pan with removable bottom, gently pressing dough into bottom and up side of pan. Remove second sheet of waxed paper. If dough cracks, gently press together. Run rolling pin over top of pan to trim excess dough. Refrigerate or freeze 10 to 15 minutes to firm pastry before baking. Prick bottom all over with fork. *Makes one 9-inch tart shell.*

EACH ⅛ PASTRY: ABOUT 200 CALORIES, 3 G PROTEIN, 20 G CARBOHYDRATE, 12 G TOTAL FAT (7 G SATURATED), 0.5 G FIBER, 58 MG CHOLESTEROL, 155 MG SODIUM.

ROLL IT RIGHT

TO FORM A SMOOTH, EVEN ROUND OF PASTRY DOUGH, ROLL THE ROLLING PIN OUTWARD FROM THE CENTER OF THE DISK OF CHILLED DOUGH, THEN GIVE THE DOUGH A QUARTER TURN AND AGAIN ROLL IT OUTWARD FROM THE CENTER. KEEP TURNING AND ROLLING THE DOUGH TO MAINTAIN AN EVEN OVERALL THICKNESS. DON'T USE THE ROLLING PIN TO STRETCH THE DOUGH, JUST TO FLATTEN IT.

Pat-in-Pan Crust for 11-Inch Tart

PREP 10 MINUTES PLUS CHILLING

1 CUP UNSALTED BUTTER (2 STICKS), SOFTENED (DO NOT
    USE MARGARINE OR SALTED BUTTER)
½ CUP SUGAR
1 LARGE EGG
1 TABLESPOON VANILLA EXTRACT
3 CUPS ALL-PURPOSE FLOUR
¼ TEASPOON SALT

In large bowl, with mixer at low speed, beat butter and sugar until blended. Increase speed to high; beat until light and creamy, scraping bowl occasionally with rubber spatula. Reduce speed to medium; beat in egg and vanilla. With wooden spoon, stir in flour and salt until mixture is crumbly. With hands, press dough together in bowl and knead a few times until flour is evenly moistened. Divide dough into 2 pieces, one slightly larger than the other; flatten into disks. Wrap each disk in plastic wrap and refrigerate 30 minutes, or until dough is firm enough to handle. *Makes one 11-inch lattice-top tart.*

EACH ¹/₁₂ PASTRY: ABOUT 290 CALORIES, 4 G PROTEIN,
32 G CARBOHYDRATE, 16 G TOTAL FAT (10 G SATURATED),
1 G FIBER, 59 MG CHOLESTEROL, 210 MG SODIUM.

Pat-in-Pan Crust for 9-Inch Tart

PREP 10 MINUTES PLUS CHILLING

¾ CUP BUTTER (1½ STICKS), SOFTENED (DO NOT USE
    MARGARINE OR SALTED BUTTER)
⅓ CUP SUGAR
1 LARGE EGG
2 TEASPOONS VANILLA EXTRACT
2 CUPS ALL-PURPOSE FLOUR
¼ TEASPOON SALT

In large bowl, with mixer at low speed, beat butter and sugar until blended. Increase speed to high; beat until light and creamy, scraping bowl occasionally with rubber spatula. Reduce speed to medium; beat in egg until blended. Beat in vanilla. With wooden spoon, stir in flour and salt until dough begins to form. With hands, press dough together. Divide dough into 2 pieces, one slightly larger than the other; flatten into disks. Wrap each disk and refrigerate 30 minutes, or until dough is firm enough to handle. *Makes one 9-inch lattice-top tart.*

EACH ⅛ PASTRY: ABOUT 310 CALORIES, 4 G PROTEIN,
32 G CARBOHYDRATE, 18 G TOTAL FAT (11 G SATURATED),
1 G FIBER, 73 MG CHOLESTEROL, 255 MG SODIUM.

No-Roll Nut Crust

PREP 10 MINUTES / BAKE 20 MINUTES

This buttery walnut crust is perfect for a banana or chocolate filling.

½ CUP WALNUTS, TOASTED
1 CUP ALL-PURPOSE FLOUR
¼ CUP SUGAR
⅓ CUP (5⅓ TABLESPOONS) COLD BUTTER OR MARGARINE,
    CUT UP

1 Preheat oven to 375° F. In food processor with knife blade attached, pulse walnuts with flour until nuts are finely ground. Add sugar; pulse to mix. Add butter and pulse until combined (mixture will appear sandy).

2 Press dough evenly into bottom and up side of 9-inch pie plate. Bake 20 minutes, or until lightly browned all over. Cool on wire rack. Fill as directed in recipe. *Makes one 9-inch crust.*

EACH ¹/₁₀ PASTRY: ABOUT 155 CALORIES, 2 G PROTEIN,
16 G CARBOHYDRATE, 10 G TOTAL FAT (4 G SATURATED),
0.1 G FIBER, 16 MG CHOLESTEROL, 65 MG SODIUM.

Coconut Pastry Crust

PREP 10 MINUTES / BAKE 20 MINUTES

Toast the coconut in a shallow pan in a 350° F oven for about 10 minutes, stirring frequently.

1 CUP ALL-PURPOSE FLOUR
½ CUP FLAKED SWEETENED COCONUT, TOASTED
6 TABLESPOONS COLD BUTTER OR MARGARINE, CUT UP
2 TABLESPOONS SUGAR
1 TABLESPOON COLD WATER

1 Preheat oven to 375° F. Grease 9-inch pie plate. In food processor with knife blade attached, combine flour, coconut, butter, sugar, and water. Pulse until dough just holds together.

2 Press dough evenly into bottom and up side of prepared pie plate, making a small rim. Bake 20 minutes, or until golden. Cover edge loosely with foil to prevent overbrowning if necessary during last 10 minutes of baking. Cool on wire rack. Fill as directed in recipe. *Makes one 9-inch crust.*

EACH ¹⁄₁₀ PASTRY: ABOUT 135 CALORIES, 1 G PROTEIN, 14 G CARBOHYDRATE, 9 G TOTAL FAT (5 G SATURATED), 0.5 G FIBER, 19 MG CHOLESTEROL, 80 MG SODIUM.

Shortbread Crust

PREP 15 MINUTES
BAKE 27 TO 30 MINUTES

Plenty of butter, mixed with confectioners' sugar and cornstarch, gives this a melt-in-your-mouth texture.

¾ CUP ALL-PURPOSE FLOUR
⅓ CUP CORNSTARCH
½ CUP BUTTER OR MARGARINE (1 STICK), SOFTENED
⅓ CUP CONFECTIONERS' SUGAR
1 TEASPOON VANILLA EXTRACT

1 Preheat oven to 325° F. In medium bowl, stir together flour and cornstarch. In large bowl, with mixer at medium speed, beat butter and confectioners' sugar until light and fluffy. Beat in vanilla. Reduce speed to low and beat in flour mixture until combined. Scrape dough into 9-inch tart pan with removable bottom.

2 For ease of handling, place sheet of plastic wrap over dough and smooth dough over bottom and up side of pan. Remove and discard plastic wrap. Prick dough all over with fork. Bake 27 to 30 minutes, until lightly golden. Cool in pan on wire rack. Fill as directed in recipe. *Makes one 9-inch crust.*

EACH ⅛ PASTRY: ABOUT 185 CALORIES, 1 G PROTEIN, 19 G CARBOHYDRATE, 12 G TOTAL FAT (7 G SATURATED), 0.5 G FIBER, 31 MG CHOLESTEROL, 120 MG SODIUM.

Baked Graham-Cracker Crumb Crust

PREP 10 MINUTES / BAKE 10 MINUTES

Here's the quick classic, with two variations. For an almost-instant dessert, fill the cooled crust with scoops of ice cream and top with hot fudge or a berry sauce.

1¼ CUPS GRAHAM-CRACKER CRUMBS (11 RECTANGULAR GRAHAM CRACKERS)
4 TABLESPOONS BUTTER OR MARGARINE, MELTED
1 TABLESPOON SUGAR

1 Preheat oven to 375° F. In 9-inch pie plate, with fork, mix crumbs, butter, and sugar. With hand, press mixture into bottom and up side of pie plate, making small rim.

2 Bake 10 minutes. Cool on wire rack. Fill as directed in recipe. *Makes one 9-inch crust.*

EACH ¹⁄₁₀ CRUST: ABOUT 110 CALORIES, 1 G PROTEIN, 13 G CARBOHYDRATE, 6 G TOTAL FAT (3 G SATURATED), 0.5 G FIBER, 12 MG CHOLESTEROL, 140 MG SODIUM.

BAKED VANILLA-WAFER CRUMB CRUST Prepare as above but use *1¼ cups vanilla-wafer cookie crumbs (about 35 cookies)* for the graham-cracker crumbs. Bake and cool as directed.
EACH ¹⁄₁₀ CRUST: ABOUT 90 CALORIES, 1 G PROTEIN, 9 G CARBOHYDRATE, 6 G TOTAL FAT (3 G SATURATED), 0 G FIBER, 12 MG CHOLESTEROL, 80 MG SODIUM.

BAKED CHOCOLATE-WAFER CRUMB CRUST Prepare as above but use *1¼ cups chocolate-wafer cookie crumbs (about 24 cookies)* for the graham-cracker crumbs. Bake and cool as directed.
EACH ¹⁄₁₀ CRUST: ABOUT 110 CALORIES, 1 G PROTEIN, 12 G CARBOHYDRATE, 7 G TOTAL FAT (3 G SATURATED), 0.5 G FIBER, 13 MG CHOLESTEROL, 130 MG SODIUM.

Pie Tops

WINDOW

Prepare Pastry for Double-Crust Pie (page 206). Roll large disk into 12-inch round. Line pie plate with crust; fill. Roll top crust into 12-inch round; place over filling. Trim edge, leaving 1-inch overhang; pinch to make high edge and shape decorative edge. Cut 4-inch "X" in center of crust; fold back points to make square opening. As well as being decorative, this "window" will allow steam to escape during baking.

SIMPLE LATTICE

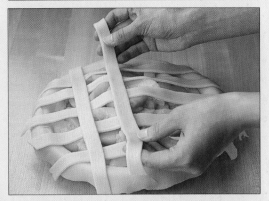

Prepare Pastry for Double-Crust Pie (page 206). Line pie plate with crust; fill. Trim dough, leaving 1-inch overhang. Roll top crust into 12-inch round; cut into ½-inch strips. Moisten edge of bottom crust with water. Place pastry strips about I inch apart across pie; press each strip at both ends to seal. Repeat with an equal number of strips placed at right angles to first ones to make lattice design. Turn overhang up over ends of strips; pinch to seal. Make high, stand-up edge that will hold juices in; flute. To make high edge, see page 212.

WOVEN LATTICE

Make lattice-crust pie (above right), but place first layer of strips on pie; do not seal ends. Fold every other strip back halfway from center. Place center cross strip on pie and replace folded part of strips. Now fold back alternate strips; place second cross strip in place. Repeat to weave cross strips into lattice. Seal ends; make high, fluted edge.

APPLIQUÉ

Prepare and fill Pastry for Double-Crust Pie, reserving trimmings. Roll out trimmings. Use small knife to cut free-form shapes, such as apple, heart, or leaves (use back of knife to mark veins in leaves); brush with water. Place, wet side down, on top of pie. Then cut several 1-inch slits as steam vents.

Decorative Edges

These borders add a professional finish to homemade pies and tarts. The forked, fluted, crimped, and rope edges are pretty on any pie, whether single- or double-crust. The appliqué heart or leaf edge is best for single-crust pies, but you will need enough pastry for a double-crust pie. For best results, chill the dough so that it is firm when you work with it.

Follow these instructions before decorating the edges of the crust.

1 Trim dough edge or top crust for double-crust pie with kitchen shears, leaving 1-inch overhang. For forked or leaf edge, trim edge even with rim of pie plate; omit Step 2 below.

2 Fold overhang under; pinch to make stand-up edge. Shape decorative edge as desired.

FORKED

Trim dough edge as in Step 1 (left) but cut it even with rim of pie plate. With floured fork, press dough to rim of plate; repeat around edge.

FLUTED

Push one index finger against outside edge of rim; with index finger and thumb of other hand, press to make ruffle. Repeat around edge, leaving ¼-inch space between ruffles.

CRIMPED

Push one index finger against inside edge of rim; with index finger and thumb of other hand, pinch to make flute. Repeat, moving outer index finger into impression made by thumb.

ROPE FOR PIE CRUST

Press thumb into dough edge at an angle, then pinch dough between thumb and knuckle of index finger. Place thumb in groove left by index finger; pinch as before. Repeat.

ROPE FOR TART SHELL

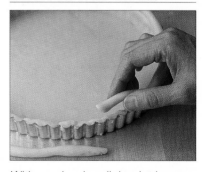

With your hands, roll dough trimmings into ¼-inch-thick ropes. Press ropes around edge of tart to create finished edge

TURRET

Trim dough, leaving 1-inch overhang; fold overhang under to make stand-up edge. With knife, make cuts down through edge to rim of pie plate, spacing cuts ½ inch apart. Fold pieces alternately toward center and rim.

HEART OR LEAF

Prepare Pastry for Double-Crust Pie (page 206). Trim bottom crust even with rim of pie plate. Roll remaining dough ⅛ inch thick. With knife or small cookie cutter, cut out hearts or leaves. Lightly brush edge of piecrust with water. Press shapes, side by side, onto edge.

FRUIT PIES

The fruit pie celebrates each season in turn, from the spring's first rosy rhubarb to autumn's crisp apples. Each pie has its own distinguishing features—a lattice crust or a streusel topping; a touch of cream or a squeeze of lemon juice; a handful of raisins or a sprinkling of chopped nuts.

Strawberry-Rhubarb Pie

PREP 30 MINUTES PLUS CHILLING
BAKE 1 HOUR 35 TO 45 MINUTES

Because rhubarb (a vegetable masquerading as a fruit) is very tart, it's often combined with strawberries as a sweet complement. It's a match made in heaven.

PASTRY FOR DOUBLE-CRUST PIE (PAGE 206)
¼ CUP CORNSTARCH
1 CUP PLUS 1 TABLESPOON SUGAR
1 PINT STRAWBERRIES, HULLED AND EACH CUT IN HALF IF LARGE
1¼ POUNDS RHUBARB, TRIMMED AND CUT INTO ½-INCH PIECES (4 CUPS)
2 TABLESPOONS BUTTER OR MARGARINE, CUT UP

1 Prepare dough as directed through chilling.

2 Preheat oven to 425° F. In large bowl, mix cornstarch and 1 cup sugar. Add strawberries and rhubarb; toss to combine.

3 Roll out larger disk of dough and line 9-inch pie plate. Spoon filling into piecrust; dot with butter. Roll top crust; cut center circle and 1-inch slits to allow steam to escape during baking, and place on filling as directed; make decorative edge (see photos opposite). Sprinkle with remaining 1 tablespoon sugar.

4 Place pie on nonstick or foil-lined cookie sheet to catch any overflow during baking. Bake 20 minutes. Turn oven control to 375° F; bake 1 hour 15 to 25 minutes longer, until filling bubbles in center. Cool on wire rack 1 hour to serve warm, or cool completely to serve later. *Makes 10 servings.*

EACH SERVING: ABOUT 375 CALORIES, 4 G PROTEIN, 53 G CARBOHYDRATE, 17 G TOTAL FAT (8 G SATURATED), 2 G FIBER, 31 MG CHOLESTEROL, 235 MG SODIUM.

Blueberry Pie

PREP 25 MINUTES PLUS CHILLING
BAKE 1 HOUR 20 MINUTES

Add a pinch of cinnamon to the filling to bring out the natural spiciness of the blueberries. And, if the berries are not very flavorful, add a little grated lemon zest as well. If you're using wild blueberries (lucky you!), increase the amount of cornstarch to ⅓ cup.

PASTRY FOR DOUBLE-CRUST PIE (PAGE 206)
¾ CUP SUGAR
¼ CUP CORNSTARCH
PINCH SALT
6 CUPS BLUEBERRIES, PICKED OVER
1 TABLESPOON FRESH LEMON JUICE
2 TABLESPOONS BUTTER OR MARGARINE, CUT UP

1 Prepare dough as directed through chilling.

2 Preheat oven to 425° F. In large bowl, combine sugar, cornstarch, and salt. Add blueberries (with water still clinging to them) and lemon juice; toss until well mixed.

3 Roll out larger disk of dough and line 9-inch pie plate. Spoon filling into piecrust; dot with butter. Roll top crust, cut center circle and 1-inch slits to allow steam to escape during baking, and place on filling as directed (or make woven lattice top); make decorative edge (see photos opposite).

4 Place pie on nonstick or foil-lined cookie sheet to catch any overflow during baking. Bake 20 minutes. Turn oven control to 375° F; bake 1 hour longer, or until filling bubbles in center and crust is golden. If necessary, cover edges of pie loosely with foil to prevent overbrowning. Cool on wire rack 1 hour to serve warm, or cool pie completely to serve later. *Makes 10 servings.*

EACH SERVING: ABOUT 380 CALORIES, 4 G PROTEIN, 54 G CARBOHYDRATE, 17 G TOTAL FAT (8 G SATURATED), 3 G FIBER, 31 MG CHOLESTEROL, 255 MG SODIUM.

Apple Galette

PREP **40** MINUTES PLUS CHILLING / BAKE **45** MINUTES

This country-style galette is a free-form tart, with the apple slices handsomely arrayed.

PASTRY FOR SINGLE-CRUST PIE (PAGE 206)
2 POUNDS GOLDEN DELICIOUS APPLES (5 MEDIUM)
¼ CUP SUGAR
2 TABLESPOONS BUTTER OR MARGARINE, CUT UP
2 TABLESPOONS APRICOT JAM, MELTED

1 Prepare dough as directed through chilling. Preheat oven to 425° F.

2 On lightly floured surface, with floured rolling pin, roll dough into 15-inch round. Transfer to large cookie sheet.

3 Peel apples; cut each in half; remove cores. Cut crosswise into ¼-inch-thick slices. Arrange slices in concentric circles on dough, leaving 1½-inch border. Fold dough up around slices (see photo at right).

4 Place 2 sheets of foil under cookie sheet; crimp edges to form rim to catch any overflow during baking. Bake 45 minutes, or until apples are tender. Place cookie sheet on wire rack. Brush apples with jam. Cool slightly to serve warm. *Makes 8 servings.*

EACH SERVING: ABOUT 415 CALORIES, 4 G PROTEIN,
54 G CARBOHYDRATE, 21 G TOTAL FAT (11 G SATURATED),
3 G FIBER, 39 MG CHOLESTEROL, 295 MG SODIUM.

Apple Galette

Fan the apple slices in concentric circles on the dough round, leaving a 1½-inch border. Sprinkle apples evenly with sugar and dot with butter. Fold the border up around the apples.

Apple Pie

PREP **35** MINUTES PLUS CHILLING
BAKE **1** HOUR **20** MINUTES

Try more than one variety of apple per pie. Different apples have different textures when baked: Some hold their shape, others cook down almost to applesauce.

PASTRY FOR DOUBLE-CRUST PIE (PAGE 206)
⅔ CUP SUGAR
2 TABLESPOONS ALL-PURPOSE FLOUR
½ TEASPOON GROUND CINNAMON
⅛ TEASPOON SALT
3 POUNDS COOKING APPLES (9 MEDIUM), PEELED, CORED,
    AND THINLY SLICED
1 TABLESPOON FRESH LEMON JUICE
1 TABLESPOON BUTTER OR MARGARINE, CUT UP

1 Prepare dough as directed through chilling.

2 Preheat oven to 425° F. In large bowl, combine sugar, flour, cinnamon, and salt. Add apples and lemon juice; toss to combine.

3 Roll out larger disk of dough and line 9-inch pie plate. Spoon filling into piecrust; dot with butter. Roll top crust, cut 1-inch slits to allow steam to escape during baking, and place on filling as directed; make decorative edge (see photos on page 212).

GALETTES GALORE

THE FRENCH WORD "GALETTE" IS APPLIED TO MANY DIFFERENT FOODS—ALL OF THEM ROUND AND FLAT. THE FRENCH TWELFTH-NIGHT CAKE, CALLED GALETTE DU ROI, OR KING'S CAKE, IS MADE OF FLAKY PASTRY; A LUCKY BEAN (OR SMALL PORCELAIN FIGURINE) IS BAKED INTO THE CAKE. IN EASTERN BRITTANY, BOTH FLOUR CRÊPES AND BUCKWHEAT CRÊPES ARE CALLED GALETTES, WHILE IN BURGUNDY, GALETTES FLAMANDES ARE ORANGE-FLAVORED HAZELNUT TARTLETS. A FLAT CAKE FORMED OF THIN POTATO SLICES IS A GALETTE DE POMMES DE TERRE.

4 Place on nonstick or foil-lined cookie sheet to catch any overflow during baking. Bake 20 minutes. Turn oven control to 375° F; bake 1 hour longer, or until filling is bubbly in center. If necessary, cover pie loosely with foil during last 20 minutes of baking to prevent overbrowning. Cool pie on wire rack 1 hour to serve warm, or cool completely to serve later. *Makes 10 servings.*

EACH SERVING: ABOUT 375 CALORIES, 4 G PROTEIN, 56 G CARBOHYDRATE, 16 G TOTAL FAT (8 G SATURATED), 3 G FIBER, 28 MG CHOLESTEROL, 250 MG SODIUM.

APPLE-GINGER PIE Prepare as for Apple Pie but omit cinnamon and add *2 tablespoons coarsely chopped crystallized ginger* to apple mixture. Bake as directed.
EACH SERVING: ABOUT 385 CALORIES, 4 G PROTEIN, 58 G CARBOHYDRATE, 16 G TOTAL FAT (8 G SATURATED), 3 G FIBER, 28 MG CHOLESTEROL, 255 MG SODIUM.

APPLE-BLACKBERRY PIE Prepare as for Apple Pie but use *3 tablespoons cornstarch* for flour, *1½ pounds apples,* and *1 pint blackberries.* Bake as directed.
EACH SERVING: ABOUT 360 CALORIES, 4 G PROTEIN, 52 G CARBOHYDRATE, 16 G TOTAL FAT (8 G SATURATED), 3 G FIBER, 28 MG CHOLESTEROL, 250 MG SODIUM.

Caramelized Apple Crostata

PREP 1 HOUR 20 MINUTES PLUS CHILLING
BAKE 1 HOUR

This luscious crostata (Italian for lattice-topped tart) is also delicious made with Bosc pears.

PAT-IN-PAN CRUST FOR 11-INCH TART (PAGE 209)
3 TABLESPOONS BUTTER OR MARGARINE
2½ POUNDS GRANNY SMITH APPLES (ABOUT 5 LARGE), PEELED, CORED, AND CUT INTO ¼-INCH-THICK SLICES
⅓ CUP PACKED LIGHT BROWN SUGAR
¼ CUP PLUS 1 TABLESPOON WATER
1 LARGE EGG YOLK

1 Prepare dough as directed through chilling.

2 In 12-inch nonstick skillet, melt butter over medium heat. Add apples, brown sugar, and ¼ cup water, and cook, stirring occasionally, 20 to 25 minutes,

until apples are lightly browned and tender. Transfer apples to pie plate; refrigerate until chilled, about 30 minutes.

3 Meanwhile, with floured hands, press larger disk of dough into bottom and halfway up side of 11-inch round tart pan with removable bottom. Refrigerate 15 minutes.

4 Remove smaller disk of dough from refrigerator. On lightly floured waxed paper, roll remaining piece of dough into 12-inch round. With pastry wheel or knife, cut dough into twelve 1-inch-wide strips. Refrigerate 15 minutes.

5 Preheat oven to 375° F.

6 Spread chilled apple filling over dough in tart pan to within ½ inch of edge. Make lattice top (see photo on page 212): Place 5 dough strips, 1 inch apart, across tart, trimming ends even with side of tart pan; repeat with 5 more strips placed diagonally across first ones to make diamond lattice pattern. Trim ends and reserve trimmings.

7 Make rope edge for tart shell (see photo on page 211); with hands, roll trimmings and remaining 2 strips of dough into about ¼-inch-thick ropes. Press ropes around edge of tart to create finished edge. (If rope pieces break, just press pieces together.)

8 In cup, beat egg yolk with remaining 1 tablespoon water. Brush egg-yolk mixture over lattice and edge of tart.

9 Bake 1 hour, or until crust is golden. Cover tart loosely with foil to prevent overbrowning during last 15 minutes of baking. Cool in pan on wire rack. Remove tart from pan to serve. *Makes 12 servings.*

EACH SERVING: ABOUT 390 CALORIES, 4 G PROTEIN, 50 G CARBOHYDRATE, 20 G TOTAL FAT (12 G SATURATED), 2 G FIBER, 85 MG CHOLESTEROL, 240 MG SODIUM.

Apple Crumb Pie

PREP **40** MINUTES PLUS CHILLING
BAKE **1** HOUR **35** TO **45** MINUTES

*You may know this as French apple pie. Our own
enriching touch is a cup of sour cream in the filling.*

PASTRY FOR SINGLE-CRUST PIE (PAGE 206)
⅔ CUP SUGAR
3 TABLESPOONS CORNSTARCH
½ TEASPOON GROUND CINNAMON
3 POUNDS GRANNY SMITH APPLES (ABOUT 7 LARGE),
    PEELED, CORED, AND CUT INTO ¾-INCH PIECES
⅓ CUP DARK SEEDLESS RAISINS
CRUMB TOPPING (BELOW)
1 CONTAINER (8 OUNCES) SOUR CREAM
1 TEASPOON VANILLA EXTRACT

1 Prepare dough as directed through chilling.

2 In large bowl, combine sugar, cornstarch, and cinnamon. Add apples and raisins; toss until well
combined.

3 Preheat oven to 400° F. Roll out dough and line
9½-inch deep-dish pie plate; make decorative edge
(see photos on page 212). Refrigerate or freeze 10 to
15 minutes to firm pastry.

4 While crust is chilling, prepare Crumb Topping.

5 Add sour cream and vanilla to apple mixture and
toss well to coat evenly. Spoon apple mixture into
chilled crust. Sprinkle top of apples evenly with
crumb mixture.

6 Place pie on nonstick or foil-lined cookie sheet to
catch any overflow during baking. Bake pie 1 hour.
Turn oven control to 350° F; bake 35 to 45 minutes
longer, until filling bubbles in center. If necessary,
cover pie loosely with foil during last 20 minutes of
baking to prevent overbrowning. Cool pie slightly on
wire rack to serve warm, or cool completely to serve
later. *Makes 10 servings.*

EACH SERVING: ABOUT 375 CALORIES, 4 G PROTEIN,
64 G CARBOHYDRATE, 13 G TOTAL FAT (7 G SATURATED),
3 G FIBER, 22 MG CHOLESTEROL, 120 MG SODIUM.

CRUMB TOPPING In medium bowl, stir together ⅔
cup all-purpose flour, ⅓ cup packed brown sugar,
and ¼ teaspoon ground cinnamon. With pastry
blender or 2 knives used scissor-fashion, cut in 3
tablespoons cold butter or margarine until mixture
resembles coarse crumbs.

French Apple Tart

PREP **1** HOUR **30** MINUTES
BAKE **1** HOUR **12** TO **20** MINUTES

*Thin apple slices are arranged over a filling of freshly-
made applesauce and glazed with apricot preserves.*

BAKED SWEET PASTRY CRUST FOR 11-INCH TART
    (PAGE 208)
2 LEMONS
4 LARGE GRANNY SMITH APPLES (2 POUNDS), PEELED AND
    CORED
4 LARGE GOLDEN DELICIOUS APPLES (2 POUNDS), PEELED
    AND CORED
6 TABLESPOONS BUTTER OR MARGARINE
½ CUP PLUS 2 TABLESPOONS SUGAR
1½ TEASPOONS VANILLA EXTRACT
¼ TEASPOON GROUND NUTMEG
⅓ CUP APRICOT PRESERVES, PRESSED THROUGH A SIEVE

1 Prepare dough as directed through chilling in
11-inch fluted tart pan. Line and weight tart shell,
bake, and cool as directed.

2 From lemons, finely grate 1½ teaspoons peel and
squeeze 2 tablespoons juice. Reserve 2 Granny
Smiths and 1 Golden Delicious apple for top. Slice
remaining apples. In large skillet, melt 4 tablespoons
butter over medium-high heat. Add sliced apples and
cook 5 minutes. Cover, reduce heat to medium, and
cook 15 minutes, or until very tender. Stir in lemon
peel and juice, ½ cup sugar, vanilla, and nutmeg.
Cook, stirring frequently, 25 to 30 minutes until
puree is very thick and has reduced to 2¼ cups. Cool
to room temperature.

3 Meanwhile, preheat oven to 375° F.

4 Thinly slice remaining apples. Spoon puree into
tart shell and spread evenly. Arrange apple slices,
overlapping in concentric circles, on puree. Melt
remaining 2 tablespoons butter. Brush apples slices
with butter and sprinkle with remaining 2 tablespoons sugar.

5 Bake 45 to 50 minutes, until apples are tender
when pierced with a knife. Cool tart on wire rack 10
minutes. Remove side of pan and cool completely.
When cool, brush apple slices with sieved preserves.
Makes 12 servings.

EACH SERVING: ABOUT 355 CALORIES, 2 G PROTEIN,
52 G CARBOHYDRATE, 16 G TOTAL FAT (10 G SATURATED),
3 G FIBER, 59 MG CHOLESTEROL, 210 MG SODIUM.

Rustic Apricot Crostata

PREP **45** MINUTES PLUS CHILLING
BAKE **40** TO **45** MINUTES

½ CUP BLANCHED ALMONDS, TOASTED
3 TABLESPOONS CORNSTARCH
2½ CUPS ALL-PURPOSE FLOUR
¼ TEASPOON SALT
1 CUP BUTTER (2 STICKS), SOFTENED (DO NOT USE
    MARGARINE)
½ CUP PLUS 2 TEASPOONS SUGAR
1 LARGE EGG PLUS 1 LARGE EGG YOLK
2 TEASPOONS VANILLA EXTRACT
1 JAR (12 OUNCES) APRICOT PRESERVES (ABOUT 1 CUP)
1 TABLESPOON WATER

1 In food processor with knife blade attached, finely grind toasted almonds with cornstarch. In medium bowl, combine nut mixture, flour, and salt.

2 In large bowl, with mixer at high speed, beat butter and ½ cup sugar until creamy. Add egg and vanilla; beat until almost combined (mixture will look curdled). With wooden spoon, stir in flour mixture until dough begins to form. With hands, press dough together in bowl. Shape dough into 2 disks, one slightly larger than the other. Wrap each in plastic wrap and refrigerate 1 hour 30 minutes to 2 hours.

3 Preheat oven to 375° F. Remove both pieces of dough from refrigerator. On lightly floured surface, with floured rolling pin, roll out larger disk of dough into 11-inch round. Press dough into bottom and up side of 11-inch tart pan with removable bottom.

4 On lightly floured waxed paper, roll remaining disk of dough into 12-inch round. With pastry wheel or knife, cut dough into twelve 1-inch-wide strips. Refrigerate 15 minutes.

5 Spread preserves over dough in tart pan to within ½ inch of edge. Make lattice top (see photo on page 211): Place 5 dough strips, 1 inch apart, across tart, trimming ends even with side of tart pan; repeat with 5 more strips placed diagonally across first ones to make diamond lattice pattern. Trim ends and reserve trimmings.

6 Make rope edge for tart shell (see photo on page 212): With hands, roll trimmings and remaining 2 strips of dough into ¼-inch-thick ropes. Press ropes around edge of tart to create finished edge.

7 In cup, beat egg yolk with water. Brush egg-yolk mixture over lattice and edge of tart; sprinkle with remaining 2 teaspoons sugar.

8 Bake 40 to 45 minutes, until crust is deep golden. Check tart occasionally during first 30 minutes of baking; if crust puffs up, prick with tip of knife. Cool on wire rack. Remove side of from pan to serve. *Makes 12 servings.*

EACH SERVING: ABOUT **390** CALORIES, **5** G PROTEIN,
50 G CARBOHYDRATE, **20** G TOTAL FAT (**10** G SATURATED),
2 G FIBER, **77** MG CHOLESTEROL, **220** MG SODIUM.

Apple-Spice Pie

PREP **40** MINUTES PLUS CHILLING
BAKE **1** HOUR **20** MINUTES

PASTRY FOR DOUBLE-CRUST PIE (PAGE **206**)
1 LEMON
⅔ CUP PACKED LIGHT BROWN SUGAR
2 TABLESPOONS ALL-PURPOSE FLOUR
1 TEASPOON GROUND CINNAMON
½ TEASPOON GROUND GINGER
¼ TEASPOON GROUND NUTMEG
⅛ TEASPOON SALT
9 MEDIUM COOKING APPLES (3 POUNDS), PEELED, CORED,
    AND THINLY SLICED
½ CUP DARK SEEDLESS OR GOLDEN RAISINS
2 TABLESPOONS BUTTER OR MARGARINE

1 Prepare dough as directed through chilling.

2 Preheat oven to 425° F. From lemon, grate ½ teaspoon peel and squeeze 1 tablespoon juice. In large bowl, combine sugar, flour, cinnamon, ginger, nutmeg, and salt. Add lemon peel and juice, apples, and raisins; toss to combine.

3 Roll out larger disk of dough and line 9-inch pie plate. Spoon mixture into piecrust; dot with butter. Roll top crust; cut center circle and 1-inch slits, and place on filling as directed; make decorative edge (see photos on page 212).

4 Place pie on nonstick or foil-lined cookie sheet to catch any overflow during baking. Bake 20 minutes. Turn oven control to 375° F; bake 1 hour longer, or until filling bubbles in center. Cool on wire rack 1 hour to serve warm, or cool completely to serve later. *Makes 10 servings.*

EACH SERVING: ABOUT **410** CALORIES, **4** G PROTEIN,
63 G CARBOHYDRATE, **17** G TOTAL FAT (**9** G SATURATED),
3 G FIBER, **31** MG CHOLESTEROL, **270** MG SODIUM.

Rustic Apricot Crostata

Apricot Pie with Almond Streusel

PREP 1 HOUR PLUS CHILLING AND COOLING
BAKE 1 HOUR 15 TO 20 MINUTES

In order for delicate apricots to survive shipping, they're picked unripe, and most of the time they do not develop much flavor. However, if you can buy locally grown apricots, stock up so you have plenty of these juicy jewels for eating fresh and also enough to make this delicious and very special pie.

PASTRY FOR SINGLE-CRUST PIE (PAGE 206)
1 CUP ALL-PURPOSE FLOUR
6 TABLESPOONS BUTTER OR MARGARINE, SLIGHTLY
  SOFTENED
⅓ CUP PACKED LIGHT BROWN SUGAR
½ CUP SLICED NATURAL ALMONDS
2 POUNDS APRICOTS, PITTED AND QUARTERED (ABOUT
  6 CUPS)
1 TO 1¼ CUPS SUGAR
3 TABLESPOONS CORNSTARCH
2 TEASPOONS FRESH LEMON JUICE

1 Prepare dough as directed through chilling. Roll out dough and line 9-inch pie plate; make decorative edge (see photos on page 212).

2 Preheat oven to 425° F. Line pie shell with foil; fill with pie weight, dry beans, or uncooked rice. Bake 15 minutes. Remove foil and weights and bake 5 to 10 minutes longer, until golden. If crust puffs up during baking, gently press it to pie pan with back of spoon. Transfer to wire rack.

3 In medium bowl, with fingertips, combine flour, butter, and brown sugar until mixture almost holds together. Add nuts.

4 In large bowl, toss apricots with sugar, cornstarch, and lemon juice. Spoon apricot filling into cooled piecrust. Crumble topping over filling.

5 Place pie on nonstick or foil-lined cookie sheet to catch any overflow during baking. Bake about 55 minutes, or until filling bubbles in center. If necessary, cover loosely with foil after about 10 minutes to prevent overbrowning. Cool on wire rack 1 hour to serve warm, or cool completely to serve later. *Makes 10 servings.*

EACH SERVING: ABOUT 425 CALORIES, 5 G PROTEIN,
65 G CARBOHYDRATE, 17 G TOTAL FAT (8 G SATURATED),
2 G FIBER, 31 MG CHOLESTEROL, 180 MG SODIUM.

Warm Banana-Pecan Tart

PREP 45 MINUTES PLUS CHILLING/
BAKE/BROIL 31 TO 32 MINUTES

If you love banana cream pie but would like to serve something a bit more elegant, try this tart. A layer of sliced bananas is topped with pecan pastry cream and a sprinkling of sugar, and broiled until the sugar caramelizes slightly. You can bake the crust and prepare the pecan cream a day ahead of time. Assemble the tart just before serving.

PASTRY FOR 11-INCH TART (PAGE 207)
½ CUP PECANS, TOASTED
½ CUP PLUS 1 TABLESPOON SUGAR
3 LARGE EGG YOLKS
1 TABLESPOON CORNSTARCH
¾ CUP HALF-AND-HALF OR LIGHT CREAM
2 TABLESPOONS BUTTER OR MARGARINE
1 TEASPOON VANILLA EXTRACT
5 RIPE MEDIUM BANANAS (ABOUT 2 POUNDS), THINLY
  SLICED ON THE DIAGONAL

1 Prepare dough as directed through chilling. Line tart pan with dough; prick all over with fork to prevent puffing during baking; chill as directed.

2 In food processor with knife blade attached, combine toasted pecans with ¼ cup sugar; pulse until nuts are very finely ground.

3 In small bowl, with wire whisk, mix egg yolks, cornstarch, and ¼ cup sugar until blended. In 2-quart saucepan, heat half-and-half to simmering over medium heat. While constantly beating with wire whisk, gradually pour about half of simmering cream into bowl with egg-yolk mixture. Reduce heat to low. Return egg-yolk mixture to saucepan and cook 4 to 5 minutes, stirring constantly, until thickened (do not boil). Stir in toasted pecan mixture, butter, and vanilla. Transfer toasted pecan cream to medium bowl; cover surface directly with plastic wrap, and refrigerate at least 30 minutes.

4 Preheat oven to 425° F. Line tart shell with foil; fill with pie weights, dry beans, or uncooked rice. Bake 20 minutes. Remove foil and weights and bake 10 minutes longer, or until golden. If crust puffs up during baking, gently press it to tart pan with back of spoon. Transfer pan to wire rack. Turn oven control to broil.

5 Arrange banana slices, overlapping slightly, in tart shell. Spoon toasted pecan cream on top of bananas and sprinkle with remaining 1 tablespoon sugar. Cover edge of crust with foil to prevent overbrowning. Place tart on oven rack at position closest to heat source and broil until top is lightly caramelized, 1 to 2 minutes. Cool slightly on wire rack. Remove side of pan and serve warm. *Makes 12 servings.*

EACH SERVING: ABOUT 310 CALORIES, 4 G PROTEIN, 35 G CARBOHYDRATE, 18 G TOTAL FAT (8 G SATURATED), 1 G FIBER, 85 MG CHOLESTEROL, 205 MG SODIUM.

Cherry Pie

PREP 1 HOUR PLUS CHILLING
BAKE 1 HOUR 20 TO 30 MINUTES

Fresh tart cherries (sometimes called pie cherries) are not easy to find. If you manage to find some, why not buy extra and freeze what you don't need.

PASTRY FOR DOUBLE-CRUST PIE (PAGE 206)
1 CUP SUGAR
¼ CUP CORNSTARCH
PINCH SALT
2¼ POUNDS TART CHERRIES, PITTED (6 CUPS)
1 TABLESPOON BUTTER OR MARGARINE, CUT UP

1 Prepare dough as directed through chilling.

2 Preheat oven to 425° F. In large bowl, stir together sugar, cornstarch, and salt. Add cherries; toss to combine.

3 Roll out larger disk of dough and line 9-inch pie plate. Spoon filling into piecrust; dot with butter. Roll top crust; cut center circle and 1-inch slits to allow steam to escape during baking; place over filling; make decorative edge (see photos on page 212).

4 Place pie on nonstick or foil-lined cookie sheet to catch any overflow during baking. Bake 20 minutes. Turn oven control to 375° F; bake 1 hour to 1 hour 10 minutes, until filling bubbles in center. If necessary, cover edges loosely with foil to prevent overbrowning during baking. Cool on wire rack 1 hour to serve warm, or cool completely to serve later. *Makes 10 servings.*

EACH SERVING: ABOUT 385 CALORIES, 4 G PROTEIN, 58 G CARBOHYDRATE, 16 G TOTAL FAT (8 G SATURATED), 1 G FIBER, 28 MG CHOLESTEROL, 240 MG SODIUM.

Canned Cherry Pie

PREP 25 MINUTES PLUS CHILLING
BAKE 1 HOUR 20 MINUTES

Water-packed canned cherries make a perfectly fine pie, especially if you jazz them up with a bit of cinnamon and vanilla. Have vanilla ice cream on hand—some folks are sure to ask for a scoop with their pie.

PASTRY FOR DOUBLE-CRUST PIE (PAGE 206)
2 CANS (16 OUNCES EACH) PITTED TART CHERRIES PACKED IN WATER
¾ CUP SUGAR
¼ CUP CORNSTARCH
⅛ TEASPOON GROUND CINNAMON
PINCH SALT
½ TEASPOON VANILLA EXTRACT

1 Prepare dough as directed through chilling.

2 Preheat oven to 425° F. Drain cherries, reserving ½ cup juice. In medium bowl, combine sugar, cornstarch, cinnamon, and salt; stir in reserved cherry juice, cherries, and vanilla.

3 Roll out larger disk of dough and line 9-inch pie plate. Spoon filling into piecrust; dot with butter. Roll top crust; cut center circle and 1-inch slits to allow steam to escape during baking; place over filling; make decorative edge (see photos on page 212).

4 Place pie on nonstick or foil-lined cookie sheet to catch any overflow during baking. Bake 20 minutes. Turn oven control to 375° F; bake 1 hour longer, or until filling bubbles in center. If necessary, cover loosely with foil to prevent overbrowning during last 20 minutes of baking. Cool on wire rack 1 hour to serve warm, or cool pie completely to serve later. *Makes 10 servings.*

EACH SERVING: ABOUT 345 CALORIES, 4 G PROTEIN, 50 G CARBOHYDRATE, 15 G TOTAL FAT (7 G SATURATED), 1 G FIBER, 25 MG CHOLESTEROL, 230 MG SODIUM.

Farm-Stand Cherry Tart

PREP 45 MINUTES PLUS CHILLING
BAKE 45 TO 50 MINUTES

Although sweet cherries are plentiful in season, they're rarely used in baked goods. We say, "seize the day!" and bake this wonderful and easy free-form tart.

1½ CUPS ALL-PURPOSE FLOUR
⅓ CUP PLUS 1 TABLESPOON CORNMEAL
⅔ CUP PLUS 1 TEASPOON SUGAR
½ TEASPOON PLUS ⅛ TEASPOON SALT
½ CUP COLD BUTTER OR MARGARINE (1 STICK), CUT UP
4 TO 5 TABLESPOONS ICE WATER
2 TABLESPOONS PLUS 1 TEASPOON CORNSTARCH
1½ POUNDS DARK SWEET CHERRIES, PITTED
1 LARGE EGG WHITE

1 In medium bowl, mix flour, ⅓ cup cornmeal, ⅓ cup sugar, and ½ teaspoon salt. With pastry blender or 2 knives used scissor-fashion, cut in butter until mixture resembles coarse crumbs. Sprinkle water, 1 tablespoon at a time, into flour mixture, mixing with hands until dough holds together (it will feel dry at first). Shape into disk.

2 Sprinkle large cookie sheet with remaining 1 tablespoon cornmeal. (If your cookie sheet has 4 rims, invert and use upside down.) Place dampened towel under cookie sheet to prevent it from slipping.

With floured rolling pin, roll dough, directly on cookie sheet, into 13-inch round. With long metal spatula, gently loosen round from cookie sheet.

3 In large bowl, combine ⅓ cup sugar with cornstarch. Sprinkle half of sugar mixture over center of dough round, leaving 2½-inch border all around. Add cherries and any cherry juice to sugar mixture remaining in bowl; toss well. With slotted spoon, spoon cherry mixture over sugared area on dough round; reserve any cherry-juice mixture in bowl. Fold dough up around cherries, leaving a 4-inch opening in center. Pinch dough to seal any cracks.

4 In small cup, mix egg white with remaining ⅛ teaspoon salt. Brush egg-white mixture over dough. Sprinkle dough with remaining 1 teaspoon sugar. Pour cherry-juice mixture through opening in top of tart. Refrigerate until well chilled, about 30 minutes.

5 Preheat oven to 425° F. Bake 45 to 50 minutes, until crust is golden brown and cherry mixture is gently bubbling. If necessary, cover loosely with foil to prevent overbrowning during last 20 minutes of baking.

6 As soon as tart is done, use long metal spatula to loosen it from cookie sheet to prevent sticking. Cool 15 minutes on cookie sheet, then slide tart onto rack to cool completely. *Makes 8 servings.*

EACH SERVING: ABOUT 350 CALORIES, 5 G PROTEIN, 56 G CARBOHYDRATE, 13 G TOTAL FAT (7 G SATURATED), 2 G FIBER, 31 MG CHOLESTEROL, 310 MG SODIUM.

Farm-Stand Cherry Tart

Sprinkle the mixture of granulated sugar and cornstarch onto the middle of the round of dough. Spoon the pitted cherries on top.

Fold up the edges of the dough to make a rounded, free-form package; sprinkle the dough with granulated sugar to help the pastry brown nicely.

Cranberry-Raisin Pie

PREP 45 MINUTES PLUS CHILLING
BAKE 1 HOUR 5 MINUTES

Once you taste a slice, you may want to make this recipe a new tradition to add to your Thanksgiving pumpkin and mince pies.

PASTRY FOR DOUBLE-CRUST PIE (PAGE 206)
1 CUP SUGAR
1 TABLESPOON CORNSTARCH
¼ CUP WATER
¾ CUP LIGHT CORN SYRUP
1 BAG (12 OUNCES) CRANBERRIES (ABOUT 3 CUPS)
1 CUP DARK SEEDLESS RAISINS
⅛ TEASPOON GROUND ALLSPICE
2 TABLESPOONS BUTTER OR MARGARINE, CUT UP

1 Prepare dough as directed through chilling.

2 In 3-quart saucepan, combine sugar and cornstarch, add water and corn syrup, and stir until well blended. Heat to boiling over medium heat, stirring. Stir in cranberries, raisins, and allspice. Cover and cook until cranberry skins pop, about 7 minutes. Remove saucepan from heat; stir in butter. Set aside to cool slightly; refrigerate to cool completely.

3 Preheat oven to 425° F. Roll out larger disk of dough and line 9-inch pie plate. Spoon filling into piecrust; dot with butter. Roll top crust, cut 1-inch slits to allow steam to escape during baking, and place on filling as directed; make decorative edge (see photos on page 212).

4 Place pie on nonstick or foil-lined cookie sheet to catch any overflow during baking. Bake 20 minutes. Turn oven control to 375° F; bake 45 minutes longer, or until crust is golden. Cool on wire rack 1 hour to serve warm, or cool completely to serve later. *Makes 10 servings.*

EACH SERVING: ABOUT 470 CALORIES, 4 G PROTEIN,
79 G CARBOHYDRATE, 17 G TOTAL FAT (8 G SATURATED),
3 G FIBER, 31 MG CHOLESTEROL, 265 MG SODIUM.

Cranberry-Pear Pie

PREP 45 MINUTES PLUS CHILLING
BAKE 1 HOUR 20 TO 30 MINUTES

You'll need ripe, sweet pears to help counter the tartness of the cranberries, so be sure to buy the pears a few days ahead of time, as they'll likely need time to ripen.

PASTRY FOR DOUBLE-CRUST PIE (PAGE 206)
3 TABLESPOONS CORNSTARCH
⅛ TEASPOON GROUND CINNAMON
¾ CUP PLUS 1 TABLESPOON SUGAR
1½ CUPS CRANBERRIES, COARSELY CHOPPED
3 POUNDS FULLY-RIPE PEARS (6 LARGE), PEELED, CORED, AND SLICED
2 TABLESPOONS BUTTER OR MARGARINE, CUT UP
1 LARGE EGG WHITE, LIGHTLY BEATEN

1 Prepare dough as directed through chilling.

2 Preheat oven to 425° F. In large bowl, mix cornstarch, cinnamon, and ¾ cup sugar. Add cranberries and pears; toss to combine.

3 Roll out larger disk of dough and line 9-inch pie plate. Spoon filling into piecrust; dot with butter. Roll top crust, cut 1-inch slits to allow steam to escape during baking, and place on filling as directed; make decorative edge (see photos on page 212). Brush crust with beaten egg white; sprinkle with remaining 1 tablespoon sugar.

4 Place pie on nonstick or foil-lined cookie sheet to catch any overflow during baking. Bake 20 minutes. Turn oven control to 375° F; bake 60 to 70 minutes longer, until filling bubbles in center. If necessary, cover loosely with foil during last 20 minutes of baking to prevent overbrowning. Cool on wire rack 1 hour to serve warm, or cool completely to serve later. *Makes 10 servings.*

EACH SERVING: ABOUT 415 CALORIES, 4 G PROTEIN,
63 G CARBOHYDRATE, 17 G TOTAL FAT (9 G SATURATED),
4 G FIBER, 31 MG CHOLESTEROL, 240 MG SODIUM.

CRANBERRY-APPLE PIE Prepare dough and filling as above but use *3 pounds Golden Delicious or Gala apples*, peeled, cored, and sliced, for pears. Bake and cool as directed.

EACH SERVING: ABOUT 410 CALORIES, 4 G PROTEIN,
62 G CARBOHYDRATE, 17 G TOTAL FAT (9 G SATURATED),
4 G FIBER, 31 MG CHOLESTEROL, 240 MG SODIUM.

Mixed Berry Pie

If there's anything better than a blueberry pie, it could only be this four-berry pie, which has strawberries, raspberries, and blackberries in it, too. This is a very juicy pie, and the juices may bubble up and spill over during baking. So be sure to place a sheet of foil under the pie plate. Don't cover the entire oven rack with foil, however—that inhibits heat circulation.

PASTRY FOR DOUBLE-CRUST PIE (PAGE 206)
1 CUP PLUS 2 TEASPOONS SUGAR
¼ CUP CORNSTARCH
⅛ TEASPOON SALT
1 PINT STRAWBERRIES, HULLED AND QUARTERED
3 CUPS BLUEBERRIES, PICKED OVER
1 CUP RASPBERRIES
1 CUP BLACKBERRIES
1 TABLESPOON FRESH LEMON JUICE

1 Prepare dough as directed through chilling.

2 Preheat oven to 425° F. In large bowl, stir together 1 cup sugar, cornstarch, and salt until blended. Add strawberries, blueberries, raspberries, blackberries, and lemon juice; stir gently to combine.

3 Roll out larger disk of dough and line 9-inch pie plate. Spoon filling into piecrust; dot with butter. Roll top crust, cut 1-inch slits to allow steam to escape during baking, and place on filling as directed; make fluted edge (see photos on page 212). Sprinkle crust with remaining 2 teaspoons sugar.

4 Place pie on nonstick or foil-lined cookie sheet to catch any overflow during baking. Bake 20 minutes. Turn oven control to 375° F; bake 55 to 60 minutes longer, until crust is brown and filling bubbles in center. If necessary, cover edges loosely with foil to prevent overbrowning during baking. Cool on wire rack 1 hour to serve warm, or cool pie completely to serve later. *Makes 10 servings.*

EACH SERVING: ABOUT 380 CALORIES, 4 G PROTEIN,
59 G CARBOHYDRATE, 15 G TOTAL FAT (7 G SATURATED),
4 G FIBER, 25 MG CHOLESTEROL, 245 MG SODIUM.

Plum Frangipane Tart

Almonds and plums, two members of the same botanical family, are natural partners. Frangipane is an almond pastry filling named for an Italian marquis who lived in Paris in the sixteenth century.

PASTRY FOR 11-INCH TART (PAGE 207)
1 TUBE OR CAN (7 TO 8 OUNCES) ALMOND PASTE,
   CRUMBLED
4 TABLESPOONS BUTTER OR MARGARINE, SOFTENED
½ CUP SUGAR
¼ TEASPOON SALT
2 LARGE EGGS
2 TEASPOONS VANILLA EXTRACT
¼ CUP ALL-PURPOSE FLOUR
1¼ POUNDS RIPE PLUMS (ABOUT 5 MEDIUM), PITTED AND
   EACH CUT INTO 6 WEDGES

1 Prepare dough as directed through chilling. Line tart pan with dough; chill as directed.

2 Preheat oven to 375° F. Line tart shell with foil; fill with pie weights, dry beans, or uncooked rice. Bake 20 minutes. Remove foil and weights; bake 8 to 10 minutes longer, until golden. If crust puffs up during baking, gently press it to tart pan with back of spoon. Transfer pan to wire rack.

3 Meanwhile, in large bowl, with mixer at low speed, beat almond paste, butter, sugar, and salt until crumbly. Increase speed to medium-high and beat until combined, scraping bowl frequently with rubber spatula, about 3 minutes. (There will be tiny lumps.) Add eggs and vanilla; beat until smooth. With spoon, stir in flour.

4 Pour filling into warm tart shell. Arrange plums in concentric circles over filling. Bake 50 to 60 minutes, until golden. Cool on wire rack. When cool, remove side of pan. *Makes 12 servings.*

EACH SERVING: ABOUT 340 CALORIES, 6 G PROTEIN,
37 G CARBOHYDRATE, 20 G TOTAL FAT (8 G SATURATED),
2 G FIBER, 66 MG CHOLESTEROL, 275 MG SODIUM.

APPLE OR PEAR FRANGIPANE TART Prepare dough and filling as above but use *1½ pounds Golden Delicious or Granny Smith apples or Bartlett or Anjou pears,* peeled and thinly sliced, for plums. Bake as directed.
EACH SERVING: ABOUT 340 CALORIES, 5 G PROTEIN,
37 G CARBOHYDRATE, 20 G TOTAL FAT (8 G SATURATED),
1 G FIBER, 66 MG CHOLESTEROL, 275 MG SODIUM.

Mixed Berry Pie

PEACH OR NECTARINE FRANGIPANE TART Prepare dough and filling as for Plum Frangipane Tart (page 224) but use *5 peaches (1¼ pounds)*, peeled, pitted, and thinly sliced, or *5 nectarines (1¼ pounds)*, pitted and thinly sliced, for plums. Bake as directed.
EACH SERVING: ABOUT 330 CALORIES, 5 G PROTEIN, 34 G CARBOHYDRATE, 19 G TOTAL FAT (8 G SATURATED), 1 G FIBER, 66 MG CHOLESTEROL, 275 MG SODIUM.

TART CHERRY FRANGIPANE TART Prepare dough and filling as for Plum Frangipane Tart (page 224) but use *1 quart tart cherries (1½ pounds)*, pitted and drained, for plums. Bake as directed.
EACH SERVING: ABOUT 330 CALORIES, 5 G PROTEIN, 34 G CARBOHYDRATE, 20 G TOTAL FAT (8 G SATURATED), 0.5 G FIBER, 66 MG CHOLESTEROL, 275 MG SODIUM.

APRICOT FRANGIPANE TART Prepare dough and filling as for Plum Frangipane Tart (page 224) but use *1 pound fresh apricots*, pitted and each cut into 4 wedges, for plums. Bake as directed.
EACH SERVING: ABOUT 330 CALORIES, 6 G PROTEIN, 34 G CARBOHYDRATE, 20 G TOTAL FAT (8 G SATURATED), 1 G FIBER, 66 MG CHOLESTEROL, 275 MG SODIUM.

Mince Pie

PREP 25 MINUTES PLUS CHILLING
BAKE 30 TO 40 MINUTES

Storebought mincemeat is very dense and benefits from being lightened with fresh fruit, nuts, and lemon juice.

PASTRY FOR DOUBLE-CRUST PIE (PAGE 206)
1 JAR (28 OUNCES) READY-TO-USE MINCEMEAT
1 COOKING APPLE, PEELED, CORED, AND FINELY CHOPPED
1 CUP WALNUTS, COARSELY BROKEN
½ CUP PACKED BROWN SUGAR
2 TABLESPOONS BRANDY OR RUM (OPTIONAL)
1 TABLESPOON FRESH LEMON JUICE
HARD SAUCE (PAGE 363) OR SLICED CHEDDAR CHEESE

1 Prepare dough as directed through chilling.

2 Preheat oven to 425° F. In medium bowl, stir mincemeat, apple, walnuts, brown sugar, brandy, if desired, and lemon juice until well mixed.

3 Roll out larger disk of dough and line 9-inch pie plate. Spoon filling into piecrust; dot with butter. Roll top crust, cut 1-inch slits to allow steam to escape during baking, and place on filling as directed; make decorative edge (see photos on page 212).

4 Place pie on nonstick or foil-lined cookie sheet. Bake 30 to 40 minutes, until golden. Cool on wire rack 1 hour to serve warm, or cool completely to serve later. Top with Hard Sauce or Cheddar. *Makes 10 servings.*

EACH SERVING WITH HARD SAUCE: ABOUT 645 CALORIES, 6 G PROTEIN, 89 G CARBOHYDRATE, 30 G TOTAL FAT (11 G SATURATED), 2 G FIBER, 41 MG CHOLESTEROL, 490 MG SODIUM.

Peach Pie

PREP 35 MINUTES PLUS CHILLING
BAKE 1 HOUR 5 TO 20 MINUTES

If you bake only one fruit pie all summer, this is the one to choose. Make it with a double crust, as suggested below, or with an open lattice top (see page 211).

PASTRY FOR DOUBLE-CRUST PIE (PAGE 206)
¾ CUP SUGAR
¼ CUP CORNSTARCH
PINCH SALT
3 POUNDS RIPE PEACHES, PEELED, PITTED, AND SLICED (ABOUT 7 CUPS)
1 TABLESPOON FRESH LEMON JUICE
1 TABLESPOON BUTTER OR MARGARINE, CUT UP

1 Prepare dough as directed through chilling.

2 Preheat oven to 425° F. In large bowl, stir together sugar, cornstarch, and salt. Add peaches and lemon juice; toss gently to combine.

3 Roll out larger disk of dough and line 9-inch pie plate. Spoon filling into piecrust; dot with butter. Roll top crust, cut 1-inch slits to allow steam to escape during baking, and place on filling as directed; make decorative edge (see photos on page 212).

4 Place pie on nonstick or foil-lined cookie sheet to catch any overflow during baking. Bake 20 minutes. Turn oven control to 375° F; bake 45 to 60 minutes longer, until filling bubbles in center. If necessary, cover loosely with foil to prevent overbrowning during last 20 minutes of baking. Cool on wire rack 1 hour to serve warm, or cool completely to serve later. *Makes 10 servings.*

EACH SERVING: ABOUT 365 CALORIES, 4 G PROTEIN, 53 G CARBOHYDRATE, 16 G TOTAL FAT (8 G SATURATED), 3G FIBER, 28 MG CHOLESTEROL, 235 MG SODIUM.

PLUM PIE Prepare as for Peach Pie but use *3 pounds tart plums*, pitted and sliced, for peaches and *1 cup sugar*. Bake and cool as directed.

EACH SERVING: ABOUT 410 CALORIES, 4 G PROTEIN, 64 G CARBOHYDRATE, 17 G TOTAL FAT (8 G SATURATED), 3.5 G FIBER, 28 MG CHOLESTEROL, 235 MG SODIUM.

PEAR PIE Prepare as for Peach Pie but use *3 pounds ripe pears*, peeled, and sliced, for peaches; add *⅛ teaspoon ground nutmeg* to sugar mixture. Bake and cool as directed.

EACH SERVING: ABOUT 395 CALORIES, 4 G PROTEIN, 61 G CARBOHYDRATE, 16 G TOTAL FAT (8 G SATURATED), 4 G FIBER, 28 MG CHOLESTEROL, 235 MG SODIUM.

CARDAMOM-PEAR PIE Prepare pie as above but use *½ teaspoon ground cardamom* for nutmeg. Bake and cool as directed.

EACH SERVING: ABOUT 395 CALORIES, 4 G PROTEIN, 61 G CARBOHYDRATE, 16 G TOTAL FAT (8 G SATURATED), 4 G FIBER, 28 MG CHOLESTEROL, 235 MG SODIUM.

Pineapple Tart

PREP 45 MINUTES PLUS CHILLING AND COOLING
BAKE 35 TO 40 MINUTES

PAT-IN-PAN CRUST FOR 9-INCH TART (PAGE 209)
1 CAN (20 OUNCES) CRUSHED PINEAPPLE IN
   UNSWEETENED PINEAPPLE JUICE
⅓ CUP PACKED LIGHT BROWN SUGAR
2 TABLESPOONS FRESH LEMON JUICE
1 TABLESPOON BUTTER OR MARGARINE, SOFTENED
1 LARGE EGG YOLK
1 TABLESPOON WATER
1 TEASPOON GRANULATED SUGAR

1 Prepare dough as directed through chilling.

2 Meanwhile, in 10-inch skillet, heat pineapple with its juice, brown sugar, and lemon juice to boiling over medium-high heat. Cook, stirring often, until liquid has evaporated, about 15 minutes; stir in butter. Spoon pineapple mixture into medium bowl; cover and refrigerate until cool.

3 Preheat oven to 375° F. Remove both pieces of dough from refrigerator. With floured hands, press larger disk of dough into bottom and up side of 9-inch round tart pan with removable bottom. Refrigerate shell at least 15 minutes, until chilled.

4 Meanwhile, on sheet of lightly floured waxed paper, roll remaining disk of dough into 10-inch

round. With pastry wheel or knife, cut dough into ten ¾-inch-wide strips. Refrigerate 15 minutes.

5 Spread chilled pineapple filling over dough in tart pan to within ½ inch of edge. Make lattice top (see photo on page 211): Place 5 dough strips, 1 inch apart, across tart, trimming ends even with side of tart pan; repeat with 5 more strips placed diagonally across first ones to make diamond lattice pattern. Trim ends and reserve trimmings.

6 Make rope edge for tart shell (see photo on page 212); with hands, roll trimmings and remaining 2 strips of dough into ¼-inch-thick ropes. Press ropes around edge of tart to create finished edge. (If rope pieces break, just press pieces together.)

7 In small cup, beat egg yolk with remaining tablespoon water. Brush egg-yolk mixture over lattice and edge of tart; sprinkle with granulated sugar.

8 Bake 35 to 40 minutes, until crust is golden. Cover tart loosely with foil to prevent overbrowning during last 15 minutes of baking. Cool in pan on wire rack. Remove tart from pan to serve. *Makes 10 servings.*

EACH SERVING: ABOUT 335 CALORIES, 4 G PROTEIN, 44 G CARBOHYDRATE, 16 G TOTAL FAT (10 G SATURATED), 1 G FIBER, 83 MG CHOLESTEROL, 220 MG SODIUM.

OFF-SEASON FRUIT PIES

WHEN FRESH FRUIT WAS UNAVAILABLE, NINETEENTH-CENTURY COOKS DEVISED THE MOCK APPLE PIE OUT OF SODA CRACKERS, SUGAR, VINEGAR, AND SPICES. HERE ARE SOME MODERN "OFF-SEASON PIES." THE PINEAPPLE TART AT LEFT IS MADE WITH CANNED FRUIT, AS IS THE CANNED CHERRY PIE ON PAGE 221. RHUBARB PIE, PAGE 229, CAN BE MADE WITH FROZEN RHUBARB, AND IF YOU FREEZE A FEW BAGS OF CRANBERRIES DURING THE HOLIDAYS, WHEN THEY'RE SURE TO BE AVAILABLE, YOU CAN MAKE CRANBERRY-RAISIN PIE, PAGE 223, AT ANY TIME OF YEAR. THE DRIED FRUIT TART ON PAGE 230 IS ANOTHER OPTION FOR "OFF-SEASON" BAKING.

Buttery Plum Tart

PREP 20 MINUTES / BAKE 45 MINUTES

European plum varieties—the small, oval bluish-purple ones—are freestone, so they'll save you some time as you prepare the ingredients for this tart. Also called prune plums or Italian plums, these egg-size fruits are very dense-fleshed and flavorful.

1¼ CUPS PLUS 1 TABLESPOON PLUS 1 TEASPOON
    ALL-PURPOSE FLOUR

¼ CUP PLUS ⅓ CUP SUGAR

½ TEASPOON GROUND CINNAMON

7 TABLESPOONS BUTTER OR MARGARINE, SOFTENED

1 POUND PLUMS (ABOUT 5), PITTED AND EACH CUT INTO
    ½-INCH-THICK SLICES

¼ CUP SLIVERED BLANCHED ALMONDS

½ CUP HEAVY OR WHIPPING CREAM (OPTIONAL)

1 Preheat oven to 375° F. In medium bowl, stir together 1¼ cups flour, ¼ cup sugar, and ¼ teaspoon cinnamon. Add butter; with hand, knead mixture until blended. Press pastry into 9-inch tart pan or into bottom and 1 inch up side of 9-inch springform pan.

2 In medium bowl, combine remaining ⅓ cup sugar, remaining 1 tablespoon plus 1 teaspoon flour, and remaining ¼ teaspoon cinnamon. Add plums and toss to combine. Arrange plum slices, closely overlapping, to form concentric circles in pan. Sprinkle with almonds.

3 Place tart on nonstick or foil-lined cookie sheet. Bake 45 minutes, or until pastry is golden and plums are tender. Cool on wire rack. Carefully remove side of pan to serve. Pass heavy cream to pour over servings, if desired. *Makes 10 servings.*

EACH SERVING WITHOUT CREAM: ABOUT 220 CALORIES, 3 G PROTEIN, 31 G CARBOHYDRATE, 10 G TOTAL FAT (5 G SATURATED), 1 G FIBER, 22 MG CHOLESTEROL, 85 MG SODIUM.

Buttery Plum Tart

Rhubarb Pie

PREP 35 MINUTES PLUS CHILLING
BAKE 1 HOUR 20 TO 40 MINUTES

Pie bakers anxiously await the appearance of rhubarb in mid-April. Its translucent pink stalks become a welcome spring tonic when baked into a pie. If spring is months away—or if fresh rhubarb never appears in your local market—you can make the pie with frozen rhubarb, which is sold cut up, in bags. Mix the frozen rhubarb with the sugar, cornstarch, and salt, and let stand until it's at least partially thawed—until the juices mingle with the sugar.

PASTRY FOR DOUBLE-CRUST PIE (PAGE 206)
1½ CUPS SUGAR
¼ CUP CORNSTARCH
PINCH SALT
2 POUNDS RHUBARB, TRIMMED AND CUT INTO ½-INCH
    PIECES (ABOUT 7 CUPS)
1 TABLESPOON BUTTER OR MARGARINE, CUT UP

1 Prepare dough as directed through chilling.

2 Preheat oven to 425° F. In large bowl, stir together sugar, cornstarch, and salt. Add rhubarb; toss to combine.

3 Roll out larger disk of dough and line 9-inch pie plate. Spoon filling into piecrust; dot with butter. Roll top crust, cut center circle and 1-inch slits to allow steam to escape during baking, and place on filling as directed; make decorative edge (see photos on page 212).

4 Place pie on nonstick or foil-lined cookie sheet to catch any overflow during baking. Bake 20 minutes. Turn oven control to 375° F; bake 1 hour to 1 hour 20 minutes, until filling bubbles in center and crust is golden. If necessary, cover loosely with foil to prevent overbrowning during baking. Cool on wire rack 1 hour to serve warm, or cool completely to serve later. *Makes 10 servings.*

EACH SERVING: ABOUT 400 CALORIES, 4 G PROTEIN,
61 G CARBOHYDRATE, 16 G TOTAL FAT (8 G SATURATED),
1 G FIBER, 28 MG CHOLESTEROL, 240 MG SODIUM.

Double Raspberry Pie

PREP 35 MINUTES / BAKE 20 TO 25 MINUTES

Raspberries are so delicate in texture and flavor that they really don't need much cooking—if any—to make a great pie. Here, an intense berry puree is made with frozen raspberries (cheaper than fresh); a bountiful quantity of fresh berries is folded into the puree, and the filling is poured into a prebaked crust.

PASTRY FOR SINGLE-CRUST PIE (PAGE 206)
1 PACKAGE (10 OUNCES) FROZEN RASPBERRIES IN HEAVY
    SYRUP, THAWED
½ CUP PLUS 1 TABLESPOON SUGAR
2 TABLESPOONS CORNSTARCH
2 TABLESPOONS BUTTER OR MARGARINE
5 CUPS FRESH RASPBERRIES
1 CUP HEAVY OR WHIPPING CREAM
½ TEASPOON VANILLA EXTRACT

1 Prepare dough as directed through chilling. Roll out dough and line 9-inch pie plate; make decorative edge (see photos on page 212). Refrigerate or freeze 15 minutes to firm pastry.

2 Preheat oven to 425° F. Line pie shell with foil; fill with pie weights, dry beans, or uncooked rice. Bake 15 minutes. Remove foil and weights; bake 5 to 10 minutes longer, until golden. Cool on wire rack.

3 In food processor with knife blade attached, pulse frozen raspberries and syrup until smooth. Strain through sieve set over a bowl; discard seeds.

4 In 2-quart saucepan, combine ½ cup sugar and cornstarch; stir until well blended. Add puree and stir to dissolve sugar. Cook over medium heat, stirring constantly, until mixture boils. Boil 2 minutes, stirring. Pour into a large bowl; stir in butter until melted. Let cool to room temperature.

5 Gently fold fresh raspberries into puree until combined. Turn raspberry mixture into baked pie shell and spread evenly. Refrigerate pie 3 hours, or up to 6 hours, until set.

6 In small bowl, with mixer on high speed, beat remaining 1 tablespoon sugar, cream, and vanilla until soft peaks form. Garnish top of pie with whipped cream. *Makes 10 servings.*

EACH SERVING: ABOUT 340 CALORIES, 3 G PROTEIN,
41 G CARBOHYDRATE, 19 G TOTAL FAT (10 G SATURATED),
3 G FIBER, 51 MG CHOLESTEROL, 135 MG SODIUM.

Classic Jam Crostata

PREP **45** MINUTES PLUS CHILLING
BAKE **35** TO **40** MINUTES

This simplest of Italian desserts, the crostata di marmellata, consists of a rich, sweet crust filled with jam. In place of raspberry jam, try apricot, blueberry, cherry, or strawberry jam, or black cherry preserves.

PAT-IN-PAN CRUST FOR 9-INCH TART (PAGE 209)
1 CUP SEEDLESS RASPBERRY JAM
1 TEASPOON FRESH LEMON JUICE
½ TEASPOON VANILLA EXTRACT
1 LARGE EGG YOLK
1 TABLESPOON WATER

1 Prepare dough as directed through chilling.

2 In small bowl, stir together jam, lemon juice, and vanilla.

3 Remove both disks of dough from refrigerator. With floured hands, press larger disk of dough into bottom and up side of 9-inch round tart pan with removable bottom. Refrigerate 15 minutes.

4 Roll remaining disk of dough into 10-inch round. With pastry wheel or knife, cut dough into ten ¾-inch-wide strips. Refrigerate 15 minutes, or until easy to handle.

5 Preheat oven to 375° F. Spread jam over dough in tart pan to ½-inch of edge. Make lattice top (see photo on page 211): Place 5 dough strips, 1 inch apart, across tart, trimming ends even with side of tart pan; repeat with 5 more strips placed diagonally across first ones to make diamond lattice pattern. Trim ends and reserve trimmings.

6 Make rope edge for tart shell (see photo on page 212); with hands, roll trimmings and remaining 2 strips of dough into about ¼-inch-thick ropes. Press ropes around edge of tart to create finished edge. (If rope pieces break, just press pieces together.)

7 Beat egg yolk and water. Brush over lattice and edge. Bake 35 to 40 minutes, until crust is golden. Cool in pan on wire rack. When cool, carefully remove side of pan. *Makes 10 servings.*

EACH SERVING: ABOUT 335 CALORIES, 4 G PROTEIN, 47 G CARBOHYDRATE, 15 G TOTAL FAT (9 G SATURATED), 0.5 G FIBER, 80 MG CHOLESTEROL, 220 MG SODIUM.

Dried Fruit Tart

PREP **40** MINUTES PLUS CHILLING
BAKE **40** TO **45** MINUTES

A touch of rum gives this dessert a holiday flavor. You can keep all the ingredients on hand and make the tart on short notice at any time of year.

PASTRY FOR 11-INCH TART (PAGE 207)
1½ CUPS MIXED DRIED FRUIT (8 OUNCES), CHOPPED
⅔ CUP APPLE JUICE
½ CUP PACKED LIGHT BROWN SUGAR
⅓ CUP LIGHT CORN SYRUP
1 TABLESPOON BUTTER OR MARGARINE, MELTED
2 TEASPOONS CORNSTARCH
1 TABLESPOON RUM
2 LARGE EGGS, LIGHTLY BEATEN
1 TABLESPOON MILK
1 TEASPOON GRANULATED SUGAR

1 Prepare dough as directed, shaping one-third into small disk and remaining dough in larger disk; chill. Use larger disk to line 9-inch tart pan with removable bottom; prick all over with fork to prevent puffing during baking; chill as directed.

2 In 1-quart saucepan, heat dried fruit and apple juice to boiling over high heat. Reduce heat to low; cook, stirring occasionally, until all apple juice has been absorbed. Spoon fruit mixture into medium bowl; cool slightly.

3 Preheat oven to 375° F.

4 Stir brown sugar, corn syrup, melted butter, cornstarch, rum, and eggs into dried fruit until well mixed. Spoon filling into shell.

5 Roll remaining disk into 9-inch round. With pastry wheel or knife, cut ten ½-inch-wide strips. Make woven lattice top (see photo on page 211): Place 5 dough strips, 1 inch apart, across tart. With 5 more strips weave across first ones. Trim ends evenly with side of tart pan. Brush strips with milk and sprinkle with remaining 1 tablespoon granulated sugar.

6 Bake 40 to 45 minutes, until filling begins to bubble and crust is golden. If necessary, cover tart with foil to prevent overbrowning during last 10 minutes of baking. Cool in pan on wire rack. When cool, carefully remove from pan. *Makes 12 servings.*

EACH SERVING: ABOUT 280 CALORIES, 3 G PROTEIN, 42 G CARBOHYDRATE, 12 G TOTAL FAT (6 G SATURATED), 2 G FIBER, 59 MG CHOLESTEROL, 215 MG SODIUM.

Apple Hand Pies

PREP 1 HOUR PLUS CHILLING / BAKE 35 TO 40 MINUTES

PASTRY FOR DOUBLE-CRUST PIE (PAGE 206)

3 TABLESPOONS PLUS ⅓ CUP GRANULATED SUGAR

2 TABLESPOONS BUTTER OR MARGARINE

2 LARGE GRANNY SMITH APPLES (1½ POUNDS), EACH
    PEELED, CORED, AND CUT INTO ½-INCH PIECES

1 TABLESPOON CORNSTARCH

¼ TEASPOON GROUND CINNAMON

PINCH SALT

1 TEASPOON FRESH LEMON JUICE

1 LARGE EGG, BEATEN

1 CUP CONFECTIONERS' SUGAR

2 TABLESPOONS WARM WATER

2 TEASPOONS LIGHT CORN SYRUP

½ TEASPOON VANILLA EXTRACT

1 Prepare dough through chilling but, in Step 1, add 2 tablespoons granulated sugar with flour.

2 In 10-inch skillet, melt butter over medium-high heat; add apples, ⅓ cup granulated sugar, cornstarch, cinnamon, and salt; cook, stirring, 8 minutes, until apples are tender. Add lemon juice; cool mixture.

3 On lightly floured surface, with floured rolling pin, roll one disk of dough into round about ⅛ inch thick. Using 5-inch round plate as a guide, cut out 5 circles. Repeat with remaining dough; reroll trimmings. You should have 14 circles in all.

4 Preheat oven to 400° F. Grease 2 large cookie sheets. Onto half of each pastry circle, spoon 1 heaping tablespoon apple filling; fold dough over filling. With fork, firmly press edges together to seal. Place pies, 2 inches apart, on prepared cookie sheets. With pastry brush, brush pies with beaten egg; sprinkle with remaining 1 tablespoon granulated sugar. Make two 1-inch slits in top of each pie to allow steam to escape during baking. Bake 15 minutes. Turn oven control to 350° F; bake 20 to 25 minutes longer, until golden brown. Cool on wire racks.

5 Meanwhile, combine confectioners' sugar, water, corn syrup, and vanilla to spreading consistency. Drizzle icing over cooled pies; let icing dry before serving. *Makes 14 pies.*

EACH PIE: ABOUT 290 CALORIES, 3 G PROTEIN,
41 G CARBOHYDRATE, 13 G TOTAL FAT (6 G SATURATED),
1 G FIBER, 37 MG CHOLESTEROL, 185 MG SODIUM.

Apple Hand Pies

Apple Tarte Tatin

PREP 45 MINUTES PLUS CHILLING
BAKE 25 MINUTES

Les Demoiselles Tatin were two sisters who ran a restaurant near the French city of Orléans. Their skillet-cooked caramelized-apple tart is now a classic.

PASTRY FOR 11-INCH TART (PAGE 207)
1 CUP SUGAR
6 TABLESPOONS BUTTER OR MARGARINE
1 TABLESPOON FRESH LEMON JUICE
3¾ POUNDS GOLDEN DELICIOUS APPLES (9 MEDIUM),
    PEELED, CORED, AND EACH CUT IN HALF

1 Preheat oven to 425° F. Prepare dough as directed but roll into 12-inch round. Transfer to cookie sheet and refrigerate until ready to use.

2 In heavy 12-inch skillet with oven-safe handle (or wrap handle in double thickness of foil), heat sugar, butter, and lemon juice over medium-high heat until mixture boils.

3 Place apples in skillet on their sides, overlapping if necessary. Cook 10 minutes. Carefully turn apples over; cook 8 to 12 minutes longer, until syrup is caramelized and thickened.

4 Place dough on top of apples in skillet; fold edge of dough under to form rim around edge of apples. Cut six ¼-inch-long slits in top to allow steam to escape during baking. Bake 25 minutes, or until crust is golden.

5 To unmold, place large platter over top of tart. Quickly turn skillet upside down to invert tart. Cool on wire rack 30 minutes to serve warm, or cool completely to serve later. *Makes 10 servings.*

EACH SERVING: ABOUT 395 CALORIES, 2 G PROTEIN,
56 G CARBOHYDRATE, 19 G TOTAL FAT (11 G SATURATED),
3 G FIBER, 43 MG CHOLESTEROL, 280 MG SODIUM.

PEACH TARTE TATIN Prepare dough and filling as above but use *3¾ pounds slightly ripe peaches (11 medium)*, peeled, halved, and pitted, for apples. Bake and cool as directed.
EACH SERVING: ABOUT 365 CALORIES, 3 G PROTEIN,
49 G CARBOHYDRATE, 19 G TOTAL FAT (11 G SATURATED),
3 G FIBER, 43 MG CHOLESTEROL, 280 MG SODIUM.

PEAR TARTE TATIN Prepare dough and filling as above but use *3¾ pounds firm, slightly ripe Bosc pears (about 7)*, peeled, cored, and halved lengthwise, for apples. Bake and cool as directed.

EACH SERVING: ABOUT 405 CALORIES, 3 G PROTEIN,
58 G CARBOHYDRATE, 19 G TOTAL FAT (11 G SATURATED),
4 G FIBER, 43 MG CHOLESTEROL, 280 MG SODIUM.

NUT PIES

Among the richest of all desserts are nut pies, packed with pecans, hazelnuts, pine nuts, almonds, or walnuts. The Southern variety is very sweet, made with both corn syrup and brown sugar, while the Austrian Linzertorte is sweetened up with raspberry jam. Our Chocolate Walnut Pie is like a brownie in a crust. Serve nut pies in slender slices, accompanied with mugs of hot coffee or tall glasses of ice-cold milk.

Southern Pecan Pie

PREP 25 MINUTES PLUS CHILLING
BAKE 1 HOUR 5 TO 10 MINUTES

Pecans are native American nuts, and the South is the main source of commercially grown pecans. In a perfect pie, plenty of coarsely chopped pecans are suspended in a dark, sweet filling, while entire nut halves "float" on top. Pecans are relatively sweet, but in contrast with this filling, their "nuttier" side comes through.

PASTRY FOR SINGLE-CRUST PIE (PAGE 206)
1¾ CUPS PECAN HALVES
¾ CUP DARK CORN SYRUP
½ CUP PACKED DARK BROWN SUGAR
4 TABLESPOONS BUTTER OR MARGARINE, MELTED
1 TEASPOON VANILLA EXTRACT
3 LARGE EGGS

1 Prepare dough as directed through chilling.

2 Roll out dough and line 9-inch pie plate; make decorative edge (see photos on page 212). With fork, prick all over with fork to prevent puffing during baking. Refrigerate or freeze 10 to 15 minutes to firm pastry.

3 Preheat oven to 425° F. Line pie shell with foil; fill with pie weights, dry beans, or uncooked rice. Bake 10 minutes. Remove foil and weights; bake 10 minutes longer, or until lightly browned. If crust puffs up during baking, gently press it to pie plate with back of spoon. Cool on wire rack at least 10 minutes. Turn oven control to 350° F.

4 Coarsely chop 1 cup pecans; reserve remaining pecan halves.

5 In large bowl, with wire whisk, mix corn syrup, brown sugar, melted butter, vanilla, and eggs until blended. Stir in chopped pecans and pecan halves.

6 Pour filling into crust. Bake 45 to 50 minutes, until edges of filling are set (center will jiggle slightly). Cool completely on wire rack. *Makes 12 servings.*

EACH SERVING: ABOUT 355 CALORIES, 4 G PROTEIN, 39 G CARBOHYDRATE, 22 G TOTAL FAT (7 G SATURATED), 1 G FIBER, 74 MG CHOLESTEROL, 175 MG SODIUM.

CHOCOLATE-PECAN PIE Prepare crust and filling as for Southern Pecan Pie but use ¾ *cup packed dark brown sugar* and add *2 squares (2 ounces) unsweetened chocolate,* melted, to filling with butter. Bake as directed.
EACH SERVING: ABOUT 400 CALORIES, 5 G PROTEIN, 44 G CARBOHYDRATE, 24 G TOTAL FAT (8 G SATURATED), 2 G FIBER, 74 MG CHOLESTEROL, 180 MG SODIUM.

NUTTY AND SWEET

BECAUSE NUTS CONTAIN A LOT OF FAT, THEY CAN BECOME RANCID IF IMPROPERLY STORED. IF THE FAT DOES BECOME RANCID, THE NUTS WILL HAVE AN UNPLEASANT, STALE FLAVOR AND ODOR. THEY MAY ALSO SEEM SOFT AND LIMP RATHER THAN BREAKING WITH A CRISP SNAP. IF NUTS BECOME RANCID, SOME OF THEIR NUTRITIONAL BENEFITS WILL BE LOST AS WELL. IT'S PREFERABLE TO BUY NUTS IN THE SHELL—THEY'LL STAY FRESH THE LONGEST—BUT SHELLING CAN BE QUITE A CHORE. NEXT BEST IS TO BUY WHOLE, NOT CHOPPED NUTS. KEEP THEM IN A TIGHTLY SEALED CONTAINER (USE A ZIP-TIGHT PLASTIC FREEZER BAG AFTER OPENING THE ORIGINAL CONTAINER) AND STORE THEM IN THE FREEZER. THERE'S NO NEED TO THAW NUTS BEFORE CHOPPING THEM OR USING THEM IN BAKING.

Pine Nut Tart

PREP 30 MINUTES PLUS CHILLING / BAKE 50 MINUTES

The sweet, oily teardrop-shaped seeds of several types of pine tree, pine nuts (pignoli) are a favorite baking ingredient in Italy; they're also a major component of pesto. Here, they're sprinkled over a buttery almond filling just before the tart is baked.

PASTRY FOR 11-INCH TART (PAGE 207)
¾ CUP SLIVERED BLANCHED ALMONDS
¼ CUP CORNSTARCH
½ TEASPOON BAKING POWDER
¼ TEASPOON SALT
⅔ CUP SUGAR
6 TABLESPOONS BUTTER OR MARGARINE, SOFTENED
3 LARGE EGGS
2 TEASPOONS VANILLA EXTRACT
¼ TEASPOON ALMOND EXTRACT
1 CUP PINE NUTS (PIGNOLI), TOASTED

1 Prepare dough as directed through chilling; line tart pan with dough; prick all over with fork to prevent puffing during baking; chill as directed.

2 Preheat oven to 425° F. Line tart shell with foil; fill with pie weights, dry beans, or uncooked rice. Bake 20 minutes. Remove foil and weights; bake 10 minutes longer, or until golden. If crust puffs up during baking, gently press it to tart pan with back of spoon. Turn oven control to 375° F.

3 Meanwhile, in food processor with knife blade attached, combine almonds, cornstarch, baking powder, and salt; pulse until nuts are very finely ground.

4 In large bowl, with mixer at low speed, beat almond mixture, sugar, and butter until crumbly. Increase speed to medium-high; beat until well combined, about 3 minutes, scraping bowl frequently with rubber spatula. Add eggs, 1 at a time, beating well after each addition, and vanilla and almond extracts; beat until smooth.

5 Pour filling into warm shell. Sprinkle pine nuts evenly over filling. Bake 20 minutes, or until golden and filling is firm. Cool in pan on wire rack. When cool, remove side of pan. *Makes 12 servings.*

EACH SERVING: ABOUT 380 CALORIES, 8 G PROTEIN, 29 G CARBOHYDRATE, 27 G TOTAL FAT (11 G SATURATED), 2 G FIBER, 89 MG CHOLESTEROL, 320 MG SODIUM.

Classic Linzer Tart

PREP 30 MINUTES PLUS CHILLING
BAKE 35 TO 40 MINUTES

This Austrian specialty, associated with the city of Linz, is a tart filled with raspberry jam. Modest, perhaps, by Austrian standards (for starters, there's no whipped cream on or in it), the Linzertorte is nonetheless a beloved tradition. Criss-crossed with strips of rich nut pastry, the diamonds of ruby-red jam peek through like jewels. Although usually made with almonds, this pastry is delicious when hazelnuts are used instead.

⅔ CUP HAZELNUTS (FILBERTS)
1¼ CUPS ALL-PURPOSE FLOUR
⅓ CUP PACKED LIGHT BROWN SUGAR
6 TABLESPOONS BUTTER OR MARGARINE, SLIGHTLY
    SOFTENED
1 LARGE EGG
½ TEASPOON VANILLA EXTRACT
¼ TEASPOON GROUND CINNAMON
¼ TEASPOON SALT
¼ TEASPOON BAKING POWDER
¾ CUP SEEDLESS RASPBERRY JAM
CONFECTIONERS' SUGAR (OPTIONAL)

1 Preheat oven to 350° F. Place hazelnuts in 9" by 9" metal baking pan. Bake 15 minutes, or until toasted. Wrap hot hazelnuts in clean cloth towel. With hands, roll hazelnuts back and forth to remove most of skins. Cool completely. Turn off oven.

2 In food processor with knife blade attached, or in blender, pulse nuts with ¼ cup flour until nuts are finely ground.

3 In large bowl, with mixer at low speed, beat brown sugar and butter until blended. Increase speed to medium-high; beat until creamy, about 3 minutes, scraping bowl with rubber spatula.

4 Reduce speed to medium and beat in egg and vanilla until smooth, about 1 minute. Reduce speed to low. Add ground nut mixture, cinnamon, salt, baking powder, and remaining 1 cup flour; beat just until combined.

5 With floured hands, press two-thirds of dough into bottom and up side of 9-inch tart pan with removable bottom (¼ inch below edge of pan). Wrap tart shell and remaining dough in plastic wrap and refrigerate 30 minutes, or until firm.

6 Preheat oven to 375° F. Spread raspberry jam over bottom of tart shell to ¼ inch from edge. Divide remaining dough into 10 equal pieces. On lightly floured surface, with floured hands, roll each piece into an 8½-inch-long rope. Place 5 ropes, about 1½ inches apart, over filling; do not seal ends. Following instructions on page 211, make lattice top with remaining 5 ropes. Trim ends of ropes even with edge of tart; press ends to seal. With any remaining trimmings, make rope for tart shell and press around inside edge of tart (see photo on page 212). Make decorative edge with fork, if desired.

7 Bake 35 to 40 minutes, until filling is hot and bubbly and crust is lightly browned. Cool on wire rack at least 1 hour. Sprinkle tart with confectioners' sugar, if desired. When cool, carefully remove side of pan. *Makes 12 servings.*

EACH SERVING: ABOUT 225 CALORIES, 3 G PROTEIN, 32 G CARBOHYDRATE, 10 G TOTAL FAT (4 G SATURATED), 1 G FIBER, 33 MG CHOLESTEROL, 130 MG SODIUM.

CRANBERRY-RASPBERRY LINZER TART Prepare tart shell as above but make cranberry-raspberry filling: In 1-quart saucepan, heat *1 cup cranberries*, picked over, *¼ cup packed light brown sugar*, *¼ cup cranberry juice cocktail*, and *a pinch of salt* to boiling over medium-high heat. Reduce heat to medium and cook, uncovered, stirring occasionally, 6 minutes, or until berries pop and mixture thickens slightly. Stir in *¾ cup seedless raspberry jam*. Cool before using. Fill tart shell, make lattice top, and bake as directed.
EACH SERVING: ABOUT 205 CALORIES, 3 G PROTEIN, 25 G CARBOHYDRATE, 10 G TOTAL FAT (4 G SATURATED), 1 G FIBER, 33 MG CHOLESTEROL, 140 MG SODIUM.

HELP WITH HAZELNUTS

THE MARBLE-SIZE NUTS CALLED HAZELNUTS OR FILBERTS HAVE A PAPERY, DARK-BROWN SKIN THAT CLINGS TIGHTLY TO THE NUTMEATS. TO REMOVE THE SKIN, WHICH IS BITTER, TOAST THE NUTS IN A 350° F OVEN FOR 10 TO 15 MINUTES, UNTIL FRAGRANT. PLACE THE HOT NUTS IN A KITCHEN TOWEL AND RUB OFF AS MUCH OF THE SKIN AS YOU CAN. DON'T WORRY IF A FEW SPECKS OF SKIN REMAIN—YOU WON'T NOTICE THE FLAVOR IN THE FINISHED DISH.

Chocolate Walnut Pie

PREP 45 MINUTES PLUS COOLING
BAKE 57 TO 60 MINUTES

*Imagine an ultra-rich, walnutty fudge brownie
baked in a shortbread crust. Sound good? Here's the
recipe. All you have to decide is whether to serve it
warm or cool, and whether to add a big spoonful of
whipped cream or a scoop of vanilla or coffee ice cream.*

SHORTBREAD CRUST (PAGE 210)
½ CUP BUTTER OR MARGARINE (1 STICK)
3 SQUARES (3 OUNCES) UNSWEETENED CHOCOLATE
½ CUP GRANULATED SUGAR
½ CUP PACKED LIGHT BROWN SUGAR
2 LARGE EGGS
¾ CUP ALL-PURPOSE FLOUR
1 TEASPOON VANILLA EXTRACT
⅛ TEASPOON SALT
¾ CUP WALNUTS, COARSELY CHOPPED

1 Prepare crust, bake, and cool as directed.

2 Preheat oven to 325° F. In 3-quart saucepan, melt
butter and chocolate over low heat, stirring occasionally. Remove from heat and stir in granulated
and brown sugars. Add eggs, 1 at a time, stirring well
after each addition. Stir in flour, vanilla, salt, and nuts
until blended. Pour into cooled baked piecrust.

3 Bake 30 minutes, or until top is just set. Cool
on wire rack 1 hour to serve warm, or cool completely to serve later. *Makes 12 servings.*

EACH SERVING: ABOUT 385 CALORIES, 5 G PROTEIN,
39 G CARBOHYDRATE, 25 G TOTAL FAT (13 G SATURATED),
2 G FIBER, 77 MG CHOLESTEROL, 195 MG SODIUM.

CHEESE, CUSTARD & CREAM PIES

Call these the *crème de la crème* of pies—all feature
creamy, velvety, silky, or deliciously dense fillings. We start
with cheese pies, a great discovery if you love cheesecake
but can't find the time to bake it (these pie fillings are not
as dense and bake in less time than cakes). The custard
and cream pies, rich with eggs, run the gamut from spicy
Pilgrim Pumpkin to eye-opening Key Lime to the everpop-
ular Banana Cream; richest of all is the devastating
Chocolate Truffle Tart.

Deluxe Cheese Pie

PREP 35 MINUTES PLUS COOLING / BAKE 45 MINUTES

BAKED GRAHAM-CRACKER CRUMB CRUST (PAGE 210)
1½ PACKAGES (8 OUNCES EACH) CREAM CHEESE,
    SOFTENED
½ CUP PLUS 2 TABLESPOONS SUGAR
2 LARGE EGGS
½ TEASPOON VANILLA EXTRACT
1 CONTAINER (8 OUNCES) SOUR CREAM

1 Prepare crust, bake, and cool as directed.

2 Preheat oven to 350° F. In small bowl, with mixer
at low speed, beat cream cheese and ½ cup sugar
until smooth, scraping bowl with rubber spatula.
Add eggs and vanilla; beat just until mixed.

3 Pour cheese filling into cooled piecrust. Bake 30
minutes, or until set. Transfer to wire rack.

4 Mix remaining 2 tablespoons sugar with sour
cream. Spread mixture over top of hot pie. Bake 5
minutes, or until set. Cool on wire rack. Refrigerate
pie at least 2 hours before serving. *Makes 10 servings.*

EACH SERVING: ABOUT 340 CALORIES, 6 G PROTEIN,
28 G CARBOHYDRATE, 24 G TOTAL FAT (14 G SATURATED),
0.5 G FIBER, 102 MG CHOLESTEROL, 265 MG SODIUM.

STRAWBERRY-CHEESE PIE Prepare as above but omit
sour-cream topping. Cool pie on wire rack. Arrange
1½ pints fresh strawberries, hulled and halved, on top
of pie. In small saucepan, melt *⅓ cup red-currant jelly*
over low heat; brush melted jelly over strawberries.
EACH SERVING: ABOUT 325 CALORIES, 5 G PROTEIN,
35 G CARBOHYDRATE, 19 G TOTAL FAT (11 G SATURATED),
2 G FIBER, 92 MG CHOLESTEROL, 260 MG SODIUM.

Ricotta Pie

PREP 50 MINUTES PLUS CHILLING
BAKE 35 TO 40 MINUTES

Italians particularly enjoy cheese pies and tarts at Easter time, but you can serve this one anytime—plain or with fresh fruit.

PAT-IN-PAN CRUST FOR 9-INCH TART (PAGE 209)
1 PACKAGE (8 OUNCES) CREAM CHEESE, SOFTENED
¾ CUP SUGAR
¼ TEASPOON GROUND CINNAMON
1 CONTAINER (32 OUNCES) RICOTTA CHEESE
5 LARGE EGG WHITES, BEATEN

1 Prepare dough as directed but shape dough into 1 disk. Wrap and refrigerate 30 minutes, or until firm enough to handle.

2 Meanwhile, in large bowl, with mixer at low speed, beat cream cheese, sugar, and cinnamon until blended. Increase speed to high; beat until light and creamy. Reduce speed to medium. Add ricotta and all but 1 tablespoon egg whites and beat just until blended.

3 Preheat oven to 400° F. Lightly grease 13" by 9" glass baking dish.

4 With lightly floured hands, press dough evenly into bottom and up side of prepared baking dish. Brush reserved egg white over bottom and sides of dough. Pour in ricotta filling; spread evenly. With fingers, gently push edge of dough into scalloped design around top of filling.

5 Bake 25 minutes. Turn oven control to 350° F. Bake 10 to 15 minutes longer, until center barely jiggles. Cool completely in dish on wire rack. Cover and refrigerate 6 hours, or overnight until well chilled. *Makes 20 servings.*

EACH SERVING: ABOUT 280 CALORIES, 9 G PROTEIN, 22 G CARBOHYDRATE, 17 G TOTAL FAT (11 G SATURATED), 0.5 G FIBER, 65 MG CHOLESTEROL, 190 MG SODIUM.

Custard Pie

PREP 20 MINUTES PLUS CHILLING AND COOLING
BAKE 55 MINUTES

PASTRY FOR SINGLE-CRUST PIE (PAGE 206)
2 CUPS MILK
4 LARGE EGGS
½ CUP SUGAR
¼ TEASPOON SALT
1 TEASPOON VANILLA EXTRACT
½ TEASPOON BUTTER OR MARGARINE, SOFTENED
PINCH GROUND NUTMEG

1 Prepare dough through chilling. Roll out dough; line 9-inch pie plate; and make decorative edge (see photos on page 212). Refrigerate 10 to 15 minutes.

2 Preheat oven to 425° F. Line pie shell with foil; fill with pie weights, dry beans, or uncooked rice. Bake 20 minutes. Remove foil and weights; bake 10 minutes, or until golden. Cool on wire rack. Turn oven control to 350° F.

3 Meanwhile, in 2-quart saucepan, heat milk over medium heat until bubbles form at edge. In medium bowl, whisk eggs, sugar, salt, and vanilla. Slowly pour milk into egg mixture, whisking rapidly.

4 Butter a second 9-inch pie plate; set plate in shallow baking pan on oven rack. Pour egg mixture into prepared pie plate; sprinkle with nutmeg. Pour enough *boiling water* into baking pan to come halfway up side of pie plate. Bake 25 minutes, or until knife inserted 1 inch from edge comes out clean. Transfer plate to wire rack to cool.

5 When custard is cool, loosen from side of pie plate with spatula; shake gently to loosen bottom. Hold far edge of plate over far edge of baked piecrust; tilt custard gently; as it slips into crust, pull plate back quickly until custard rests in crust. Let filling settle a few minutes before serving. *Makes 8 servings.*

EACH SERVING: ABOUT 290 CALORIES, 7 G PROTEIN, 32 G CARBOHYDRATE, 14 G TOTAL FAT (7 G SATURATED), 0.5 G FIBER, 132 MG CHOLESTEROL, 270 MG SODIUM.

Pilgrim Pumpkin Pie

PREP 25 MINUTES PLUS CHILLING
BAKE 1 HOUR 10 TO 15 MINUTES

Pumpkin-pie spice from the supermarket would do the trick here, but if you mix your own spices you can tailor the flavor to your preferences. Toss in a pinch of ground cloves, perhaps, or use a little less nutmeg. Or, for a spicier pie, try adding ⅛ teaspoon of ground white pepper.

PASTRY FOR SINGLE-CRUST PIE (PAGE 206)
1 CAN (16 OUNCES) SOLID PACK PUMPKIN (NOT PUMPKIN-PIE MIX) OR 2 CUPS MASHED COOKED PUMPKIN
1 CAN (12 OUNCES) EVAPORATED MILK
2 LARGE EGGS
¾ CUP PACKED BROWN SUGAR
1 TEASPOON GROUND CINNAMON*
½ TEASPOON GROUND GINGER*
¼ TEASPOON GROUND NUTMEG*
½ TEASPOON SALT

1 Prepare dough as directed through chilling. Roll out dough and line 9-inch pie plate; make turret edge (see photo on page 212). Refrigerate or freeze 10 to 15 minutes to firm pastry.

2 Preheat oven to 425° F. Line pie shell with foil; fill with pie weights, dry beans, or uncooked rice. Bake 15 minutes. Remove foil and weights; bake 5 to 10 minutes longer, until golden. If crust puffs up during baking, gently press it to pie plate with back of spoon. Cool on wire rack. Turn oven control to 375° F.

3 In large bowl, combine pumpkin, evaporated milk, eggs, sugar, cinnamon, ginger, nutmeg, and salt and beat until well mixed. Place prepared pie plate on oven rack; pour in pumpkin mixture. Bake 50 minutes, or until knife inserted 1 inch from edge comes out clean. Cool on wire rack about 1 hour. Serve with whipped cream, if you like. *Makes 10 servings.*

*Instead of cinnamon, ginger, and nutmeg, use 1½ teaspoons pumpkin-pie spice.

EACH SERVING: ABOUT 270 CALORIES, 6 G PROTEIN, 37 G CARBOHYDRATE, 11 G TOTAL FAT (6 G SATURATED), 1 G FIBER, 66 MG CHOLESTEROL, 280 MG SODIUM.

Lemon Soufflé Tart

PREP 45 MINUTES PLUS CHILLING
BAKE 45 TO 50 MINUTES

PASTRY FOR 11-INCH TART (PAGE. 207)
4 LARGE LEMONS
6 LARGE EGGS, SEPARATED
1 TABLESPOON ALL-PURPOSE FLOUR
⅔ CUP SUGAR
1 TABLESPOON BUTTER OR MARGARINE
¼ TEASPOON CREAM OF TARTAR
⅛ TEASPOON SALT

1 Prepare dough as directed through chilling. Roll out dough and line 11-inch tart pan with removable bottom. Refrigerate or freeze 10 to 15 minutes.

2 Preheat oven to 425° F. Line tart shell with foil; fill with pie weights, dry beans, or uncooked rice. Bake 15 minutes. Remove foil and weights; bake 10 minutes longer, until golden. If crust puffs up during baking, gently press it to tart pan with back of spoon. Cool on wire rack. Turn oven control to 350° F.

3 From lemons, grate 2 teaspoons peel and squeeze ¾ cup juice. In small bowl, with mixer at high speed, beat egg yolks, flour, and ⅓ cup sugar until very thick and lemon-colored and mixture forms ribbon when beaters are lifted, about 10 minutes. Transfer mixture to 2-quart saucepan; stir in lemon peel and juice. Cook over medium-low heat, whisking constantly until thick and mixture mounds slightly, 10 to 20 minutes. Beat in butter.

4 In large bowl, with mixer at high speed, beat egg whites with cream of tartar and salt until soft peaks form. Beat at high speed, gradually add remaining ⅓ cup sugar, beating until sugar dissolves and whites hold stiff peaks when beaters are lifted.

5 With wire whisk, fold one-third of beaten whites into yolk mixture. Fold yolk mixture into remaining whites. Spoon into tart shell; smooth top. Bake 20 to 25 minutes, until lightly browned. Cool on wire rack 15 minutes to serve warm, or serve at room temperature. Remove side of pan. Garnish with raspberries and sprinkle with confectioners' sugar, if you like. *Makes 12 servings.*

EACH SERVING: ABOUT 240 CALORIES, 5 G PROTEIN, 25 G CARBOHYDRATE, 13 G TOTAL FAT (7 G SATURATED), 0.5 G FIBER, 130 MG CHOLESTEROL, 240 MG SODIUM.

Chocolate Truffle Tart

PREP 20 MINUTES PLUS COOLING
BAKE 50 MINUTES

Not your old-fashioned custard pie, this wickedly rich chocolate tart is adorned with white-chocolate hearts.

PASTRY FOR 9-INCH TART (PAGE 207)

6 SQUARES (6 OUNCES) SEMISWEET CHOCOLATE, COARSELY CHOPPED

½ CUP BUTTER OR MARGARINE (1 STICK)

¼ CUP SUGAR

1 TEASPOON VANILLA EXTRACT

½ CUP HEAVY OR WHIPPING CREAM

3 LARGE EGGS

WHITE-CHOCOLATE HEARTS (PAGE 365)

1 Prepare dough through chilling. Line fluted 9-inch tart pan with removable bottom; prick with fork; chill as directed to firm pastry.

2 Preheat oven to 400° F. Line tart shell with foil; fill with pie weights, dry beans, or uncooked rice. Bake 20 minutes. Remove foil and weights; bake 10 minutes longer, or until golden. If crust puffs up during baking, press it to tart pan with back of spoon. Cool in pan on wire rack. Turn oven control to 350° F.

3 Meanwhile, in heavy 2-quart saucepan, melt semisweet chocolate and butter over very low heat, stirring frequently. Stir in sugar and vanilla. In small bowl, with fork or wire whisk, lightly beat cream and eggs. Blend some chocolate mixture into egg mixture; stir egg mixture back into chocolate mixture.

4 Pour mixture into tart shell. Bake 20 minutes, or until custard is just set (center will appear jiggly). Cool on wire rack; refrigerate to serve chilled.

5 Prepare White-Chocolate Hearts and garnish tart. Remove side of pan to serve. *Makes 12 servings.*

EACH SERVING: ABOUT 325 CALORIES, 4 G PROTEIN, 24 G CARBOHYDRATE, 25 G TOTAL FAT (14 G SATURATED), 1 G FIBER, 103 MG CHOLESTEROL, 210 MG SODIUM.

Chocolate Truffle Tart

Chess Pie

PREP 25 MINUTES PLUS CHILLING
BAKE 1 HOUR 5 TO 10 MINUTES

Opinions vary about how chess pies (longtime Southern favorites) got their name. Some suspect that the pies took their name from the cabinet (pie chest) where they were stored; and others cite the reply of someone who was asked what kind of pie she had served. "Jes' pie," she replied. The name probably comes from the word "cheese." In seventeenth-century England and Colonial America, desserts with this texture were called "cheese pies."

PASTRY FOR 9-INCH TART (PAGE 207)
5 TABLESPOONS BUTTER OR MARGARINE
3 LARGE EGGS
1¼ CUPS SUGAR
½ CUP MILK
2 TABLESPOONS ALL-PURPOSE FLOUR
2 TABLESPOONS CORNMEAL
1 TEASPOON VANILLA EXTRACT
¼ TEASPOON SALT
⅛ TEASPOON GROUND NUTMEG PLUS ADDITIONAL FOR
   SPRINKLING

1 Prepare dough as directed. Line 9-inch tart pan with removable bottom; prick dough all over with fork to prevent puffing during baking; chill as directed.

2 Preheat oven to 425° F. Line tart shell with foil; fill with pie weights, dry beans, or uncooked rice. Bake 15 minutes. Remove foil and weights; bake 5 to 10 minutes longer, until golden. If crust puffs up during baking, gently press it to tart pan with back of spoon. Cool on wire rack. Turn oven control to 375° F.

3 In 2-quart saucepan, melt butter over low heat. With wire whisk or fork, beat in eggs, sugar, milk, flour, cornmeal, vanilla, salt, and ⅛ teaspoon nutmeg until blended.

4 Pour egg mixture into cooled tart shell; sprinkle with nutmeg. Bake 45 minutes, or until knife inserted 1 inch from edge comes out clean. Cool on wire rack. Serve at room temperature, or refrigerate to serve chilled. Remove side of pan to serve. *Makes 12 servings.*

EACH SERVING: ABOUT 255 CALORIES, 3 G PROTEIN,
32 G CARBOHYDRATE, 13 G TOTAL FAT (7 G SATURATED),
0.5 G FIBER, 83 MG CHOLESTEROL, 225 MG SODIUM.

Buttermilk Pie

PREP 40 MINUTES PLUS CHILLING AND COOLING
BAKE 1 HOUR 10 MINUTES

This variation on the chess pie—and there are many— boasts a mildly tangy flavor, not just from the buttermilk but from a few spoonfuls of lemon juice.

PASTRY FOR SINGLE-CRUST PIE (PAGE 206)
1 CUP SUGAR
3 TABLESPOONS ALL-PURPOSE FLOUR
3 LARGE EGGS
1 LARGE EGG YOLK
1¼ CUPS BUTTERMILK
2 TABLESPOONS BUTTER OR MARGARINE, MELTED AND
   COOLED
2 TEASPOONS FRESH LEMON JUICE
1½ TEASPOONS VANILLA EXTRACT
⅛ TEASPOON GROUND NUTMEG
PINCH SALT

1 Prepare dough as directed through chilling. Roll out dough and line 9-inch pie plate; make decorative edge (see photos on page 212).

2 Preheat oven to 425° F. Line pie shell with foil; fill with pie weights, dry beans, or uncooked rice. Bake 20 minutes. Remove foil and weights; bake 5 minutes longer, or until golden. If crust puffs up during baking, gently press it to pie plate with back of spoon. Cool on wire rack at least 10 minutes. Turn oven control to 350° F.

3 In large bowl, with wire whisk, combine sugar and flour. In medium bowl, beat eggs and egg yolk. Add buttermilk, melted butter, lemon juice, vanilla, nutmeg, and salt and whisk until blended. Whisk egg mixture into sugar mixture until combined.

4 Pour filling into cooled piecrust. Bake about 45 minutes, until knife inserted halfway between edges and center comes out clean. Cool on wire rack 2 hours to serve warm. *Makes 10 servings.*

EACH SERVING: ABOUT 275 CALORIES, 5 G PROTEIN,
37 G CARBOHYDRATE, 12 G TOTAL FAT (6 G SATURATED),
0.5 G FIBER, 105 MG CHOLESTEROL, 195 MG SODIUM.

Grandma's Sweet-Potato Pie

Spiced mashed sweet potato tastes very much like pumpkin, and this pie would make a nice change for the Thanksgiving menu. If you're using canned potatoes, be sure to buy the water-packed variety, not those in a sweet, heavy syrup.

PASTRY FOR SINGLE-CRUST PIE (PAGE 206)
2 MEDIUM SWEET POTATOES (ABOUT 1 POUND), UNPEELED, OR 2 CANS (16 TO 17 OUNCES EACH) SWEET POTATOES, DRAINED
1½ CUPS HALF-AND-HALF OR LIGHT CREAM
¾ CUP PACKED DARK BROWN SUGAR
1 TEASPOON GROUND CINNAMON
¾ TEASPOON GROUND GINGER
¼ TEASPOON GROUND NUTMEG
½ TEASPOON SALT
3 LARGE EGGS

1 Prepare dough as directed through chilling.

2 Meanwhile, if using fresh sweet potatoes, in 3-quart saucepan, heat sweet potatoes and enough water to cover to boiling over high heat. Reduce heat; cover and simmer 30 minutes, or until fork-tender. Drain. Cool potatoes until easy to handle; peel and cut into chunks. In large bowl, with mixer at low speed, beat sweet potatoes until smooth. Add half-and-half, brown sugar, cinnamon, ginger, nutmeg, salt, and eggs; beat until well blended.

3 Preheat oven to 425° F. Line pie shell with foil; fill with pie weights, dry beans, or uncooked rice. Bake 10 minutes. Remove foil and weights; bake 10 minutes longer, or until golden. If crust puffs up during baking, gently press it to pan with back of spoon. Cool on wire rack Turn oven control to 350° F.

4 Spoon sweet-potato mixture into cooled piecrust. Bake 40 minutes, or until knife inserted 1 inch from edge comes out clean. Cool on wire rack 1 hour to serve warm, or cool slightly, then refrigerate to serve chilled. *Makes 10 servings.*

EACH SERVING: ABOUT 295 CALORIES, 5 G PROTEIN, 39 G CARBOHYDRATE, 13 G TOTAL FAT (7 G SATURATED), 1 G FIBER, 89 MG CHOLESTEROL, 265 MG SODIUM.

Lemon Meringue Pie

Be sure to spread the meringue all the way out to the edge of the crust—it should touch the crust all around. Otherwise, the meringue will shrink as it bakes.

PASTRY FOR SINGLE-CRUST PIE (PAGE 206)
4 TO 5 MEDIUM LEMONS
⅓ CUP CORNSTARCH
¼ TEASPOON PLUS PINCH SALT
1½ CUPS SUGAR
1½ CUPS WATER
3 LARGE EGG YOLKS
2 TABLESPOONS BUTTER OR MARGARINE
4 LARGE EGG WHITES
¼ TEASPOON CREAM OF TARTAR

1 Prepare dough as directed through chilling.

2 Preheat oven to 425° F. Line pie shell with foil; fill with pie weights, dry beans, or uncooked rice. Bake 10 minutes. Remove foil and weights; bake 10 minutes longer, or until golden. If crust puffs up during baking, press it to pie plate with back of spoon. Cool on wire rack. Turn oven control to 400° F.

3 Meanwhile, from lemons, grate 1 tablespoon peel and squeeze ¾ cup juice. In 2-quart saucepan, mix cornstarch, ¼ teaspoon salt, and 1 cup sugar; stir in water. Cook over medium heat, stirring constantly, until mixture thickens and boils. Boil 1 minute, stirring constantly. Remove saucepan from heat.

4 In small bowl, whisk egg yolks. Stir in small amount of hot cornstarch mixture until blended; slowly pour egg-yolk mixture back into hot cornstarch mixture in saucepan, stirring rapidly to prevent curdling. Place saucepan over low heat and cook, stirring constantly, about 4 minutes, until filling is very thick. Remove saucepan from heat; stir in butter until melted. Gradually stir in lemon juice and peel. Pour into cooled piecrust.

5 In small bowl, with mixer at high speed, beat egg whites, cream of tartar, and pinch of salt until soft peaks form when beaters are lifted. Gradually sprinkle in remaining ½ cup sugar, 2 tablespoons at a time, beating until sugar has completely dissolved and egg whites stand in stiff, glossy peaks when beaters are lifted.

6 Spread meringue over filling to edge of crust. Swirl meringue with back of spoon to make attractive top. Bake 10 minutes, or until meringue

is golden. Cool pie on wire rack away from draft. Refrigerate at least 3 hours before serving. *Makes 10 servings.*

EACH SERVING: ABOUT 310 CALORIES, 4 G PROTEIN, 49 G CARBOHYDRATE, 11 G TOTAL FAT (5 G SATURATED), 0.5 G FIBER, 82 MG CHOLESTEROL, 225 MG SODIUM.

LIME MERINGUE PIE Prepare crust and filling as for Lemon Meringue Pie but use *2 teaspoons freshly grated lime peel* for lemon peel and *½ cup fresh lime juice* for fresh lemon juice. Bake and cool as directed.
EACH SERVING: ABOUT 305 CALORIES, 4 G PROTEIN, 48 G CARBOHYDRATE, 11 G TOTAL FAT (5 G SATURATED), 0.5 G FIBER, 82 MG CHOLESTEROL, 225 MG SODIUM.

Shaker Lemon Pie

PREP 15 MINUTES PLUS STANDING OVERNIGHT
BAKE 1 HOUR 2 TO 10 MINUTES

For this early American pie, use small thin-skinned lemons, and remove all the seeds!

PASTRY FOR SINGLE-CRUST PIE (PAGE 206)
3 LARGE LEMONS
1½ CUPS SUGAR
4 LARGE EGGS

1 Slice 1 lemon paper-thin, discarding seeds. Cut off peel and white pith from remaining 2 lemons; slice paper-thin, discarding seeds. In medium bowl, combine lemons and sugar. Cover and let stand overnight until lemons are soft and sugar dissolves.

2 The next day, prepare dough and line 9-inch pie plate as directed.

3 Preheat oven to 425° F. Line pie shell with foil; fill with pie weights, dry beans, or uncooked rice. Bake 15 minutes. Remove foil and weights; bake 7 to 10 minutes longer, until golden. If crust puffs up during baking, gently press it to plate with back of spoon. Cool on wire rack. Turn oven control to 375° F.

4 Meanwhile, in medium bowl, whisk eggs. Remove 1 tablespoon beaten egg to cup for brushing later. Stir lemon mixture into bowl with beaten eggs until combined. Pour into cooled piecrust. With fork, arrange lemon slices decoratively on surface. Brush edge of pastry with reserved egg. Bake 40 to 45 minutes, or until filling is slightly puffed and lightly golden. Cool on wire rack. *Makes 8 servings.*

EACH SERVING: ABOUT 350 CALORIES, 6 G PROTEIN, 59 G CARBOHYDRATE, 12 G TOTAL FAT (5 G SATURATED), 0.5 G FIBER, 122 MG CHOLESTEROL, 165 MG SODIUM.

Lemon Tart

PREP 20 MINUTES PLUS CHILLING AND COOLING
BAKE 52 TO 57 MINUTES

Note that this tart requires a very high rim, which should extend above the edge of the pan.

PASTRY FOR 9-INCH TART (PAGE 207)
4 TO 6 LEMONS
4 LARGE EGGS
1 CUP GRANULATED SUGAR
⅓ CUP HEAVY OR WHIPPING CREAM
CONFECTIONERS' SUGAR

1 Prepare dough through chilling; line 9-inch tart pan with removable bottom, pressing dough up sides to form ¼-inch rim above edge of pan. Freeze 15 minutes to prevent puffing during baking.

2 Preheat oven to 425° F. Line tart shell with foil; fill with pie weights, dry beans, or uncooked rice. Bake 15 minutes. Remove foil and weights; bake 7 to 12 minutes longer, until golden. If crust puffs up during baking, gently press it to tart pan with back of spoon. Cool on wire rack. Turn oven control to 350° F.

3 From lemons, grate 1½ teaspoons peel and squeeze ⅔ cup juice. In medium bowl, with wire whisk or fork, beat eggs, granulated sugar, and lemon peel and juice until well combined. Whisk in cream.

4 Carefully pour lemon mixture into cooled tart shell. Place on cookie sheet and bake 30 minutes, or until barely set. Cool completely on wire rack. Just before serving, remove side of pan; sprinkle with confectioners' sugar. *Makes 8 servings.*

EACH SERVING: ABOUT 325 CALORIES, 5 G PROTEIN, 40 G CARBOHYDRATE, 17 G TOTAL FAT (9 G SATURATED), 0.5 G FIBER, 143 MG CHOLESTEROL, 195 MG SODIUM.

RASPBERRY-TOPPED LEMON TART Prepare tart as above. Cool. Before serving, scatter *1 pint fresh raspberries* over top of tart.
EACH SERVING: ABOUT 340 CALORIES, 5 G PROTEIN, 43 G CARBOHYDRATE, 17 G TOTAL FAT (9 G SATURATED), 2 G FIBER, 143 MG CHOLESTEROL, 195 MG SODIUM.

Caramel Walnut Tart

PREP 45 MINUTES PLUS CHILLING
BAKE 53 TO 60 MINUTES

The layer of filling in this tart is not very deep, but it is devilishly rich. Follow the instructions for caramelizing the sugar with particular care. Be sure to use a large enough pan, as the caramel syrup can quickly bubble up to several times its original volume.

SWEET PASTRY CRUST FOR 9-INCH TART (PAGE 208) OR
   PASTRY FOR 9-INCH TART (PAGE 207)
1 CUP SUGAR
¼ TEASPOON FRESH LEMON JUICE
¾ CUP HEAVY OR WHIPPING CREAM
1 TABLESPOON BUTTER OR MARGARINE
1 LARGE EGG
½ TEASPOON VANILLA EXTRACT
1 CUP WALNUTS, TOASTED

1 Prepare dough as directed through chilling; line fluted tart pan with removable bottom with dough; chill as directed.

2 Preheat oven to 375° F. Line tart shell with foil; fill with pie weights, dry beans, or uncooked rice. Bake 15 minutes. Remove foil and weights; bake 8 to 10 minutes longer, until golden brown. Transfer to wire rack. Turn oven control to 350° F.

3 In 2-quart heavy saucepan, stir sugar and lemon juice together to the consistency of wet sand. Heat over low heat, stirring gently, until sugar melts. Increase heat to medium and cook until amber in color. With pastry brush dipped in water, occasionally wash down side of pan to prevent sugar from crystallizing. Remove saucepan from heat. Carefully add cream to pan gradually, stirring constantly (mixture will bubble and lump up vigorously). Add butter, return pan to heat, and stir until caramel dissolves. Set saucepan aside to cool.

4 Preheat oven to 350° F. In large bowl, whisk egg and vanilla until smooth. Add cooled caramel mixture and whisk until blended.

5 Sprinkle walnuts over cooled shell. Pour caramel mixture on top. Bake 30 to 35 minutes, until bubbly at edges and set but still slightly jiggly in center. Cool on wire rack 10 minutes. Carefully remove side of pan; cool completely. *Makes 16 servings.*

EACH SERVING: ABOUT 245 CALORIES, 3 G PROTEIN,
24 G CARBOHYDRATE, 16 G TOTAL FAT (7 G SATURATED),
0.5 G FIBER, 59 MG CHOLESTEROL, 95 MG SODIUM.

Key Lime Pie

PREP 20 MINUTES PLUS COOLING AND CHILLING
BAKE 25 TO 30 MINUTES

The original Key Lime Pie, which dates back to the turn of the twentieth century, is filled with a tart citrus custard made with a then-new miracle ingredient—sweetened condensed milk. Canned milk is no novelty to us today, but this recipe lingers deliciously on. If you can't get key limes—grown in the Florida Keys and not widely available—regular limes will do.

BAKED GRAHAM-CRACKER CRUMB CRUST (PAGE 210)
6 TO 8 LIMES, PREFERABLY KEY LIMES
1 CAN (14 OUNCES) SWEETENED CONDENSED MILK
2 LARGE EGGS, SEPARATED
GREEN FOOD COLORING (OPTIONAL)
½ CUP HEAVY OR WHIPPING CREAM
LIME SLICES (OPTIONAL)

1 Prepare crust, bake, and cool as directed.

2 Preheat oven to 375° F. From limes, grate 2 teaspoons peel and squeeze ½ cup juice. In medium bowl, with wire whisk or fork, combine sweetened condensed milk with lime peel and juice, and egg yolks until mixture thickens. Add a few drops green food coloring, if you like.

3 In small bowl, with mixer at high speed, beat egg whites until stiff peaks form when beaters are lifted. With rubber spatula or wire whisk, gently fold egg whites into lime mixture.

4 Pour filling into cooled piecrust; smooth top. Bake 15 to 20 minutes, just until filling is firm. Cool on wire rack, then refrigerate 3 hours, or until well chilled.

5 In small bowl, with mixer at medium speed, beat cream until stiff peaks form. Pipe or spoon whipped cream around edge of filling. Place lime slices on top of filling, if desired. *Makes 10 servings.*

EACH SERVING: ABOUT 300 CALORIES, 6 G PROTEIN,
36 G CARBOHYDRATE, 15 G TOTAL FAT (8 G SATURATED),
0.5 G FIBER, 85 MG CHOLESTEROL, 210 MG SODIUM.

Caramel Walnut Tart

Squash Pie

Butternut squash is close kin to pumpkin, so it's no wonder that it makes a delicious pie. As a shortcut— and nobody will ever guess—use frozen pureed winter squash. For 2 cups, you'll need to buy two 10-ounce packages; you will have a little bit of squash left over.

PASTRY FOR 11-INCH TART (PAGE 207)
1 SMALL BUTTERNUT SQUASH (2 POUNDS), PEELED AND
    CUT INTO 2-INCH CHUNKS
¼ CUP WATER
3 LARGE EGGS, LIGHTLY BEATEN
¾ CUP PACKED LIGHT BROWN SUGAR
6 TABLESPOONS BUTTER OR MARGARINE, MELTED AND
    COOLED
1 CUP HEAVY OR WHIPPING CREAM
1 TEASPOON VANILLA EXTRACT
1 TEASPOON GROUND CINNAMON
¾ TEASPOON GROUND GINGER
¼ TEASPOON GROUND ALLSPICE
1 TEASPOON FRESHLY GRATED ORANGE PEEL

1 Prepare dough as directed through chilling.

2 Preheat oven to 425° F. Place squash and water in 13" by 9" glass baking dish; cover with foil. Bake 35 minutes, or until tender. With slotted spoon, transfer squash to food processor with knife blade attached. Process squash until smooth (you should have 2 cups puree).

3 Roll dough into 14-inch round and line deep-dish 9-inch pie plate; make decorative edge (see photos on page 212). Line pie shell with foil; fill with pie weights, dry beans, or uncooked rice. Bake 15 minutes. Remove foil and weights; bake 10 minutes longer, or until golden. Turn oven control to 350° F.

4 In large bowl, combine beaten eggs, brown sugar, and melted butter. Add cream, vanilla, cinnamon, ginger, allspice, orange peel, and squash and whisk until well combined and smooth.

5 Pour filling into cooled piecrust. Bake 55 minutes, or until toothpick inserted 1 inch from edge comes out clean. Cool on wire rack 1 hour to serve warm, or cool completely to serve later. *Makes 10 servings.*

EACH SERVING: ABOUT 435 CALORIES, 5 G PROTEIN, 41 G CARBOHYDRATE, 29 G TOTAL FAT (17 G SATURATED), 2 G FIBER, 140 MG CHOLESTEROL, 320 MG SODIUM.

Italian Easter Grain Pie

The filling for pastiera, a traditional Easter dessert from Naples, is made with wheat berries for a slightly chewy texture. The ricotta filling is scented with orange-flower water and orange peel, which shows the ancient Middle-Eastern influence on the cuisine of this part of Italy.

½ CUP PEELED OR HULLED WHEAT BERRIES, (8 OUNCES)
¼ TEASPOON SALT
PASTRY CREAM FOR 9-INCH TART (PAGE 360)
ITALIAN SWEET PASTRY (PAGE 207)
1 CONTAINER (15 OUNCES) RICOTTA CHEESE
¼ CUP SUGAR
2 LARGE EGGS
½ TEASPOON ORANGE-FLOWER WATER OR VANILLA EXTRACT
1 TEASPOON FRESHLY GRATED ORANGE PEEL
2 TABLESPOONS FINELY CHOPPED CANDIED CITRON OR
    CANDIED LEMON PEEL
⅛ TEASPOON GROUND CINNAMON

1 One day ahead, in large bowl, cover wheat berries in *4 cups water*; cover with plastic wrap and refrigerate 24 hours. Early the next day, drain berries and rinse. In 4-quart saucepan, heat softened berries, salt, and *3 cups water* to boiling over high heat; reduce heat to low, cover, and simmer 1 hour 45 minutes to 2 hours, or until berries are tender. Drain and refrigerate until ready to use.

2 Prepare pastry cream and dough as directed but shape dough into 2 equal pieces. Wrap and refrigerate 30 minutes or overnight.

3 Place ricotta in sieve lined with paper towel set over bowl; cover and refrigerate 1 hour. Transfer drained ricotta to large bowl, discarding liquid. With mixer at medium speed, beat ricotta and sugar about 3 minutes, until creamy. Reduce speed to low; beat in 1 egg, orange-flower water, and pastry cream. With rubber spatula, stir in orange peel, candied citron, cinnamon, and cooled wheat berries.

4 Preheat oven to 350° F. On lightly floured surface, with well-floured rolling pin, roll half of dough into 14-inch round. Gently ease into 9-inch springform pan. Spoon filling evenly into pastry.

5 Between 2 sheets of waxed paper, roll remaining dough into 10-inch round. Place on small cookie sheet. In small bowl, beat remaining egg. Remove top sheet of waxed paper. Brush beaten egg on pastry. With pastry wheel or knife, cut into ten 1-inch-wide strips. Freeze 5 minutes, or until firm.

6 Make lattice top (see photo on page 211). Place 5 pastry strips, 1 inch apart, over filling. Place remaining 5 strips diagonally across first ones to make lattice pattern. Trim edge of dough to ½ inch above lattice strips; fold dough in over strips and brush with beaten egg to seal. Bake 1 hour 5 minutes, or until top crust is golden. Cool in pan on wire rack. Run small thin knife around edge of pie and remove side of pan. Serve at room temperature, or refrigerate to serve chilled. *Makes 14 servings.*

EACH SERVING: ABOUT 350 CALORIES, 11 G PROTEIN, 45 G CARBOHYDRATE, 15 G TOTAL FAT (8 G SATURATED), 3 G FIBER, 129 MG CHOLESTEROL, 255 MG SODIUM.

WHEAT BERRIES

TO MAKE THE ITALIAN EASTER GRAIN PIE (AT LEFT), YOU'LL NEED WHEAT BERRIES, WHICH ARE WHOLE, UNPROCESSED KERNELS OF WHEAT. FOR THE BERRIES TO SOFTEN WITHIN THE SPECIFIED TIME— AND FOR THE PIE FILLING TO DEVELOP THE RIGHT TEXTURE AS IT BAKES—THEY SHOULD BE SOFT WHITE WHEAT, NOT HARD RED WINTER WHEAT. LOOK FOR WHEAT BERRIES AT A HEALTH-FOOD STORE OR ITALIAN GROCERY, AND ASK FOR HELP IF THEY'RE NOT CLEARLY IDENTIFIED.

Chocolate Pudding Pie with Coconut Crust

PREP 20 MINUTES PLUS CHILLING
BAKE 20 MINUTES

You could "cheat" by using a packaged pudding mix, but the flavor wouldn't compare to that of the filling we've devised for this pie.

COCONUT PASTRY CRUST (PAGE 210)
¾ CUP SUGAR
⅓ CUP CORNSTARCH
½ TEASPOON SALT
3¾ CUPS MILK
5 LARGE EGG YOLKS
3 SQUARES (3 OUNCES) UNSWEETENED CHOCOLATE, MELTED
2 TEASPOONS VANILLA EXTRACT
2 TABLESPOONS BUTTER OR MARGARINE
1 CUP HEAVY OR WHIPPING CREAM
¼ CUP FLAKED SWEETENED COCONUT, TOASTED

1 Prepare crust, bake, and cool as directed.

2 In 3-quart saucepan, stir together sugar, cornstarch, and salt; stir in milk until smooth. Cook, stirring constantly over medium heat, until mixture is thickened and boils; boil 1 minute. In small bowl, with wire whisk or fork, beat egg yolks lightly. Beat small amount of hot milk mixture into yolk mixture. Slowly pour yolk mixture back into milk mixture, stirring rapidly to prevent lumping. Cook over low heat 2 minutes, stirring constantly, until very thick, or an instant-read thermometer registers 160° F when placed in custard.

3 Remove saucepan from heat and stir in melted chocolate, vanilla, and butter; blend well. Pour filling into cooled piecrust. Place plastic wrap on surface of filling. Refrigerate 4 hours, or until filling is set.

4 In chilled bowl, with mixer at medium speed, whip cream until stiff peaks form. Pipe or spoon whipped cream over filling. Sprinkle toasted coconut on top. *Makes 10 servings.*

EACH SERVING: ABOUT 455 CALORIES, 7 G PROTEIN, 41 G CARBOHYDRATE, 31 G TOTAL FAT (18 G SATURATED), 2 G FIBER, 177 MG CHOLESTEROL, 285 MG SODIUM.

Banana Cream Pie

PREP 30 MINUTES PLUS CHILLING / BAKE 10 MINUTES

If you're searching for a coconut cream pie recipe, look below—we've given it as a variation of Banana Cream.

BAKED VANILLA-WAFER CRUMB CRUST (PAGE 210)
¾ CUP SUGAR
⅓ CUP CORNSTARCH
¼ TEASPOON SALT
3¾ CUPS MILK
5 LARGE EGG YOLKS
1¾ TEASPOONS VANILLA EXTRACT
2 TABLESPOONS BUTTER OR MARGARINE
3 RIPE MEDIUM BANANAS
¾ CUP HEAVY OR WHIPPING CREAM

1 Prepare crust, bake, and cool as directed.

2 In 3-quart saucepan, stir together sugar, cornstarch, and salt; stir in milk until smooth. Cook, stirring constantly, over medium heat, until mixture has thickened and boils; boil 1 minute. In small bowl, beat egg yolks lightly; beat in small amount of hot milk mixture. Slowly pour yolk mixture back into milk mixture, stirring rapidly to prevent lumping. Cook over low heat, stirring constantly, 2 minutes, or until very thick.

3 Remove saucepan from heat and stir in 1½ teaspoons vanilla and butter. Pour half of filling into piecrust. Slice 2 bananas and arrange sliced bananas on top; spoon remaining filling over bananas. Place plastic wrap on surface of filling. Refrigerate pie at least 4 hours, or overnight.

4 In small chilled bowl, with mixer at medium speed, beat cream and remaining ¼ teaspoon vanilla until stiff peaks form; spread over filling. Slice remaining banana; arrange around edge of pie. *Makes 10 servings.*

EACH SERVING: ABOUT 385 CALORIES, 6 G PROTEIN, 45 G CARBOHYDRATE, 21 G TOTAL FAT (12 G SATURATED), 1 G FIBER, 162 MG CHOLESTEROL, 275 MG SODIUM.

COCONUT CREAM PIE Prepare crust and filling as above but omit bananas. Fold *¾ cup flaked sweetened coconut* into filling before pouring into piecrust. Refrigerate and top with whipped cream as directed. Sprinkle with *¼ cup flaked sweetened coconut*, toasted.
EACH SERVING: ABOUT 390 CALORIES, 6 G PROTEIN, 40 G CARBOHYDRATE, 23 G TOTAL FAT (14 G SATURATED), 1 G FIBER, 162 MG CHOLESTEROL, 295 MG SODIUM.

Italian-Style Fresh Berry Tart

PREP 40 MINUTES PLUS CHILLING AND COOLING
BAKE 27 TO 30 MINUTES

You can take this festive dessert a step at a time: Bake the crust in advance, and prepare the filling through the end of Step 2. Follow step 3 close to serving time.

BAKED SWEET PASTRY CRUST FOR 11-INCH TART
   (PAGE 208)
3 LARGE EGG YOLKS
⅓ CUP GRANULATED SUGAR
2 TABLESPOONS CORNSTARCH
1 CUP MILK
2 TABLESPOONS BUTTER OR MARGARINE
1 TEASPOON VANILLA EXTRACT
½ CUP HEAVY OR WHIPPING CREAM
2 CUPS FRESH BLUEBERRIES
2 CUPS FRESH RASPBERRIES
2 CUPS FRESH BLACKBERRIES
CONFECTIONERS' SUGAR

1 Prepare tart shell, bake, and cool as directed.

2 Meanwhile, in small bowl, with wire whisk, mix egg yolks and granulated sugar until blended. Stir in cornstarch until smooth. In 2-quart saucepan, heat milk to simmering over medium heat. While constantly beating with wire whisk, gradually pour about half of simmering milk into egg-yolk mixture. Return egg-yolk-mixture to saucepan and cook, whisking constantly, until pastry cream has thickened and boils; reduce heat and cook, stirring, 1 minute. Remove saucepan from heat; stir in butter and vanilla. Transfer pastry cream to medium bowl; cover surface directly with plastic wrap to prevent skin from forming and refrigerate until cold, at least 2 hours.

3 Up to 2 hours before serving, in small bowl, with mixer at medium speed, beat cream just until stiff peaks form. Whisk pastry cream until smooth; fold in whipped cream.

4 Spoon pastry-cream mixture into baked tart shell and spread evenly; top with berries and sprinkle with confectioners' sugar. Remove side of pan to serve. *Makes 12 servings.*

EACH SERVING: ABOUT 285 CALORIES, 4 G PROTEIN, 29 G CARBOHYDRATE, 18 G TOTAL FAT (10 G SATURATED), 3 G FIBER, 95 MG CHOLESTEROL, 210 MG SODIUM.

TARTLETS

A platter of tiny tarts, filled with fresh fruit or an ultra-rich almond or hazelnut cream, is a real show-stopper. Each tartlet is a two-bite jewel, and nobody can eat just one. Because the filling is the real star of the show, choose ripe, fragrant fruit. Keep small berries whole; cut strawberries, bananas, kiwifruit, peaches, and plums into bite-size pieces. Some fruits—apples, pears, peaches, nectarines, and bananas—should be brushed with orange or lemon juice to prevent browning. You can also brush the fruits with liqueur for extra flavor.

Fruit Tartlets

PREP 45 MINUTES PLUS CHILLING AND COOLING
BAKE 15 MINUTES

For elegant individual desserts, make up plates of four tartlets each. At Christmastime, the color combination of kiwifruit and strawberries is especially festive.

PASTRY FOR 9-INCH TART (PAGE 207)
1 CONTAINER (8 OUNCES) SOFT CREAM CHEESE
3 TABLESPOONS SUGAR
1 TABLESPOON MILK
¾ TEASPOON VANILLA EXTRACT
2 CUPS FRUIT, SUCH AS SLICED KIWIFRUIT, HALVED
  STRAWBERRIES, CANNED MANDARIN-ORANGE SECTIONS,
  AND SMALL SEEDLESS RED AND GREEN GRAPE HALVES
MINT LEAVES

1 Prepare dough as directed through chilling.

2 Preheat oven to 425° F. Divide dough in half. Roll each half into 12-inch rope; cut each rope into twelve 1-inch pieces. Press each piece of dough evenly into bottom and up side of 24 mini muffin-pan cups. Prick each shell several times with toothpick. Bake 15 minutes, or until golden. Cool in pans on wire rack 5 minutes. Remove shells from pans; cool completely on wire rack.

3 Meanwhile, in small bowl, with fork, beat cream cheese, sugar, milk, and vanilla until blended. Refrigerate until ready to serve.

4 Fill each tartlet shell with about 2 teaspoons filling; top with fruit; garnish with mint leaves. *Makes 2 dozen tartlets.*

EACH TARTLET: ABOUT 100 CALORIES, 1 G PROTEIN,
8 G CARBOHYDRATE, 7 G TOTAL FAT (4 G SATURATED),
0.5 G FIBER, 18 MG CHOLESTEROL, 80 MG SODIUM.

Almond Tartlets

PREP 1 HOUR PLUS CHILLING / BAKE 15 MINUTES

PASTRY FOR SINGLE-CRUST PIE (PAGE 206)
1 CUP BLANCHED ALMONDS, TOASTED
1 CUP CONFECTIONERS' SUGAR PLUS ADDITIONAL FOR
  SPRINKLING
1 LARGE EGG
3 TABLESPOONS BUTTER OR MARGARINE, SOFTENED
1 TEASPOON VANILLA EXTRACT

1 Prepare dough as directed through chilling.

2 Preheat oven to 400° F. In food processor with knife blade attached, pulse almonds with 1 cup confectioners' sugar until nuts are very finely ground. Add egg, butter, and vanilla; process until smooth.

3 On lightly floured surface, roll dough paper-thin (thinner than ¹⁄₁₆ inch thick). With 2½-inch round cutter, cut out 36 pastry rounds (if necessary, reroll scraps). Fit each round into 36 mini muffin-pan cups or 1¾-inch tartlet molds.

4 Spoon almond filling to ¼ inch of rim into each tartlet shell. Bake 15 minutes, or until golden. Remove tartlets from pans; cool completely on wire racks. Sift confectioners' sugar over tartlets, if you like. *Makes 3 dozen tartlets.*

EACH TARTLET: ABOUT 85 CALORIES, 2 G PROTEIN,
8 G CARBOHYDRATE, 5 G TOTAL FAT (2 G SATURATED),
0.5 G FIBER, 12 MG CHOLESTEROL, 40 MG SODIUM.

HAZELNUT TARTLETS Prepare tartlet shells and filling as above but use *1 cup hazelnuts*, toasted and skinned, for almonds. Bake and cool as directed.
EACH TARTLET: ABOUT 80 CALORIES, 1 G PROTEIN,
8 G CARBOHYDRATE, 5 G TOTAL FAT (2 G SATURATED),
0.5 G FIBER, 12 MG CHOLESTEROL, 40 MG SODIUM.

Lemon Curd & Fruit Tartlets

PREP 35 MINUTES PLUS CHILLING / BAKE 15 MINUTES

These tiny tarts, seemingly fresh from a French pastry shop, will evoke "oohs" and "aahs" when you bring them to the table. A layer of lemon curd (which can be cooked and chilled well in advance) makes a lovely foil for a few perfect berries.

PASTRY FOR 9-INCH TART (PAGE 207)

LEMON CURD (PAGE 361)

1½ PINTS BERRIES, SUCH AS RASPBERRIES, BLUEBERRIES, OR STRAWBERRIES, HULLED

¼ CUP APRICOT JAM

1 Prepare dough as directed through chilling.

2 Preheat oven to 425° F. Divide dough in half. Roll each half into 12-inch rope; cut each rope into twelve 1-inch pieces. Press each piece of dough evenly into bottom and up side of 24 mini muffin-pan cups. Prick each shell several times with toothpick. Bake 15 minutes, or until golden. Cool in pans on wire rack 5 minutes. Remove shells from pans; cool completely on wire rack.

3 Meanwhile, prepare Lemon Curd; chill as directed.

4 Fill each tartlet shell with about 2 teaspoons curd. Top with fresh berries of your choice. Warm apricot jam just until melted; strain and drizzle over berries on each tartlet. *Makes 2 dozen tartlets.*

EACH TARTLET: ABOUT 115 CALORIES, 1 G PROTEIN, 12 G CARBOHYDRATE, 7 G TOTAL FAT (4 G SATURATED), 1 G FIBER, 42 MG CHOLESTEROL, 85 MG SODIUM.

Lemon Curd & Fruit Tartlets

SAVORY PIES & TARTS

Don't reserve your pastry-making skills for sweets; use your expertise in creating tender, flaky crusts to produce an international array of dramatic main dishes. Quiches and savory tarts, pies and turnovers need only a salad accompaniment to make them a meal. Cut into smaller portions, these tarts make excellent appetizers.

Wild Mushroom Quiche

PREP 45 MINUTES PLUS CHILLING
BAKE 50 TO 55 MINUTES

Fortunately, once-scarce wild mushrooms are now cultivated and widely available at reasonable prices. They're ever so much more flavorful than white button mushrooms.

PASTRY FOR SINGLE-CRUST PIE (PAGE 206)
2 TABLESPOONS BUTTER OR MARGARINE
4 OUNCES SHIITAKE MUSHROOMS, STEMS REMOVED AND
  CAPS THINLY SLICED
4 OUNCES CREMINI MUSHROOMS, THINLY SLICED
2 LARGE SHALLOTS, FINELY CHOPPED
¼ TEASPOON DRIED THYME
¼ TEASPOON SALT
¼ TEASPOON COARSELY GROUND BLACK PEPPER
PINCH GROUND NUTMEG
¼ CUP DRY WHITE WINE
2 CUPS HALF-AND-HALF OR LIGHT CREAM
3 LARGE EGGS
4 OUNCES GRUYÈRE OR JARLSBERG CHEESE, SHREDDED
  (1 CUP)

1 Prepare dough as directed through chilling. Roll out dough and line 9-inch pie plate; make decorative edge (see photos on page 212). Refrigerate or freeze 10 to 15 minutes to firm pastry.

2 Preheat oven to 425° F. Line pie shell with foil; fill with pie weights, dry beans, or uncooked rice. Bake 10 minutes. Remove foil and weights; bake 5 minutes longer, or until lightly golden. If crust puffs up during baking, press it to plate with back of spoon. Cool on wire rack. Turn oven control to 350° F.

3 In nonstick 12-inch skillet, melt butter over medium-high heat. Add mushrooms and cook, stirring occasionally, 8 to 10 minutes, until lightly browned and all liquid has evaporated. Stir in shallots, thyme,

salt, pepper, and nutmeg; cook 2 to 3 minutes longer, until shallots are golden. Add wine; cook, stirring, 1 to 2 minutes, until all liquid has evaporated.

4 In large bowl, with wire whisk or fork, mix half-and-half and eggs until well blended.

5 Place cheese and mushroom mixture in baked piecrust. Pour egg mixture over cheese and mushroom mixture. Place sheet of foil underneath pie plate; crimp edges to form rim to catch any overflow during baking. Bake 35 to 40 minutes, until knife inserted in center of quiche comes out clean. Cool on wire rack 15 minutes. Serve hot or at room temperature. *Makes 8 main-dish servings.*

EACH SERVING: ABOUT 355 CALORIES, 11 G PROTEIN,
21 G CARBOHYDRATE, 25 G TOTAL FAT (14 G SATURATED),
1 G FIBER, 141 MG CHOLESTEROL, 330 MG SODIUM.

Sweet Onion Tart

PREP 1 HOUR PLUS CHILLING / BAKE 55 MINUTES

Our adaptation of an Alsatian onion tart is topped with onions that have been slowly simmered in butter until they're soft, golden, and sweet.

3 CUPS ALL-PURPOSE FLOUR
2 TEASPOONS SALT
½ CUP VEGETABLE SHORTENING
½ CUP (1 STICK) PLUS 3 TABLESPOONS COLD BUTTER OR
  MARGARINE
7 TO 8 TABLESPOONS COLD WATER
2 POUNDS SWEET ONIONS, THINLY SLICED
2½ CUPS MILK
5 LARGE EGGS
¾ CUP FRESHLY GRATED PARMESAN CHEESE
2 TEASPOONS CHOPPED FRESH THYME OR ½ TEASPOON
  DRIED THYME
1 TABLESPOON CHOPPED FRESH PARSLEY
½ TEASPOON COARSELY GROUND BLACK PEPPER

1 In large bowl, with fork, stir together flour and 1 teaspoon salt. With pastry blender or 2 knives used scissor-fashion, cut in shortening and ½ cup butter until mixture resembles coarse crumbs. Sprinkle cold water, 1 tablespoon at a time, into flour mixture, mixing lightly with fork after each addition, until mixture is just moist enough to hold together. With hands, shape dough into ball.

2 On lightly floured surface, with floured rolling pin, roll dough into rectangle about 18" by 13". Gently fold rectangle into fourths and carefully center in ungreased 15½" by 10½" jelly-roll pan; unfold. Lightly press dough into bottom and up sides of pan. Trim dough, leaving ½-inch overhang. Fold overhang under and pinch to form decorative edge level with rim of pan. Wrap and refrigerate tart shell about 30 minutes.

3 Meanwhile, in deep 12-inch skillet, melt remaining 3 tablespoons butter over medium-high heat. Add onions and cook, stirring frequently, about 25 minutes, until onions are golden. Remove from heat.

4 Preheat oven to 425° F. Line tart shell with foil; fill with pie weights, dry beans, or uncooked rice. Bake 20 minutes. Remove foil and weights; bake 10 minutes longer, or until golden. Transfer to wire rack to cool. Turn oven control to 400° F.

5 In large bowl, whisk together milk, eggs, Parmesan, thyme, parsley, pepper, and remaining 1 teaspoon salt until blended.

6 Spread cooked onions evenly over baked tart shell. Pour egg mixture over onions. Bake 25 minutes, or until egg mixture is set and tart is nicely browned. Serve hot. Or cool on wire rack; then wrap and refrigerate to serve cold later. Cut into 32 pieces. *Makes 32 appetizers.*

EACH APPETIZER: ABOUT 155 CALORIES, 4 G PROTEIN, 13 G CARBOHYDRATE, 9 G TOTAL FAT (4 G SATURATED), 1 G FIBER, 48 MG CHOLESTEROL, 250 MG SODIUM.

Sweet Onion Tart

Leek, Tomato & Goat Cheese Tart

PREP 55 MINUTES / BAKE 50 TO 55 MINUTES

The irresistible tang of goat cheese, or chèvre, makes this savory tart a real treat. All you need for the recipe is a 4-ounce log of the cheese.

6 MEDIUM LEEKS (2½ POUNDS)
2 TABLESPOONS OLIVE OIL
¼ TEASPOON SALT
¼ TEASPOON GROUND BLACK PEPPER
PASTRY FOR 11-INCH TART (PAGE 207)
½ CUP FINELY SHREDDED PARMESAN CHEESE
3 SMALL RIPE TOMATOES (¾ POUND)
1 TEASPOON FRESH THYME
¼ POUND GOAT CHEESE

1 Trim leeks, reserving white and pale green portions only. Slice leeks, rinse, and let drain. In a large skillet, heat 1 tablespoon oil over medium-high heat. Add leeks, reduce heat to medium; cover and cook 10 minutes, stirring occasionally. Uncover and cook 5 minutes longer, until leeks are soft and any moisture has evaporated. Stir in ⅛ teaspoon salt and ⅛ teaspoon pepper.

2 Ease dough into 11" by 1" round tart pan with removable bottom. Fold overhang in and press against side of tart pan to form rim ⅛ inch above pan edge.

3 Line tart shell with foil; fill with pie weights, dry beans, or uncooked rice. Bake 20 minutes. Remove foil and weights; bake 5 to 10 minutes longer, until golden brown. Cool on wire rack.

4 Slice tomatoes. Sprinkle bottom of tart shell with Parmesan. Spread with leeks. Arrange tomatoes on top. Sprinkle with remaining ⅛ teaspoon salt and ⅛ teaspoon pepper. Sprinkle with thyme and drizzle remaining 1 tablespoon oil over filling. Crumble goat cheese over top.

5 Bake 25 minutes, or until goat cheese is lightly browned. Cool on wire rack 5 minutes. Remove side of pan and cool tart 10 minutes longer. Cut into wedges to serve. *Makes 10 appetizer or 6 main-course servings.*

EACH APPETIZER: ABOUT 295 CALORIES,
8 G PROTEIN, 23 G CARBOHYDRATE, 20 G TOTAL FAT
(10 G SATURATED), 2 G FIBER, 38 MG CHOLESTEROL,
430 MG SODIUM.

Ricotta & Tomato Pie

PREP 35 MINUTES PLUS CHILLING
BAKE 1 HOUR 2 TO 5 MINUTES

This is a summer dish, for one simple reason: The tomato slices that cover the ricotta filling must be truly ripe, red, and tasty. If luscious tomatoes are not available, you can still make the tart: Simply serve it plain or with our Pizza Sauce (page 142).

PASTRY FOR SINGLE-CRUST PIE (PAGE 206)
1 CONTAINER (15 OUNCES) RICOTTA CHEESE
¾ CUP GRATED PECORINO ROMANO CHEESE
½ TEASPOON GROUND BLACK PEPPER
3 LARGE EGGS, LIGHTLY BEATEN
2 MEDIUM TOMATOES, CORED AND THINLY SLICED
¼ CUP FRESH BASIL, SHREDDED

1 Prepare dough as directed through chilling. Roll out dough and line 9-inch pie plate; make high fluted edge (see photo on page 212). Refrigerate or freeze 10 to 15 minutes to firm pastry.

2 Preheat oven to 425° F. Line pie shell with foil; fill with pie weights, dry beans, or uncooked rice. Bake 15 minutes. Remove foil and weights; bake 7 to 10 minutes longer, until golden. If crust puffs up during baking, gently press it to pie plate with back of spoon. Cool on wire rack 15 minutes. Turn oven control to 350° F.

3 While crust is cooling, prepare filling: In medium bowl, whisk together ricotta, Pecorino, and pepper. Add eggs and whisk to combine.

4 Pour filling into cooled piecrust. With paper towel, pat tomatoes dry; arrange tomato slices on top of cheese mixture, overlapping if necessary. Sprinkle basil over top. Bake 40 minutes, or until set and lightly puffed. Cool on wire rack 30 minutes before serving. Serve warm or at room temperature. *Makes 8 first-course servings.*

EACH SERVING: ABOUT 315 CALORIES, 14 G PROTEIN,
20 G CARBOHYDRATE, 20 G TOTAL FAT (11 G SATURATED),
1 G FIBER, 130 MG CHOLESTEROL, 290 MG SODIUM.

Leek, Tomato & Goat Cheese Tart

Quiche Lorraine

PREP 20 MINUTES PLUS CHILLING
BAKE 1 HOUR 10 TO 15 MINUTES

This creamy custard tart, which took the States by storm in the 1960s, has settled into its rightful place as a favorite American adoptee. For the fullest and most authentic flavor, use a good French Gruyère.

PASTRY FOR SINGLE-CRUST PIE (PAGE 206)
4 SLICES BACON, CHOPPED
2 CUPS HALF-AND-HALF OR LIGHT CREAM
4 LARGE EGGS
½ TEASPOON SALT
⅛ TEASPOON GROUND BLACK PEPPER
PINCH NUTMEG
4 OUNCES GRUYÈRE OR SWISS CHEESE, COARSELY
  SHREDDED (1 CUP)

1 Prepare dough as directed through chilling. Roll out dough and line 9-inch pie plate; make decorative edge (see photos on page 212). Refrigerate or freeze 10 to 15 minutes to firm pastry.

2 Preheat oven to 425° F. Line pie shell with foil; fill with pie weights, dry beans, or uncooked rice. Bake 10 minutes. Remove foil and weights; bake 5 minutes longer, or until lightly golden. If crust puffs up during baking, gently press it to pie plate with back of spoon. Transfer to wire rack to cool. Turn oven control to 350° F.

3 In 2-quart saucepan, cook bacon over medium-low heat about 5 minutes, until brown. With slotted spoon, transfer bacon to paper towels to drain.

4 In medium bowl, with wire whisk or fork, mix half-and-half, eggs, salt, pepper, and nutmeg until well blended.

5 Sprinkle bacon and cheese over cooled piecrust. Pour half-and-half mixture over bacon and cheese. Place sheet of foil underneath pie plate; crimp foil edges to form rim to catch any overflow during baking. Bake 55 to 60 minutes, or until knife inserted in center comes out clean. Cool on wire rack 15 minutes before serving. Serve hot or at room temperature. *Makes 8 main-dish servings.*

EACH SERVING: ABOUT 350 CALORIES, 12 G PROTEIN,
19 G CARBOHYDRATE, 25 G TOTAL FAT (13 G SATURATED),
0.5 G FIBER, 162 MG CHOLESTEROL, 430 MG SODIUM.

ASPARAGUS QUICHE Prepare and bake piecrust; make half-and-half mixture as above but omit bacon.

Trim *1 pound asparagus* and cut into ¾-inch pieces (2½ cups). Cook in boiling water, 6 to 8 minutes, until tender. Drain and rinse asparagus with cold running water to cool slightly. Sprinkle asparagus and cheese over piecrust. Pour in half-and-half mixture. Bake 40 to 45 minutes, or until knife in center comes out clean. Cool and serve as directed.

EACH SERVING: ABOUT 340 CALORIES, 13 G PROTEIN,
21 G CARBOHYDRATE, 23 G TOTAL FAT (12 G SATURATED),
1 G FIBER, 160 MG CHOLESTEROL, 380 MG SODIUM.

Pizza Rustica

PREP 40 MINUTES / BAKE 1 HOUR 10 MINUTES

You may be surprised to see that this country-style Italian cheese pie calls for a sweet pastry crust, but the slight sweetness makes a delicious contrast to the robust filling, with its chunks of salami and prosciutto.

ITALIAN SWEET PASTRY (PAGE 207)
3 CUPS RICOTTA CHEESE
⅓ CUP FRESHLY GRATED PECORINO ROMANO
4 LARGE EGGS
½ TEASPOON GROUND BLACK PEPPER
8 OUNCES MOZZARELLA CHEESE, SHREDDED (2 CUPS)
2 OUNCES SALAMI, COARSELY CHOPPED (¾ CUP)
2 OUNCES PROSCIUTTO, COARSELY CHOPPED (½ CUP)
1 TEASPOON WATER

Pizza Rustica

Gently fit the dough into the springform pan, easing it into the angle at the bottom. Don't trim the excess dough around the rim: You'll use it to seal the top crust onto the pie.

1 Prepare pastry as directed but use only 1 tablespoon sugar and shape dough into 2 disks, one slightly larger than the other. Preheat oven to 350° F. On floured surface, roll larger disk into 14-inch round. Fit dough into bottom and up side of 9-inch round springform pan.

2 In large bowl, stir together ricotta, Pecorino, 3 eggs, and pepper. Spoon one-third of cheese mixture into bottom of pan. Sprinkle half of mozzarella, salami, and prosciutto over cheese. Top with half of remaining cheese mixture and sprinkle remaining mozzarella, salami, and prosciutto on top. Top with remaining cheese mixture.

3 Trim edge of dough in pan even with top of pan. Roll small pastry disk into 9-inch round. Place on top of cheese mixture.

4 In small bowl, whisk together remaining egg and water. Brush edges of 9-inch round with egg mixture and fold dough from sides of pan in to cover edges. Brush top with egg mixture. Bake 1 hour 10 minutes, or until golden brown and set. Cool in pan on wire rack 20 minutes. Run thin metal spatula around edge; remove side of pan. Serve warm or at room temperature. *Makes 12 first-course servings.*

EACH SERVING: ABOUT 400 CALORIES, 19 G PROTEIN, 24 G CARBOHYDRATE, 25 G TOTAL FAT (14 G SATURATED), 0.5 G FIBER, 183 MG CHOLESTEROL, 520 MG SODIUM.

Spicy Empanadas

PREP 1 HOUR / BAKE 30 MINUTES

Enjoyed in many countries of Latin America, empanadas are filled with meat, vegetables, or both. Miniatures—empanaditas—are wonderful party fare.

PASTRY:

2½ CUPS ALL-PURPOSE FLOUR
½ CUP YELLOW CORNMEAL
1 TEASPOON SALT
¼ TEASPOON GROUND RED PEPPER (CAYENNE)
1 CUP COLD BUTTER (2 STICKS), CUT UP
1 CONTAINER (8 OUNCES) SOUR CREAM

FILLING:

8 OUNCES BONELESS PORK LOIN, TRIMMED
2 TABLESPOONS OLIVE OIL
8 OUNCES LEAN GROUND BEEF

1 MEDIUM ONION, CHOPPED (1 CUP)
1 SMALL GREEN PEPPER, FINELY CHOPPED (¾ CUP)
1 SMALL RED PEPPER, FINELY CHOPPED (¾ CUP)
4 LARGE GARLIC CLOVES, FINELY CHOPPED
2 PICKLED JALAPEÑO CHILES, FINELY CHOPPED
⅓ CUP PIMIENTO-STUFFED GREEN OLIVES, CHOPPED
⅓ CUP DRIED CURRANTS
1 TEASPOON GROUND CUMIN
¾ TEASPOON SALT
¼ TEASPOON GROUND BLACK PEPPER
¼ TEASPOON GROUND CINNAMON
¼ TEASPOON GROUND RED PEPPER (CAYENNE)
2 MEDIUM TOMATOES, CHOPPED (1½ CUPS)
1 LARGE EGG, LIGHTLY BEATEN

1 Prepare Pastry: In a food processor with knife blade attached, combine flour, cornmeal, salt, and ground red pepper. Add butter and process until mixture resembles fine crumbs. Add sour cream and pulse until dough begins to hold together. Turn dough out onto surface, gather together, and divide in half. Press each half into disk. Wrap and refrigerate at least 2 hours or up to 2 days.

2 Prepare Filling: Finely chop pork. In 12-inch skillet, heat 1 tablespoon oil over high heat. Add pork and beef. Cook 5 minutes, until browned and any liquid has evaporated. Transfer to plate.

3 Add remaining 1 tablespoon oil, onion, and green and red peppers to skillet Cook over medium-high heat 5 minutes, or until vegetables have softened. Add garlic, jalapeños, olives, currants, cumin, salt, pepper, cinnamon, and ground red pepper. Cook over medium heat 5 minutes. Add meat and tomatoes. Heat to a simmer, partially cover, and cook 10 minutes, until flavors are blended. Turn filling into large bowl, cover loosely, and refrigerate until cold.

4 On floured surface, with floured rolling pin, roll 1 disk into 24" by 8" rectangle. Cut crosswise into six 8" by 4" rectangles. Place ⅓ cup filling on one end of each rectangle, about ½ inch from end and sides. Brush edges with beaten egg. Fold pastry over to cover filling. Press edges together and press with floured fork to seal. Transfer to large cookie sheet; refrigerate. Repeat with remaining dough and filling.

5 Preheat oven to 400° F. Brush tops of empanadas with beaten egg. Bake 30 minutes, rotating sheets between upper and lower racks halfway through baking, until browned. Transfer to wire rack to cool. Serve warm or room temperature. *Makes 12 servings.*

EACH EMPANADA: ABOUT 435 CALORIES, 13 G PROTEIN 34 G CARBOHYDRATE, 28 G TOTAL FAT (14 G SATURATED), 2 G FIBER, 93 MG CHOLESTEROL, 665 MG SODIUM.

Specialty Pastry

Specialty Pastry

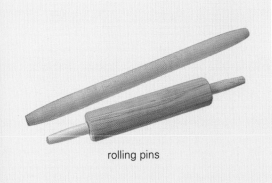

rolling pins

pastry bag

pastry brush

pastry wheels

"It's all in the wrist," they say of astonishing acts that seem deceptively easy. Pastry-making does require some sleight of hand, but the right equipment helps, too. There are two types of **rolling pins:** American-style pins have a cylindrical roller that turns on two handles; the best have ball-bearing action. A French, or European, rolling pin, turned from a single piece of wood, may be straight or tapered. Rather than gripping handles, you roll the whole pin under your palms. Whichever you prefer, get a smooth, heavy hardwood pin. To pipe choux pastry into shapes, and to fill the puffs after baking, you'll need a **pastry bag.** Today's plastic-lined bags are much easier to wash than the traditional fabric ones. You'll also need an assortment of tips, which are sold individually and in sets. Use a **pastry brush,** which has sterilized natural or nylon bristles, for glazing dough with an egg wash or brushing phyllo with melted butter. A pastry brush is great for basting meat and poultry, too, but keep a separate one for desserts. The implement that looks like a pizza cutter or wheel is a **pastry wheel.** Use it for cutting and trimming puff pastry or phyllo dough (and for dividing up a pizza). The smaller cutter is a type of pastry wheel called a jagger; it leaves a toothed edge like that created by pinking shears.

Previous page: Cream Puffs

Basic techniques

PUFF PASTRY

Flatten the cold butter into a uniformly thick square by rolling it between two sheets of waxed paper.

Center the slab of butter diagonally atop the larger square of chilled dough.

Fold the four corners of the dough over the butter as if you were creating an envelope. Seal the seams by flattening them with a rolling pin.

Roll the packet of butter and dough into an 18" by 12" rectangle (it will be quite thick).

Fold the two short sides into the center as if you were folding a letter. Seal the seam together with your fingers.

Give the folded dough a quarter turn, then roll it out into a 15" by 8" rectangle. Fold the dough in thirds again, then wrap and chill before continuing.

CHOUX PASTRY

After melting the butter in boiling water, stir in the flour all at once. Stir it vigorously until it forms a ball and leaves the sides of the pan.

Add the eggs one at a time. At first the egg won't combine with the dough, but after brief beating, you'll have a thick, satiny mixture.

PHYLLO DOUGH

Work with one sheet of phyllo at a time, leaving the others covered to keep them from drying out. Brush the phyllo with melted butter.

PUFF PASTRY

Making puff pastry is the crowning achievement of the baker's art. Once you've mastered it, you can truly call yourself an accomplished baker. The pastry's myriad of flaky layers are created by repeatedly folding and rolling a block of chilled butter into a sheet of dough. Here, we offer recipes for *tea. demi-feuilletée*—sometimes called simple puff pastry. It's not as labor-intensive or time-consuming as full-fledged *pâte feuilletée* but will do you proud in tarts, palmiers, cheese straws, and other sophisticated desserts and party snacks.

Puff Pastry

PREP 1 HOUR 30 MINUTES PLUS CHILLING

If you don't have a cool marble slab to work on, chill the countertop with an ice-filled jelly-roll pan.

3 CUPS ALL-PURPOSE FLOUR
1 CUP CAKE FLOUR (NOT SELF-RISING)
1 TEASPOON SALT
2 CUPS (4 STICKS) COLD UNSALTED BUTTER (DO NOT USE
    SALTED BUTTER OR MARGARINE)
1 CUP ICE WATER

1 In large bowl, stir together all-purpose and cake flours and salt. With pastry blender or fingertips, work ½ cup butter into flour mixture until coarse crumbs form. With fork, gradually stir in ice water, 1 tablespoon at a time, until soft dough forms, adding more water if necessary. Wrap dough in plastic wrap; refrigerate 30 minutes. Meanwhile, between 2 sheets of waxed paper, with rolling pin, pound and roll remaining 1½ cups butter into 6-inch square; wrap and refrigerate.

2 On lightly floured surface, with floured rolling pin, roll dough into 12-inch square; place butter square diagonally in center. Fold corners of dough over butter so they meet in the center, overlapping slightly (see photos for Puff Pastry, page 261). Press with rolling pin to seal. Roll dough into 18" by 12" rectangle. From one short side, fold one-third of dough over center, then fold opposite one-third over first, letter-style, to form 6" by 12" rectangle; press seam to seal.

3 Give dough quarter turn. Roll dough into 15" by 8" rectangle; fold into thirds to form 5" by 8"

rectangle. Wrap in plastic wrap; refrigerate at least 1 hour. Repeat, rolling dough into 15" by 8" rectangle and folding into thirds, 2 more times. Wrap and refrigerate 30 minutes. Repeat rolling, folding, and refrigerating 2 more times, or 6 times in all. After sixth time, wrap well and refrigerate at least 1 hour or up to 3 days (or freeze up to 1 month) before using. *Makes about 2½ pounds dough.*

Palmiers

PREP 30 MINUTES PLUS PREPARING PASTRY AND CHILLING
BAKE 14 MINUTES PER BATCH

The step-by-step photographs opposite will help you form these scrolled "palm leaves." Serve palmiers with fresh berries and cups of coffee or fine te

¼ RECIPE PUFF PASTRY (AT LEFT) OR 1 SHEET FROZEN
    PUFF PASTRY (HALF OF 17¼-OUNCE PACKAGE), THAWED
⅓ CUP SUGAR

1 Prepare Puff Pastry as directed. Sprinkle sugar on surface. Place puff pastry on sugared surface. With floured rolling pin, roll dough into 16" by 10" rectangle, incorporating as much sugar as possible into dough. Using side of your hand, make indentation lengthwise down center of dough (see top photo opposite). Starting at one long side, roll dough tightly up to indentation (see middle photo opposite). Repeat with other long side until it meets first in center. Wrap scroll in plastic wrap and refrigerate 30 minutes, or until chilled enough to slice and sugar has dissolved.

2 Preheat oven to 400° F. Line large cookie sheet with foil. With knife, cut scroll crosswise into ¼-inch-thick slices (see bottom photo opposite). Place slices, 1 inch apart, on prepared cookie sheet. Bake 7 minutes. Turn cookies over and bake 7 minutes longer, or until sugar has caramelized and cookies are deep golden. Cool 1 minute on cookie sheet. With wide spatula, transfer cookies to wire rack to cool.

3 Repeat with remaining dough. *Makes about 5 dozen palmiers.*

EACH PALMIER: ABOUT 25 CALORIES, 0 G PROTEIN,
3 G CARBOHYDRATE, 2 G TOTAL FAT (1 G SATURATED),
0 G FIBER, 4 MG CHOLESTEROL, 10 MG SODIUM.

Making Palmiers

After rolling the sheet of puff pastry into a 16" by 10" rectangle, use the side of your hand to make a shallow indentation down the middle of the dough.

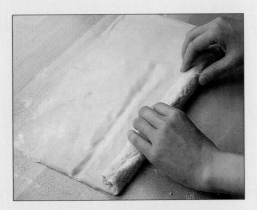

Roll one long side of the sheet of dough inward toward the center, then roll the other side in until they meet. Wrap and chill the scroll so that it holds its shape.

After chilling, slice the dough crosswise into ¼-inch-thick slices. When baked, the rolls of dough will become crisp, delicate double scrolls coated with caramelized sugar.

Gruyère Palmiers

PREP 20 MINUTES PLUS PREPARING PASTRY AND CHILLING
BAKE 15 MINUTES PER BATCH

Instead of cheese straws or wafers, offer these savory palmiers at your next party—and be sure everyone knows that you made them yourself! Flavor the palmiers with nutty-sweet Gruyère or with Parmesan. If the latter, be sure to use freshly grated cheese and not the pre-grated kind sold in cartons.

¼ RECIPE PUFF PASTRY (OPPOSITE) OR 1 SHEET FROZEN
    PUFF PASTRY (HALF OF 17¼-OUNCE PACKAGE), THAWED
4 OUNCES GRUYÈRE CHEESE, SHREDDED (1 CUP)

1 Prepare Puff Pastry as directed. Place puff pastry on lightly floured surface. With floured rolling pin, roll dough into 16" by 10" rectangle. Using side of your hand, make indentation lengthwise down center of dough. Sprinkle cheese over dough (see top photo at left). Starting at one long side, roll dough tightly up to indentation (see middle photo at left). Repeat with other long side until it meets first in center. Wrap scroll in plastic wrap and refrigerate 30 minutes, or until chilled enough to slice.

2 Preheat oven to 400° F. With knife, cut scroll crosswise into ¼-inch-thick slices (see bottom photo at left). Place slices, 1 inch apart, on ungreased large cookie sheet. Bake 15 minutes, or until golden brown. Cool 1 minute on cookie sheet on wire rack. With wide spatula, transfer to wire rack to cool.

3 Repeat with remaining dough. *Makes about 5 dozen palmiers.*

EACH PALMIER: ABOUT 30 CALORIES, 1 G PROTEIN,
2 G CARBOHYDRATE, 2 G TOTAL FAT (1 G SATURATED),
0 G FIBER, 6 MG CHOLESTEROL, 15 MG SODIUM.

PARMESAN PALMIERS Prepare as above but use ½ *cup freshly grated Parmesan cheese* for Gruyère. Bake as directed.
EACH PALMIER: ABOUT 25 CALORIES, 1 G PROTEIN,
2 G CARBOHYDRATE, 2 G TOTAL FAT (1 G SATURATED),
0 G FIBER, 5 MG CHOLESTEROL, 25 MG SODIUM.

Cinnamon-Sugar Straws

PREP 20 MINUTES PLUS PREPARING PASTRY AND CHILLING
BAKE 15 MINUTES

A variation on the French pastry twists called sacristains, these pretty sweets emerge from the oven with a coating of caramelized cinnamon sugar.

¼ RECIPE PUFF PASTRY (PAGE 262) OR 1 SHEET FROZEN
   PUFF PASTRY (HALF OF 17¼-OUNCE PACKAGE), THAWED
½ CUP SUGAR
2 TEASPOONS GROUND CINNAMON

1 Prepare Puff Pastry as directed. Preheat oven to 400° F. Line 2 large cookie sheets with foil. Mix sugar and cinnamon. Sprinkle half of sugar mixture on surface. Place dough on sugared surface. Roll into 15" by 10" rectangle, sprinkling remaining sugar mixture under and over dough to prevent sticking.

2 With sharp knife, cut dough crosswise into ¾-inch-wide strips. Twist each strip 2 or 3 times, and place, ½ inch apart, on prepared cookie sheets. Bake 15 minutes, rotating sheets between upper and lower racks halfway through baking, or until sugar has caramelized. With wide spatula, loosen straws and cool completely on cookie sheets on wire racks. *Makes 20 straws.*

EACH STRAW: ABOUT 85 CALORIES, 1 G PROTEIN,
10 G CARBOHYDRATE, 5 G TOTAL FAT (3 G SATURATED),
0 G FIBER, 12 MG CHOLESTEROL, 30 MG SODIUM.

Spicy Cheese Straws

PREP 30 MINUTES / BAKE 20 TO 22 MINUTES PER BATCH

1 TABLESPOON PAPRIKA
½ TEASPOON DRIED THYME
¼ TO ½ TEASPOON GROUND RED PEPPER (CAYENNE)
¼ TEASPOON SALT
1 PACKAGE (17¼ OUNCES) FROZEN PUFF PASTRY, THAWED
1 LARGE EGG WHITE, SLIGHTLY BEATEN
8 OUNCES SHARP CHEDDAR CHEESE, SHREDDED (2 CUPS)

1 Preheat oven to 375° F. In small bowl, stir together paprika, thyme, ground red pepper, and salt. Grease 2 large cookie sheets.

2 On lightly floured surface, unfold 1 puff-pastry sheet. With floured rolling pin, roll dough into 14-inch square. Lightly brush dough with beaten egg white. Sprinkle half of paprika mixture on dough. Sprinkle half of cheese on one half of dough. Fold dough over to cover cheese, forming 7" by 14" rectangle. With rolling pin, lightly roll over dough to seal layers.

3 With pizza cutter or sharp knife, cut dough crosswise into ½-inch-wide strips. Place strips, ½ inch apart, on prepared cookie sheets, twisting each strip twice and pressing ends against cookie sheet to prevent strips from uncurling during baking.

4 Bake 20 to 22 minutes, until golden. With wide spatula, carefully transfer straws to wire racks to cool.

5 Repeat with remaining dough, beaten egg white, paprika mixture, and cheese. *Makes about 4 dozen cheese straws.*

EACH STRAW: ABOUT 80 CALORIES, 2 G PROTEIN,
5 G CARBOHYDRATE, 6 G TOTAL FAT (2 G SATURATED),
2 G FIBER, 5 MG CHOLESTEROL, 70 MG SODIUM.

Pithiviers

PREP 20 MINUTES PLUS PREPARING PASTRY AND CHILLING
BAKE 30 TO 35 MINUTES

Named for a town south of Paris, this impressive pastry "cake" has a rich almond-paste filling.

½ RECIPE PUFF PASTRY (PAGE 262), CUT INTO 2 PIECES,
   OR 1 PACKAGE (17¼ OUNCES) FROZEN PUFF PASTRY,
   THAWED
2 LARGE EGGS
1 TABLESPOON WATER
1 TUBE OR CAN (7 TO 8 OUNCES) ALMOND PASTE
1 TABLESPOON VANILLA EXTRACT
2 TEASPOONS SUGAR

1 Prepare Puff Pastry as directed. In medium bowl, with fork, beat eggs. Transfer 1 tablespoon egg to cup; mix in water; set aside. In food processor with knife blade attached, pulse almond paste until fine crumbs form. Add almond paste and vanilla to eggs in bowl; with fork, mix until smooth.

Pithiviers

2 Lightly flour large cookie sheet. Place damp towel under cookie sheet to prevent it from moving. Place 1 piece fresh puff pastry (or 1 thawed sheet, unfolded) on cookie sheet. With floured rolling pin, roll dough into 13-inch square.

3 Invert 11-inch round dish or bowl onto dough, lightly pressing on it to make mark of a circle. With pastry wheel or sharp knife, trim dough to 12-inch circle, leaving 1-inch border around dish; use trimmings for Palmiers (page 262), if desired.

4 With small spatula, spread almond mixture to cover 11-inch circle. Lightly flour another large cookie sheet; on it, roll, mark, and trim remaining piece of puff pastry as in Steps 2 and 3. Refrigerate about 15 minutes, or until chilled enough to move without losing its shape.

5 Preheat oven to 400° F. With pastry brush, brush some reserved egg mixture on border around almond mixture. Place chilled dough circle on top of almond mixture; press all around edge to seal.

6 With tip of sharp knife, cut ½-inch triangles, 2 inches apart, from edge of dough; discard triangles.

7 With tip of knife, lightly score top circle with curved lines, starting at center and working toward edge (do not cut all the way through). Brush circle

with remaining egg mixture; sprinkle with sugar. (Dessert can be prepared to this point and refrigerated up to 4 hours before baking.) Bake 10 minutes. Turn oven control to 350° F; bake 20 to 25 minutes longer, until no part of dough remains white, covering pastry loosely with foil to prevent overbrowning. Cool on wire rack at least 30 minutes before serving. *Makes 12 servings.*

EACH SERVING: ABOUT 265 CALORIES, 5 G PROTEIN, 23 G CARBOHYDRATE, 17 G TOTAL FAT (8 G SATURATED), 0 G FIBER, 66 MG CHOLESTEROL, 85 MG SODIUM.

APPLE-ALMOND PITHIVIERS Prepare dough as for Pithiviers; prepare filling as directed but use *1 large egg, ½ tube or can almond paste,* and *2 teaspoons vanilla extract;* spread on dough. Top with *1 pound Golden Delicious apples (3 medium),* peeled, cored, thinly sliced, and tossed with *2 teaspoons all-purpose flour.* Top filling with remaining dough circle. Cut triangles in edge, score top, brush top with egg mixture, sprinkle with sugar, and bake as directed. *Makes 10 servings.*

EACH SERVING: ABOUT 265 CALORIES, 4 G PROTEIN, 23 G CARBOHYDRATE, 17 G TOTAL FAT (9 G SATURATED), 1 G FIBER, 59 MG CHOLESTEROL, 95 MG SODIUM.

Napoleon

PREP 25 MINUTES PLUS PREPARING PASTRY AND CHILLING
BAKE 25 TO 30 MINUTES

One of the most eye-catching items in a pastry shop, these pastry-and-custard "sandwiches" are made in a variety of ways. Use homemade or frozen puff pastry, fill with pastry cream, and top with a simple dusting of confectioners' sugar (or glaze with the traditional chevron-patterned icing).

½ RECIPE PUFF PASTRY (PAGE 262) OR 1 PACKAGE
   (17¼ OUNCES) FROZEN PUFF PASTRY, THAWED
VANILLA OR CHOCOLATE PASTRY CREAM (PAGE 360)
1 CUP CONFECTIONERS' SUGAR
2 TABLESPOONS WATER
½ SQUARE (½ OUNCE) SEMISWEET CHOCOLATE, MELTED

1 Prepare Puff Pastry as directed. Preheat oven to 400° F. On lightly floured surface, with floured rolling pin, roll dough into rectangle ⅛ inch thick. (The rectangle will be about 13" by 17" if using fresh puff pastry and 12" by 14" if using thawed frozen puff pastry.) Transfer rectangle to large cookie sheet and prick with fork. Cover with another cookie sheet. Bake fresh puff pastry 25 minutes; bake frozen variety 20 minutes. Remove top cookie sheet, and bake about 5 minutes longer, or until golden. Cool on wire rack.

2 Cut baked puff pastry lengthwise into thirds.

3 Prepare Vanilla or Chocolate Pastry Cream and chill as directed.

4 Turn 1 puff-pastry strip over on cooling rack. Mix confectioners' sugar with water, stirring until smooth. Pour over strip and smooth with spatula. Quickly pour stripes of melted chocolate lengthwise over glaze and drag knife crosswise through chocolate to make decorative top. Let glazed strip stand about 30 minutes, until dry.

5 With wire whisk, beat pastry cream just until smooth. Place 1 unglazed puff-pastry strip on serving platter. Spread half of pastry cream on top. Top with second unglazed pastry strip and spread with remaining pastry cream. Place glazed puff-pastry strip on top. Chill at least 1 hour, or until pastry cream is firm, or up to 3 hours. To serve, slice with serrated knife. *Makes 12 servings.*

EACH SERVING WITH VANILLA PASTRY CREAM: ABOUT 375 CALORIES, 5 G PROTEIN, 46 G CARBOHYDRATE, 19 G TOTAL FAT (11 G SATURATED), 0.5 G FIBER, 119 MG CHOLESTEROL, 125 MG SODIUM.

EACH SERVING WITH CHOCOLATE PASTRY CREAM: ABOUT 480 CALORIES, 4 G PROTEIN, 45 G CARBOHYDRATE, 32 G TOTAL FAT (19 G SATURATED), 0.5 G FIBER, 181 MG CHOLESTEROL, 215 MG SODIUM.

PEAR NAPOLEON Prepare puff pastry as for Napoleon through Step 2. Use pear filling for pastry cream; omit glaze: In 6-quart Dutch oven, melt *½ cup butter or margarine* (1 stick) over medium-high heat. Add *6 pounds ripe Anjou or Packham pears*, peeled, cored, and cut into 1-inch pieces, and heat to boiling. Stir in *⅔ cup granulated sugar*. Cook, stirring occasionally, about 1 hour, or until pears begin to brown. Reduce heat to medium-low and cook about 30 minutes longer, stirring frequently, until mixture has reduced to about 3¾ cups. Transfer to jelly-roll pan and refrigerate until completely cool. (If not thick enough to spread, return to Dutch oven and cook until thickened.) Place 1 pastry strip on serving platter. Spread half of pear mixture on top. Top with second pastry strip and spread with remaining pear mixture. Top with remaining pastry strip. Sprinkle with *confectioners' sugar*. Make decorative design, if desired: Wearing an oven mitt to protect hand, heat end of metal skewer directly over high heat until hot. Lightly drag skewer across top of Napoleon to caramelize sugar. Repeat, making cross-hatch design. Serve immediately, or let stand at room temperature up to 3 hours. To serve, slice with serrated knife.
EACH SERVING: ABOUT 455 CALORIES, 3 G PROTEIN, 61 G CARBOHYDRATE, 24 G TOTAL FAT (14 G SATURATED), 6 G FIBER, 62 MG CHOLESTEROL, 180 MG SODIUM.

RASPBERRY NAPOLEON Prepare puff pastry as for Napoleon through Step 2. Omit pastry cream and glaze. With mixer at high speed, beat *1 cup heavy or whipping cream, 3 tablespoons sugar,* and *1 teaspoon vanilla extract* until stiff. Place 1 puff-pastry strip on serving platter. Spread with ⅔ cup whipped cream and scatter *½ pint of raspberries* on top. Spread scant ⅓ cup whipped cream over second pastry strip; invert onto berries. Spread ⅔ cup whipped cream and scatter additional *½ pint raspberries* on top. Spread remaining whipped cream on third pastry strip and invert on top. Sprinkle with *confectioners' sugar*. Serve immediately, or refrigerate up to 2 hours. To serve, slice with serrated knife.
EACH SERVING: ABOUT 310 CALORIES, 3 G PROTEIN, 24 G CARBOHYDRATE, 23 G TOTAL FAT (14 G SATURATED), 1 G FIBER, 69 MG CHOLESTEROL, 105 MG SODIUM.

Raspberry Napoleon

Elegant Puff-Pastry Tarts

PREP 1 HOUR PLUS PREPARING PASTRY AND CHILLING
BAKE 40 MINUTES

The tart shells can be made through Step 2 and frozen, then baked straight from the freezer. The filling is not cooked in the shells, so you can use a variety of different fruits. For example, you could make four of each: cherry, raspberry, blueberry, and strawberry.

PUFF PASTRY (PAGE 262)
1 LARGE EGG, BEATEN
1½ CUPS HEAVY OR WHIPPING CREAM
3 TABLESPOONS SUGAR
1½ TEASPOONS VANILLA EXTRACT
4 CUPS FRESH FRUITS AND BERRIES, CUT UP

1 Prepare Puff Pastry as directed. Cut dough crosswise in half. On lightly floured surface, with floured rolling pin, roll 1 half of dough into 20½" by 10½" rectangle, gently lifting dough occasionally to prevent sticking. With pastry wheel or sharp knife, trim edges to make 20" by 10" rectangle. Cut rectangle into eight 5-inch squares; place on ungreased large cookie sheet. Refrigerate 30 minutes. Repeat with remaining dough half.

2 For each tart, fold 1 dough square diagonally in half to form triangle. Starting at folded side, cut ½-inch border strip on both sides of triangle, leaving dough uncut at triangle point so strips remain attached (see top photo at right). Unfold triangle (see middle photo at right). Lift up both loose border strips and slip one under the other, gently pulling to match corners on base (see bottom photo at right). Attach points with a drop of water. Refrigerate on cookie sheet 30 minutes.

3 Preheat oven to 400° F. Bake tarts 20 minutes. Turn oven control to 375° F; brush top of borders with beaten egg. Rotate sheets between upper and lower racks; bake 20 minutes longer, or until centers of tarts are lightly browned. Cool tarts on wire rack.

4 To serve, in small bowl, with mixer at medium speed, beat cream, sugar, and vanilla until soft peaks form. Fill tarts with whipped cream; top with fruit of choice. *Makes 16 tarts.*

EACH TART: ABOUT 440 CALORIES, 5 G PROTEIN,
34 G CARBOHYDRATE, 32 G TOTAL FAT (20 G SATURATED),
1 G FIBER, 106 MG CHOLESTEROL, 160 MG SODIUM.

Puff Pastry Tarts

Start with eight 5-inch squares of chilled puff pastry. Fold one square diagonally in half. Starting near the fold, make a cut ½ inch from the edge without cutting through either the fold.

When you unfold the dough, it should look like this. Lift up one border strip and cross it over, aligning it with the opposite edge.

Cross the other border strip over the dough and match it to the opposite edge. Brush a drop of water under the point of each strip and press gently to help the two layers adhere.

Brie in Puff Pastry

PREP 20 MINUTES PLUS STANDING
BAKE 30 TO 35 MINUTES

A wheel of Brie is enclosed in puff pastry and baked until golden. It is easier to make than you think and perfect for entertaining. Allow time for it to cool before serving, or the cheese will be too runny.

1 PACKAGE (17¼ OUNCES) FROZEN PUFF PASTRY, THAWED
1 LARGE EGG YOLK
1 TABLESPOON WATER
1 WHEEL (8 INCHES IN DIAMETER) BRIE CHEESE
  (2 POUNDS)
GREEN AND RED SEEDLESS GRAPES FOR GARNISH

1 On lightly floured surface, unfold 1 puff-pastry sheet. With floured rolling pin, roll into 13" by 10" rectangle. From rectangle, cut 13" by 1½" strip and 8½-inch circle. Repeat with remaining sheet.

2 In cup, with fork, beat egg yolk and water.

3 Preheat oven to 425° F. Place 1 dough circle on ungreased large cookie sheet; center Brie on circle. Brush side of Brie with some egg-yolk mixture. Wrap the 2 long dough strips around side of Brie; press strips firmly against Brie so that they adhere during baking. Brush strips with some egg-yolk mixture.

4 Place remaining dough circle on top of Brie. Press edges of circles to dough strips to seal Brie completely in puff pastry.

5 With tip of knife, lightly score top of dough with 1-inch squares. Brush top and side of dough with remaining egg-yolk mixture.

6 Bake 30 to 35 minutes, until pastry is golden brown. Cool on wire rack 1 hour 30 minutes to 2 hours to firm to serving consistency.

7 To serve, with spatula, transfer Brie to large deep platter; garnish with small clusters of grapes. *Makes 24 servings.*

EACH SERVING WITHOUT GRAPES: ABOUT 230 CALORIES,
9 G PROTEIN, 9 G CARBOHYDRATE, 17 G TOTAL FAT
(1 G SATURATED), 0 G FIBER, 47 MG CHOLESTEROL, 280 MG
SODIUM.

CHOUX PASTRY

The "other" puff pastry, choux pastry, or *pâte à choux* (pronounced "pot-a-SHOE") is used for such festive pastries as cream puffs and éclairs, as well as for savory gougères. As desserts, choux-paste shells can hold flavored, sweetened whipped creams, custard, or ice cream. Filled with chicken or crab salad, creamed seafood, or herbed cream cheese, they make very tempting hors d'oeuvres. Compared with the more elaborate form of puff pastry (see page 262), choux pastry is almost laughably easy to make. The dough is mixed by hand in a saucepan. The trickiest part of it all may be convincing yourself, as you beat in the eggs, that the wet, curdled-looking mixture will quickly turn into a thick, satiny dough.

Choux Pastry

PREP 10 MINUTES / COOK 5 MINUTES

"Choux" means cabbages; the recipe takes its name from the plump, round shape of cream-puff shells—the most familiar use of this versatile dough.

1 CUP WATER
½ CUP (1 STICK) BUTTER OR MARGARINE
¼ TEASPOON SALT
1 CUP ALL-PURPOSE FLOUR
4 LARGE EGGS

1 In 3-quart saucepan, heat water, butter, and salt to boiling over medium heat until butter has melted. Remove saucepan from heat. With wooden spoon, vigorously stir in flour all at once until mixture forms ball and leaves side of pan.

2 Add eggs, 1 at a time, beating well after each addition, until batter is smooth and satiny. Shape warm batter as directed in recipes. *Makes 8 large cream puffs, 22 small puffs, or 30 éclairs.*

Cream Puffs

You can bake these puffs a few days ahead of time, then recrisp them in a preheated 325° F oven for 10 minutes. After cooling, fill them with softened ice cream, as we do here, or with pastry cream or ricotta filling, as in the following recipe.

CHOUX PASTRY (PAGE 269)
SUBLIME HOT FUDGE SAUCE (PAGE 362)
1 QUART VANILLA ICE CREAM, SLIGHTLY SOFTENED

1 Preheat oven to 400° F. Grease and flour large cookie sheet. Prepare Choux Pastry. Using slightly rounded ¼-cup measure, drop batter in 8 large mounds, 3 inches apart, onto prepared cookie sheet. With moistened finger, gently smooth tops to round.

2 Bake 40 to 45 minutes, until deep golden. Remove cookie sheet from oven; with knife, poke hole into side of each puff to release steam. Turn off oven. Return cookie sheet to oven and let puffs stand in oven 10 minutes. Transfer puffs to wire rack to cool.

3 With serrated knife, cut each cooled puff horizontally in half; remove and discard any moist dough inside.

4 Prepare Hot Fudge Sauce. To serve, place ½-cup scoop vanilla ice cream in bottom half of each puff; replace tops. Spoon hot fudge sauce over puffs. *Makes 8 large cream puffs.*

EACH PUFF: ABOUT 630 CALORIES, 9 G PROTEIN,
56 G CARBOHYDRATE, 44 G TOTAL FAT (26 G SATURATED),
3 G FIBER, 215 MG CHOLESTEROL, 320 MG SODIUM.

CROQUEMBOUCHE

THIS FESTIVE CREATION IS THE TRADITIONAL FRENCH WEDDING CAKE, A TAPERING TOWER OF TINY, FILLED CREAM PUFFS "GLUED" TOGETHER WITH WARM CARAMEL. AFTER THE CARAMEL SETS, THE STRUCTURE STANDS ON ITS OWN AND IT CAN BE ADORNED WITH FLOWERS, SMALL FRUITS, CANDIES, AND A VEIL OF SPUN SUGAR. CROQUEMBOUCHE IS ALSO A FAVORITE CENTERPIECE FOR CHRISTMAS BUFFETS.

Small Cream Puffs

Children adore these bite-size "minis." For dessert lovers of any age, arrange the pastries on pretty plates and garnish with Raspberry Sauce (page 363).

VANILLA OR CHOCOLATE PASTRY CREAM (PAGE 360),
PRALINE PASTRY CREAM (PAGE 361), OR RICOTTA
FILLING (PAGE 362)
CHOUX PASTRY (PAGE 269)
CONFECTIONERS' SUGAR

1 Prepare filling of choice; cover and chill until ready to use.

2 Preheat oven to 400° F. Grease 2 large cookie sheets. Prepare Choux Pastry. Spoon batter, by rounded tablespoons, 1½ inches apart, onto prepared cookie sheets to make 22 mounds. (Or with pastry bag, pipe batter to make 22 mounds.)

3 Bake 35 minutes, rotating sheets between upper and lower racks halfway through baking, or until deep golden. Transfer puffs to wire racks to cool.

4 With serrated knife, cut each cooled puff horizontally almost in half, leaving one side attached. Whisk filling until smooth. Spoon 2 tablespoons filling into bottom half of each puff; replace top of puff and sprinkle with confectioners' sugar. *Makes 22 small cream puffs.*

EACH PUFF WITH VANILLA PASTRY CREAM: ABOUT 135
CALORIES, 3 G PROTEIN, 14 G CARBOHYDRATE, 7 G TOTAL
FAT (4 G SATURATED), 0 G FIBER, 92 MG CHOLESTEROL,
95 MG SODIUM.

EACH PUFF WITH CHOCOLATE PASTRY CREAM: ABOUT 160
CALORIES, 3 G PROTEIN, 17 G CARBOHYDRATE, 9 G TOTAL
FAT (5 G SATURATED), 0.5 G FIBER, 92 MG CHOLESTEROL,
95 MG SODIUM.

EACH PUFF WITH PRALINE PASTRY CREAM: ABOUT 210
CALORIES, 4 G PROTEIN, 25 G CARBOHYDRATE, 11 G TOTAL
FAT (4 G SATURATED), 0.5 G FIBER, 92 MG CHOLESTEROL,
95 MG SODIUM.

EACH PUFF WITH RICOTTA FILLING: ABOUT 175 CALORIES, 6
G PROTEIN, 13 G CARBOHYDRATE, 11 G TOTAL FAT (6 G
SATURATED), 0 G FIBER, 71 MG CHOLESTEROL,
115 MG SODIUM.

Paris-Brest

PREP 50 MINUTES PLUS CHILLING AND COOLING
BAKE 55 MINUTES

This dessert was created for the famed bicycle race between the cities of Paris and Brest. The pastry is intended to resemble a bicycle tire.

3 LARGE EGG YOLKS
⅔ CUP GRANULATED SUGAR
3 TABLESPOONS CORNSTARCH
2 CUPS MILK
2 TEASPOONS VANILLA EXTRACT
CHOUX PASTRY (PAGE 269)
¼ CUP WATER
½ CUP SLICED NATURAL ALMONDS, TOASTED
1 CUP HEAVY OR WHIPPING CREAM
1 TABLESPOON CONFECTIONERS' SUGAR PLUS ADDITIONAL
   FOR SPRINKLING

1 Prepare pastry cream: In medium bowl, with wire whisk, beat egg yolks, ⅓ cup granulated sugar, and cornstarch until blended. In 3-quart saucepan, heat milk to simmering over medium-high heat. Gradually pour about half of simmering milk into yolk mixture, beating constantly with wire whisk. Return egg-yolk mixture to saucepan and cook, whisking constantly, until mixture thickens and boils; reduce heat to low and cook, stirring, 2 minutes. Remove saucepan from heat; stir in vanilla. Pour pastry cream into heatproof container; cover and refrigerate at least 2 hours, until cold.

2 Preheat oven to 425° F. Grease and flour large cookie sheet. Using 8-inch cake pan or plate as guide, with toothpick, trace circle in flour on cookie sheet.

3 Prepare Choux Pastry. Spoon batter into pastry bag fitted with ½-inch plain tip (or zip-tight bag with corner cut). Using tracing as guide, pipe dough in 1-inch-wide ring just inside circle on cookie sheet. Pipe another 1-inch-wide ring outside of first, making sure both are touching. With remaining batter, pipe another ring on top along center seam of first 2 rings (see photo at right). With moistened finger, gently smooth dough rings where ends meet.

4 Bake "wreath" 20 minutes. Turn oven control to 375° F; bake 25 minutes longer, or until deep golden. Remove wreath from oven; poke sides in several places with toothpick to release steam, and bake 10

minutes longer. Remove wreath from cookie sheet and cool completely on wire rack.

5 While wreath is cooling, prepare almond praline: Lightly grease cookie sheet. In 1-quart saucepan, heat remaining ⅓ cup granulated sugar and water to boiling over medium-high heat, swirling pan occasionally to help dissolve sugar. Boil mixture 5 to 7 minutes, without stirring, until golden. Remove pan from heat. Stir in ⅓ cup almonds. Stir mixture over low heat just until it reliquefies. Immediately pour praline mixture onto cookie sheet; spread with back of spoon to ½-inch thickness. Let praline cool on cookie sheet on wire rack 10 minutes, until firm.

6 Break praline into small pieces. In food processor with knife blade attached, process praline until ground into fine powder.

7 With long serrated knife, cut cooled wreath horizontally in half. Pull out some of the wet "eggy" mixture inside wreath and discard. In small bowl, with mixer at medium speed, beat cream and 1 tablespoon confectioners' sugar until stiff peaks form. With rubber spatula, gently fold praline into pastry cream; spoon into bottom of wreath. Top with whipped cream. Replace top of wreath.

8 To serve, sprinkle with confectioners' sugar; garnish with reserved almonds. *Makes 12 servings.*

EACH SERVING: ABOUT 325 CALORIES, 6 G PROTEIN,
26 G CARBOHYDRATE, 22 G TOTAL FAT (11 G SATURATED),
0 G FIBER, 180 MG CHOLESTEROL, 175 MG SODIUM.

Piping a Wreath

Use a large plain tip on your pastry bag to pipe three rings of choux pastry onto the prepared cookie sheet: two concentric rings and a third ring along the center seam on top.

Cream-Puff Ring

PREP 45 MINUTES PLUS CHILLING AND COOLING
BAKE 40 MINUTES

*This wreath-shaped dessert is ideal for a Christmas
party. Use Chocolate Pastry Cream, if you prefer.*

VANILLA PASTRY CREAM (PAGE 360)
CHOUX PASTRY (PAGE 269)
½ CUP HEAVY OR WHIPPING CREAM
CHOCOLATE GLAZE (PAGE 360)

1 Prepare Vanilla Pastry Cream; cover and refrigerate
until ready to use.

2 Preheat oven to 400° F. Lightly grease and flour
large cookie sheet. Using 7-inch plate as guide, with
toothpick, trace circle in flour on cookie sheet.
Prepare Choux Pastry. Drop batter by heaping tablespoons into 12 mounds inside circle to form ring.
Mounds should be touching.

3 Bake 40 minutes, or until deep golden. Turn off
oven. Let ring stand in oven 15 minutes. Transfer
ring to wire rack to cool.

4 With long serrated knife, cut cooled ring horizontally in half. In small bowl, with mixer at medium
speed, beat cream until soft peaks form. With wire
whisk, beat pastry cream until smooth. With rubber
spatula, fold whipped cream, one third at a time, into
pastry cream; spoon into bottom of ring. Replace top.

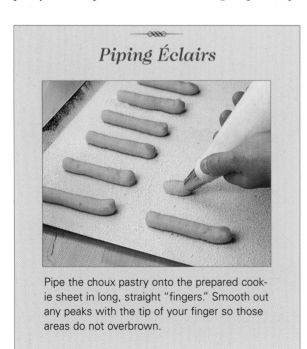

Piping Éclairs

Pipe the choux pastry onto the prepared cookie sheet in long, straight "fingers." Smooth out
any peaks with the tip of your finger so those
areas do not overbrown.

5 Prepare Chocolate Glaze. Spoon glaze over ring.
Let stand until glaze sets. *Makes 12 servings.*

EACH SERVING: ABOUT 350 CALORIES, 7 G PROTEIN,
33 G CARBOHYDRATE, 22 G TOTAL FAT (12 G SATURATED),
1 G FIBER, 190 MG CHOLESTEROL, 210 MG SODIUM.

Éclairs

PREP 45 MINUTES PLUS CHILLING AND COOLING
BAKE 40 MINUTES

*Baked, unfilled shells can be frozen. After filling and
frosting, éclairs can be refrigerated for up to 3 hours.*

VANILLA OR CHOCOLATE PASTRY CREAM (PAGE 360)
CHOUX PASTRY (PAGE 269)
CHOCOLATE GLAZE (PAGE 359)

1 Prepare pastry cream of choice; cover and refrigerate until ready to use.

2 Preheat oven to 400° F. Grease and flour large
cookie sheet. Prepare Choux Pastry. Spoon batter
into large pastry bag fitted with ½-inch round tip.
Pipe batter into strips about 3½" by ¾", 1 inch apart,
onto prepared cookie sheet to make 30 éclairs (see
photo at left). With fingertip dipped in water, smooth
any peaks.

3 Bake 40 minutes, or until deep golden. Transfer
pastries to wire racks to cool.

4 With serrated knife, cut each cooled éclair horizontally almost in half, leaving one side attached.
With small knife, make hole in each end. Whisk
pastry cream until smooth; spoon into large pastry
bag fitted with ¼-inch round tip. Pipe into bottom
halves of split éclairs or pipe into both ends of whole
éclairs.

5 Prepare Chocolate Glaze. Dip top of each éclair
into glaze, smoothing with small metal spatula if
necessary. Let stand until glaze sets. *Makes 30 éclairs.*

EACH ÉCLAIR WITH VANILLA PASTRY CREAM: ABOUT 125
CALORIES, 3 G PROTEIN, 13 G CARBOHYDRATE, 7 G TOTAL
FAT (4 G SATURATED), 0 G FIBER, 71 MG CHOLESTEROL,
80 MG SODIUM.

EACH ÉCLAIR WITH CHOCOLATE PASTRY CREAM: ABOUT 140
CALORIES, 3 G PROTEIN, 15 G CARBOHYDRATE, 8 G TOTAL
FAT (5 G SATURATED), 1 G FIBER, 71 MG CHOLESTEROL,
80 MG SODIUM.

Saint-Honoré

PREP 2 HOURS / BAKE 40 MINUTES

Saint Honoré, the patron saint of French bakers, is honored with this lavish creation: a glorious construct of pastry ringed with cream-filled puffs and the center filled with cream filling, and drizzled with caramel.

VANILLA PASTRY CREAM (PAGE 360)
PASTRY FOR 9-INCH TART (PAGE 207)
CHOUX PASTRY (PAGE 269)
1 CUP HEAVY OR WHIPPING CREAM
1½ CUPS SUGAR
¼ CUP WATER

1 Prepare Vanilla Pastry Cream through chilling; cover and refrigerate until ready to use. Prepare Pastry for 9-Inch Tart. On lightly floured surface, with floured rolling pin, roll dough into 12-inch circle, trim edges. Place dough on ungreased large cookie sheet, prick with fork, and refrigerate.

2 Preheat oven to 400° F. Grease and flour large cookie sheet. Prepare Choux Pastry through Step 2. Spoon batter into large pastry bag fitted with ½-inch round tip. Pipe batter into 16 mounds 1½" wide and 1" high, 2 inches apart, onto prepared cookie sheet.

With fingertip dipped in water, smooth any peaks. Fill pastry bag with remaining batter and pipe around edge of the dough circle to form rim.

3 Bake puffs 40 minutes and pastry circle 25 minutes, until golden, rotating sheets between upper and lower racks after 20 minutes of baking. Transfer puffs to wire rack to cool. Cool pastry circle on cookie sheet on wire rack.

4 In small bowl, with mixer at high speed, beat cream until stiff peaks form. Spoon 1¼ cups pastry cream into large pastry bag fitted with a ¼-inch round tip. Fold whipped cream into remaining 1½ cups pastry cream; refrigerate.

5 Insert tip of pastry bag into side of each puff and pipe in pastry cream to fill halfway.

6 In 2-quart saucepan, heat sugar and water to boiling over medium-high heat. Boil until mixture turns amber in color. Immediately pour hot caramel into small bowl to stop cooking. Carefully dip bottom of each puff in caramel and attach on top of rim in a ring around edge of pastry. Drizzle remaining caramel over puffs. Spread pastry-cream mixture evenly in center of circle. Refrigerate up to 6 hours before serving. *Makes 16 servings.*

EACH SERVING: ABOUT 390 CALORIES, 6 G PROTEIN, 46 G CARBOHYDRATE, 20 G TOTAL FAT (11 G SATURATED), 0.5 G FIBER, 159 MG CHOLESTEROL, 215 MG SODIUM.

Saint-Honoré

Mini Gougères

PREP 20 MINUTES / BAKE 30 TO 35 MINUTES

The gougère is a specialty of the Burgundy region of France. This savory choux pastry, made with Gruyère, or a similar cheese, is baked as individual puffs or in a large ring. Traditionally served at wine tastings, individual gougères are an appealing party food. Our two-bite versions can be made a few hours ahead and reheated in a 400° F oven for 5 minutes.

6 OUNCES GRUYÈRE OR SWISS CHEESE
1 CUP WATER
6 TABLESPOONS BUTTER OR MARGARINE, CUT UP
1½ TEASPOONS DIJON MUSTARD
½ TEASPOON HOT PEPPER SAUCE
¼ TEASPOON SALT
1 CUP ALL-PURPOSE FLOUR
4 LARGE EGGS

1 Preheat oven to 400° F. Grease and flour 2 large cookie sheets. Shred 1 cup cheese; finely dice remaining cheese.

2 In 3-quart saucepan, heat water, butter, mustard, hot pepper sauce, and salt to boiling. Remove saucepan from heat. With wooden spoon, vigorously stir in flour all at once until mixture forms ball and leaves side of pan.

3 Add eggs, 1 at a time, beating well after each addition, until batter is smooth and satiny. Stir in shredded and diced cheese. Drop batter by rounded teaspoons, about 2 inches apart, onto prepared cookie sheets.

4 Bake 30 to 35 minutes, rotating sheets between upper and lower racks halfway through baking, until deep golden. Transfer puffs to wire racks to cool. Serve warm or at room temperature. *Makes about 3 dozen puffs.*

EACH PUFF: ABOUT 60 CALORIES, 3 G PROTEIN,
3 G CARBOHYDRATE, 4 G TOTAL FAT (2 G SATURATED),
0 G FIBER, 34 MG CHOLESTEROL, 65 MG SODIUM.

Black Pepper Puffs with Goat-Cheese Filling

PREP 30 MINUTES / BAKE 35 MINUTES

Here's an hors d'oeuvre that will positively establish your reputation as a baker—a contemporary finger food that's worlds away from the usual crackers and chips. The peppery puffs hold a mixture of cream cheese and goat cheese, freshened with chopped parsley. Blue-cheese fans will find a pleasing variation below.

1 TEASPOON BLACK PEPPERCORNS
CHOUX PASTRY (PAGE 269)
8 OUNCES GOAT CHEESE, SOFTENED
1 PACKAGE (3 OUNCES) CREAM CHEESE, SOFTENED
2 TABLESPOONS MILK
1 TABLESPOON CHOPPED FRESH PARSLEY

1 Place peppercorns in zip-tight plastic bag. Crush with rolling pin.

2 Preheat oven to 400° F. Grease 2 large cookie sheets. Prepare Choux Pastry; stir in crushed peppercorns. Drop batter by rounded teaspoons, 1½ inches apart, onto prepared cookie sheets.

3 Bake 35 minutes, rotating sheets between upper and lower racks halfway through baking, or until deep golden. Transfer puffs to wire racks to cool.

4 In medium bowl, combine goat cheese, cream cheese, milk, and parsley until blended. Spoon filling into pastry bag fitted with ¼-inch round tip. Insert tip into side of each cooled puff and pipe in filling to fill halfway. *Makes about 4 dozen puffs.*

EACH PUFF: ABOUT 60 CALORIES, 2 G PROTEIN,
2 G CARBOHYDRATE, 5 G TOTAL FAT (3 G SATURATED),
0 G FIBER, 29 MG CHOLESTEROL, 65 MG SODIUM.

BLACK PEPPER PUFFS WITH BLUE-CHEESE FILLING
Prepare puffs as above and cool. Use blue-cheese filling for goat cheese filling: In bowl, combine *1 package (8 ounces) cream cheese*, softened, *3 ounces blue cheese*, crumbled, *2 tablespoons milk*, and *1 tablespoon chopped fresh parsley* until blended. Fill as directed.
EACH PUFF: ABOUT 55 CALORIES, 2 G PROTEIN,
2 G CARBOHYDRATE, 5 G TOTAL FAT (3 G SATURATED),
0 G FIBER, 29 MG CHOLESTEROL, 75 MG SODIUM.

Cheddar Curry Puffs

PREP 20 MINUTES / BAKE 25 TO 30 MINUTES

Here's an innovative example of "fusion cuisine." French puff pastry meets English Cheddar cheese and Indian curry seasonings. Serve these powerfully flavored puffs alongside a platter of chilled raw vegetable sticks and cherry tomatoes for a refreshing contrast.

2 TEASPOONS CURRY POWDER
½ TEASPOON GROUND CORIANDER
½ TEASPOON GROUND CUMIN
¼ TEASPOON GROUND RED PEPPER (CAYENNE)
1 CUP WATER
6 TABLESPOONS BUTTER OR MARGARINE, CUT UP
½ TEASPOON SALT
1 CUP ALL-PURPOSE FLOUR
4 LARGE EGGS
4 OUNCES CHEDDAR CHEESE, SHREDDED (1 CUP)

1 Preheat oven to 400° F. Grease 2 large cookie sheets.

2 In 3-quart saucepan, heat curry powder, coriander, cumin, and ground red pepper over medium heat, stirring constantly, 1 minute, or until very fragrant. Stir in water, butter, and salt; heat to boiling over high heat. Remove saucepan from heat. With wooden spoon, vigorously stir in flour all at once; place over medium-low heat, and stir constantly until mixture forms ball and leaves side of pan. Remove saucepan from heat.

3 Add eggs, 1 at a time, beating well after each addition, until batter is smooth and satiny. Stir in cheese. Spoon batter into large bag fitted with large writing tip (about ½-inch diameter). Pipe batter, about 1 inch apart, onto prepared cookie sheets, forming mounds 1" wide by ¾" high. Or, drop batter by teaspoons, forming small mounds. With fingertip dipped in water, gently smooth peaks.

4 Bake 25 to 30 minutes, rotating sheets between upper and lower racks halfway through baking, until deep golden. Transfer to wire racks to cool. Serve puffs warm or at room temperature.

5 Repeat with remaining batter. *Makes about 8 dozen puffs.*

EACH PUFF: ABOUT 20 CALORIES, 1 G PROTEIN,
1 G CARBOHYDRATE, 1 G TOTAL FAT (1 G SATURATED),
0 G FIBER, 12 MG CHOLESTEROL, 30 MG SODIUM.

PHYLLO DOUGH

One of the best things about phyllo (filo) dough is that you don't have to make it yourself! These paper-thin leaves of pastry—a Greek and Middle-Eastern specialty—are sold ready-made, either refrigerated or frozen. A one-pound package contains about 30 sheets of dough, which is made from flour, water, oil, and salt. If you buy it frozen, thaw the whole package for several hours, or until you can separate the leaves. When you're ready to start baking, remove only as many leaves as you need, wrap the remainder in plastic wrap, and refreeze them for another time. If the pastry sheets dry out, they will become too brittle to handle, so always keep phyllo covered with a damp kitchen cloth as you work with it.

Phyllo Tart Shell

PREP 10 MINUTES / BAKE 15 MINUTES

Brushed with melted butter, the layers of phyllo bake up crisp and delicate. This 9-inch shell is suitable for sweet or savory fillings.

3 TABLESPOONS BUTTER OR MARGARINE, MELTED
5 SHEETS (16" BY 12" EACH) FRESH OR FROZEN
  (THAWED) PHYLLO

1 Preheat oven to 375° F. Lightly brush 9-inch pie plate, including rim, with melted butter.

2 On surface, brush 1 phyllo sheet with some melted butter. Keep remaining phyllo covered with plastic wrap to prevent it from drying out. Place sheet over prepared pie plate; gently pat onto bottom and side of pie plate. Brush second phyllo sheet with some melted butter. Place second sheet over pie plate at slight angle on top of first sheet. Gently pat sheet onto bottom and side of pie plate. Repeat layering with remaining phyllo and melted butter, placing each sheet at slight angle from previous one. Roll overhang toward center to form rim.

3 Bake 15 minutes, or until golden. Cool on wire rack. Fill with desired filling. *Makes one 9-inch shell.*

EACH 1/10 PASTRY: ABOUT 60 CALORIES, 1 G PROTEIN,
5 G CARBOHYDRATE, 4 G TOTAL FAT (2 G SATURATED),
0 G FIBER, 9 MG CHOLESTEROL, 80 MG SODIUM.

Baklava

Packaged phyllo makes this deservedly famous Greek pastry easy to prepare at home. Just layer the sheets of phyllo with the sweet, cinnamony walnut filling, bake, and then soak the whole pan of pastry with warm honey. Food of the gods!

4 CUPS WALNUTS (ABOUT 16 OUNCES), FINELY CHOPPED
½ CUP SUGAR
1 TEASPOON GROUND CINNAMON
1 PACKAGE (16 OUNCES) FRESH OR FROZEN (THAWED) PHYLLO (ABOUT 16 SHEETS)
¾ CUP BUTTER OR MARGARINE (1½ STICKS), MELTED
1 CUP HONEY

1 Preheat oven to 300° F. Grease 13" by 9" glass or ceramic baking dish. In large bowl, combine walnuts, sugar, and cinnamon.

2 Trim phyllo sheets into 13" by 9" rectangles. Cover phyllo with plastic wrap to prevent it from drying out. In prepared baking dish, place 1 phyllo sheet; brush with some melted butter. Repeat to make 5 more layers of phyllo; sprinkle 1 cup walnut mixture over phyllo.

3 Place 1 phyllo sheet in baking dish over walnut mixture; brush with some melted butter. Repeat to make at least 6 layers of phyllo, overlapping small strips of phyllo to make rectangles, if necessary. Sprinkle 1 cup walnut mixture over phyllo. Repeat layering 2 more times, ending with walnut mixture.

4 Place remaining phyllo on top of walnut layer; brush with some melted butter. With sharp knife, cut lengthwise just halfway through layers into 3 equal strips; cut each strip crosswise into 4 rectangles; then cut each rectangle diagonally into 2 triangles. Bake 1 hour 25 minutes, or until top is golden brown.

5 Meanwhile, in small saucepan, heat honey over medium-low heat until hot but not boiling. Spoon hot honey evenly over hot baklava. Cool baklava in pan on wire rack at least 1 hour. Cover and let stand at room temperature until serving.

6 To serve, with sharp knife, cut all the way through triangles. *Makes 24 servings.*

EACH SERVING: ABOUT 265 CALORIES, 4 G PROTEIN, 25 G CARBOHYDRATE, 18 G TOTAL FAT (5 G SATURATED), 1 G FIBER, 16 MG CHOLESTEROL, 115 MG SODIUM.

Phyllo Tartlets

A creamy filling is best for these crisp, light shells (see box below for some suggestions). Pop the shells out of the pan carefully, using the tip of a small knife if they don't come out easily.

2 TABLESPOONS BUTTER OR MARGARINE, MELTED
6 SHEETS (16" BY 12" EACH) FRESH OR FROZEN (THAWED) PHYLLO

1 Preheat oven to 375° F.

2 On surface, brush 1 phyllo sheet with some melted butter. Cover remaining phyllo with plastic wrap to prevent it from drying out. Cover with second phyllo sheet; brush with some melted butter. Repeat with third sheet of phyllo. With long sharp knife, cut phyllo into twelve 4-inch squares. Gently pat 1 square onto bottom and up side of twelve 2½-inch muffin-pan cups.

3 Repeat buttering, layering, and cutting into squares with remaining 3 phyllo sheets and melted butter. Arrange 1 square at a right angle on top of each phyllo square in muffin-pan cups.

4 Bake 12 minutes, or until phyllo is crisp and golden. Cool in pan on wire rack. Carefully remove from pan. Fill just before serving. *Makes 12 tartlet shells.*

EACH SHELL: ABOUT 45 CALORIES, 1 G PROTEIN, 5 G CARBOHYDRATE, 2 G TOTAL FAT (1 G SATURATED), 0 G FIBER, 5 MG CHOLESTEROL, 65 MG SODIUM.

TARTLET FILLINGS

BAKE A BATCH OF PHYLLO TARTLETS AND CREATE YOUR OWN FILLINGS FOR THEM: SPOON IN A SWEETENED OR FLAVORED WHIPPED CREAM, PASTRY CREAM, OR SWEETENED RICOTTA. GARNISH WITH BERRIES, SLICED FRESH FRUIT, CHOCOLATE CURLS, CHOCOLATE MINI-CHIPS, CHOPPED CRYSTALLIZED GINGER, OR MINT SPRIGS. OR FILL THE SHELLS WITH FRESH FRUIT AND PIPE WHIPPED CREAM DECORATIVELY ON TOP.

Phyllo Tartlets

Apple Strudel

PREP 1 HOUR PLUS COOLING / BAKE 35 TO 40 MINUTES

One of the trickiest jobs in baking is making strudel dough, which includes hand-stretching a tissue-sheer piece of dough to the size of a tabletop. Packaged phyllo eliminates all that intensive labor but does not sacrifice the light delicate pastry.

½ CUP BUTTER OR MARGARINE (1 STICK)
4 POUNDS GRANNY SMITH APPLES (8 LARGE), PEELED,
   CORED, AND CUT INTO ½-INCH PIECES
½ CUP DARK SEEDLESS RAISINS
⅔ CUP PLUS ¼ CUP GRANULATED SUGAR
¼ CUP WALNUTS, TOASTED AND GROUND
¼ CUP PLAIN DRIED BREAD CRUMBS
½ TEASPOON GROUND CINNAMON
¼ TEASPOON GROUND NUTMEG
8 SHEETS (16" BY 12" EACH) FRESH OR FROZEN
   (THAWED) PHYLLO
CONFECTIONERS' SUGAR

1 In 12-inch skillet, melt 2 tablespoons butter over medium heat. Add apples, raisins, and ⅔ cup sugar. Cook, uncovered, stirring occasionally, 15 minutes. Increase heat to medium-high and cook 15 minutes longer, or until liquid has evaporated and apples are tender but not brown. Remove skillet from heat; cool completely.

2 Meanwhile, in small bowl, stir together remaining ¼ cup sugar, walnuts, bread crumbs, cinnamon, and nutmeg until thoroughly combined.

3 Preheat oven to 400° F. In small saucepan, melt remaining 6 tablespoons butter. Cut two 24-inch-long sheets of waxed paper; arrange sheets overlapping 2 long sides by about 2 inches. Place 1 sheet of phyllo on waxed paper. Brush phyllo with melted butter. Cover remaining phyllo with plastic wrap to prevent it from drying out. Sprinkle phyllo sheet with 2 scant tablespoons bread-crumb mixture. Top with another sheet of phyllo and brush lightly with butter; sprinkle with 2 scant tablespoons crumb mixture. Continue layering phyllo, brushing each sheet with melted butter and sprinkling with scant 2 tablespoons crumb mixture. Reserve 1 tablespoon melted butter.

4 Spoon cooled apple filling along long side furthest from you, leaving about ¾-inch border from edges; cover about one-third of phyllo rectangle. Using waxed paper to help lift roll, from the side furthest from you, roll up phyllo jelly-roll fashion. Place roll,

seam side down, diagonally on large cookie sheet. Tuck in ends of roll. Brush with remaining 1 tablespoon melted butter.

5 Bake 35 to 40 minutes, or until phyllo is golden and filling is hot (cover with foil during the last 10 minutes of baking if strudel is overbrowning). Cool on cookie sheet on wire rack about 20 minutes before slicing. Before serving, sprinkle with confectioners' sugar. *Makes 10 servings.*

EACH SERVING: ABOUT 340 CALORIES, 2 G PROTEIN,
58 G CARBOHYDRATE, 13 G TOTAL FAT (6 G SATURATED),
4 G FIBER, 25 MG CHOLESTEROL, 190 MG SODIUM.

APPLE-CRANBERRY STRUDEL Use apple-cranberry filling for apple filling: In 12-inch skillet, melt *4 tablespoons butter or margarine* over medium heat. Add *3 pounds Golden Delicious apples (about 6 large)*, peeled, cored, and cut into ½-inch pieces, *1½ cups cranberries, ½ cup dark seedless raisins, ½ teaspoon ground cinnamon*, and *½ cup sugar*. Cook, uncovered, stirring occasionally, 12 minutes. Increase heat to medium-high and cook about 10 minutes longer, until liquid has evaporated and apples are tender but not brown. Remove skillet from heat; cool completely. Prepare phyllo as for Apple Strudel and bake as directed.
EACH SERVING: ABOUT 285 CALORIES, 2 G PROTEIN,
44 G CARBOHYDRATE, 13 G TOTAL FAT (7 G SATURATED),
3 G FIBER, 31 MG CHOLESTEROL, 190 MG SODIUM.

PEAR STRUDEL Use pear filling for apple filling: Prepare filling as directed but use *4 pounds Bartlett pears*, peeled, cored, and cut into ½-inch pieces, for apples and only *½ cup sugar*. In Step 1, cook pear filling 35 minutes in all; cool completely. Prepare phyllo as for Apple Strudel and bake as directed.
EACH SERVING: ABOUT 320 CALORIES, 3 G PROTEIN,
52 G CARBOHYDRATE, 13 G TOTAL FAT (6 G SATURATED),
5 G FIBER, 25 MG CHOLESTEROL, 190 MG SODIUM.

CHERRY STRUDEL Use cherry filling for apple filling: In 4-quart saucepan, heat *2 cans (16 ounces each) tart cherries packed in water*, drained (½ cup liquid reserved), *1 cup sugar, ¼ cup cornstarch, 1 tablespoon fresh lemon juice*, and *¼ teaspoon ground cinnamon* to boiling over medium-high heat, stirring occasionally. Reduce heat to medium-low; boil 1 minute. Remove saucepan from heat; stir in *½ teaspoon vanilla extract*; cool completely. Prepare phyllo as for Apple Strudel and bake as directed.
EACH SERVING: ABOUT 230 CALORIES, 2 G PROTEIN,
40 G CARBOHYDRATE, 8 G TOTAL FAT (4 G SATURATED),
0 G FIBER, 19 MG CHOLESTEROL, 150 MG SODIUM.

DRIED FRUIT STRUDEL Use dried fruit filling for apple filling: In 2-quart saucepan, heat *2 cups mixed dried fruit*, cut into 1-inch pieces, *1 cup dried figs*, cut into 1-inch pieces, *2 strips (3" by 1" each) lemon peel*, *1 cinnamon stick (3 inches)*, and *1¾ cups water* to boiling over high heat, stirring occasionally. Reduce heat to medium; cook 20 minutes, or until all liquid has been absorbed; cool. Remove lemon peels and cinnamon stick. Prepare phyllo as for Apple Strudel and bake as directed.

EACH SERVING: ABOUT 235 CALORIES, 3 G PROTEIN, 42 G CARBOHYDRATE, 8 G TOTAL FAT (4 G SATURATED), 4 G FIBER, 19 MG CHOLESTEROL, 150 MG SODIUM.

CHEESE STRUDEL Use cheese filling: In large bowl, with mixer at medium speed, beat *1 package (8 ounces) cream cheese*, softened, *¼ cup sugar*, and *1 tablespoon cornstarch* 1 minute, until blended. Fold in *1 cup ricotta cheese, 1 teaspoon freshly grated lemon peel*, and *½ teaspoon vanilla.* Cover and refrigerate. Prepare phyllo as for Apple Strudel and fill with cheese filling. Place 2 sheets of foil under cookie sheet; crimp edges to form rim to catch any overflow during baking. Bake as directed.

EACH SERVING: ABOUT 255 CALORIES, 6 G PROTEIN, 16 G CARBOHYDRATE, 19 G TOTAL FAT (11 G SATURATED), 0 G FIBER, 56 MG CHOLESTEROL, 230 MG SODIUM.

Mushroom-Potato Strudel

PREP 45 MINUTES PLUS COOLING
BAKE 40 TO 45 MINUTES

For a tasty appetizer, serve half slices on a bed of greens topped with sour cream and fresh chives.

1½ POUNDS BAKING POTATOES (3 LARGE), PEELED AND THICKLY SLICED

1½ TEASPOONS SALT

9 TABLESPOONS BUTTER OR MARGARINE

2 GARLIC CLOVES, FINELY CHOPPED

8 OUNCES SHIITAKE MUSHROOMS, STEMS REMOVED AND CAPS COARSELY CHOPPED

8 OUNCES WHITE MUSHROOMS, STEMS TRIMMED AND CAPS COARSELY CHOPPED

2 TABLESPOONS SNIPPED CHIVES

6 SHEETS (16" BY 12" EACH) FRESH OR FROZEN (THAWED) PHYLLO

3 TABLESPOONS PLAIN DRIED BREAD CRUMBS

1 In 2½-quart saucepan, combine potatoes and cold *water* to cover by 1 inch. Heat to boiling, add 1 teaspoon salt, and boil 15 minutes, or until potatoes are tender. Drain, reserving 2 tablespoons potato cooking liquid. Return potatoes to saucepan. Add 2 tablespoons butter and reserved potato cooking liquid; with potato masher, mash until smooth.

2 Meanwhile, in 12-inch skillet, melt 2 tablespoons butter over low heat. Add garlic and cook, stirring frequently, 2 minutes, or until tender. Add shiitake mushrooms, increase heat to medium, and cook, stirring frequently, 5 minutes, or until almost tender. Stir in white mushrooms and remaining ½ teaspoon salt and cook, stirring frequently, 5 minutes, or until tender and dry. Stir mushroom mixture and chives into potato mixture.

3 In small saucepan, melt remaining 5 tablespoons butter over low heat. Cool to room temperature.

4 Preheat oven to 375° F. Grease 15½" by 10½" jelly-roll pan. Lay 1 phyllo sheet on kitchen towel with long side facing you. Brush with some melted butter and top with second phyllo sheet. Brush with some melted butter and sprinkle with 1 tablespoon bread crumbs. Top with 2 more phyllo sheets, brushing each with some melted butter. Sprinkle with 1 tablespoon bread crumbs. Top with remaining 2 phyllo sheets, brushing each with some melted butter. Sprinkle with remaining 1 tablespoon bread crumbs.

5 Spoon mushroom-potato mixture along long side furthest from you, leaving 1-inch border at top and ends. Flatten mixture slightly. Fold ends over filling. Using the towel as your guide, roll phyllo up from the long side furthest from you to form a log. Roll log, seam side down, off towel onto prepared jelly-roll pan. With serrated knife, make slashes at 1-inch intervals down length of log. Brush with remaining melted butter.

6 Bake 40 to 45 minutes, until golden brown. Cool. To serve, cut into 8 slices. *Makes 8 main-dish servings.*

EACH SERVING: ABOUT 235 CALORIES, 4 G PROTEIN, 24 G CARBOHYDRATE, 15 G TOTAL FAT (8 G SATURATED), 2 G FIBER, 35 MG CHOLESTEROL, 520 MG SODIUM.

Strawberry Napoleons

PREP **45** MINUTES / BAKE **10** MINUTES

These are easier to make than traditional Napoleons and are a pleasant change from strawberry shortcake.

1 LARGE EGG WHITE

PINCH SALT

1 TEASPOON WATER

4 SHEETS (16" BY 12" EACH) FRESH OR FROZEN
 (THAWED) PHYLLO

3 TABLESPOONS BUTTER OR MARGARINE, MELTED

⅓ CUP PLUS 1 TABLESPOON SUGAR

½ CUP SLICED NATURAL ALMONDS

¾ CUP HEAVY OR WHIPPING CREAM

½ TEASPOON VANILLA EXTRACT

1 PINT STRAWBERRIES, HULLED AND SLICED

1 Preheat oven to 375° F. In small bowl, lightly beat egg white and salt with water. Lay 1 phyllo sheet on surface; brush with some melted butter and sprinkle with about 1 rounded tablespoon sugar. Top with second phyllo sheet; brush with some melted butter and sprinkle with 1 rounded tablespoon sugar. Repeat layering with third phyllo, some melted butter, and sugar. Top with remaining phyllo and brush with egg-white mixture.

2 With sharp knife or pizza wheel, cut phyllo lengthwise into 3 equal strips, then cut each strip crosswise into 4 squares. Cut each square diagonally in half to make 24 triangles. Place phyllo triangles on ungreased large cookie sheet; sprinkle with sliced almonds and 1 rounded tablespoon sugar. Bake 10 minutes, or until golden. With wide spatula, transfer to wire racks to cool.

3 Just before serving, in small bowl, with mixer at medium speed, beat cream with vanilla and remaining 1 tablespoon sugar until stiff peaks form.

Strawberry Napoleons

4 To assemble, place 1 phyllo triangle in center of each of 8 dessert plates. Top each with about 1 tablespoon whipped cream and about 1 rounded tablespoon sliced strawberries. Place a second phyllo triangle on top of each, rotating it so that points of second triangle are angled slightly away from points of first triangle. Top triangles with remaining whipped cream and strawberries, dividing them equally; top each dessert with third triangle. Serve immediately. *Makes 8 napoleons.*

EACH NAPOLEON: ABOUT 230 CALORIES, 3 G PROTEIN, 20 G CARBOHYDRATE, 16 G TOTAL FAT (8 G SATURATED), 1 G FIBER, 42 MG CHOLESTEROL, 125 MG SODIUM.

Galatoboureko

PREP 50 MINUTES PLUS COOLING / BAKE 35 MINUTES

This Greek dessert consists of a thick vanilla custard between phyllo crusts; the pastry is soaked with lemon syrup while still warm. Serve warm or chilled.

6 CUPS MILK

2 STRIPS (3" BY 1" EACH) ORANGE PEEL

¾ CUP QUICK-COOKING ENRICHED FARINA CEREAL

¾ CUP SUGAR

4 LARGE EGGS

2 TEASPOONS VANILLA EXTRACT

8 OUNCES (ABOUT 16 SHEETS) FRESH OR FROZEN
   (THAWED) PHYLLO

½ CUP BUTTER OR MARGARINE (1 STICK), MELTED

LEMON SYRUP (AT RIGHT)

1 Preheat oven to 350° F. Grease 13" by 9" glass or ceramic baking dish. In 3-quart saucepan, heat milk and orange peel to boiling over medium-high heat. In small bowl, combine farina and sugar; gradually sprinkle into milk mixture, stirring with spoon; heat to boiling. Reduce heat to medium-low and cook, stirring, 5 minutes, or until mixture thickens slightly. Remove saucepan from heat. Discard orange peel.

2 In large bowl, with mixer at high speed, beat eggs and vanilla well. Reduce speed to medium and gradually beat in farina mixture.

3 Place 1 phyllo sheet in prepared baking dish, allowing it to extend up side of dish; brush with some melted butter. Repeat to make 5 more layers,

brushing each with melted butter. Pour farina mixture into phyllo-lined dish.

4 Cut remaining phyllo into approximately 13" by 9" rectangles. Place 1 phyllo sheet on farina; brush with some melted butter. Repeat with remaining phyllo and butter, overlapping phyllo to make rectangles, if necessary. With sharp knife, cut top phyllo layers only lengthwise into 4 equal strips; then cut each strip crosswise into 6 pieces. Bake 35 minutes, or until top is golden and puffy.

5 Meanwhile, prepare Lemon Syrup. Pour hot syrup evenly over hot dessert. Cool in pan on wire rack at least 2 hours before serving.

6 To serve, with sharp knife, cut all the way through layers. Serve warm or cover and refrigerate to serve chilled. *Makes 24 servings.*

EACH SERVING: ABOUT 180 CALORIES, 4 G PROTEIN, 25 G CARBOHYDRATE, 7 G TOTAL FAT (4 G SATURATED), 0 G FIBER. 54 MG CHOLESTEROL, 140 MG SODIUM.

LEMON SYRUP In 1-quart saucepan, heat ¾ cup sugar, ⅓ cup water, and 4 strips lemon peel (3" by 1" each) to boiling over medium heat, stirring occasionally. Reduce heat and simmer 8 minutes, or until syrup thickens slightly. Discard peel and stir in 1 tablespoon fresh lemon juice. *Makes about ¾ cup.*
EACH TABLESPOON: ABOUT 24 CALORIES, 0 G PROTEIN, 6 G CARBOHYDRATE, 0 G TOTAL FAT (0 G SATURATED), 0 G FIBER. 0 MG CHOLESTEROL, 0 MG SODIUM.

GREEK DESSERTS

THE PASTRIES, CAKES, AND COOKIES OF THE GREEK ISLANDS ARE OFTEN FLAVORED WITH ORANGE OR LEMON, HONEY, BRANDY, OR CINNAMON, AND MADE WITH WALNUTS, ALMONDS, OR PISTACHIOS. ALONG WITH BAKLAVA (PAGE 276) AND GALATOBOUREKO (AT LEFT), SOME OTHER FAVORITES ARE KOURAMBIEDES (RICH LITTLE BUTTER COOKIES); YAOURTINI (A BRANDIED YOGURT CAKE); AND KADAIFI (FILLED "BIRD'S NESTS" MADE WITH A SHREDDED PHYLLO-LIKE DOUGH THAT RESEMBLES SHREDDED WHEAT).

Bisteeya

PREP 1 HOUR 30 MINUTES / BAKE 45 MINUTES

One of the defining dishes of Moroccan cuisine, bisteeya is an elaborate banquet dish consisting of layers of fine, flaky pastry, cut-up squab, eggs, and a sweetened almond filling. A classic bisteeya is prepared with 20-inch rounds of a special pastry called "warka," but packaged phyllo dough makes an excellent substitute. To approximate a Moroccan feast—considerably scaled down—follow the bisteeya with a dessert of fresh fruit salad flavored with rosewater (or a platter of dried figs, apricots, dates, and nuts); accompany the fruit with simple butter cookies and sweetened mint tea.

CHICKEN FILLING:

4 POUNDS CHICKEN LEG QUARTERS
1 MEDIUM ONION, FINELY CHOPPED
⅓ CUP FRESH CILANTRO LEAVES, CHOPPED
1 CINNAMON STICK (3 INCHES)
1 TEASPOON COARSELY GROUND BLACK PEPPER
¾ TEASPOON GROUND GINGER
½ TEASPOON SALT
¼ TEASPOON GROUND TURMERIC
PINCH SAFFRON THREADS

ALMOND FILLING:

8 OUNCES NATURAL OR BLANCHED ALMONDS, TOASTED
½ CUP CONFECTIONERS' SUGAR
2 TEASPOONS GROUND CINNAMON
3 TABLESPOONS UNSALTED BUTTER, MELTED

EGG FILLING:

¼ CUP FRESH LEMON JUICE
10 LARGE EGGS, LIGHTLY BEATEN
¼ TEASPOON SALT

PHYLLO LAYERS:

5 TABLESPOONS UNSALTED BUTTER, MELTED
8 SHEETS (16" BY 12" EACH) FRESH OR FROZEN
  (THAWED) PHYLLO

GARNISH:

2 TEASPOONS CONFECTIONERS' SUGAR
1 TEASPOON GROUND CINNAMON

1 Prepare Chicken Filling: In 5-quart Dutch oven, combine Chicken Filling ingredients and *3 cups water*; heat to boiling over high heat. Reduce heat to low; cover and simmer 30 minutes, or until chicken loses its pink color throughout. With slotted spoon, transfer chicken to large plate; cool until easy to han-

dle. Skim fat and reserve broth. Discard cinnamon stick. Shred chicken into small pieces; discard skin and bones.

2 Prepare Almond Filling: In food processor with knife blade attached, pulse toasted almonds, confectioners' sugar, and cinnamon until nuts are finely ground. Transfer to small bowl and stir in melted butter.

3 Prepare Egg Filling: In Dutch oven, heat reserved broth to boiling over high heat. Boil broth 20 to 30 minutes, until reduced to 2 cups. Reduce heat to low and stir in lemon juice. Pour beaten eggs into simmering broth, stirring frequently, until eggs are set. Pour egg mixture into colander to drain excess liquid. Transfer egg mixture to plate to cool; sprinkle with salt.

4 Prepare Phyllo Layers: Preheat oven to 400° F. Brush 13" by 9" metal baking pan with some melted butter. Remove phyllo from package; cover with plastic wrap to prevent it from drying out. On waxed paper, lightly brush 1 phyllo sheet with some melted butter. Place sheet crosswise in half of the pan, allowing phyllo to drape over sides and one end of pan. Place a second phyllo sheet crosswise in other end of pan. Top each sheet with 1 more phyllo sheet, but do not brush with butter. Repeat layering one more time to make 2 layers, 4 sheets in all.

5 Place cooled shredded chicken pieces over phyllo; top with cooled egg mixture and sprinkle with almond filling. Fold overhanging edges of phyllo over filling. Place 1 phyllo sheet lengthwise over filling, tucking edges in to fit top; do not brush with butter. Repeat with another phyllo sheet; lightly brush this sheet with some melted butter. Repeat layering 1 more time, to make 4 sheets in all.

6 Bake pie 25 minutes, or until lightly golden. Remove pan from oven; cover with large baking sheet and invert hot pie onto baking sheet. Bake pie 20 minutes longer, or until golden.

7 To garnish pie, cut 1-inch-wide strips of waxed paper. Place strips diagonally, 1 inch apart, on top of pie. In cup, mix confectioners' sugar and cinnamon. Sprinkle spaces between strips with some sugar mixture. Carefully remove strips and discard. *Makes 16 servings.*

EACH SERVING: ABOUT 310 CALORIES, 21 G PROTEIN, 14 G CARBOHYDRATE, 19 G TOTAL FAT (6 G SATURATED), 2 G FIBER, 200 MG CHOLESTEROL, 250 MG SODIUM.

Bisteeya

Spanakopita

PREP 1 HOUR / BAKE 35 TO 40 MINUTES

You can prepare the spinach filling for this popular Greek pastry a day ahead of time; refrigerate it, covered, until needed. Let the filling come to room temperature while you prepare the bottom crust.

6 TABLESPOONS BUTTER OR MARGARINE
1 JUMBO ONION (1 POUND), FINELY CHOPPED
4 PACKAGES (10 OUNCES EACH) FROZEN CHOPPED
   SPINACH, THAWED AND SQUEEZED DRY
8 OUNCES FETA CHEESE, CRUMBLED
1 CUP PART-SKIM RICOTTA CHEESE
½ CUP CHOPPED FRESH DILL
¼ TEASPOON SALT
¼ TEASPOON COARSELY GROUND BLACK PEPPER
3 LARGE EGGS
10 SHEETS (16" BY 12" EACH) FRESH OR FROZEN
   (THAWED) PHYLLO

1 In 12-inch skillet, melt 2 tablespoons butter over medium-high heat until hot. Add onion and cook, stirring occasionally, about 15 minutes, until tender and lightly browned.

2 Transfer onion to large bowl. Stir in spinach, feta, ricotta, dill, salt, pepper, and eggs until combined.

3 Preheat oven to 400° F. Melt remaining 4 tablespoons butter. Cover phyllo with plastic wrap to prevent it from drying out. Lightly brush bottom and sides of 11" by 7" glass or ceramic baking dish with some melted butter. On waxed paper, lightly brush 1 phyllo sheet with some melted butter. Place phyllo sheet into prepared baking dish, pressing against sides of dish and allowing edges to overhang sides. Lightly brush second phyllo sheet with some melted butter; place over first sheet. Repeat, buttering and layering 3 more times, for a total of 5 sheets. Spread spinach filling evenly over phyllo

4 Fold overhanging edges of phyllo over filling. Cut remaining 5 phyllo sheets crosswise in half. On waxed paper, lightly brush 1 phyllo piece with some melted butter. Place on top of filling. Repeat with remaining cut phyllo, brushing each piece lightly with butter.

5 Bake 35 to 40 minutes, hot in center and phyllo is golden. Cool slightly. *Makes 16 appetizers.*

EACH APPETIZER: ABOUT 175 CALORIES, 8 G PROTEIN,
13 G CARBOHYDRATE, 10 G TOTAL FAT (6 G SATURATED),
2 G FIBER, 69 MG CHOLESTEROL, 380 MG SODIUM.

Spring Vegetable Pie

PREP 35 MINUTES / BAKE 40 TO 45 MINUTES

½ CUP BUTTER OR MARGARINE (1 STICK)
6 GREEN ONIONS, THINLY SLICED (1 CUP)
2 POUNDS THIN ASPARAGUS, TRIMMED AND CUT INTO
   1-INCH PIECES
1 TEASPOON SALT
1 TEASPOON DRIED MINT
1 CONTAINER (32 OUNCES) PART-SKIM RICOTTA CHEESE
⅔ CUP FRESHLY GRATED PARMESAN CHEESE
3 LARGE EGGS
½ TEASPOON GROUND BLACK PEPPER
8 SHEETS (16" BY 12" EACH) FRESH OR FROZEN
   (THAWED) PHYLLO
10½ TEASPOONS PLAIN DRIED BREAD CRUMBS

1 In 12-inch skillet, melt 2 tablespoons butter over medium heat. Add green onions and cook 2 minutes, or until tender. Add asparagus, ½ teaspoon salt, and ½ teaspoon mint and cook, stirring frequently, 10 minutes, or until tender. Cool to room temperature.

2 Preheat oven to 375° F. Butter 13" by 9" metal baking pan. In large bowl, stir together ricotta, Parmesan, eggs, pepper, remaining ½ teaspoon salt, and remaining ½ teaspoon mint. Stir in asparagus mixture until combined.

3 In small saucepan, melt remaining 6 tablespoons butter. Fit 1 phyllo sheet into bottom and up sides of prepared pan. Brush with some melted butter and sprinkle with 1½ teaspoons bread crumbs. Repeat layering, buttering, and sprinkling with bread crumbs until you have 5 layers of phyllo. Spread ricotta mixture over phyllo.

4 Top with 1 phyllo sheet, brush with butter, and sprinkle with 1½ teaspoons bread crumbs. Top with another sheet of phyllo, brush with melted butter, and sprinkle with remaining 1½ teaspoons bread crumbs. Top with remaining sheet of phyllo and brush with remaining melted butter. With knife, make several slashes into top layers of phyllo, cutting through to filling.

5 Bake 40 to 45 minutes, or until filling is set and phyllo is golden brown. Cool in pan on wire rack 10 minutes. *Makes 8 main-dish servings.*

EACH SERVING: ABOUT 420 CALORIES, 23 G PROTEIN,
23 G CARBOHYDRATE, 27 G TOTAL FAT (15 G SATURATED),
1 G FIBER, 154 MG CHOLESTEROL, 850 MG SODIUM.

Parmesan Pepper Sticks

PREP 30 MINUTES / BAKE 5 TO 8 MINUTES PER BATCH

Scrolled pastry sticks rich with Parmesan are a cut above the usual breadsticks. Serve these with soup or salad, or as a party snack. They can be prepared ahead of time and baked just before serving.

12 SHEETS (16" BY 12" EACH) FRESH OR FROZEN
  (THAWED) PHYLLO
4 TABLESPOONS BUTTER OR MARGARINE, MELTED
½ CUP FRESHLY GRATED PARMESAN CHEESE
1½ TABLESPOONS COARSELY GROUND BLACK PEPPER

Phyllo Triangles

Make a "sandwich" of two sheets of phyllo (depending on the recipe, there may be something in between). Use a pastry wheel to cut the phyllo into five long, narrow strips. Place a spoonful of filling at the short end of one strip.

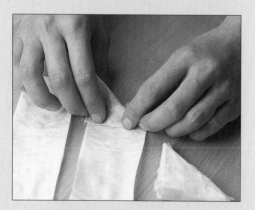

Fold the short end diagonally over the filling so that it meets the long side. Flip this triangle upward. Continue folding until you have a small triangular packet. If you've ever folded the flag at camp, this will be very familiar!

1 On sheet of waxed paper, place 1 phyllo sheet and brush with some melted butter. Cover remaining phyllo with plastic wrap to prevent it from drying out. Sprinkle 2 teaspoons Parmesan and ⅛ teaspoon pepper over sheet. Fold sheet in half crosswise. Starting from long open side, roll phyllo up tightly, jelly-roll fashion, toward folded side. Cut roll crosswise to make 4 sticks. Place sticks, seam side down, 1 inch apart, on large cookie sheet; brush with some melted butter.

2 Repeat with remaining phyllo, butter, cheese, and pepper, making 48 sticks in all. If not serving right away, cover sticks with foil and refrigerate.

3 Preheat oven to 425° F. Bake sticks 5 to 8 minutes, until golden brown. Serve hot or at room temperature. *Makes 4 dozen sticks.*

EACH STICK: ABOUT 30 CALORIES, 1 G PROTEIN,
3 G CARBOHYDRATE, 2 G TOTAL FAT (1 G SATURATED),
0 G FIBER, 3 MG CHOLESTEROL, 50 MG SODIUM.

Black Bean & Cheese Triangles

PREP 35 MINUTES / BAKE 15 MINUTES PER BATCH

The phyllo is brushed with spiced oil instead of butter to add extra Mexican flavor to these turnovers. The photos at left show how to fold the triangles.

½ CUP OLIVE OIL
¼ TEASPOON GROUND CUMIN
¼ TEASPOON GROUND RED PEPPER (CAYENNE)
1 CAN (15 TO 16 OUNCES) BLACK BEANS, WELL DRAINED
4 OUNCES MONTEREY JACK CHEESE, FINELY CHOPPED
½ CUP FRESH CILANTRO, CHOPPED
1 LARGE PLUM TOMATO, FINELY CHOPPED
1 LARGE PICKLED JALAPEÑO CHILE, MINCED
24 SHEETS (16" BY 12" EACH) FRESH OR FROZEN
  (THAWED) PHYLLO

1 Preheat oven to 375° F. In small saucepan, combine oil, cumin, and ground red pepper over low heat until warm.

2 In medium bowl, combine beans, cheese, cilantro, tomato, and pickled jalapeño. With back of large spoon, mash beans against side of bowl, stirring until mixture holds together.

3 Place 1 phyllo sheet on surface with a short end facing you. Cover remaining phyllo with plastic wrap to prevent it from drying out. Brush sheet with oil mixture. Top with second phyllo sheet and brush with oil mixture. With pastry wheel or sharp knife, cut phyllo lengthwise into 5 equal strips (see top photo opposite). Place rounded teaspoon of filling at end of one strip. Fold one corner of strip diagonally over filling so that short edge meets long edge of strip, forming a right angle. Continue folding over at right angles to form a triangular-shaped package (see bottom photo opposite). Place, seam side down, on large cookie sheet. Brush lightly with oil mixture. Repeat with remaining phyllo, oil, and filling, placing triangles 1 inch apart.

4 Bake 15 minutes, or until golden brown and crisp. (Filling may leak out in a few spots.) With wide spatula, transfer triangles to wire rack to cool slightly. Serve warm. *Makes 5 dozen triangles.*

EACH TRIANGLE: ABOUT 50 CALORIES, 1 G PROTEIN, 5 G CARBOHYDRATE, 3 G TOTAL FAT (1 G SATURATED), 0.5 G FIBER, 2 MG CHOLESTEROL, 75 MG SODIUM.

Mushroom-Hazelnut Triangles

PREP 40 MINUTES / BAKE 15 MINUTES PER BATCH

This wonderful combination of shiitake and portobello mushrooms, garlicky cheese, and the surprise of sweet hazelnuts fills these festive hors d'oeuvres.

⅔ CUP HAZELNUTS (FILBERTS)

3 TABLESPOONS CHOPPED FRESH PARSLEY

1 CONTAINER (10 OUNCES) WHITE MUSHROOMS, HALVED

8 OUNCES PORTOBELLO MUSHROOM CAPS, CUT INTO
    1-INCH PIECES

8 OUNCES SHIITAKE MUSHROOMS, STEMS REMOVED AND
    CAPS ROUGHLY CHOPPED

¾ CUP BUTTER OR MARGARINE (1½ STICKS)

2 SHALLOTS, MINCED (¼ CUP)

½ TEASPOON SALT

¼ TEASPOON GROUND BLACK PEPPER

1 PACKAGE (4 TO 5 OUNCES) SOFT SPREADABLE CHEESE
    WITH GARLIC AND HERBS

1 PACKAGE (16 OUNCES) FRESH OR FROZEN (THAWED)
    PHYLLO

1 Preheat oven to 350° F. Place hazelnuts in 9" by 9" metal baking pan. Bake 15 minutes, or until toasted. Wrap hot hazelnuts in clean cloth towel. With hands, roll hazelnuts back and forth to remove most of skins. Cool completely. In food processor with knife blade attached, finely chop hazelnuts. In small bowl, combine hazelnuts and parsley.

2 Turn oven control to 375° F. In food processor with knife blade attached, finely chop white, portobello, and shiitake mushrooms in batches.

3 In large skillet, melt 2 tablespoons butter over medium heat. Add shallots and cook 3 minutes, or until softened. Add mushrooms, salt, and pepper; increase heat to medium-high, and cook, stirring frequently, until mushrooms are dry and any liquid has evaporated. Transfer filling to bowl and refrigerate until cool. Add cheese and stir until well blended.

4 In small saucepan, melt remaining 10 tablespoons butter. Place 1 phyllo sheet on surface with a short end facing you. Cover remaining phyllo with plastic wrap to prevent it from drying out. Brush sheet lightly with some melted butter. Sprinkle with 2 teaspoons hazelnut mixture. Top with second phyllo sheet and brush lightly with some melted butter. With pastry wheel or sharp knife, cut phyllo lengthwise into 5 equal strips (see top photo opposite). Place rounded measuring teaspoon of filling at the end of one strip. Fold one corner of strip diagonally over filling so that short edge meets long edge of strip, forming a right angle. Continue folding over at right angles to form a triangular-shaped package (see bottom photo opposite). Place, seam side down, on large cookie sheet. Brush lightly with some melted butter. Repeat with remaining phyllo, melted butter, hazelnut mixture, and mushroom filling, placing triangles 1 inch apart.

5 Bake 15 minutes, or until golden brown and crisp. With wide spatula, transfer triangles to wire rack to cool. Serve warm. *Makes 70 triangles.*

EACH TRIANGLE: ABOUT 55 CALORIES, 1 G PROTEIN, 5 G CARBOHYDRATE, 4 G TOTAL FAT (2 G SATURATED), 0 G FIBER, 7 MG CHOLESTEROL, 85 MG SODIUM.

Greek Cheese Pastries

PREP 2 HOURS 30 MINUTES / BAKE 15 TO 20 MINUTES

This recipe gives you a choice of three ways to shape these "bourekakia me tyri." Choose one—tidy rolls, flag-folded triangles, or plump little bundles—or divide up the phyllo sheets and make some of each. To prepare the pastries ahead of time, shape and fill them, then freeze them in jelly-roll pans until firm. Transfer the frozen pastries to freezer boxes, separating the layers with waxed paper. At serving time, bake the unthawed pastries in a preheated oven (400° F) for 20 minutes, or until golden.

1 PACKAGE (8 OUNCES) FETA CHEESE
1 CUP PART-SKIM RICOTTA CHEESE
¼ CUP CHOPPED FRESH PARSLEY
½ TEASPOON COARSELY GROUND BLACK PEPPER
2 LARGE EGGS
1 POUND (ABOUT 30 SHEETS) FRESH OR FROZEN
  (THAWED) PHYLLO
½ CUP BUTTER OR MARGARINE (1 STICK), MELTED

1 In medium bowl, with fork, finely crumble feta; stir in ricotta, parsley, pepper, and eggs.

2 With knife, cut phyllo as directed for Rolls, Triangles, and Bundles (see below). Place cut phyllo on waxed paper, then cover with plastic wrap to prevent it from drying out.

3 Grease 15½" by 10½" jelly-roll pans. Prepare appetizers as directed below. Place, about 1 inch apart, on prepared jelly-roll pans. Brush pastries with some melted butter. If not serving right away, cover with plastic wrap and refrigerate.

4 Preheat oven to 400° F. Bake pastries 15 to 20 minutes, until golden. (If Bundles brown too quickly, cover loosely with foil partway through cooking.) *Makes about 6 dozen appetizers.*

EACH APPETIZER: ABOUT 40 CALORIES, 1 G PROTEIN,
3 G CARBOHYDRATE, 3 G TOTAL FAT (2 G SATURATED),
0 G FIBER, 13 MG CHOLESTEROL, 75 MG SODIUM.

ROLLS Cut stack of 6 phyllo sheets crosswise into 4 strips. Brush 1 strip lightly with some melted butter. Place 1 rounded teaspoon filling on center at end of strip. Roll strip with filling one-third of way, then fold left and right sides over roll; continue rolling to end. Repeat to make 24 rolls.

TRIANGLES Cut stack of 5 sheets phyllo lengthwise into 5 strips (see top photo, page 286). Brush 1 strip lightly with melted butter. Place 1 rounded teaspoon filling at end of strip. Fold one corner of strip diagonally over filling. Continue folding over at right angles to form a triangular-shaped package (see bottom photo, page 286). Repeat to make 25 triangles.

BUNDLES Cut stack of 5 sheets phyllo lengthwise into 4 strips, then cut each strip crosswise into 5 squares. Place 2 squares on top of each other, brush top lightly with melted butter. Layer 2 more squares crosswise over first 2; brush with melted butter. Place 1 rounded teaspoon filling in center; crimp phyllo around filling. Repeat to make 25 bundles.

Spinach Cigars

PREP 1 HOUR / BAKE 20 TO 22 MINUTES PER BATCH

Hold the matches—these are for eating, not smoking! They're mini phyllo rolls stuffed with a ricotta-and-spinach mixture seasoned with Middle-Eastern herbs and spices.

1 PACKAGE (10 OUNCES) FROZEN CHOPPED SPINACH,
  THAWED
1 CUP PART-SKIM RICOTTA CHEESE
2 OUNCES CRUMBLED FETA CHEESE (½ CUP)
¼ CUP FRESHLY GRATED PARMESAN CHEESE
1 LARGE EGG
3 GREEN ONIONS, CHOPPED
½ TEASPOON DRIED MINT
½ TEASPOON GROUND CUMIN
¼ TEASPOON GROUND CORIANDER
¼ TEASPOON GROUND RED PEPPER (CAYENNE)
¼ TEASPOON GROUND BLACK PEPPER
12 SHEETS (16" BY 12" EACH) FRESH OR FROZEN
  (THAWED) PHYLLO
½ CUP BUTTER OR MARGARINE (1 STICK), MELTED

1 Squeeze spinach dry. In large bowl, combine spinach, ricotta, feta, Parmesan, egg, green onions, mint, cumin, coriander, and ground red and black peppers. Stir until blended.

2 Preheat oven to 375° F. Place 1 phyllo sheet on surface with a short end facing you. Cover remaining phyllo with plastic wrap to prevent it from drying out. Brush lightly with some melted butter. Top with second phyllo sheet and brush with some melted butter.

3 With pastry wheel or sharp knife, cut phyllo in half crosswise and lengthwise to make 4 rectangles. Place 1 rounded tablespoon filling in strip at one short end of each rectangle, ½ inch from end and sides. Roll phyllo up loosely. Place, seam side down, on ungreased large cookie sheet. Brush lightly with some melted butter. Repeat with remaining phyllo, melted butter, and filling.

4 Bake 20 to 22 minutes, until golden brown. With wide spatula, transfer to wire rack to cool. Serve warm. *Makes 24 cigars.*

EACH CIGAR: ABOUT 95 CALORIES, 3 G PROTEIN, 6 G CARBOHYDRATE, 6 G TOTAL FAT (4 G SATURATED), 0.5 G FIBER, 25 MG CHOLESTEROL, 155 MG SODIUM.

Samosas

PREP 35 MINUTES / BAKE 15 MINUTES PER BATCH

A favorite first course in Indian restaurants, samosas are little fried turnovers filled with spicy ground meat (keema samosa) or highly seasoned potatoes and peas (aloo samosa). For these simplified samosas, phyllo replaces homemade pastry. With a nod to today's health-conscious cooking, these filled pastries are baked, rather than deep-fried.

3 BAKING POTATOES, (1½ POUNDS), PEELED AND CUT INTO
   1-INCH CHUNKS
1¼ TEASPOONS SALT
1 TEASPOON CUMIN SEEDS
¼ CUP OLIVE OIL
1 MEDIUM ONION, FINELY CHOPPED (1 CUP)
2 LARGE GARLIC CLOVES, MINCED
¼ TEASPOON GROUND BLACK PEPPER
¼ TEASPOON GROUND RED PEPPER (CAYENNE)
⅛ TEASPOON GROUND TURMERIC
⅛ TEASPOON GROUND CARDAMOM
½ CUP FROZEN PEAS
⅓ CUP LOW-FAT PLAIN YOGURT
½ CUP BUTTER OR MARGARINE (1 STICK), MELTED
1 PACKAGE (16 OUNCES) FRESH OR FROZEN (THAWED)
   PHYLLO

1 In 3-quart saucepan, cover potatoes with *water*, add ½ teaspoon salt, and heat to boiling. Reduce heat and simmer, covered, until tender, about 15 minutes.

2 While potatoes are cooking, toast cumin seeds in a 10-inch skillet over medium-low heat, shaking skillet frequently, until fragrant, about 4 minutes.

3 In skillet, heat 2 tablespoons oil over medium-low heat. Add onion and cook, stirring frequently, until golden brown, about 10 minutes. Stir in remaining ¾ teaspoon salt, garlic, black and ground red peppers, turmeric, cardamom, and peas. Cook, stirring frequently, 2 minutes. Remove skillet from heat.

4 Drain potatoes well and while still hot, add to skillet. With potato masher, mash potatoes, leaving some chunks. Stir in yogurt. Transfer mixture to bowl and cover loosely. Refrigerate about 1 hour, until cool.

5 Preheat oven to 375° F. Stir remaining 2 tablespoons oil into melted butter. Place 1 phyllo sheet on surface with a short end facing you. Cover remaining phyllo with plastic wrap to prevent it from drying out. Brush lightly with some butter mixture. Top with second phyllo sheet. With pastry wheel or sharp knife, cut sheets lengthwise into 5 equal strips (see top photo, page 286). Place a heaping measuring teaspoon of filling at the end of strip. Fold one corner of strip diagonally over filling so that short edge meets long edge of strip, forming a right angle. Continue folding over at right angles to form a triangular-shaped package (see bottom photo, page 286). Place, seam side down, 1 inch apart, on large cookie sheet. Brush lightly with butter mixture. Repeat with remaining phyllo, butter mixture, and filling, placing triangles 1 inch apart. Use 32 sheets of phyllo in all.

6 Bake 15 minutes, or until golden brown and crisp. With wide spatula, transfer to wire rack to cool. Serve warm or room temperature. *Makes 80 samosas.*

EACH SAMOSA: ABOUT 40 CALORIES, 1 G PROTEIN, 5 G CARBOHYDRATE, 2 G TOTAL FAT (1 G SATURATED), 0 G FIBER, 3 MG CHOLESTEROL, 70 MG SODIUM.

Cakes

layer cake pans

Bundt pan

jelly-roll pan

springform pan

tube pan

Cakes

To give your cakes their due, use good-quality pans. Heavy-gauge aluminum ones are among the best. Look for pans with well-sealed seams (if any) and nicely rounded edges. A non-stick surface is useful on some bakeware, such as Bundt and tube pans, but for layer pans such a finish is not necessary or desirable. **Layer cake pans** are kitchen basics—both round and square, in 8- and 9-inch sizes. You'll need at least two round layer pans—three if you make three-layer cakes. European baking traditions are echoed in the **Bundt pan,** a large, deeply fluted tube pan. A 12-cup (10-inch) Bundt pan has the same capacity as a 10-inch tube pan (Bundt cake recipes can also be baked in two 9" by 5" loaf pans). The **jelly-roll pan** is, appropriately enough, used for baking thin sheet cakes that are to be rolled around fillings. It can also be used, upside down, as a cookie sheet. The **springform pan,** used for cheesecakes and some tortes, has a removable side that closes tightly with a clasp. When the cake has been baked and cooled, the side is unfastened and removed, and the cake is served on the base. For baking chiffon and angel-food cakes, you'll need a **tube pan** (10-inch is the standard size) with a removable bottom, which makes it easier to remove these delicate cakes from the pan.

Previous page: Classic Devil's Food Cake

Basic techniques

GÉNOISE

The eggs and sugar have been beaten long enough when the mixture is very thick. It should fall in a thick ribbon when the beaters are lifted.

To add dry ingredients, sift half over the beaten egg mixture, and then gently fold in; repeat with remaining half. Do not stir or beat the batter.

Many génoise recipes require the layers to be halved horizontally. Using a long, serrated knife, cut through the cake with a sawing motion.

JELLY-ROLL CAKES

Loosen the cake for a jelly roll from the sides of the pan, then flip it out onto a kitchen towel that has been sprinkled with confectioners' sugar.

Starting at one short end, roll the still-warm cake up in the towel. Letting the cake cool this way makes it easier to roll the filled cake.

ANGEL-FOOD CAKE

Cool angel-food or chiffon cake upside down. If the pan doesn't have "feet" to stand it on, slip the tube of the pan onto the neck of a bottle.

Slide a paring knife around the edge of the pan to loosen any parts that might stick. Then turn the cake out.

LAYERS, LOAVES & SPECIAL CAKES

Here's your basic "wardrobe" of cakes, including chocolate, carrot, devil's food, and gingerbread, as well as special-occasion desserts such as Chocolate Truffle Cake and Greek Walnut Cake. If you're new to cake-baking from scratch, start with the Yellow Cake recipe below, and then try some of the variations that follow. For perfect results, always be sure to use the pan size called for in the recipe.

Yellow Cake

PREP 35 MINUTES PLUS COOLING / BAKE 30 MINUTES

There are few desserts as straightforward and purely good as a slice of all-American yellow cake filled and topped with chocolate frosting. Except, maybe, your own personal yellow cupcake iced with that same frosting. Our coconut, orange, and "tweed" variations are also sure to please.

2 CUPS ALL-PURPOSE FLOUR
2 TEASPOONS BAKING POWDER
1 TEASPOON SALT
½ CUP VEGETABLE SHORTENING OR ½ CUP BUTTER OR
    MARGARINE (1 STICK), SOFTENED
1¼ CUPS SUGAR
3 LARGE EGGS
1 TEASPOON VANILLA EXTRACT
1 CUP MILK
CHOCOLATE BUTTER FROSTING (PAGE 353) OR DESIRED
    FROSTING

1 Preheat oven to 350° F (325° F if baking 9" by 9" cake). Grease and flour two 8-inch round cake pans, or one 9" by 9" metal baking pan.

2 In medium bowl, stir together flour, baking powder, and salt.

3 In large bowl, with mixer at medium speed, beat shortening and sugar until light and fluffy, about 5 minutes. Add eggs, 1 at a time, beating well after each addition. Beat in vanilla. Reduce speed to low; add flour mixture alternately with milk, beginning and ending with flour mixture. Beat just until smooth, scraping bowl frequently with spatula.

4 Spoon batter into prepared pans. Bake 8-inch layers about 30 minutes, 9" by 9" cake 40 to 45 min-

utes, until toothpick inserted in center of cake comes out clean. Cool in pans on wire racks 10 minutes. With small knife, loosen layers from sides of pans; invert onto wire racks to cool completely.

5 Meanwhile, prepare Chocolate Butter Frosting. Place 1 cake layer, rounded side down, on cake plate; spread with ⅔ cup frosting. Top with second layer, rounded side up. Frost side and top of cake with remaining frosting. *Makes 12 servings.*

EACH SERVING: ABOUT 540 CALORIES, 5 G PROTEIN, 82 G CARBOHYDRATE, 23 G TOTAL FAT (10 G SATURATED), 1 G FIBER, 78 MG CHOLESTEROL, 385 MG SODIUM.

COCONUT CAKE Prepare batter as for Yellow Cake and bake in two 8-inch round cake pans as directed. Prepare Fluffy White Frosting (page 359). From *1 package (7 ounces) flaked sweetened coconut*, measure out 1 cup and, in bowl, combine with 1 cup frosting. Spread on cake layer. Top with remaining cake layer and frost as above with remaining frosting. Sprinkle top and sides of cake with remaining coconut.
EACH SERVING: ABOUT 425 CALORIES,6 G PROTEIN, 64 G CARBOHYDRATE, 17 G TOTAL FAT(8 G SATURATED), 2 G FIBER, 56 MG CHOLESTEROL,355 MG SODIUM.

FRESH ORANGE CAKE Prepare batter as for Yellow Cake and add *1 teaspoon freshly grated orange peel* with vanilla. Bake in two 8-inch round cake pans and cool as directed. Frost with Orange Butter Frosting (page 353) or Fluffy White Frosting (page 359).
EACH SERVING WITH ORANGE BUTTER FROSTING: ABOUT 495 CALORIES, 5 G PROTEIN, 77 G CARBOHYDRATE, 19 G TOTAL FAT (8 G SATURATED), 0.5 G FIBER, 77 MG CHOLESTEROL, 385 MG SODIUM.

TWEED CAKE Prepare batter as for Yellow Cake and fold in *4 squares (4 ounces) semisweet chocolate*, grated on coarse side of grater. Bake and frost as directed.
EACH SERVING WITH CHOCOLATE BUTTER FROSTING: ABOUT 585 CALORIES, 6 G PROTEIN, 88 G CARBOHYDRATE, 25 G TOTAL FAT (11 G SATURATED), 1 G FIBER, 78 MG CHOLESTEROL, 385 MG SODIUM.

CUPCAKES Prepare batter as for Yellow Cake. Line twenty-four 2½-inch muffin-pan cups with fluted paper liners. Pour batter into cups and bake 20 to 25 minutes, until toothpick inserted in center of cupcake comes out clean. Cool; frost tops with Chocolate Butter Frosting (page 353), or frosting of choice. *Makes 24 cupcakes.*
EACH CUPCAKE WITH CHOCOLATE BUTTER FROSTING: ABOUT 265 CALORIES, 3 G PROTEIN, 41 G CARBOHYDRATE, 11 G TOTAL FAT (5 G SATURATED), 0.5 G FIBER, 39 MG CHOLESTEROL, 190 MG SODIUM.

Coconut Cake

Blitz Torte

PREP 25 MINUTES PLUS COOLING
BAKE 20 TO 25 MINUTES

"Blitz" means lightning, and this is one of the quickest cakes around. You'd never guess, though, by tasting it. The yellow-cake layers are crowned with meringue and filled with sweetened whipped cream and raspberries. Don't make the cake only with berries, though—try it with peaches, substituting sour cream sweetened with brown sugar for the whipped cream.

1 CUP ALL-PURPOSE FLOUR
1 TEASPOON BAKING POWDER
¼ TEASPOON SALT
⅓ CUP MILK
2 TEASPOONS VANILLA EXTRACT
1¼ CUPS PLUS 1 TABLESPOON SUGAR
½ CUP BUTTER OR MARGARINE (1 STICK), SOFTENED
3 LARGE EGGS, SEPARATED
¼ CUP SLICED ALMONDS
½ CUP HEAVY OR WHIPPING CREAM
½ PINT RASPBERRIES

1 Preheat oven to 350° F. Grease and flour two 8-inch round cake pans. In medium bowl, stir together flour, baking powder, and salt. In measuring cup, mix milk and 1½ teaspoons vanilla.

2 In large bowl, with mixer at low speed, beat ½ cup sugar and butter until blended. Increase speed to high; beat 2 minutes, or until creamy. Reduce speed to medium-low; add yolks, 1 at a time, beating well after each addition. Reduce speed to low; add flour mixture alternately with milk mixture, beginning and ending with flour mixture. Beat until smooth, scraping bowl occasionally with rubber spatula. Divide batter evenly between prepared pans.

3 In large bowl, with mixer at high speed, beat egg whites until soft peaks form when beaters are lifted. Sprinkle ¾ cup sugar, 2 tablespoons at a time, into egg whites, beating well after each addition, until sugar dissolves and whites stand in stiff glossy peaks when beaters are lifted.

4 Divide meringue evenly between pans, smoothing with small spatula. Sprinkle almonds over meringue layers. Bake 20 to 25 minutes, until meringue is golden and toothpick inserted in center of layers comes out clean. Cool in pans on wire racks 10 minutes. With small knife, loosen layers from sides of pans; invert gently onto wire racks; then invert again so that meringue sides are up. Cool completely.

5 Just before serving, in medium bowl with mixer at high speed, beat cream, remaining 1 tablespoon sugar, and remaining ½ teaspoon vanilla until soft peaks form.

6 Place 1 cake layer, meringue side down, on serving plate; spread with whipped cream. Top with berries. Top with second layer, meringue side up. *Makes 10 servings.*

EACH SERVING: ABOUT 335 CALORIES, 5 G PROTEIN,
40 G CARBOHYDRATE, 18 G TOTAL FAT (9 G SATURATED),
1 G FIBER, 106 MG CHOLESTEROL, 230 MG SODIUM.

Lemon Cake

PREP 1 HOUR PLUS COOLING AND CHILLING
BAKE 30 MINUTES

For a pastel four-layer cake, suitable for springtime celebrations, two layers of Yellow Cake are split and custardy Lemon Filling spread between them. The top and sides of the cake are then lavished with Lemon Butter Frosting.

LEMON FILLING (PAGE 361)
YELLOW CAKE (PAGE 294)
2 TEASPOONS FRESHLY GRATED LEMON PEEL
LEMON BUTTER FROSTING (PAGE 353)

1 Prepare Lemon Filling; cover and refrigerate until cold, about 3 hours.

2 Prepare batter for Yellow Cake and stir in grated lemon peel until combined. Divide batter between two greased and floured 8-inch round cake pans. Bake and cool as directed.

3 Meanwhile, prepare Lemon Butter Frosting. With serrated knife, split each cake layer in half horizontally, making 4 layers. Place 1 layer, cut side up on cake plate; spread with half of lemon filling up to ¼-inch from edge. Top with another layer, cut side down; spread with ½ cup frosting. Repeat with remaining 2 layers and filling. Frost side and top of cake with remaining frosting. Refrigerate cake until serving time. *Makes 12 servings.*

EACH SERVING: ABOUT 620 CALORIES, 6 G PROTEIN,
91 G CARBOHYDRATE, 27 G TOTAL FAT (12 G SATURATED),
0.5 G FIBER, 164 MG CHOLESTEROL, 445 MG SODIUM.

Golden Butter Cake

PREP **45** MINUTES PLUS COOLING
BAKE **23** TO **28** MINUTES

Imagine the buttery flavor of a pound cake, only lighter. This cake is luscious with any frosting. Or, fill it with jam, then dust it with confectioners' sugar.

3 CUPS CAKE FLOUR (NOT SELF-RISING)
1 TABLESPOON BAKING POWDER
½ TEASPOON SALT
1 CUP MILK
2 TEASPOONS VANILLA EXTRACT
2 CUPS SUGAR
1 CUP BUTTER OR MARGARINE (2 STICKS), SOFTENED
4 LARGE EGGS
SILKY ORANGE BUTTER FROSTING (PAGE 354) OR DESIRED FROSTING

1 Preheat oven to 350° F. Grease three 8-inch round cake pans or two 9-inch cake pans. Line bottoms with waxed paper; grease and flour paper.

2 In medium bowl, stir together flour, baking powder, and salt. In measuring cup, mix milk and vanilla.

3 In large bowl, with mixer at medium-high speed, beat sugar and butter until light and creamy, about 5 minutes. Add eggs, 1 at a time, beating well after each addition. Reduce speed to low; add flour mixture alternately with milk mixture, beginning and ending with flour mixture. Beat just until smooth, scraping bowl occasionally with rubber spatula.

4 Divide batter evenly among prepared pans. Stagger pans on 2 oven racks, placing 2 on upper rack and 1 on lower rack, so that pans are not directly above one another. Bake 23 to 28 minutes for 8-inch cake pans, or 23 to 25 minutes for 9-inch cake pans, until toothpick inserted in center of cake comes out clean. Cool on wire racks 10 minutes. With small knife, loosen layers from sides of pans; invert onto racks. Remove waxed paper; cool completely.

5 Meanwhile, prepare Silky Orange Butter Frosting. Place 1 cake layer on cake plate; spread with ⅔ cup frosting or whipped cream and berries, if you like. Top with second layer, ⅔ cup frosting, and remaining cake layer. Frost side and top of cake. *Makes 16 servings.*

EACH SERVING: ABOUT **485** CALORIES, **5** G PROTEIN, **58** G CARBOHYDRATE, **26** G TOTAL FAT (**16** G SATURATED), **0** G FIBER, **120** MG CHOLESTEROL, **430** MG SODIUM.

Whipped Cream Cake

PREP **15** MINUTES PLUS COOLING
BAKE **20** TO **25** MINUTES

Heavy or whipping cream takes the place of butter in this recipe, and you can "gild the lily" by filling and topping the cake with whipped cream. Serve with berries or sliced nectarines. Or, fill and frost the cake with your favorite butter frosting.

1½ CUPS CAKE FLOUR (NOT SELF-RISING)
2 TEASPOONS BAKING POWDER
½ TEASPOON SALT
¾ CUP SUGAR
2 LARGE EGGS
1 CUP HEAVY OR WHIPPING CREAM
1 TEASPOON VANILLA EXTRACT

1 Preheat oven to 350° F. Grease and flour two 8-inch round cake pans. In medium bowl, combine flour, baking powder, and salt.

2 In large bowl, with mixer at low speed, beat sugar and eggs until they form a ribbon when beaters are lifted. Add cream and vanilla and beat until thick and light (batter will not come to soft peaks).

3 Sift half of flour mixture over cream mixture; with rubber spatula, fold in just until blended. Repeat with remaining flour mixture.

4 Divide batter evenly between prepared pans. Bake 20 to 25 minutes, until cake pressed lightly with finger in middle springs back. Cool in pans on wire racks 10 minutes. With small knife, loosen layers from sides of pans; invert onto wire racks and cool completely. *Makes 10 servings.*

EACH SERVING: ABOUT **230** CALORIES, **3** G PROTEIN, **30** G CARBOHYDRATE, **11** G TOTAL FAT (**6** G SATURATED), **0** G FIBER, **75** MG CHOLESTEROL, **235** MG SODIUM.

Cardamom Buttermilk Cake

PREP 25 MINUTES PLUS COOLING / BAKE 30 MINUTES

Cardamom is often used in Scandinavian baking. This cake has a thin, crunchy pecan crust that beautifully complements the berry-and-cream filling.

2 TABLESPOONS PLUS ¾ CUP BUTTER OR MARGARINE
  (1½ STICKS), SOFTENED
¾ CUP PECANS, FINELY CHOPPED
1¼ CUPS PLUS 2 TABLESPOONS GRANULATED SUGAR
1 ORANGE
2 CUPS ALL-PURPOSE FLOUR
1 TEASPOON BAKING SODA
½ TEASPOON SALT
½ TEASPOON GROUND CARDAMOM
½ TEASPOON GROUND GINGER
1 CUP BUTTERMILK
1½ TEASPOONS VANILLA EXTRACT
½ CUP PACKED LIGHT BROWN SUGAR
2 LARGE EGGS
½ CUP HEAVY OR WHIPPING CREAM
½ PINT RASPBERRIES

1 Preheat oven to 350° F. Use the 2 tablespoons butter to generously grease two 9-inch round cake pans. In small bowl, stir together pecans and ¼ cup granulated sugar. Coat prepared pans with pecan mixture. From orange, grate ½ teaspoon peel and squeeze 2 tablespoons juice.

2 In bowl, stir together flour, baking soda, salt, cardamom, ginger, and orange peel. In second bowl, mix buttermilk, orange juice, and 1 teaspoon vanilla.

3 In large bowl, with mixer at medium speed, beat butter until smooth. Add 1 cup granulated sugar and brown sugar, beating until combined. Reduce speed to low. Add eggs, 1 at a time, beating well after each addition. Add flour mixture alternately with buttermilk mixture, beginning and ending with flour mixture. Beat until smooth, scraping bowl occasionally with rubber spatula.

4 Spoon batter into prepared pans. Bake 30 minutes or until toothpick inserted in center of layers comes out clean. Cool in pans on wire racks 10 minutes. With small knife, loosen layers from sides of pans; invert layers onto racks to cool completely.

5 In medium bowl, combine cream, remaining 2 tablespoons granulated sugar, and remaining ½ tea-spoon vanilla. With mixer at high speed, beat until stiff peaks form. Fold in raspberries.

6 Place 1 cake layer, nut side down, on cake plate. Spoon whipped-cream mixture over cake. Top with remaining layer, nut side up. Garnish with additional whipped cream and raspberries, if desired. Serve immediately, or refrigerate for up to 4 hours. *Makes 12 servings.*

EACH SERVING: ABOUT 420 CALORIES, 5 G PROTEIN, 52 G CARBOHYDRATE, 22 G TOTAL FAT (10 G SATURATED), 1 G FIBER, 81 MG CHOLESTEROL, 360 MG SODIUM.

Peanut Butter Cake

PREP 30 MINUTES PLUS COOLING
BAKE 35 TO 40 MINUTES

2 CUPS ALL-PURPOSE FLOUR
2 TEASPOONS BAKING POWDER
¾ CUP CREAMY PEANUT BUTTER
½ CUP BUTTER OR MARGARINE (1 STICK), SOFTENED
1 CUP GRANULATED SUGAR
½ CUP PACKED BROWN SUGAR
2 LARGE EGGS
2 TEASPOONS VANILLA EXTRACT
¾ CUP MILK
MILK CHOCOLATE FROSTING (PAGE 356)

1 Preheat oven to 350° F. Grease and flour 13" by 9" metal baking pan. In medium bowl, stir together flour and baking powder.

2 In large bowl, with mixer at medium speed, beat peanut butter, butter, and granulated and brown sugars 3 minutes, or until creamy. Add eggs, 1 at a time, beating well after each addition. Beat in vanilla. Reduce speed to low; add flour mixture alternately with milk, beginning and ending with flour mixture.

3 Turn batter into prepared pan and spread evenly. Bake 35 to 40 minutes, until toothpick inserted in center of cake comes out almost clean. Cool cake completely in pan on wire rack.

4 Meanwhile, prepare Milk Chocolate Frosting. Frost top of cake. *Makes 12 servings.*

EACH SERVING: ABOUT 615 CALORIES, 9 G PROTEIN, 67 G CARBOHYDRATE, 36 G TOTAL FAT (18 G SATURATED), 2 G FIBER, 103 MG CHOLESTEROL, 425 MG SODIUM.

Lazy Daisy Cake

PREP 25 MINUTES / BAKE 35 TO 40 MINUTES

Of course you're not lazy, but you're probably busy! The broiled-on coconut-pecan topping saves time and an extra step of making a separate frosting.

1⅓ CUPS ALL-PURPOSE FLOUR
1½ TEASPOONS BAKING POWDER
½ TEASPOON SALT
¾ CUP PLUS 2 TABLESPOONS MILK
6 TABLESPOONS BUTTER OR MARGARINE
3 LARGE EGGS
1 CUP GRANULATED SUGAR
1½ TEASPOONS VANILLA EXTRACT
½ CUP PACKED LIGHT BROWN SUGAR
½ TEASPOON GROUND CINNAMON
½ CUP PECANS, FINELY CHOPPED
½ CUP FLAKED SWEETENED COCONUT

1 Preheat oven to 350° F. Grease and flour 9" by 9" metal baking pan. Into small bowl, sift flour, baking powder, and salt.

2 In saucepan, heat ¾ cup milk and 2 tablespoons butter over low heat until butter melts.

3 In small bowl, with mixer at medium-high speed, beat eggs 2 minutes, or until pale yellow. Gradually beat in granulated sugar. Beat 2 minutes, or until thick. Beat in vanilla. Transfer egg mixture to bowl.

4 Reduce speed to low; add flour mixture alternately with hot milk mixture, beginning and ending with flour mixture. Beat just until smooth, scraping bowl frequently with rubber spatula. Immediately pour batter into prepared pan.

5 Bake 35 to 40 minutes, until toothpick inserted in center of cake comes out clean. Place pan on wire rack while you make topping. Preheat broiler.

6 In medium saucepan, combine remaining 2 tablespoons milk, remaining 4 tablespoons butter, brown sugar, and cinnamon. Heat to boiling over medium heat, stirring occasionally. Remove saucepan from heat. Stir in pecans and coconut. Spoon topping over hot cake and spread to cover evenly.

7 Place pan in broiler 5 inches from heat, and broil 1 to 2 minutes, watching carefully and rotating pan, until topping is bubbly and browned. Cool completely on wire rack. *Makes 12 servings.*

EACH SERVING: ABOUT 280 CALORIES, 4 G PROTEIN, 40 G CARBOHYDRATE, 12 G TOTAL FAT (6 G SATURATED), 1 G FIBER, 71 MG CHOLESTEROL, 250 MG SODIUM.

Marmalade Cake

PREP 35 MINUTES PLUS COOLING
BAKE 25 TO 30 MINUTES

Many old American cake recipes include jam or jelly, either as an ingredient or as a filling. Here, orange marmalade is mixed into the batter. Decorate the frosted cake with bow knots, using long, thin slivers of orange peel, if you like.

2 CUPS ALL-PURPOSE FLOUR
½ TEASPOON BAKING POWDER
½ TEASPOON BAKING SODA
¼ TEASPOON SALT
½ CUP BUTTER OR MARGARINE (1 STICK), SOFTENED
1 CUP SUGAR
3 LARGE EGGS
1 CUP ORANGE MARMALADE
½ CUP BUTTERMILK
FLUFFY WHITE FROSTING (PAGE 359) OR SILKY ORANGE
   BUTTER FROSTING (PAGE 354)

1 Preheat oven to 350° F. Grease two 9-inch round cake pans. Line bottoms with waxed paper; grease and flour paper.

2 In medium bowl, stir together flour, baking powder, baking soda, and salt.

3 In large bowl, with mixer at medium speed, beat butter and sugar until light and creamy, about 5 minutes. Add eggs, 1 at a time, beating well after each addition. Beat in marmalade. Reduce speed to low; add flour mixture alternately with buttermilk, beginning and ending with flour mixture. Beat just until combined.

4 Pour batter evenly into prepared pans. Bake 25 to 30 minutes, until toothpick inserted in center of layers comes out clean. Cool in pans on wire racks 10 minutes. With small knife, loosen layers from sides of pans; invert onto racks. Remove waxed paper; cool completely.

5 Meanwhile, prepare Fluffy White Frosting. Place 1 cake layer on cake plate; spread with heaping 1 cup frosting. Place second layer on top; frost side and top of cake with remaining frosting. *Makes 12 servings.*

EACH SERVING WITH FLUFFY WHITE FROSTING: ABOUT 370 CALORIES, 5 G PROTEIN, 68 G CARBOHYDRATE, 10 G TOTAL FAT (5 G SATURATED), 0.5 G FIBER, 74 MG CHOLESTEROL, 250 MG SODIUM.

Banana Layer Cake

PREP 40 MINUTES PLUS COOLING / BAKE 30 MINUTES

The cake's flavor depends on the sweetness of the bananas, so use really ripe ones. If you like, garnish the cake with banana slices dipped in fresh lemon juice to maintain their color.

1 CUP MASHED FULLY RIPE BANANAS (2 TO 3 BANANAS)
¼ CUP BUTTERMILK
1 TEASPOON VANILLA EXTRACT
2 CUPS CAKE FLOUR (NOT SELF-RISING)
1 TEASPOON BAKING POWDER
½ TEASPOON BAKING SODA
¼ TEASPOON SALT
⅛ TEASPOON GROUND NUTMEG
1¼ CUPS SUGAR
½ CUP BUTTER OR MARGARINE (1 STICK), SOFTENED
2 LARGE EGGS
CREAM CHEESE FROSTING (PAGE 357)

1 Preheat oven to 350° F. Grease three 8-inch round cake pans. Line bottoms with waxed paper; grease and flour paper.

2 In small bowl, mix bananas, buttermilk, and vanilla. In medium bowl, stir together flour, baking powder, baking soda, salt, and nutmeg.

3 In large bowl, with mixer at medium speed, beat sugar and butter 5 minutes, or until light and creamy. Add eggs, 1 at a time, beating well after each addition. Reduce speed to low; add flour mixture alternately with banana mixture, beginning and ending with flour mixture. Beat just until smooth, scraping bowl occasionally with rubber spatula.

4 Divide batter evenly among prepared pans. Stagger pans on 2 oven racks, placing 2 on upper rack and 1 on lower rack, so that pans are not directly above one another. Bake 30 minutes, or until toothpick inserted in centers of layers comes out clean. Cool in pans on wire racks 10 minutes. With small knife, loosen layers from sides of pans; invert onto wire racks. Remove waxed paper; cool completely.

5 Meanwhile, prepare Cream Cheese Frosting. Place 1 cake layer on cake plate; spread with ½ cup frosting. Top with second layer, ½ cup frosting, and remaining layer. Frost side and top of cake with remaining frosting. *Makes 16 servings.*

EACH SERVING: ABOUT 355 CALORIES, 3 G PROTEIN,
53 G CARBOHYDRATE, 15 G TOTAL FAT (9 G SATURATED),
0 G FIBER, 66 MG CHOLESTEROL, 250 MG SODIUM.

Carrot Cake

PREP 40 MINUTES PLUS COOLING
BAKE 55 TO 60 MINUTES

2½ CUPS ALL-PURPOSE FLOUR
2 TEASPOONS BAKING SODA
2 TEASPOONS GROUND CINNAMON
1 TEASPOON BAKING POWDER
1 TEASPOON SALT
½ TEASPOON GROUND NUTMEG
4 LARGE EGGS
1 CUP GRANULATED SUGAR
¾ CUP PACKED LIGHT BROWN SUGAR
1 CUP VEGETABLE OIL
¼ CUP MILK
1 TABLESPOON VANILLA EXTRACT
3 CUPS LIGHTLY PACKED SHREDDED CARROTS (ABOUT 6 MEDIUM)
1 CUP WALNUTS, CHOPPED
¾ CUP DARK SEEDLESS RAISINS
CREAM CHEESE FROSTING (PAGE 357)

1 Preheat oven to 350° F. Grease 13" by 9" metal baking pan. Line bottom with waxed paper; grease paper. Dust with flour. Or, grease and flour 10-inch Bundt pan.

2 In medium bowl, stir together flour, baking soda, cinnamon, baking powder, salt, and nutmeg.

3 In large bowl, with mixer at medium-high speed, beat eggs and granulated and brown sugars 2 minutes, scraping bowl frequently with rubber spatula. Beat in oil, milk, and vanilla. Reduce speed to low; add flour mixture and beat until smooth, about 1 minute, scraping bowl frequently. Fold in carrots, walnuts, and raisins.

4 Pour batter into prepared pan. Bake 55 to 60 minutes for 13" by 9" cake, about 1 hour for Bundt cake, until toothpick inserted in center of cake comes out almost clean, with a few moist crumbs attached. Cool in pan on wire rack 10 minutes. With small knife, loosen cake from sides of pan; invert onto rack. Remove waxed paper; cool completely.

5 Meanwhile, prepare Cream Cheese Frosting. Place cake on large platter; spread frosting over top and sides of cake. *Makes 16 servings.*

EACH SERVING: ABOUT 550 CALORIES, 6 G PROTEIN,
71 G CARBOHYDRATE, 28 G TOTAL FAT (8 G SATURATED),
2 G FIBER, 77 MG CHOLESTEROL, 445 MG SODIUM.

Cranberry Upside-Down Cake

PREP 35 MINUTES
BAKE 1 HOUR TO 1 HOUR 10 MINUTES

This is an easy-to-prepare holiday dessert or brunch cake. Use unthawed frozen cranberries to save time.

¾ CUP BUTTER OR MARGARINE (1½ STICKS), SOFTENED

⅔ CUP PACKED LIGHT BROWN SUGAR

2 CUPS FRESH OR FROZEN CRANBERRIES

½ CUP PECANS, COARSELY CHOPPED

1½ CUPS ALL-PURPOSE FLOUR

2 TEASPOONS BAKING POWDER

3 LARGE EGGS, SEPARATED

1 CUP GRANULATED SUGAR

1 TEASPOON VANILLA EXTRACT

½ CUP MILK

1 Preheat oven to 350° F. Line inside of 9-inch springform pan with foil. Grease foil. Melt ¼ cup butter and pour into pan; tilt to coat bottom evenly. Sprinkle with brown sugar. Sprinkle with cranberries and pecans, spreading cranberries evenly. In medium bowl, stir together flour and baking powder.

2 In small bowl, with mixer at medium speed, beat egg whites until foamy. Increase speed to medium-high and beat until soft peaks form when beaters are lifted. Gradually beat in ¼ cup granulated sugar and beat until stiff peaks form when beaters are lifted.

3 In large bowl, with mixer at low speed, beat remaining ½ cup butter and remaining ¾ cup granulated sugar until blended. Increase speed to medium; beat 2 minutes, or until fluffy. Beat in egg yolks until well blended. Beat in vanilla.

4 Reduce speed to low. Beat in flour mixture alternately with milk just until blended. Stir in 1 large

Cranberry Upside-Down Cake

spoonful of beaten whites. In two additions, fold in remaining whites just until blended.

5 Turn batter into prepared pan and spread evenly. Bake 1 hour to 1 hour 10 minutes, until toothpick inserted in center of cake comes out clean. Cool in pan on wire rack 15 minutes. Invert cake onto cake plate, and remove sides of pan and foil. Cool completely. *Makes 12 servings.*

EACH SERVING: ABOUT 340 CALORIES, 4 G PROTEIN, 45 G CARBOHYDRATE, 17 G TOTAL FAT (8 G SATURATED), 1 G FIBER, 86 MG CHOLESTEROL, 225 MG SODIUM.

Pumpkin-Spice Cake

PREP 25 MINUTES PLUS COOLING
BAKE 55 TO 60 MINUTES

Canned solid pack pumpkin isn't just for pies. You can use it in baking muffins, cookies, and this luscious, sweetly glazed Bundt cake. The pumpkin makes the cake exceptionally moist, and pumpkin-pie spice adds that familiar and favorite fall flavor.

CAKE:
3½ CUPS ALL-PURPOSE FLOUR
1 TABLESPOON PUMPKIN-PIE SPICE
2 TEASPOONS BAKING POWDER
1 TEASPOON BAKING SODA
½ TEASPOON SALT
1 CAN (16 OUNCES) SOLID PACK PUMPKIN (NOT PUMPKIN-PIE MIX)
¼ CUP MILK
2 TEASPOONS VANILLA EXTRACT
1¾ CUPS GRANULATED SUGAR
1 CUP BUTTER OR MARGARINE (2 STICKS), SOFTENED
4 LARGE EGGS

BROWN BUTTER GLAZE:
6 TABLESPOONS BUTTER OR MARGARINE
½ CUP PACKED LIGHT BROWN SUGAR
2 TABLESPOONS MILK
1 TEASPOON VANILLA EXTRACT
1 CUP CONFECTIONERS' SUGAR

1 Preheat oven to 350° F. Grease and flour 10-inch Bundt pan.

2 Prepare Cake: In medium bowl, stir together flour, pumpkin-pie spice, baking powder, baking soda, and salt. In small bowl, mix pumpkin, milk, and vanilla.

3 In large bowl, with mixer at low speed, beat granulated sugar and butter until blended, scraping bowl frequently with rubber spatula. Increase speed to high; beat until creamy, about 5 minutes, scraping bowl occasionally. Reduce speed to low; add eggs, 1 at a time, beating well after each addition. Add flour mixture alternately with pumpkin mixture, beginning and ending with flour mixture. Beat just until smooth, scraping bowl occasionally.

4 Pour batter into prepared pan. Bake 55 to 60 minutes, until toothpick inserted in center of cake comes out almost clean. Cool in pan on wire rack 15 minutes. With small spatula, loosen cake from side of pan; invert onto wire rack. Cool completely.

5 When cake is cool, prepare Brown Butter Glaze: In 2-quart saucepan, heat butter over medium heat, stirring occasionally, until melted and golden brown, about 3 to 5 minutes. Add brown sugar and milk and whisk over low heat until sugar dissolves, about 2 minutes. Remove saucepan from heat; whisk in vanilla. Gradually whisk in confectioners' sugar, whisking until smooth, about 3 minutes. Cool glaze until slightly thickened, about 5 minutes, whisking occasionally.

6 Place cake on cake plate; pour glaze over cake, letting glaze drip down sides. *Makes 20 servings.*

EACH SERVING: ABOUT 340 CALORIES, 4 G PROTEIN, 49 G CARBOHYDRATE, 15 G TOTAL FAT (8 G SATURATED), 1 G FIBER, 77 MG CHOLESTEROL, 320 MG SODIUM.

PUMPKIN-PIE SPICE

A READY-MADE BLEND OF "WARM" SPICES FOR BAKING, PUMPKIN-PIE SPICE IS SOLD IN MOST SUPERMARKETS. BUT YOU CAN ALSO MIX UP YOUR OWN: COMBINE 1½ TEASPOONS GROUND CINNAMON, 1 TEASPOON GROUND GINGER, ¼ TEASPOON GROUND NUTMEG, AND ⅛ TEASPOON GROUND CLOVES. STIR TO COMBINE. THIS MAKES ROUGHLY 1 TABLESPOON—ENOUGH FOR THE RECIPE AT LEFT.

Spice Cake

PREP 30 MINUTES PLUS COOLING
BAKE 25 TO 30 MINUTES

Chocolate lovers alert: This fragrant, tender spice cake pairs beautifully with Silky Chocolate Butter Frosting (page 354).

2 CUPS ALL-PURPOSE FLOUR
1½ TEASPOONS GROUND CINNAMON
1 TEASPOON BAKING POWDER
½ TEASPOON BAKING SODA
½ TEASPOON GROUND GINGER
¼ TEASPOON GROUND NUTMEG
¼ TEASPOON SALT
½ CUP BUTTER OR MARGARINE (1 STICK), SOFTENED
½ CUP PACKED BROWN SUGAR
½ CUP GRANULATED SUGAR
2 LARGE EGGS
¼ CUP LIGHT (MILD) MOLASSES
½ CUP SOUR CREAM
½ CUP MILK
BURNT BUTTER FROSTING (PAGE 353)

1 Preheat oven to 350° F. Grease two 9-inch round cake pans. Line bottoms with waxed paper; grease and flour paper. In medium bowl, stir together flour, cinnamon, baking powder, baking soda, ginger, nutmeg, and salt.

2 In large bowl, with mixer at low speed, beat butter and brown and granulated sugars until blended. Increase speed to medium-high; beat 2 minutes, until creamy. Add eggs, 1 at a time, beating well after each addition. Beat in molasses until combined.

3 In measuring cup, with fork, mix sour cream and milk. Reduce speed to low. In three additions, add flour mixture alternately with sour-cream mixture, beginning and ending with flour mixture.

4 Divide batter between prepared pans; spreading it evenly. Bake 25 to 30 minutes, until toothpick inserted in center of layers comes out clean. Cool in pans on wire racks 10 minutes. With small knife, loosen layers from sides of pans; invert layers onto rack. Remove waxed paper; cool completely.

5 Meanwhile, prepare Burnt Butter Frosting. Place 1 cake layer on cake plate. Spread with ½ cup frosting. Top with second layer. Frost top and side with remaining frosting. *Makes 12 servings.*

EACH SERVING: ABOUT 495 CALORIES, 4 G PROTEIN,
77 G CARBOHYDRATE, 20 G TOTAL FAT (12 G SATURATED),
0.5 G FIBER, 83 MG CHOLESTEROL, 325 MG SODIUM.

Applesauce Spice Cake

PREP 20 MINUTES PLUS COOLING / BAKE 40 MINUTES

Served straight from the pan, this should be quite a hit with the after-school crowd. And a square or two of applesauce cake will be much appreciated by brown-baggers, unexpected guests, or midnight snackers.

2 CUPS ALL-PURPOSE FLOUR
1½ TEASPOONS GROUND CINNAMON
1 TEASPOON BAKING POWDER
½ TEASPOON BAKING SODA
½ TEASPOON GROUND GINGER
¼ TEASPOON GROUND NUTMEG
½ TEASPOON SALT
½ CUP BUTTER OR MARGARINE (1 STICK), SOFTENED
1 CUP PACKED DARK BROWN SUGAR
¼ CUP GRANULATED SUGAR
2 LARGE EGGS
1¼ CUPS UNSWEETENED APPLESAUCE
½ CUP DARK SEEDLESS RAISINS
CONFECTIONERS' SUGAR

1 Preheat oven to 350° F. Grease and flour 9" by 9" metal baking pan.

2 In medium bowl, stir together flour, cinnamon, baking powder, baking soda, ginger, nutmeg, and salt.

3 In large bowl, with mixer at low speed, beat butter and brown and granulated sugars until blended. Increase speed to medium-high; beat 3 minutes until well combined. Add eggs, 1 at a time, beating well after each addition. Reduce speed to low. Beat in applesauce (mixture may appear curdled). Beat in flour mixture until smooth, scraping bowl occasionally with rubber spatula. Stir in raisins.

4 Scrape batter into prepared pan and spread evenly. Bake 40 minutes, or until toothpick inserted in center of cake comes out clean. Cool completely in pan on wire rack. Before serving, sprinkle with confectioners' sugar. *Makes 9 servings.*

EACH SERVING: ABOUT 370 CALORIES, 5 G PROTEIN,
63 G CARBOHYDRATE, 12 G TOTAL FAT (7 G SATURATED),
2 G FIBER, 75 MG CHOLESTEROL, 385 MG SODIUM.

Honey Cake

PREP 15 MINUTES / BAKE 45 TO 55 MINUTES

Dark and glossy but not terribly rich, this cake is traditionally enjoyed during the Jewish New Year, when honey is eaten as a symbolic "sweetener" of the coming year. You might like to decorate the top (before baking) with a few whole blanched almonds, a traditional adornment for this cake

3 CUPS ALL-PURPOSE FLOUR
2½ TEASPOONS BAKING POWDER
1 TEASPOON BAKING SODA
½ TEASPOON SALT
½ TEASPOON GROUND CLOVES
¼ TEASPOON GROUND ALLSPICE
1 CUP HONEY
¾ CUP PACKED LIGHT BROWN SUGAR
¾ CUP STRONG BLACK COFFEE
¼ CUP VEGETABLE OIL
2 TABLESPOONS WHISKEY
2 TEASPOONS FRESHLY GRATED LEMON PEEL
3 LARGE EGGS
1 LARGE EGG YOLK

1 Preheat oven to 325° F. Grease two 8½" by 4½" metal loaf pans.

2 In medium bowl, stir together flour, baking powder, baking soda, salt, cloves, and allspice.

3 In large bowl, with mixer at medium speed, beat honey, brown sugar, coffee, oil, whiskey, and lemon peel until light and creamy. Beat in eggs and egg yolk, 1 at a time, beating well after each addition. Reduce speed to low. Beat in flour mixture just until combined.

4 Divide batter between prepared pans. Bake 45 to 55 minutes, until tops spring back when lightly touched and a toothpick inserted in center of loaves come out clean (tops may be a bit sticky). With small knife, loosen loaves from sides of pans; invert loaves onto wire racks. Turn loaves right side up and cool completely. *Makes 2 loaves, 12 slices each.*

EACH SLICE: ABOUT 160 CALORIES, 3 G PROTEIN,
31 G CARBOHYDRATE, 4 G TOTAL FAT (1 G SATURATED),
0.5 G FIBER, 35 MG CHOLESTEROL, 165 MG SODIUM.

Greek Walnut Cake

PREP 25 MINUTES / BAKE 35 TO 40 MINUTES

Toasted walnuts lend rich flavor to this cake, which is soaked with a warm honey-orange syrup after it's baked. If you chop the nuts in a food processor, use brief pulses so that the nuts do not become walnut butter.

CAKE:
2 CUPS ALL-PURPOSE FLOUR
1½ TEASPOONS BAKING POWDER
½ TEASPOON BAKING SODA
½ TEASPOON SALT
½ TEASPOON CINNAMON
¼ TEASPOON GROUND CLOVES
1 CUP BUTTER OR MARGARINE (2 STICKS), SOFTENED
1 CUP SUGAR
6 LARGE EGGS
1 TABLESPOON FRESHLY GRATED ORANGE PEEL
1 CONTAINER (8 OUNCES) PLAIN LOW-FAT YOGURT
1 CUP WALNUTS, TOASTED AND FINELY CHOPPED

SYRUP:
1 CUP SUGAR
½ CUP HONEY
¾ CUP WATER
FRESHLY GRATED PEEL OF 1 ORANGE

1 Preheat oven to 350° F. Grease 13" by 9" metal baking pan. Prepare Cake: In large bowl, stir together flour, baking powder, baking soda, salt, cinnamon, and cloves.

2 In large bowl, with mixer at medium speed, beat butter and sugar until light and fluffy. Add eggs, 1 at a time, beating well after each addition. Beat in orange peel. Reduce speed to low; add flour mixture alternately with yogurt, beginning and ending with flour mixture. Fold in walnuts.

3 Spoon batter into prepared pan, and smooth with rubber spatula. Bake 35 to 40 minutes, until toothpick inserted in center of cake comes out clean. Cool in pan on wire rack.

4 Meanwhile, prepare Syrup: In 1-quart saucepan, stir together sugar, honey, water, and orange peel. Bring to boiling over medium heat, stirring constantly. Simmer 5 minutes. Spoon lukewarm syrup over cake. Cool before slicing. *Makes 16 servings.*

EACH SERVING: ABOUT 375 CALORIES, 6 G PROTEIN,
49 G CARBOHYDRATE, 19 G TOTAL FAT (8 G SATURATED),
1 G FIBER, 112 MG CHOLESTEROL, 310 MG SODIUM.

Gingerbread

Gingerbread

PREP **10** MINUTES / BAKE **45** TO **50** MINUTES

Dense, old-fashioned gingerbread is perfect with a dollop of whipped cream. For a more cakelike result, beat the batter with an electric mixer for 2 minutes.

2 CUPS ALL-PURPOSE FLOUR

½ CUP SUGAR

2 TEASPOONS GROUND GINGER

1 TEASPOON GROUND CINNAMON

½ TEASPOON BAKING SODA

½ TEASPOON SALT

1 CUP LIGHT (MILD) MOLASSES

½ CUP BUTTER OR MARGARINE (1 STICK), CUT INTO 4
    PIECES

¾ CUP BOILING WATER

1 LARGE EGG

WHIPPED CREAM (OPTIONAL)

1 Preheat oven to 350° F. Grease and flour 9" by 9" metal baking pan.

2 In large bowl, stir together flour, sugar, ginger, cinnamon, baking soda, and salt.

3 In small bowl, combine molasses and butter. Add boiling water and stir until butter melts. Add molasses mixture and egg to flour mixture; whisk until blended.

4 Pour batter into prepared pan. Bake 45 to 50 minutes, until toothpick inserted in center of cake comes out clean. Cool in pan on wire rack. Serve warm or at room temperature with whipped cream, if desired. *Makes 9 servings.*

EACH SERVING WITHOUT WHIPPED CREAM: ABOUT 350 CALORIES, 4 G PROTEIN, 59 G CARBOHYDRATE, 12 G TOTAL FAT (7 G SATURATED), 1 G FIBER, 51 MG CHOLESTEROL, 325 MG SODIUM.

CHOCOLATE CAKES

Many people believe that chocolate cake is more deserving than apple pie as "America's #1 Dessert". One thing that chocolate cakes certainly have in their favor is that they come in so many "styles," from darkest Devil's Food to light German's Chocolate Cake with its rich coconut-pecan topping, to a flourless, confectionlike Chocolate Truffle Cake. Dedicated chocoholics will want chocolate filling and chocolate frosting with their chocolate layers. For a change, you might "lighten up" a bit with a vanilla-flavored, peanut-butter, or mocha frosting. For a special taste treat, have fresh raspberries in raspberry puree over a plain slice of a very rich chocolate cake and garnish with a dollop of fresh whipped cream.

Rich Chocolate Cake

PREP **45** MINUTES PLUS COOLING
BAKE **40** TO **45** MINUTES

Look no further: This delicious chocolate cake recipe makes the quintessential birthday cake.

2 CUPS ALL-PURPOSE FLOUR
1 CUP UNSWEETENED COCOA
2 TEASPOONS BAKING POWDER
1 TEASPOON BAKING SODA
½ TEASPOON SALT
1⅓ CUPS MILK
2 TEASPOONS VANILLA EXTRACT
2 CUPS SUGAR
1 CUP BUTTER OR MARGARINE (2 STICKS), SOFTENED
4 LARGE EGGS
FLUFFY WHITE FROSTING (PAGE **359**) OR DESIRED
    FROSTING

1 Preheat oven to 350° F. Grease 13" by 9" metal baking pan or three 8-inch round cake pans. Line bottom(s) with waxed paper; grease and flour paper.

2 In medium bowl, stir together flour, cocoa, baking powder, baking soda, and salt. In measuring cup, mix milk and vanilla.

3 In large bowl, with mixer at low speed, beat sugar and butter until blended. Increase speed to high; beat until creamy, about 5 minutes. Reduce speed to medium-low; add eggs, 1 at a time, beating well after

each addition (mixture may appear grainy). Reduce speed to low; add flour mixture alternately with milk mixture, beginning and ending with flour mixture. Beat until batter is smooth, scraping bowl occasionally with rubber spatula.

4 Pour batter into prepared pan(s). Bake 40 to 45 minutes for 13" by 9" cake, 30 minutes for 8-inch cake layers, or until toothpick inserted in center of cake comes out almost clean. Cool in pan on wire rack 10 minutes. With small knife, loosen sides of 13" by 9" cake or 8-inch layers from sides of pan, then invert cake onto wire rack to cool completely.

5 Meanwhile, prepare Fluffy White Frosting. Frost side and top of 13" by 9" cake; or use to fill and frost layer cake. *Makes one 13" by 9" cake, 16 servings. or one 8-inch 3-layer cake, 16 servings.*

EACH SERVING OF 13" BY 9" CAKE: ABOUT 355 CALORIES, 5 G PROTEIN, 54 G CARBOHYDRATE, 15 G TOTAL FAT (8 G SATURATED), 2 G FIBER, 87 MG CHOLESTEROL, 365 MG SODIUM.

MEXICAN CHOCOLATE-SPICE CAKE Prepare batter as for Rich Chocolate Cake but use only *⅔ cup milk* and add *⅔ cup strong black coffee*; add *1 teaspoon ground cinnamon* and *⅛ teaspoon ground cloves* with flour mixture. Bake and frost as directed.
EACH SERVING OF 13" BY 9" CAKE: ABOUT 350 CALORIES, 5 G PROTEIN, 54 G CARBOHYDRATE, 14 G TOTAL FAT (8 G SATURATED), 2 G FIBER, 86 MG CHOLESTEROL, 360 MG SODIUM.

RICH CHOCOLATE CUPCAKES Prepare batter as for Rich Chocolate Cake. Line thirty-six 2½-inch muffin-pan cups with fluted paper liners. Pour batter into prepared pans. (Do not bake all cupcakes at once. Bake only as many as will fit on center rack of oven.) Bake 25 minutes, or until toothpick inserted in center comes out clean. Repeat with remaining batter. Cool in pans on wire rack 10 minutes. Remove cupcakes from pans to cool completely. Frost tops of cupcakes with Fluffy White Frosting or desired frosting. *Makes 36 cupcakes.*
EACH CUPCAKE WITH FLUFFY WHITE FROSTING: ABOUT 155 CALORIES, 2 G PROTEIN, 24 G CARBOHYDRATE, 6 G TOTAL FAT (4 G SATURATED), 1 G FIBER, 39 MG CHOLESTEROL, 160 MG SODIUM.

One-Bowl Chocolate Cake

PREP 20 MINUTES PLUS COOLING / BAKE 30 MINUTES

One-bowl recipes are lifesavers when you need to bake a party-pretty layer cake in record time. The only trick is to be sure to have the butter soft enough to blend easily into the batter.

2 CUPS ALL-PURPOSE FLOUR
1 CUP GRANULATED SUGAR
¾ CUP BROWN SUGAR
⅔ CUP UNSWEETENED COCOA
1½ TEASPOONS BAKING POWDER
½ TEASPOON BAKING SODA
½ TEASPOON SALT
1½ CUPS MILK
½ CUP BUTTER OR MARGARINE (1 STICK), SOFTENED
2 LARGE EGGS
2 TEASPOONS VANILLA EXTRACT
PEANUT BUTTER FROSTING (PAGE 356) OR DESIRED
    FROSTING

1 Preheat oven to 350° F. Grease two 9-inch round cake pans.

2 In large bowl, combine flour, granulated and brown sugars, cocoa, baking powder, baking soda, salt, milk, butter, eggs, and vanilla. With mixer at low speed, beat until dry ingredients are moistened. Increase speed to high; beat 3 minutes, until smooth.

3 Divide batter between prepared pans. Bake 30 minutes, or until toothpick inserted in center of layers comes out clean. Cool layers in pans on wire racks 10 minutes. With small knife, loosen layers from side of pans; invert onto racks; cool completely.

4 Meanwhile, prepare Peanut Butter Frosting. Place 1 cake layer on cake plate; spread with ½ cup frosting. Top with remaining layer. Frost side and top of cake with remaining frosting. *Makes 12 servings.*

EACH SERVING: ABOUT 550 CALORIES, 9 G PROTEIN, 72 G CARBOHYDRATE, 27 G TOTAL FAT (13 G SATURATED), 3 G FIBER, 90 MG CHOLESTEROL, 470 MG SODIUM.

Classic Devil's Food Cake

PREP 35 MINUTES PLUS COOLING
BAKE 30 TO 35 MINUTES

Devil's Food is the rich, dense, and chocolate opposite of the delicate, yolkless, butterless Angel Food.

2 CUPS ALL-PURPOSE FLOUR
1 CUP UNSWEETENED COCOA
1½ TEASPOONS BAKING SODA
½ TEASPOON SALT
½ CUP BUTTER OR MARGARINE (1 STICK), SOFTENED
1 CUP PACKED LIGHT BROWN SUGAR
1 CUP GRANULATED SUGAR
3 LARGE EGGS
1½ TEASPOONS VANILLA EXTRACT
1½ CUPS BUTTERMILK
CHOCOLATE BUTTER FROSTING (PAGE 353) OR FLUFFY
    WHITE FROSTING (PAGE 359)

1 Preheat oven to 350° F. Grease three 8-inch round cake pans. Line bottoms with waxed paper; grease paper. Dust pans with flour.

2 In medium bowl, stir together flour, cocoa, baking soda, and salt.

3 In large bowl, with mixer at low speed, beat butter and brown and granulated sugars until blended. Increase speed to high; beat 5 minutes. Reduce speed to medium-low; add eggs, 1 at a time, beating well after each addition. Add vanilla and beat until mixed. Add flour mixture alternately with buttermilk, beginning and ending with flour mixture; beat just until batter is smooth, scraping bowl occasionally with rubber spatula.

4 Divide batter equally among prepared pans. Bake 30 to 35 minutes, until toothpick inserted in center of layers comes out clean. Cool layers in pans on wire racks 10 minutes. With small knife, loosen layers from side of pans; invert onto wire racks. Remove waxed paper; cool completely.

5 Meanwhile, prepare Chocolate Butter Frosting. Place 1 cake layer on cake plate; spread with ⅓ cup frosting. Top with second layer; spread with ⅓ cup frosting. Place remaining layer on top. Frost side and top with remaining frosting. *Makes 16 servings.*

EACH SERVING: ABOUT 450 CALORIES, 5 G PROTEIN, 74 G CARBOHYDRATE,17 G TOTAL FAT (10 G SATURATED), 2 G FIBER, 72 MG CHOLESTEROL, 355 MG SODIUM.

Checkerboard Cake

PREP 50 MINUTES PLUS COOLING / BAKE 20 MINUTES

Cookware shops sell special pans for making this cake. However, you can turn out a handsome specimen without them. You will need two pastry bags and three 8-inch round pans.

2¼ CUPS CAKE FLOUR (NOT SELF-RISING)
2 TEASPOONS BAKING POWDER
½ TEASPOON SALT
¾ CUP PLUS 1 TABLESPOON MILK

1½ TEASPOONS VANILLA EXTRACT
1½ CUPS SUGAR
¾ CUP BUTTER OR MARGARINE (1½ STICKS), SOFTENED
3 LARGE EGGS
2 SQUARES (2 OUNCES) SEMISWEET CHOCOLATE, MELTED
1 SQUARE (1 OUNCE) UNSWEETENED CHOCOLATE, MELTED
SILKY CHOCOLATE BUTTER FROSTING (PAGE 354)

1 Preheat oven to 350° F. Grease three 8-inch round cake pans. Line bottoms with waxed paper; grease paper. Dust pans with flour.

2 In medium bowl, stir together flour, baking powder, and salt. In 1-cup measuring cup, mix ¾ milk and vanilla.

Checkerboard Cake

Making a Checkerboard Cake

The checkerboard effect is created by piping alternating rings of chocolate and vanilla batter into three pans. To begin, pipe a band of chocolate batter around the edge of one pan

Use the second decorating bag, filled with the vanilla batter, to pipe a white ring inside the chocolate ring.

Fill in the center with chocolate batter. Fill a second pan in the same way, then do the third pan in reverse—with vanilla batter at the outer edge and center. When stacked, the layers will produce the checkerboard effect.

3 In large bowl, with mixer at low speed, beat sugar and butter until blended. Increase speed to high; beat 5 minutes, until light and creamy. Reduce speed to medium-low; add eggs, 1 at a time, beating well after each addition. Reduce speed to low; add flour mixture alternately with milk mixture, beginning and ending with flour mixture. Beat just until smooth, scraping bowl occasionally with rubber spatula.

4 Spoon half of batter into medium bowl. Into batter remaining in large bowl, with rubber spatula, stir in melted chocolates and remaining 1 tablespoon milk.

5 Spoon vanilla batter into 1 large decorating bag with ½-inch opening (or use heavy-duty zip-tight plastic bag with corner cut to make ½-inch opening). Repeat with chocolate batter and a second large decorating bag with ½-inch opening. Pipe 1½-inch-wide band of chocolate batter around inside edge of 2 prepared cake pans, then pipe 1½-inch-wide band of vanilla batter next to each chocolate band (see photos at left). Pipe enough chocolate batter to fill in the center of each pan. In third pan, repeat piping, alternating rings of batter, but start with vanilla batter around inside edge of pan.

6 Stagger cake pans on 2 oven racks, placing 2 on upper rack and 1 on lower rack, so that pans are not directly above one another. Bake 20 minutes, or until toothpick inserted in center of layers come out almost clean. Cool in pans on wire racks 10 minutes. With small knife, loosen layers from sides of pans; invert onto wire racks. Remove waxed paper; cool completely.

7 Meanwhile, prepare Silky Chocolate Butter Frosting. Place 1 of the 2 identical cake layers on cake plate; spread with ½ cup frosting. Top with the reverse-design cake layer. Spread with another ½ cup frosting. Top with remaining cake layer; frost side and top of cake with remaining frosting. *Makes 16 servings.*

EACH SERVING: ABOUT 455 CALORIES, 4 G PROTEIN, 51 G CARBOHYDRATE, 27 G TOTAL FAT (16 G SATURATED), 1 G FIBER, 98 MG CHOLESTEROL, 365 MG SODIUM.

Double-Chocolate Bundt Cake

PREP 30 MINUTES PLUS COOLING / BAKE 45 MINUTES

There is no comparing this to a Bundt cake made with a mix. Only a from-scratch cake could be this moist and rich. The mocha glaze is an indulgence; you can also sprinkle the cake with confectioners' sugar, if you like.

2¼ CUPS ALL-PURPOSE FLOUR

1½ TEASPOONS BAKING SODA

½ TEASPOON BAKING POWDER

½ TEASPOON SALT

¾ CUP UNSWEETENED COCOA

1 TEASPOON INSTANT ESPRESSO-COFFEE POWDER

¾ CUP HOT WATER

2 CUPS SUGAR

⅓ CUP VEGETABLE OIL

2 LARGE EGG WHITES

1 LARGE EGG

1 SQUARE (1 OUNCE) UNSWEETENED CHOCOLATE, MELTED

2 TEASPOONS VANILLA EXTRACT

½ CUP BUTTERMILK

MOCHA GLAZE (OPTIONAL, AT RIGHT)

CHOOSING CHOCOLATE

YOU'LL FIND SEVERAL DIFFERENT TYPES OF BAKING CHOCOLATE IN THE SUPERMARKET: UNSWEETENED, SEMISWEET OR BITTERSWEET—INTERCHANGEABLE IN MOST RECIPES—AND DARK SWEET. (MILK CHOCOLATE, AMERICA'S FAVORITE, IS RARELY USED FOR BAKING.) YOU MAY WANT TO GO BEYOND THE SUPERMARKET VARIETIES AND EXPERIMENT WITH FINER CHOCOLATES, WHICH HAVE A HIGHER PROPORTION OF CHOCOLATE LIQUOR. WHITE CHOCOLATE, SOLD IN BARS AND CHIPS, IS NOT TECHNICALLY CHOCOLATE BECAUSE IT CONTAINS NO CHOCOLATE LIQUOR. FOR THE BEST-QUALITY CHOCOLATE, LOOK FOR A BRAND THAT CONTAINS COCOA BUTTER RATHER THAN OTHER VEGETABLE FATS.

---

1 Preheat oven to 350° F. Grease 12-cup Bundt pan.

2 On sheet of waxed paper, stir together flour, baking soda, baking powder, and salt.

3 In 2-cup measuring cup, mix cocoa, espresso-coffee powder, and hot water until blended; set aside.

4 In large bowl, with mixer at low speed, beat sugar, oil, egg whites, and whole egg until blended. Increase speed to high; beat until creamy, about 2 minutes. Reduce speed to low; beat in cocoa mixture, chocolate, and vanilla. Add flour mixture alternately with buttermilk, beginning and ending with flour mixture. Beat just until combined, scraping bowl occasionally with rubber spatula.

5 Pour batter into prepared pan. Bake 45 minutes, or until toothpick inserted in center of cake comes out clean. Cool in pan on wire rack 10 minutes. With small knife, loosen cake from side of pan; invert onto wire rack. Cool completely.

6 Meanwhile, prepare Mocha Glaze. Place cake on cake plate; pour glaze over top of cooled cake letting it run down sides. Allow glaze to set before serving. *Makes 16 servings.*

EACH SERVING WITH MOCHA GLAZE: ABOUT 280 CALORIES, 4 G PROTEIN, 53 G CARBOHYDRATE, 7 G TOTAL FAT (2 G SATURATED), 2 G FIBER, 14 MG CHOLESTEROL, 230 MG SODIUM.

EACH SERVING WITHOUT MOCHA GLAZE: ABOUT 235 CALORIES, 4 G PROTEIN, 42 G CARBOHYDRATE, 7 G TOTAL FAT (2 G SATURATED), 2 G FIBER, 14 MG CHOLESTEROL, 225 MG SODIUM.

MOCHA GLAZE In medium bowl, combine ¼ teaspoon instant espresso-coffee powder and 2 tablespoons hot water; stir until dissolved. Stir in 3 tablespoons unsweetened cocoa, 3 tablespoons dark corn syrup, and 1 tablespoon coffee-flavored liqueur until blended. Stir in 1 cup confectioners' sugar until smooth. *Makes about 1 cup.*

EACH TABLESPOON: ABOUT 45 CALORIES, 0 G PROTEIN, 11 G CARBOHYDRATE, 0 G TOTAL FAT (0 G SATURATED), 0.5 G FIBER, 0 MG CHOLESTEROL, 5 MG SODIUM.

German's Chocolate Cake

PREP 45 MINUTES PLUS COOLING / BAKE 30 MINUTES

Contrary to what most people think, this beloved chocolate cake is not a German creation. The correct name is German's, and it comes from the brand name of an American baking chocolate that first created it.

2 CUPS ALL-PURPOSE FLOUR

1 TEASPOON BAKING SODA

¼ TEASPOON SALT

1¼ CUPS BUTTERMILK

1 TEASPOON VANILLA EXTRACT

3 LARGE EGGS, SEPARATED

1½ CUPS SUGAR

¾ CUP BUTTER OR MARGARINE (1½ STICKS), SOFTENED

4 SQUARES (4 OUNCES) SWEET BAKING CHOCOLATE, MELTED

COCONUT-PECAN FROSTING (PAGE 356)

1 Preheat oven to 350° F. Grease three 8-inch round cake pans. Line bottoms with waxed paper; grease and flour paper.

2 In small bowl, combine flour, baking soda, and salt. In 2-cup measuring cup, mix buttermilk and vanilla.

3 In medium bowl, with mixer at medium-high speed, beat egg whites until frothy. Gradually sprinkle in ¾ cup sugar, 1 tablespoon at a time, and beat until soft peaks form when beaters are lifted.

4 In large bowl, with mixer at medium speed, beat butter until light and fluffy. Add remaining ¾ cup sugar and beat until well blended. Reduce speed to medium-low; add egg yolks, 1 at a time, beating well after each addition. Beat in melted chocolate.

5 Reduce speed to low; add flour mixture alternately with buttermilk mixture, beginning and ending with flour mixture. Beat until smooth, scraping bowl occasionally. With rubber spatula, fold half of beaten whites into batter; gently fold in remaining whites.

6 Divide batter among prepared pans. Stagger pans on 2 oven racks, placing 2 pans on upper rack and 1 on lower rack, so that pans are not directly above one another. Bake 30 minutes, or until toothpick inserted in center comes out almost clean. Cool in pans on racks 10 minutes. With knife, loosen layers from pans; invert onto racks. Remove waxed paper; cool completely.

7 Meanwhile, prepare Coconut-Pecan Frosting. Place 1 layer on cake plate; spread with 1 cup frosting. Top with second cake layer and another cup of frosting. Top with remaining layer. Frost side and top of cake with remaining frosting. *Makes 16 servings.*

EACH SERVING: ABOUT 505 CALORIES, 5 G PROTEIN, 53 G CARBOHYDRATE, 31 G TOTAL FAT (16 G SATURATED), 1.5 G FIBER, 140 MG CHOLESTEROL, 320 MG SODIUM.

Chocolate Truffle Cake

PREP 1 HOUR PLUS OVERNIGHT TO CHILL
BAKE 35 MINUTES

This devilishly dense flourless chocolate dessert should be baked a day ahead and refrigerated overnight to let it firm up. Adorn the top with hearts, stars, crescent moons, or other shapes, made with stencils (below).

14 SQUARES (14 OUNCES) SEMISWEET CHOCOLATE

2 SQUARES (2 OUNCES) UNSWEETENED CHOCOLATE

1 CUP (2 STICKS) BUTTER (DO NOT USE MARGARINE)

9 LARGE EGGS, SEPARATED

½ CUP GRANULATED SUGAR

¼ TEASPOON CREAM OF TARTAR

CONFECTIONERS' SUGAR

Simple Cake Stencils

To decorate a cake with stars or other simple shapes, make a stencil by cutting the shape from a square of lightweight cardboard (a manila file folder works well). Hold the stencil over the top of the cake and sift unsweetened cocoa, confectioners' sugar, or cinnamon sugar over it. Repeat for desired pattern.

Chocolate Truffle Cake

1 Preheat oven to 300° F. Remove bottom from 9-inch springform pan and cover with foil, wrapping foil around to the back (this will make it easier to remove cake from pan). Replace bottom. Grease and flour foil bottom and side of pan.

2 In heavy 2-quart saucepan, combine semisweet and unsweetened chocolates and butter and melt over very low heat, stirring frequently, until smooth. Pour chocolate mixture into large bowl.

3 In small bowl, with mixer at high speed, beat egg yolks and granulated sugar until very thick and lemon-colored, about 5 minutes. Add egg-yolk mixture to chocolate mixture, stirring with rubber spatula until blended.

4 In another large bowl, with clean beaters, with mixer at high speed, beat egg whites and cream of tartar until soft peaks form when beaters are lifted. With rubber spatula or wire whisk, fold beaten egg whites into chocolate mixture, one-third at a time.

5 Pour batter into prepared pan; spread evenly. Bake 35 minutes. (Do not overbake; the cake will firm up while standing and chilling.) Cool cake completely in pan on wire rack. Refrigerate overnight in pan.

6 To remove cake from pan, run a hot knife around edge of cake, then lift off side of pan. Invert cake onto cake plate; unwrap foil from back of bottom and lift off bottom of pan. Peel foil from cake.

7 Let cake stand 1 hour at room temperature before serving. To decorate top of cake, using fine sieve, sprinkle with confectioners' sugar. Or, place stencil on top of cake; sprinkle confectioners' sugar heavily over stencil, and lift off carefully. *Make 20 servings.*

EACH SERVING: ABOUT 250 CALORIES, 4 G PROTEIN, 19 G CARBOHYDRATE, 19 G TOTAL FAT (11 G SATURATED), 2 G FIBER, 120 MG CHOLESTEROL, 125 MG SODIUM.

Reine de Saba

PREP 1 HOUR PLUS COOLING / BAKE 25 TO 28 MINUTES

Named for the darkly beautiful Queen of Sheba—"Reine de Saba" in French—this intense chocolate-almond torte is equally tempting made with hazelnuts.

6 SQUARES (6 OUNCES) SEMISWEET CHOCOLATE
1 SQUARE (1 OUNCE) UNSWEETENED CHOCOLATE
⅔ CUP BLANCHED ALMONDS, TOASTED
½ CUP CAKE FLOUR (NOT SELF-RISING)
½ CUP BUTTER OR MARGARINE (1 STICK), SLIGHTLY
    SOFTENED
⅓ CUP PLUS 4 TABLESPOONS SUGAR
3 LARGE EGGS, SEPARATED
1 TEASPOON VANILLA EXTRACT
¼ TEASPOON CREAM OF TARTAR
⅓ CUP HEAVY OR WHIPPING CREAM
1 TEASPOON LIGHT CORN SYRUP

1 Preheat oven to 325° F. Grease and flour 8-inch round cake pan.

2 In small heavy saucepan, melt 3 squares semisweet chocolate and unsweetened chocolate over low heat, stirring frequently, until smooth. Remove saucepan from heat; cool.

3 In food processor with knife blade attached, or in blender, chop ½ cup toasted nuts and flour until nuts are very finely ground (reserve remaining nuts for garnish).

4 In large bowl, with mixer at low speed, beat butter and ⅓ cup sugar just until blended. Increase speed to high; beat until light and fluffy, about 2 minutes. Reduce speed to low; beat in egg yolks, vanilla, and melted chocolate mixture until blended, about 1 minute, scraping bowl often with rubber spatula.

5 In small bowl, with clean beaters and mixer at high speed, beat egg whites and cream of tartar until soft peaks form. Gradually sprinkle in remaining 4 tablespoons sugar and beat until whites hold stiff, glossy peaks when beaters are lifted.

6 With rubber spatula, fold nut mixture into yolks mixture just until blended. Gently fold beaten egg whites into yolk mixture, one-third at a time.

7 Spread batter evenly in prepared pan. Bake 25 to 28 minutes, until toothpick inserted in cake about 2 inches from edge comes out clean. (The center of cake will still be slightly soft.) Cool cake in pan on wire rack 15 minutes. With small knife, loosen cake from side of pan; invert onto wire rack to cool com-

pletely. (The recipe can be prepared up to this point 2 days in advance. If not using cake right away, wrap well with plastic wrap and refrigerate.)

8 Coarsely chop remaining 3 squares semisweet chocolate; place in small bowl. In small saucepan, heat cream just to boiling over low heat. Pour hot cream over chopped chocolate; let stand 1 minute. Gently stir until chocolate melts; stir in corn syrup. Let stand at room temperature until glaze begins to thicken, about 5 minutes. Meanwhile, coarsely chop reserved nuts.

9 Place cake on cake plate. Tuck strips of waxed paper under edge of cake to keep plate clean when glazing. Pour chocolate glaze over cake. With metal spatula, spread glaze to completely cover top and side of cake. Sprinkle chopped nuts around top edge of cake. Chill cake 20 minutes to set glaze. Remove and discard waxed-paper strips. Refrigerate cake if not serving right away. *Makes 12 servings.*

EACH SERVING: ABOUT 285 CALORIES, 4 G PROTEIN,
24 G CARBOHYDRATE, 21 G TOTAL FAT (10 G SATURATED),
2 G FIBER, 83 MG CHOLESTEROL, 100 MG SODIUM.

Molten Chocolate Cakes

PREP 20 MINUTES / BAKE 8 TO 9 MINUTES

These incredibly rich chocolate cakelets should be served hot from the oven while the centers are still molten! Real show stoppers, they are the perfect party dessert because the batter can be made ahead of time, poured into custard cups, and refrigerated for 24 hours (or even frozen for up to two weeks). Bake refrigerated batter for 10 minutes, or frozen batter—straight from the freezer—for 16 minutes. Serve with whipped cream or ice cream.

½ CUP BUTTER OR MARGARINE (1 STICK)
4 SQUARES (4 OUNCES) SEMISWEET CHOCOLATE
¼ CUP HEAVY OR WHIPPING CREAM
½ TEASPOON VANILLA EXTRACT
¼ CUP ALL-PURPOSE FLOUR
2 LARGE EGGS
2 LARGE EGG YOLKS
¼ CUP SUGAR
WHIPPED CREAM OR VANILLA ICE CREAM (OPTIONAL)

1 Preheat oven to 400° F. Grease eight 6-ounce custard cups. Sprinkle with granulated sugar.

2 In 3-quart saucepan, combine butter, chocolate, and cream and heat over low heat, stirring occasionally, until melted and smooth. Remove saucepan from heat. Whisk in vanilla and flour just until smooth.

3 In medium bowl, with mixer at high speed, beat eggs, egg yolks, and sugar until thick and lemon-colored, about 10 minutes. Fold egg mixture, one-third at a time, into chocolate mixture.

4 Divide batter evenly among prepared custard cups. Place cups on jelly-roll pan for easier handling and bake 8 to 9 minutes, until edge of cakes is set but center still jiggles. Cool in pan on wire rack 3 minutes. With small knife, loosen cakes from sides of each cup and turn each out onto individual dessert plates. Serve immediately with whipped cream or ice cream, if desired. *Makes 8 servings.*

EACH SERVING WITHOUT WHIPPED CREAM OR ICE CREAM: ABOUT 300 CALORIES, 4 G PROTEIN, 22 G CARBOHYDRATE, 23 G TOTAL FAT (13 G SATURATED), 1 G FIBER, 148 MG CHOLESTEROL, 140 MG SODIUM.

POUND CAKES

In the old days—when it wasn't worth firing up the oven unless you baked several cakes—pound cake recipes called for one pound each of butter, sugar, flour, and eggs. The butter and sugar, then the eggs, had to be laboriously creamed until perfectly smooth, light, and fluffy, because the beaten eggs had to serve as leavening (baking soda or powder were not used), and the batter had to be as light as possible to enable the eggs to do their work. Today, most folks are happy to bake one pound cake at a time, and electric mixers, baking soda, baking powder, and other modern conveniences make whipping up a pound cake almost effortless. Still, you do want to cream the butter and sugar for a good long time, until it feels smooth, and not grainy, between your fingers. A slice of pound cake can be the base for all sorts of fresh berry and fruit toppings with or without whipped cream. Try pound cake with a scoop of your favorite ice cream and topping. Two pound cakes are the basis for our whimsical Fire Truck Cake (page 342) that will enthrall the youngster in your family on his or her birthday.

Pound Cake

PREP 20 MINUTES / BAKE 1 HOUR

Here's a basic recipe plus two variations. Be sure to try the black pepper version: The spices give the cake a slightly hot "kick" that's really something special.

2 CUPS CAKE FLOUR (NOT SELF-RISING)
1 TEASPOON BAKING POWDER
½ TEASPOON SALT
1 CUP BUTTER OR MARGARINE (2 STICKS), SOFTENED
1 CUP SUGAR
4 LARGE EGGS
1½ TEASPOONS VANILLA EXTRACT

1 Preheat oven to 325° F. Grease and flour 9" by 5" metal loaf pan.

2 In medium bowl, stir together flour, baking powder, and salt. In large bowl, with mixer at medium speed, beat butter until creamy. Add sugar, and beat 5 minutes, or until light and creamy. Add eggs, 1 at a time, beating well after each addition. Beat in vanilla. Reduce speed to low; beat in flour mixture just until combined.

3 Turn batter into prepared pan and spread evenly. Bake 1 hour, or until cake pulls away from sides of pan and toothpick inserted in center of cake comes out clean. Cool in pan on wire rack 10 minutes. With small knife, loosen cake from sides of pan; invert onto wire rack; invert again right side up to cool completely. *Makes 12 servings.*

EACH SERVING: ABOUT 300 CALORIES, 4 G PROTEIN, 32 G CARBOHYDRATE, 17 G TOTAL FAT (10 G SATURATED), 0 G FIBER, 112 MG CHOLESTEROL, 315 MG SODIUM.

SPICE POUND CAKE Prepare batter as above but use *⅓ cup dark brown sugar* and only *⅔ cup granulated sugar.* Add *1 teaspoon ground cinnamon, ½ teaspoon ground ginger, ⅛ teaspoon ground black pepper,* and *⅛ teaspoon ground allspice* to flour mixture. Bake as directed.
EACH SERVING: ABOUT 300 CALORIES, 4 G PROTEIN, 32 G CARBOHYDRATE, 17 G TOTAL FAT (10 G SATURATED), 0 G FIBER, 112 MG CHOLESTEROL, 315 MG SODIUM.

BLACK PEPPER POUND CAKE Prepare batter as for Pound Cake and add *¾ teaspoon ground black pepper* and *a pinch ground allspice* to flour mixture. Bake as directed.
EACH SERVING: ABOUT 300 CALORIES, 4 G PROTEIN, 32 G CARBOHYDRATE, 17 G TOTAL FAT (10 G SATURATED), 0 G FIBER, 112 MG CHOLESTEROL, 315 MG SODIUM.

Bourbon Brown Sugar Pound Cake

Bourbon Brown Sugar Pound Cake

PREP 30 MINUTES / BAKE 1 HOUR 20 MINUTES

The rich flavor of butter is so important to the overall quality of this cake that it would be a shame to make it with anything else (i.e., margarine or shortening).

3 CUPS ALL-PURPOSE FLOUR

¾ TEASPOON SALT

½ TEASPOON BAKING POWDER

½ TEASPOON BAKING SODA

¾ CUP MILK

2 TEASPOONS VANILLA EXTRACT

6 TABLESPOONS BOURBON

1½ CUPS PACKED DARK BROWN SUGAR

½ CUP PLUS ⅓ CUP GRANULATED SUGAR

1 CUP BUTTER (2 STICKS), SOFTENED (DO NOT USE MARGARINE)

5 LARGE EGGS

2 TABLESPOONS ORANGE JUICE

1 Preheat oven to 325° F. Grease and flour 12-cup fluted tube pan.

2 In medium bowl, stir together flour, salt, baking powder, and baking soda. In 1-cup measuring cup, mix milk, vanilla, and 4 tablespoons bourbon.

3 In large bowl, with mixer at medium speed, beat brown sugar, ½ cup granulated sugar, and butter; increase speed to high, and beat until light and creamy, about 5 minutes. Add eggs, 1 at a time, beating well after each addition. Reduce speed to low; add flour mixture alternately with milk mixture, beginning and ending with flour mixture, scraping bowl occasionally with rubber spatula.

4 Pour batter into prepared pan. Bake 1 hour 20 minutes, or until cake springs back when lightly touched with finger and toothpick inserted in center of cake comes out clean. Cool in pan 10 minutes. Loosen cake from side and center of pan; remove from pan; place on wire rack over waxed paper.

5 In small bowl, combine orange juice, remaining ⅓ cup granulated sugar, and remaining 2 tablespoons bourbon; brush mixture all over warm cake. Cool cake completely. *Makes 20 servings.*

EACH SERVING: ABOUT 280 CALORIES, 4 G PROTEIN, 40 G CARBOHYDRATE, 12 G TOTAL FAT (6 G SATURATED), 1 G FIBER, 79 MG CHOLESTEROL, 250 MG SODIUM.

Seed Cake

PREP 25 MINUTES / BAKE 1 HOUR 5 MINUTES

This favorite Victorian tea cake is best when cooled and then wrapped overnight. During this "resting time," the citrus and caraway perfume the entire cake.

2 CUPS ALL-PURPOSE FLOUR
1 TEASPOON BAKING POWDER
¼ TEASPOON GROUND NUTMEG
¼ TEASPOON SALT
½ CUP BUTTER OR MARGARINE (1 STICK), SOFTENED
¾ CUP SUGAR
2 LARGE EGGS
1 TEASPOON VANILLA EXTRACT
⅔ CUP MILK
1 TEASPOON FRESHLY GRATED LEMON PEEL
1 TEASPOON FRESHLY GRATED ORANGE PEEL
1½ TEASPOONS CARAWAY SEEDS
½ CUP DRIED CURRANTS

1 Preheat oven to 350° F. Grease and flour 8" by 4" metal loaf pan.

2 In small bowl, stir together flour, baking powder, nutmeg, and salt.

3 In large bowl, with mixer at low speed, beat butter and sugar until creamy. Add eggs, 1 at a time, beating well after each addition. Beat in vanilla. Add flour mixture alternately with milk, beginning and ending with flour mixture. Beat in lemon and orange peels, caraway seeds, and currants.

4 Pour batter into prepared pan. Bake 1 hour 5 minutes, or until toothpick inserted in center of loaf comes out clean. Cool in pan on wire rack 10 minutes. Invert onto wire rack, and invert again, right side up, to cool completely. *Makes 1 loaf, 12 servings.*

EACH SERVING: ABOUT 240 CALORIES, 4 G PROTEIN, 34 G CARBOHYDRATE, 10 G TOTAL FAT (5 G SATURATED), 1 G FIBER, 58 MG CHOLESTEROL, 185 MG SODIUM.

Cornmeal Pound Cake

PREP 20 MINUTES / BAKE 1 HOUR 5 MINUTES

Cornmeal adds a slightly crunchy texture to this cake.

1 CUP ALL-PURPOSE FLOUR
½ CUP YELLOW CORNMEAL
½ TEASPOON BAKING POWDER
¼ TEASPOON SALT
1 CUP BUTTER OR MARGARINE (2 STICKS), SOFTENED
1 CUP SUGAR
4 LARGE EGGS
1 TEASPOON FRESHLY GRATED ORANGE PEEL
1 TEASPOON VANILLA EXTRACT

1 Preheat oven to 325° F. Grease and flour 6-cup fluted tube pan or 9" by 5" metal loaf pan.

2 In medium bowl, stir together flour, cornmeal, baking powder, and salt.

3 In large bowl, with mixer at medium speed, beat butter and sugar until light and creamy, about 5 minutes. Add eggs, 1 at a time, beating well after each addition. Beat in orange peel and vanilla. Reduce speed to low; beat in flour mixture just until combined, scraping bowl with rubber spatula.

4 Pour batter into prepared pan. Bake 1 hour 5 minutes, or until cake pulls away from sides of pan and toothpick inserted in center of cake comes out clean. Cool in pan on wire rack 10 minutes. With small knife, loosen cake from sides of pan; invert onto wire rack to cool completely *Makes 10 servings.*

EACH SERVING: ABOUT 355 CALORIES, 5 G PROTEIN, 36 G CARBOHYDRATE, 21 G TOTAL FAT (12 G SATURATED), 1 G FIBER, 135 MG CHOLESTEROL, 295 MG SODIUM.

Chocolate Pound Cake

PREP 30 MINUTES PLUS COOLING
BAKE 1 HOUR 20 TO 25 MINUTES

*Unlike some of the more extravagant chocolate
creations, this tube cake sneaks up on you with its rich
chocolate flavor. The coarsely grated chocolate, added
last to the batter, is a unique accent. Use the large holes
on the grater, so that you have small bits of chocolate
rather than a fine powder.*

3 CUPS ALL-PURPOSE FLOUR
1 CUP UNSWEETENED COCOA
½ TEASPOON BAKING POWDER
1½ CUPS BUTTER OR MARGARINE (3 STICKS), SOFTENED
2¾ CUPS SUGAR
2 TEASPOONS VANILLA EXTRACT
5 LARGE EGGS
1½ CUPS MILK
2 OUNCES BITTERSWEET CHOCOLATE, GRATED

1 Preheat oven to 350° F. Grease and flour 10-inch
tube pan with removable bottom. Line outside of
pan with foil. In medium bowl, sift flour, cocoa, and
baking powder.

2 In large bowl, with mixer at medium speed, beat
butter until creamy. Gradually beat in sugar; beat 3
minutes, until fluffy. Beat in vanilla. Add eggs, 1 at a
time, beating well after each addition until blended.
Reduce speed to low; beat in flour mixture alternately with milk, beginning and ending with flour
mixture. Stir in grated chocolate.

3 Spoon batter into prepared pan, spreading evenly.
Bake 1 hour 20 to 25 minutes, until toothpick inserted in center of cake comes out clean. Cool in pan on
wire rack 10 minutes. With small knife, loosen cake
from side and center of pan. Remove pan side and
let cool completely. Run a thin knife around bottom
of cake to remove pan bottom. *Makes 20 servings.*

EACH SERVING: ABOUT 360 CALORIES, 5 G PROTEIN,
47 G CARBOHYDRATE, 18 G TOTAL FAT (10 G SATURATED),
2 G FIBER, 93 MG CHOLESTEROL, 180 MG SODIUM.

CHIFFON & ANGEL-FOOD CAKES

The chiffon cake is a true American original. First devised
in the 1940s, the chiffon cake recipe was revolutionary in
its use of oil rather than butter or other solid shortening.
Angel-food cake, an earlier creation, is even more singular
among cakes: It's made with egg whites only, and no
shortening—so it starts out fat free.

Vanilla Chiffon Cake

PREP 20 MINUTES / BAKE 1 HOUR 15 MINUTES

2¼ CUPS CAKE FLOUR (NOT SELF-RISING)
1½ CUPS GRANULATED SUGAR
1 TABLESPOON BAKING POWDER
1 TEASPOON SALT
½ CUP VEGETABLE OIL
5 LARGE EGGS, SEPARATED
1 TABLESPOON VANILLA EXTRACT
¾ CUP COLD WATER
2 LARGE EGG WHITES
½ TEASPOON CREAM OF TARTAR
CONFECTIONERS' SUGAR

1 Preheat oven to 325° F. In large bowl, stir together flour, 1 cup granulated sugar, baking powder, and
salt. Make a well in center. Add oil, 5 egg yolks,
vanilla, and water; whisk into dry ingredients.

2 In another large bowl, with mixer at high speed,
beat 7 egg whites and cream of tartar until soft peaks
form when beaters are lifted. Gradually sprinkle in
remaining ½ cup granulated sugar, 2 tablespoons at
a time, and beat until whites just stand in stiff peaks
when beaters are lifted. With rubber spatula, gently
fold one-third of whites into egg-yolk mixture, then
fold in remaining whites.

3 Pour batter into ungreased 9- to 10-inch tube pan.
Bake 1 hour 15 minutes, or until top springs back
when touched with finger. Invert cake in pan on metal funnel or bottle; cool completely. With small knife,
carefully loosen cake from side and center of pan.
Transfer to cake plate. Sprinkle with confectioners'
sugar. *Makes 16 servings.*

EACH SERVING: ABOUT 220 CALORIES, 4 G PROTEIN,
32 G CARBOHYDRATE, 9 G TOTAL FAT (1 G SATURATED),
0 G FIBER, 66 MG CHOLESTEROL, 265 MG SODIUM.

CITRUS CHIFFON CAKE Prepare batter as for Vanilla Chiffon Cake but use *1 tablespoon freshly grated orange peel* and *1 teaspoon freshly grated lemon peel* in place of vanilla. Use *½ cup fresh orange juice* and *¼ cup fresh lemon juice* in place of cold water. Bake cake, cool, and remove from pan as directed. In small bowl, combine *1 cup confectioners' sugar, 1 teaspoon freshly grated lemon peel, ¼ teaspoon vanilla extract,* and about *5 teaspoons orange juice* until smooth. Spoon glaze over cooled cake.

EACH SERVING: ABOUT 250 CALORIES, 4 G PROTEIN, 40 G CARBOHYDRATE, 9 G TOTAL FAT (1 G SATURATED), 0 G FIBER, 66 MG CHOLESTEROL, 265 MG SODIUM.

Angel-Food Cake

PREP 30 MINUTES / BAKE 35 TO 40 MINUTES

Unparalleled in its pristine delicacy, angel-food cake is also perfect when served with fresh fruit, bright scoops of sorbet, or a divinely decadent chocolate sauce. Or use some of the yolks to make our luscious Custard Sauce (page 363) for a topping.

1 CUP CAKE FLOUR (NOT SELF-RISING)
½ CUP CONFECTIONERS' SUGAR
1⅔ CUPS EGG WHITES (12 TO 14 LARGE EGG WHITES)
1½ TEASPOONS CREAM OF TARTAR
½ TEASPOON SALT
1¼ CUPS GRANULATED SUGAR
2 TEASPOONS VANILLA EXTRACT
½ TEASPOON ALMOND EXTRACT

1 Preheat oven to 375° F. Sift flour and confectioners' sugar through sieve into medium bowl.

2 In large bowl, with mixer at medium speed, beat egg whites, cream of tartar, and salt until foamy. Increase speed to medium-high; beat until soft peaks form when beaters are lifted. Gradually sprinkle in granulated sugar, 2 tablespoons at a time, and beat until egg whites just stand in stiff peaks when beaters are lifted. Beat in vanilla and almond extracts.

3 Transfer egg-white mixture to larger bowl. Sift flour mixture, one-third at a time, into whites, folding with rubber spatula or wire whisk just until flour mixture disappears. Do not overmix.

4 Turn batter into ungreased 9- to 10-inch tube pan. Bake 35 to 40 minutes, until cake springs back when lightly touched. Invert cake in pan on metal funnel

or bottle; cool completely in pan. With small knife, carefully loosen cake from side and center of pan; remove cake from pan and place on cake plate. *Makes 12 servings.*

EACH SERVING: ABOUT 155 CALORIES, 4 G PROTEIN, 34 G CARBOHYDRATE, 0 G TOTAL FAT (0 G SATURATED), 0 G FIBER, 0 MG CHOLESTEROL, 155 MG SODIUM.

CAPPUCCINO ANGEL-FOOD CAKE Prepare batter as for Angel-Food Cake and add *4 teaspoons instant espresso-coffee powder* and *½ teaspoon ground cinnamon* to egg whites before beating; use *1½ teaspoons vanilla extract* and omit almond extract. Bake cake, cool, and remove from pan as directed. In small cup, mix *1 tablespoon confectioners' sugar* with *⅛ teaspoon ground cinnamon*; sprinkle over cooled cake.

EACH SERVING: ABOUT 155 CALORIES, 4 G PROTEIN, 34 G CARBOHYDRATE, 0 G TOTAL FAT (0 G SATURATED), 0 G FIBER, 0 MG CHOLESTEROL, 155 MG SODIUM.

FLUFFING AND FOLDING

THERE ARE TWO VITAL STEPS IN PREPARING AN ANGEL-FOOD CAKE: BEATING THE EGG WHITES PROPERLY AND THEN FOLDING THE DRY INGREDIENTS INTO THE STIFFLY BEATEN WHITES. A WORD OR TWO ABOUT EGG WHITES: IT'S MUCH EASIER TO SEPARATE EGGS WHEN THEY ARE COLD. BREAK EACH EGG OVER A SMALL BOWL, LETTING THE WHITE DROP INTO THE BOWL. CHECK TO MAKE SURE THERE IS NO YOLK IN THE WHITE. EVEN A SMALL AMOUNT OF YOLK WILL PREVENT THE WHITES FROM GAINING MAXIMUM VOLUME. THEN ADD THE PRISTINE WHITE TO THE MIXING BOWL AND SEPARATE THE NEXT EGG. THE WHITES WILL RISE TO GREATER VOLUME WHEN THEY'RE BEATEN AT ROOM TEMPERATURE. FOLD DRY INGREDIENTS INTO STIFF, GLOSSY EGG WHITES ABOUT A THIRD AT A TIME. THE FOLDING PROCESS IS ALL-IMPORTANT; THE DRY INGREDIENTS MUST BE INCORPORATED INTO THE STIFFLY BEATEN EGG WHITES WITHOUT DEFLATING THEM TOO MUCH, AS IT IS THE AIR TRAPPED IN THE EGG WHITES THAT GIVES THE VOLUME TO THE CAKE.

Chocolate Angel-Food Cake

PREP 30 MINUTES / BAKE 35 TO 40 MINUTES

Here's how to have your chocolate cake and eat it too— with virtually no fat! Using cocoa powder, rather than solid chocolate, makes the magic possible. Serve the cake with a sprinkling of confectioners' sugar, if you like.

¾ CUP CAKE FLOUR (NOT SELF-RISING)
½ CUP UNSWEETENED COCOA
1½ CUPS SUGAR
1⅔ CUPS EGG WHITES (12 TO 14 LARGE EGG WHITES)
1½ TEASPOONS CREAM OF TARTAR
½ TEASPOON SALT
1½ TEASPOONS VANILLA EXTRACT

1 Preheat oven to 375° F. Sift flour, cocoa, and ¾ cup sugar through sieve into medium bowl.

2 In large bowl, with mixer at medium speed, beat egg whites, cream of tartar, and salt until foamy. Increase speed to medium-high; beat until soft peaks form when beaters are lifted. Gradually sprinkle in remaining ¾ cup sugar, 2 tablespoons at a time, and beat until egg whites just stand in stiff peaks when beaters are lifted. Beat in vanilla.

3 Sift cocoa mixture, one-third at a time, into whites, folding with rubber spatula or wire whisk just until cocoa mixture disappears. Do not overmix.

4 Turn batter into ungreased 9- to 10-inch tube pan. Bake 35 to 40 minutes, until cake springs back when lightly touched. Invert cake in pan on metal funnel or bottle; cool cake completely. With small knife, carefully loosen cake from side and center of pan; remove from pan and place on cake plate. *Makes 12 servings.*

EACH SERVING: ABOUT 149 CALORIES, 5 G PROTEIN, 33 G CARBOHYDRATE, 1 G TOTAL FAT (0 G SATURATED), 1 G FIBER, 0 MG CHOLESTEROL, 155 MG SODIUM.

SPONGE CAKES & CAKE ROLLS

Versatile sponge cake can be baked as layers, in a tube pan, or in a rectangular sheet (to be rolled around a filling for a scrumptious cake roll). Like angel-food cakes, sponge cakes require well-beaten eggs, but sponge cakes are made with whole eggs, rather than egg whites alone. And sponge cakes, unlike angel-food, contain at least a small amount of fat. French sponge cake, called génoise, actually originated in Italy (it is named for the city of Genoa). Génoise is the basis for many of the spectacular desserts you'll see in a French pâtisserie. This cake is made with just a little melted butter, but the cake is enhanced after baking by brushing it with a flavored sugar syrup, or by sprinkling it with liqueur.

Boston Cream Pie

PREP 35 MINUTES / BAKE 20 MINUTES

Why this very special New England dessert is called a pie is anyone's guess: It is, in fact, two layers of golden sponge cake, sandwiched with a dense custard filling and slathered with a thick chocolate glaze. One of Boston's greatest hotels, the Parker House, actually takes credit for this version; a simpler Boston Cream Pie is unglazed and sprinkled with confectioners' sugar.

3 LARGE EGGS
1½ CUPS ALL-PURPOSE FLOUR
1½ TEASPOONS BAKING POWDER
¼ TEASPOON SALT
3 TABLESPOONS BUTTER OR MARGARINE
½ CUP WATER
1½ TEASPOON VANILLA EXTRACT
1⅓ CUPS SUGAR
PASTRY CREAM FOR 9-INCH TART (PAGE 360)
CHOCOLATE GLAZE (PAGE 360)

1 Preheat oven to 350° F. Grease two 8-inch round cake pans. Line with waxed paper; grease and flour.

2 In medium bowl, stir together flour, baking powder, and salt. In large bowl, with mixer at high speed, beat eggs 5 minutes, or until light and tripled in volume.

3 Meanwhile, combine water and butter in small saucepan; heat to boiling. Remove from heat; add vanilla. Gradually beat sugar into eggs, beat 2 to 8 minutes, until thick and lemon-colored and mixture forms ribbon when beaters are lifted, scraping bowl occasionally with rubber spatula. In two additions, fold in flour mixture until just blended; pour in water mixture and gently blend.

4 Divide batter evenly between prepared pans. Bake 20 minutes, or until toothpick inserted in centers of layers come out clean. With small knife, loosen layers from sides of pans; invert onto wire rack. Remove waxed paper; cool completely.

5 Meanwhile, prepare Pastry Cream for 9-Inch Tart.

6 When cake is cool, prepare Chocolate Glaze.

7 Place one cake layer, rounded side down, on cake plate; top with pastry cream. Top with second cake layer, rounded side up. Pour glaze over top. With small metal spatula; spread the glaze evenly to edges allowing it to drip down sides of cake. Let glaze set. *Makes 12 servings.*

EACH SERVING: ABOUT 325 CALORIES, 5 G PROTEIN, 50 G CARBOHYDRATE, 12 G TOTAL FAT (7 G SATURATED), 1 G FIBER, 110 MG CHOLESTEROL, 210 MG SODIUM.

Boston Cream Pie

Passover Almond Sponge Cake

PREP 25 MINUTES / BAKE 45 MINUTES

During Passover, wheat flour and leavening are forbidden, so this traditional cake is made with matzo meal and is lightened only with beaten eggs.

2 LEMONS
1½ TEASPOONS VANILLA EXTRACT
¼ TEASPOON ALMOND EXTRACT
9 LARGE EGGS, SEPARATED
1½ CUPS SUGAR
¾ CUP SLIVERED ALMONDS, TOASTED
1⅓ CUPS MATZO MEAL
¼ TEASPOON SALT

1 Preheat oven to 350° F. From lemons grate 1½ teaspoons peel; reserve. Squeeze 3 tablespoons lemon juice. In cup, combine lemon juice and vanilla and almond extracts.

2 In large bowl, with mixer at high speed, beat egg whites until soft peaks form when beaters are lifted. Sprinkle in ¾ cup sugar, 2 tablespoons at a time, and beat until sugar dissolves and whites stand in stiff, glossy peaks form when beaters are lifted.

3 In food processor with knife blade attached, process almonds and 2 tablespoons matzo meal until finely ground. Add remaining 1¼ cups matzo meal, and process until nuts are finely ground.

4 In another large bowl, with mixer at high speed, with same beaters, beat egg yolks with remaining ¾ cup sugar until thick and lemon-colored and mixture forms ribbon when beaters are lifted, scraping bowl occasionally with rubber spatula. In three additions, fold in flour mixture until just blended; fold in lemon-juice mixture and peel. In three additions, fold whites into yolk mixture.

5 Pour batter into ungreased 9- to 10-inch tube pan. Bake 45 minutes, or until skewer inserted in center of cake comes out clean. Cool in pan 10 minutes. Invert cake in pan on metal funnel or bottle; cool completely in pan. With small knife, carefully loosen cake from side and center of pan. Remove cake from pan and place on cake plate. *Makes 16 servings.*

EACH SERVING: ABOUT 195 CALORIES, 6 G PROTEIN, 30 G CARBOHYDRATE, 6 G TOTAL FAT (1 G SATURATED), 0.5 G FIBER, 120 MG CHOLESTEROL, 70 MG SODIUM.

Hot-Water Sponge Cake

PREP 20 MINUTES / BAKE 35 TO 40 MINUTES

This fail-safe cake is traditionally baked in a tube pan, but you can use two 9-inch round pans. Fill with Lemon Filling (page 361) and dust the top with confectioners' sugar. Also, try Whipped Cream Frosting (page 358) and serve with fresh berries.

6 LARGE EGGS
1¾ CUPS ALL-PURPOSE FLOUR
2 TEASPOONS BAKING POWDER
½ TEASPOON SALT
½ CUP WATER
4 TABLESPOONS BUTTER OR MARGARINE, CUT INTO 4 PIECES
1 CUP SUGAR
1½ TEASPOONS VANILLA EXTRACT

1 Preheat oven to 350° F. Grease bottom of 9- to 10-inch tube pan without removable bottom. Or grease bottoms of two 9-inch round cake pans; line bottoms with waxed paper, and grease paper.

2 Place eggs in bowl of warm water; let stand 10 minutes. Sift flour, baking powder, and salt onto a sheet of waxed paper.

3 In large bowl, with mixer at high speed, beat eggs until very foamy and doubled in volume, about 5 minutes. While beating eggs, combine water and butter in small saucepan and heat to boiling; remove from heat. Gradually sprinkle sugar into eggs, 2 tablespoons at a time, and beat 2 minutes, until eggs thicken slightly. Reduce speed to low. Sift flour mixture over eggs and beat until blended and no lumps of flour remain, scraping bowl frequently. Add hot-water mixture and beat until blended, scraping bowl frequently.

4 Pour batter into prepared pan. Bake 35 to 40 minutes for tube cake, or about 25 minutes for 9-inch layers, until toothpick inserted in center of cake comes out clean. Invert cake in tube pan on metal funnel or bottle; cool completely. For 9-inch layers, remove from pans immediately to cool on wire racks. With small knife, loosen tube cake from side and center of pan. Remove cake from pan and place on cake plate. *Makes 16 servings.*

EACH SERVING: ABOUT 155 CALORIES, 4 G PROTEIN, 23 G CARBOHYDRATE, 5 G TOTAL FAT (3 G SATURATED), 0.5 G FIBER, 87 MG CHOLESTEROL, 185 MG SODIUM.

Sand Torte

PREP 20 MINUTES / BAKE 40 TO 45 MINUTES

Denser than a sponge cake, but lighter than pound cake, this German specialty is flavored with lemon and brandy. Serve thick slices of the cake with poached dried fruit in the winter, and fresh berries in berry puree in the summer.

¾ CUP (1½ STICKS) PLUS 1 TABLESPOON BUTTER OR
    MARGARINE, SOFTENED
1 CUP PLUS 1 TABLESPOON SUGAR
5 LARGE EGGS
2 CUPS CAKE FLOUR (NOT SELF-RISING)
1 TEASPOON BAKING POWDER
¼ TEASPOON SALT
1 TEASPOON VANILLA EXTRACT
1 TABLESPOON BRANDY (OPTIONAL)
½ TEASPOON FRESHLY GRATED LEMON PEEL

1 Preheat oven to 350° F. Butter 9-inch tube pan; sprinkle with some sugar.

2 In large bowl, with mixer at low speed, beat ¾ cup butter and 1 cup sugar until blended. Increase speed to high; beat 1 minute, or until creamy. Reduce speed to medium-low; add eggs, 1 at a time, beating well after each addition. Add flour, baking powder, and salt; beat until batter is smooth. Add vanilla, brandy, if you like, and lemon peel; beat 5 minutes, until batter is light and fluffy.

3 Spoon batter into prepared pan; smooth with rubber spatula. Bake 40 to 45 minutes, until cake springs back slightly when touched. Immediately turn cake out of pan onto wire rack. Melt remaining 1 tablespoon butter; brush over top of hot cake. Sprinkle cake with remaining 1 tablespoon sugar. Cool completely on wire rack. *Makes 16 servings*

EACH SERVING: ABOUT 210 CALORIES, 3 G PROTEIN,
24 G CARBOHYDRATE, 11 G TOTAL FAT (7 G SATURATED),
0 G FIBER, 93 MG CHOLESTEROL, 185 MG SODIUM.

Génoise

PREP 20 MINUTES PLUS COOLING
BAKE 15 TO 20 MINUTES

This light, fine-grained sponge cake can be iced with any flavor of buttercream, filled with whipped cream and fresh fruit, or glazed and decorated with fresh flowers (see box, page 345).

6 LARGE EGGS
1 CUP SUGAR
1 CUP ALL-PURPOSE FLOUR
½ TEASPOON SALT
2 TEASPOONS VANILLA EXTRACT
6 TABLESPOONS BUTTER OR MARGARINE, MELTED AND
    COOLED
FLAVORED SIMPLE SYRUP (PAGE 363)
FRESH BUTTERCREAM (PAGE 352)

1 Preheat oven to 350° F. Grease and flour either three 8-inch round cake pans or two 9-inch round cake pans.

2 In large metal bowl, with wire whisk, mix eggs and sugar. Place egg mixture over a large pan with water over medium heat. Stirring occasionally, heat until mixture is lukewarm and sugar has dissolved. Remove mixture from heat.

3 With mixer at high speed, beat egg mixture about 10 minutes, until thick and lemon-colored and mixture forms ribbon when beaters are lifted, scraping bowl occasionally with rubber spatula. In small bowl, mix flour and salt. In two additions, sift flour mixture over egg mixture and fold in until just blended; fold in vanilla and melted butter.

4 Divide batter evenly among prepared pans. Bake 15 to 20 minutes or until cake is golden and springs back when lightly touched. With small knife, loosen layers from sides of pans; immediately invert onto wire rack to cool.

5 Meanwhile, prepared Flavored Simple Syrup and Fresh Buttercream.

6 Place 1 layer on plate; brush with flavored syrup and spread with ½ cup buttercream. Repeat layering with remaining 2 layers, syrup, and buttercream. Frost side of cake with remaining buttercream. *Makes 16 servings.*

EACH SERVING: ABOUT 335 CALORIES, 4 G PROTEIN,
33 G CARBOHYDRATE, 20 G TOTAL FAT (11 G SATURATED),
0 G FIBER, 177 MG CHOLESTEROL, 150 MG SODIUM.

Lemon Génoise Prepare batter as for Génoise (page 325) and add *1 teaspoon freshly grated lemon peel* and *2 tablespoons fresh lemon juice* with melted butter. Bake as directed.
Each serving: About 335 calories, 4 g protein, 33 g carbohydrate, 20 g total fat (11 g saturated), 0 g fiber, 177 mg cholesterol, 150 mg sodium.

Orange Génoise Prepare batter as for Génoise (page 325) and add *1 teaspoon freshly grated orange peel* and *2 tablespoons fresh orange juice* with melted butter. Bake as directed.
Each serving: About 335 calories, 4 g protein, 33 g carbohydrate, 20 g total fat (11 g saturated), 0 g fiber, 177 mg cholesterol, 150 mg sodium.

Almond Génoise Prepare batter as for Génoise (page 325) and add *¼ teaspoon almond extract* with vanilla extract. Bake as directed.
Each serving: About 335 calories, 4 g protein, 33 g carbohydrate, 20 g total fat (11 g saturated), 0 g fiber, 177 mg cholesterol, 150 mg sodium.

Chocolate Génoise with Ganache

PREP 50 MINUTES PLUS COOLING / BAKE 25 MINUTES

This may be the ultimate in elegant chocolate cakes—the one that you'd serve with demitasse as the finale to your most festive dinner party. Note that the eggs and sugar need to be whipped until the batter falls in ribbons from the beater (see photo, page 293). A heavy-duty stand mixer is a great help here, as this process may take 30 minutes or more.

7 LARGE EGGS

1¼ CUPS GRANULATED SUGAR

1½ TEASPOONS VANILLA EXTRACT

¾ CUP CAKE FLOUR (NOT SELF-RISING)

¾ CUP UNSWEETENED COCOA PLUS ADDITIONAL FOR
   DUSTING PANS

½ TEASPOON SALT

½ CUP BUTTER OR MARGARINE (1 STICK), MELTED AND
   COOLED TO LUKEWARM

GANACHE (PAGE 359)

CONFECTIONERS' SUGAR

1 Preheat oven to 350° F. Grease two 9-inch round cake pans. Line bottoms with waxed paper; grease paper. Dust pans with cocoa.

2 In large bowl, with mixer at high speed, beat eggs, granulated sugar, and vanilla until mixture has increased in volume about 4 times and is the consistency of whipped cream. This will take anywhere from 5 to 35 minutes.

3 Meanwhile, in medium bowl, stir together flour, cocoa, and salt until blended. In four additions, sift flour mixture over egg mixture, and fold gently.

4 Divide batter evenly between prepared pans. Bake 25 minutes, or until layers spring back when lightly touched and pull away from sides of pan. Cool in pans on wire racks 10 minutes. With small knife, loosen layers from sides of pans; invert onto wire racks. Remove waxed paper; cool completely.

5 Meanwhile, prepare Ganache; let stand at room temperature 30 minutes before using.

6 With serrated knife, cut each layer horizontally in half. Place bottom half of 1 layer, cut side up, on cake plate; spread with ⅓ cup ganache. Top with second layer and another ⅓ cup ganache. Repeat layering to make 4 layers of cake and 3 layers of ganache in all. Sprinkle top of cake with confectioners' sugar. Frost sides with remaining ganache. *Makes 20 servings.*

Each serving: About 260 calories, 4 g protein, 29 g carbohydrate, 16 g total fat (9 g saturated), 2 g fiber, 104 mg cholesterol, 140 mg sodium.

Jelly Roll

For a real old-fashioned jelly roll, simply spread the cake with strawberry jam (or raspberry, or another favorite flavor). If the jelly is very stiff, warm it slightly so that it will spread smoothly without tearing the cake. Lemon Filling (page 361), or whipped cream and sliced strawberries are other options.

5 LARGE EGGS, SEPARATED
½ CUP GRANULATED SUGAR
1 TEASPOON VANILLA EXTRACT
½ CUP ALL-PURPOSE FLOUR
CONFECTIONERS' SUGAR
⅔ CUP STRAWBERRY JAM

1 Preheat oven to 350° F. Grease 15½" by 10½" jelly-roll pan. Line with waxed paper; grease paper.

2 In large bowl, with mixer at high speed, beat egg whites until soft peaks form when beaters are lifted. At high speed, gradually sprinkle in ¼ cup granulated sugar, 1 tablespoon at a time, and beat until whites hold stiff peaks when beaters are lifted.

3 In small bowl, with mixer at high speed, beat egg yolks, remaining ¼ cup granulated sugar, and vanilla until very thick and lemon-colored, 5 to 10 minutes; stir in flour. With rubber spatula, gently fold egg-yolk mixture into beaten egg whites.

4 Spread batter in prepared pan. Bake 10 to 15 minutes, until top of cake springs back when lightly touched with finger.

5 Meanwhile, sift confectioners' sugar onto clean kitchen towel. With small knife, loosen edges of cake from sides of pan; invert onto towel. Carefully peel off waxed paper. Trim ¼ inch from edges of cake. Starting from one short side, roll cake, jelly-roll fashion, in towel. Cool completely on wire rack.

6 Unroll cooled cake. Spread with jam. Starting from same short side, roll cake without towel and transfer, seam side down, to cake platter. Sprinkle with confectioners' sugar. *Makes 10 servings.*

EACH SERVING: ABOUT 160 CALORIES, 4 G PROTEIN, 30 G CARBOHYDRATE, 3 G TOTAL FAT (1 G SATURATED), 0.5 G FIBER, 106 MG CHOLESTEROL, 40 MG SODIUM.

Angel-Food Cake Roll

This super-light, pure white cake roll has a faint almond flavor. It's delicious with the Lemon Curd Cream, or you could use Stabilized Whipped Cream (page 358) instead. Another idea: Fill the cake with Chocolate Pastry Cream (page 360) and frost it with Amaretto Buttercream (page 353), if you like.

¾ CUP CAKE FLOUR (NOT SELF-RISING)
¾ CUP CONFECTIONERS' SUGAR
9 LARGE EGG WHITES
¼ TEASPOON SALT
¾ CUP GRANULATED SUGAR
1½ TEASPOONS VANILLA EXTRACT
¼ TEASPOON ALMOND EXTRACT
LEMON CURD CREAM (PAGE 361)

1 Preheat oven to 325° F. Grease 15½" by 10½" jelly-roll pan. Line with waxed paper; grease and flour paper. Sift flour and confectioners' sugar into small bowl.

2 In large bowl, with mixer at medium speed, beat egg whites and salt until foamy. Increase speed to medium-high; beat until soft peaks form when beaters are lifted. Sprinkle in granulated sugar, 2 tablespoons at a time, and beat until whites just stand in stiff peaks when beaters are lifted. Beat in vanilla and almond extracts.

3 In two additions, sift flour mixture into egg whites, folding with rubber spatula just until flour mixture disappears. Do not overmix.

4 Turn batter into prepared jelly-roll pan. Bake 30 minutes, or until cake springs back when lightly touched. Cool completely in pan on wire rack. Invert cake onto surface. Carefully peel off waxed paper.

5 Meanwhile, prepare Lemon Curd Cream.

6 Spread lemon curd cream evenly over cake, leaving ½-inch border on all sides. Starting from one long side, roll cake and transfer, seam side down, to long platter. Refrigerate until ready to serve. *Makes 14 servings.*

EACH SERVING: ABOUT 205 CALORIES, 3 G PROTEIN, 30 G CARBOHYDRATE, 8 G TOTAL FAT (4 G SATURATED), 0 G FIBER, 65 MG CHOLESTEROL, 130 MG SODIUM.

Brandied Bûche de Noël

PREP 1 HOUR 30 MINUTES PLUS COOLING AND CHILLING
BAKE 10 MINUTES

This is our variation on the traditional French Yule Log. Instead of using all chocolate buttercream, we've chosen our Brandied Butter Frosting.

⅓ CUP ALL-PURPOSE FLOUR

¼ CUP UNSWEETENED COCOA

1 TEASPOON GROUND CINNAMON

¾ TEASPOON GROUND GINGER

PINCH GROUND CLOVES

PINCH SALT

5 LARGE EGGS, SEPARATED

¼ TEASPOON CREAM OF TARTAR

½ CUP GRANULATED SUGAR

2 TABLESPOONS BUTTER OR MARGARINE, MELTED AND
    COOLED SLIGHTLY

TWO-TONE BRANDIED BUTTER FROSTING (PAGE 355)

MERINGUE MUSHROOMS (OPTIONAL, PAGE 198)

CONFECTIONERS' SUGAR (OPTIONAL)

1 Preheat oven to 375° F. Grease 15½" by 10½" jelly-roll pan. Line with waxed paper; grease and flour paper. On sheet of waxed paper, stir together flour, cocoa, cinnamon, ginger, cloves, and salt.

2 In bowl, with mixer at high speed, beat egg whites and cream of tartar until soft peaks form when beaters are lifted. Gradually sprinkle in ¼ cup granulated sugar and beat until egg whites hold stiff peaks.

3 In large bowl, using same beaters and with mixer at high speed, beat egg yolks and remaining ¼ cup granulated sugar until very thick and lemon-colored, 5 to 10 minutes. With rubber spatula, gently fold beaten whites into beaten yolks, one-third at a time. Gently fold flour mixture, one-third at a time, into egg mixture. Fold in melted butter just until combined.

4 Spread batter evenly in prepared pan. Bake 10 minutes, or until top of cake springs back when lightly touched with finger. Meanwhile, sprinkle clean cloth towel with confectioners' sugar. Immediately invert onto sugared towel. Carefully peel off waxed paper. Starting from one long side, roll cake, jelly-roll fashion, with towel. Transfer roll, seam side down, to wire rack and cool completely, about 1 hour.

5 Prepare Two-Tone Brandied Butter Frosting.

6 Gently unroll cooled cake. With metal spatula, spread white frosting almost to edges. Starting from same long side, roll up cake without towel. Cut 1½-inch-thick diagonal slice off each end of roll. Place cake, seam side down, on platter. Spread chocolate frosting over roll. Place each end piece on sides of roll to resemble branches. Spread remaining chocolate frosting over roll and branches. Swirl frosting to resemble bark of tree. Refrigerate cake at least 2 hours before serving. Garnish platter with Meringue Mushrooms and sprinkle lightly with confectioners' sugar, if desired. *Makes 14 servings.*

EACH SERVING: ABOUT 190 CALORIES, 3 G PROTEIN, 20 G CARBOHYDRATE, 11 G TOTAL FAT (6 G SATURATED), 0.5 G FIBER, 99 MG CHOLESTEROL, 120 MG SODIUM.

Bûche de Noël

Roll the cake around the white frosting and cut both ends off on a diagonal. Save the cut pieces to use as "branches."

Spread some chocolate frosting over the roll, then attach the two cut-off diagonal ends to the roll, and frost.

Fallen Chocolate Soufflé Roll

PREP 25 MINUTES PLUS COOLING AND CHILLING
BAKE 15 MINUTES

This roulade (as it's called in France) is made with a delicate soufflé mixture baked in a jelly-roll pan. The "cake" puffs, then falls, resulting in a thin layer with a cloudlike texture. For a Mexican twist, cinnamon and cloves flavor the chocolate cake.

5 SQUARES (5 OUNCES) SEMISWEET CHOCOLATE

1 SQUARE (1 OUNCE) UNSWEETENED CHOCOLATE

1 TEASPOON INSTANT ESPRESSO-COFFEE POWDER,
    DISSOLVED IN 3 TABLESPOONS HOT WATER

6 LARGE EGGS, SEPARATED

6 TABLESPOONS GRANULATED SUGAR

1 TEASPOON VANILLA EXTRACT

¾ TEASPOON GROUND CINNAMON

¼ TEASPOON SALT

⅛ TEASPOON GROUND CLOVES

1½ CUPS HEAVY OR WHIPPING CREAM

¼ CUP COFFEE-FLAVORED LIQUEUR

5 TABLESPOONS CONFECTIONERS' SUGAR PLUS ADDITIONAL
    FOR SPRINKLING

1 Preheat oven to 350° F. Grease 15½" by 10½" jelly-roll pan. Line with waxed paper; grease and flour paper.

2 In top of double boiler set over simmering water, melt semisweet and unsweetened chocolates with coffee, stirring often.

3 In large bowl, with mixer at high speed, beat egg whites until soft peaks form when beaters are lifted. Gradually sprinkle in 3 tablespoons granulated sugar, 1 tablespoon at a time, and beat until whites hold stiff peaks when beaters are lifted.

4 In small bowl, with mixer at high speed, beat egg yolks with remaining 3 tablespoons granulated sugar until very thick and lemon-colored, 5 to 10 minutes. Reduce speed to low; beat in vanilla, cinnamon, salt, and cloves. With rubber spatula, fold chocolate mixture into egg-yolk mixture. Gently fold one-third of egg whites into chocolate mixture; fold chocolate mixture into remaining egg whites.

5 Spread batter evenly in prepared pan. Bake 15 minutes, or until firm to the touch. Cover cake with dampened, clean cloth towel; cool in pan on wire rack 30 minutes.

6 Meanwhile, in large bowl, with mixer at medium speed, beat cream until soft peaks form. Beat in coffee liqueur and 3 tablespoons confectioners' sugar; beat until stiff peaks form.

7 Remove towel from cake; sift remaining 2 tablespoons confectioners' sugar over cake. With small knife, loosen cake from sides of pan. Cover cake with sheet of foil and a large cookie sheet; invert cake onto cookie sheet. Carefully peel off waxed paper.

8 Spread whipped cream evenly over cake, leaving ½-inch border. Starting from a long side and using foil to help lift cake, roll cake jelly-roll fashion (cake may crack). Place rolled cake, seam side down, on long platter. Refrigerate at least 1 hour, until ready to serve. Just before serving, sprinkle with confectioners' sugar. *Makes 16 servings.*

EACH SERVING: ABOUT 200 CALORIES, 3 G PROTEIN, 16 G CARBOHYDRATE, 14 G TOTAL FAT (8 G SATURATED), 1 G FIBER, 110 MG CHOLESTEROL, 70 MG SODIUM.

Cannoli Cake Roll

PREP 1 HOUR 30 MINUTES PLUS COOLING AND CHILLING
BAKE 10 TO 15 MINUTES

You'll recognize the ricotta filling in this cake roll if you've ever eaten cannoli, the crisp, tube-shaped Italian pastry. For an out-of-the-ordinary Christmas dessert, you can follow the directions for assembling the Brandied Bûche de Noël (page 328) using this cake and filling. For the tree-bark effect, use a brown frosting rather than a white one. Meringue Mushrooms (page 198), the classic garnish for a yule log, are optional, but festive.

CAKE ROLL:

JELLY ROLL (PAGE 327), WITHOUT JAM

2 TABLESPOONS ORANGE-FLAVORED LIQUEUR

1 TABLESPOON WATER

1 TABLESPOON GRANULATED SUGAR

RICOTTA FILLING:

1¼ CUPS RICOTTA CHEESE

4 OUNCES REDUCED-FAT CREAM CHEESE (NEUFCHÂTEL)

½ CUP CONFECTIONERS' SUGAR

½ TEASPOON VANILLA EXTRACT

¼ TEASPOON GROUND CINNAMON

¼ CUP SEMISWEET CHOCOLATE MINI-CHIPS

FROSTING:

¾ CUP HEAVY OR WHIPPING CREAM

3 TABLESPOONS CONFECTIONERS' SUGAR

2 TABLESPOONS ORANGE-FLAVORED LIQUEUR

½ TEASPOON VANILLA EXTRACT

¼ CUP PISTACHIO NUTS, CHOPPED

1 TABLESPOON SEMISWEET CHOCOLATE MINI-CHIPS

ORNAMENTAL ORANGES FOR GARNISH (OPTIONAL)

1 Prepare and bake Jelly Roll as directed. Meanwhile, in cup, mix liqueur, water, and granulated sugar until sugar dissolves.

2 Sprinkle clean cloth towel with confectioners' sugar. When cake is done, immediately invert hot cake onto towel. Carefully peel off waxed paper. Brush cake with orange-liqueur mixture. Starting from a long side, roll cake with towel jelly-roll fashion. Cool cake roll, seam side down, on wire rack until completely cool, about 1 hour.

3 Meanwhile, prepare Ricotta Filling: In food processor with knife blade attached, process ricotta, cream cheese, confectioners' sugar, vanilla, and cinnamon until smooth. Transfer filling to bowl; stir in chocolate chips. Cover and refrigerate filling while cake cools.

4 Assemble cake: Gently unroll cooled cake. With metal spatula, spread filling over cake almost to edges. Starting from same long side, roll cake without towel. Place rolled cake, seam side down, on long platter.

5 Prepare Frosting: In small bowl, with mixer at medium speed, beat cream and confectioners' sugar until soft peaks form. With rubber spatula, fold in orange liqueur and vanilla. With metal spatula, spread whipped-cream frosting over cake. Refrigerate cake at least 2 hours before serving. Sprinkle top of cake with chopped pistachios and chocolate chips just before serving. Garnish platter with ornamental oranges, if desired. *Makes 14 servings.*

EACH SERVING: ABOUT 250 CALORIES, 7 G PROTEIN, 24 G CARBOHYDRATE, 14 G TOTAL FAT (7 G SATURATED), 0.5 G FIBER, 110 MG CHOLESTEROL, 80 MG SODIUM.

Cannoli Cake Roll

FRUITCAKES

The legendary holiday fruitcake that has passed from relative to relative year after year bears no resemblance to these tender, moist, spicy cakes. The first is a dark Christmas cake worthy of Dickens; laden with brandy-soaked fruit, it's baked as twelve little loaves, perfect for gifts. The second is a Scottish recipe that's lighter and more delicate. The Christmas cake benefits from weeks of aging; the Dundee cake is ready to eat the next day.

Dark Christmas Fruitcake

PREP 1 HOUR 30 MINUTES PLUS 8 HOURS TO SOAK
PLUS 1 MONTH TO STAND
BAKE 1 HOUR 30 TO 35 MINUTES

There's a full cup of brandy in this recipe, but for even more of a kick, you can periodically sprinkle the cakes with more brandy while they age. Unless you have an extremely cool pantry (almost unheard of these days), be sure to store the cakes in the refrigerator.

3 CUPS DRIED FIGS, STEMMED AND CHOPPED
2 CUPS PITTED DATES, CHOPPED
2 CUPS GOLDEN RAISINS
2 CUPS DARK SEEDLESS RAISINS
1 BOX (10 OUNCES) DRIED CURRANTS (2 CUPS)
1½ CUPS DICED CANDIED CITRON
1 CUP DICED CANDIED PINEAPPLE
1 CUP RED CANDIED CHERRIES, COARSELY CHOPPED
1 CUP DICED CANDIED ORANGE PEEL
1 CUP BRANDY
3 CUPS ALL-PURPOSE FLOUR
½ TEASPOON GROUND CINNAMON
¼ TEASPOON BAKING SODA
¼ TEASPOON GROUND ALLSPICE
¼ TEASPOON GROUND CLOVES
2 CUPS BUTTER OR MARGARINE (4 STICKS), SOFTENED
1 BOX (16 OUNCES) DARK BROWN SUGAR
6 LARGE EGGS
⅓ CUP DARK MOLASSES
⅔ CUP MILK
5 CUPS PECANS OR WALNUTS

1 In large bowl, mix figs, dates, golden raisins, dark raisins, currants, citron, pineapple, cherries, orange peel, and brandy. Cover and let stand 8 hours or overnight, stirring a few times.

2 Preheat oven to 275° F. Grease twelve 5¾" by 3¼" by 2" mini loaf pans. Line bottoms with waxed paper; grease paper.

3 In medium bowl, stir together flour, cinnamon, baking soda, allspice, and cloves.

4 In large bowl, with mixer at low speed, beat butter and brown sugar until blended. Increase speed to medium-high; beat 5 minutes, scraping bowl frequently, until light and creamy. Reduce speed to medium. Beat in eggs, 1 at a time, beating well after each addition. Beat in molasses. Reduce speed to low, and beat in flour mixture alternately with milk, beginning and ending with flour mixture, until blended, scraping bowl. Turn batter into larger bowl for easier mixing. Stir in fruit mixture, including any brandy not absorbed by fruit, and nuts.

5 Spoon batter into prepared pans, spreading evenly. Bake cakes 1 hour 30 to 35 minutes, until toothpick inserted in centers of cakes comes out clean. Cool cakes in pans on wire racks 15 minutes. With small knife, loosen cakes from sides of pans and invert onto wire racks. Turn top sides up and cool completely. Remove waxed paper. Wrap in plastic wrap and then in foil. Let stand in a cool place or refrigerate at least 1 month before serving. Refrigerate up to 6 months. *Makes 12 cakes, 4 servings each.*

EACH SERVING: ABOUT 395 CALORIES, 4 G PROTEIN, 61 G CARBOHYDRATE, 17 G TOTAL FAT (6 G SATURATED), 3 G FIBER, 48 MG CHOLESTEROL, 125 MG SODIUM.

Dundee Cake

PREP 35 MINUTES PLUS OVERNIGHT TO STAND
BAKE 2 HOURS TO 2 HOURS 15 MINUTES

Somewhat more subtle than a holiday fruitcake, this popular Scottish teacake is topped with whole almonds and lightly flavored with orange.

2 CUPS ALL-PURPOSE FLOUR
1 TEASPOON BAKING POWDER
¼ TEASPOON SALT
¼ TEASPOON GROUND ALLSPICE
¼ TEASPOON GROUND CINNAMON
⅔ CUP BLANCHED WHOLE ALMONDS
1 CUP SUGAR

⅔ CUP GOLDEN RAISINS

⅔ CUP DRIED CURRANTS

½ CUP DICED CANDIED CITRON

½ CUP DICED CANDIED ORANGE OR LEMON PEEL

½ CUP RED CANDIED CHERRIES, CHOPPED

1 CUP BUTTER OR MARGARINE (2 STICKS), SOFTENED

4 LARGE EGGS

2 TABLESPOONS ORANGE-FLAVORED LIQUEUR

1 Preheat oven to 300° F. Grease and flour 8-inch springform pan.

2 In medium bowl, stir together flour, baking powder, salt, allspice, and cinnamon.

3 In food processor with knife blade attached, combine ⅓ cup almonds and ¼ cup sugar. Process until almonds are finely ground. In medium bowl, mix ground-almond mixture, raisins, currants, citron, orange peel, and cherries.

4 In large bowl, with mixer at low speed, beat remaining ¾ cup sugar and butter until blended.

Increase speed to medium-high and beat 5 minutes, or until light and creamy. Add eggs, 1 at a time, beating well after each addition. Beat in orange liqueur. Reduce speed to low; beat in flour mixture until blended, scraping bowl (batter will be thick). Stir in fruit mixture.

5 Spoon batter into prepared pan, spreading evenly. Arrange remaining ⅓ cup almonds on top of batter. Bake 2 hours to 2 hours 15 minutes, until toothpick inserted in center of cake comes out clean. Cover pan loosely with foil after 1 hour to prevent top from overbrowning. Cool in pan on wire rack 20 minutes. With small knife, loosen cake from side of pan; remove pan side. Cool completely on wire rack. When cool, remove pan bottom and wrap cake in plastic wrap and then in foil. Let stand overnight before serving. *Makes 20 servings.*

EACH SERVING: ABOUT 290 CALORIES, 4 G PROTEIN,
40 G CARBOHYDRATE, 13 G TOTAL FAT (6 G SATURATED),
1 G FIBER, 67 MG CHOLESTEROL, 180 MG SODIUM.

Dundee Cake

CHEESECAKES

You can make quick cheesecakes ("baked" in the refrigerator) and low-fat cheesecakes (substituting yogurt or tofu for the cream cheese), but the fact is they will never reach the blissful richness of the real thing.

New York-Style Cheesecake

PREP 20 MINUTES PLUS RESTING AND CHILLING
BAKE 1 HOUR 5 TO 10 MINUTES

Purists will insist on devouring this cake unadorned, while the more adventurous will enjoy our variations. A garnish of fresh berries on top of the cake always makes it look festive.

GRAHAM-CRACKER CRUMB CRUST (PAGE 210), UNBAKED
3 PACKAGES (8 OUNCES EACH) CREAM CHEESE, SOFTENED
¾ CUP SUGAR
1 TABLESPOON ALL-PURPOSE FLOUR
1½ TEASPOONS VANILLA EXTRACT
3 LARGE EGGS
1 LARGE EGG YOLK
¼ CUP MILK

1 Preheat oven to 375° F. Prepare Graham-Cracker Crumb Crust in 8½- to 9-inch springform pan. With hand, press mixture firmly onto bottom and up side of pan. Bake 10 minutes; cool on wire rack. Turn oven control to 300° F.

2 In large bowl, with mixer at medium speed, beat cream cheese and sugar until smooth and fluffy. Beat in flour and vanilla until well combined.

3 Reduce speed to low and beat in eggs and egg yolk, 1 at a time, beating well after each addition. Beat in milk just until blended.

4 Pour batter into pan. Bake cake 55 to 60 minutes until set and 3 inches from center is slightly wet and cake is lightly golden and set. Cool completely on wire rack. Refrigerate overnight before serving. To serve, remove side of pan. Place cake on plate; garnish with fruits, if desired. *Makes 16 servings.*

EACH SERVING: ABOUT 275 CALORIES, 5 G PROTEIN,
19 G CARBOHYDRATE, 20 G TOTAL FAT (12 G SATURATED),
0.5 G FIBER, 108 MG CHOLESTEROL, 230 MG SODIUM.

APRICOT SWIRL CHEESECAKE Prepare and bake Graham-Cracker Crumb Crust as for New York-Style Cheesecake. In 1-quart saucepan, combine *¾ cup (5 ounces) dried apricots, ¾ cup water*, and *2 tablespoons sugar*. Bring to boiling over medium heat. Reduce to simmer, cover, and cook 15 to 20 minutes, until apricots are very soft; puree in food processor. Prepare batter as directed for New York-Style Cheesecake but omit milk. Spoon batter into prepared pan; spoon apricot mixture on top in several dollops. Using knife, swirl apricot mixture through cheesecake batter. Bake cake, cool, and chill as directed.
EACH SERVING: ABOUT 300 CALORIES, 6 G PROTEIN,
26 G CARBOHYDRATE, 20 G TOTAL FAT (12 G SATURATED),
1 G FIBER, 108 MG CHOLESTEROL, 225 MG SODIUM.

GINGER CHEESECAKE Prepare crust as for New York-Style Cheesecake but use *9 ounces gingersnaps*, crushed, for graham crackers; bake as directed in Step 1. Prepare batter as directed for New York-Style Cheesecake and add *⅓ cup minced crystallized ginger* and *1 teaspoon freshly grated lemon peel*. Bake cake, cool, and chill as directed.
EACH SERVING: ABOUT 320 CALORIES, 6 G PROTEIN,
29 G CARBOHYDRATE, 21 G TOTAL FAT (12 G SATURATED),
0 G FIBER, 108 MG CHOLESTEROL, 280 MG SODIUM.

AMARETTO CHEESECAKE Prepare crust as for New York-Style Cheesecake but use *6 ounces amaretti cookies*, crushed, for graham crackers and omit sugar; bake as directed in Step 1. Prepare batter as directed for New York-Style Cheesecake but use only *2 tablespoons milk* and add *2 tablespoons amaretto (almond-flavored liqueur)*. Bake cake, cool, and chill as directed.
EACH SERVING: ABOUT 280 CALORIES, 5 G PROTEIN,
20 G CARBOHYDRATE, 20 G TOTAL FAT (12 G SATURATED),
0 G FIBER, 110 MG CHOLESTEROL, 175 MG SODIUM.

CHOCOLATE MARBLE CHEESECAKE Prepare Chocolate-Wafer Crumb Crust (page 210) and bake as directed. Prepare batter as directed for New York-Style Cheesecake but omit milk. Melt *2 ounces (2 squares) semisweet chocolate*. In small bowl, stir together melted chocolate and 1 cup cheesecake batter. Pour plain cheesecake batter into prepared pan. Spoon chocolate batter over top in several dollops. Using knife, swirl chocolate batter through plain batter. Bake cake, cool, and chill as directed.
EACH SERVING: ABOUT 290 CALORIES, 5 G PROTEIN,
21 G CARBOHYDRATE, 21 G TOTAL FAT (12 G SATURATED),
0.5 G FIBER, 108 MG CHOLESTEROL, 220 MG SODIUM.

Chocolate Cheesecake

PREP 25 MINUTES PLUS COOLING AND CHILLING
BAKE 1 HOUR TO 1 HOUR 5 MINUTES

Diehard chocolate lovers, raise your forks! With a pound and a half of cream cheese and a half-pound of chocolate, this is not a cake for the faint of heart.

CHOCOLATE-WAFER CRUMB CRUST (PAGE 210)

3 PACKAGES (8 OUNCES EACH) CREAM CHEESE, SOFTENED

1 CUP SUGAR

¼ CUP UNSWEETENED COCOA

4 LARGE EGGS

¾ CUP SOUR CREAM

1½ TEASPOONS VANILLA EXTRACT

8 SQUARES (8 OUNCES) SEMISWEET CHOCOLATE, MELTED AND COOLED

1 Preheat oven to 325° F. Prepare Chocolate-Wafer Crumb Crust in 9-inch springform pan. Press mixture firmly onto bottom of pan (see photo at right). Bake 10 minutes. Cool on wire rack.

2 In large bowl, with mixer at medium speed, beat cream cheese until smooth. Beat in sugar and cocoa until blended, scraping bowl occasionally with rubber spatula. Reduce speed to low. Add eggs, 1 at a time, beating after each addition, just until blended, scraping side of bowl frequently. Beat in sour cream and vanilla. Add melted chocolate and beat until well blended.

3 Pour batter into cooled crust. Bake 50 to 55 minutes, until cheesecake is set 2 inches in from sides, with the center jiggly and shiny. Turn off oven; let cheesecake remain in oven with door ajar 1 hour.

4 Remove cake from oven and cool completely in pan on wire rack. Cover loosely and refrigerate until well chilled, at least 6 hours before serving. To serve, remove side of pan and place cake on plate. Cut with a knife dipped in warm water, wiping knife between slices. *Makes 16 servings.*

EACH SERVING: ABOUT 380 CALORIES, 7 G PROTEIN,
31 G CARBOHYDRATE, 27 G TOTAL FAT (16 G SATURATED),
2 G FIBER, 113 MG CHOLESTEROL, 230 MG SODIUM.

Creamy Lemon-Ricotta Cheesecake

PREP 20 MINUTES PLUS COOLING AND CHILLING
BAKE 1 HOUR 25 MINUTES

This is cheesecake all'Italiana—the filling is made with ricotta. The original is made with a cookie-dough crust, but the vanilla-wafer crust is easier to prepare.

4 LARGE LEMONS

4 TABLESPOONS BUTTER OR MARGARINE

1 CUP VANILLA-WAFER CRUMBS (ABOUT 30 COOKIES)

1¼ CUPS SUGAR

¼ CUP CORNSTARCH

2 PACKAGES (8 OUNCES EACH) CREAM CHEESE, SOFTENED

1 CONTAINER (15 OUNCES) RICOTTA CHEESE

4 LARGE EGGS

2 CUPS HALF-AND-HALF OR LIGHT CREAM

2 TEASPOONS VANILLA EXTRACT

1 Preheat oven to 375° F. From lemons, grate 4 teaspoons peel and squeeze ⅓ cup juice. In small saucepan, melt butter over low heat; stir in 1 teaspoon lemon peel. Pour butter mixture into 9-inch springform pan. Add wafer crumbs and stir until moistened. With hand, press mixture firmly onto bottom of pan (see photo below). Bake 10 minutes, or until golden. Cool on wire rack about 30 minutes. Wrap outside of pan with heavy-duty foil.

Making a Crumb Crust

The springform pan allows you to unmold a cheesecake with the crumb crust intact. Press the buttered crumbs evenly and firmly onto the bottom of the pan. Some recipes call for the crumbs to be pressed up the side of the pan as well.

2 Turn oven control to 325° F. In small bowl, combine sugar and cornstarch until blended. In large bowl, with mixer at medium speed, beat cream cheese and ricotta until smooth, about 5 minutes; slowly beat in sugar mixture. Reduce speed to low; beat in eggs, half-and-half, lemon juice, vanilla, and remaining 3 teaspoons lemon peel just until blended, scraping bowl often with rubber spatula.

3 Pour batter into crust. Bake 1 hour 15 minutes. Turn off oven; let cheesecake remain in oven 1 hour.

4 Remove cake from oven; discard foil and cool completely in pan on wire rack. Cover and refrigerate until well chilled, at least 6 hours or overnight. To serve, remove side of pan and place cake on plate. Cut with a knife dipped in warm water, wiping knife between slices. *Makes 16 servings.*

EACH SERVING: ABOUT 325 CALORIES, 8 G PROTEIN, 25 G CARBOHYDRATE, 22 G TOTAL FAT (13 G SATURATED), 0 G FIBER, 117 MG CHOLESTEROL, 180 MG SODIUM.

Lime Cheesecake

PREP 20 MINUTES PLUS COOLING AND CHILLING
BAKE 1 HOUR TO 1 HOUR 12 MINUTES

The sour cream and lime juice combine to give the filling a refreshing tang. This cheesecake is a bit lighter than most, but it's still rich and delicious.

1¼ CUPS VANILLA-WAFER CRUMBS (ABOUT 35 COOKIES)
3 TABLESPOONS BUTTER OR MARGARINE, MELTED
3 LARGE LIMES
2 PACKAGES (8 OUNCES EACH) CREAM CHEESE, SOFTENED
1¼ CUPS SUGAR
1 CONTAINER (16 OUNCES) SOUR CREAM
1 TEASPOON VANILLA EXTRACT
3 LARGE EGGS
LIME SLICES FOR GARNISH (OPTIONAL)

1 Preheat oven to 350° F. In 9" springform pan, combine wafer crumbs and melted butter; stir with fork until moistened. With hand, press mixture firmly onto bottom of pan (see photo opposite). Tightly wrap outside of pan with heavy-duty foil to prevent leakage when baking in water bath. Bake 10 to 12 minutes, until deep golden. Cool on wire rack.

2 From limes, grate 1 tablespoon peel and squeeze ⅓ cup juice. In large bowl, with mixer at medium speed, beat cream cheese until smooth; slowly beat in sugar until blended. Reduce speed to low; beat in sour cream, lime juice and peel, and vanilla. Add eggs, 1 at a time, beating after each addition, just until blended.

3 Pour batter into crust and place pan in large roasting pan. Place pan on oven rack. Carefully pour enough *boiling water* into roasting pan to come halfway up side of springform pan. Bake 50 to 60 minutes, until edge is set but center still jiggles. Turn off oven; let cheesecake remain in oven with door ajar 30 minutes.

4 Remove cake from water bath; discard foil. With small knife, loosen cheesecake from side of pan to help prevent cracking during cooling. Cool cheesecake completely in pan on wire rack. Cover and refrigerate until well chilled, at least 6 hours or overnight. Remove side of pan and place cake on plate to serve. Garnish with lime slices, if you like. *Makes 16 servings.*

EACH SERVING: ABOUT 285 CALORIES, 5 G PROTEIN, 23 G CARBOHYDRATE, 20 G TOTAL FAT (12 G SATURATED), 0 G FIBER, 89 MG CHOLESTEROL, 155 MG SODIUM.

SERVE YOURSELF RIGHT

FOR A BAKERY-PERFECT CHEESECAKE PRESENTATION, CHILL THE CAKE THOROUGHLY, PREFERABLY OVERNIGHT. TIGHTLY WRAP IT SO THE FILLING DOES NOT PICK UP AROMAS FROM OTHER FOODS IN THE REFRIGERATOR. AT SERVING TIME, PLACE THE PAN ON A SERVING PLATTER. CAREFULLY OPEN THE CLASP AND REMOVE THE SIDE OF THE PAN. BRUSH AWAY ANY CRUMBS THAT FALL ONTO THE PLATTER. USE A LARGE, SHARP KNIFE TO SLICE THE CAKE INTO WEDGES. WIPE THE BLADE CLEAN AFTER MAKING EACH CUT, THEN DIP THE BLADE IN HOT WATER, DRY IT OFF QUICKLY, AND CUT THE NEXT SLICE.

# Beginner's Guide to Cake Art

Decorating Tools

DECORATING BAG Polyester or plastic-coated canvas is best; disposable plastic is good for bright icings, which can stain. (Uncoated canvas bags are clumsier to use, and the fat from frosting or whipped cream can ooze right through the fabric.) Buy 8- or 10-inch bags, which accept all standard decorating tips.

COUPLER This collarlike plastic cap has a hole in the middle to hold the decorating tip. It forms a tight seal between the bag and the decorating tip, and lets you switch tips without changing bags when using the same frosting.

TIPS These cone-shaped metal nozzles have a design cut out of the point to form various shapes and textures as the frosting is pushed through. Do some practice piping onto waxed paper before you start on a cake; you can spoon the frosting back into the bag and try again. You'll find that your results vary depending upon the angle at which you hold the tip and on how hard you squeeze the bag.

Note: Wash bag, couplers, and tips in hot soapy water after using, turning bags inside out. Rinse well. Dry tips immediately to prevent rusting.

TO FILL A DECORATING BAG

To fill a decorating bag: With coupler and tip in place, place bag in tall glass; fold top half of bag down to form cuff. Using a rubber spatula, fill bag halfway with frosting, gently pushing frosting down as you go. After you unfold cuff, shake frosting down (to eliminate air pockets), twist top, and you're ready to pipe. (For best results when piping any design, hold bag with twisted end between thumb and index finger of your writing hand; use other hand to guide and squeeze lower part of bag.)

STAR TIP

Makes stars and ropes. For stars: Hold bag at 90° angle with tip slightly above surface of cake. Squeeze bag to form star, then stop squeezing and pull bag away. The size of the star depends on the amount of pressure applied as well as on the size of the tip opening. For rope: Hold bag at 45° angle and pipe a partial S curve (don't drag the tail down to complete the S) tuck tip under top portion of S curve and repeat, joining curves to form a rope.

PLAIN TIP

Pipes dots, lines, squiggles, or messages. For dots: Hold bag at 90° angle with tip slightly above surface of cake. Squeeze bag, without lifting the tip, until dot is size you like. Stop squeezing and pull bag away. If dot gets a little "tail" at top, smooth it gently with finger dipped in confectioners' sugar or cornstarch. For lines, squiggles, or written messages: Hold bag at 45° angle. Squeeze bag with steady, even pressure while piping. Stop squeezing before lifting bag.

BASKET-WEAVE TIP

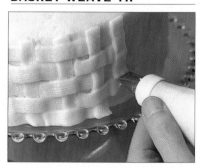

Looks like it's really woven, but it's not. Position bag so that serrated side of tip is facing up. Beginning at top edge of cake, pipe one vertical strip down side of cake. Then pipe horizontal bars across that vertical strip, each about one tip-width apart. Pipe a second vertical strip down side of cake, just slightly overlapping ends of horizontal bars. Pipe additional horizontal bars across second vertical strip in spaces between bars on first vertical strip. Repeat all around cake.

Classic Birthday Cake

PREP 1 HOUR 30 MINUTES PLUS COOLING
BAKE 20 TO 25 MINUTES

Every bit as pretty as a cake from the bakery, and so much more delicious! Both the cake and frosting are made with butter for an unmistakable homemade taste. The cake is frosted and simply decorated with a shell border, but if you like, try the frosting roses (see directions at right). For this, you'll need a few "flower nails," which look like oversized thumbtacks and are available wherever cake-decorating equipment is sold. For that special personal touch, make a small amount of Ornamental Frosting (page 358), tint it with food-color paste, and use a small writing tip ($^1/_{16}$-inch opening) to pipe a name or message on the cake.

SPECIAL EQUIPMENT:
LARGE METAL SPATULA
SMALL METAL SPATULA
STAR TIP (¼-INCH OPENING)
DECORATING BAG WITH COUPLER

CAKE:
GOLDEN BUTTER CAKE (PAGE 297)
BIG-BATCH BUTTER FROSTING (PAGE 354)
FROSTING ROSES (OPTIONAL; DIRECTIONS AT RIGHT)

1 Prepare Golden Butter Cake as directed for three 8-inch round baking pans. Bake and cool as directed.

2 Prepare Big-Batch Butter Frosting. Transfer 1 cake layer, bottom side up, to large plate. With large metal spatula, spread top with about ½ cup frosting, top with second layer; spread with ½ cup more frosting. Frost flat top and side of cake with 1¼ cups frosting. Spoon remaining frosting into decorating bag fitted with small star tip.

3 For shell border: Hold bag at 45° angle with the tip slightly above surface of cake. Squeeze bag with a lot of pressure and lift the tip slightly as frosting builds and fans out. Relax pressure as you pull the tip down toward you to make a small tail. Start each new shell behind the tail of the previous shell. Repeat to cover the top and bottom edge of cake. (If icing becomes too soft, refrigerate bag a few minutes until firm enough to pipe.) Refrigerate cake.

4 Make Frosting Roses, if desired. Place roses on cake. *Makes 16 servings.*

EACH SERVING WITHOUT FROSTING ROSES: ABOUT 765 CALORIES, 5 G PROTEIN, 101 G CARBOHYDRATE, 39 G TOTAL FAT (23 G SATURATED), 0 G FIBER, 154 MG CHOLESTEROL, 555 MG SODIUM.

MAKING A FROSTING ROSE Begin by making a recipe Ornamental Frosting (page 358). Using pink and green food-color paste, tint 2 cups frosting pink (for roses) and remaining frosting green (for leaves, see below).

Prepare roses: Spoon pink icing into decorating bag fitted with just a coupler. In left hand, hold 1 medium flower nail (1½ inches wide) between thumb and fingers so it will twirl easily. Place dab of icing in center of nail. Press 2" square piece of waxed paper onto dab of frosting. Holding bag vertically a little above center of nail, squeeze out beehive-shaped base of rose. When beehive of icing is a little higher than it is wide at the bottom, release pressure completely and lift bag away.

Attach 1 small rose tip (½-inch opening). With smaller side facing up, at 45° angle, touch larger end of tip opening to a point about one-third down base slightly covering top of base, squeeze out ribbon of icing while turning nail counterclockwise. Make one full turn of nail. The two ends of ribbon should be overlapping slightly.

Now to make petals, you must turn the smaller top end of tip opening 45° to right. Squeeze out ribbon of icing while turning nail counterclockwise, but make only one-third of a complete turn. Start next petal about halfway along curve of last one, so they overlap. Continue squeezing out more petals as you rotate nail and complete rose. Transfer waxed paper to a wire rack and let roses dry slightly. Repeat two more times to make 3 roses total.

MAKING FROSTING LEAVES When ready to put roses on cake, make leaves: Spoon green icing into a decorating bag fitted with a small leaf tip (¼-inch opening). Place roses on cake, off from the center. Pipe a few leaves between roses: Holding bag at an angle to counter with edge of tip lightly touching, squeeze with firm pressure so that icing fans into wide base. Then relax pressure as you pull tube away, slowly raising and lowering it to form curved leaf, stop squeezing, and pull up and away to form leaf.

Dotted Swiss Almond Cake

PREP 1 HOUR PLUS COOLING / BAKE 35 MINUTES

Inspired by the delicate fabric with the little raised dots—the stuff of little girls' party dresses—this almond-flavored 4-layer cake is filled with both raspberry preserves and Amaretto Buttercream.

2½ CUPS ALL-PURPOSE FLOUR
2½ TEASPOONS BAKING POWDER
½ TEASPOON SALT
½ CUP BUTTER OR MARGARINE (1 STICK), SOFTENED
1 TUBE OR CAN (7 TO 8 OUNCES) ALMOND PASTE, CRUMBLED
1½ CUPS SUGAR
5 LARGE EGG WHITES
1 TABLESPOON VANILLA EXTRACT
1¼ CUPS MILK
AMARETTO BUTTERCREAM (PAGE 353)
6 TABLESPOONS SEEDLESS RED RASPBERRY PRESERVES OR JAM

1 Preheat oven to 350° F. Grease and flour two 8" by 8" metal baking pans. Line bottoms with waxed paper; grease paper. Dust pans with flour.

2 In medium bowl, stir together flour, baking powder, and salt.

3 In large bowl, with mixer at low speed, beat butter, almond paste, and sugar until combined, about 2 to 3 minutes, scraping bowl often with rubber spatula. Increase speed to medium; beat until well mixed, about 2 to 3 minutes, scraping bowl often (mixture may look crumbly). Gradually beat in egg whites and vanilla just until blended. Reduce speed to low; add flour mixture alternately with milk, beginning and ending with flour mixture, scraping bowl occasionally with rubber spatula.

4 Pour batter into prepared pans. Bake 35 minutes, or until toothpick inserted in center of cakes comes out clean. Cool layers in pans on wire racks 10 minutes. With small knife, loosen layers from sides of pans; invert onto wire racks. Remove waxed paper; cool completely.

5 Meanwhile, prepare Amaretto Buttercream. Spoon 1 cup buttercream into decorating bag fitted with very small plain tip (about ⅛-inch diameter); set aside for decorating frosted cake.

6 With serrated knife, cut each cake layer horizontally in half. Place bottom half of 1 layer, cut side up, on cake plate; spread with 2 tablespoons raspberry preserves. Spread ⅓ cup buttercream on top. Repeat layering 2 times, ending with a cake layer.

7 With metal spatula, spread remaining buttercream on sides and top of cake. Use frosting in bag to pipe small clusters of dots on top of cake. With slightly larger plain tip (about ⅜-inch diameter), pipe dots around bottom and top borders of cake. Refrigerate cake until serving time. *Makes 24 servings.*

EACH SERVING: ABOUT 375 CALORIES, 4 G PROTEIN, 40 G CARBOHYDRATE, 22 G TOTAL FAT (12 G SATURATED), 0.5 G FIBER, 54 MG CHOLESTEROL, 175 MG SODIUM.

Clown Cupcakes

PREP 1 HOUR PLUS COOLING / BAKE 20 TO 25 MINUTES

When it's time to bake cupcakes for your child's class party, create some colorful clown faces made from candies. Feel free to substitute other sweets for the ones we've suggested, as long as the shapes work.

SPECIAL EQUIPMENT:
SMALL METAL SPATULA

CUPCAKES:
YELLOW CAKE (PAGE 294)
BIG-BATCH BUTTER FROSTING (PAGE 354)
24 ORANGE OR RED FRUIT SLICES, HALVED LENGTHWISE
48 BITE-SIZE FRUIT CANDIES
24 GUM BALLS OR JAW BREAKERS
12 RED GUMMY ROUNDS, CUT IN HALF

1 Prepare batter for Yellow Cake as directed for 24 cupcakes. Bake and cool as directed.

2 Prepare Big-Batch Butter Frosting. With small metal spatula, frost tops of cupcakes. Place 2 fruit slices on either side of each cupcake for the clown's hair. Place 2 bite-size fruit candies for eyes and 1 gum ball for the nose. Cut each gummy round piece into a mouth shape and place on cupcake. *Makes 24 cupcakes.*

EACH CUPCAKE WITHOUT CANDIES: ABOUT 325 CALORIES, 2 G PROTEIN, 48 G CARBOHYDRATE, 14 G TOTAL FAT (7 G SATURATED), 0.5 G FIBER, 51 MG CHOLESTEROL, 230 MG SODIUM.

Dotted Swiss Almond Cake

Fire Truck Cake

PREP 1 HOUR 30 MINUTES / BAKE 1 HOUR 10 MINUTES

Cut and assemble the cakes as shown, and go to town with brightly colored frosting and decorations. To highlight a birthday, you could pipe a number on the door of the truck (#4, for instance) to indicate the "Engine Company" and your child's age.

SPECIAL EQUIPMENT:

SMALL METAL SPATULA

3 DECORATING BAGS WITH COUPLERS, EACH WITH SMALL
    WRITING TIP (⅛-INCH OPENING)

CAKE:

2 RECIPES POUND CAKE (PAGE 317)

BIG-BATCH BUTTER FROSTING (PAGE 354)

RED, BLACK, AND YELLOW FOOD-COLOR PASTE

6 YELLOW CANDY-COATED CHOCOLATES

6 CHOCOLATE-SANDWICHED COOKIES

1 PRETZEL STICK (2 INCHES)

2 PIECES BLACK SHOESTRING LICORICE (4 INCHES EACH)

1 Prepare Pound Cakes; bake and cool as directed.

2 Prepare Big-Batch Butter Frosting. Tint 2½ cups frosting deep red. Tint ¼ cup black. Tint ¼ cup deep yellow. Leave remaining frosting white. Spoon black, yellow, and white frostings into decorating bags fitted with writing tips.

3 Reserve 1 whole loaf for the back of the fire truck. Cut remaining loaf as directed at right (see top photo). Shave a thin sliver off the tops of both loaves for a flatter surface.

4 On long platter, with small metal spatula, join pieces of fire truck with red frosting (see bottom photo). Frost front, cab, and back of truck with red frosting.

5 With toothpick, trace outlines in frosting to resemble a large window on the front of cab and doors and windows on the sides of cab. Pipe rows of white frosting to fill in outline of each window; smooth with small metal spatula. Use decorating bag with black frosting to pipe outline around windows and doors. Press 4 yellow-coated candies to the top of the cab and attach two yellow candies on the front of the cab for headlights. Outline headlights with black frosting. Pipe 4 lines along bottom third of the front of the cab as the front bumper. Set decorating bag with black icing aside.

6 Use decorating bag with yellow frosting and pipe 2 ladders on top of back of fire truck. With white frosting, pipe a small circle in the center of each cookie for the wheels. Attach wheels to front, middle, and back of truck sides. Use the remaining black frosting to outline tops of each wheel.

7 Cut pretzel stick in half. Wrap licorice strings around length of each pretzel half and attach with toothpicks to the side of the fire truck. Refrigerate until ready to serve. *Makes 24 servings.*

EACH SERVING WITHOUT CANDY, COOKIES, OR PRETZEL:
ABOUT 485 CALORIES, 4 G PROTEIN, 60 G CARBOHYDRATE,
26 G TOTAL FAT (15 G SATURATED), 0 G FIBER,
135 MG CHOLESTEROL, 395 MG SODIUM.

Fire Truck Cake

Leave one cake whole. Cut the other cake in half crosswise, then cut one of those halves into two equal pieces. Cut one of these pieces in half again. There should be four pieces total: one half, one quarter, and two eighths.

Use the quarter-piece for the front of the truck. Set the half-piece on end for the cab. Line up the two small pieces behind the "cab," and rest the whole cake on them, as shown.

Spring Bonnet Cake

PREP **45** MINUTES PLUS COOLING
BAKE ABOUT **40** MINUTES

This delightful lemon-iced cake is just the thing for Easter or Mother's Day, or for the birthday of a sweet lady at any age. Coordinate the colors of the icing "ruffle," the ribbon, and the fresh flowers to the rest of the party decor.

SPECIAL EQUIPMENT AND SUPPLIES:
DECORATING BAG WITH COUPLER
MEDIUM RIBBON OR PETAL TIP (½-INCH OPENING)
1 PIECE WIDE SATIN RIBBON (ABOUT 1¼ YARDS LONG)
FREESIA AND/OR OTHER EDIBLE FLOWERS (SEE BOX ON
    OPPOSITE PAGE)

CAKE:
WHIPPED CREAM CAKE (PAGE 297)
BIG-BATCH BUTTER FROSTING (PAGE 354)
2 TABLESPOONS FRESH LEMON JUICE
1 TEASPOON FRESHLY GRATED LEMON PEEL
RED AND YELLOW FOOD-COLOR PASTE
ASSORTED NONTOXIC FLOWERS

1 Grease and flour 1-quart ovensafe bowl and 11-inch round tart pan with removable bottom. Prepare batter for Whipped Cream Cake.

2 Spread 2½ cups cake batter in prepared tart pan; place remaining batter in prepared bowl. Bake cake in tart pan 20 minutes, cake in bowl 40 minutes, or until toothpick inserted in centers comes out clean. Cool as recipe directs.

3 Prepare Big-Batch Butter Frosting but use 2 tablespoons lemon juice for half-and-half and add grated

Spring Bonnet Cake

lemon peel. Transfer ½ cup frosting to small bowl; tint pale pink. Tint remaining frosting pale yellow.

4 Assemble cake: For brim, place 11-inch cake layer on flat cake plate or tray. With metal spatula, spread some yellow frosting over top and side of brim. For crown, trim uneven bottom of cake baked in bowl. Place crown on center of brim. Spread remaining yellow frosting over cake.

5 Spoon pink frosting into decorating bag fitted with ribbon or petal tip. Pipe ruffled edge around edge of cake brim.

6 Tie ribbon around base of crown; make bow. Garnish cake with fresh flowers or frosting roses. *Makes 16 servings.*

EACH SERVING: ABOUT 425 CALORIES, 2 G PROTEIN, 62 G CARBOHYDRATE, 19 G TOTAL FAT (11 G SATURATED), 0 G FIBER, 81 MG CHOLESTEROL, 270 MG SODIUM.

FLORAL FANTASY CAKES

FRESH FLOWERS AND LEAVES ARE A FINE FINISHING TOUCH FOR A CAKE. BUT BE CAREFUL WHICH BLOOMS YOU USE—SOME TYPES ARE TOXIC (SEE BELOW). ALTHOUGH IT'S UNLIKELY THAT ANYONE WILL TRY TO EAT THE FLOWERS, THEY MUST BE NONTOXIC IF THEY TOUCH THE CAKE. FLOWERS AND LEAVES MUST ALSO BE FREE OF PESTICIDES, HERBICIDES, AND FUNGICIDES. BLOSSOMS FROM YOUR OWN GARDEN MAY FIT THIS DESCRIPTION; THOSE FROM A FARMER'S MARKET MAY ALSO QUALIFY (ASK THE GROWER). FOR A SAFE, PRETTY CAKE, SELECT FROM AMONG ORANGE, LEMON, OR APPLE BLOSSOMS; ROSES, NASTURTIUMS, ENGLISH DAISIES, FREESIAS, HONEYSUCKLE, LILACS, PANSIES, WOOD VIOLETS, GARDENIAS, CHRYSANTHEMUMS, AND MARIGOLDS.

DO NOT USE: FOXGLOVES, TIGER LILIES, CALLA LILIES, LILIES OF THE VALLEY, LARKSPUR, MOUNTAIN LAUREL, BUTTERCUPS, SWEET PEAS, OLEANDER, PHILODENDRON LEAVES, CHERRY LEAVES, MISTLETOE, HOLLY BERRIES, OR POINSETTIAS.

Sweetheart Cake

PREP 40 MINUTES PLUS COOLING
BAKE 20 TO 25 MINUTES

Valentine's Day is the obvious occasion for a heart-shaped dessert, but this pretty pink cake is equally appropriate for an anniversary or romantic dinner. You don't need heart-shaped pans for this—the cake is baked in one round and one square pan.

SPECIAL EQUIPMENT:

DECORATING BAG WITH COUPLER
SMALL WRITING TIP (¹/₁₆-INCH OPENING)

CAKE:

GOLDEN BUTTER CAKE (PAGE 297)
BIG-BATCH BUTTER FROSTING (PAGE 354)
PINK FOOD-COLOR PASTE

1 Preheat oven to 350° F. Prepare Golden Butter Cake as directed but divide batter between one 8-inch square baking pan and one 8-inch round cake pan and bake 20 to 25 minutes. Cool as directed.

2 Meanwhile prepare Big-Batch Butter Frosting. Tint 2½ cups light pink. Leave remaining frosting white.

3 Assemble cake on large platter or cutting board covered with cellophane or foil. Place square cake on center of board, forming a diamond shape. Cut round cake in half to form 2 semicircles. Place semicircles on both sides of upper half of square to form heart shape.

4 With large metal spatula, spread top and sides of cake with pink frosting. Fit decorating bag with small writing tip (¹/₁₆-inch opening). Keeping tip slightly above surface of cake, pipe a continuous string of frosting, curve it up, down, and around until area is covered, taking care that scrolls do not overlap. *Makes 20 servings.*

EACH SERVING: ABOUT 610 CALORIES, 4 G PROTEIN, 81 G CARBOHYDRATE, 31 G TOTAL FAT (19 G SATURATED), 0 G FIBER, 123 MG CHOLESTEROL, 440 MG SODIUM.

Carousel Cake

PREP 1 HOUR PLUS COOLING / BAKE 25 MINUTES

What child wouldn't be delighted with the appearance of this spectacular merry-go-round on the birthday menu? One cautionary note: Put candles on the cake after removing the dome and the straw supports.

SPECIAL EQUIPMENT AND SUPPLIES:
4 DECORATING BAGS WITH COUPLERS
4 SMALL WRITING TIPS (1/16-INCH OPENING)
LARGE METAL SPATULA
11 PLASTIC DRINKING STRAWS
STAPLER
1 COLORED PLASTIC PLATE (ABOUT 10½ INCHES)
NARROW CURLING RIBBON IN ASSORTED COLORS
COLORFUL ANIMAL STICKERS

CAKE:
GOLDEN BUTTER CAKE (PAGE 297)
BIG-BATCH BUTTER FROSTING (PAGE 354)
2 BOXES (2⅛ OUNCES EACH) ANIMAL CRACKERS
ABOUT 1 CUP BITE-SIZE FRUIT CANDIES
RED, GREEN, YELLOW, AND BLUE FOOD-COLOR PASTE

1 Preheat oven to 350° F. Prepare batter for Golden Butter Cake and bake in 2 prepared 9-inch round cake pans as directed. Cool.

2 Prepare Big-Batch Butter Frosting. Tint ¼ cup frosting red. Tint ¼ cup frosting green. Tint ¼ cup frosting yellow. Tint ¼ cup frosting blue. Leave remaining frosting white. Spoon each colored frosting into decorating bag fitted with small writing tip. Decorate animal crackers as you like; let set.

3 Transfer 1 layer, bottom side up, to large plate. With large metal spatula, spread top with about ½ cup white frosting, top with second layer. Frost top and side of cake with remaining white frosting. Press crackers and candies around side of cake.

4 With scissors, cut 8 straws to measure 6 inches each. Insert 6-inch straws, 1 inch from edge, evenly spaced around cake; insert 3 remaining straws touching in center of cake.

5 With scissors, make 8 evenly spaced cuts in paper plate, from edge to ¼ inch from center. With plate bottom side up, proceed around plate overlapping cut sections by ½ inch and stapling each overlap at edge of plate to form dome-shaped top for carousel.

6 Attach colorful stickers around edge of dome. With ribbon, make curled streamers; tape them to top center of dome. Set dome on straws and insert remaining cookies leaning against straws. *Makes 14 servings.*

EACH SERVING WITHOUT CRACKERS OR CANDY: ABOUT 875 CALORIES, 6 G PROTEIN, 116 G CARBOHYDRATE, 44 G TOTAL FAT (27 G SATURATED), 0 G FIBER, 176 MG CHOLESTEROL, 630 MG SODIUM.

Mouse Cupcakes

PREP 1 HOUR 30 MINUTES PLUS COOLING
BAKE 20 TO 25 MINUTES

With a few adjustments in the facial features and ears (use different cookies), these cupcakes can become dogs, cats, bears, or bunnies. Tint the base frosting brown or tabby-orange (for the kitties), or leave it white.

SPECIAL EQUIPMENT:
2 DECORATING BAGS WITH COUPLERS
2 SMALL WRITING TIPS (1/16-INCH OPENING AND ⅛-INCH OPENING)

CAKE:
YELLOW CAKE (PAGE 294)
BIG-BATCH BUTTER FROSTING (PAGE 354)
BLACK AND PINK FOOD-COLOR PASTE
48 VANILLA WAFERS
BLACK SHOESTRING LICORICE, CUT INTO
    1-INCH PIECES

1 Prepare batter for Yellow Cake as directed for 24 cupcakes. Bake and cool as directed.

2 Prepare Big-Batch Butter Frosting. Tint 2½ cups frosting gray. Tint ½ cup frosting black and remaining ¾ cup frosting light pink. Frost tops of all 24 cupcakes with gray butter cream. Place 2 vanilla wafers on top third of each cupcake to form ears; frost ears with gray frosting.

3 Spoon black frosting into decorating bag fitted with 1/16-inch opening. Pipe 2 eyes on each mouse. Spoon pink frosting into decorating bag, fitted with ⅛-inch opening. Pipe a nose, a mouth, and center of ears with pink frosting. Use licorice pieces for mouse whiskers. *Makes 24 cupcakes.*

EACH CUPCAKE WITHOUT LICORICE: ABOUT 325 CALORIES, 2 G PROTEIN, 48 G CARBOHYDRATE, 14 G TOTAL FAT (7 G SATURATED), 0.5 G FIBER, 51 MG CHOLESTEROL, 230 MG SODIUM.

Carousel Cake

Sunflower Cupcakes

PREP ABOUT 1 HOUR 30 MINUTES PLUS COOLING
BAKE 20 TO 25 MINUTES

Celebrate a summer cookout or picnic with these sunny cupcakes. The glorious golden-yellow petals surround chocolate-chip "sunflower seeds."

SPECIAL EQUIPMENT:

DECORATING BAG WITH COUPLER
SMALL STAR TIP (¼-INCH OPENING)

CAKE:

YELLOW CAKE (PAGE 294)
BIG-BATCH BUTTER FROSTING (PAGE 354)
YELLOW AND ORANGE FOOD-COLOR PASTE
½ CUP SEMISWEET CHOCOLATE CHIPS

1 Prepare batter for Yellow Cake as directed for 24 cupcakes. Bake and cool as directed.

2 Prepare Big-Batch Butter Frosting. Tint deep yellow (use both yellow and orange food-color paste). With small metal spatula, frost tops of cupcakes. Spoon remaining frosting into decorating bag fitted with small star tip. Starting ¾ inch from edge of cupcake, pipe sunflower petals by squeezing frosting from bag while slowly pulling slightly past edge of cupcake, gradually releasing pressure. Run a layer of petals around cupcake and an overlapping layer in the seams between the petals of the first layer. Fill the center with 1 teaspoon semisweet chocolate chips. Repeat with remaining cupcakes, frosting, and chocolate chips. *Makes 24 cupcakes.*

EACH CUPCAKE: ABOUT 340 CALORIES, 3 G PROTEIN, 50 G CARBOHYDRATE, 15 G TOTAL FAT (7 G SATURATED), 0.5 G FIBER, 51 MG CHOLESTEROL, 230 MG SODIUM.

COLOR UP YOUR CAKES

FOR TINTING FROSTINGS AND ICINGS, THE PROS PREFER PASTE FOOD COLORS (ALSO CALLED ICING COLORS), WHICH DO NOT DILUTE THE FROSTING AS LIQUID COLORS CAN. ADD PASTE COLORING A TINY BIT AT A TIME, USING THE TIP OF A TOOTHPICK: THE COLORS ARE EXTREMELY INTENSE.

Black & White Cupcakes

PREP 1 HOUR 30 MINUTES PLUS COOLING
BAKE: 20 TO 25 MINUTES

The ever-welcome treat of homemade cupcakes takes on an artistic air when they are decorated with "black" (really dark chocolate) and white frostings in a variety of patterns. See page 338 for how to use decorating tips and use the photo at right for inspiration; then create your own designs. Of course you can use other color combinations, too!

SPECIAL EQUIPMENT:

2 DECORATING BAGS WITH COUPLERS
2 WRITING TIPS (¼-INCH OPENING)
2 STAR TIPS (¼-INCH OPENING)
2 SMALL BASKET-WEAVE TIPS (⅛-INCH OPENING)

CAKE:

GOLDEN BUTTER CAKE (PAGE 297)
SILKY VANILLA BUTTER FROSTING (PAGE 354)
2 SQUARES (2 OUNCES) UNSWEETENED CHOCOLATE,
   MELTED AND COOLED
1 SQUARE (1 OUNCE) SEMISWEET CHOCOLATE, MELTED AND
   COOLED

1 Preheat oven to 350° F. Line twenty-four 2½-inch muffin-pan cups with fluted paper liners. Prepare Golden Butter Cake batter as directed. Pour batter into prepared cups; bake 20 to 25 minutes. Cool.

2 Prepare Silky Vanilla Butter Frosting. Remove 1½ cups frosting and set aside. To frosting remaining in bowl, beat in melted unsweetened and semisweet chocolates until blended. Spoon each frosting into decorating bag fitted with a coupler.

3 Using the two frostings with suggested decorating tips, and small spatula, decorate tops of cupcakes with designs of your choice. *Makes 24 cupcakes.*

EACH CUPCAKE: ABOUT 460 CALORIES, 4 G PROTEIN, 50 G CARBOHYDRATE, 27 G TOTAL FAT (16 G SATURATED), 0.5 G FIBER, 103 MG CHOLESTEROL, 375 MG SODIUM.

Frostings, Fillings & Flourishes

Fresh Buttercream

PREP 15 MINUTES PLUS COOLING / COOK 5 MINUTES

Only the pure flavor of unsalted butter will do here.

⅔ CUP MILK

4 LARGE EGG YOLKS

¾ CUP SUGAR

1 CUP UNSALTED BUTTER (2 STICKS), SOFTENED (DO NOT
  USE SALTED BUTTER OR MARGARINE)

2 TEASPOONS VANILLA EXTRACT OR 2 TABLESPOONS
  FAVORITE FLAVORED LIQUEUR OR BRANDY

1 In 1-quart saucepan, heat milk to boiling over medium heat. Meanwhile, in small bowl, whisk egg yolks with sugar until blended. Gradually whisk hot milk into yolk mixture. Return mixture to saucepan; cook over medium heat, stirring constantly, just until thickened slightly and mixture coats back of wooden spoon well. (Do not boil or custard will curdle.) Remove pan from heat. Strain custard through sieve into clean large bowl. Cool to room temperature.

2 With mixer at medium speed, beat softened butter into custard, 1 tablespoon at a time, beating until completely smooth after each addition. (If mixture begins to appear oily, refrigerate 20 minutes, or place bowl in larger bowl of ice water 10 minutes, then proceed. If butter does not incorporate perfectly and small flecks remain, let stand 15 minutes, then beat at high speed until smooth before proceeding.) Beat in vanilla or liqueur. *Makes about 2⅓ cups.*

FIGURING FROSTING

HERE'S HOW MUCH FROSTING YOU'LL NEED FOR

VARIOUS CAKE SIZES:

8-INCH ROUND, TWO LAYERS	2¼ CUPS
8-INCH ROUND, THREE LAYERS	2¾ CUPS
9-INCH ROUND, TWO LAYERS	2⅔ CUPS
8-INCH SQUARE, ONE LAYER	1⅓ CUPS
9-INCH SQUARE, ONE LAYER	2 CUPS
13- BY 9-INCH, ONE LAYER	2⅓ CUPS
10-INCH TUBE CAKE	2¼ CUPS
24 CUPCAKES	2¼ CUPS

EACH TABLESPOON: ABOUT 70 CALORIES, 0 G PROTEIN,
4 G CARBOHYDRATE, 6 G TOTAL FAT (3 G SATURATED), 0 MG
FIBER, 0 G FIBER, 37 MG CHOLESTEROL, 5 MG SODIUM.

Meringue Buttercream

PREP 30 MINUTES PLUS COOLING / COOK 15 MINUTES

1½ CUPS SUGAR

¾ CUP WATER

4 LARGE EGG WHITES

¼ TEASPOON CREAM OF TARTAR

2 CUPS UNSALTED BUTTER (4 STICKS), SOFTENED (DO NOT
  USE SALTED BUTTER OR MARGARINE)

1½ TEASPOONS VANILLA EXTRACT

PINCH SALT

1 In 2-quart saucepan, heat 1 cup sugar and ½ cup water to boiling over high heat, without stirring. Cover and cook 2 minutes longer. Remove cover; set candy thermometer in place and continue cooking, without stirring, until temperature reaches 248° to 250° F, or hard-ball stage.

2 Meanwhile, in top of double boiler or in large stainless-steel bowl set over 4-quart saucepan, over 1-inch simmering water (double-boiler top or bowl should be about 2 inches from water), with hand-held mixer at high speed, beat egg whites, remaining ½ cup sugar, remaining ¼ cup water, and cream of tartar 5 minutes, or until soft peaks form. Reduce speed to low; slowly pour hot syrup in thin stream into egg-white mixture. Increase speed to high; beat until meringue forms stiff peaks and mixture reaches 160° F on thermometer. Remove double-boiler top or bowl from saucepan, and beat until cool to touch, about 10 minutes.

3 When meringue is cool, reduce speed to medium. Gradually add softened butter, 1 tablespoon at a time, beating after each addition. (If buttercream appears to curdle, increase speed to high and beat until mixture comes together, then reduce speed to medium and continue adding softened butter.) When buttercream is smooth, reduce speed to low and beat in vanilla and salt. *Makes about 4 cups.*

EACH TABLESPOON: ABOUT 70 CALORIES, 0 G PROTEIN,
5 G CARBOHYDRATE, 6 G TOTAL FAT (4 G SATURATED),
0 G FIBER, 16 MG CHOLESTEROL, 5 MG SODIUM.

Amaretto Buttercream

PREP 35 MINUTES PLUS COOLING / COOK 5 MINUTES

This meringue-based buttercream is flavored with almond liqueur (substitute almond extract if you'd rather not use alcohol). Try it on a chocolate cake or any layer cake made with nuts.

1 CUP SUGAR

⅓ CUP WATER

4 LARGE EGG WHITES

2 CUPS UNSALTED BUTTER (4 STICKS), SOFTENED (DO NOT USE SALTED BUTTER OR MARGARINE)

¼ CUP AMARETTO (ALMOND-FLAVORED LIQUEUR) OR ½ TEASPOON ALMOND EXTRACT

PINCH SALT

1 In 1-quart saucepan, heat ¾ cup sugar and water to boiling over high heat, without stirring. Cover and cook 2 minutes longer. Remove cover; set candy thermometer in place and continue cooking, without stirring, until temperature reaches 248° to 250° F, or hard-ball stage. Remove saucepan from heat.

2 Just before syrup is ready (temperature will be about 220° F), in large bowl, with mixer at high speed, beat egg whites until foamy. Gradually beat in remaining ¼ cup sugar and continue beating until soft peaks form.

3 With mixer at low speed, slowly pour hot syrup in thin stream into beaten egg-white mixture. Increase speed to high; beat until meringue forms stiff peaks and mixture is cool to the touch, about 15 minutes.

4 When meringue is cool, reduce speed to medium. Gradually add softened butter, 1 tablespoon at a time, beating after each addition. (If buttercream appears to curdle, increase speed to high and beat until mixture comes together, then reduce speed to medium and continue adding softened butter, 1 tablespoon at a time.) When buttercream is smooth, reduce speed to low; beat in amaretto or extract and salt until incorporated. *Makes about 4 cups.*

EACH TABLESPOON: ABOUT 65 CALORIES, 0 G PROTEIN, 3 G CARBOHYDRATE, 6 G TOTAL FAT (4 G SATURATED), 0 G FIBER, 16 MG CHOLESTEROL, 5 MG SODIUM.

Small-Batch Butter Frosting

PREP 10 MINUTES

The variations below offer five different frosting flavors for a standard (8- or 9-inch) layer cake.

1 PACKAGE (16 OUNCES) CONFECTIONERS' SUGAR

½ CUP BUTTER OR MARGARINE (1 STICK), SOFTENED

4 TO 6 TABLESPOONS MILK OR HALF-AND-HALF

1½ TEASPOONS VANILLA EXTRACT

In large bowl, with mixer at medium-low speed, beat confectioners' sugar, softened butter, and 3 tablespoons milk until smooth and blended. Beat in additional milk as needed for easy spreading consistency. Increase speed to medium-high; beat until light and fluffy. *Makes about 2⅓ cups.*

EACH TABLESPOON: ABOUT 70 CALORIES, 0 G PROTEIN, 12 G CARBOHYDRATE, 3 G TOTAL FAT (2 G SATURATED), 0 G FIBER, 7 MG CHOLESTEROL, 25 MG SODIUM.

LEMON BUTTER FROSTING Prepare as above but use *2 tablespoons milk, 2 tablespoons fresh lemon juice,* and *1 teaspoon grated lemon peel.* Use only *1 to 2 tablespoons milk* as needed for easy spreading consistency.
EACH TABLESPOON: ABOUT 70 CALORIES, 0 G PROTEIN, 12 G CARBOHYDRATE, 3 G TOTAL FAT (2 G SATURATED), 0 G FIBER, 7 MG CHOLESTEROL, 25 MG SODIUM.

ORANGE BUTTER FROSTING Prepare as above but use *2 tablespoons orange juice* for lemon juice and *1 teaspoon grated orange peel* for lemon peel.
EACH TABLESPOON: ABOUT 70 CALORIES, 0 G PROTEIN, 12 G CARBOHYDRATE, 3 G TOTAL FAT (2 G SATURATED), 0 G FIBER, 7 MG CHOLESTEROL, 25 MG SODIUM.

BURNT BUTTER FROSTING In small skillet, cook ½ cup butter over medium heat until lightly browned; cool. Prepare frosting as for Small-Batch Butter Frosting but use cooled browned butter for butter.
EACH TABLESPOON: ABOUT 70 CALORIES, 0 G PROTEIN, 12 G CARBOHYDRATE, 3 G TOTAL FAT (2 G SATURATED), 0 G FIBER, 7 MG CHOLESTEROL, 25 MG SODIUM.

CHOCOLATE BUTTER FROSTING Prepare as for Small-Batch Butter Frosting but beat in either *4 squares (4 ounces) bittersweet chocolate,* melted and cooled, or *3 squares (3 ounces) semisweet chocolate plus 1 square (1 ounce) unsweetened chocolate,* melted and cooled. *Makes about 2¾ cups.*
EACH TABLESPOON: ABOUT 75 CALORIES, 0 G PROTEIN, 12 G CARBOHYDRATE, 3 G TOTAL FAT (2 G SATURATED), 0 G FIBER, 6 MG CHOLESTEROL, 20 MG SODIUM.

Big-Batch Butter Frosting

PREP 10 MINUTES

This makes a cup and a half more frosting than the small-batch version, enough to fill and frost festive desserts such as the Fire Truck Cake (page 342).

1 CUP BUTTER OR MARGARINE (2 STICKS), SOFTENED
6 CUPS CONFECTIONERS' SUGAR (ABOUT ONE AND ONE-
   HALF 16-OUNCE PACKAGES)
½ CUP HALF-AND-HALF OR LIGHT CREAM
1 TABLESPOON VANILLA EXTRACT

In large bowl, with mixer at low speed, beat all ingredients just until blended. Increase speed to medium; beat until frosting is smooth and fluffy, about 1 minute, scraping bowl constantly with rubber spatula. *Makes about 3¾ cups.*

EACH TABLESPOON: ABOUT 75 CALORIES, 0 G PROTEIN,
11 G CARBOHYDRATE, 3 G TOTAL FAT (2 G SATURATED),
0 G FIBER, 9 MG CHOLESTEROL, 30 MG SODIUM.

Silky Vanilla Butter Frosting

PREP 10 MINUTES PLUS COOLING / COOK 8 MINUTES

This fine-textured frosting is made by beating together softened butter and a thick, saucelike base. The base should be completely cool before the two are combined.

1 CUP SUGAR
½ CUP ALL-PURPOSE FLOUR
1⅓ CUPS MILK
1 CUP BUTTER OR MARGARINE (2 STICKS), SOFTENED
1 TABLESPOON VANILLA EXTRACT

1 In 2-quart saucepan, stir together sugar and flour until evenly combined. Gradually stir in milk until smooth. Cook over medium-high heat, stirring often, until mixture thickens and boils. Reduce heat to low; cook 2 minutes, stirring constantly. Remove saucepan from heat; cool completely.

2 In large bowl, with mixer at medium speed, beat softened butter until creamy. Gradually beat in milk mixture and vanilla. *Makes about 3¼ cups.*

EACH TABLESPOON: ABOUT 55 CALORIES, 0 G PROTEIN,
5 G CARBOHYDRATE, 4 G TOTAL FAT (2 G SATURATED),,
0 G FIBER, 10 MG CHOLESTEROL, 40 MG SODIUM.

SILKY LEMON BUTTER FROSTING Prepare as for Silky Vanilla Butter Frosting but omit vanilla extract and add *1 tablespoon freshly grated lemon peel.*
EACH TABLESPOON: ABOUT 55 CALORIES, 0 G PROTEIN,
5 G CARBOHYDRATE, 4 G TOTAL FAT (2 G SATURATED),
0 G FIBER, 10 MG CHOLESTEROL, 40 MG SODIUM.

SILKY ORANGE BUTTER FROSTING Prepare as for Silky Vanilla Butter Frosting but omit vanilla extract and add *1 teaspoon freshly grated orange peel.*
EACH TABLESPOON: ABOUT 55 CALORIES, 0 G PROTEIN,
5 G CARBOHYDRATE, 4 G TOTAL FAT (2 G SATURATED),
0 G FIBER, 10 MG CHOLESTEROL, 40 MG SODIUM.

Silky Chocolate Butter Frosting

PREP 10 MINUTES PLUS COOLING / COOK 8 MINUTES

This is our basic "silky" frosting in an intense chocolate mode. Cocoa replaces some of the flour, and there are 4 ounces of semisweet chocolate in the recipe, too. For a classic combination, use it on Yellow Cake (page 294).

¾ CUP SUGAR
¼ CUP ALL-PURPOSE FLOUR
3 TABLESPOONS UNSWEETENED COCOA
1 CUP MILK
1 CUP BUTTER OR MARGARINE (2 STICKS), SOFTENED
1 TABLESPOON VANILLA EXTRACT
4 SQUARES (4 OUNCES) SEMISWEET CHOCOLATE, MELTED
   AND COOLED

1 In 2-quart saucepan, stir together sugar, flour, and cocoa until evenly combined. Gradually stir in milk until smooth. Cook over medium heat, stirring, until mixture thickens and boils. Reduce heat to low; cook 2 minutes, stirring constantly. Remove saucepan from heat; cool completely.

2 In large bowl, with mixer at medium speed, beat softened butter until creamy. Gradually beat in cooled milk mixture, vanilla, and melted chocolate. *Makes about 3 cups.*

EACH TABLESPOON: ABOUT 65 CALORIES, 0 G PROTEIN, 6 G CARBOHYDRATE, 5 G TOTAL FAT (3 G SATURATED), 0 G FIBER, 11 MG CHOLESTEROL, 40 MG SODIUM.

Two-Tone Brandied Butter Frosting

PREP 15 MINUTES PLUS COOLING / COOK 10 MINUTES

1 CUP SUGAR
½ CUP ALL-PURPOSE FLOUR
1 CUP MILK
1 SQUARE (1 OUNCE) SEMISWEET CHOCOLATE
1 SQUARE (1 OUNCE) UNSWEETENED CHOCOLATE
1 CUP BUTTER OR MARGARINE (2 STICKS), SOFTENED
2 TABLESPOONS BRANDY
1 TEASPOON VANILLA EXTRACT

1 In 2-quart saucepan, combine sugar and flour. With wire whisk, mix in milk until smooth. Cook over medium-high heat, stirring often, until mixture thickens and boils. Reduce heat to low and cook 2 minutes, stirring constantly. Cool completely, about 45 minutes. Meanwhile, melt chocolates over low heat, stirring frequently; cool slightly.

2 In large bowl, with mixer at medium speed, beat butter until creamy. Gradually beat in cooled flour mixture. When mixture is smooth, beat in brandy and vanilla until blended. Spoon half of frosting into small bowl; stir cooled chocolate into frosting remaining in large bowl. *Makes 1½ cups of each flavor.*

EACH TABLESPOON (VANILLA): ABOUT 60 CALORIES, 0 G PROTEIN, 5 G CARBOHYDRATE, 4 G TOTAL FAT (2 G SATURATED), 0 G FIBER, 11 MG CHOLESTEROL, 40 MG SODIUM.

EACH TABLESPOON (CHOCOLATE): ABOUT 70 CALORIES, 0 G PROTEIN, 6 G CARBOHYDRATE, 5 G TOTAL FAT (3 G SATURATED), 0 G FIBER 11 MG CHOLESTEROL, 40 MG SODIUM.

Molasses Butter Frosting

PREP 10 MINUTES

Cream cheese and molasses give this frosting a slight tang. It's wonderful on spice, pumpkin, or apple cake.

1 CUP BUTTER OR MARGARINE (2 STICKS), SOFTENED
1 PACKAGE (8 OUNCES) LIGHT CREAM CHEESE (NEUFCHÂTEL), SLIGHTLY SOFTENED
1 PACKAGE (16 OUNCES) CONFECTIONERS' SUGAR
¼ CUP LIGHT (MILD) MOLASSES

In large bowl, with mixer at high speed, beat softened butter and cream cheese until smooth. Reduce speed to low. Beat in confectioners' sugar and molasses until blended. Increase speed to medium high; beat until smooth and frosting has easy spreading consistency. *Makes about 3¾ cups.*

EACH TABLESPOON: ABOUT 70 CALORIES, 0 G PROTEIN, 8 G CARBOHYDRATE, 4 G TOTAL FAT (2 G SATURATED), 0 G FIBER, 11 MG CHOLESTEROL, 50 MG SODIUM.

White Chocolate Butter Frosting

PREP 15 MINUTES

You can't tell that this is a chocolate frosting until you taste it. But oh, what a scrumptious surprise!

1 CUP BUTTER (2 STICKS), SOFTENED (DO NOT USE MARGARINE)
3 TABLESPOONS MILK
2 CUPS CONFECTIONERS' SUGAR
6 OUNCES WHITE CHOCOLATE, SWISS CONFECTIONERY BARS, OR WHITE BAKING BARS, MELTED AND COOLED

In large bowl, with mixer at low speed, beat softened butter, milk, confectioners' sugar, and melted white chocolate just until blended. Increase speed to high; beat 2 minutes, or until light and fluffy, scraping bowl often with rubber spatula. *Makes about 3½ cups.*

EACH TABLESPOON: ABOUT 60 CALORIES, 0 G PROTEIN, 6 G CARBOHYDRATE, 4 G TOTAL FAT (3 G SATURATED), 0 MG FIBER, 9 MG CHOLESTEROL, 35 MG SODIUM.

Milk Chocolate Frosting

PREP 15 MINUTES

3 MILK-CHOCOLATE CANDY BARS (1.55 OUNCES EACH),
    MELTED AND COOLED
¾ CUP BUTTER (1½ STICKS), SOFTENED
1½ CUPS CONFECTIONERS' SUGAR
3 TO 4 TABLESPOONS MILK

In large bowl, with mixer at low speed, beat melted chocolate and softened butter until blended. Add confectioners' sugar and 3 tablespoons milk. Beat until smooth, adding remaining 1 tablespoon milk as needed. Increase speed to medium-high and beat 1 minute, or until fluffy. *Makes about 2¾ cups.*

EACH TABLESPOON: ABOUT 70 CALORIES, 0 G PROTEIN,
6 G CARBOHYDRATE, 5 G TOTAL FAT (3 G SATURATED),
0 G FIBER, 12 MG CHOLESTEROL, 45 MG SODIUM.

Peanut Butter Frosting

PREP 10 MINUTES

Here's how to make a dessert lover's dreams come true. Serve up Cocoa Brownies (page 31), One-Bowl Chocolate Cake (page 308), or Banana Layer Cake (page 301) lavished with this creamy frosting.

½ CUP BUTTER OR MARGARINE (1 STICK), SOFTENED
½ CUP CREAMY PEANUT BUTTER
1 PACKAGE (3 OUNCES) CREAM CHEESE, SOFTENED
1 TEASPOON VANILLA EXTRACT
2 CUPS CONFECTIONERS' SUGAR
2 TO 3 TABLESPOONS MILK

1 In large bowl, with mixer at medium speed, beat softened butter, peanut butter, cream cheese, and vanilla until smooth and fluffy.

2 Add confectioners' sugar and 2 tablespoons milk. Beat until blended. Increase speed to medium-high; beat 2 minutes, or until fluffy, adding remaining 1 tablespoon milk as needed for easy spreading consistency. *Makes about 2¾ cups.*

EACH TABLESPOON: ABOUT 65 CALORIES, 1 G PROTEIN,
6 G CARBOHYDRATE, 4 G TOTAL FAT (2 G SATURATED),
0 G FIBER, 8 MG CHOLESTEROL, 40 MG SODIUM.

Coconut-Pecan Frosting

PREP 5 MINUTES / COOK 15 MINUTES

This unique cooked frosting is an absolute must for German's Chocolate Cake (page 314); you can also spread it on any chocolate layer or sheetcake.

½ CUP BUTTER OR MARGARINE (1 STICK), CUT UP
1 CUP HEAVY OR WHIPPING CREAM
1 CUP PACKED LIGHT BROWN SUGAR
3 LARGE EGG YOLKS
1 TEASPOON VANILLA EXTRACT
1 CUP FLAKED SWEETENED COCONUT
1 CUP PECANS, CHOPPED

In 2-quart saucepan, combine butter, cream, and brown sugar. Heat almost to boiling over medium-high heat, stirring occasionally. Meanwhile, place egg yolks in medium bowl. Slowly pour about ½ cup sugar mixture into egg yolks, whisking. Reduce heat to medium-low. Add egg-yolk mixture to saucepan and whisk until thickened (do not boil). Remove saucepan from heat. Stir in vanilla, coconut, and pecans until combined. Cool to room temperature. *Makes about 3 cups.*

EACH TABLESPOON: ABOUT 80 CALORIES, 1 G PROTEIN,
6 G CARBOHYDRATE, 6 G TOTAL FAT (3 G SATURATED),
0 G FIBER, 25 MG CHOLESTEROL, 30 MG SODIUM.

Butterscotch Frosting

PREP 5 MINUTES / COOK 5 MINUTES

This old-fashioned frosting is wonderful on banana or spice cake. It makes enough to fill and frost the top of an 8- or 9-inch layer cake, but not enough to cover the sides. But that's the old-fashioned way to ice a cake.

1 CUP PACKED BROWN SUGAR
⅓ CUP BUTTER OR MARGARINE, CUT UP
⅓ CUP HEAVY OR WHIPPING CREAM

1 In 1-quart saucepan, heat brown sugar, butter, and cream to boiling over high heat, stirring occasionally. Set candy thermometer in place and continue cooking until temperature reaches 240° F or soft-ball stage (when small amount of mixture dropped into very cold water forms a soft ball which flattens on removal from water).

2 Transfer mixture to small bowl. With mixer at medium speed, beat 3 minutes, until thickened and frosting is of spreading consistency. *Makes 1 cup plus 2 tablespoons.*

EACH TABLESPOON: ABOUT 90 CALORIES, 0 G PROTEIN, 12 G CARBOHYDRATE, 5 G TOTAL FAT (3 G SATURATED), 0 G FIBER, 15 MG CHOLESTEROL, 40 MG SODIUM.

Caramel Frosting

PREP 5 MINUTES / COOK 5 MINUTES

With a lighter caramel flavor than the Butterscotch Frosting (opposite page), this is a great match for the Tweed Cake (page 294). The frosting is a little sticky, but if you grease the icing spatula with a little oil or nonstick vegetable cooking spray, the frosting will be easier to spread.

1¾ CUPS SUGAR
½ CUP BUTTER (1 STICK), CUT UP (DO NOT USE MARGARINE)
¾ CUP MILK, PLUS ADDITIONAL, IF NEEDED

1 In heavy 3-quart saucepan, heat sugar and butter over high heat until sugar has dissolved, stirring occasionally. Stir in milk. Set candy thermometer in place and continue cooking until temperature reaches 240° F on candy thermometer or soft-ball stage (when small amount of mixture dropped into very cold water forms a soft ball which flattens on removal from water).

2 Transfer mixture to small bowl. With mixer at high speed, beat 2 to 3 minutes, until thickened and frosting is of spreading consistency. If frosting becomes too thick to spread, stir in additional milk, 1 teaspoon at a time, until thinned to desired consistency. *Makes about 1½ cups.*

EACH TABLESPOON: ABOUT 95 CALORIES, 0 G PROTEIN, 15 G CARBOHYDRATE, 4 G TOTAL FAT (3 G SATURATED), 0 G FIBER, 11 MG CHOLESTEROL, 45 MG SODIUM.

Maple Frosting

PREP 3 MINUTES / COOK 10 MINUTES

For a change of pace with your favorite applesauce, pumpkin, spice, or carrot cake, try this fluffy frosting. Use real maple syrup—the lower grades, if you can get them, have a more pronounced maple flavor.

2 LARGE EGG WHITES
1½ CUPS MAPLE OR MAPLE-FLAVORED SYRUP
⅛ TEASPOON SALT
1 TEASPOON VANILLA EXTRACT

In top of double boiler, over simmering water, with hand-held mixer at high speed, beat egg whites, maple syrup, and salt 7 to 10 minutes, until soft peaks form. Remove double-boiler top from saucepan. Add vanilla and beat 1 to 2 minutes, until thickened and of easy spreading consistency. *Makes about 6 cups.*

EACH TABLESPOON: ABOUT 15 CALORIES, 0 G PROTEIN, 3 G CARBOHYDRATE, 0 G TOTAL FAT (0 G SATURATED), 0 G FIBER, 0 MG CHOLESTEROL, 5 MG SODIUM.

Cream Cheese Frosting

PREP 10 MINUTES

The favorite of many cake lovers, cream cheese frosting is the traditional topping for Carrot Cake and is delicious on Banana Layer Cake, too (both recipes, page 301). Decorate the cake with chopped walnuts.

3 CUPS CONFECTIONERS' SUGAR
2 PACKAGES (3 OUNCES EACH) CREAM CHEESE, SLIGHTLY SOFTENED
6 TABLESPOONS BUTTER OR MARGARINE, SOFTENED
1½ TEASPOONS VANILLA EXTRACT

In large bowl, with mixer at low speed, beat confectioners' sugar, cream cheese, softened butter, and vanilla just until blended. Increase speed to medium; beat 1 minute, or until smooth and fluffy, scraping bowl often with rubber spatula. *Makes about 2½ cups.*

EACH TABLESPOON: ABOUT 65 CALORIES, 0 G PROTEIN, 9 G CARBOHYDRATE, 3 G TOTAL FAT (2 G SATURATED), 0 G FIBER, 9 MG CHOLESTEROL, 30 MG SODIUM.

Whipped Cream Frosting

PREP 5 MINUTES

This makes enough to fill and frost a 2-layer cake or a tube cake, a 13" by 9" cake, or 2 dozen cupcakes. Keep the frosted cake refrigerated until serving time.

2 CUPS HEAVY OR WHIPPING CREAM
¼ CUP CONFECTIONERS' SUGAR
1 TEASPOON VANILLA EXTRACT

In large bowl, with mixer at medium speed, beat cream, confectioners' sugar, and vanilla until stiff peaks form. *Makes about 4 cups.*

EACH TABLESPOON: ABOUT 30 CALORIES, 0 G PROTEIN, 1 G CARBOHYDRATE, 3 G TOTAL FAT (2 G SATURATED), 0 G FIBER, 10 MG CHOLESTEROL, 5 MG SODIUM.

COFFEE WHIPPED CREAM FROSTING Prepare as for Whipped Cream Frosting but dissolve *2 teaspoons instant coffee powder* in *2 teaspoons hot water*, cool. Beat into whipped cream.
EACH TABLESPOON: ABOUT 30 CALORIES, 0 G PROTEIN, 1 G CARBOHYDRATE, 3 G TOTAL FAT (2 G SATURATED), 0 G FIBER, 10 MG CHOLESTEROL, 5 MG SODIUM.

COCOA WHIPPED CREAM FROSTING Prepare as for Whipped Cream Frosting but use *½ cup confectioners" sugar* and add *½ cup unsweetened cocoa*.
EACH TABLESPOON: ABOUT 30 CALORIES, 0 G PROTEIN, 1 G CARBOHYDRATE, 3 G TOTAL FAT (2 G SATURATED), 0 G FIBER, 10 MG CHOLESTEROL, 5 MG SODIUM.

Stabilized Whipped Cream

PREP 10 MINUTES

Adding gelatin to whipped cream stabilizes the mixture so that it does not break down and "weep."

2 CUPS HEAVY OR WHIPPING CREAM
1 TEASPOON VANILLA EXTRACT
1¼ TEASPOONS UNFLAVORED GELATIN
2 TABLESPOONS COLD WATER
⅓ CUP CONFECTIONERS' SUGAR

1 In large bowl, combine cream and vanilla. In small saucepan, evenly sprinkle gelatin over cold water; let stand 1 minute to soften. Cook over medium-low heat until gelatin completely dissolves, stirring frequently, about 2 minutes (do not boil). Remove saucepan from heat.

2 With mixer at medium-high speed, immediately begin beating cream mixture. Beat about 1 minute, until thickened and soft peaks just begin to form. Beat in confectioners' sugar, then beat in dissolved gelatin in a thin steady stream. Beat until stiff peaks form but mixture is still soft and smooth; do not overbeat. *Makes about 4 cups.*

EACH TABLESPOON: ABOUT 30 CALORIES, 0 G PROTEIN, 1 G CARBOHYDRATE, 3 G TOTAL FAT (2 G SATURATED), 0 G FIBER, 10 MG CHOLESTEROL, 5 MG SODIUM.

Ornamental Frosting

PREP 10 MINUTES

This hard-drying icing, tinted with food coloring, is used to decorate cookies—to put the smiles and buttons on Gingerbread Cut-Outs (page 60) or to write names on Ultimate Sugar Cookies (page 63). We've used meringue powder in order to avoid raw egg whites in this uncooked frosting. Meringue powder is available wherever cake-decorating equipment is sold.

1 PACKAGE (16 OUNCES) CONFECTIONERS' SUGAR
3 TABLESPOONS MERINGUE POWDER
⅓ CUP WARM WATER
ASSORTED FOOD COLORINGS (OPTIONAL)

1 In bowl, with mixer at medium speed, beat confectioners' sugar, meringue powder, and water until blended and mixture is so stiff that knife drawn through it leaves a clean-cut path, about 5 minutes.

2 If you like, tint frosting with food colorings as desired; keep covered with plastic wrap to prevent drying out. Use small metal spatula, artists' paintbrushes, or decorating bags with small writing tips to decorate with frosting. (You may need to thin frosting with a little warm water to obtain the right spreading or piping consistency.) *Makes about 3 cups.*

EACH TABLESPOON: ABOUT 40 CALORIES, 0 G PROTEIN, 10 G CARBOHYDRATE, 0 G TOTAL FAT (0 G SATURATED), 0 G FIBER, 0 MG CHOLESTEROL, 0 MG SODIUM.

Fluffy White Frosting

PREP 15 MINUTES / COOK 7 MINUTES

This classic American "Seven-Minute Frosting" has a marshmallow-like texture. It's recommended for Marmalade Cake (page 300) or for chocolate cakes. If using it on a chocolate cake, omit the lemon juice.

2 LARGE EGG WHITES
1 CUP SUGAR
¼ CUP WATER
2 TEASPOONS FRESH LEMON JUICE (OPTIONAL)
1 TEASPOON LIGHT CORN SYRUP
¼ TEASPOON CREAM OF TARTAR

1 In top of double boiler, or in medium stainless-steel bowl set over 3- to 4-quart saucepan, over 1-inch simmering water (double-boiler top or bowl should be about 2 inches from water), with hand-held mixer at high speed, beat egg whites, sugar, water, lemon juice, if using, corn syrup, and cream of tartar until soft peaks form and temperature reaches 160° F on candy thermometer, about 7 minutes.

2 Remove double-boiler top or bowl from saucepan; beat mixture 5 to 10 minutes longer, until stiff peaks form. *Makes about 3 cups.*

EACH TABLESPOON: ABOUT 15 CALORIES, 0 G PROTEIN, 4 G CARBOHYDRATE, 0 G TOTAL FAT (0 G SATURATED), 5 G FIBER, 0 MG CHOLESTEROL, 5 MG SODIUM.

HARVEST MOON FROSTING Prepare as above but use *1 cup packed dark brown sugar* for white sugar and omit lemon juice.
EACH TABLESPOON: ABOUT 20 CALORIES, 0 G PROTEIN, 5 G CARBOHYDRATE, 0 G TOTAL FAT (0 G SATURATED), 0 G FIBER, 0 MG CHOLESTEROL, 5 MG SODIUM.

Ganache

PREP 5 MINUTES / COOK 5 MINUTES

Ganache is the richest of all chocolate frostings— virtually a spreadable fudge. It's traditionally used to complement a not-so-rich cake, such as Chocolate Génoise (page 326). Use a fine-quality chocolate for this recipe because it's the chocolate that will make or break the frosting. If the ganache is too thick to spread when you take it out of the refrigerator, let it stand at room temperature until softened.

1 CUP HEAVY OR WHIPPING CREAM
2 TABLESPOONS SUGAR
2 TEASPOONS BUTTER OR MARGARINE
10 SQUARES (10 OUNCES) SEMISWEET CHOCOLATE, COARSELY CHOPPED
1 TEASPOON VANILLA EXTRACT
1 TO 2 TABLESPOONS BRANDY OR ORANGE- OR ALMOND-FLAVORED LIQUEUR (OPTIONAL)

1 In 2-quart saucepan, combine cream, sugar, and butter and heat to boiling over medium-high heat; remove saucepan from heat.

2 Add chocolate to cream mixture and whisk until melted and smooth. Stir in vanilla and brandy or liqueur, if you like. Pour into jelly-roll pan and place in refrigerator to cool. *Makes about 2 cups.*

EACH TABLESPOON: ABOUT 75 CALORIES, 1 G PROTEIN, 7 G CARBOHYDRATE, 6 G TOTAL FAT (3 G SATURATED), 0.5 G FIBER, 11 MG CHOLESTEROL, 5 MG SODIUM.

WHIPPED GANACHE Prepare and cool as above. Bring cooled ganache to room temperature; spoon into medium bowl. With hand-held mixer, whip ganache until light in color and mixture is of easy spreading consistency.

Chocolate Glaze

PREP 5 MINUTES / COOK 3 TO 5 MINUTES

Pour or spread the warm (not hot) glaze over Boston Cream Pie (page 322) and Éclairs (page 272). The glaze will thicken and set as it cools.

3 SQUARES (3 OUNCES) SEMISWEET CHOCOLATE, COARSELY CHOPPED
3 TABLESPOONS BUTTER
1 TABLESPOON LIGHT CORN SYRUP
1 TABLESPOON MILK

In heavy 1-quart saucepan, heat chocolate with butter, corn syrup, and milk over low heat, stirring occasionally, until smooth. *Makes about ½ cup.*

EACH TABLESPOON: ABOUT 100 CALORIES, 1 G PROTEIN, 9 G CARBOHYDRATE, 8 G TOTAL FAT (5 G SATURATED), 0.5 G FIBER, 12 MG CHOLESTEROL, 50 MG SODIUM.

Vanilla Pastry Cream

PREP 5 MINUTES PLUS CHILLING / COOK 10 MINUTES

2¼ CUPS MILK
4 LARGE EGG YOLKS
⅔ CUP SUGAR
¼ CUP CORNSTARCH
¼ CUP ALL-PURPOSE FLOUR
2 TEASPOONS VANILLA EXTRACT

1 In 3-quart saucepan, heat 2 cups milk to boiling over high heat. Meanwhile, in large bowl, with wire whisk, beat egg yolks, remaining ¼ cup milk, and sugar until smooth; whisk in cornstarch and flour until combined. Gradually whisk hot milk into egg-yolk mixture.

2 Return mixture to saucepan; cook over medium-high heat, whisking constantly, until mixture thickens and boils. Reduce heat to low and cook, whisking, 2 minutes.

3 Remove saucepan from heat; stir in vanilla. Pour pastry cream into shallow dish. Press plastic wrap onto surface of pastry cream to keep skin from forming as it cools. Cool to room temperature. Refrigerate at least 2 hours, or overnight. *Makes about 2¾ cups.*

EACH TABLESPOON: ABOUT 30 CALORIES, 1 G PROTEIN, 5 G CARBOHYDRATE, 1 G TOTAL FAT (0 G SATURATED), 0 G FIBER, 21 MG CHOLESTEROL, 5 MG SODIUM.

CHOCOLATE PASTRY CREAM Prepare as for Vanilla Pastry Cream and add *3 squares (3 ounces) semisweet chocolate* and *1 square (1 ounce) unsweetened chocolate,* melted, with vanilla. *Makes about 3 cups.*
EACH TABLESPOON: ABOUT 40 CALORIES, 1 G PROTEIN, 6 G CARBOHYDRATE, 2 G TOTAL FAT (1 G SATURATED), 0 G FIBER, 19 MG CHOLESTEROL, 5 MG SODIUM.

Pastry Cream for 9-Inch Tart

PREP 5 MINUTES PLUS CHILLING / COOK 8 MINUTES

Spread this firmer pastry cream in a tart shell, then top it with sliced fruit or whole berries. This is also the traditional filling for Boston Cream Pie (page 322).

1 CUP PLUS 2 TABLESPOONS MILK
2 LARGE EGG YOLKS
⅓ CUP SUGAR
2 TABLESPOONS ALL-PURPOSE FLOUR
2 TABLESPOONS CORNSTARCH
1 TABLESPOON BUTTER OR MARGARINE
1 TEASPOON VANILLA EXTRACT

1 In 1-quart heavy saucepan, heat ¾ cup milk to boiling over medium heat. Meanwhile, in large bowl, with wire whisk, beat egg yolks, remaining milk, and sugar until smooth; whisk in flour and cornstarch until combined. Gradually whisk hot milk into egg-yolk mixture.

2 Return mixture to saucepan; cook over medium heat, whisking constantly, 4 minutes, or until mixture thickens and boils. Reduce heat to low and cook, whisking, 2 minutes.

3 Remove saucepan from heat; stir in butter and vanilla. Pour pastry cream into shallow dish. Press plastic wrap onto surface of pastry cream to keep skin from forming as it cools. Cool to room temperature. Refrigerate at least 2 hours, or overnight. *Makes about 1½ cups.*

EACH TABLESPOON: ABOUT 30 CALORIES, 1 G PROTEIN, 4 G CARBOHYDRATE, 1 G TOTAL FAT (1 G SATURATED), 0 G FIBER, 21 MG CHOLESTEROL, 10 MG SODIUM.

Praline Pastry Cream

PREP 15 MINUTES PLUS CHILLING / COOK 25 MINUTES

VANILLA PASTRY CREAM (OPPOSITE PAGE)
1 CUP SUGAR
⅓ CUP WATER
1 CUP SLIVERED BLANCHED ALMONDS, TOASTED

1 Prepare Vanilla Pastry Cream; refrigerate until cold.

2 Grease jelly-roll pan. In 2-quart saucepan, heat sugar and water, stirring gently, over low heat until sugar dissolves. Increase heat to medium and boil rapidly. With pastry brush dipped in water, occasionally wash down side of pan to prevent sugar from crystallizing. Cook, swirling pan occasionally, about 7 minutes, until syrup turns a light amber.

3 Working quickly, stir in almonds. Spread almond mixture in thin layer on prepared jelly-roll pan; cool until hardened. Break praline into small pieces.

4 In food processor with knife blade attached, process praline until finely ground. In medium bowl, combine pastry cream and praline until blended. *Makes about 3¼ cups.*

EACH TABLESPOON: ABOUT 55 CALORIES, 1 G PROTEIN,
8 G CARBOHYDRATE, 2 G TOTAL FAT (0 G SATURATED),
0 G FIBER, 18 MG CHOLESTEROL, 5 MG SODIUM.

Lemon Curd

PREP 5 MINUTES / COOK 12 TO 15 MINUTES

A time-honored British teatime tradition (they often serve it on toast), lemon curd is a smooth, velvety citrus custard that also makes a wonderful filling for tarts. Lemon Curd Cream is a super-rich variation.

2 LEMONS
½ CUP SUGAR
6 TABLESPOONS BUTTER OR MARGARINE
3 LARGE EGG YOLKS

1 From lemons, grate 1½ teaspoons peel and squeeze ⅓ cup juice. In 1-quart saucepan, cook lemon peel and juice, sugar, butter, and yolks over low heat, stirring constantly with wooden spoon,

until mixture thickens and coats back of spoon, or temperature on candy thermometer reads 140° F for 5 minutes. (Do not boil or yolks will curdle.)

2 Pour mixture into medium bowl. Press plastic wrap onto surface of curd to keep skin from forming as it cools. Cool to room temperature. Refrigerate 1 hour, or up to 2 days. *Makes about 1 cup.*

EACH TABLESPOON: ABOUT 75 CALORIES, 1 G PROTEIN,
7 G CARBOHYDRATE, 5 G TOTAL FAT (3 G SATURATED),
0 G FIBER, 52 MG CHOLESTEROL, 45 MG SODIUM.

LEMON CURD CREAM Prepare and cool Lemon Curd as directed. Beat *¼ cup heavy or whipping cream* to soft peaks. Fold into curd. *Makes about 1⅔ cups.*
EACH TABLESPOON: ABOUT 55 CALORIES, 0 G PROTEIN,
4 G CARBOHYDRATE, 4 G TOTAL FAT (2 G SATURATED),
0 G FIBER, 35 MG CHOLESTEROL, 30 MG SODIUM.

Lemon Filling

PREP 15 MINUTES / COOK 8 MINUTES

This "sturdier" cornstarch-thickened version of lemon curd works as a filling for a layer cake or jelly roll.

3 LARGE LEMONS
1 TABLESPOON CORNSTARCH
6 TABLESPOONS BUTTER OR MARGARINE
¾ CUP SUGAR
4 LARGE EGG YOLKS

1 From lemons, grate 1 tablespoon peel and squeeze ½ cup juice. In 2-quart saucepan, with wire whisk, mix cornstarch and lemon peel and juice until smooth. Add butter and sugar. Heat to boiling over medium heat; boil 1 minute, stirring constantly.

2 In small bowl, beat egg yolks lightly. Into egg yolks, beat small amount of hot lemon mixture; pour egg mixture back into lemon mixture in saucepan, beating rapidly. Reduce heat to low; cook, stirring constantly, 5 minutes, or until thick (do not boil).

3 Pour mixture into medium bowl. Press plastic wrap onto surface to keep skin from forming as it cools. Cool to room temperature. Refrigerate 3 hours, or up to 3 days. *Makes about 1 cup.*

EACH TABLESPOON : ABOUT 95 CALORIES, 1 G PROTEIN,
11 G CARBOHYDRATE, 6 G TOTAL FAT (3 G SATURATED),
0 G FIBER, 65 MG CHOLESTEROL, 45 MG SODIUM.

Ricotta Filling

PREP **5** MINUTES

Vary this super-quick filling by stirring in chopped dried fruit, finely chopped semisweet chocolate, or chocolate mini-chips.

1 CONTAINER (32 OUNCES) RICOTTA CHEESE
1⅓ CUPS CONFECTIONERS' SUGAR
1 TEASPOON FRESHLY GRATED ORANGE PEEL
2 TEASPOONS VANILLA EXTRACT
⅛ TEASPOON GROUND CINNAMON

In food processor with knife blade attached, pulse ricotta until smooth. Add confectioners' sugar, orange peel, vanilla, and cinnamon; pulse to combine. *Makes about 4 cups.*

EACH TABLESPOON: ABOUT 35 CALORIES, 2 G PROTEIN, 3 G CARBOHYDRATE, 2 G TOTAL FAT (1 G SATURATED), 0 G FIBER, 7 MG CHOLESTEROL, 10 MG SODIUM.

Streusel Topping

PREP **10** MINUTES

Sprinkle this buttery, crumbly topping over the batter before baking muffins, coffee cakes, and quick breads. Or use it as a topping for fruit pie, in place of a crust. If you're a serious streusel-lover, make a double batch for a thicker layer; save any extra to swirl into portions of pudding or slightly softened ice cream.

½ CUP ALL-PURPOSE FLOUR
⅓ CUP PACKED BROWN SUGAR
4 TABLESPOONS COLD BUTTER OR MARGARINE, CUT UP

In medium bowl, combine flour, brown sugar, and butter. With pastry blender or 2 knives used scissor-fashion, cut in butter until mixture resembles coarse crumbs. Use fingers to crumble topping when using. *Makes about ¾ cup.*

EACH TABLESPOON: ABOUT 75 CALORIES, 1 G PROTEIN, 10 G CARBOHYDRATE, 4 G TOTAL FAT (2 G SATURATED), 0 G FIBER, 10 MG CHOLESTEROL, 40 MG SODIUM.

Sublime
Hot Fudge Sauce

PREP **5** MINUTES / COOK **10** MINUTES

Old-fashioned fudge sauce has become a "gourmet" item—as you know if you've priced any lately. We have come up with a superb homemade version. Keep the sauce refrigerated for up to one week; spoon out as much as you need and heat it in the microwave.

1 CUP HEAVY OR WHIPPING CREAM
¾ CUP SUGAR
4 SQUARES (4 OUNCES) UNSWEETENED CHOCOLATE, CHOPPED
2 TABLESPOONS LIGHT CORN SYRUP
2 TABLESPOONS BUTTER OR MARGARINE
2 TEASPOONS VANILLA EXTRACT

1 In heavy 2-quart saucepan, heat cream, sugar, chocolate, and corn syrup to boiling over medium heat, stirring occasionally. Cook 4 to 5 minutes, stirring constantly, until sauce thickens slightly (mixture should be gently boiling).

2 Remove saucepan from heat. Stir in butter and vanilla until smooth and glossy. Serve immediately, or let cool completely, cover, and refrigerate. (Do not cover sauce until it is completely cool or condensation will collect on the wrap and make the sauce grainy.) *Makes about 1¾ cups.*

EACH TABLESPOON: ABOUT 85 CALORIES, 1 G PROTEIN, 8 G CARBOHYDRATE, 6 G TOTAL FAT (4 G SATURATED), 0.5 G FIBER, 14 MG CHOLESTEROL, 15 MG SODIUM.

MICRO-MELTING CHOCOLATE

TO MELT CHOCOLATE IN A MICROWAVE, PLACE CHOCOLATE IN A BOWL. COOK AT MEDIUM POWER UNTIL THE SURFACE OF THE CHOCOLATE LOOKS SHINY—NOTE THAT IT WILL NOT LOSE ITS SHAPE UNTIL YOU STIR IT. CHECK AFTER 1 MINUTE TO SEE IF THE CHOCOLATE HAS MELTED. IF NOT, GIVE IT A BIT MORE TIME, BUT CONTINUE TO CHECK IT OFTEN.

Custard Sauce (Crème Anglaise)

PREP 5 MINUTES / COOK 15 MINUTES

Spoon this classic "pouring custard" over a slice of plain cake or a wedge of fruit pie, a bowl of berries, or a serving of apple crisp. For a flavor switch, replace the vanilla with 1 tablespoon brandy or liqueur.

1¼ CUPS MILK
4 LARGE EGG YOLKS
¼ CUP SUGAR
1 TEASPOON VANILLA EXTRACT

1 In 2-quart saucepan, heat milk to boiling over medium heat. Meanwhile, in medium bowl, whisk egg yolks with sugar until smooth. Gradually whisk hot milk into egg-yolk mixture.

2 Return mixture to saucepan; cook over medium heat, stirring constantly (do not boil or mixture will curdle), just until mixture thickens slightly and coats back of wooden spoon. (A finger run across custard-coated spoon should leave a track.)

3 Remove saucepan from heat. Strain custard through sieve into clean bowl. Stir in vanilla. Serve warm or cover and refrigerate up to 2 days to serve chilled. *Makes about 1¾ cups.*

EACH TABLESPOON: ABOUT 20 CALORIES, 1 G PROTEIN, 2 G CARBOHYDRATE, 1 G TOTAL FAT (0 G SATURATED), 0 G FIBER, 32 MG CHOLESTEROL, 5 MG SODIUM.

Raspberry Sauce

PREP 5 MINUTES / COOK 5 MINUTES

1 CONTAINER (10 OUNCES) FROZEN RASPBERRIES IN SYRUP, THAWED
2 TABLESPOONS RED CURRANT JELLY
2 TEASPOONS CORNSTARCH

1 Press thawed raspberries through sieve into 2-quart saucepan. Stir in jelly and cornstarch. Heat to boiling over medium heat, stirring; boil 1 minute.

2 Pour sauce into bowl; cover and refrigerate. *Makes about 1 cup.*

EACH TABLESPOON: ABOUT 25 CALORIES, 0 G PROTEIN, 7 G CARBOHYDRATE, 0 G TOTAL FAT (0 G SATURATED), 0 G FIBER, 0 MG CHOLESTEROL, 0 MG SODIUM.

Flavored Simple Syrup

PREP 2 MINUTES / COOK 5 MINUTES

Brush this syrup over fine-grained cakes (such as Génoise, page 325) to add flavor and moistness. For this recipe, choose a liqueur that is clear and pale in color, not a creamy one.

¼ CUP SUGAR
¼ CUP WATER
2 TABLESPOONS FAVORITE-FLAVOR LIQUEUR OR BRANDY

In 1-quart saucepan, heat sugar and water over high heat, stirring occasionally, until sugar dissolves. Remove saucepan from heat and stir in liqueur. *Makes about ⅓ cup.*

EACH TABLESPOON: ABOUT 55 CALORIES, 0 G PROTEIN, 10 G CARBOHYDRATE, 0 G TOTAL FAT (0 G SATURATED), 0 G FIBER, 0 MG CHOLESTEROL, 0 MG SODIUM.

Hard Sauce

PREP 10 MINUTES

Never serve a Christmas pudding without hard sauce! The sauce is firm enough to scoop up in a spoon but melts on contact with warm pudding or mince pie.

1 CUP CONFECTIONERS' SUGAR
⅓ CUP BUTTER OR MARGARINE, SOFTENED
½ TEASPOON VANILLA EXTRACT

In small bowl, with mixer at medium speed, beat confectioners' sugar with softened butter until creamy; beat in vanilla. Spoon into small bowl; refrigerate, covered, if not serving immediately. *Makes about ⅔ cup.*

EACH TABLESPOON: ABOUT 100 CALORIES, 0 G PROTEIN, 12 G CARBOHYDRATE, 6 G TOTAL FAT (4 G SATURATED), 0 G FIBER, 16 MG CHOLESTEROL, 60 MG SODIUM.

Flourishes

Chocolate Wedges

PREP 10 MINUTES PLUS COOLING
COOK 5 MINUTES

Stand these wedges atop a frosted cake or a whipped-cream-topped pie to literally add an extra dimension to the dessert.

½ CUP SEMISWEET CHOCOLATE CHIPS
2 TEASPOONS VEGETABLE
    SHORTENING

On 10-inch-long sheet of waxed paper, with toothpick, trace circle using bottom of 9-inch round cake pan; cut out circle. Place cake pan, bottom side up, on surface; moisten slightly with *water*. Place waxed-paper circle on pan (water will keep paper from sliding). With large metal spatula, evenly spread melted chocolate mixture on waxed paper. Refrigerate until chocolate is firm, about 30 minutes. Heat blade of long knife in hot water; wipe dry. Quickly but gently, cut chocolate into wedges. Use wedges to garnish cakes and pies. *Makes 16 wedges.*

You can cut the chocolate round into as many wedges as you wish.

Chocolate Curls

PREP 15 MINUTES PLUS COOLING
COOK 5 MINUTES

It's best to make these just before you plan to use them.

1 PACKAGE (6 OUNCES) SEMISWEET
    CHOCOLATE CHIPS
2 TABLESPOONS VEGETABLE
    SHORTENING

1 Melt chocolate with shortening as for Chocolate Wedges (at left). Pour chocolate mixture into foil-lined or disposable 5¾" by 3¼" loaf pan. Refrigerate until chocolate is set, about 2 hours.

2 Remove chocolate from pan. Using vegetable peeler, draw blade across surface of chocolate to make large curls. If chocolate appears too brittle to curl, let stand at room temperature 30 minutes to soften slightly. To avoid breaking curls, use toothpick to lift and transfer. *Makes enough to cover top of 9-inch cake.*

It's easiest to shave long curls if the chocolate is slightly warm.

Chocolate Leaves

PREP 20 MINUTES PLUS COOLING
COOK 5 MINUTES

These decorations are made by spreading melted chocolate onto real leaves. Leaves from the following plants are safe (nontoxic) and sturdy enough to be suitable: gardenia, grape, lemon, magnolia, nasturtium, rose, wood violet. Before using the leaves, wash them with warm, soapy water; rinse and dry them thoroughly.

½ CUP SEMISWEET CHOCOLATE CHIPS
2 TEASPOONS VEGETABLE
    SHORTENING
6 MEDIUM LEMON LEAVES

Turn each leaf over and spread melted chocolate on the underside.

After chilling, peel the leaf off the chocolate, not the other way around.

1 In heavy 1-quart saucepan, heat chocolate chips and shortening over very low heat until melted and smooth, stirring frequently. Meanwhile, rinse lemon leaves and pat dry with paper towels.

2 With pastry brush or small metal spatula, spread a layer of melted chocolate mixture on underside of leaves (using underside will give more distinct leaf design). Refrigerate chocolate-coated leaves until chocolate is firm, about 30 minutes.

3 With cool hands, carefully peel each leaf from chocolate. Use leaves to garnish cakes and pies. *Makes 6 chocolate leaves.*

Chocolate Ruffles

PREP 20 MINUTES PLUS COOLING
COOK 5 MINUTES

If the temperature of the chocolate is just right, the ruffles will fold nicely.

8 SQUARES (8 OUNCES) SEMISWEET
CHOCOLATE, CHOPPED

1 In heavy 1-quart saucepan, melt chocolate over low heat, stirring constantly. Spoon about ¼ cup melted chocolate onto inverted 15½" by 10½" jelly-roll pan. With metal spatula, spread chocolate to cover pan bottom evenly. Refrigerate just until chocolate is firm, about 10 minutes.

2 Make ruffles. Place chocolate-covered jelly-roll pan, with 10½-inch side toward you, on damp cloth to keep it from moving. With blade of wide spatula, starting at the far right corner, scrape up about a 3-inch-wide strip of chocolate toward you, pulling spatula with right hand, gathering left side of chocolate strip with left hand, and allowing right side to fan out. (Consistency of chocolate is very important. If it is too soft, it will gather into a mush; if too hard, it will break and crumble. If chocolate is too firm, let stand at room temperature a few minutes until soft enough to work with; if too soft, return to refrigerator.) Place ruffles on cookie sheet; refrigerate until firm.

3 Continue making ruffles with chocolate on pan. Repeat with remaining melted chocolate, using a clean jelly-roll pan each time. (The more jelly-roll pans you have, the faster you can make ruffles.) If ruffles break while making, return chocolate to saucepan and melt again, heating only until melted. *Makes enough to cover top of 9-inch cake.*

Hold one side of the ruffle together as the other side fans out.

White Chocolate Hearts

PREP 15 MINUTES
COOK 3 MINUTES

These open designs are very striking when used on Chocolate Truffle Tart (page 240). They are also appropriate, especially on Valentine's Day, on a special chocolate cake.

1½ OUNCES WHITE CHOCOLATE,
COARSELY CHOPPED

1 With pencil, draw outline of 12 hearts, each about 1½" by 1½", on piece of waxed paper. Place waxed paper, pencil-side down, on cookie sheet; tape to cookie sheet.

2 In top of double boiler over simmering water, melt white chocolate, stirring, until smooth. Spoon warm chocolate into small decorating bag fitted with small writing tube; use to pipe heart-shaped outlines on waxed paper. Let hearts stand until set. *Makes 12 hearts.*

White chocolate hearts look spectacular on a dark chocolate cake.

Chocolate Butterflies

PREP 15 MINUTES PLUS COOLING
COOK 5 MINUTES

You can also use this technique to make 3-dimensional shapes of your own devising.

2 SQUARES (2 OUNCES) SEMISWEET
CHOCOLATE, CHOPPED
1 TEASPOON VEGETABLE SHORTENING

1 Cut waxed paper into ten 4" by 2½" rectangles. Fold each rectangle crosswise in half to form 2" by 2½" rectangle. With pencil, draw outline of half a butterfly on each folded rectangle, using center fold for butterfly body (the pressure of the pencil point will mark the bottom half of paper as well). Unfold rectangles and place on clean flat surface, tracing side down. Tape rectangles to heavy surface, about 2 inches apart, with small pieces of cellophane or masking tape.

2 In heavy 1-quart saucepan, heat chocolate and shortening over low heat until chocolate is melted and smooth, stirring constantly. Cool 10 minutes. Spoon mixture into small decorating bag with small plain tip. Pipe some chocolate mixture onto each waxed-paper rectangle in thin continuous line over tracing and along centerfold to make a butterfly. Repeat with remaining chocolate to make 10 butterflies in all.

Use a small plain piping tip to pipe chocolate butterfly shapes on the folded squares of waxed paper.

3 Remove and discard tapes. With wide spatula, carefully lift each piece of waxed paper and place, chocolate side up, in 2½-inch muffin-pan cup or in section of empty egg carton so that waxed paper is slightly bent on center fold. Refrigerate at least 1 hour, or until chocolate is set. With cool hands, carefully peel off waxed paper. Use butterflies to garnish cakes or pies. *Makes 10 chocolate butterflies.*

Letting the shapes cool on the slightly folded paper will produce "flying" butterflies.

Index

Index

METRIC CONVERSIONS

LENGTH

If you know:	Multiply by:	To find:
INCHES	25	MILLIMETERS
INCHES	2.5	CENTIMETERS
FEET	30	CENTIMETERS
YARDS	0.9	METERS
MILES	1.6	KILOMETERS
MILLIMETERS	0.04	INCHES
CENTIMETERS	0.4	INCHES
METERS	3.3	FEET
METERS	1.1	YARDS
KILOMETERS	0.6	MILES

VOLUME

If you know:	Multiply by:	To find:
TEASPOONS	5	MILLILITERS
TABLESPOONS	15	MILLILITERS
FLUID OUNCES	30	MILLILITERS
CUPS	0.24	LITERS
PINTS	0.47	LITERS
QUARTS	0.95	LITERS
GALLONS	3.8	LITERS
MILLILITERS	0.03	FLUID OUNCES
LITERS	4.2	CUPS
LITERS	2.1	PINTS
LITERS	1.06	QUARTS
LITERS	0.26	GALLONS

WEIGHT

If you know:	Multiply by:	To find:
OUNCES	28	GRAMS
POUNDS	0.45	KILOGRAMS
GRAMS	0.035	OUNCES
KILOGRAMS	2.2	POUNDS

TEMPERATURE

If you know:	Multiply by:	To find:
DEGREES FAHRENHEIT	0.56 (AFTER SUBTRACTING 32)	DEGREES CELSIUS
DEGREES CELSIUS	1.8 (THEN ADD 32)	DEGREES FAHRENHEIT